A Passage for Dissent

A Passage for Dissent: The Best of *Sipapu*, 1970–1988

by
Noel Peattie

with a foreword by
SANFORD BERMAN

McFarland & Company, Inc., Publishers
Jefferson, North Carolina, and London

Author's note: The Columbia University Libraries classify *Sipapu* (or did as of 1974) under Library of Congress class HX, "Communism, Socialism and Anarchism." *Who says this isn't a "Movement" publication?* (Now, where's the "Movement"?)

British Library Cataloguing-in-Publication data available

Library of Congress Cataloguing-in-Publication Data

Peattie, Noel.
   A passage for dissent : the best of Sipapu, 1970–1988 / Noel Peattie.
      p.   cm.
   Includes index.
   ISBN 0-89950-399-3 (lib. bdg. : 50# alk. paper) ⊗
   1. Publishers and publishing—United States. 2. Freedom of the press—United States. 3. Underground press—United States. 4. Little presses—United States. 5. Ethnic press—United States. 6. Dissenters—United States.   I. Title.
Z471.P4   1989
071'.3—dc19   88-43490
                                                                            CIP

© 1973, 1974, 1975, 1976, 1977, 1978, 1979, 1980, 1981, 1982, 1983, 1984, 1985, 1986, 1987, 1988, 1989 Noel Peattie. All rights reserved.

Printed in the United States of America.

McFarland & Company, Inc., Publishers,
   Box 611, Jefferson, North Carolina 28640

Table of Contents

Foreword (by Sanford Berman)	ix
Introduction; something about the editor/publisher	1
1 : 1 Origin of the name; the meeting in the Happy Valley Bar	3
1 : 2 Further through the tunnel	9
2 : 1 Oracular revealings — an interview with Steve Levine of the late *San Francisco Oracle*	11
2 : 2 Charging for subscriptions	21
3 : 1 The new prisoner: interview with Jay Halford	23
3 : 2 Sanford Berman's challenge; the life, death, and resurrection of the littlemag (interview with Len Fulton)	28
4 : 1 Leamer and the Movement press (interview with Laurence Leamer); rjs and the cultural anarchism of the East, by Hugh Fox	43
4 : 2 With me along the strip of herbage strown (interview with Lime Saddle); that just divides the desert from the sown (Barbara Pruitt at UFWU headquarters); where name of slave and sultan is forgot (Berman reforms the subject headings); and peace to Mahmud on his golden throne *(The Spiritual Community Guide);* damnation DAMP; with Father Dollen at the front; the fortunes of *Synergy*	60
5 : 1 Get out your Tablut (a game of chess from Lapland)	72
5 : 2 OXOMOXO! (interview with Walter Medeiros); the trumpet's silver sound is still (David McPhail on the Sonoma County *Bugle*); Estren's *History of Underground Comics* is Sipapu's book of the year	76
6 : 1 Stumped for an answer (the Sonoma County *Stump*); Mother knows best *(The Mother Earth News);* women of letters (with Diane Kruchkow at a convocation of	

	women writers); Hugh Fox on the underground; a symposium on Chicano literature	90
6 : 2	Asian-American writers' conference; Women's Collection Development Conference; will Pudge *ever* get laid? (interview with Lee Marrs); from the conferences; my love gave me a turtle tag; tell me not here, it needs not saying (review of Callenbach's *Ecotopia*)	107
7 : 1	The nightingales are singing near (interview with Tobie Lurie); from the conferences; COSMEPologists of the world, unite!	125
7 : 2	Rise up so early in the morn (interview with Jackie Eubanks)	136
8 : 1	Beyond baroque art in Venice (interview with Alexandra Garrett and George Drury Smith); San Francisco International Book Fair (with A.D. Winans); ALA resolute?; the new age and its dictionary; and all the morning stars shouted for joy!	142
8 : 2	Quiet, please, we're doing a revolution (interview with Carole Leita and the Women Library Workers); well, what technology is appropriate?; National Women's Studies Conference (with Nancy Osborne); CLA forum on publishers and libraries; underground comix; old libraries	162
9 : 1	Interview with Joseph Bruchac III; CLA and *The Speaker* film; turtle time again; Alex Jack as poet; E.F. Schumacher obituary	182
9 : 2	Proposition 13; poet as printer as poet (interview with Judyl Mudfoot); *The Speaker* again; t-shirts and turtle pins; transcendental meditation and *Class Struggle*	207
10 : 1	A gentle word from Philadelphia (interview with Elliot Shore); independent no more (Deck Hazen on the Santa Cruz *Independent*); reviews of books on the Ohlone people and the Loch Ness monster	221
10 : 2	The bookdealer as scholar, printer, poet (interview with Jack Shoemaker); conference on conferences	232
11 : 1	¡Paracaidismo! (interview with Dan Poynter); the whole problem of peace (review of *Time Bomb*)	248
11 : 2	"Is there anybody there?" said the traveller (interview with John Wilcock); Black Hills Alliance Gathering (with Janet Mercurio and Isao Fujimoto); *Winds of Change*	254

Table of Contents

12 : 1	ALA West; COSMEP; reviews; National Nude Days; Three Mile Island Creamy Mushroom Dressing	266
12 : 2	CLA in San Francisco; Mid-Continent Forum for the Future of Literature	279
13 : 1	Conference on the San Francisco Renaissance and interview with Michael Davidson of the Archive for New Poetry at UC San Diego; Brutus vs. Caesar in South Africa (by Judith Getts); the bear is the prosecutor, the taiga is the law (book review); Winters joins the peace movement	286
13 : 2	Interview with Brad Chambers; "the train of the dead" with Diane Callum	302
14 : 1	Interview with Karl Kempton; statement to support the CIBC; underground publications in Puerto Rico (with Luisin Medina); Peace Pilgrim	320
14 : 2	Disciples of the Beat angels (interview with Arthur and Kit Knight); reviews	340
15 : 1	The Data Center (Oakland, California); data beyond the Center (interview with Zoia Horn); publishing in the Netherlands	352
15 : 2	Lands without banners (interview with Theresa Vinciguerra)	372
16 : 1	Publishing as a total erotic experience (interview with Lily Pond); conferences briefly tackled (CLA and David McCalden, ALA Midwinter); the new undergrounds; specialties (review of *Black Box Magazine*)	378
16 : 2	The indexers (interview with the Alternative Press Index collective); "truth" and consequences; ALA Chicago '85; reviews; where poets fear to tread (Diane Callum returns from Nicaragua via U.S. Customs)	407
17 : 1	Meanwhile, back at the ranch (interview with Art Cuelho); libraries and the life of the mind (CLA 1985); ceremonies for Bob Kaufman (with A.D. Winans); review of Benetta's *Crusade of the Credulous*	430
17 : 2	Cardinal Mazarin is dead?! (McCalden again; review of an article by John Swan); reviews	462
18 : 1	California small press issue (with David Scott Peattie)	472
18 : 2	CLA 1987; reviews; a poetic manifesto in one sentence, plus a digression	481
Index		485

Foreword

by Sanford Berman

Okay. I confess to being a magazine junkie. So much so, in fact, that I seldom read whole books any more. No time. But to get directly to the point: of all the rags that regularly jam my mailbox, *Sipapu* is one of the few I feel a compulsion to devour right away. Like instantly. Even if it means an hourlong, pre-dawn stint on the downstairs couch. (Among the other periodicals that affect me the same way: *Shmate, Z Magazine, Maledicta, Cultural Survival Quarterly,* and *The Skeptical Inquirer.*)

Why this addiction to such a homespun-looking, twice-yearly "newsletter for librarians, collectors, and others interested in the alternative press, which includes small and 'underground' presses, Third World, dissent, feminist, peace, and all forms of indescribable publishing in general"? Why forego sleep over a mag largely composed of ruminations and reviews by *one* guy? Well, because the topics are inherently "hot," intriguing, and important. And that "one guy" just happens to be the closest thing we've got in librarianship to a "Renaissance Man," although his roots, style, and interests stem more from 60s/70s California than 15th century Italy. Noel Peattie is at once librarian, poet, raconteur, reporter, printer, editor, aesthete, social activist, philosopher, essayist, critic, publisher, and eccentric. That's a description that frankly doesn't fit anyone else in the library profession. And maybe never did.

Begun in 1970 as "a tunnel between two worlds," *Sipapu* has actually proven to be a continuing tunnel between *many* worlds, making necessary and useful connections among counterculturists, people of color, avant-garde/out-of-the-mainstream artists and sages, all kinds of radicals, and, of course, library types. Yet all of this—the interviews, musings, conference reports, and bountiful reviews—wouldn't "work" if it weren't informed by Peattie's own values and craft, by his "special" personality. For Noel Peattie *cares* about things like racism, sexism, antisemitism, and inequality. He's personally involved with publishing and the alternative press. He writes with grace, candor, and wit. And he has a well-developed critical sense. *Sipapu* fairly exudes Noel's own humanity, taste, and good humor. In short, it's a "good read," even an "exciting read."

There's one more aspect to the Peattie persona that Noel himself might never admit. Possibly he'd deny it. That quality, simply stated, is *courage,* another rare trait in librarianship as well as most other professions. For it was courageous to print uncensored interviews with cartoonists and editors like Lee Marrs and Lily Pond who produce sex-positive, no-apologies-please erotica. It was courageous to run lengthy, revealing conversations with such libraryland "pariahs" (or heroes) as Right-to-Know advocate Zoia Horn (once jailed for refusing to testify against peace activists) and prejudice-fighter Brad Chambers (vilified by Nat Hentoff as "the direct descendant of Cotton Mather"). And it was courageous to challenge the library world's Holy Canons of Intellectual Freedom, brilliantly demonstrating that the Gospel According to Judy Krug is at once simplistic and insensitive.

Oddly, Peattie's 19-year labor has not spawned numberless awards and honors from his peers. Sure, his faithful subscribers appreciate him. So do his colleagues within the American Library Association's Social Responsibilities Round Table. And he *has* won kudos from people like Jim Danky ("*Sipapu* is alive with Peattie's personality and wit and exemplifies the creative energy that pervades the alternative press"), Valerie Wheat ("Noel's nose for petite detail and Jane Austenian sensibility make *Sipapu* unique"), and Judson Jerome ("*Sipapu* is distinguished by its candid, scholarly and critical tone"). But mostly he hasn't received the public recognition he richly deserves. (Indeed, despite repeated appeals, H.W. Wilson still refuses to index *Sipapu* in *Library Literature.*) McFarland, to its credit, has somewhat remedied this scandalous inattention by publishing not only *Passage for Dissent,* but also *The Freedom to Lie: A Debate About Democracy* (1989), coauthored by Peattie and John Swan.

As further redress, however, I now propose that:

- every *Sipapu* fan write Wilson, demanding that the mag be indexed (both in the future and retrospectively)
- the Social Responsibilities Round Table of the American Library Association present Noel with a special, once-only award for outstanding lifetime achievement in promoting cultural diversity and social justice
- either *American Libraries, Wilson Library Bulletin,* or *Library Journal* publish an in-depth interview with Noel himself.

Introduction

A *sipapu* is a tunnel: in the Hopi language of the Southwest, and in other people's beliefs, it's the place of emergence: where Spider Woman led the human race from underground captivity, to the upper air. To some Apache people, it's a metaphor for the birth canal, the tunnel we all passed through. For me, who chanced on the word, only dimly understanding its significance, it's a personal passage.

I'm not a Native American, but I took twenty hours in coming through my mother's birth canal, and barely made it. Now I emerge once again, into the existence of print. If I have borrowed the term unfairly, at least I made my *Sipapu* a place of emergence for others: contributors, poets, and raisers of issues.

Culling from my own work, and cutting as the publisher's needs demanded, has proved a correcting experience for me. It once seemed very important to explore some problems which are now no longer interesting. Many conferences, almost all book reviews, and a couple of interviews are no longer relevant or readable. Those who would use *Sipapu* as a mirror of the seventies and eighties will either want to consult the whole film (microfilms are available from the Doheny Library, University of Southern California), or explore other periodicals and books of the period.

Those who read here, furthermore, should remember that this is a review and interview journal for librarians, who can find elsewhere coverage of the world's daily news, and editorial opinions. *Sipapu* is not the kind of underground paper that purports to solve the problems of the Middle East or Southeast Asia; it is, or started out to be, an underground paper about underground papers, and became one librarian's exploration of the lesser-known islands of the world of print.

Readers will also pick up on changes in the direction of the magazine: from a collector's jumble of news, to a coverage of small press activity, to an emphasis on intellectual freedom issues seen from a social responsibility standpoint. And here, too, my viewpoint has changed over the years: what seemed gospel once, later seems questionable.

A periodical becomes a responsibility and an identity, like a child or a house. It will be hard to let go of it upon retirement, a few years from now. Perhaps it will continue under other hands, who knows? But living with it has been such a joy and a burden, that it will be hard to imagine life without it.

I am pleased to acknowledge help: from my contributors, illustrators, critics (friendly and harsh); and above all to my printer, Douglas Galbraith, doing business as The Printer, Davis. With one exception, all the issues are from his hands. His advice has been invaluable; his prices, the lowest. Thanks too to Sandy Berman for his friendship and his foreword.

Last of all, my unexpected publisher: Robert Franklin. He was central in convincing me that this project could and should be done. I had doubts based on previous disappointments: he gave me every encouragement, and proof of his sincerity.

Noel Peattie
Fall 1988

1 : 1

This selection comprises the first two pages of Sipapu, *v. 1, no. 1; there were six pages in all. The other pages included the outline of a classification scheme for the collector of underground and counter-cultural papers; it was never used.*

The meaning of the term sipapu *is clearly explained in the text, but why was this term chosen? In October 1969 I drove across the country to visit my brother in Princeton and to sell my car. On the south rim of the Grand Canyon I came across the excavation of a* kiva, *neatly labelled by the National Park Service, which explained what a* sipapu *is and what it stands for. I found the concept intriguing, and thought, "What a wonderful name for a mysterious paper or periodical!" because at that time I had been collecting underground papers, such as the San Francisco* Oracle *and the Haight-Ashbury* Love Street, *admiring their "psychedelic" designs and bold use of color obtainable from a web press. I also had been going on peace marches in San Francisco, stuffing my pockets with literature handed out by everyone on the sidelines — Diggers, Anarchists, Trotskyites or Technocrats.*

It occurred to me that somebody ought to be keeping track of all this stuff, and apparently it occurred to several other people too: Russell Benedict, a "volunteer curator" of a "Collectors' Network" at the University of Nevada–Reno Library; Sol Behar, of the University of California, Berkeley; and W.P. Allan, from Stanford. A visit to Berkeley to set up a preliminary meeting at the California Library Association's upcoming conference in San Francisco was soon joined by others, and we were on our way. Benedict, who couldn't be there, had suggested some sort of newsletter (although he had his own Collector's Network News), *and at the end of the historic meeting in the Happy Valley Bar described here, I volunteered to do the newsletter. I remembered the* sipapu *while driving home, and* Sipapu *was conceived, being actually born in the first week of January, 1970.*

The pompously named "conference" never amounted to much, nor did its successors. The newsletter outlived the group. The reason for this was that others were not really interested in submitting copy. Since I certainly did not want to write the whole paper for myself, even though I never expected to have more than a hundred subscribers, I sent a copy of this issue to the California Library Association, asking them to help find me contributors.

To my surprise, CLA simply reproduced the first page of Sipapu, *just as you see it here, in the February 1970 issue of their* Newsletter. *They then appended a note telling their readers that I wanted copy, and that* Sipapu *could be had* gratis.

I had neither copyright, business license, nor funds beyond my salary and savings. I thought I would be running an esoteric fanzine for a few years until somebody else offered to take it over or it died. Consequently I was astounded when I received in the mail, dozens of requests for free copies of Sipapu *from libraries all over the Golden State. They were eager, desperate for information on the counter-cultural explosion, and I found myself running off more copies, running to the post office to buy more stamps, and starting a paper file of requesting libraries.*

A wild surmise entered my head. I knew William R. Eshelman, who after hiring me for my first library job at Los Angeles State University (now California State University–Los Angeles), had gone on to become editor of Wilson Library Bulletin. *I sent him a copy, with a similar announcement, not failing to add that the magazine was free for the asking.*

What happened next seems in retrospect like one of those lucky events that turn the fortunes of the poor and aspiring, from Dick Whittington to today's hero. I started getting requests for Sipapu *from all over the United States. In a fortnight I had 700 (nonpaying) subscribers, aside from the few friends I have always shared* Sipapu *with. As a marketing test it was an expensive strategy, but as a goldmine—or Pandora's box—it was overwhelming.*

It must be remembered that I had no experience in editing a paper and my only writing before this had been unsaleable fiction and derivative poetry. (That is, aside from a collaboration, at age 17, with my father on a book of essays, A Cup of Sky, *published by Houghton Mifflin in 1950.) I had also no knowledge of how to run a newsletter business. Finally I had not the slightest idea of what the whole continuing labor would mean in terms of money, time, and emotional stamina. It was a good thing that I knew nothing: or I never would have got started.*

I was 37 and while I had a very good job at the University of California–Davis, my lit'ry career existed mostly in my head. Even then I did not realize that instead of writing one more pleasant but forgettable novel I had started to create my own instrument of expression. Of course there have been one-man papers before; I.F. Stone's Weekly *and* Manas *come to mind, as well as the large number of little magazines, but* Sipapu *is neither a showcase for poets nor a political commentary (though at times it has approached both). Rather it is a personal vision of cultural upheaval, written for librarians, and others, by a librarian. The fact of having a continuous and definable audience, even if that is not an audience of the rich and famous, has been the one essential in keeping* Sipapu *alive. Simply to have sounded off, giving my cockalorum opinions on various subjects to anyone and no one, as I had been doing since I was a small boy, would have never garnered requests for my paper from all over the country (another difference between me and I.F. Stone: Stone was in daily contact with people of power). My "better mousetrap" was and is actually my subscribers: trying to keep them interested is my yearly concern.*

Pam Scrutton did the layout (the marginal decorations). On the advice of Jean

Stalnaker, who did the layout for the succeeding issue, I offered Pam $75 — which she at first refused, having never been paid for her art work before. I persuaded her to accept the payment, and she went on to marriage and a fine artistic career. After a while I stopped asking artists to do my margins and started collecting graphics from bookdealers' catalogs; at present my use of graphics is next to nil.

Vol. I, No. 1   January 1970

A newsletter for librarians, scholars, editors and others concerned with ethnic studies, the counter-culture, and the underground press. published irregularly, distributed free (for the present), and edited by Noel Peattie, Collection Development Section, University Library, University of California, Davis, California 95616. Home address: Rt. 1, Box 216 Winters, Calif. 95694

(Not a publication of the University of California.)

SIPAPU: A TUNNEL CONNECTING TWO WORLDS: In the kivas of the Southwest, the round huts used by Pueblo and other Indians for religious ceremonies, are two holes: one to receive the sacred fire, and the other, the sipapu, for a tunnel to the other world. Through this underground passage the ancestors of the pueblos are said to have emerged from a subterranean prison; through it the spirits of the dead pass; and to this day the sipapu connects the world of spirit and the world of everyday reality. We hope the name SIPAPU will connect in our readers' minds the world of the ethnic minority and radical with the mystical world of the hippie, and the world of the librarian and scholar alert to the subterranean shift in our country's life.

page 1.

The editor therefore welcomes the aid of librarians and others in cooperating with each other through us, keeping us abreast of new publications, and coordinating their efforts in preserving and making available their collections in this field to present and future researchers. Please send us your descriptions of what you are collecting in this undercountry; what you plan for the future; and how you think you could best help each other and perhaps also as lovers of intellectual freedom, the publishers and distributors of underground presses. For the present, expenses will be borne by the editor, but if *Sipapu* gets too popular, outside help will be sought. Distribution will be chiefly to librarians, but we are interested in everyone's help. We hope to become an underground paper about underground papers. "Get you below!"

GETTING IT ALL TOGETHER: The First California Conference on Ethnic Studies and the Counter-Culture met at the registration desk of the Annual Conference of the California Library Association, in the Sheraton Palace Hotel, San Francisco, at 11:15 a.m. PST, 11 December 1969. After waiting around for other members for fifteen minutes, the group wandered back to the general membership meeting, and finding it hopelessly entangled in a parliamentary snafu, was suddenly stricken with collective drought and adjourned to the hotel's Happy Valley Bar, a few steps away. Present were: Sol Behar and Kit Lyons, of UC Berkeley, Gerta Maskaleris of the Bancroft Library at UC Berkeley, and Celeste West and Mike Spence, of San Francisco Public Library, as well as Noel Peattie of UC Davis.

The following action was taken: At the suggestion of Sol Behar, the association of librarians interested in his area was to remain independent of UC, CLA, and ALA, and informal—not dependent on fixed schedules. *Hang Loose* was the motto of the meeting. News of our work was to be placed in SF Public Library's *Synergy* and the CLA *Newsletter,* as the best way of interesting others without getting shipwrecked in administrative channels. Noel Peattie agreed to serve as a clearinghouse and to publish a newsletter, with the hope that out of this future meetings might grow.

(*Sipapu* is this newsletter. The editor chose the name himself on the way home.)

It was agreed that librarians would send descriptions of their work and interests to the editor. Among the persons to whom the newsletter might be sent, Bill Allan of Stanford was named. (The editor met Anne Mitchell of UCLA at another CLA meeting the following day, and she expressed regret at having missed us, so she gets one too.) The notes of Noel Peattie on the possible scope of our work were approved as amended by Kit Lyons.

Information was exchanged as to the following ongoing work in this field: Laird Wilcox's *Guide to the Left,* a comprehensive publication of which the organization was considered not quite satisfactory; and the *Radical Reader's Guide,* an index published by Robert Stilger, of Carleton College,

Northfield, Minnesota 55057. Someone mentioned that AMS Press was going to microfilm a number of underground newspapers. A subsequent visit to AMS's booth at the CLA conference revealed that their brochure will not be ready until January 1970; the editor got his name on their mailing list. The meeting concluded, at the suggestion of Mike Spence, with a singing of "Solidarity Forever," and cries of "Power to the People!" and "Peace!"

Subsequently the editor heard from a former colleague at CSC/LA that a Mr. Spreitzer at USC was microfilming radical papers. The editor will try to contact Mr. Spreitzer and see what he is doing.

1 : 2

Our v. 1, no. 2, was drawn in elegant black and printed on tan paper. Jean Stalnaker's animals curved round the text, but as can be seen by reading it, I was still writing practically all of it myself. And at my own expense!

SIPAPU: FURTHER THROUGH THE TUNNEL: Since our first issue, dated January 1970, we have received easily a hundred requests for copies, and perhaps, without prejudice to our learned readers, they were attracted by those words in *Wilson Library Bulletin* and in CLA *Newsletter* "a free subscription!" Three scholars, indeed, sent a dollar apiece—which was silently pocketed, but will here be acknowledged with thanks. Actually we needed not money (well, since you insist), but copy—which, truth to tell, a few were in a position to supply. Most libraries are trying to build up a counter-ethnic-underground collection and are just getting started, so that they have little to report. It turns out, then, that America is peopled chiefly by folks trying to find out what's happening in America. And that's better than the blissful ignorance of not long past.

For those of you who came in late, and are wondering what the hell is a sipapu, we recommend the *Webster's Third International,* or better yet, a trip through the National Parks of our great Southwest. Anyone who has just heard of *Sipapu,* will get v. 1, no. 2, and also v. 1, no. 1, as long as the supply lasts. For the rest of you, be assured that we have saved all your request letters and we will try to supply you with new issues as they come out. And all those who were going to send us copy and didn't, should do so now. It's to your own benefit that your splendid collection be publicized.

Perhaps this is a good time to make our intention plain. We are not competing with the *Berkeley Tribe, Amistad, The Black Scholar, New Serial Titles,* or "Births, deaths and magazine notes" in *Bulletin of Bibliography.* We are not a general Movement paper; we lack the time and staff to act as a checklist of the underground press, and are primarily interested in reporting library programs and collections and new publishing ventures. The periodicals mentioned are all doing a splendid job, and nobody is doing exactly what we are doing, to our knowledge.

We will describe important papers, as they are born, transmogrified, or killed off; and we do welcome articles of strong opinion. We also encourage, even at some risk, the subscription to controversial (including Movement) papers.

That ethnic and underground papers are controversial, and that librarians have lost their jobs by subscribing to them, there is no doubt. But that young people, particularly Third World people, need them, is also true. You can always say, "Let them subscribe at home, or buy them on the street; I have a job to protect"; and we cannot tell you to sacrifice your career. But consider, also, that the duty of a librarian is to increase the flow of information, not to impede it, and that self-censorship is the most dangerous form of censorship. It has no limits and it accelerates under the pressure of fear of the unknown. Someone, somewhere, will have to lay his job on the line in subscribing to those papers, and the recent retreats from intellectual freedom in California, Texas, and Missouri are a threat that librarians everywhere will have to face—or be prepared to abandon all freedom altogether.

A number of colleges and universities have reported their efforts to build up ethnic studies collections, but few have told *how* they did it or what obstacles they encountered. Mr. John Smith, University Librarian at the University of California at Irvine, tells us that he has been trying to collect underground newspapers in Orange County, where they are really driven underground, as was *Sherwood Forest.* We are not sure of its continued existence; but we do know that *Plain Wrapper,* a Resistance paper from Palo Alto, and the *San Francisco Oracle,* lately published in Larkspur, California, are dead. The usual cause of death—lack of funds.

2 : 1

Beginning with v. 2, no. 1, I started numbering consecutively: this became "consecutive issue no. 3." (Librarians: your catalog card should include a note: v. 2, no. 1—also numbered consecutively: no. 3— .)

This issue was illustrated by José and Miriam Argüelles, who introduced me to my first interviewee, Steven Levine, former editor of the San Francisco Oracle. *The UC Davis Library had just bought, on my recommendation, a complete set of the* Oracle, *plus its layovers, and I visited Levine at his in-laws', borrowing for the purpose a tape recorder from the University. Steve was suffering from low back pain and was under medication, and the resulting tape needed professional transcription available only at Berkeley. UCD has the original tape; the (thoroughly edited) interview appears below.*

Interviews became my mainstay for many years. I used to wonder: "Who shall I interview next?" While I have not given up the idea, interviewing has become less important as readers voice their preference for reviews, and interviews fade under the pressure of time's changing occasions. Some interviews have been dropped from this anthology because they were not important, or because the interviewees were not happy with the result, or because the situation of the interviewees changed so drastically that I decided that it would be a misrepresentation to reprint the interviews that they had endured under different circumstances. "The rhythms change, they do not close."

ORACULAR REVEALINGS: The *City of San Francisco Oracle,* hereinafter described as the *Oracle,* was perhaps the best of the hippie papers that grew out of the "San Francisco Renaissance" in its later, post–Beat phase. The *Oracle* was published by one group in Haight Street, San Francisco, and later by another group in Larkspur, Marin County, California; the two incarnations of the paper had little to do with each other. The Library of the University of California, Davis, has purchased the backfiles of both series and the artwork of the first, from Stephen Levine, one of the earliest editors of the paper. The *Oracle,* which used a different name *(P.O. Frisco)* for its first issue, changed rapidly from a radical magazine to an "Aquarian" paper; the difference being that between those who seek to change society, and those who try to alter man's inner landscape. With our purchase came overlays and sketches, while correspondence and other papers have been promised us. No edition in reprint of the *Oracle* can be considered truly complete, whatever announcements you may hear; the reason being that the paper carried several variants in each issue, depending on the needs of the editors and the results of the variant printings. We supply here excerpts from an interview with Mr. Levine, taken 22 August 1970, to help our readers visualize what goes on in the minds of those who are putting out an "underground paper":

SIPAPU: Steve, roughly when did the *Oracle* begin, and for how long were you associated with it?

LEVINE: The *Oracle* began in early fall of 1966. I was living in the woods when the first issue came out. I got a letter from Ron Thelan, originator of the first "psychedelic" shop in the country, the man who contributed the first $250 to start the *Oracle*. He had asked for some of my work to publish, so I brought them a column I was doing. We were then living in a cabin right above the San Andreas Fault, so the column was called "Notes from the San Andreas Fault." That was published in the third issue, and so when I came to San Francisco I was involved as a writer from the third issue, and more and more as an editor in later issues. Finally I went to the editorial desk from about the fourth issue to the last, which would be number twelve.

SIPAPU: In short, you were involved in it from fall '66 to perhaps spring '68.

LEVINE: Spring '68 was the last issue.

SIPAPU: You ended up, finally, as editor?

LEVINE: Yes, so to speak. The paper was a very cooperative outfit, where there wasn't necessarily *an* editor. Allen Cohen had been involved with it from its inception, and there was a big switch-over about the third issue, when I became involved. By the third and fourth issues I was helping them get material, and doing a little copy-editing. We were in a back room over the Print Mint on Haight Street and we moved the office. We had no desks up until that time. There were only tables for layout. And when we got two desks, Allen took one and I took the other, and we were there most of the time. But there were a number of other people who brought in or passed on copy: Steve Leiper, George Tsongas, Harry Monroe, Bill Dodd; and others who dropped by or recommended material: Allen Ginsberg, Michael McClure, Gary Snyder, Lew Welch. You see, the term "editor" is really a nineteenth-century idea, not applicable here, because we didn't edit. We were just the channels that the energy came through.

We had a poem Gary Snyder had sent us. He was in Kyoto at the time. It was called "A curse on the men in Washington," and there was a lot of discussion about that poem. The discussion centered around the whole idea of a curse, of sending out destruction of the old, as some people saw it. Other people saw it as an insight into the cosmic circuitry of things. And I remember there were a couple of FBI agents up, looking for a deserter from the service — whom they'd just passed on the stairs coming up to the office and hadn't even recognized. And I showed *them* the poems and asked them what *they* thought.

So everybody was really an editor; it was really the Collective Cortex as editor, part of the common consciousness. I don't think there was ever any single issue that everybody who was considered an editor wholly agreed on. If somebody felt strongly about a piece, and nobody else had a strong objection to it, it went in, generally. Sometimes everybody felt very strongly about it and thought it should be in. The artwork was often done right on the boards; but because the technology limited us to 48 pages of black and white, or 32 pages with two colors, or 24 pages with three colors, the machines edited the paper too, sometimes allowing what could be left in and what couldn't.

SIPAPU: You seem to have had a spiritual, collective operation. So, you left in February of 1968.

LEVINE: No, somewhat later. I was publishing a book in Mexico City, and Allen Cohen went down with me there; I was there for six weeks, while Allen stayed for three weeks and then came back. And just before I split, Peter Tork, one of the Monkees, loaned us $5000 on request. The *Oracle,* I might add, was in severe financial difficulties, although the banks would lend us money; we borrowed $3000 and repaid it; later we borrowed $4500 and were having trouble repaying. We left that loan with our staff to produce *Oracle* number 12; most of it was already on the boards and the rest had been selected for inclusion. There were three people: Harry Monroe, George Tsongas and Garry Goldhill, who had been one of the editors in the beginning — I say three, although there was never any single number, because it changed daily. These were the men who took over to produce issue no. 12.

Thus Allen Cohen and I had split the last week in January, leaving the $5000 there with the other people to produce the last issue. When we came back the last issue was out, but for various reasons we felt we had had enough. And so Allen and I left the *Oracle,* leaving the rest of that money with the staff to produce issue no. 13 — which never appeared. We left because we felt the Haight-Ashbury was changing; and the tremendous energy stream, which made us work sometimes ten or twelve hours a day, had left us exhausted after a year and a half of that intensity.

Have you ever read Gurdjieff's *Meetings with Remarkable Men?* He had to travel all over the world to meet those men. We only had to sit in that office, and people came in whom we admired tremendously. Buckminster Fuller came there, and Robert Thiebald, and Tim Leary, and Herb Alpert, and

Ralph Metzner, and Chinmayananda, and Rolling Thunder (a Shoshone medicine man), or any number of remarkable beings.

People in Des Moines or Oshkosh would write us and say, "How groovy that the *Oracle* exists, because it reaffirms my interior seekings." But the *Oracle*, as much as it was an oracle for them, was an oracle for us, too, because we learned a tremendous amount from the people. The best part of the *Oracle* never got published.

SIPAPU: Well, that's always the way. The best part of any life can never be expressed in its outward achievements. The *Oracle* in the series that folded in November 1969, was a different crowd, right? Did you have anything to do with them at all?

LEVINE: Sam Lewis, a Sufi Master who had many young followers, had asked us about a continuation, at one point near the end of the *Oracle*. We were at Gavin Arthur's house one day when I met Sam. We folded in the spring; then the second series came out several months later. No, we had nothing to do with it, except we gave it our blessings—our blessings! Just as it moved through us, it moved through them, and as it wasn't ours and we didn't own it, so we had nothing to say. And they did a super thing. It was a different thing, yet it couldn't be different altogether, because it was so universal, what each of us were up to; but their paper was more Sufi-oriented. But it was an *Oracle* too, just as there was a *Southern California Oracle*. And those are just the names of the papers. I think all of the underground press (which was misnamed, because it was really the over-ground press), even the press of the violent revolutionaries, had partaken in the idea of brotherhood. Sometimes the idea was in a crystal ball, sometimes in nerve circuits, in a pill you dropped, or in a gun barrel. Some were revolutionaries who said, "Fuck the pigs," while other said, "Have nothing to do with that. Meditating in a cave affects consciousness as strongly as throwing a bomb in the streets." So that each of the underground presses, in my opinion, were just aspects of the collective mind.

SIPAPU: I think you have very correctly described the essentially tribal nature of what's going on, and the sense that virtually everybody has, who has any sympathetic contact with this, of being in contact with an enormous source of energy. It's as if we were plugged into a galaxy, and when it went around, we went around too. As I understand it, therefore, the term *Southern California Oracle* is a coincidence.

LEVINE: No. Joe Dana, who was the main energy-mover for that paper, was up in the office fairly early in the life of the *San Francisco Oracle*, in the days when we were still over the Print Mint. This was about the time of the Human Be-In. You see, that's the turning-point for us—the Be-In issue, no. 5. It was the first one where we really got into the use of color and super-overlays. Joe was there, and I believe he had some source of money and certainly a vision, and he asked if he could use "The Oracle" as a name. We let him, and financed it in part. I think we gave him $1200 worth of papers to sell, and let him keep the money toward the printing of his own first issue.

Notice, please: whenever I say "his" that is just a means of putting it into language, but the whole point was that there never were any individual underground papers. I'm not sure if there were newspapers that were one man's trip, and certainly even some of those were run as time and opportunity dictated; whoever was around a paper at a given time, edited it.

SIPAPU: Now, the present *Oracle*. I have seen the masthead or logo, or whatever you call it, on a paper in The Tides Bookshop, Sausalito.

LEVINE: Yes. It's the same logo.

SIPAPU: Who owns the logo?

LEVINE: Well, you see, that's interesting. Nobody does. Nobody owns an "Oracle" of any sort. We started with $250, our first printing was just 2500, because those web presses click it off so quickly that that was the least you could do, the most reasonable to do. We went from 2500 to well over 100,000, and got play from everybody. Everybody reviewed it, from *Playboy* to the *Wall Street Journal*. Everybody was enthralled by the technology being used for something new. Most of the advancement in color usage had occurred first in advertising layout. Some printers had already used moiré patterns and color work, so as to give a third-dimensional effect; but these had appeared chiefly in commercial art. They were not common in newsprint, and until fairly recently, we did not have colored pictures on the front pages of newspapers. So we took something that was present, and applied it to what we were up to, to our state of mind.

SIPAPU: Now: you have mentioned technical processes, you have mentioned financing. For the benefit of others who might want to start a paper of this scope, would you please point out one or two pitfalls that everybody ought to avoid, and at least some triumphs that you think others could learn to imitate?

LEVINE: "Starting a paper of that scope"? The thing is, we were the right thing at the right time. That's why we were so successful. There might be other papers that might not do as well.

We were never harassed by the police at all — maybe because we scarcely got into politics at all. There was talk about "exorcising" the Pentagon, but the Pentagon was just the object of an exorcism which each of us was trying within himself. The *I Ching* says, "Don't attack an enemy until you've cleared that same motivation from yourself." And that's a lifetime work.

I can remember that I felt, and I can remember saying this more than once, that the criteria for inclusion of material in the *Oracle* were honesty, beauty and joy. These words are so imprecise that our decisions were very intuitive. I would look at a piece and tell Allen, "This doesn't look like *Oracle* material." And Allen would say, "What is *Oracle* material? If we publish it, it's *Oracle* material." And he was right. Just do whatever you want, and not get hung up in your own way; and always change, as the Beatles did. Follow the process, and not what seems to be successful; don't get sidetracked by what happened yesterday.

SIPAPU: I'm speaking of something more specific; for example, some of the details of the web process and other graphic processes involved. I don't think everybody knows that, and everybody who sees a copy of the *Oracle* might be tempted to say, "Oh, I can do that!" What is the web process in brief, and how does one prepare to handle it?

LEVINE: The web process is an off-shoot of lithography. In working with color, first of all you'd lay out your page and see what overlays were needed, and what overlays what. In doing this, you would have to remember that when you're laying it out, page 1 is not next to page 2. Page 1 may be next to page 16, while page 2 is on another web. This problem didn't arise in the first issues, because we didn't have color. Color came when we had more money and energy and skill. I can remember times when we were at the printers' and we didn't know what it was going to look like. We'd say, "Okay, we want to use gold and scarlet," and we'd see that when it hit the finish of the paper we were using, it would look terrible. So while it was still on the press, somebody would run up to the scarlet and put blue in it while it was still running, so there was a difference in what the first thousand and the last thousand of that printing of 20,000 copies looked like. It was a very on-going process.

Registration, the impression falling cleanly so that overlays weren't blurry or off-center, is the ideal cleanliness of perfect printing. But on web presses you don't have quite that perfection, no real fine tuning for a single page; the press runs so fast that the paper slackens or stretches just slightly, and so you lose registration and get blurry edges — a technical limitation. Cleanliness can be attained with care, however, by having enough paper and taking enough time until it gets just right.

There are different papers to use, and through them you get different intensities of color. We'd look at the page, and we'd say, "Okay, there it is — black on white. But using those colors is just our habit." That was the whole problem of the underground press on every level — to break conditioning. (This involves everything from fasting and meditation to psychedelics, none of which are fully separated from any of the others.) You'd see what you had to work with: white background and colored ink. Then we'd say, "Why not take these and reverse them? Why not leave the ink the color of the paper and print everything else, in other words, print in negative?" I can think of a Tom Weir photo that we did this way, a picture of one of the Grateful Dead holding a huge spider — and we made a very surrealistic picture out of it. We printed it in brown, and then instead of doing an outline, we just covered the whole page in yellow. One plate had an image of the photograph, the black part of the photograph in negative reverse; the other plate was just a whole sheet. So where the yellow fell over the brown it changed it to gold, and the rest of the page was yellow. So it saved us time doing an acetate overlay, and we realized that there were all kinds of things we could do. Whole pages, whole overlays could be a solid color and we could print something over it. The solid color would still come out and the overlay would look like three colors, because the combination of whites and overlay would produce double colors without half-toning.

Here's a good instance: We have two colors to use, that is, two plates hitting the paper. This would normally give two colors, but we put dividers in where the ink goes and run five colors on that one plate, and keep changing them. That's called a split font. Do a split font in the background and a split font in the other plate, and you end up with ten colors. You end up with mud, though, if you're not careful. You can't tell until it's on the press, without experience. You could look at the first thousand of a run, or the last or middle thousand, and they were changing; each issue changed as each moment changed, and each copy of each issue is slightly different. I don't think you could find two issues that were exactly alike without a close analysis of them.

SIPAPU: That's the result of the way you went at it, and that's why the *Oracle* was one of the best papers that the underground press produced. Tell us more about financing.

LEVINE: When we got up to 100,000 copies, it cost $5000 per issue. Finally we did a tape with Timothy Leary, Alan Watts, Allen Ginsberg and Gary Snyder, and printed that as a 52-page issue, all in as much color as possible — and that was it. We blew it financially, which was fine; but we never quite caught up with that. It was the turn-on issue, the one that got everybody excited, but it was also the issue that broke us. But that was what the paper was for! It wasn't to make money.

When the taxes were paid, I don't think anybody drew more than $1500. And the one person who got that $1500 was only involved in one issue; but then he had five kids, and he needed the money. Other people who were involved for a year and a half, or more, got $500. I don't think anybody who was there consistently got $1000, anyone at all. It was just food and rent money.

One of the good things that happened while we were doing the *Oracle* was that things suddenly became free for almost everybody who was involved. We still had to pay rent, we still had to pay for food, but we could go almost anywhere for free — the jazz clubs let us in for free. That whole paper was really San Francisco — the best of what was happening, the best of what was being thought. And the worst, too. And it supported everybody.

But at last some people felt that others were getting more than they deserved, while they themselves were going without. Once a person starts thinking he went without, that means he's *not* going without. He's confused, he's no longer doing his work just to do it. So a few were thinking about what they were getting paid for it; and that was because they were tired. People were so tired that they were *thinking,* so tired they were *reasoning:* the energy wasn't coming through as clearly. Some people became so tired that they were exasperated—that was it. And rather than drown in that energy which we had all learned so much from, we just said: "We don't want to do it anymore, but anyone else who wants to do it—here's some money, here's a subscription list, here's machinery (a couple of electric typewriters and a rent-free pad)—it's yours." But issue no. 13 never came out, even though it got all the way to negatives.

Still, while it lasted, we had this vision, a point beyond ourselves. We'd have arguments about who was art director, and still we would be doing a mindful job. You can see the City of God, and put out a beautiful paper, even through the arguments. Allen and I had the final word as editors and still had to contend with loud and joyous mutinies every once in a while. So between the vision and the struggle, the *Oracle* kept straightening itself out.

SIPAPU: Of course the way you went at it, and the place your heads were at, made it possible for the *Oracle* to straighten itself out. The *Oracle,* however, closed—and increasingly I'm disinclined to call it a failure—simply because the continuing energy, the stream of protons, as it were, had exhausted this particular set of bodies and minds, and it was now time for someone else to get in the way of the radiation,—right?

LEVINE: Yes. And there was something ancient about it. You remember the Twelve Tribes of Israel? The Cohens were the priests, and the Levites—I being a Levine—were the guardians of the Temple, the Torah and the Law. [See Numbers 2: 50-53.] So Allen Cohen was prime energy-mover, and prime insight—he of all of us was truly oracular. Of course, oracles were always very vague, and it took the priests to interpret them. And until recently we lived in the woods about fifty feet away from each other; and he has a dome, and I had a tent, among thirty other people in Mendocino.

Allen's insight was such that the *Oracle* went on. However, the energy that was used up in putting out the paper was so tremendous that I can remember us just sitting there sometimes,—dazed. Somebody would come up and say, "Oh, there are the two guys that are..." and ask us some question, and we say "Huh?" And they would think "Oh, they're really stoned." But we weren't stoned at all. We were just exhausted. Which was good because at that point they had to answer their own questions.—And that was perfect!

That's all the *Oracle* ever did. That's what the *I Ching* does; it gives you a mirror, and you answer your own questions.

SIPAPU: Right. Just like Tarot cards or any other divinatory method, all it does and all it is intended to do is to open out the insides of people.

LEVINE: Yes.

SIPAPU: And this is what the famous oracles of Delphi and Dodona did. I remember when I talked to the staff of the second avatar, which included some very delightful people —

LEVINE: Do you mean the newspaper *The Avatar?*

SIPAPU: No, I'm talking about the second series of the *Oracle.*

LEVINE: There were also two newspapers called *The Avatar* that came out on the same day. Did you know that? Talk about the synchronicity of the underground press! One day we went out on the street for lunch — and we saw a newspaper called *The Avatar* about half a block from the office — and it was from Seattle, I believe. About two blocks down we came across another paper that had reached San Francisco at exactly the same time, and *it* was called *The Avatar,* and *it* was from Boston. Neither knew of the other's existence!

SIPAPU: Actually, I was speaking of the Larkspur series or edition, because it was published out of Larkspur, in Marin County. They too had some of your difficulties. The artist, Eduardo Arditi, told me, "We love doing this, but we get completely exhausted, and at the end of the month we just have to scatter in different directions and rest up."

LEVINE: *We* never got a chance to do that.

SIPAPU: Speaking of other papers, were you aware of a paper published in Portland, Oregon, called *The Seer?*

LEVINE: Oh, yes, we saw that.

SIPAPU: We subscribed to it at Davis, but we never got any copies. I think it died too soon. [*Ed. note: The Seer* did close after one issue.]

Can you tell us what has become of some of the other artists, writers and contributors, and where they are now?

LEVINE: Almost everybody's out of the city. Allen's living in the woods, Steve Leiper has been living in Sonoma County for a while. Most of the people are doing organic gardening, raising animals, building their own houses, delivering their own children, writing their own poetry, publishing a bit here and there. I think the most successful people — meaning those who were lucky enough to be able to trust their vision — went out and started living it.

For a lot of people their art became peripheral. They were no longer "artists" — that 18th-century concept of art above everything else — and they recognized that art was just a vehicle for chronicling their genes. And a lot of people went to the woods to live, or with groups of people in communes, but certainly in some form of communion with their brothers.

Where we have been living until now there's Gene Grimm, who laid out a few issues, and did some writing. He wrote some articles entitled "Teonanachtl," which is the Nahuatl name for the sacred mushroom.

Of some twenty people who were deeply involved in the *Oracle,* more than half have had children at almost exactly the same time. Allen's child and my child were born five days apart. Gene Grimm now has two children, Allen has a child, I have a child and another coming; Travis, I believe, has another child now. Hedy McGee, an extraordinary artist who did a number of covers and centerfolds for the *Oracle,* has had another child (at the time she had one who was then about six or seven). I saw her picture in *Horizon* not so long ago; she was also in *Alice's Restaurant.* Marty Linhart, who did a lot of the business work, is up in a commune in Northern California. George Tsongas, I believe, is still in the city. Harry Monroe's lady is about to have a baby now. A lot of life came out of all that.

SIPAPU: This then is the ultimate success of an artistic movement — that love is central to it and provides a lot of the energy for it, and that beautiful, happy children are born out of it. This was the way of Shelley's generation, of Renoir's. The California environment is as good as any other to produce such a movement, and that is why I was interested in the *Oracle.* — Have you a last word for us?

LEVINE: The Chinese of centuries back said that a work to be displayed should be good enough to be carved in bamboo. Today in our new mechanical Ice Age, one might measure their work against the heart-value of the tree which must be cut in order to print our papers.

Peace. Let your love-light shine.

SIPAPU: Peace to all of us, and thank you very much, Steve.

2 : 2

The cost of publishing Sipapu *having risen to several hundred dollars an issue, it seemed obvious that I could no longer give it away while paying for it out of my own pocket. Either I would have to charge, or find outside funding. I applied for a grant from the Council on Library Resources, but they were not interested, and their annual report showed how much they preferred getting libraries involved with the first steps to automation. I then devised a circular, "SIPAPU CAN NO LONGER BE DISTRIBUTED GRATIS," in which I explained to my seven hundred readers that I would no longer be able to pass the magazine out free, and that subscribers would receive two issues a year for two dollars. Making the price that cheap was a mistake; few people will pay less than ten dollars for a magazine, and I have had to double the price twice since then. But the magazine was short, and I wanted to get it to "the people," so I kept it at two dollars for several years.*

I seem to have lost all my copies of the flyer, but it contained the first prototype of my logo — SIPAPU stood in huge angular letters over a lonely wall of angular desert mountains — a setting full moon, a volcano streaming a thin line of smoke on a south wind. The design reappeared in v. 8, no. 2.

SIPAPU AND THE PANIC OF 1971: Our circulation over the past eighteen months has risen to unheard-of heights (at least we never heard of it until it happened). Over 700 libraries, librarians and freepress people in 48 States of the Union, six Provinces of Canada and several foreign countries demanded free copies of *Sipapu* the minute they read about it in *Library Journal, Wilson Library Bulletin, The Los Angeles Free Press* and the California Library Association's *Newsletter*. Even with an overrun of 200 copies of v. 2, no. 1, the stock was quickly exhausted, and hence there are NO BACKFILES of *Sipapu* left. We have found that some libraries that *should* have backfiles *don't* have them: they were misplaced, and in some cases, librarians wrote on official letterheads for copies — which they then took with them when they switched jobs. If your library is thus deprived, write us and we'll tell you where you can find backfiles to copy.

Meanwhile, back at the ranch, the costs had gone *way* outasite: over $900 for three issues. You all received copies of our circular asking for subscriptions of $2 a year; we have now received checks from about 160 subscribers, beginning with Fr. Charles Dollen of the University of San Diego,—on whom we invoke divine blessings. The money received will enable us to go on for at least another year; we are grateful to everyone who has helped *Sipapu* keep going.

3 : 1

I no longer remember how I met Jay Halford, the ex-prisoner who published The Anvil, *and I have lost track of him since. I hope he is free and well. At the time, interviewing former prisoners seemed a very risky thing to do; now that we have writing programs in prisons, and presidential aides find themselves behind bars, knowing "cons" is not only not risky, it's fashionable.*

THE NEW PRISONER: "The prisons are now developing three kinds of men," says Jay Halford, former editor of *The Anvil,* a publication of the United Prisoners' Union; "psychopaths, mystics and hard-core revolutionaries." We are fortunate to have a chance to interview Mr. Halford. It should be explained that *The Anvil* ran to only three issues—all rather hard to get; the complete set is at the U.C. Davis Library, and the successor paper, following a reorganization, is *The Outlaw.*

There are times in an editor's life when his duty is *not to edit.* In order to preserve not only the viewpoint, but also the language, of Mr. Halford's responses, textual editing has been confined to an absolute minimum,— mostly punctuation. Whether you are inclined to agree with his ideas or to challenge his statements,—we hope that you will agree that he should have a place to speak his mind. Accordingly, we present Halford's words unretouched:

SIPAPU: What has been happening in prisons since ca. 1955?

HALFORD: Up to 1955, prisoners were largely racist and apolitical, enough so that prisons did not require adjustment centers. All the violence that has taken place since 1955 has happened inside adjustment centers. Cons were "conwise": involved in a cycle of conscious crime and conscious retribution, they figured that if they got caught, they'd do their time. But Malcolm X, Eldridge Cleaver, Tim Leary, George Jackson, exemplified the new type of prisoner. They were men who came out of prisons politically conscious as to why prisons exist. Now prisoners, perhaps more than people on the outside have dealt with their racism and are united against the oppressor, which is capitalism and its bureaucrats. (An adjustment center is a prison within a prison, designed specifically to hold political prisoners and those who rebelled as prisoners—prisoners who rose up against thousands of unconstitutional prison rules.) The philosophy of the prison system in America has been based on the premise that you can physically and psychologically intimidate men and make them conform. The application of this premise is ludicrous, in that you are dealing with men who had to be taken off the streets because they wouldn't conform.

SIPAPU: Where are you at and what are your purposes?

HALFORD: My experience in prison brought me to being a Marxist. G.B. Shaw said: "You'll never know what kind of a country you live in until you go to its prisons." When I was in the county jail, a lot of the men there became aware of the incredible inequities of the system. For in jail, if you don't have the finances you can't bail out, and you can't get a good attorney, and consequently the chances are overwhelming that you'll go to prison. As for myself, right now I am committed to a lifelong struggle against a system that oppresses millions of people. I'm writing plays, poems, and short stories, and I see these as vehicles for directing change and raising the consciousness of the people. The poverty I knew outside was one thing, but the degradation I knew in prison was what crystallized my opinions. I am a white, and prison is the closest whites come to knowing and realizing what it is to be black.

SIPAPU: How did the paper start? What about the name?

HALFORD: The conception of a Prisoners' Union is an old dream, fostered by thousands of convicts for many years. But in the summer of 1970, about twelve ex-convicts, with a total of about 200 years' incarceration between them, had a meeting and decided that it was time the Convicted Class was born. We wrote a constitution and a preamble over four or five weekends; this constitution and preamble alluded to a "Bill of Rights of the Convicted Class." This demanded everything from the abolition of corporal punishment to the right to unionize and form labor unions in prison. More than anything, we envisioned a radical political labor union of prisoners. We wanted to institute conjugal visits to combat the homosexuality that we were being forced into due to the absence of women; and we demanded the abolition of prison slave-labor sweatshops, where prisoners are forced to work for two cents an hour—or go to solitary confinement. The paper, *The Anvil* (an anvil being a piece of steel on which you can break chains), was devoted to two major tasks: 1) informing the people about the cycle of poverty, prison, parole, and more poverty, in which thousands of people are trapped; and 2) arousing the indignation of the prisoners in order that they might see themselves as the most brutalized and oppressed minority in all the world. It was our belief that no one had ever scientifically set down and tried to determine the effects of incarceration on men. We personally knew incarceration to be the most dehumanizing form of punishment on earth; and *The Anvil* was devoted to bringing all that to an end. We went out of our way to make the paper a lucid document: no obscenities, no "off the pig," etc. Although we did not advocate violence, the paper became an object of fear and hate on the part of prison officials. They banned it after the execution of George Jackson. Men who were caught in possession of the paper were transferred to opposite ends of the state of California. In the paper we tried to deal with the whole spectrum of the effects of incarceration, from the human interest of a wife suffering on welfare outside, to the husband being sent to solitary confinement for kissing his wife too long during visiting hours. We tried to show the excruciating ordeal of a parolee trying to survive in capitalist society to the prison system driving men to suicide to the unsung heroism of an ex-felon who got killed trying to help his fellow-men. Another thing that we exposed was the conscious racism of prison bureaucrats.

SIPAPU: Why you as editor? How did you prepare?

HALFORD: Out of the founding group I was the most qualified writer. So the task fell to me, and I saw it as an exciting challenge—it afforded me the opportunity to get in some long-desired blows against the prison empire, for what they had done to me and to my brothers during the four years I was in Soledad State Prison for armed robbery. When I was in prison, the prison officials constantly confiscated my writings, forced me to live in solitary confinement for ninety days and nights, and (the most bitter of all that I can recall), when I had defended myself against the physical coercion of a berserk prison official, they took me to the adjustment center, forced me to strip in the midst of about eight prison officials, and all present poked me with sticks and made fun of my body. All the foregoing abuses made me eager to undertake the editorship of *The Anvil*.

SIPAPU: How was it run and who was the "censor?"

HALFORD: The only restriction we had on the paper was that there would be no excessive obscenity. We put the emphasis on telling the truth: the evil was so pervasive that we didn't have to lie about it. When the paper went to the galleys, I was the last person to approve it. All of us had known each other for years, and they knew that my literary judgment was good, and they trusted me; so it was just a question of disseminating the truth. One of the decisions which we made very early was never to take advertising, even if we got into financial difficulties; we weren't going to follow the capitalist path of exploitation.

SIPAPU: Were the articles written in prison, or on parole?

HALFORD: Save for four exceptions,—Don Jackson, a freelance writer, Dr. Richard Korn, a criminologist at U.C. Berkeley, Dr. James Hillman and Dr. Frank Rundle, former psychiatrists at Soledad,—the rest of the paper was written by myself, prisoners inside, ex-convicts outside, and families of prisoners. Jerry Helland, a young radical, was primarily responsible for the layout.

SIPAPU: What hassles did you encounter? Printer, police...?

HALFORD: Our first issue was printed at Woody's Press Shop in Sacramento. He printed it on credit; the remaining issues were printed by Local No. 1 in Long Beach. I took the third issue in and the guy wanted to "peruse" it—in effect, to censor it. I asked him why, and he answered, "We don't want to get into trouble with anyone." I asked him who did he think he would get into trouble with, and he evaded the issue. They started acting funny and I decided to look for another printer. The police were watching us. One prisoner in San Quentin intercepted a memo to the warden from the Department of Corrections, which claimed that *The Anvil* was on the verge of exciting to violence. We were inciting men to unionize, not to violence.

SIPAPU: How was *The Anvil* distributed?

HALFORD: It was distributed in four ways. 1) It was smuggled into prison; 2) sent into prison by mail—but the recipients paid for it!; 3) sold at penology/criminology conventions, public events, Unitarian churches, hawked at schools; 4) through bookstores, head shops, etc. We printed 1500 copies for the first issue, 3000 for the second, 5000 for the third. We got letters from prisoners, and from their relatives; we got checks from prisoners "to use in the struggle against the prison system." There is no doubt that this paper set a precedent: this was the first organ of the convicted class in America. I know that this paper sparked off revolts in prisons around the country; it was in county jails and in Attica too. It was a cry for unity, struggle, and class solidarity against the oppressor. We saw ourselves as Third World, and now prisoners will never again be held down by intimidation and physical oppression. The political revolt for change and humanity has started, and it cannot be stopped.

SIPAPU: What is the future of the paper and who "owns" the paper?

HALFORD: The future of the paper will be left up to those who emerged out of the inferno of prison life and who decided that the paper is their struggle. The prisoners who have political consciousness and the personal courage to do something about it are the owners of the paper.

SIPAPU: What other prison papers exist in California?

HALFORD: None. Unless you mean the institutional papers approved by the warden. Those editors and writers I have little respect for; they are writers for death. They do not believe what they are saying; they are just "doing their number." In 1967 and 1968, there were two precursors to *The Anvil*. These were the *San Quentin Outlaw*—over a hundred guys shipped out of San Quentin for this; and the *Soledad Rebel,* whose writers suffered a similar fate.

SIPAPU: What are your future plans?

HALFORD: Freelance writing, and the continuing struggle to realize myself; perhaps largely as a consequence of prison, I will be forever committed against capitalism, and the thousand inhumanities it perpetrates.

COMMENT ON PRISON PAPERS: Halford is not quite correct in saying that there are no other papers devoted to the interests of prisoners. We have seen: *The Outlaw,* successor to *The Anvil,* published by the United Prisoners' Union at 1348 Seventh Avenue, San Francisco, CA 94122, a paper very much like its predecessor; the Committee for Prisoner Humanity and Justice *Newsletter,* a mimeo available from Room 37, 1029 Fourth Street, San Rafael, CA 94901; and *The Cage and the Doorkey,* a montage of articles and letters, from 21275 Casa Correo, Concord, CA 94921. *Corrections* is a mimeo published at 3189 Sixteenth Street, San Francisco, CA 94103. Largest, and possibly the best edited, is *The Penal Digest International,* a full tabloid of reports. Get it, 12 for $9, from P.O. Box 89, Iowa City, IA 52240. Volume 1, no. 3 has a questionnaire for librarians.

3 : 2

This selection comprises almost the whole of v. 3, no. 2, and is important because in it I meet three friends who have greatly influenced my later life.

Sanford Berman was working in Zambia when he published Prejudices and Antipathies, *and our correspondence began when he sent me a review copy. That correspondence has continued ever since. I warned him, as I warn all who ask me to review their work, that I would have to call the shots as I saw them; but he had no difficulty with that, and so the review, largely favorable, appeared just as it appears here. In retrospect I think I made too much of geographical conflicts, and my final philosophizing is not very helpful. Some changes I suggested have been made, by both Berman (now at Hennepin County Library, Minnesota) and the Library of Congress. In spite of occasional disagreements we have kept in touch, and in spite of initial resistance by the library leadership, Berman was finally given the Margaret Mann Citation for excellence in cataloging and classification (see* Sipapu, *v. 12, no. 1, p. 268).*

Len Fulton was a new friend when I drove up to his lovely home in Paradise, California. His wife had recently died in an automobile crash, which accounts for the vaguely apocalyptic tone of the whole interview. Len and I have also kept in touch, although his enterprise has greatly expanded and he has also got into local politics, so that he has little time for confidential chats any more. He has been enormously sustaining in times of trouble, critical when necessary, and as a small press figure he is towering and irreplaceable.

The illustrations for this issue were done by an old friend, Walt Stevens, whom I have known for over thirty years. He also did v. 10, no. 1. He and his wife Tuck live in Eugene, Oregon.

SANFORD BERMAN'S CHALLENGE: Berman, Sanford. *Prejudices and Antipathies: A Tract on the LC Subject Heads Concerning People.* Metuchen, NJ, The Scarecrow Press, 1971. — This is one of the most important books written for librarians in this decade. If we criticize it, we nevertheless suggest that every librarian read it attentively.

Tersely stated, Berman's point about the *Library of Congress Subject Headings* (7th edition, 1966; hereinafter called *LCSH*) is:

the LC list can only "satisfy" parochial, jingoistic Europeans and North Americans, white-hued, at least nominally Christian (and preferably Protestant) in faith, comfortably situated in the middle- and higher-income brackets, largely domiciled in suburbia, fundamentally loyal to the Established Order, and heavily imbued with the transcendent, incomparable glory of Western civilization. Further, it reflects a host of untenable—indeed obsolete and arrogant—assumptions with regard to young people and women. And exudes something less than sympathy or even fairness toward organized labor and the sexually unorthodox or "avant-garde."

Berman *proves* his point. And *how* he proves it: 228 pages of reasoned, devastating, witty and patient explanation of the one text that many librarians have found most difficult of all to master. A wealth of footnotes attends every other sentence; each contains extensive bibliographical references; nobody can say that Berman hasn't done his homework.

Berman's method is to isolate an *"Item"* or subject heading; criticize the heading or its cross- or other references for their ignorance of, or bias toward or against, creeds, races, sexes, life-styles, countries or events; and then suggest a *remedy,* in the form of a cancellation, a new heading, or a new reference. He supports his remedies by quotations or explanations, often derived from members of the group adversely affected. Thus he recommends AFRO-AMERICAN instead of NEGRO, rearranges the headings under WOMEN, and shows the persistence of stereotypes in headings relating to JEWS.

We cheered with delight as Berman, simplifying and clearing away deadwood, knocked down one obstacle after another: CHILDREN—MANAGEMENT, which suggests an illustration to Dickens; DISCOVERY AND EXPLORATION, with its suggestion that only whites discover things (how many have read Duyvendak's essay on China's discovery of East Africa during the Ming Dynasty, or seen the Chinese painting of a giraffe?); CONVERTS, with its implication that Christianity is the thing that you ought to get converted to; COMMUNIST STRATEGY, with its implication of a Great Red Spider in the Kremlin; MIXED BLOODS, which is patently bad biology; and dozens of others. Berman's critique, in short, merits our wholehearted approval, and we criticize him not for his good works, but for his failure to follow his own conclusions through to the end.

We will begin with what we perceive as problems, and go on to the ultimately revolutionary implications of his work,—implications which perhaps he has not completely understood. (Page references are to his book; his own page references are to *LCSH.*)

Item: YELLOW PERIL (p. 29). Berman says, "Such phraseology is of a piece with 'slope,' 'gook,' or 'chink,'" and recommends abolishing it without even a cross-reference. The phrase is even more dangerous than that. Berman should look up the term in *Webster's Third International Dictionary:* he would see that not even under EAST AND WEST or PAN-PACIFIC RELATIONS (his remedies), is there a heading adequate for this "scare tactic." *Remedy:* Introduce a heading: SCARE TACTICS (POLITICAL PSYCHOLOGY), and make this heading, YELLOW PERIL, xx references, while introducing a scope note, based on Webster's definition, under YELLOW PERIL.

Item: PAGANISM; PAGANISM IN LITERATURE; CIVILIZATION, PAGAN (p. 43). Berman considers the term "Christian chauvinist." If he will order a copy of the *Green Egg*, P.O.B. 2953, St. Louis, MO 63130, he will get the surprise of his life—and a chance to introduce some new subject headings.

Item: CHURCH, CHURCH HISTORY (p. 53). Again, a "Christian-centered" term. But one only used to denote a Christian community or a Christian building. A Moslem building is a *mosque;* the Buddhist community is the *Sangha.* Why not go all the way, and introduce comparable terms from the vernacular of other religions?

Item: GABRIEL PROSSER'S SLAVE REVOLT ... DENMARK VESEY'S SLAVE REVOLT; etc. (p. 70). Berman deserves acclaim for his wish to bring forward the names of Prosser, Vesey, and others, as revolutionaries. But putting the subject headings in this form means that the reader would look under VESEY, DENMARK for his life, and under DENMARK (!) for his revolt! How about WELLINGTON'S VICTORY, WATERLOO, 1815? No, battles in LC are rightly listed by place, not by victor, loser or participants. (We bet you don't even look under "Daniel" for Daniel SHAYS'S REBELLION.) A subject heading is not an index or an analytic, although specific cards may have added entries for significant leaders.

Item: INSULAR POSSESSIONS, TERRITORIAL POSSESSIONS, COLONIES (p. 96–9). Berman is right in saying that the U.S. has also undergone an imperialist era, and that many in the Virgin Islands, Puerto Rico, and Micronesia are intensely aware of it. Still, Britain calls her remaining dependent areas, or some of them, "colonies," and the U.S. still uses the terms "insular possessions." What's a colony, what's a possession? Take Hawaii: since 1960 a State of the Union, it was once an independent Polynesian kingdom, and today a significant proportion of its population is of Asian descent. Most of its wealth, however, is in the hands of whites. Is it in law a State, in fact a colony? What is the *exact* implication of each term?

Item: LEGENDS, ORIENTAL (p. 130). Berman does not go far enough. ORIENTAL, in most of its forms, and ORIENTALS, should be dropped entirely. The proper geographical form is ASIA, EASTERN. EAST (FAR EAST) should also be dropped. See Fodor's *Guide to Japan and East Asia, 1965* (New York, McKay, 1965), p. 15.

Item: WOMEN—RIGHTS OF WOMEN (p. 178). Berman can relax: as of September 1971, WOMEN'S LIBERATION MOVEMENT has been introduced as a new subject heading. But he better tauten up again: there's an x-reference from WOMEN'S LIB. A slang term as a cross-reference? Ridiculous!

Item: UNDERGROUND PRESS (p. 216). We prefer ALTERNATIVE PRESS or better yet FREEPRESS (one word: admittedly a neologism), for publications such as *Berkeley Tribe,* and *East Village Other,* which are anti-Establishment but circulated freely, and CLANDESTINE PRESS, CLANDESTINE LITERATURE, for publications which almost automatically expose their authors, publishers, and distributors to arrest.

Item: SINGLE PEOPLE: xx Chastity, Virginity (p. 226). Does Berman think this is a definition, or even an injunction? Or perhaps "this mournful truth is everywhere confessed," that single people have to stay chaste *faute de mieux.*

Clearly, Berman has opened a lot of windows. But has he opened enough? For example, in correcting white views about African civilization, he has said nothing about white misapprehensions about white civilization, as reflected in *LCSH.* Examples follow:

Item: CAUCASIAN RACE. sa Aryans; Mediterranean race; Semites; Teutonic race. x Caucasians; . . . White race.

Do white people come from the Caucasus Mountains? Is there anyone who can say in what part of the globe the races of man first appeared? When the period of European expansion first started, white people were found from Ireland to Japan (the Ainus). The idea of associating them with the Caucasus is surely outmoded; therefore our *remedy* is to cancel CAUCASIAN RACE, and to substitute (with sweeping and truly Bermanesque simplicity) WHITE RACE as the common subject heading, with appropriate cross-references.

Item: ANGLO-SAXON RACE. "Here are entered works on the nations of Anglo-Saxon descent."—If there's one thing we're tired of, it's the overuse of the term "Anglo-Saxon," and its slang derivative, "W.A.S.P." The Anglo-Saxons were a people who invaded Britain about the fourth century and held it till the Norman Conquest; philologists call their language Old English. We

suggest that the term be restricted accordingly, as it is in ANGLO-SAXON CIVILIZATION. English people today, and their kinfolk overseas, are a mixture of stocks: Celtic, Teutonic, Scandinavian, French and Flemish, and latterly Jewish, Indian and African. Anglo-Saxons, Berman, aren't the half of it. *Remedy:* Cancel ANGLO-SAXON RACE. Refer to COMMONWEALTH OF NATIONS, and introduce a new heading, ENGLISH-SPEAKING PEOPLES, with appropriate cross-references.

Mention of England and its peoples brings us to geographic headings. Neither *LCSH* nor Berman ever comes to grips with this problem, which touches the related question of author entries. For example, take the entry: "Russia *(1923-   U.S.S.R.).*" Visitors to American libraries from that country have pointed out the absurdity of that entry: the state established by Lenin is obviously here to stay. Nobody, after all, would make an author entry such as: "North America *(1776-   United States).*" Others have pointed out that the USSR contains many non-Russian peoples, as Letts, Lithuanians, Estonians, Kirghiz, etc. When you turn to the subject headings, all you find is RUSSIA, RUSSIA—HISTORY—REVOLUTION, 1917-1923, and RUSSIA—HISTORY—1923-   . None of these give any indication of the real name of the country today; if we use UNITED STATES, and GREAT BRITAIN, surely the equivalent form, is SOVIET UNION. The *remedy,* therefore, is to introduce SOVIET UNION as a subject heading, for works on Russia published since 1923, and as an author entry where similarly appropriate.

Item: ANGOLA (Berman, p. 114-120). Berman criticizes LC for not subdividing this heading by the terms—COLONIAL PERIOD and—NATIONAL LIBERATION MOVEMENT, and suggests introducing a see-reference from "Namibia" to AFRICA, SOUTHWEST, and another from "Zimbabwe (territory)" to RHODESIA. It is a pity that LC does not publish a geographical name authority file, with a history of the changes of names among certain countries (e.g. Zambia, Zaïre, Guyana). It might well have trouble doing so, for in many cases of disputed or unsettled territories the "right" name is a matter of violent controversy, one of what Berman calls "the colossal demands of our revolutionary age." (Berman, p. xii.) The librarian who responds to the cry of "Which side are you on?" (Berman, p. x) will be asked to choose between headings, or to choose which will be the main heading and which the cross-reference. Whichever he gives priority to, some party will be offended; if he avoids the issue, he will offend the party whose interests appear to be neglected. All right, class, which side are you on?

RHODESIA	or	ZIMBABWE?
BORINQUÉN	or	PUERTO RICO?
SOUTHWEST, NEW	or	AZTLÁN?
AZANIA	or	SOUTH AFRICA?
SOUTH TIROL	or	UPPER ADIGE?
NORTHERN IRELAND	or	ULSTER?
CHINA (REPUBLIC)	or	CHINA (PEOPLE'S REPUBLIC)?
ISRAEL	or	PALESTINE – HISTORY – ZIONIST OCCUPATION, 1948– ?
EDUCATION – INDIA – KASHMIR	or	EDUCATION – PAKISTAN – KASHMIR?
SOUTHERN STATES (U.S.)	or	REPUBLIC OF NEW AFRICA?

And don't forget, that in a large research library catalog, every time those areas are used as subdivisions they will have to be tracked down and altered.

It may seem as if we are inventing or multiplying difficulties. But if we are to recognize the "demands of our revolutionary age," they will have to be faced, and faced squarely. If we are to take the demands of Black nationalists in the southern U.S. seriously, we shall have to make some kind of entry or cross-reference for REPUBLIC OF NEW AFRICA. If we do so, we will run into possible objections from Southern taxpayers. Which side *are* we on?

From all this, it should be clear that to "Bermanize" the subject headings in a large library, the librarian will be obliged to follow one of a number of possible directions:

1. He may elect to change subject headings only, either by erasing and retyping, or by moving blocks of cards intact and typing and filing guide cards and cross-references. This will be most particularly opportune if the catalog is to be divided. Even so, this will be a large and on-going project;

as we have shown, Berman has only begun the task of exposing racism, sexism, and other prejudices and antipathies in *LCSH*. In doing so he will be undoubtedly taking sides; if he eliminates the xx references to "Criminal law" and "Offenses against the person" under ABORTION, he will delight some and enrage others. He must be prepared to face this.

2. He may elect to change *some* author and geographical headings, with the result that many cards using geographical subdivisions will have to be tracked down and altered.

3. He will have to prepare and defend a budget allocation of staff time and resources, for this long-term project. Unfortunately, Berman nowhere gives cost details of his own experience in this work, nor explains how current books can be added to the shelf while at least some time is devoted to recataloging. A comparative study in this direction would be useful. The librarian will also have to overcome their (usually hidden) prejudices and antipathies in order to gain their full support for the project. Hiring and promotions will follow accordingly.

4. Finally, he may elect to close the catalog: a term meaning, "We did it this way up to 1 July 1972; since then, all cards have been done differently, but we won't go back and change the old ones." This compromise may be adopted by many larger libraries; a rumor is circulating that the Library of Congress may close its own catalog (see "Overdue," *Wilson Library Bulletin,* April 1972).

What the individual librarian may do we cannot predict. We noted with interest, however, some less-publicized features of Berman's book,—namely the quotations on p. iii. One of these is from Sidney L. Jackson: "It is high time to tackle the subject headings." With this we can all agree; there are problems even with less controversial headings (e.g. EUROPEAN WAR, 1914-1918, and its many subdivisions). The other two are from Confucius (or a Confucian proverb) and from Bertolt Brecht.

Both Confucius and Brecht were profoundly human-hearted men with a great trust in common sense and decency; still, the differences in their lifestyles, the difference between the advisor to monarchs and the exiled man of the theatre, are almost as great as their resemblances. We discern a touch of both in Berman; sometimes he clears away simple obfuscation and ignorance, and decently calls things by their right names; sometimes he invites us to take sides, to place ourselves fearlessly in alignment with the revolutionary demands of our age, and to refuse to pander to other people's outworn prejudices. Which side is Berman on?

Perhaps he is on the side of challenge and change. In this regard he strikes us as being oddly like Marshall MacLuhan, although he might well disclaim the comparison. Yet both of them have learned, from their experience in a region far from the traditional centers of Western culture, or (in Berman's case) in the center of a different culture, that Western culture diminishes in force as its peripheries are approached. Both of them have published books to tell us of their important discoveries, and in each case their styles—aphoristic in the one, populist in the other—are part of their messages.

To sum up: The implications of Berman's book are clear. Words are fighting words, even (or especially) words on subject cards; the individual librarian has a responsibility to do something about them, even if this means a reordering of priorities. He must not pander to the social backgrounds and intellectual levels of his more ignorant or badly-brought-up or brainwashed readers, but take the lead in dispelling their prejudices and antipathies by a thorough, if long-term, housecleaning of his subject catalog.

We reply that this housecleaning, while in many ways highly desirable, is much larger than even Berman has suggested; that it will affect far more than a single department of a large library, or more than a few cards; and that it should be undertaken only after careful consideration and debate, both within a single library and in the profession at large.

Sipapu cannot sustain this debate. We simply haven't the space. We therefore invite our larger, better-funded sister publications, such as *Library Journal, Synergy,* and *Wilson Library Bulletin,* to devote an issue to Berman's question, with contributions from the most eminent scholars, and ample space for Berman to refute and elucidate. Short reviews (like this one) are not enough. We join with Berman in a plea for *dialogue* and *action.*

EXTERMINATION OF THE TRIBE: We interrupt this program to announce the death of the *Berkeley Tribe.* Born out of the *Berkeley Barb* in 1969, and initially more successful than the *Barb,* it formally announced its own end in an undated issue published some time in early May, 1972. Reasons for folding: the difficulties a very idealistic staff had in relating to each other, plus the fact that sales dropped from 45,000 to 7,000. The people, more liberal or perhaps more skeptical than the editors, simply stopped reading the *Tribe;*

at any rate, they were not into the issue-oriented organizing that the *Tribe* seemed to urge on them. The Red Mountain Tribe still exists, as does the *Barb*. We predict that the RMT will split to do their own thing.

THE LIFE, DEATH, AND RESURRECTION OF THE LITTLEMAG: *DUSTbooks* is a small-press imprint that covers three lines of publishing activity: a literary periodical *(DUST)*, a series of chapbooks of both prose and poetry, and a series of trade periodicals which detail information about the books, literary magazines, authors and editors of the small and underground presses. Since the early sixties, the publisher, Len Fulton, has been fully committed to getting contemporary literature into print, and to researching and defining its sources and vehicles.

Mr. Fulton's name is well known to librarians throughout the United States and Canada, for with the 7th edition of his *Directory of Little Magazines and Small Presses*, he continues an invaluable service to the Republic of Letters. A fascinating article by him on the small presses of the sixties, with special attention to concrete poetry and the "meat poets," appeared under the title "Anima rising: little magazines in the sixties," in the January 1971 issue of *American Libraries*. It contained a 113-item bibliography, as well as a plea to librarians not to ignore the littlemags, nor to expect of them the bibliographical consistency you expect of large popular magazines. It makes essential reading for all librarians, especially those who stopped reading poetry with the death of T.S. Eliot.

Instead of quoting from that article, surely available at your nearest library, we give you some words that appeared in his own periodical, *Small Press Review*, in January 1970: "The main point of disjunction between the old and the new where we are lodged seems to me to be a vision of man as an extension of structure, of form, on the one hand, and a vision of him as an extension of energy, or process, on the other. This is an interface to which science adjusted itself long ago, at least in part, going from static to dynamic theories. . . . The mind at work is more like a movie camera than a still one. You do not stop a river to know its character, or the wind, or freeze the heart motionless."

Fulton is a tall slender man with a mustache, who lives in a foothill town in northern California, and who is frequently seen astride a horse. We take you now to 5218 Scottwood Road, Paradise, CA 95969, for an interview with Len Fulton:

SIPAPU: Tell us your essentials: birth, parentage, education, and how you got started in littlemags.

FULTON: Two people were born in Lowell, Massachusetts: Jack Kerouac and myself. My father is a Scotsman from Canada, my mother of French extraction from Pennsylvania. I lived in 17 towns before I was 17, spent two years at the University of Maine, and went broke publishing three weekly newspapers in that State. I worked for the first offset daily in New

York, and then came West: B.A. 1961 at the University of Wyoming, later graduate work in psychology in Berkeley. I broke off a Ph.D. program there because I was tired of rat mazes and Skinner boxes, and preferred the subject of Freud's literary roots. I had a family, so I went to work as a biostatistician in the California Department of Public Health in Berkeley, and stayed there seven years. I've recently started fooling with a master's at Chico State College in English. — How did I get into littlemags? It's hard to say why you do these things: fortunately most people don't plan their lives but just seem to find themselves involved in something. In 1963 I and a half-dozen other people started a little magazine named *DUST*, the same year the underground press started with the *L.A. Free Press*. Something was cooking. Littlemags exploded all over at about the same time. I wrote twenty articles for Kunkin of the *Free Press* on the small press scene. Not long after I got into *DUST*, I discovered that a small press is essentially a one-man life-style; the essence of an individual. The small press is the outgrowth of a person's experience and outlook. As a result, trying to do *DUST* with six people, even though it was intended to be cosmic in its implications, we broke down; ultimately the most dominant person tended to impose his viewpoint on the magazine. And so, in the ten years since its inception, *DUST* has really had only one publisher: me.

SIPAPU: You're editing other things now . . . *Small Press Review, Directory of Little Magazines:* how did you get into these?

FULTON: Somewhere back there I became self-consciously interested in the *production of literature.* My concerns enlarged on me — almost without my knowing it. I found it terribly agreeable to be in touch with other small pressmen, to know what they were doing. Something in me dispermits my holding focus on just my own things. My sights inevitably rise. The human drama of *how* literature gets produced is fascinating and vital as an art form laid over other art forms. So anyway I have been plotting this publishing process; and some of what gets done around here is the rudimentary form of it — like the *Directory of Little Magazines* which started in 1964–5, or the *Directory of Editors* which started three or four years ago, or the *Small Press Record of Books.* You can't do anything without knowledge. Some of what I do on the other hand is more fully a part of the very process which it seems to plot — like the *Small Press Review,* which started in 1966, and which has sought to show stages, energies and directions in this process. The Committee of Small Magazine Editors and Publishers (COSMEP) is an outgrowth of this too — I'm not alone, you know, in these self-conscious interests. When Jerry Burns moved to Berkeley in mid-1967 the idea of a conference of editors was about the first thing that came up between us. Incidentally Burns also typeset the 3d edition of the magazine directory and a couple of issues of the *Small Press Review.* It took us 13 months to go from idea to happening with the first COSMEP conference (Berkeley, 1968). The organization itself came out of a panel on distribution: Harry Smith, Hugh Fox, D.R. Wagner, Doug Blazek, and myself. We later sat in Larry Blake's Rathskeller and wrote up a proposal for a $15,000 grant (which we didn't get) to establish a distribution agency for little magazines. Later that year Burns, Richard Morris and I set the thing up formally. Incorporation was blocked in California for technical reasons, but was completed in New York in December, 1971. We've had conferences each year: Ann Arbor, 1969: Buffalo, 1970; San Diego, 1971; Madison, Wisconsin, June 6–10, 1972. We have about 300 member presses.

And so, plotting a drama. At some level I suppose I'm literariopathic—more interested in the *how* than the *what* of literature. I'd rather err on the side of inclusion—it's too easy to become aesthetically constipated. Life's too short to be a bigot. I've been working out an aesthetic theory for years, and have developed a notion about artistic process and form which I call a "psychogeometry." This will be the central notion in my theory if I ever finish it. But I'll be damned if I'll let such a thing make a narrow-minded elitist out of me—I'll leave that to critical theory. Learning stops where dogma begins. Habit is the ballast that chains the dog to his vomit, says Samuel Beckett.

SIPAPU: When and why did you move to Paradise?

FULTON: We came here in January, 1969. I have to spend at least half my life outdoors or my system rebels. That happened to me one day in Los Angeles in 1968. The bureaucracy had chewed me up in some neurological fashion—so I quit. We looked all over Oregon and northern California and finally settled here as a place we could afford. It's an interesting old town, a gold-mining town originally, and gambling. It's name was Pair o' Dice.

SIPAPU: Staff? technical and financial details?

FULTON: Staff: high school and freshman college women, paid by the hour. I had a paid editor for *DUST* for seventeen months. Printing is farmed out. Typesetting is done on an IBM Selectric; layout, paste-up and design is done by me, although occasionally I will buy artwork. Financial details: I earned money from the bureaucracy, and have poured it into this work, and I am still pouring. The only thing that I've ever done that has broken even is the *Directory of Little Magazines,* and that is because it combines the best of all possible worlds; it's useful, and also it's done with some sense of quality. Quantity is secondary; also it's done with some sense of quality. Quantity is secondary; I want accuracy of information. I sell advertising in it, and sell it wholesale to jobbers and agents. It is also being used in creative writing classes. It defrays some expenses on other trade items I publish: *Small Press Record of Books, Directory of Small Magazine Editors and Publishers*—this last a companion volume to the *Directory of Little Magazines.* The *Directory of Small Magazine Editors and Publishers* gives information not found in the *Directory of Little Magazines:* the editors' views of themselves and their work. The *Small Press Record of Books* is arranged by author, gives publisher, size, price, etc., the 2d edition (March, 1972) is more comprehensive and more international.

I do an annual survey to keep listings current and edit the answers. Much of the information is in my head — I can tell what is still alive, which mag died two years ago, etc.

SIPAPU: In your head? What happens if the Great Hand descends and spirits you away from us?

FULTON: Die, you mean...

SIPAPU: Yes, I've wondered that with *Sipapu* even. What if my BMW takes it in mind to run into the big ditch on Road 31?

FULTON: Hmm. Maybe you should sell insurance! I can't worry about death because it would mess me up in life. One of Alan Watts's more likely wisdoms is that death has elements of glory only if it is taken as the last step in life. He does not say, as I happen to think, that it is also absurd. But then, glory itself is one of the most imposing of absurdities. So, if you ruin your life worrying about dying, then you are just absurd — no trace of glory remains. My wife, as you know, was killed in an auto accident at 31, so I've been as close to death as anyone. The romantic part of death disappeared for me right then. Death is one of the great literary themes, but for me it is an empty, hollow reduction to nothingness in the final Beckett sense. When it really happens to you, the whole literary side of death seems to evaporate. But the world goes on when I die or you die — and that includes the littlemags.

SIPAPU: We understand you have a war with the U.S. Postal Service.

FULTON: I guess you could call it that, though locally I've been able to get along, once we've established just which of us knows more about his trade. But the Postal Service doesn't work — not just for the small presses, but for the American people. By raising postage, especially first class and other special classes, the Government impedes our communication with each other. When you get down to the third and fourth classes, used by the small independent presses, usurious rates violate our freedom of the press, because this freedom implies being able to get stuff out to those who want it, as well as just to print it. Just being able to print it is like saying free speech means you're just free to say what you want in your own house. The small press is the actualization of the free-press guarantee because its *raison d'être* is dissent from some established view. And free speech belongs exclusively to the dissenter. The right to agree is nothing.

I've asked the ACLU in New York to help me enter a class suit against the U.S. Postal Service to make it stop violating these First Amendment rights of the small presses. I claim that the Postal Service makes money on first class, and third class junk mail. Second class — and we speak here of *Life, Look* and *Time* — represents an over-500-million-dollar deficit. The lobbyists for the big magazines have been successful for decades in seeing to it that everyone but them paid for their tonnage. Now, as that lobbying program seems to be collapsing, they are mounting a very effective public tear-jerking campaign about their plight—well before that alleged 123% in second class service goes through. There is even a cadaver to show: *Look.* This will probably blunt the public's sense of their own plight with first class. That is the design anyway, and I hope it doesn't work. I've had correspondence with *Life* over the issue: they are very brilliant in their own defense. I make it a habit never to underestimate the genius these big magazines can call up. If I didn't know that they've made billions in this century getting us all to pay for these second-class privileges I would almost be moved to pity.

SIPAPU: So what do you think should be done?

FULTON: Second-class mail, or some of it, should be privately incorporated by the users, a whole separate postal system. The rest of the postal service should be simply subsidized by taxes. A first-class letter should be a nickel at most—6 cents for air mail because air mail is cheap—the cost has always been under the price. I'll have a special issue of *Small Press Review* on the subject, as I have made a good sample-survey of the small presses, and I am convinced that we are all in the same troubled waters.

I think the employees should be paid better and the work humanized. My friend John Bennett of *Vagabond* has written a grim account of his personal experiences working for the U.S. Postal Service, which will be in that *SPR* issue. These employees are strictly fourth class in a Federal scheme that *does* pay some bureaucrats very well. The U.S. Postal Service is simply a giant American corporation that has tried to legislate its competitors out of business.

SIPAPU: Have you a word for us librarians?

FULTON: I've always assumed, and found it to be true, that librarians are among our most intelligent, likeable and peaceful people. Their hearts are good, their spirits right. They are human and essentially egalitarian, and I think we swell pressmen have in the past accused them unjustly of being obeisant or weak. As much as anybody else running a small press I'd like to find a *bête noire*, but personal experience tells me its *not* a librarian.

There is in a library, as you know better than I, a demand for compulsion. A library practically embodies the obsessive-compulsive force of a culture. All the rigor a taxonomic society can muster comes to a head in the library, as well it ought to, otherwise we have chaos among the very records of our learning. Still, a library is a great place for hanky-panky, frivolous

frolicking through the great tiers of the best insulation in the world! It is an erotic environment, right there at the very thalamus of rational man! Libraries are a turn-on. Is that weird? But as regards the littlemags, I do think a compulsive serials syndrome is handicapping. Some librarians no doubt see *us* as the *bête noire;* and it is a testament to their perspicuity and our perseverance that we get into libraries at all. A serials librarian would do well to remember that the origin of the small press is in dissent, and that vitality is more valued than consistency of any kind.

One thing I bet—librarians read a lot more out of the small mags than out of the other stuff they get in. One time I walked into the Harriman Library in Buffalo to see why the hell they were always claiming issues of *DUST* or *Small Press Review*. I mentioned *DUST* and about three clerks hollered from down the line, so I walked over and asked them if they read it. They said they did when no one was looking. I take it library employees can't read on the job or something. Crazy! Like working in a brewery but being scolded for taking a swig now and again. Libraries should offer bonuses to people who will read what they file a couple hours a day.

I know librarians are up against the money problem, but in the case of a small mag, if they have reasonable assurance of its existence they should just risk the subscription money and not spend twice that amount verifying or claiming. A once-a-year claim on all overdue stuff should get as much result as four times a year. As a publisher I frown very darkly on librarians who send claims for stuff actually stolen. I think every library ought to have experts on small press material—people who know the sources and are at least passingly familiar with the contents. I've always wanted to make an odyssey for a year or more just going from library to library and holding seminars on the small presses. Do you think it would work?

SIPAPU: Why not? If you have no staff, the assaults of the library bureaucracy are like the hours mentioned in the old sundial motto: *Vulnerant omnes, ultima necat:* all wound, the last mortally. But before we all expire, what do you think is the future of the littlemag movement as related to the freepress and the counter-culture generally?

FULTON: In spirit of course the underground press papers are our allies in a cause. In the so-called marketplace they are competitors. They produce content with sensation and mercantility. They shove us off the newsstands—one friend of mine insists they are an enemy and will have to be contended with. It is dismaying to go from bookstore to bookstore looking for a small press book or magazine and find in each place the stands and shelves groaning with newspapers. They certainly do pack a social wallop that is often confused as a cultural one. The best of them are often done by ex-magazine people, like Robert Head of *Nola Express*. The now-defunct *Nickel Review* was more *like* a magazine. Kois of *Kaleidoscope* did a magazine before he did a newspaper. A little magazine seems to be a process wherein lie the elements of future artistic *form;* in the freepress lie those early elements of future artistic *content.* Power rules the moment but thought rules the ages, someone said. The little magazine is a more sluggish genre than the paper, and it will endure ages of experimental journalism. As regards this, if we are still talking to librarians, they should remember to be less trendy, and understand that a newspaper has a lot less future library value than a magazine—but that the magazine collection is every bit as hard—harder—to assemble after the fact. A librarian came here from The Netherlands and was astonished when I let him go through my newspapers and take what he wanted. He spent a great deal of time searching and sorting. It's wrongheaded.

SIPAPU: Advice to anybody starting a little magazine...?

FULTON: First of all, I believe that every single individual in the world ought to publish his own magazine, just as everyone should write his own poems. But beyond that, if a person has to ask that question and take the answer seriously, than he's not ready to do his own magazine. A littlemag is something you do, not because you want to, but because you must. Every man his own organ.

SIPAPU: An organ is something you use to express life...

FULTON: Hey, do you know what the French word for orgasm is? *Un peu de mort.*

NOTES TO OUR FEATURE ARTICLES: 100 copies only have been printed of: *Subject Headings Employed at the Makarere Institute of Social Research Library, A Select List, February 1972,* compiled by Sanford Berman. Write P.O. Box 16022, Kampala, Uganda. — For a further discussion of the small magazines vs. the U.S. Postal Service, see pp. 42-43 of *Newsweek,* 3 July 1972 (the one with Joseph Papp on the cover). We are advised that the unnamed House subcommittee that heard the reports will not be printing them until August at the earliest; nor does it say whether Fulton was there, and at press time we were unable to reach him. But the case for the littlemag seems to have been spelled out well enough, if *Newsweek* can be trusted. — *Free,* the magazine of travelling, living, and being, is not free. You have to shell out $2.98 for 4 seasonal issues. It is a thumb-tripper's and easy rider's periodical, whose most valuable part is a Crashers' Directory. No. 1, Spring/Summer 1972, comes from 704 Santa Monica Boulevard, Santa Monica, CA 90401 (you were expecting Avon, SD?) — The 11th issue, v. 3, no. 3, of Fulton's *Small Press Review* is done entirely by and for women. It is superb. Begin with this issue if you are not already a subscriber.

4 : 1

The interview with Laurence Leamer was done by mail, he answering from his home in Maryland. I've never met Leamer, and regret having lost track of him.

Hugh Fox, a small press publisher from way back, and a frequent member of COSMEP's Board of Directors, sent me a contribution which was unsolicited and welcomed anyway. He was astounded when I paid him for it. Fox teaches English at Michigan State University.

I don't think that the California Library Association will ever meet at Disneyland again. We were promised that we would have the place all to ourselves one evening — just CLA and "one other group" — but this group, designated only by a string of initials, turned out to be a huge mob of grammar-school kids, ages roughly 8 to 12, thousands of them, mobbing entrances, jamming exits, screaming and pushing. It was like the French Revolution in miniature, with all the participants no taller than five feet. The librarians, many of whom were no longer young and therefore unable to cope, fled. The only compensation for this conference was that I first met Sanford Berman. I think the reason he wore a badge saying "People's Librarian" was that he was currently unemployed.

This issue was consecutive issue no. 7, January 1973.

THE RETURN OF SANFORD BERMAN: Our long essay-review, in the last issue, of Sanford Berman's *Prejudices and Antipathies* provoked a friendly reply, followed by clippings and annotations, from that redoubtable author. He sticks by his guns in criticizing the Library of Congress subject heading YELLOW PERIL; and indicates that in his revised list of subject headings, for use in the Library of the Makarere Institute of Social Research, Makarere University, Kampala, Uganda, the term ORIENTAL ... was replaced by ASIA, ... ASIAN. We also have been given to understand that the MISR Library's *Bulletin,* of which he was the editor, has been suspended "for reasons of finance and integrity." A supplement to his book appears in a periodical entitled *Ugandan Libraries* (v. 1, no. 1, September 1972) which would be of general interest to those who care about the profession in tropical countries. (Address: East African School of Librarianship, Makarere

University, P.O. Box 7062, Kampala, Uganda). Berman and his family returned to the U.S. about the time that issue was published.

LEAMER AND THE MOVEMENT PRESS: *Sipapu*'s Book of the Year for 1972 is Laurence Leamer's *The Paper Revolutionaries: The Rise of the Underground Press* (N.Y.: Simon and Schuster, 1972). In our opinion, it supersedes all previous accounts of this, our central subject, and amounts to a definitive statement of where we are now in the freepress field, as described by a man of integrity and sense who has apparently seen the Movement press from the inside.

"The history of the underground press," writes Leamer, "is not a simple success story. 'We blew it,' says Captain Billy American in *Easy Rider,* and his remark could stand as an epitaph for each generation of underground papers. They blew it by accepting the hippie myth. They blew it by thinking drugs could be a panacea. They blew it by jumping at the idea of a Marxist revolution. They fail, and they fail, and they fail again, and they move on, taking something from each experience, learning more about freedom and how to create an indigenous radicalism, and carrying with them a richer and more varied Movement" (p. 19). Leamer, in short, is neither uncritical nor cynical.

Leamer's opening chapters tell us about the early days of John Wilcock, Max Scherr, Paul Krassner, about the papers they founded and their importance as "Originators" and "Precursors." There are anecdotes and quotations from their tabloids, as well as illustrations of sample pages, but in each case there is an analysis of the contents of each paper, the stands the editors took, and the consequences for their audience. For example, when Leamer comes to Arthur Kunkin and the *Los Angeles Free Press* (p. 27), he gives you the exact date that Kunkin started distributing the *Freep,* — May Day 1964, describes Kunkin's background with *The Militant,* correctly analyzes the "weekend leftist" character of his audience, mentions the paper's rise in seven years to the rank of second-largest paid circulation among weekly newspapers in the U.S., critiques the paper for style and content, and summarizes its contents and achievements before moving on, briskly, to Max Scherr and the *Berkeley Barb.* The eventual fate of both the publishers and their papers is told in "Postmortem on the First Generation": from becoming successful one-man journalists they became unsuccessful entrepreneurs, — their staffs in revolt, their books in the red, denounced as "pigs" by Movement journalists and many of their audience. Thus the First Generation "blew it" on the leadership question: how could you preach revolution or even socialism and still be a boss with a score of employees and a profit motive? You couldn't, and out of the failure of the single capitalist approach the communal tribal paper was born.

In the meanwhile, a strain had arisen between "The Heads and the Fists," as Leamer calls them: the cultural underground, with its visions of trees, grass, music, and love vs. the political underground, the angry students of Marx, Marcuse and Fanon, who printed papers attacking the President and the police, glorified the urban guerrilla and waved the flags of North Vietnam and the National Liberation Front. Typical of the cultural underground was the *San Francisco Oracle,* whose original "Human Be-In" on New Year's Day, 1967, was strictly apolitical, and frustrating to the radicals who were present. Typical of the political underground was the Liberation News Service, founded in 1967 as a split-off from the anarchic Underground Press Service by Ray Mungo and the late Marshall Bloom. Both LNS and UPS are still going, but the LNS acts as a news distribution service, and is serious about its Marxist politics; the UPS remains a cooperative of various underground or semi-straight hip papers. The *Oracle,* meanwhile, switched hands and subsequently died, its editors moved into meditation or small press publishing, and the Haight-Ashbury it had helped build up became (not by its intention) a hideous slum of teen-age drug addicts.

In the second phase of the underground press, described by Leamer in "The Arming of the Cultural Vision" and "The Arming of the Political Vision," the Marxists took over and organized campuses and cities, using their papers as a base. Leamer makes the point that in many places the Movement was the paper, the paper was the Movement: publishing a paper was the way you made revolution. These chapters analyze the rise of the Yippie movement, and its varying expression in the *Rag* (Austin, Texas), the *Rat* (Columbia University), the *Berkeley Tribe* (a staffers' paper splitting off from the *Barb* in revolt against Max Scherr). For some, the nucleus was a local SDS chapter; for others, a local anti-war movement *(The Great Speckled Bird,* Atlanta, whose title is ultimately derived from Jeremiah 12:9). Here are accounts of Tom Forcade's great pie-throw at the President's Commission on Obscenity and Pornography (May 1970), of the strike at Columbia, and of a lamentable non-interview with Janis Joplin. ("What do I want with an interview in a little old hippie publication?" she told her visitors from *Rat.* She had already talked with *Life, Look, Time* and *Holiday* over the past two days in New York. "Look, if you can convince my publicity manager it's important, I'll do it." The underground journalists gave up and went back to Texas.)

In "Post-mortem on the Second Generation" Leamer points out how the Marxist revolutionary papers slowly got ahead of the people. Those who applauded the Weathermen because their acts would force the middle class "to make an existential choice—either for or against the revolution" (p. 115), found that not only the middle class but their own workers made a choice *against* the revolution when it appeared that the revolution could only be bought at the price of bombings. Even the Weathermen eventually repudiated their "military error," and the Red Mountain Tribe found that their paper's circulation was falling, as the "street people" on Berkeley's Telegraph Avenue, for whom it was written, gradually lost interest in it. After contrasting (with examples) the *Tribe*'s style with that of the old *New Masses,* Leamer writes "In their passion, the *Tribe*'s revolutionary journalists had forgotten that fundamental distinction between rhetoric and reportage.... The paper was full of the casual invective that calls a cop a 'pig' and thinks it has said something." A long quotation, "Life in the Movement," from *Old Mole* (Boston), sums up the personal and psychological problems of revolutionary journalism brilliantly.

However, don't get the idea that Leamer is out to put the freepress down. In the chapter "Repression," and again in "The Mass Media and the Underground Press," Leamer writes of the attempted suppression of the *Los Angeles Free Press,* followed by hasslings and censorship in San Diego, Houston, Atlanta, and other cities. He documents and denounces the casual and even contemptuous attitude of straight pressmen toward the underground press. The city editor of the *Los Angeles Times* said of the *Los Angeles Free Press,* at the opening of the trial of Kunkin's paper for publishing the names of the agents of the California State Bureau of Narcotics: "For what they did they got what was coming to them." It took conviction and appeal in that case before the *Times* realized that what happened to the *Freep* might happen to them too. Here and elsewhere, Leamer makes the point that cannot be made too often: that if an underground newspaper had published the Pentagon Papers, the Papers would have been confiscated, the freepressmen would have been hurried off to prison, and we would have little more knowledge of Daniel Ellsberg's revelations than we do of early Etruscan literature.

Speaking of Awful Revelations, one of Leamer's most appalling is about *Newsweek* (for which Leamer once worked). He gives a long excerpt from its issue of 12 October 1970, detailing life in a Colorado training camp for guerrillas, said to be so high in the mountains that it is "above the clouds most of the time." Up there, supposedly, the young revolutionaries were being trained for The Day. Although *Newsweek* is, as Leamer admits, "one of our best and most innovative magazines," the long story falls of its own weight: how were the guerrillas managing to survive up in the stratosphere? (To our knowledge, the only mountains with near-permanently cloud-free tops are in the tropics, such as Mauna Kea with its astronomical observatory. Even Mount Everest collects clouds.) Besides, wouldn't the Cloud 9 activity have been spotted by jet pilots from (among other places) the U.S. Air Force Academy at Colorado Springs? Frankly the whole story has a touch of the comic strip: Shangri-La seized by Trashman. It would all be very funny if *Newsweek* did not have a reputation for integrity and accuracy to maintain. Somebody was high, all right, but it was way up above the clouds on Madison Avenue.

Finally, Leamer takes up "The Cosmetic Bohemians": *Screw, The New York Review of Sex, Rags,* and other publications which degrade "the revolution of the spirit" from grooving together and making love down to buying cassettes and drinking Coke: the co-opt cadres. Quite properly he begins with Du Maurier's *Trilby,* and goes on to a shrewd analysis of *Rolling Stone's* adventures into politics (they were least appreciated by their audience when they were most perceptive), and then to the rise and demise of *Rags,* the hip fashion mag. Here the acid in his pen etches details clearly.

And the Third Generation of the underground press? Leamer says it has only begun. Writing in early 1972 he says, "These days there are many soothsayers of doom predicting the imminent demise of the Movement and the underground press. What they forget is that the Movement has fallen into discouragement and despair . . . only to be reborn . . . with renewed energy and strength. . . . There may still be a revolution coming." Too shrewd to give us a timetable of change, he admits that the revolution "may be successfully resisted," and warns us against falling too easily into the cultural anarchism in which the dopehead, happy with his friends, can forget about the war. He warns us too, against believing in the ultimate triumph of the good guys: the cultural and political freaks alike might be driven into a corner, talking only to themselves and lashing out at everybody else.

Still, Leamer's note is one of optimism. Have twelve months destroyed or dulled it? Mr. Leamer has kindly answered our questions, written from his pad (high above the clouds?) in Maryland:

SIPAPU: Let's begin at the beginning, go on till we come to the end, then stop. Your birth, parentage, education? Are you any relation to Laurence E. Leamer, the economist? How did you learn to write?

LEAMER: I was born in Chicago at the beginning of the Second World War. Yeah, that's my father, he's an economist. So's my brother, who's 3 years younger. My little brother just graduated from college. I guess I learned to write by writing. I went to Antioch. My friends were in the hip literary set, you might say, but I was always too awed by those New York City types ever really to try to write. My father was teaching at Harpur College in upstate New York and I was very much a small town boy. When I graduated I went into the Peace Corps to go to Nepal, — that was in 1964, — more out of a sense of adventure than of idealism. I was stationed in what was probably the most remote placement in the Peace Corps: two days' walk from the nearest road, one day's walk from any kind of communication. I really dug Nepal; smoked a lot of good stuff, walked so many places: one summer 500 miles to the top of the country to live with Sherpas. I love Nepal so, even now: they are a blessed people and gave me so much joy. When I got out I got this Ford Fellowship that was to be used at the University of Oregon. That's where I met Eliana, my wife, who's a teacher of emotionally disturbed people, and that's where I started to write. I was grossed out by graduate school. I wrote a piece about the anti-war activities of returned PCV's; we leafletted, talked, did stuff like that. Then I did a piece for the *New Republic* on George

Wallace, which whetted my appetite for writing, so I went to Columbia Journalism School. I didn't have any bread, but I guess they liked the idea of giving a fellowship to somebody from Oregon. My book, by the way, is dedicated to a dear old friend of mine from Antioch who OD'd in the Haight a few months before the Summer of Love.

SIPAPU: Your connection with the Movement?

LEAMER: My connections with the Movement? I guess, in the first place, to have gone to Antioch in the 1960's was like being in boot camp for the counter-culture. There were the kinds of cultural and political concerns there that a few years later would become a mass movement. I'm really not ashamed of having served in the Peace Corps; I learned a great deal, though, from what we know now, — or should know now, about American foreign policy; I sure wouldn't recommend it any longer. I returned to this country and found it ever so much nearer to Vietnam than Nepal ever was. Those napalmed bodies looked a lot like the people I lived with. I didn't have the guts to be a draft resister, — few of us did; and I believe that if we had, thousands of us, — the war would have been over long ago. I was over in Bangladesh earlier this year and I saw what a nation of young people can do. Shit, I don't mean picking up the gun in the U.S.; I mean as a moral force, in this country a much better weapon, when fortified with political courage and energy. I did some stuff in the anti-war movement, — not anything I would ever tell my children about, — but some stuff.

SIPAPU: Your account is entirely concerned with the middle-class white rebels. Did you exclude the others because you found it would have doubled the size of the book, or because you were rejected by women and Third World people?

LEAMER: No, my book was specifically about the lily-white youth culture movement. I really didn't have enough time to deal with other elements. I did talk to some women's papers but that was just emerging when I finished my research.

SIPAPU: Did you publish at Antioch?

Did you split from *Newsweek* over a crisis, or did the grant from the Twentieth Century Fund just come along?

LEAMER: No, as I said, I never wrote until I was out in Oregon. *Newsweek* and I didn't hit it off too well. That experience radicalized me, for I saw what enormous harm this mass media pabulum was doing. I saw what bullshit it was, how everybody with any integrity left realized it was bullshit, but that it just continued. I saw that nobody had any power, nobody any true responsibility. The whole thing was not to be wrong: fuck being right. I was lucky to get the grant from the Twentieth Century Fund. I was supposed to go to India to write a biography of Indira Gandhi at that time; but I did the underground press book instead.

SIPAPU: Cultural vs. political revolution is a big theme of yours. In the light of the Nixon re-election, which way do you predict for the Movement? Or is the whole issue dead for another ten or twenty years?

LEAMER: Wow! I like that quote in the book by John Dos Passos: that the Movement is that wave of insurgency that has kept this country free. I *don't* think things are dead for twenty years; but I think things are going to be quiet. The Movement depended so much on the media that it became convinced it was so much bigger than it ever was. Things are happening all over, though: new ideas, new papers, new people. Once that vision of apocalypse is gone, — of immediate apocalypse anyway, — maybe we're better off. We really need information right now, — ideas, themes. That's why librarians and libraries, books and magazines, and the media, are so important. All kinds of things are happening in this country, and we need ways and tools to find out what they are, — to communicate.

SIPAPU: If you were given the capital, would you found another paper now? What would you do with it, and whom would you ask to help you?

LEAMER: I guess my quarrel with the Movement, with editors, with the Establishment, is that I like to say what I like to say and that's that. I would like to see a paper that truly was unfettered in its ideology, a Whole Earth Paper, that sought ideas and feeling, that cared deeply about writing, because that writing could carry these ideas; that cared deeply about reporting because only then could the people know. Whom to assist me? Everybody!

SIPAPU: What work are you presently engaged in?

LEAMER: I'm a free-lance writer. Really. I've been writing mainly for that great Maoist sheet, *Harper's*. I worked for a month in a coal mine last year and did a piece for them on that. They're the ones who sent me to Bangladesh. That piece is in the August issue. I've got a piece in the *New York Times Magazine* about the reform in the United Mine Workers. Right now I'm doing pieces for several magazines.

SIPAPU: What future (next eight years or so) do you predict for the U.S.? Is the Movement dead as a result of the recent election?

LEAMER: The institutions of this society are so deadened with boredom, bureaucracy, corruption and cant that new ideas rarely emerge. To me the Movement is that new energy, that vitality, that truth that is the last best hope for all of us. It's a long, long journey and the old New Left has only one lousy beacon; and we just can't be afraid wherever we lead ourselves. We can't fear truth and have a movement that discourages truth, that masks and distorts reality in the name of political or cultural purpose. No, of course the Movement isn't dead. Some of the people in the early Movement are dead, dead inside, but the Movement isn't dead. Let the media go elsewhere. Let the scabs feed off something else. But the Movement isn't dead.

SIPAPU: What contact have you had with librarians? What are their opportunities with regard to the underground press?

LEAMER: The librarians hold one of the keys to the kingdom. Several months ago I was doing research in the Library of Congress, and this good old librarian turned me on to the Temporary National Economic Committee (TNEC) hearings in the 1930's. They were the most thorough look at the economic and business structure of this country that anyone has ever taken. And practically nobody knows about them. This spring somebody told me that my book was reviewed in the Kirkus Service so I checked it out. And there I find reviews for dozens of books that I had never seen, or even heard of; books that didn't get reviewed elsewhere. The idea of counter-culture librarians blows my mind. What fantastic possibilities! What an opportunity! Imagine what a library could be.

RJS AND THE CULTURAL ANARCHISM OF THE EAST: In 1967 there arrived unsolicited at the Library of the University of California at Davis, one issue of a four-page underground newspaper from Cleveland, Ohio, with the amazing title of *The Buddhist Third-Class Junkmail Oracle.* The paper was a collage of pictures, poems and statements about the underground press in that city, and it combined news stories of crackdowns and persecutions with mystic ritual invocations.

The name of the editor, d. a. levy, was not then as well known to us as it has become since the poet's death in 1971. It turns out that one of the main presences behind levy was a poet known to us only as RJS. RJS, who is apparently still alive and living in Cleveland, is the purest type of cultural anarchist, and one of a Cleveland group of beat/hip poets, including T.L.

Kryss, Kent Taylor, and Tom Ferguson, much less well known than the San Francisco tribe. Their headquarters is Jim Lowell's Asphodel Book Shop in Cleveland. Tom Ferguson is now reported to be putting out the *BTCJO;* we haven't seen any recent copies. Whatever the whole truth about RJS may be, here is an article about him by Hugh Fox (Michigan State University, Lansing), editor of *Ghost Dance,* which shows RJS as the representative of a movement that is already beginning to seem part of the past, for better or for worse:

RJS: Non-paranoid prophet in persecution territory:

At its simplest, RJS's message is pure hippyism: transform the world through love:

fuk it/
cleveland
im not teachin yr children to hate u
(this uve alreadi taught them)
now its
GIVE A COP A ROSE
& dig love
(which is buried sumwher)
in the mEYEnds
of yr few delinquent children

(In "Forever Worship the Second Coming,"
for Gene Bloom, Steve Richmond, and RJS, 1968)

Even here, though, RJS's hippyism has its own kind of communication-obsessed slant. The key, the use of *mEYEnds* instead of *minds,* is mostly indicative of RJS's whole slant on the relationship between eye and mind, between freedom and communication, mind and "outside control" structures.

RJS has a very special concern with "real reality," the reality beyond all symbols and projected messages, the penetration into reality stripped bare, the message with the medium minimized.

He is the most radical of all current underground prophets and shares with levy a horrendous vision of the U.S. as a savage police state putting down (hard!) any attempt to actually create a love-based "eye-mind" (or mind's-eye) hippy culture.

His own personal history, of course, backs up and lends credence to his far-out and radical view of the degree of U.S. totalitarianism. In 1967, he was sentenced to six months in the workhouse in Cleveland for "contributing to the delinquency of minors," while in fact what he really did (by his own account) was to provide an asylum for runaways—with a little pot and acid thrown in on the side.

Assistant Cuyahoga County Prosecutor George J. Moscarino described RJS as a "prophet of the neo-American church whose holy sacraments are

LSD and marijuana" *(Cleveland Plain Dealer,* May, 1967), and in fact RJS's whole slant was then toward drug-based liberation, an attempt at mind-stretching, out of pragmatic, realistic-naturalistic American "reality" into new worlds of inner, expanded consciousness. He was very much like levy, a Hindu mystic, a Zen master under an Anglo-Saxon skin. He genuinely believed in the U.S. as a perfect field for psychic stretching and development ... until the axe fell.

Since his workhouse experience, though, RJS's whole sensitivity has changed. He views his encounter with the straight world as a necessary and liberating trial that forced him to reevaluate the entire relation between the outsider and the inside world.

I remember at the COSMEP conference at Berkeley, California, in 1968 when RJS confronted Richard Krech and called California a "psychedelic whorehouse." For Krech and the rest of the California crowd liberation, growth, psychic development were as "natural" and as easy to come by as light and air. There was a very definite California slant of buoyant optimism. Life was all Hindu shirts and long hair, pot and Ravi Shankar and the Monterey Folk and Jazz Festivals, light shows and Golden Gate Park, surf, sun and love. In the late sixties Haight-Ashbury bloomed and Berkeley became the site of the People's Park. So far the entire outward, optimistic wave of transcendental mysticism had flowed on unimpeded by any strong official displeasure. But when he went to California in 1968, RJS went with another kind of American reality already in his bones. He anticipated the whole anti-hippy, anti-youth movement which spread to California in 1969. Cleveland *was* future reality, and the California stance was an unrealistic interlude that had been allowed to flourish unattached to the pressures and tensions of "real" American life.

RJS complained about all Californians, poets who had come to Cleveland flying high, making noise, attracting attention. It wasn't something you did. RJS knew. Control was growing. For every outward growth energy-exertion of the hippy mind, the Establishment was beginning to exert its own death, collapse energy. levy wrote about RJS: "He was sent to jail, not for dealing with drugs (or psychedelics), not for committing a crime. He was sent to jail because he talked too much, he was a potential leader. He was in the open too much." (In *Forever Worship the Second Coming...*").

On the level of communication theory, RJS views the entire war between the Hip and Square worlds in terms of attempted mind-control. The issue, as far as he is concerned, is primarily involved with packets of communication energy, nets of communication control. The whole U.S. is slowly being converted into a massive "control area." The military-industrial complex—the power elite—is not merely extending its own control net over U.S. consciousness, but is consciously fighting against any anti-control mechanisms that still might be operative. The media are being operated as high-energy control devices that are systematically cancelling out all spontaneous, form-seeking—but still unformed—mind-growth developments.

At the same time that he is attacking this "over-control" communication-power net, however, RJS extends the principle of "control" (and the need for spontaneity) universally over *all* potential control-areas. In an article in the *Madison Kaleidoscope* (v. 1, no. 3, 22 July 1969) entitled "RJS pegs COSMEP," for example, writing about the 1968 COSMEP conference, he hits out against the same double-level communication (real vs. apparent) that he finds in the rest of U.S. society:

> the little mag editors, "underground" publications ... its all funny (like life, etc.) everyone came and said they wouldn't spend time or hassle any more government or council forms in an attempt to get a grant for their magazine & publishing: the surface declaration of "i wont play their game." then everybody proceeded to FILL OUT a time consuming and complicated form & everyone checked the block that said "im going to play their game but i wont tell myself about it" ... ITS THE same sickness ive battled before, if i wanted to take advantage of anything id have taken a scholarship, got a degree, made lots of money, bought a swimming pool in the suburbs, sat out in the sun next to my pool, not caring at all if anyone fell in and drowned. maybe i should, it doesnt seem like anything is happening anyhow, just a lot of people substituting one illusion of security or a multiplicity of illusions, for the illusions that have existed previously. DO YOU CALL THAT PROGRESS??? a revolution which takes one turn one turn around its axis & then stops (in the same place?) or possibly one that deluded itself into believing that it was moving in the first place?

He went to California looking for "enlightenment" (always the same goal of his constant, sincerely intense quest) and found "nothing new ... & all of a sudden i'm back HOME, no cosmic joy and peace in cleveland...."

What RJS wants is communication on a totally detached, mystical, non–Yankee-pragmatic-goal-directed level. He wants to go beyond mere yak-yak words ("HOW LONG CAN WORDS GO ON???") into a kind of Tibetan intuitive person-to-person communication that transcends outer goal-seeking ("what i mean is like saying I AM HERE") and moves into a direct person-person confrontation on a delicately existential level.

He defends what he calls "healthy paranoia," a realistic appraisal of the degree of psychic-spiritual "sellout" in the whole American scene. On the one hand he finds so-called mystics talking about "cosmic joy," but is told "it's not safe to carry a wallet while walking through the Haight-Ashbury district," the focal point for the cosmic-joy community. He distrusts any kind of mystical claims that for him don't square with reality. For him the "bombs are already falling," while the California—and elsewhere this is extended to fit much more than merely California—mentality uses words as defense rather than information mechanisms:

...u've got all the information, dammit all the words; why cant you put the information u've got into actuality instead of using the words as a defense mechanism?

RJS is trying to get himself "off this planet" so he can "see what it looks like from a distance," but meanwhile he is deeply frustrated by the game he sees all around him of not only communication used for control (the game of the power elite) but also communication used as a device of *self*-deception.

He ends his attack on words as defense mechanisms with a very zen-flavored prayer:

a prayer for those who still believe,
a prayer for those who have given up believing,
a prayer for those who listen
and,
a prayer for those who hear.

Believers and non-believers, listeners and hearers, RJS's compassion extends over the whole communication-short-circuited country, to everyone who uses words to block rather than transmit thought.

In another article in the *Madison Kaleidoscope* (undated) RJS expands and deepens his attack on anti-communication to other areas of the Movement scene and also gives fuller statements of his own mystical-psychological views.

First of all he attacks *Kaleidoscope* itself, a very good example of RJS's total non- (even anti-) alignment. The grounds for the attack are especially interesting. He was supposed to write an evaluative article about *Kaleidoscope,* but then *Kaleidoscope* copped out because—as the editors put it—they didn't want to become "too self-conscious." RJS's basic starting point as a thinker, of course, is precisely a kind of totally withering self-analysis that doesn't balk even at self-annihilation if that is where truth necessarily leads it. As he says:

could it be that self-consciousness leads to self-awareness which could be self-destructive and we wouldn't want any of that would we?

He then moves into a commentary on what he calls PWD—Processes Which Define—which he claims are "the mortal enemy of ground zero multiple reality associates." RJS also calls himself Captain Zero and for a long time—before changing press names with every book printed—operated out of Ground Zero Press.

The concept of "ground zero multiple reality" here is essentially the need to stay "undefined." Definition, *per se,* is mind-limiting and forces the imagination into pre-ordained channels. RJS here not only rejects static, status-quo overground definitions, but hits at the heart of an even greater (because more subtle) enemy to underground selfness—the formation of anti-definitions that have really been called into existence by comparable overground definitions. The Square not only evokes but defines the Hippy, and this very process of defining in itself limits the Hippy and forces him away from areas of self-awareness (the primary goal) which he would have explored if he hadn't been so defined.

RJS not only rebels against overground organization rigidity but is equally sensitive to its counterpart in the underground. He prefers to remain a permanently undefined non-joiner because of the sure psychic death connected with "joining" (= definition). Joining of any kind becomes inevitably a participation in the same type of consciousness that the underground so vocally condemns.

Of course the power-anti-power structure isn't the heart of RJS's fear, but the very idea of *any* structure which impedes inner-growth. Even semantic structures are confining, and when Paul Buhle talks to RJS for a while in Madison he reacts negatively against the very structure of Buhle's language, not his thought:

> ...i felt like smashing him in the face but didn't probably because he's bigger than i am. i possibly agreed with whatever he was thinking but the words came out of his mouth in such an orderly fashion that i couldn't understand a thing he was saying.

This is RJS's furthest out break for total "unstructuring." The sequential, Indo-European language-structuring arranged in logical, syllogistic thought-structures means being "caged."

He wants to go beyond Occidental logic and move into a pure, mystical state of unstructured, intuitive immediacy. Starting from his fluid structureless core that implies a fresh, individual confrontation with each and every segment of reality, RJS's whole establishment and anti-establishment rejection is really part of a much larger rejection of the entire Occidental world-view. RJS's real value lies in the genuineness of his rejection, and in the fact that he and d.a. levy (and perhaps Ginsberg, Simon, Krech and Laffing Water ... in a way) are the only genuine "mystics" in the whole underground scene. RJS is not interested in an underground which is merely a grumpy and resentful version of the overground, but believes that if the underground is to be a workable alternative, it has to be an alternative that is different in *kind* from the overground.

The overground is highly motivated, profit-directed, ego-inflated, logical, sequential, organized, rational, conscious, work-obsessed, restless; therefore any meaningful underground alternative must be unmotivated, truth- and experience-directed, egoless, instantaneous, unorganized, intuitive, subconscious, joy-instilled (but not obsessed), totally calm, at peace with itself.

Viewed from RJS's perspective much of the forced showy "mysticism," the worn-on-the-sleeve "purity" of the new underground is totally sham, — whereas RJS himself, viewed from the standpoint of either the usual over- or under-ground is totally "out of it," directionless, meaningless, "mad."

Especially when he ends his own articles with self-destructive blanket-cancellations:

> ...the ideas & opinions expressed in this article were not necessarily those of its author. the article & its theoretical & imaginary contents are only the result of some ridiculous drive to fill up space with meaningless words and imagine that somebody is interpreting them. the drive to write is like a hangover from when i was drunk upon the idea of myself as a poet, and its still here even after i wonder what am i doing here anyhow. i dont know where i'm going & i'm probably afraid to admit to myself why i'm still moving, and before all that i was into politics.

This, of course, is the ultimate cutting-away from the Occident, the annihilation of one's public self, the ridiculing of one's own ego-image. The frightening thing is that RJS not only practices what he preaches, but actually has the wild nerve to expect the same from others. But at least with him, we have a good solid look at the East planted down unexpectedly and paradoxically in the West, and looking at the scene through his eyes we can understand the nature of the "image" (= media) war that is currently being waged. RJS's own solution, stepping into "definitionlessness," moving into total detachment from "groupness" of any kind is the closest that the U.S. has come to the development of a genuine Zen (or even Taoist) mystique.

JOIN THE CLAQUE, AND A SRRT YOURSELF: The 74th Annual Conference of the California Library Association was held in the Disneyland Hotel at Anaheim, 30 November through 4 December 1972. We can't believe we swallowed the whole thing, but we did, — and at considerable expense.

Disneyland is an expensive and anti-intellectual place to stay, and the prepaid lunches and brunches turned out to be rabbit food; no insult intended to the redoubtable Bugs Bunny. Some of the best programs turned out to be sponsored by the lively Bay Area Social Responsibilities Round Table of the American Library Association. Among the SRRT programs was one on "Action through local library groups" held on Friday, 1 December; one the next day on "Institutional racism"; and another, that evening, on "Small socially aware book and magazine publishers."

The "Action through local library groups" audience heard a history of the Bay Area SRRT given by Joyce Crooks, and an account of their newsletter given by Sue Critchfield; Joan Goddard discussed the work of the outfit in getting law books to prisoners, describing their role as *amicus curiae* in *Gilmore* vs. *Lynch,* a case which established the right of prisoners to obtain such information. Dorothy English, of San Mateo County Library, described her work as a children's librarian in reviewing new books and small press publications.

The large crowd attending the "Institutional racism" panel discussion heard Ed Cavallini, Daly City Public Library discuss institutional racism in terms of power to affect the lives of many individuals. The speech by Dr.

Mildred Dickeman, Dept. of Anthropology, California State College/Sonoma, was read (due to illness) by Joyce Crooks; it was masterly, and analyzed the paradox of group-consciousness in what claims to be an individualistic society. The schools, she insisted, act as screening devices to exclude all who do not conform to white middle-class standards; the nonconformers appear in our streets as dropouts. Joyce Sumbi, Los Angeles County Public Library System, spoke of her personal experiences as a Black woman in not obtaining the promotions she expected; she was apparently radicalized by her experience and is now one of the parties to a class action suit against the system. Jim Crayton, Pasadena City College Library, also had some criticisms of library management in general; his speech was witty and devastating. Homer Fletcher discussed the Affirmative Action Program at San Jose Public Library in terms of its success.

The panel of "Small socially aware book and magazine publishers" was directed by Sue Critchfield from under her red Spanish hat. Ruth Gottstein of Glide Publications discussed the dangers of corporate book publishers to the market for new ideas, and the response from the rapidly growing number of small publishers. She mentioned also the Book Fair to be produced by the Friends of Books and Comix in June; a resolution supporting this Fair was passed at the CLA Membership Meeting the following afternoon. Irv Thomas spoke for the philosophy of *Black Bart*, of which he is an editor. This group consists of dropouts and escapees from the system; most of them are of middle years, like Thomas himself, a handsome gentleman with a beard. Among his pieces of advice to librarians was to quit, go out fighting, — and then start your own library: — an idea which has appealed to us for years, but which poses some problems of capital as well as security. Alta, a woman who has been through Women's Liberation and even beyond, told us something of why she became a publisher (Shameless Hussy Press); she then read some of her own poems, in an intensely emotional voice which was somehow not intense at all but instead releasing and clearing. Finally Sanford Berman, the "People's Librarian" (so his badge declared him to be), emphasized to the audience the need to acquire alternative publications. For him, the literature of the Establishment obtainable from trade publishers is fundamentally right-wing and so if a librarian sticks to that in his purchasing, no real balance exists. The librarian must include small press books and underground papers if he is to achieve the objectivity he claims to strive for; the Right is already in control. His suggestions were practical and witty.

On Sunday, 3 December, we heard one of several important discussion groups, all scheduled for 10:30; this one was on "Acquisition of non-standard library material." We could quarrel with Moderator Bob Bellinger's definition of non-standard, as he included audio-visual material produced by major corporations; but not with the presentation by Elizabeth Martinez Smith (Los Angeles County Library), who gave a brilliant and passionate talk, illustrated with examples and full of solid facts, on the importance of Chicano materials. We understand that she has made this presentation to other groups; we hope so, because every California librarian should be acutely aware of the library needs of California's largest Third World minority. She pointed out the importance, not only of having Chicano materials somewhere in the library building, but of presenting them in such a fashion that Chicanos know they are there, and of having some librarian to keep up with the latest developments in Chicano and Latin-American culture and politics, particularly as reflected in magazines and newspapers published in Latin America on a wide variety of subjects. It appears that every interest of English-speaking readers is followed by some periodical in Spanish; — she urged the purchase of titles in Spanish which are familiar to Mexicans on various topics (e.g., women's magazines) at the expense (if necessary) of less-read English titles. Using the late Ruben Salazar's definition of a Chicano, as "an American of Mexican descent with a non-Anglo image of himself," she pointed out the difficulty that the Anglo librarian faces in acquiring really good books and periodicals, at a time when reprint and and other publishers are hastening to make money in the ethnic market. Central to any good periodicals program, in her view, are *Con Safos* (= "the same to you"), and *El Grito* ("The cry"); the first a magazine with a street emphasis, the second (not to be confused with *El Grito del Norte,* Tijerina's northern New Mexico paper), a scholarly historical journal. According to her, 18% of California's population is Spanish-surnamed, and of these, 60% (or 10.8% of the total) are Spanish-language *only.* (We would not have believed the latter figure so high, but it's important.) Among significant presses, whose catalogs we might do well to acquire, she mentioned Totinem Press, Denver; Mitla Press, El Paso; and Perspectivo Publications, La Puente, California.

    The other meetings of interest to our readers concerned a review (extending over two meetings) of the Illinois Plan for the recruitment of minority librarians. In that State, nearly $150,000 is currently being spent to train ten Black and other librarians noted not for their previous education so much as for their community leadership, giving them also a $6000 stipend in return for their agreement to work in an Illinois library for two years. A committee, chaired by John J. Ayala of Long Beach City College, was organized to bring the same benefits to California. — Somewhere back in our earlier issues we longed for a "Union Catalog of Far-out Publications." Part of such a catalog is now in the offing; a catalog for the University of California's 9 campuses (except Berkeley) covering radical and Third World publications, as well as historical society and anthropology papers likely to be relevant, is being published under the direction of Ms. Connie Bullock, UCLA. It is due January 1973, and a second edition (including Berkeley, which is having computer problems) is already contemplated. Watch for our notice of one or the other editions in our next issue. — Meanwhile, Russell Benedict, of the

University of Nevada's Reno campus, is anxious to hear from you on the collections of extreme Right and Left material you may have assembled. Write him c/o Special Collections Dept., Library, U. of Nevada, Reno NV 89507. — Finally, a fast curve ball was passed to our friend Fr. Charles Dollen, of the University of San Diego, in the form of a resolution introduced by Zoia Horn at the last general Membership Meeting of the CLA Conference, instructing his Intellectual Freedom Committee to investigate the U.S. Government's attempt to suppress information, as reflected in the Pentagon Papers case and other cases. Only time will tell how he will handle this one.

4 : 2

This issue is the only one done in green ink on yellow paper, and must have been very difficult to microfilm later. Lime Saddle, the commune interviewed here, has long since disappeared, as most communes of the sixties and seventies did. The headings of the first four articles form a verse (no. 11) from Fitzgerald's translation of Omar's Rubaiyat.

Barbara Pruitt has gone through several jobs since working at Keene. So far as I know, Cesar Chavez still has his headquarters there. Fr. Dollen is now a monsignor at St. Gabriel's Church, Poway, California.

Synergy was subsequently replaced by Booklegger, *a magazine put out by Celeste West and other women librarians, also living together. When that group broke up, Celeste was left alone with the Booklegger imprint, which she still occasionally uses to issue short titles.*

WITH ME ALONG THE STRIP OF HERBAGE STROWN: Lime Saddle is the beautiful name of a district in the red ridges of Butte County. It's an old mining district, and there is still much wealth in Oroville, the county seat, with its big homes and shady streets. But Lime Saddle is also the home (and the name) of a collective settlement, and the western end of a most unusual cooperative publishing venture.

Lime Saddle being a commune, cooperative or collective settlement (the term "colively" was introduced by the *San Francisco Oracle* some years ago, and we would like to see it renewed), our interview questions were directed to everybody in general and to nobody in particular. Also, since the living is rural and the style informal, with small children running in and out and goats bleating to be fed (they specialize in *kids,* you might say) — there was no reason to employ a typewriter or tape recorder; it would have been uncool. The answers are rather a composite of what we got from Vince, George, Steve and Wendy.

Having inspected the small house, the cabins and vegetable gardens, and the rocky slope which the goats love, we settled down, a glass of goat's milk in hand, and talked somewhat as follows:

SIPAPU: You say you publish this new magazine, *Communities* and yet we can't make out whether you put it out, or Twin Oaks, or Walden Three, or who. What is your connection with these other communes, anyhow?

LIME SADDLE: We aren't derived from Twin Oaks, as some folks think, but we do cooperate with them. The arrangement is open, voluntary. Here's how we work it out—situation as of May 1973, with Issue #3 of *Communities:*

Lime Saddle Oroville, CA	Community Service Yellow Springs, OH	Twin Oaks Louisa, VA	Walden Three Providence, RI

some editing
Bay Area
  distributing
	some editing
	printing
	publicity
	layout (as of #3)
		subscriptions
		address list
		accounting
			typesetting
			composing
			layout for
			  Issues #1–2

In addition, a commune in Woodhurst, Massachusetts is going to get into editing, and the typesetting and composing will probably be transferred to Yellow Springs. We're behind with our schedule—all the network—and that's because there have been delays at Walden Three.

SIPAPU: OK, but how does this relate to *The Modern Utopian, Communitarian,* and *Alternatives?*

LIME SADDLE: These don't exist any more. They're really merged into *Communities.* Vince and George used to be with the Alternatives Foundation in San Francisco. Richard Fairfield, editor of *Alternatives Newsletter,* is still publishing it as he travels around from his Maryland base; but he's independent, he has no connection with *Communities.*

SIPAPU: So the way for a library to subscribe to *Communities* is . . . ?

LIME SADDLE: . . . to write to P.O. Drawer 426, Louisa, VA 23093, and enclose $6.00 for a year. (They don't bill.) They will also send you a lot of other communal literature, directories of communes, their journal, *Leaves of Twin Oaks,* and much more, especially if you become a lifetime subscriber for $50.00. But the heart of it all is *Communities.*

SIPAPU: And how often does it appear?

LIME SADDLE: Well, we're trying to get it out every two months.

SIPAPU: And what do you call this whole network?

LIME SADDLE: Community Publications Cooperative. In addition we are setting up a Community Market, a whole-earth type listing of goods, services and ideas. It will appear in the third issue of *Communities.*

SIPAPU: We notice that you and Yellow Springs (site of Antioch College, and an old communitarian center) divide the editorial function between you. How does this work out?

LIME SADDLE: Well, here in the office we have a collection of proposed articles, on this shelf we have a file of columns, and over here are our book reviews. But the cover of the latest issue is the work of Yellow Springs. So we guess you could say that Lime Saddle collects the articles, and Yellow Springs comments on and organizes them. And vice versa.

SIPAPU: Then who sets editorial policy?

LIME SADDLE: We both do; it's a working agreement we have. If they can't fit something we have into one issue, it goes into the next. If there are more complex disagreements, we straighten it out by letter or telephone.

SIPAPU: That's a lot of long-distance telephone calls.

LIME SADDLE: Hopefully not.

SIPAPU: Then your service is to distribute here in northern California. Does that mean we get our copy from Oroville?

LIME SADDLE: No, yours comes, like ours once it's finished, from Twin Oaks. All we do, as far as distributing goes, is take copies around to bookstores in the Bay area. Local bookstores wishing to stock *Communities* should reach us here at Lime Saddle, Route 1, Box 191, Oroville, CA 95965.

SIPAPU: And that's how you get the word out.

LIME SADDLE: That, and receiving many weekend visitors—it's quiet now, but you should see this place on a weekend—and talking to our neighbors...

SIPAPU: Who, we dare say, are suspicious.

LIME SADDLE: Not at all. They can see we're at work, and we ask their advice. We've had really good feelings, good relationships, with the people in the area.

SIPAPU: And, of course, you visit other communes.

LIME SADDLE: Yes, one of us just came back from Ananda, near North Columbia, California. (Ananda Community is a large settlement founded by Swami Kriyananda, of the Self-Realization Fellowship, author of *Cooperative Communities: How to Start Them and Why.* They have a Vedanta temple and several thriving industries. North Columbia is in the Sierra foothills.) And since some of us are from Oregon, we're in touch with communities there.

SIPAPU: And then, of course, there's the big June conference in Napa...

LIME SADDLE: No, it's not in Napa any more. They don't have the facilities; we're expecting hundreds of people. We're looking for land in Mendocion County, enough so that people can camp out.

SIPAPU: A sort of camp-in, then?

LIME SADDLE: No, this is serious. We're only inviting people seriously interested in communal living ... not sightseers. There will be no drugs, alcohol, or weapons, just workshops—as on women in communes, crops and horticulture, livestock, etc. And we're the group charged with getting it started, small as we are.

SIPAPU: Of course, by the time this issue of *Sipapu* appears, your conference will already have taken place. However, our readers can doubtless read about it in future issues of *Communities*.

LIME SADDLE: Yes, but don't forget, this is only a way-station, a stopping-place, like Lime Saddle itself.

SIPAPU: You mean, there's always Something Beyond?

LIME SADDLE: Yes, there's Communitarian Village. This is a projected village of several hundred people on an essentially undeveloped section of land of about 1000 acres, preferably on the West Coast. We have come to see that although the commune is a satisfactory alternative to the nuclear family, in many ways it just exhibits the nuclear family's shortcomings at a higher level. The commune's limited size, its isolated membership, its financial and cultural limitations, have pushed us to see the advantages of a larger community, based on various compatible life-styles and living arrangements within a rural setting. We are hoping to build a technology based on a Community Land Trust, using carefully arranged zones for wilderness, agriculture, industry and settlement . . . people can write to us here at Lime Saddle for our five-page paper on the Communitarian Village.

SIPAPU: So your ultimate aim?

LIME SADDLE: Is a world society, a communitarian federation of peoples, able to live together in peace. No, we don't want to dominate anyone. We want to set up a network of communication and cooperative activity, including co-ops, free schools, child care centers, communes, radical change organizations, the underground media, which will cross national frontiers and encompass the entire world.

THAT JUST DIVIDES THE DESERT FROM THE SOWN: In a remote and semi-arid part of California, a unique library is being organized. The United Farm Workers' Union has acquired an abandoned tuberculosis sanitarium in the Tehachapi Pass country, near Keene, in Kern County, 20 miles southeast of Bakersfield; and it has turned its old wooden buildings into an administrative headquarters to assist their nationwide operations. They now plan a professional library, specializing in agricultural economics, as part of this complex.

We talked recently with the coordinator of the project, Barbara Pruett, a young woman of sense and courage, in her late twenties. She explained that since all of the UFWU's money is currently going for the strike against the growers and the Teamsters, their library must be supported totally by contributions, both of money and of basic materials. They are asking for those things that every library takes for granted: envelopes, pens, typing paper, library supplies, typewriters, fireproof filing cabinets, file folders, map cabinets, cassette tape recorders, and appropriate printed materials. They especially request funding for a microfilm program. As for Ms. Pruett herself, all she is getting from the UFWU is room and board and $5.00 a week.

Ms. Pruett is fully aware of the difficulties of her work in La Paz, as the settlement is known; but she is mature and determined. She has been working as a volunteer in support of the farm workers for about a year now; she received the library assignment from the UFWU in April. Her immediate objective is to obtain as much basic funding and material as she can in a year, and to organize the library in such a way that a union worker will be able to take it over without having had any formal library training. (This means, among other things, a special system of classification and cataloging, without reliance on LC or DC.)

"We want to have everything the growers have," said Ms. Pruett; "that means access to all the papers, documents, and periodicals that they have standing orders for." But, she added, "Our greatest need is for volunteers and basic supplies right now, so that we can get this library going as soon as possible."

Ms. Pruett does not neglect the hazards of her job. Besides the hostility of the growers, there is the rough competition of the International Brotherhood of Teamsters, which has been trying to sign grower contracts for several years and is now locked in a battle with Cesar Chavez's UFWU for representation of the farm workers. Four UFWU field offices have been burned down in the last three years during various stages of the conflict. While the pressures are continuous, Ms. Pruett feels that she has the most interesting and important position in the library profession at this time.

Ms. Pruett had but little time with us. She was at the University of California at Davis to visit our library and to call on the Chicano student organization, MECHA (= Movimiento Estudiantil CHicano de Aztlán). By the time you read this, she expects to be down at La Paz, sorting papers and receiving your appropriate donations in a landscape of wooden buildings, tumbled mountains, scrub oaks, lizards and sand. It gets up to 100° down there, and this was the area of maximum intensity of the great Kern County earthquake of 21 July 1952.

"Of course the buildings are air-conditioned," we said.

"Of course not," Ms. Pruett said firmly.

"Then at the end of the day you can relax with a cold beer," we suggested.

"Not at all," Ms. Pruett corrected us. "La Paz is *dry.* Very *dry.*" She left us gasping with admiration at her courage.

Address: Ms. Barbara Pruett, United Farm Workers' Union, P.O. Box 62, Keene, CA 93531.

WHERE NAME OF SLAVE AND SULTAN IS FORGOT: The Hennepin County Library at Minneapolis is now the home of Sanford

Berman, of Zambia and Uganda, whose works and adventures have been chronicled in earlier issues. This is the place where he is using his opportunity to remove (or at least cease using) sexist and racist headings from the Library of Congress catalog cards. He tells us that he has been circulating memoranda in his Catalog Department—he's the head of it—asking for the use of new headings: AFRO—AMERICAN instead of NEGRO, WOMEN ARTISTS instead of WOMEN AS ARTISTS, etc. In short, he has been trying to "Bermanize" the Hennepin County Library. (For a full account of his thesis and its implications, see *Sipapu,* v. 3, no. 2, July 1972.)

We make no criticisms of how other people run their libraries.

In any case, to write up this story fully, we would have to fly to Minneapolis and interview, not only Berman, but his co-workers, his boss and the public.

This is, of course, entirely beyond our powers. But it will be interesting when the Library of Congress issues the next (8th) edition of its *List of Subject Headings:* because LC has reported in its *Bulletin* that they will take Berman's suggestions seriously. If *they* change, everyone else will have to change with them, or else fall more and more out of step. Question: how seriously will they take Berman's criticisms? And will *you* have to "Bermanize" *your* library? The whole question remains more explosive by far than most libraries have realized. (Nobody has taken up our suggestion of a Great Debate on the subject.)

AND PEACE TO MAHMUD ON HIS GOLDEN THRONE: In our v. 3, no. 1, January 1972, we mention the Ommers' Directory: *The Spiritual Community Guide,* published by The Spiritual Community, Box 1080, San Rafael, CA 94902. You should be aware (completely, spiritually *aware*) that they have published a revised edition and a *Supplement.* (Make dashed-on entry, please.) The *Supplement* is unfortunately in a taller format than the original, making it harder to bind them together; it contains fewer statements and more ads, but it is still essential for any library in California or elsewhere. Otherwise, how will you answer such reference questions as "Where do I go for Zen training?" or "Where is the nearest organic food store?" Let us hope that your library is the kind of place where people feel *freed* to ask such questions.

In a different (all right, *how* different?) religious vein, we have been made very conscious of the latest edition of *The Witches' Almanac*. It is published by Grosset and Dunlap from Road 2, Box 200, Pine Bush, NY 12566, price one dollar; prepared and edited by Elizabeth Pepper and John Wilcock (editor of *Other Scenes, Mexico on $5 a Day,* and other countercultural and travel publications). *The Witches' Almanac* looks rather like the *Old Farmer's Almanac,* being just a bit taller, and reads like the OFA chanted backwards. Well, not backwards, since the days are in the right order, but the pages are arranged by zodiacal sign, not calendar month, and the text is full of advice of more interest to Tituba than to Giles Corey. Almost every day has texts for the followers of Wicca, or the Old Religion: 30 May, "Pay no heed to censure"; 4 July, "Practice art of Revery" (a hard day to practice it on, in our opinion); 23 August, "Mate not"; 14 September, "Baffle enemy with laughter." Actually the booklet is done with considerable taste, contains some very fine information on herbs (complete with Latin names, and lovely old drawings from herbals), much very down-to-earth advice on how to survive in our dehumanized culture, and a ringing prosecution of Satanism (Jesus People please note, these people are not, repeat thrice NOT, Satanists). The ads seem a little out of place, but there aren't too many of them, and the herb-lore is wholly right. Artemis, protectress of maidens and wild things, bless this almanac.

DAMNATION DAMP: The *Directory of Alternative Media Periodicals* is edited by John Noyce, and published by Smoothie Publications, 67 Vere Road, Brighton, Sussex, ENGLAND. And despite its format—stencil on soft paper—it is a joy. The second edition (1972) is very successful, and for us, very English. In the first place, it is clear that in Great Britain and Ireland there are as many alternative publications as in any comparable area of the U.S., if not more. They include fanzines, socialist/communist papers, rock sheets, literary magazines—you name it, they have it too, and don't you ever doubt it. A flourishing counter-culture, not confined to London, is indeed publishing from Brighton to Wick. Among the magazines listed, we liked these titles particularly: *The North Devon Snail* (published in Kent), *Heads & Freaks* (formerly *Brighton Heads and Freaks*—we regret the change of name, as it conjured up visions of an Edwardian gentleman on the pier inquiring, "Excuse me, Sir, but can you direct me to the office of the *Brighton Heads and Freaks?*"), and *Curiously Strong*. This last, we venture to suggest, must come from the label on a certain brand of cough drops: "The Allenburys Jujubes and Pastilles: Curiously Strong." If this is not the origin of this title, we'd like to know what the origin of it is. We know the cough drops, know them of old; if you have a better answer, pray supply. And pray supply yourselves with *DAMP,* if you want to know anything about everything happening in the British Isles to-day.

"GET YOU BELOW!" This cry, taken up in our first issue, is now being repeated by two other workers in the underground press field. Roger C. Palmer, a young librarian at the State University of New York at Buffalo, is circulating a grant proposal for an Alternative Research Center. As we go to press, his project has not been approved for funding by any group, but it aims to establish collecting space and the professional position of selector of materials. Indexing and other forms of bibliographical control, as well as reports based on the collection, are part of the project requested for funding. Mr. Palmer has already sent out form letters to some 210 Movement organizations listed in a recent issue of *Work Force,* and all but about fifty of these have responded; some forty respondents answered with long, personal letters, and of all these only one was noticeably hostile in tone. Please don't bug poor Mr. Palmer with requests for copies of his proposal; he has found it very expensive to make such copies.

Mr. James Danky, of Broken Bridge Farm, Route 3, Box 599, Fort Atkinson, WI 53538, has the ambitious scheme in mind of making a national union list of underground and alternative papers. He claims that he has picked up 3,000 titles in 175 libraries, but apparently the exact run of each title in each library is not given. He is anxious to hear from anyone who has a collection of underground papers on his/her library. This union list will be published later this year, according to Mr. Danky, by the State Historical Society of Wisconsin at Madison.

WITH FATHER DOLLEN AT THE FRONT: Fr. Charles Dollen, of the University of San Diego, was a leader in the Committee to Defeat Proposition 18, the omnibus antipornography amendment in California. Herewith his "Reflections on Proposition 18":

"IT HAS HAPPENED BEFORE; it will happen again. The forces of censorship will gather behind a new CLEAN force, or another State Senator Harmer. So, it's worth looking at the logistics of defeating the next surge of Puritans.

"ACLU alerted CLA that no argument had been alerted against Proposition 18, and the matter was referred to the California Library Association's Intellectual Freedom Committee. After hasty telephone conversations, an *ad hoc* committee agreed upon the ballot opposition format.

"Next, a public relations firm was hired, one that had experience in California's political battles. Two committees were formed immediately, — one for finances and the other to seek cooperation from Hollywood stars. Within one week, men like John Wayne and Bob Hope had been recruited. (This is, in our editorial opinion, the most astonishing part of the whole story!)

"The financial goal was to raise one million 'clean' dollars. Without too much difficulty, this goal was almost reached by election time.

"Then there were strategy sessions. The PR people really knew their job, and they set up press conferences, and radio and TV appearances. Those of us who were on the committee were made available for TV debates and radio talk shows—many, many of both. It was agreed that we would not attack the opposition or call into question their good faith, or their political or religious affiliations. (Privately, I had some doubts....)

"Above all, we had to agree on a publicity slogan. If all the voters had been academicians, we could have appealed to the First Amendment and to academic freedom. However, we had to reach the mass of the electorate in a very complicated election year.

"We agreed on: 'NO on obscenity; NO on censorship; and NO on Proposition Eighteen.' We blanketed the State with leaflets which explained that we were not defending pornography but we were against censorship, and against the real possibility for the triumph of censorship that would appear if Proposition 18 passed.

"Obviously, these fairly simple tactics worked: Proposition Eighteen was defeated by about 69% of the voters. I think we communicated the essential message, and our effectiveness was increased by never deviating from that one central position. Even when we were attacked personally, we did not rise to the occasion to say anything but our core message.

"The library profession and the media responded most generously, in every way. When the censors are ready to strike again, we must be ready to mobilize again. Isn't there something about eternal vigilance being the price for liberty?"—FR. CHARLES DOLLEN.

We give it as our private opinion, that at least in California, attempts to ban pornography are as hopeless as attempts to ban booze. People—especially males—enjoy bare bods the way they enjoy booze, and they aren't going to appreciate anyone taking either of them away. Call it male chauvinism if you like, but ultimately it weighs in on the side of freedom of expression.

THE FORTUNES OF SYNERGY: We viewed with alarm, nay, we breathed fire and indignation, in the best tradition of Far Western journalism, when we heard that California State Librarian Ethel Crockett was cutting off the funds for our sister publication, *Synergy*. Since the bad news was announced in March, the situation has cleared up somewhat, but *Synergy* is by no means safe and the claims and counter-charges have made understanding the situation more difficult.

For those of you who came in late, *Synergy* is the name of a library periodical, founded in 1967, and devoted to counter-cultural, specialized and off-beat librarianship, described in articles and bibliographies. Very much like *Sipapu* in fact, not so much of a newsletter and interview sheet, but more substantial, with really great illustrations.

Now the funding of *Synergy* has always been rather complicated. The funds are originally Federal money: the Department of Health, Education and Welfare administered them through the California State Library under Title II of the Library Services and Construction Act of 1964. The Bay Area Reference Center was accordingly set up by the California State Library at the San Francisco Public Library, using SFPL's brightest employees as its staff. Besides answering reference questions by telephone, they published *Synergy,* with the aid of a staff member working fifteen hours a week. The funds paid the printer, and consequently there was a limit on the number of subscribers: there still is a waiting list. Twice *Synergy* won a coveted library publications prize from the American Library Association, and hundreds of librarians and researchers learned to rely on its articles and bibliographies.

From what has been said about its funding, it is obvious that the funds for *Synergy,* like all federal funding for libraries, would have in any case run out on 30 June 1974. What Ms. Crockett did, on or about 15 February 1973, was say to the *Synergy* people that these funds would not be available for the publication of *Synergy* after 30 June 1973. *They* say that *she* said that the publication was "irrelevant," that she was acting on the advice of a CSL Advisory Council on Libraries, and that when they tried to get into contact with her, she refused to see them. *She* denies the whole thing (are you still with us? sound familiar?). Anyway, Ms. Crockett told the *Library Journal* that she had *never* called *Synergy* irrelevant.

However, some facts are a matter of record:

- *Synergy* was indeed denied funds for the period beginning 1 July 1973 — an indefinite period.
- It was indeed difficult for *Synergy* people to see Ms. Crockett.
- The *Synergy* staff, having not heard from Ms. Crockett since their protest letter of 16 March, circulated (21 March) a protest broadside, displaying the figure of a jawy monster with long arms pursuing, across a desolate plain, a tiny bean-like creature with two fast little legs and two big scared eyes. "*REAGAN APPOINTEE NIXES* SYNERGY!" said the broadside, and you could utter your protest below by checking any one of several boxes, including one marked "AARRGHHH!" Yes, they circulated it, and they got slapped down by John F. Anderson, Director, San Francisco Public Library.
- The protest was filled in by many people and sent in to Ms. Crockett. In addition, the Librarians' Association of the University

of California approved a resolution in defense of *Synergy,* presented by its Davis division at the statewide meeting at UC Irvine, 5 May 1973, — where it passed *nemine contradicente.*

• Ms. Crockett — whether in response to the protests, or for some other reason, we don't presume to say, — extended the life of *Synergy* through 31 December 1973, giving it three more issues. She is alleged to have explained on that occasion that her real reason for axing *Synergy* was that it was "too successful," and since it had (as she apparently believed) plenty of outside capital, it should be a profit-making venture, and it should no longer "feed at the public trough."

• The San Francisco Public Library suppressed two editorials designed to explain *Synergy's* situation to its readers, and are alleged to have blocked five different reprint offers which would have brought in some money. So *Synergy* has *no* large amount of money to continue publishing with. Meanwhile, Celeste West, editor-in-chief of *Synergy* is resigning from SFPL effective 15 July 1973, and seeking a career in the law.

Since *Library Journal* and *Wilson Library Bulletin* have stressed Ms. Crockett's side of the story, we will try to give that of Ms. West. She sent us the following statement:

"Our Stately Librarian made the autocratic, uninformed, and unpopular decision to axe *Synergy.* She claims that she was not warned that the BARC staff and readers would resist, though we did warn her; we feel that she trusted the heavy head of Titular Authority to bully through.

"We did indeed take the whole battle out into the open: asked for reasons, demanded accountability, invited the whole profession to participate. I heartily recommend the tactic of publicity. It absolutely freaks hotshot hierarchs, who are such closet queens about the whole decision-making process. By keeping everything dark and furtive, sell-outs (from professional ethics to power politics) go unremarked (and unchecked).

"Sad, but true to caste, BARC Director McNamee and SF City Librarian Anderson split with all the rest of the BARC staff (15) over the issue of challenging Crockett's divine right to dictate *Synergy* out of existence. I was forbidden to use the telephone and TWX; 'officially reprimanded' forever in my personnel file for writing to Crockett; and censored in expressing any position in *BARC Notes* and the *SF Official Bulletin.* Naturally, I am filing a grievance, with the help of the Union, against this ugly gag trip, and, yup, even a 'counter-reprimand.' Time we played turnabout with such military-school intimidation.

"Anyway, after a fine flap of publicity and marvellous letters of support for the mag, Crockett had to revise her official, hopelessly censorious, 'reasons' for cutting out *Synergy.* These had been: advice of the California State Council on Libraries and other unidentified critics. She now denies that she ever cited such causes and blames her secretary for foiling our attempt to set up some sort of dialogue.

"I wish now that we had just held a sit-in in her office. There was no personal confrontation until both sides had drawn up their lines. Crockett's feelings about eliminating *Synergy* were almost all conveyed to us through Anderson. Now Crockett says LSCA money can be used for only two years on a successful project; but to us this time limitation is false; hundreds of successful projects continue to receive support beyond two years. Besides, a federal project like BARC is not allowed to collect money for its already tax-financed activities. We would have opened up our mailing list long ago and charged if there had been any lawful machinery for doing so.

"SFPL is blithely saying, in the face of publicity, that it will take over the mag and for no one to worry. But the BARC staff categorically refuses to do a magazine under SFPL because we've been burned too often. Besides, the library has bollixed five different reprint offers which might have brought in money. It has choked creativity on the bone of prior censorship, and has suppressed our protesting editorials, plus issue #40, finished weeks ago. What does this all mean in the Infinite Scheme of things? Why, it's as serious as a butterfly's wing. And who is responsible? Those, simply, who care to respond." —CELESTE WEST.

Sipapu makes the following final comments: 1. Those who have devoted themselves passionately to a thing, will use every passionate means to defend it. 2. Government money means government control. 3. Nothing, certainly not us, will ever replace *Synergy*. Whoever is at fault, or whatever means or considerations *might* have been used, — the library world is the permanent loser.

5 : 1

The interview in this issue was with Robert Head and Darlene Fife, of the NOLA Express (New Orleans). Their paper closed down a year or so after the interview, and they moved to West Virginia. Since they're now occupied with other activities, and January 1974 is so long ago, I decided not to reprint the interview.

Most of the rest of the paper was only of passing interest. The selection here is a game which (I understand) was briefly produced for a modern market — I've seen it, but never played it.

I therefore have made the great Swedish botanist and taxonomist Carolus Linnaeus (1707-1778) one of my contributors. My father, Donald Culross Peattie (1898-1964), was a great admirer of Linnaeus and was with difficulty dissuaded from naming me Carolus Linnaeus Peattie. This might have been acceptable in gymnasium *or* lycée, *but as a monicker in America, on a school baseball diamond, it would have been a disaster. I would have had to hide behind the nickname "Chuck." At the thought of being "Chuck" my soul swoons in the vertigo of horror. I'm glad I am what I am.*

GET OUT YOUR TABLUT: Just for a giggle, we're going to teach you a game, to while away these long snowy evenings. (There's snow on the hills in Winters.) It comes from Lapland! and was discovered there by Carolus Linnaeus, on his epoch-making one-man scientific expedition to Arctic Scandinavia in 1732. The description, in his own words, is from his *Lachesis Lapponica, or A Tour in Lapland,* tr. by James Edward Smith, London, 1811, v. 2, p. 55-58. You remember the Sameh, a.k.a., the Lapps, — they're a people who came out of Central Asia ages ago and settled in extreme northern Europe; they speak a language closely related to Finnish. So this is really a Third World game, in a sense, although R.C. Bell, in his *Board and Table Games,* classes this as one of the *tafl* group, of which the most familiar is Fox & Geese. Although the Geese (or pursuers) generally win, it may be possible to adapt this "hunting game" (as apart from a "war game") so that the pursued (Fox) has a chance. The Lapps call the two unequal sides Muscovites and

Swedes, and we hope that in playing it you will enjoy a fight to the Finnish. Here goes!

TABLUT, or Lappish Chess.

The game called *Tablut* is played with a checkered board, and twenty-five pieces, or men, in the following manner.

Fig. 1 is the king, whose station is in the central square or royal castle, called *konokis* by the Laplanders, to which no other person can be admitted.

Fig. 2, represents one of the eight Swedes his subjects, who, at the commencement of the game, are stationed in the eight squares, adjoining to the royal castle, marked 2 and 3.

Fig. 3, is one of sixteen Muscovites, their adversaries, who occupy the sixteen embroidered squares, (some of them marked 4 in the cut), situated four together in the middle of each side of the field.

The vacant squares, distinguished by letters, may be occupied by any of the pieces in the course of the game.

LAWS.

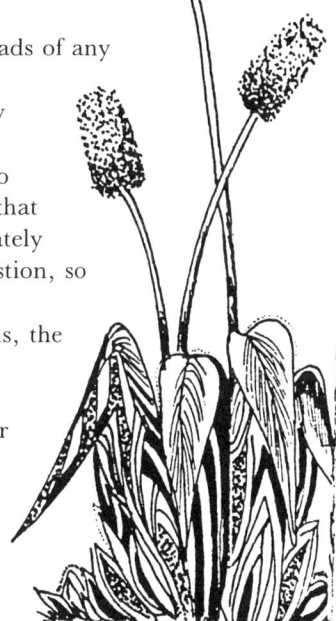

1. Any piece may move from one square to another in a straight line, as from *a* to *c;* but not corner-wise, or from *a* to *e*.

2. It is not allowed to pass over the heads of any other pieces that may be in the way, or to move, for instance, from *b* to *m,* in case any were stationed at *e* or *i*.

3. If the king should stand in *b,* and no other piece in *e, i,* or *m,* he may escape by that road, unless one of the Muscovites immediately gets possession of one of the squares in question, so as to interrupt him.

4. If the king be able to accomplish this, the contest is at an end.

5. If the king happens to be in *e,* and none of his own people or his enemies either in *f,* or *g, i,* or *m,* his exit cannot be prevented.

6. Whenever the person who moves the king perceives that a passage is free, he must call out *raichi,* and if there be two ways open, *tuichu*.

7. It is allowable to move ever so far at once, in a right line, if the squares in the way be vacant, as from *c to n*.

8. The Swedes and the Muscovites take it by turns to move.

9. If any one man gets between two squares occupied by his enemies, he is killed and taken off, except the king, who is not liable to this misfortune.

10. If the king, being in his own square or castle, is encompassed on three sides by his enemies, one of them standing on each of the squares numbered 2, he may move away by the fourth. If one of his own people happens to be in this fourth square, and one of his enemies in number 3 next to it, the soldier thus enclosed between his king and the enemy is killed. If four of the enemy gain possession of the four squares marked 2, thus enclosing the king, he becomes their prisoner.

11. If the king be in 2, with an enemy in each of the adjoining squares, *a, A,* and 3, he is likewise taken. You'll need 1 of no. 1, 8 of no. 2, and 16 of no. 3. Pawns and checkers may do it.

12. Whenever the king is thus taken or imprisoned, the war is over, and the conqueror seizes all the Swedes, the conquered party resigning all the Muscovites he has taken. —Carolus Linnaeus.

Since the Muscovites have the advantage in numbers and position, you may wish to alter the rules by permitting the king to move diagonally. Bell's book gives some details of tactics and capture in Tablut—the method is like that in Go—and the relation of the game to other ancient games of North Europe. At any rate, Tablut is a change from those crossword puzzles in *Wilson Library Bulletin.*

HAPPY NEW YEAR!

STAFF FOR THIS ISSUE: Noel Peattie, editor; Darlene Fife and Gerda Maskaleris, interviewees; Samuel Douglas, contributor; Reny Slay, art; The Printer, Davis, printing. Carolus Linnaeus, anthropologist.

5 : 2

This, Sipapu's *consecutive issue no. 10, was the first issue to contain an index. I did it myself (don't wait, dear colleagues, for someone else to do it for you), and I have had a profound respect for all indexers since.* Sipapu *has never been indexed in* Library Literature, *and* American Humanities Index *turned me down, saying it couldn't be done. However,* Alternative Press Index *eventually started indexing* Sipapu, *and* CALL *(Current Awareness of Library Literature) indexed* Sipapu *for a while, until the editor unaccountably stopped publishing.*

I have lost track of Walter Medeiros. The opening word, OXOMOXO, I thought should be AOXOMOXOA. Walter didn't have the poster at hand, and was positive it was OXOMOXO. The title is that of a Grateful Dead album. Deadheads are welcome to set us all straight.

A lot of the professional underground comic artists were far less impressed with Estren's book than I was.

The illustrations were done by Nancy Waters.

OXOMOXO! Wasn't that the name of the ancient kingdom ruled by Ozymandias!? What is the precise significance of the Dance of the Five Moons, and when and where did it take place? And who made this phrase famous: "May the baby Jesus close your mouth and open your mind"? The answers to these questions, which to find might well baffle the erudition of a regiment of reference librarians, are on the tip of the tongue of a young man of longish hair and serious countenance, who sits on the floor of a small duplex in Berkeley, waiting for someone to come along and *care* enough to ask them. For Walter P. Medeiros, sometime architect, art historian, and now collector, is probably the leading authority on rock concert posters in the world.

Sipapu has previously interviewed editors, publishers, and librarians. Yet surely their least appreciated collaborator is the collector. And Medeiros has one of the most interesting collections in our general field that we have yet seen. The rock concert posters (= hippie posters, psychedelic posters)

76

were announcements of rock concerts in San Francisco and environs during the late sixties, specifically during the period 1966-71. In this incredibly short time, as Medeiros explains in his unpublished M.A. thesis *(San Francisco Rock Concert Posters; Imagery and Meaning,* U.C. Berkeley, 1972) a whole consciousness exploded, dispersed, and left its trace in a unique form of graphic art.

Likely enough most of our friends have never seen these posters, although they must have heard rock of that age and place (Jefferson Airplane, Grateful Dead, Country Joe and the Fish, etc.). Around a hundred bands were playing in San Francisco then, mostly at the Fillmore Auditorium, presented by Bill Graham, and at the Avalon Ballroom by Chet Helms, whose company was named The Family Dog. To announce these dance-concerts, posters were designed by artists who were for the most part without formal training, but who used imagery and symbols of the past *(art nouveau, Sezession,* plus material from Egyptian, Oriental, and Amerindian art, as well as scenes from early films and advertisements). The artists themselves—Wes Wilson, Victor Moscoso, Rick Griffin, Alton Kelley, and Stanley "Mouse" Miller—are scarcely big names in the straight "fine" art world even today: nor is that their ambition. However, from their preference for disseminating art through a more popular medium, they are known in the world of design and craftsmanship—and also on record albums and underground comics.

Sipapu hasn't the facilities to reproduce the art of that era. Our printing costs are high enough without using a four-color process. To describe an art, or interview its collector, without being able to present examples, is rather like visiting a museum with the aid of a seeing-eye dog. But if we can't give you the posters, we can give you Walter Patrick Medeiros, M.A., historian of counter-culture art. We take you now to 1506 B Bonita, Berkeley, CA 94709:

SIPAPU: How did you get so intensely involved in studying and collecting the dance concert posters?

MEDEIROS: Because I got turned on to the culture that produced them. I grew up in the Bay Area, and moved to San Francisco in August 1966, after having been away for about 9 years. On returning I discovered the hippie culture, which offered a way to break through the alienation and creative frustration I was experiencing, professionally and personally. I had just gotten my architectural license then, and it was already clear that the profession was a dead end for me. I began visiting Haight Street and going to the ballrooms, and eventually the positive "hit" of happiness I got there gave me the courage to quit architecture and enroll in art history at U.C. Berkeley, in 1968. When I had to do a master's thesis, I chose an unresearched field, the SF poster art, which became a continuing field of activity, involving me in a society of mellow creative people.

SIPAPU: How did you get into this on a systematic basis?

MEDEIROS: Since 1967 I had picked up a few posters from the streets, and from going to the dances, where they were given out. And T-Lautrec, one of the printers, gave me a couple dozen. So I would study all the posters I could find for each artist, then call them and arrange an interview to discuss their art, their backgrounds, the dance hall scene, etc. Fortunately I met Randy Tuten early in my research. He's stoned on posters, and he has *the* collection. He digs talking about them, and he's generous. He gave me copies of all his own work, and some of other artists', too. He has a complete set of both Fillmore and Avalon posters in postcard format, all arranged chronologically in binders. Through Randy I had, almost immediately, access to the virtually complete works of every artist. Today it would be difficult and costly for us to assemble such collections from scratch; and without him I would not have learned much of what I know.

SIPAPU: Let us confess. Before we started *Sipapu,* we were going to do an in-print catalog of posters, to be called "Peattie's Poster Paradise." We even wrote a friend who runs a graphic arts workshop in Berkeley, for help, but we became abashed by the scope of the project. Any chance of your doing it now?

MEDEIROS: An in-print catalog is unlikely, but I have in mind, if I can find the time (i.e. the money) to do it, a *catalogue raisonné* of the roughly 500 posters produced in this period. This would require innumerable small posters in picture form, a close description of varying states and editions, etc.

SIPAPU: But how would you arrange it?

MEDEIROS: Chronologically, as in this journal. *(Produces journal of concerts and posters;* Sipapu *gasps appropriately.)* Here is a complete record of Avalon posters derived from my collection and Randy Tuten's, from October 1965 to June 1971.

SIPAPU: Ah, there's the Dance of the Five Moons; we have that one. It happened on the third and fourth of February, 1967.

MEDEIROS: The title, of course, is typical of the posters in its use of astrological symbolism. The five moons are those of the planet Uranus, associated with Aquarius.

SIPAPU: But the planet was in Leo that night.

MEDEIROS: The poster is by Victor Moscoso. And that leads to another fantasy of mine: to put together an archive of my tape-recorded interviews and a complete collection of posters on slides — in a museum, for future historians.

SIPAPU: Obviously you've tried the grant trip —

MEDEIROS: Yes, I've tried all sorts of local and national foundations, but there isn't money available, and no interest — it's considered irrelevant kid stuff in such places. I've little hope for institutional support.

SIPAPU: So what you have to offer the world is the posters, some slides such as you showed at UC Davis in conjunction with the show there, and your interview tapes.

MEDEIROS: Well, these are the materials I work with. I like to turn people on to visual awareness, both for pleasure and cultural understanding. I'm an educator, really, and I'm good at it. I'm into audiovisual methods, programs that teach what's behind images and style — not an explanation that lessens the art, but one where the meaning heightens the perception and appreciation. After all, that's what happened to me, and many of my friends have told me that I've influenced their vision and perception. These posters turned me on, and I like to share them.

SIPAPU: So you have all these projects, and no prospect of financial support. We're surprised at that, considering the interest in the UC Davis exhibit.

MEDEIROS: Correct. And I haven't been able to do much myself with the limits and distractions of hustling odd jobs (drafting and carpentry) to make ends meet. I had hoped to get a teaching job, but no luck. I have some good ideas, however — like this calendar, with a different poster for each month. I've talked to publishers about it, but those who dig it don't have the money, those with money can't see it. I've been trying to get a book together, too, but haven't been able to complete the preliminary work, so I could get a contract and advance. We seem to be in a trough: the art of that period is too close to us to develop the interest of reminiscence.

SIPAPU: How long do you think it will take?

MEDEIROS: A few years; maybe ten years from the start of the movement; that takes us to 1976. Around that time we may begin to see a revival of interest in the hippie movement and its art. Notice how the past is soon revived as a product — the media are voracious — we're getting into the Fifties' rock-and-roll scene already.

SIPAPU: What are the artists and their promoters doing now?

MEDEIROS: The artists are now into other forms of art. Wes Wilson is producing stained glass. Rick Griffin went through a fantastic trip, in which he produced posters with nonsense (= unintelligible) lettering; one of the last has the dance concert information along the lower margin, while huge yellow unreadable letters loom over a vast horizon of a junkyard, filled with radio and TV sets. It's almost as if this were the graveyard of human communication. He freaked out in southern California, joined the Jesus People for a while, and is now back where he started, doing graphic work for *Surfer Magazine*. Kelley-Mouse, a poster partnership, is now doing business as Monster Company, producing high-quality T-shirt art, some of it based on rock posters and record albums, such as the Grateful Dead T-shirt; other designs use funky, downhome subjects, such as the 1940's style Mercury and Chevy cars. Still other artists are doing record album covers. Tuten still works in the tradition of old-time commercial graphics, with a strong emphasis on lettering and design. As for the promoters, the old Fillmore and Family Dog are long gone. Bill Graham still produces dance concerts—nationwide now—but rarely uses posters, relying on radio and newspaper ads; Randy Tuten does a lot of newspaper ads for Bill. Chet Helms, who discovered the phrase "May the baby Jesus shut your mouth and open your mind," on a lavatory wall, and used it as the slogan of The Family Dog, is no longer in the promotion business.

SIPAPU: But the force that produced the posters, the consciousness of love and sharing, and the hatred of ideology and oppression alike—is that gone?

MEDEIROS: No, I don't think it's gone. I know many people whose lives are still based on those values. The energy is dispersed; you see freaks all over the country now. San Francisco was the high-energy center where it emerged, and that intensity is of course gone. But that was a natural, inevitable process. What happened there was that the classic dream of human perfectibility, of a society based on love, gentleness, freedom from fear materialized briefly in the early days of the Haight. That's the kernel of truth in the "love generation" legend. And people who reject that fact didn't experience it—if they experienced the Haight at all, it was too late, or they got burned by it, from their excessive, naive optimism. A heavy rush of idealism came down, and its creators projected it as a model for the rest of the world. It's understandable.

But of course, such a unique lifestyle couldn't survive. The rush to the

Haight brought people who were unready for it: the too eager, the immature, and hard types who exploit gentleness. Sooner or later, the creative people left for the country (some by 1967!), or other towns, and worked at getting it together, with themselves, then with families, and work in solid and realistic ways. This is still going on; not every survivor of that period is a burned-out dope freak. Out of that period, dispersing across America, came the ecology and anti-war movements. No, you can't say it's gone. It's everywhere.

SIPAPU: Yes, it's everywhere; even some straights have been affected; they wear beards and talk bop. But what have you to say to the critics of an older generation who see this art primarily in terms of its antecedents: *art nouveau*, for instance, or *art deco?* We hear a lot of this fake art-historical criticism, and it strikes us as a kind of concealed put-down.

MEDEIROS: Yes, it's a matter of ignorance or cynicism. The art of the past was regarded by those artists as a fantastic source of imagery. Although works by Ingres *(Thetis and Jupiter)* and Rossetti (drawing of Jane Burden Morris) are occasionally adapted for use in the posters, the artists owe very little to the old masters, or to Mucha and Roller. Their sources are LSD, grass, music, and above all the intense imaginative lifestyle that was the hippie scene. The hippie poster artists are populist, non-intellectual; although Victor Moscoso had been a fine-arts painter from Yale, he had reached a dead-end in painting by the mid-1960's, and was ready for something less abstract, closer to experience. Stanley "Mouse" Miller started out pinstriping and flame-painting custom cars, which is about as far as you can get from Ingres and Rossetti, however good they are. No, the "culture of the lilies" is remote from San Francisco 1967. A riot of California poppies is more like it.

Above all, there may or may not be a specific "meaning" or message within any given poster (apart from the dance-concert information given). Most important, is that the posters integrate images into a total work of *visual* art. Any idea or program with which the design began is transformed into a *visual* statement. This is difficult for scholarly or literary people to appreciate, I find. We tend to approach graphic art with a literal mindset; the artists told me that they worked on the design "till it looked right." More than any experience I had in the university, my involvement with these artists taught me how to appreciate art visually (apart from analytically, or symbolically).

SIPAPU: Well, that about sums it up ... wait a bit! What is OX-OMOXO? It isn't in our Greek lexicon!

MEDEIROS: Ah, well, it isn't a word at all. It illustrates how a very commonplace image could be transformed in poster art. It's based on the name of an English brand of bouillon cube, for oxtail soup, OXO. This was a heavy image for Rick Griffin, one he used often. The cubes came in a nice tin, with OXO on it in large funky letters, and for Griffin, it took on a cosmic symbolism. The symmetry of it—it's a palindrome—was attractive to him graphically and metaphysically. He did many variations on it, and in this case made it into a pseudo-occult word by putting "om" in the center. He made a drawing of an eyeball figure riding a surfboard through a flaming circle exclaiming: "!OXOMOXO! EYE AM THE 'I.'" That's a heavy "hoot" (= surfer's exultant cry). Griffin came out of the surfing culture.

I might add here that the pun, the metaphor is a prominent aspect of Griffin's work, as in that of other poster artists. I see it as having a common origin in the ineffable sense of unity felt when one is stoned; but it also relates to a little-known tradition of Western art. Christian art has often reflected the philosophy that the secular, the mundane, could be used as an avenue to the sacred, the knowledge and experience of God. The Buddhists, of course, came to the same conclusion. Some hippies took this sense of cosmic unity very seriously; for others it was light, like "hey, far out." Griffin's work reflects this range of response: from the flippant street kid to the reverent mystic.

SIPAPU: Wow! Talk about going through changes, starting from a simple palindrome on a bouillon cube tin. But what happens when you swallow such a fantastic bouillon cube?

MEDEIROS: Hmmm. Well, as the White Rabbit said, in the Joe McHugh poster, KEEP YOUR HEAD!

***BIBLIOGRAPHY: Actual accounts of the posters, as apart from the bands or the general hippie consciousness, are rare. We select a few titles mostly from Medeiros's M.A. thesis bibliography:

Collins, Tom. "Wes Wilson: Rock and Roll Posters as Art," Berkeley, *The Daily Californian,* 30 November 1966, p. 1.

Conklin, Lee. (Drawings) *Psychedelic Review,* Winter, 1970–71.

Medeiros, Walter P. *Electric Posters,* San Francisco rock concert memorabilia, 1966–68; guide to the exhibition. Exhibited at the University of California, Davis; Memorial Union Fourth Floor Gallery, January 9–February 15, 1974. Davis, 1974.

Walker, Cummings G., comp. *The Great Poster Trip: Art Eureka.* Editor: Cummings G. Walker. Designer: Richard O. Teater. Palo Alto, Calif., Coyne and Blanchard, 1968.

THE TRUMPET'S SILVER SOUND IS STILL: David MacPhail writes of his experiences on the *Sonoma County Bugle,* a paper whose death he witnessed:

"When I picked up my first copy of the *Sonoma County Bugle,* the spring of 1971, it had a clean professional look and, as the first serious attempt to establish an alternative, counter-culture-style newspaper in the county, it looked unusually healthy. A 16-page fortnightly tabloid, *The Bugle* had investigative stories on such subjects as PG&E's proposed nuclear power plant on fault-ridden Bodega Head and on the county's controversial predator control program, which threatened county wildlife, according to environmentalists. Besides all this, it had a charm that was engaging by its irreverence and slightly mad quality.

"A year later, however, *The Bugle* was on its knees, gasping, and by September, 1973, its third birthday, it was dead at issue #64.

"Some say *The Bugle* started after a blurred and now-forgotten barroom epiphany experienced by one of the paper's ridiculously thin editors and because another did not have a pet dog.

"'I always wanted a pet dog,' said the petless editor, 'so I could call something "Bugle."'

"Others, obviously more serious, say *The Bugle* was an attempt, like other counter-culture life-style experiments in Sonoma County as Morning Star Ranch and Wheeler Ranch, to bring some sort of alternative comprehensible order to what appeared to be the established madness of such things as Nixonomics, Vietnam, Cambodia and the Kent State killings.

"'Across the country,' one *Bugle* writer said at the paper's last rites, 'counterparts of the Kent State victims arose (in 1971) in fury and horror to seize control of their destinies.'

"*The Bugle* arose from the ashes of a Sonoma State College campus paper called *Steppes,* whose editors were rally organizers, like many radical groups. They were heard on campus, shouting 'Two, four, six, eight, organize and

smash the State.' After the college administration smashed *Steppes,* Michael Funke, Stephen Laughlin, Anthony Tusler and a handful of other Sonoma State students went off-campus, where they cranked out what they hoped would be a viable alternative for the entire county.

"Their timing was good. By 1970 Sonoma County, with a population of 210,000, was one of the fastest growing Bay Area counties. A large and steady influx of under-thirty, ex-urbanites flooded the hills and woods and, totally ignored by the established daily and weekly press, formed a potential core audience for any new counter-culture paper. In fact, according to the 1970 census, the greatest increase in Sonoma County's population — 84% — was in the 15- to 24-year-old age group.

"For its first eighteen months, *The Bugle* seemed to be in the right place at the right time. Moving from Cotati to a small skid row office in Santa Rosa, the county's administration and population center, and using a volunteer staff, the paper gathered advertisers and a consistent readership with a good coverage of environmental issues, the local anti-war movement, jail reform, plus coverage of the county's Chicano, Indian and Black minorities. By opening its pages to the alternative school movement, gay liberation and women's groups, all almost totally ignored by the conventional press, it gained their support, too.

"But by spring, 1972, *The Bugle* was on its knees, desperately pleading for help from the community to survive. It was deeply in debt, barely able to pay printing and distribution costs, much less salaries for its poverty-stricken staff. Laughlin had already quit to join two other under-thirty political hopefuls in an eventually successful takeover of the Cotati city council. Editor Funke quit for the 17th and last time; advertising and circulation were shadows of their former selves. *The Bugle's* attempt to maintain itself as an alternative paper had burned everyone out.

"Pleas for help brought fresh volunteers, new blood to the paper. I came on as writer, photographer and circulation manager (for which I was paid a commission on papers sold). Under the direction of associate editors Chuck Idelson and Bob Weinstein, everyone gritted their teeth and pulled *The Bugle* together. But as the last of a long and very irregular line of circulation managers, I came to see that *The Bugle's* demise was not a natural death but more of a suicide.

"For instance, *The Bugle* editorial staff often tended to focus on issues and views that reflected their views and those of their readers who bowed towards Cotati, the county's political counter-culture's Mecca. Yet I discovered that most of our readership was concentrated in the Russian River area and Santa Rosa, where hip culture was considerably less political.

"In 1972, River people, a loose confederation of long-haired craftsmen and hip straights, started their own paper, which immediately grabbed a readership equivalent to *The Bugle's*, though their distribution area was considerably less. They even gave us stiff competition on Cotati's streets.

"The River readers consistently told me that they liked *The Bugle,* but disliked its tendency toward 'Smash the State' politics, no matter how tongue in cheek, and felt that the paper was philosophically too much oriented toward Cotati. As soon as a non-political, but community-oriented paper came to the River, our sales started to slip.

"*The Bugle* editorial staff's somewhat limited views also reflected themselves in circulation. For reasons I have never determined, everyone seemed to think our circulation hovered around 2000. My monthly figures never showed a paid distribution more than 1500, more likely 1300 to 1400.

"Consistently, however, our press run was 2500 to 3000, leaving us with at least 1000 extra copies each time out.

"Probably the major factor in the death of *The Bugle,* however, was the editors' admitted total disinterest in the paper's business matters. 'We never claimed to be business people,' Funke said. 'I mean you can't have it too together if you have to call up an advertiser and ask if they could check to see how much they owed us.' But to me the absence of any interest in the business of *The Bugle* almost amounted to a death wish.

"*The Bugle,* like Morning Star Ranch, Wheeler Ranch and other political and social movements of the last several years, never really found a political or social base within its community. 'Yes,' said associate editor Chuck Idelson, who now works on an established weekly in Oregon, 'we made a lot of mistakes in advertising, circulation and subscriptions. But perhaps our major problem was in understanding exactly what community we were trying to serve.'

"'We tried,' according to Bob Weinstein, another associate editor who just completed his B.A. at Sonoma State, 'to be a forum for people or groups who were and are being ignored by the other media in the county. I guess the saddest thing about *The Bugle* folding is the void it will leave in Sonoma County!'

"I agree with Bob. For all the epiphany-stained madness and Smash the State psychology associated with *The Bugle,* it was much needed and much loved. I loved it and its passing is, indeed, sad."—DAVID MACPHAIL.

THE WARDER SILENT ON THE HILL: Another alternative paper folded! This is getting morbid, especially when it's the paper whose co-editor we interviewed last time around, the *NOLA Express,* of New Orleans, Darlene Fife and Robert Head, editors. From a tepee in the Appalachians Fife sends us a long letter, explaining that the proximate cause of the suspension (later a permanent closing) was eviction from their French Quarter house the day after Christmas, 1973, by an owner who wanted to divide up the space into mini-apartments. At the same time Head was acting as intervenor against the

plans of Louisiana Power and Light, who planned to build a nuclear fission power plant in the area. Head and Fife are vehemently opposed to nuclear fission power plants, and they were preparing for the latest round of hearings, and collecting money to bring an expert down from Minnesota, when the blow struck. While Darlene Fife moved into the headquarters of the Atlantis Distributing Company, Robert Head went on the road making contacts. In his travels he found the right mountain spot, and there they are now—still fighting the power plants, and circulating a petition to Congress for a moratorium on the building of same, for copies of which you should write Ms. Egan O'Connor at 305 High Street, Moorestown, NJ 08057. Although the decision in the case of LP&L went against them, they are still interested in non-polluting sources of energy (incl. solar power). Where they live now, however, they lack the electricity to run a typewriter, and they do not know when they can resume publication of *NOLA Express*. We can only regret their eviction and still more the way they were overruled on an issue affecting the health and safety of millions. Readers of Ibsen's *An Enemy of the People* will have done their preliminary homework.

SIPAPU'S BOOK OF THE YEAR is *A History of Underground Comics,* by Mark James Estren (San Francisco, Straight Arrow Books, 1974, $9.95). The only fault of this book is that it's impossible to put it down long enough to stop and review it. Otherwise, it is the most magnificent survey of a counter-cultural phenomenon ever published. The text is not secondary but rather integral to the innumerable illustrations, all of which are carefully documented in red in the margins; it winds among them, with a discussion of the origin of subversive comics, and of their progress through early violent or sexually explicit strips to the establishment of a Comics Code and the suppression of "dangerous" comics during the Fifties. There are chapters on the revival of the comics form; on violence, especially as seen in the work of S. Clay Wilson; on sexism, as exemplified in the drawing of R. Crumb; illustrations (tantalizingly few) from comics done by liberated women, such as Trina; and the story of the artists' political comment, copyright hassles, and relations with the overground society. There are also appendixes showing the early work of Harvey Kurtzman, an important influence at the start of the movement; a typical E.C. horror comic reproduced in full (this is the sort of comic that was banned in the Fifties, but the underground comic artists read such comics anyway, and like the poster artists, used the themes as raw material), a list of comic books and a bibliography. Even the poster artists get back in the act; there are a couple of OXO drawings by Griffin.

It is virtually impossible to analyze this work without quoting it, because its texture is so dense. We spent a whole day in compulsive fascination staring at the gorgeous parade of freaks, monsters, beautiful girls, hippies, caricatured political figures, lantern-jawed heroes, villains, helpless little guys, wild women, mad scientists, ghouls, crooks, holy fools, Black hipsters, cops, ducks, moose, toads, bugs who utter Hebrew letters and alive floating detached heads; who, starting with a wild house party on the outer covers and taking it indoors on the title page (address of the house is 533 Diamond; if that's San Francisco, then it's east of Twin Peaks), break up and cavort through squares and strips on every single page of this fabulous history. Indeed they *are* their history, and in this book the cartoonists' imaginary creatures break away from them, as well as from Mr. Estren, to take on a collective life of their own: a life where slimy creatures bubble up out of pools, motorcycle gangs bash and massacre each other, dirty old men cackle over a new plot, and the cartoonists themselves address you, the audience, with a clear intention of leading you up the garden path.

This is a good book for clearing the head. It not only exposes the hype of censorship, it also exposes the sexism in some of the cartoonists themselves (though not all); it faces the criticism of radical ideologues as well as the bewilderment of Middle America. The debate between Kurtzman and Gilbert Shelton (creator of the Fabulous Furry Freak Brothers), at the Alternative Media Project at Goddard College in Plainfield, VT, in June 1970, — with a man and a woman, both radicals, is very illuminating. The artists answer from an honorable position of individualism, without making any claims that they could win out in a collective society. The debate did reveal a real division or "generation gap" among comic artists and their readers; some look very seriously toward a socialist society toward which they expect the artists to join in struggle; the artists themselves wanted to let their minds float free, and comment politically only when and where they felt like it. The debate is an old one, of course, but in our minds, Kurtzman had the last word.

It occurs to us that there is a sense in which R. Crumb is anti-sexist, as S. Clay Wilson is anti-violence. To us Wilson seems to be saying: "You dream of running around in gangs beating people up — all right, you don't, but your neighbors do. This is how filthy, cruel and ultimately ridiculous it really is." And Crumb, whose character Flaky Foont lets that con man guru Mr. Natural run his mind as Angelfood McSpade lets men use her body, seems to be saying, "If you let other people take over your mind and body, you can expect to be raped. Your protests are absurd once it's happened — you let them get started on you." And when Crumb depicts a young woman showing off "the biggest knockers in the Movement," he depicts a creature that never was — but can anyone deny that personal, even sometimes sexual, vanity, is a big part of radical chic? The New Left doesn't like to hear of these things, except on occasions when it admits, at midnight, that they have still in them too much of the old unregenerate society. What they can't stand is to have a non-theoretical outsider point it out graphically with a coarse wit.

Coarse these cartoonists are, but never mean-spirited. They don't make sex look petty, or dismiss violence as trivial. These things Estren's book might bring out more sharply. There has been very little attention paid to this book. Not only the big review media, but also the library press, has ignored it or underplayed it. This is a pity, because although the price is high, Straight Arrow must have taken a big risk in publishing it. Of course, libraries don't owe it to publishers to buy their high-risk books, but it would be a pity if this one were to die. Unfortunately, the distance between the consciousness of Estren's cartoonist friends and the consciousness of most of America is to be measured in megaparsecs, and too many librarians, we fear, will fear to order it. But you, "the happy few," will not hesitate for a minute. You will order Estren's book, open a can of Tree Toad beer (a brand found only in these pages), and slurp it down as you meet the monsters and beat the heat. And a happy weekend to you.

At about the same time that we discovered Estren's history, we located an UNDERGROUND COMICS FESTIVAL in the Memorial Union of the Berkeley campus of the University of California, under the title of "Berkeley Con." The date was 17-20 April, 1974, and it wasn't just illness and other preoccupations that left us confused by the proceedings. Our notes recall for us a huge hall, tables loaded with comics, old and new, and posters like the kind Medeiros collects; some of the comics were new, some were collector's treasures, carefully preserved backfiles. The workshops and panels seem to

have been incredibly confused, with everyone talking at once and consciousnesses coming down like a tropical downpour. We can only recall the fantastic costumes, and fragments of conversation: "sex isn't sexist" . . . "Leninists in hiking boots" . . . "we reserve the right to be just as crazy as the men." The poster artists' panel, according to our colleague who taped it, was equally incoherent.

The program for other days on which we weren't able to be there was incredibly tight, with panels or workshops every hour or half an hour. Those comixfreex should learn how to run open spacey conferences from a really together outfit, say (to pick an example at random) the American Library Association.

6 : 1

Numbers 1 and 2 of volume 6 (consecutive issues nos. 11 and 12) mark the entrance and exit of Dora Biblarz as partner-contributor. Dora Biblarz was then a librarian in UC Davis's Acquisitions Department; she resigned due to other commitments on her time.

Carolyn Kimsey sold me her piece from her then home in North Carolina. I never met her nor the staff at Mother Earth News. *Diane Kruchkow, formerly Massachusetts-based editor of* Zahir, *and later, of* Small Press News, *now lives in Maine.*

STUMPED FOR AN ANSWER? Last issue we announced the silencing of the Sonoma County *Bugle,* an underground paper described by David MacPhail. He continues with a description of the *Bugle'*s successor, the Sonoma County (formerly Russian River) *Stump:*

"By the summer of 1972, Sonoma County's Russian River resort area 75 miles north of San Francisco was filled with young people. In itself, this was not unusual. For decades, young people from all over the Bay area had flocked to the redwood groves and swimming beaches bordering this cool, green river. They swam, played, smoked, romanced among the redwoods and, when summer was over, they all disappeared with the rest of the tourists, leaving the sidewalks of Guerneville and Monte Rio deserted. What was different by the summer of 1972 was the fact that the young people who now came to the area were not leaving when the summer was over. They were moving in to stay. And they weren't just from the San Francisco Bay area. They came from L.A., Long Beach, San Diego, Bakersfield and cities in other parts of the country. But if they were from different areas, they had two things in common besides their youth: their hair and their lifestyle. These young people were longhairs and they brought the counter-culture to the Russian River. What had grown up by 1972 within and around the old, established conservative communities of Guerneville, Monte Rio, Villa Grande, Rio Nido, and Cazadero was a young, hip, individualistic and amorphous conglomeration of longhaired potters, sandal makers, carpenters,

leather craftsmen, rock musicians, astrologers, toy makers, herb witches, poets, organic gardeners, wood butchers, candle makers, mystics, knaves and highwaymen. And many of these freaks had started to raise families in their redwood forest homes.

"Alienated as these hairy immigrants were from the established culture, harassed by Sheriff's deputies and local toughs, discriminated against by landlords and merchants, ignored or cursed by the local press and isolated from welfare and medical services in Santa Rosa 20 miles distant, the time was right in 1972 for an attempt at bringing this disparate mob together. — Enter the Russian River *Stump*.

"The *Stump* is a weekly tabloid-sized newspaper with a paid circulation of about 1500 and is aimed at the alternative subculture on the River. It is an excellent example of how communications, as here through the printed media, can bring people together to meet their own needs.

"The *Stump* sprouted into print in June, 1972, from donated offices overlooking the River in Monte Rio and was the first, overt, organized attempt to give some shape and identity to the counter-culture on the River. Originated by a man who called himself Jack the Carpenter and staffed by a handful of other volunteers, the *Stump* consisted of staff-written local news and commentary concerning the longhaired community, plus columns and features on astrology, organic gardening, police harassment, womens' liberation, rock music, welfare rights, ecology, craftsmen and longhaired businesses. Most of these subjects had hardly been thought of on the River before, — much less discussed openly.

"Despite such initial mistakes as oversized press runs, non-existent bookkeeping and unnecessarily high printing costs which almost killed the *Stump* within two months, the paper was devoured by longhairs hungry for news of their brothers and sisters and was an almost immediate popular success. In an editorial in the *Stump*'s first edition, Jack, who gave up the editorship after six months and, along with other original staffers, left the paper because of economic pressures, outlined the philosophy of the *Stump:*

"'We believe that inherent in any positive goal . . . is the need for survival; that in these times of megaweapons, pollution and overpopulation, survival depends on control of our environment; that this control will only come when the understanding of all people reflects concern for the collective good; and that can only come through communication. We believe that it is not enough to be not reactionary, to rebel against an apparent wrong. We believe that we must make some attempt to define and work within the limits of a popular direction. We believe that the path toward the positive must involve breaking from parasitic dependence on the mother culture.... We must learn to recycle our money and talents; to generate our own economy; we must learn to depend on ourselves.'

"And in many ways self-reliance is what happened with the advent of the *Stump*. For instance, through the *Stump*, the Mountain River Guild, a crafts guild, was formed. Previously, River craftsmen vainly competed with one another rather than cooperating for survival. The Guild brought craftsmen together and staged three successful crafts fairs, two at Monte Rio and one at Christmastime, 1972, in Santa Rosa, the area's largest marketplace. Today, many Guild craftsmen have their own successful businesses. Groups such as a food co-op, a women's center, and a badly needed health clinic were helped into life and nourished by the *Stump*. And though some proposed projects like a Monte Rio community center failed, 'these things couldn't have happened without the *Stump*,' according to Bliss Buys, the only original member still with the paper, whose current Guernewood Park offices are still staffed with volunteers (some of whom now get $3 a week for their efforts).

"The counter-culture on the River has lost some of its energy now, and crafts fairs have been banned by the powers-that-are. But the *Stump*, run now by an editorial board rather than by an editor, still tries to 'turn people on to something (in the community) they can get into,' says Bliss, and the paper still 'gives people with a beef the chance to air it,' a service not provided by other papers. No other newspaper, for instance, deals with such problems as longhairs getting beaten up by tow-truck operators when the operators answer a call to find out that the stranded motorist has long hair. The *Stump* 'is the only recourse people have in such situations,' Bliss says. 'If we show that these things are happening, maybe they'll stop.'

"The subculture on the River is smaller now, but, Bliss says, in many ways it is smaller and more tightly knit. It is becoming more powerful, she feels, as it learns new ways to deal with the power interests and entrenched county bureaucracy and thus continue to meet its needs.

"Many new things have happened on the River since 1972. And, as Bliss says, 'The *Stump* had to happen before all these things could happen.'

"We have seen a copy of the *Stump:* it is a charming, rather old-fashioned paper with an appropriately local and woodsy approach. They review films that have shown elsewhere for years and are apparently coming back for a re-run; e.g. *Zabriskie Point*. There are columns on dope and astrology, and one called 'The Growing Experience,' by Janice Broccoli. P.O. Box A, Monte Rio, CA 95462. $5.00 a year."—DAVID MACPHAIL.

MOTHER KNOWS BEST: In January 1970 the first slim, 64-page issue of *The Mother Earth News* began turning up at head shops, natural food stores, and other underground-press outlets across the United States. The pale gold cover of the magazine featured a rising sun and promised "a new beginning." Between the covers of *The Mother Earth News* were articles such as: "How to make it your way" and "Morning Glory Farm" that stressed alternative lifestyles, ecology, and the do-it-yourself, homespun philosophy of the young couple who launched the magazine, John and Jane Shuttleworth. Today, on its fifth anniversary, *The Mother Earth News* is a bimonthly of international circulation, with 165,000 paid subscribers and a standard press run of 235,000 copies for each new issue. Our interview this time took us (c/o Carolyn A. Kimsey) to Hendersonville, North Carolina to talk with Kenneth Hodges, head of the Editorial Department at *The Mother Earth News:*

SIPAPU: What is *The Mother Earth News* all about, Ken?

HODGES: The magazine's first priority is trying to find ways to do good things for the planet, to harmonize with nature. *Mother* carries articles on organic gardening, for instance, as opposed to energy-intensive, highly synthetic methods of farming. And the second priority is trying to find ways for people to live richer, more satisfying lives. Like *Mother* features home businesses as an alternative to the 9-to-5 grind.

SIPAPU: Can you sketch the beginning of *The Mother Earth News* for us?

HODGES: John and Jane Shuttleworth started the magazine just about a year after they'd met and married in Raleigh, North Carolina. They'd moved up to Madison, Ohio. John was doing promotional work for Bede Aircraft, and I think they were both free-lancing on the side for a magazine in North Carolina. But John decided that what he really wanted to do was to start his own—actually, a newsletter. It wasn't until after Jane and he began nailing together the first issue that it expanded into a magazine. They began by placing tiny ads in underground papers—such as the *East Village Other* and *L.A. Free Press.* When the ads began pulling in subscriptions they quit their jobs and in late 1969 began putting together the first *Mother.* They had about $1,500 to start with—some savings, some money from Jane's parents, some money from John's parents, and even part of it from a loan company. At the beginning it was just John and Jane, but people who were passing through Madison and knew about the magazine would drop by their cottage and help. And they worked awful hard, going for three or four days and nights at a time—straight on—without sleeping.

SIPAPU: And *The Mother Earth News* was a success right from the start?

HODGES: Yes. Well, John was raised on a dairy farm in Indiana, and

Jane grew up on a farm in North Carolina, so they knew what they were talking about in extolling the family farm type of life. Also, John has a very active mind and has always been good at whatever he did. He'd been bumming around the world ever since he dropped out of Ball State Teachers College (now Ball State University, Muncie, IN) and had worked 300 or some odd jobs. So he knows a little something about almost everything. He'd always collected information on ecology and self-sufficiency, *Mother*-type fare. And Jane backed him in starting the magazine. In fact, the name *The Mother Earth News* was Jane's idea. John's original thought was to call it something like *Chief Joseph Speaks* — in tribute to Chief Joseph of the Nez Perce Indians — but he saw there were more possibilities in the name *The Mother Earth News*. Such as, you know, "Mother."

SIPAPU: What about financing? Once the $1,500 John and Jane had scrapped together was gone, did *Mother* rely on advertising revenues?

HODGES: *Mother* immediately joined the Underground Press Syndicate (now the Alternative Press Syndicate) and got advertising in those publications right off the bat. So that helped bring in subscriptions. As far as advertisements in *Mother* went, John's idea was to keep the advertising space at 15% of the magazine — instead of the standard in the magazine business, which is 55% of each issue — and to screen all advertisers and make sure they were good people offering a worthwhile product or service, and were not just out to make money at the expense of *Mother's* readers — with the idea that readers would trust whoever advertises in the magazine.

SIPAPU: So, in effect, *The Mother Earth News* sinks or swims on the basis of circulation?

HODGES: Yes, *Mother* had ties with a national distributor in the beginning. John signed a short-term contract with Dell because they promised something like "instant national exposure." But he got out of that as soon as possible. Dell wouldn't promote the magazine, and then if they did push it and it sold, they'd keep most of the money. So John formed his own distributing company, which is still a part of *The Mother Earth News* corporation. The magazine does its own distribution — in some cases through regional outlets — so everything is controlled right here at the home office.

SIPAPU: So, what about you, Ken? How did you come to be head of the editorial department at *Mother?*

HODGES: I first started work with *Mother* in November of 1971, mainly because I knew John. I'd been a musician for the ten years prior to that, and had known John since 1964. We met when I was with the Folksters trio in Hawaii and John was — I think — working at a service station. Anyhow, we kept in touch. Then in 1966 John spent a few months with me in my apartment in New York. In December of that year my music group, the Bitter End singers, decided to play a tour through Germany and England, and John went along with us as our road manager. When we got back to the States, John and I split company, but continued to keep in touch. Then in October of 1971, when I'd decided to get out of music for a while, I called John from L.A. and asked if he would be around when I came East. "Yes," he said, and "please stop by."

Well, John had told me about publishing *Mother,* but I expected such a one-horse operation that, if I worked there, which was only a possibility, I'd moonlight at night and work during the day for free at *Mother.* But it turned out that, although quite small, the magazine was a well-organized operation. The first issue I helped on was no. 13, and neither John nor I had any idea what I could do. I had no magazine experience! Then I guess it was no. 14 when John put me on proofreading, and about no. 15 or so I became copy editor and in charge of the editorial office. At that point a couple of senior staff members left, and all of a sudden I was the senior staff member. From that day on, I've been doing basically the same job, only it's expanded quite a bit.

SIPAPU: So you started with *The Mother Earth News* when it was a struggling new enterprise in Madison. In your opinion, what's the secret of *Mother's* success?

HODGES: There's been a widespread discontent in this country for years. *Mother* tries to turn that discontent into something positive. Some counter-culture publications stress the "overthrowing the system" idea. *Mother* has a positive rather than a negative approach. Then, as far as money goes, John Shuttleworth is a manager *par excellence.* I mean he's really quite good at it. People who come here say that it's impossible for an editorial staff as small as we are to do what we do. But it's done. It's done because everyone is forced to work efficiently — you don't stand around the coffee table and talk or that kind of thing. I know *Clear Creek* had a lot of money to start with, and then got more but still failed. And that was true of *Earth* magazine also. The management was just poor. *Earth* (mentioned in *Sipapu*, no. 4, p. 4) went in for slick paper treatment, with *fashions* in there of all things! The whole *Mother* strategy is to carry as much how-to information as possible, with nothing that's flighty. Most of the magazine's articles are how-to: how to raise cattle or build your own home or something.

SIPAPU: In September of 1973, when *Mother's* circulation was just reaching over 100,000, why did the magazine pack up and move from Madison, Ohio, to Hendersonville, North Carolina?

HODGES: Because of our plans for The Mother Earth News Research Center, a kind of ecological experimentation center and living example of *Mother's* "working with nature, doing more with less" theme. We needed an area of the United States where the southern and northern types of flora overlapped and where the climate was right for farming and the altitude, etc. suitable for solar and wind power tests. The Research Center will also be involved with alternative housing, alternative transportation, and things like that.

SIPAPU: What did local Hendersonville people think when *The Mother Earth News* moved into the area?

HODGES: The townspeople basically are fine. But always there are a few who think we're a communist publication. That happened in Ohio, too—especially in Ohio, because *Mother* was a new thing back then.

SIPAPU: Does *Mother* employ any local people?

HODGES: The entire operation—the magazine, Mother's General Store and the Bookstore—employs around 65 people, and probably 50 or 55 are local folks. The editorial staff of *Mother,* including John, is about five people, and it doesn't include any local people at all.

SIPAPU: What about treatment of employees, pay rates, and benefits at *Mother?*

HODGES: All employees are treated the same. In editorial we probably get slightly higher salaries, but that's because of longevity. The editorial staff, overall, has more longevity than people in other areas of the operation. At this point, the basic starting rate at *Mother* is $2.50 per hour. Then generally, for a while, the increases come pretty rapidly in 25-cent jumps. Just up until recently the "company benefits" here were nil. But now we have five paid holidays, medical insurance and a couple of days of sick leave. Eventually, there will be a profit-sharing plan set up which all employees can participate in.

SIPAPU: And the status of women at *Mother Earth News?*

HODGES: I think it's fair to say that women get an equal chance at *Mother.* There are more women than men employed by *Mother.* Most of the department heads are women.

SIPAPU: A recent story about *The Mother Earth News* that appeared in the *Atlanta Journal and Constitution* magazine was titled: "*Mother* is a One-Man Show." Is this true? If so, in what way?

HODGES: I'd say that *Mother* is basically a one-man show, meaning John Shuttleworth's show. John started the magazine. John has a background that is more extensive and varied than anyone else's here. As I said earlier, he knows at least a little about almost everything—which is terribly important for a how-to magazine. Plus that, he is, as businessmen go, pretty darn good. So John keeps pretty tight control over all departments.

SIPAPU: What about the future of *The Mother Earth News?* And, especially, do you see the magazine getting involved with local communities?

HODGES: Well, of course, there's the Research Center, the first one right here in the Great Smoky Mountains. Our plans include a second experimental center in the Northwest in Oregon or Washington, one in Costa Rica and one in New Zealand—for a total of four in different environmental zones. We're currently expanding the magazine from 132 pages to 148 and eventually want it to peak at around 196 pages. We also have a pilot film in the works for a TV series, and, if it works out well and can be sold to a network, John and Jane will be appearing on national television. As far as getting involved with Hendersonville or any local town that we might happen to be in at some point, we haven't had time to do it. Our staff is still too small to enable anyone to have much spare time. We have been working with the classes of Professor George Ramsey at the Georgia Tech School of Architecture on designing the first Research Center, but that's about the extent of our local involvement. Things are just recently starting to look good for *The Mother Earth News*. It's been a long haul. There are a lot more things that need to be done, a lot of hard work ahead, before *Mother* will admit to success.

The Mother Earth News is an offset press publication, brought to the camera-ready stage at the home office in Hendersonville and then flown to Ohio for printing by an outside firm. Magazines are then trucked back to North Carolina by *Mother* for distribution by the home office's shipping department and dealer department. Recent issues of *The Mother Earth News* contain interviews with people active in alternative culture areas, articles on starting home businesses, small-scale farming using natural methods, experimental work in alternative energy sources, an "energy hotline" of environmental news, reviews of little magazines and new organizations, lots of letters from readers with *their* how-to tips and over 20 pages of P & S listings (contacts for getting back to the land). Subscriptions to *The Mother Earth News* are $8.00 per year, $1.50 per single issue, from *The Mother Earth News,* P.O. Box 70, Hendersonville, NC 28739. —CAROLYN A. KIMSEY.

WOMEN OF LETTERS: Diane Kruchkow, poet, editor of *Zahir,* and Chair One of COSMEP (Committee of Small Magazine/press Editors and Publishers), reports from America's first known conference of women writers, held at Bridgeport, Connecticut, 3-4 August 1974:

"Convocation: Women in Writing," sponsored by the N.O.W. (National Organization for Women) task force on Women and the Arts, and coordinated by COSMEP member Valerie Harms of Magic Circle Press, began Friday night with a brief introduction by Valerie, after which Sharon Spencer talked of how she saw her first-priority identity change from college teacher (Montclair State College, Upper Montclair, New Jersey) to novelist. Sharon read from one of her books, *The Space Between,* and then read a "Manifesto of a Woman Writer."

There was a lot of discussion afterwards about women's role in academia, women finding time for their art, women's relationships with publishers (this prompted one woman to remark, "Being rejected by a male editor is not failure; it may be incredible success"). The alternatives to the commercial publishing world were also discussed as talk centered around the small presses. After the discussion, some women read brief selections from their poems. Among them were Louise Matledge, Donna Ippolito, Binnie Klein and Jenine Dobbs.

Saturday morning Megan Terry talked on playwriting and life in the theater. Megan, a well-known dramatist who works with the Magic Theater in Omaha, shared the Obie in 1970 for her play, *Approaching Simone* (Simone Weil, the great French writer) which could not find a publisher until the Feminist Press came along. A recent work is *Babes in the Big House,* a prison fantasy. Megan talked about the necessity of taking control of one's own writing—trying to get money through grants; taking over a TV station for women's plays, etc. Her plays, she said, were produced on radio only abroad, not in the U.S. She emphasized that women have to work actively to make their own destiny as artists. That includes turning to small press publishing and creating new independent presses. Some playwrights of special note she mentioned were Irene Furness, Rosalyn Drexler, Adrienne Kennedy, Kathleen Kimball and Judith Katz.

Later in the morning seven women participated in a panel called "Wonder Women in Publishing and Marketing." They were: Valerie Harms, Magic Circle Press; Rochelle Holt, Ragnarok Press; Donna Ippolito, Black Maria Magazine and Swallow Press; Donna Loercher, Feminist Book Mart; Anne Pride, KNOW, Inc. (a Director of COSMEP); Verne Moberg, Feminist Press; and Lele Stephens, Erato Publications. These women mostly summarized their involvements, many of which are familiar to small press publishers. Valerie showed some beautiful books her press had done, one a celebration with Anais Nin, and mentioned that J. Philip O'Hara (the poet Frank O'Hara's brother) of Chicago, recently said that he'd distribute these books. Rochelle Holt talked about the hassles and rewards not only of publishing but also of printing. Donna Loercher has put together a distribution company for feminist books. Anne Pride began KNOW in 1969 by printing pamphlets; then expanded into books. Verne Moberg began the Feminist Press in 1970 after working in commercial publishing.

As a result of a lot of energy fermenting in different directions Saturday morning, discussion groups on 11 topics were set up to meet during lunch and supper. The topics were: creative energy; fantasy and solitude vs. reality; feminist vs. establishment presses and agents; spiritual development in writing; guerilla theater; poetry; novel writing; illustrating; identity through writing; journalism; and experimental forms. Most met for an hour or so before the evening session and good conversation, if nothing else, got accomplished.

Saturday afternoon the rains came and the talk drifted. There was a brief mention of 1975-1976 being the United Nations Year of the Woman, complete with a one-half million-dollar International Women's Arts Festival. The co-ordinator for this is Marilyn Boll, 330 E. 33d Street New York, NY 10016. It was suggested that something be done for women in writing, as for example an international women's writing conference. 8 March 1975 will be International Women's Day, by the way. The International Organization of Women in the Arts will also try to help out. For more information we were directed to: Linda Heddle, Lowell Hall, University of Wisconsin, 610 Langdon Street,

Madison, WI 53706. Other Bicentennial addresses are Government Bicentennial Office, American Revolution Bicentennial Administration, 736 Jackson Place NW, Washington, DC 20276; and more importantly, People's Bicentennial, Dupont Circle Building, 1344-46 Connecticut Avenue, NW, Washington, DC 20036.

Carol Cote, managing editor of *The Writer* and an officer of NOW, stayed for a few hours Saturday afternoon. The talk turned to NOW politics, and people began drifting out. Much of the talk centered on volunteerism vs. payment, which is sometimes a concern of COSMEP, too. Carol did mention that the NOW Legal Defense Fund has some money and will help people write grant proposals, although one would have to be a NOW member to work through them. Valerie mentioned that there is a women's retreat called "Emma's Place" at Hearst Castle, P.O. Box 717, Grover City, CA 93433 (805-409-9633) which costs $3.00 a night. There's also a women's village in Santa Fe, NM, in which women are doing the construction.

Saturday night we saw a film, "Anais Observed" by Robert Snyder. This was followed by another poetry reading. Before her reading, Sue Silvermarie announced that Elizabeth Gould Davis, author of *The First Sex* and other feminist books, had committed suicide a few days before. She was Dita Beard's sister. This event changed the direction of the whole conference and strengthened the emphasis of putting control of writing into the writers' hands. The effect of Ms. Davis's suicide was still very strong Sunday morning. In the meeting the groups worked on a statement demanding: that writers get a subsidy from the Federal government; that we research how other governments (as Sweden) support the arts (Siv Cedering Fox gave a brief but impassioned talk on this at the COSMEP conference in New York); that we apply for a grant to support the researchers; and that we work with NOW lawyers to draft how to do this. We also decided to dedicate an anthology which would come out of the conference to Ms. Davis, and to publish Sue Silvermarie's poem in broadside form (the staff of *Gravida* will work on this).

As we got onto other topics, Anne McGovern talked about the politics of children's literature—how the stereotyped views of boys and girls are slowly changing with the help of aware writers and illustrators. Anne is now working on a book on Deborah Sampson, a book on sharks (who, it has been shown, prefer to eat men to women, 20 to 1), a book on lions called *Is the King of Beasts a Queen?* (for the female seems to do most of the work), and a book in which the captain of the baseball team is female.

The formal conference (and my attendance thereat) ended with a talk and slide show by Miriam Arguelles on "The Re-emergence of the Goddess" in which we saw how some ancient and contemporary works of art relate to women. Ms. Arguelles has written a fine article, "The Goddess and the Astronaut" for *Maitreya,* no. 4, an issue devoted to women, which was

reprinted in the August 1974 issue of *East-West Journal*. (She and her husband Jose illustrated *Sipapu*, v. 2, no. 1, consecutive issue no. 3, January 1971.)

Altogether, the conference brought many women together who expressed a frustrating sense of isolation in their art. Many women from New York City began talking of meeting regularly and planning action groups. Other women came away with a renewed sense of their place and their art. I came away from this, my first writers' conference, (although this probably strictly wasn't one) and my first extensive women's meeting, a little tired, a little upset at the lack of edible food, and a little frustrated at the many weaknesses I still saw. But when I got home I was caught by a picture on my calendar of a Mexican woman at a United Farm Workers' rally lifting up her arms in the jubilation and strength of her integrity. I stared at the picture for a long time and felt the strength of this woman and all women. And then I reflected upon the conference and felt a stirring somewhere within me. And I knew, as others too were learning, that Elizabeth Gould Davis did not die in vain. — DIANE KRUCHKOW.

FOX ON THE UNDERGROUND: From the introduction to the latest work of Hugh Fox, author of *The Living Underground*, comes the following analysis of the alternative press scene as of now:

Mid-1970's: the counter-culture literary thrust of the 60's, muted, low-keyed, all but invisible as protest, has become institutionalized as a permanent fixture on the cultural scene. The magazines and books continue to emerge, there are two big counter-culture reviews, *Margins* and *Small Press Review*, while many if not most of the small presses have entered into organizations (COSMEP, Alternative Press Syndicate), Coordinating Council of Literary Magazines, and the concern of the small press world is *itself*, its own dynamics. Its identity is no longer derived from concentrating on a counter-identity. George Drury Smith's *(Beyond Baroque)* recent suggestion that the whole terminology of "small press" and "counter-culture" be transformed into "independent" is crucial. . . .

Some months ago I was asked by the editor of *Confrontation* for an essay on the image of the hero in the contemporary American novel, meaning *(his* meaning) the contemporary commercial-sector novel. I couldn't write the article because valid criticism of any literature implies that there is a "literature" to criticize and the tighter the control-squeeze to conform to any given control-model, the less "writing" becomes "literature." Literature as pamphleteering (the "accepted" Soviet writing) as well as literature as pork-sausage (the NYC "manufactured-novel") do not freely reflect the spirit, the psychology, the whole flavor of a people or a time, but express merely the boxed-in formalisms of a particular group imposing a particular doctrine on art.

After the Romantics, we can't really return blithely back to the idea of artist as anonymous servant of the church or state, and that is precisely what the commercial sector is asking the artist to do: disappear as a genetically, organically complex individual and fit his art to the uses of someone else's bankroll. The Romantics erased the idea of 13th century anonymity and made every artist a school, a movement, a total world; and any attempt to reverse the direction of art back to the artist as handmaiden of any one creed or doctrine always results in an underground: whether in the Soviet Union or the United States. The underground emerges when any *official* program, private or public, dictates: This is the way art is, what it is, how it is to be done.

Of course it's really much more mysterious than that. I'm thinking of the Akamba in East Africa, back in the 1920's. The idea of "writer/poet" didn't exist as a function. There are Medicine ("Wise") Men, and the Medicine Men are really only the members of the tribe who in any way function *like* the modern "writer"—as a conduit between the Tribe and the Supernatural: curing sickness, telling "fortunes," and in general keeping the Tribe in benign alignment with the Dream-World, the Unknown-World, the World of the Dead, the World of the Future (divination).

The writer in the U.S. in the 1970's basically should fulfill this shamanistic function; he is the Seer, the Oracle; in his work he materializes the way things will be, divines, predicts the Future, exorcises her evil, is prescriptively prophetic, not merely pointing out the way things *are* going, but the way they *should* go....

By turning writing into product, this shamanistic, seer function is blocked, and Art no longer serves as mirror, omen, prophecy, prescription. And so the society that depends on the shaman's function for diagnosis, no longer knows *what* it is nor where it is (or should be) going. Which nicely describes the U.S. today; involved with product-images that do not reveal the true state of the nation, but rather a falsely benign state of misleading optimism. We become involved solely with ephemera, trivia, surface; and the dimensions of change outside our conglomerate information-world are completely lost to us. Our information is "buy me" information, ersatz, confusing and especially negative because it substitutes a seeming-something instead of just leaving a gaping blank. We're eating chalk and we think it's ham sandwiches.

The individualistic, non-formulized writer, then, is of necessity a psycho-social historian. The various individualities of various "free" writers become a data-bank of the psycho-social history of an era; because literary history, after all, *is* nothing more than the Time-Spirit given voice and form. — HUGH FOX.

THE FIRST NATIONAL SYMPOSIUM ON CHICANO LITERATURE was held 21–22 November 1974 at New Mexico Highlands University in Las Vegas, NM, an old town on the Santa Fe Trail that until had two governments, one Anglo and one Hispano. The town, and this symposium, were and are divided in sympathies.

The symposium was very hastily organized, for while the idea had been in the works for some time, a firm commitment for money from the National Educational Task Force — La Raza was received less than a month before.

This resulted, of course, in a smaller attendance, both in terms of speakers and audience, than might otherwise have been possible. Organization was in the hands of David Conde, Highlands' Ethnic Studies chief, and Phil Ortega, managing editor of *La Luz* magazine (360 S. Monroe St., Denver, CO 80209. A list of his publications on Chicano literature is available from this address). The conference drew 230 participants from 11 States and from 22 different universities, although a good chunk of the body count was local faculty and students. The local Chicano students' organization put a lot of effort into the affair. There was an organizing meeting at which it was announced that "we need some girls to staff the registration tables" (oh-oh!) while the assignment of people to discuss issues at the cocktail party with the visiting speakers was mostly given to men, until not enough of them would volunteer and someone commented that "this could even be done by some of you ladies." In fairness, some consciousness began to dawn. About half the invited speakers were women, and there were some quasi-embarrassed remarks made about *machismo*. For Las Vegas, NM, this was progress.

Sylvia Gonzales led off the first morning after a welcoming speech by Dr. Frank Angel, the President of Highlands University and the first Chicano to hold such a position in this country. Dr. Gonzales, who works at San José, spoke on national character vs. universality in Chicano poetry. Her point was that styles are universal, that works are the creation of unique personal vision, a response to the human condition. She made an analogy with the beginnings of American literature, which (she said) first concerned itself with Britain (the past, the roots of the people), then moved on to descriptions of the American scene and finally, when society was more stable, moved to universal themes. Chicano literature is going through the same phases, she said. Unfortunately, at this point she degenerated into some quasi-genetic jazz about Chicanos being mixtures of European rationality and Asian (via Amerindian) spirituality, and thus more fit to govern than whites.

It seemed to me that the analogy we drew was very apt. If there was a first national symposium on American literature it must have been very much like this one on Chicano literature. A lot of term-defining, yes-there-is-a-Chicano-literature-and-don't-let-anyone-tell-you-differently arguments, a lot of pride in the existence of the conference and the progress of the nation which that implied; etc., etc.

The next speaker was Tino Villaneuva of Boston University, who, unfortunately for me spoke in very fast Spanish. I went out to get coffee and met my office mate Gilbert Rivera. He said that Villaneuva must be from Texas or Cuba because he spoke so fast, and he left because the guy was too much of a strain on his northern New Mexico, which is an enclave relatively untouched by the outside world, would clash with the culture of the big city and of the border groups; as we shall note.

José Renya spoke on the humor of Texas Chicanos. He told a few of the jokes he had collected. One good one: a recent Mexican immigrant goes up to a Coke machine and puts in 15 cents, not realizing that the price is now a quarter. A light comes on that says "Dime." He looks furtively around, and when no one is watching, whispers to the machine, "Give me a Coke!" — Charlotte Cardenas spoke on the novel *Bless Me, Ultima,* by Anaya. She praised the book in general, but criticized the portrayal of Ultima herself, who she said had no human qualities and in particular seemed to be sexless. Cardenas felt such undeveloped characters had no place in modern literature. This drew a very heated response from the audience. I talked to Cardenas afterwards, and she said that as *Ultima* is somewhat of a sacred cow in northern New Mexico, she has chosen it as a nice target to draw some response. I asked her if Ultima's sexlessness wasn't just an outcropping of a more general problem: the portrayal of women in general. She thought so, and said that in fact women are not people in Chicano literature. Indeed, "it is worse than that," according to Cardenas. Still, she said, this wasn't a cause of concern. Most Chicano novels are (so far) first novels; first novels tend to be autobiographical; and most of the authors had not, in their lives, seen any women doing anything but being mothers and going to church. Cardenas's talk was the only one which was a "typical" literature talk, about a specific topic, and not generalized bullshit. When I asked people in the audience for their impressions, most of them said that the conference should have contained more material like Cardenas's talk.

I missed most of the rest of the talks due to my teaching job, but my spies tell me that there was a talk on the poem, "Yo soy Joaquin," by Donaldo Castro, and a showing of a film made about the poem. Also there were speeches by Juan Bruce Novoa; Guillermo Rojas, from *Sipapu*'s home turf, UC Davis (Spanish Dept.) and Tomás Ibarra Fausto. The last afternoon was devoted to a panel, featuring a table of critics and an audience of local people, most of whom were by now doing a slow burn because the conference had not been what they imagined. This panel discussion comes to you filtered through me, who understood the slower Spanish of the locals much better than that of the fast-speaking panelists; so although I may have some of the ideas recorded incorrectly, here is what went down:

Betsy Tapia, a local student, read some of her poetry, and we all dug it. The panel never did get on to discussing her literature or anybody else's, however. The audience went after the panel with arguments like these: criticism of literature is a luxury that the poor can't afford; literature itself does nothing for the poor; the panelists are copping out by surviving in a university environment; what is really needed is to talk to the older people, preserving their wisdom, to conserve our ancient heritage and get back to the land and fight for La Raza. The panel fired back with these facts: most Chicanos (85%) live in cities, not in the backwoods of New Mexico; the "ancient heritage" is a bunch of romanticized hogwash; the ancient ones and their wisdom aren't relevant to the L.A. barrios and besides some people *are* doing that kind of collecting; the locals aren't seeing the big picture; and finally, literature *is* relevant, so there! The panel was caught somewhat off-balance by this unexpected audience venom and so didn't argue as effectively as they might have. For example, no one bothered to point out that Tom Paine, Karl Marx, etc. were not exactly irrelevant to their Movements; or that literature, in reflecting reality, can affect people in profound ways and produce real pride in their culture and insight into their lives.

Altogether, this panel discussion was a sophomoric bore, probably just like the one at the (hypothetical) "First American National Lit" meeting. The cause of this was undoubtedly local frustration. The leaders of the local Chicano groups felt frustrated over several things: the general nature of the talks; the academic English-teachers'-meeting tone, the lack of human contacts. But most of all, I felt it was local culture and the local conception of what it means to be a Chicano hitting national reality head on. But still, here in Las Vegas, NM, in the crisp, cold, fall weather, with the incomparable chili and mountain air to inspire one and all, at one of the home bases of the Hispanic people, was a good place for the first symposium on Chicano literature. There were a lot of good vibrations, especially on the first day; a feeling that it was great that this was happening at all. In that sense, it was a sign of progress and stability. A collection of papers presented is being prepared, but general availability (outside of participants) is undecided. However, there is a new publications distributor, which put on a nice display of books at the conference: their address: El Camino Real, Bldg. 41, Denver Federal Center, Denver, CO 80225. — PAUL DUBOIS.

6 : 2

This issue of Sipapu *was originally done in green on white, with illustrations by Meg Hehner. A loss of some issues necessitated an overrun of black on white.*
Ours was the first review of Callenbach's Ecotopia. *Our impression is that this book has finally sunk into the earth, — where it will fertilize further "green" movements. Its faults are obvious, its intention worthy. The essay title is the first line of a Housman poem.*
Lee Marrs, creator of Pudge, *has not been heard from in recent years.*
There now is a Women's Studies Program at U.C. Davis.

THE ASIAN-AMERICAN WRITERS' CONFERENCE is here described by Dean Lan, a student at UC Davis:

"Recognition of historic injustice and cautious optimism marked the mood at the Asian-American Writers' Conference held 24-29 March 1975, at the Oakland Museum. The stated objective of the Conference was to 'encourage creative expression, and also to provide an occasion for the exchange of ideas, resources and experiences among the Asian-American community, thereby reestablishing the tradition and continuity of Asian-American writing that was broken during and after World War II.'

"The conference, organized by the Combined Asian-American Resources Project, Inc. (CAMP), with the Oakland Museum and the Guild for Cultural and Ethnic Affairs, drew participants from as far away as Indiana, according to Jeff Chan, faculty member of California State University, San Francisco. Audiences averaging over a hundred daily attended the drama, fiction and poetry readings and workshops as well as the lectures on the history of Asian-American writing. Short films were shown, including 'Dupont Guy, the Schiz of Grant Avenue,' and 'I Told You So,' a documentary of the poet Lawson Inada, now of Oregon. Panel topics included Filipino-American literature, Autobiography, and Stereotypes. The panel on Stereotypes, in particular, included Pat Nakano and Connie Yu, who discussed examples of the general exclusion, and Christopher Chow, one of the first Asian television reporters, narrating videotaped examples of the media coverage of Asians. Dr. Ben Tong, the fourth member of the panel, warned of the severe psychological and physiological consequences of negative self-image.

"The diverse meanings of the term *Asian-American,* one of the main recurring themes at workshops and lectures, were brought into focus at sell-out performances of Frank Chin's first play, 'Chickencoop Chinaman,' the first Asian-American work produced by the New York stage. Chin's definition of the situation of his people, 'I'm neither Chinese nor American; I'm a Chinaman,' captures the dilemma confronting the minority writer in a white-dominated writers' world in America.

"The conference represented a historic first step in the recognition of Asian-American writing as an authentic and unique force in American literature. The logo on the announcement was equally striking: a Japanese actor in samurai costume, wielding a giant pencil instead of a sword, against a ruled background of legal-sized paper: black on yellow."—DEAN LAN.

WOMEN'S COLLECTION DEVELOPMENT CONFERENCE: The Collection Section of the Chapter of Academic and Research Libraries, California Library Association, was opened in the Faculty Club of the University of California, Davis, 25 April 1975, by Dora Biblarz, Northern California coordinator of this group. There were thirty-four women and four men in the clubroom that morning when the meeting started at 10:20.

The setting and style were informal; without table or gavel, Ms. Biblarz simply called everyone together and introduced Helen Remick, academic coordinator of the UC Davis Women's Center. Ms. Remick described the evolution of the Center, which was rather different from many similar campus centers; it started out as a peer counselling group, became an administrative department, and at last acquired an academic coordinator. Ms. Remick holds an appointment in the Department of Psychology; there is no overall program of women's studies at UC Davis, although several related courses, or courses with a feminist consciousness, on campus, notably in Psychology and History, are available. Ms. Remick's appointment with the Women's Center is a half-time appointment.

Its library has also developed slowly. Few books are in it; most of these are in the Shields Library, the main one on campus. Instead, the Women's Center library consists of vertical file material and newspaper clippings; these are keyed by number to a subject list of headings. A true list of articles, or retrieval system, is yet to come. The clientele of the Center has also been studied, and astonishingly enough includes few undergraduates. Young women between the ages of 17 and 22 are still not frequent visitors to the Center, and for two reasons, Ms. Remick believed; first of all, they still have faith in the system, in the security of marriage and the ease of a (part-time) career, and secondly, women have been affected by the return to traditional values characteristic of the seventies. It's only when they have been out in the world and have been exposed to the edge of discrimination, or when divorce becomes a possibility, that they turn to the Center. Hence most of the visitors are women over 22. High school students have been off limits hitherto, but with the aid of a grant from off-campus, directed especially toward community work, the Center hopes to try to reach high school women and women in outlying areas.

Ms. Remick avoided the temptation (which probably many men in her place would have found irresistible) to make a long speech, and instead questions flowed naturally from the audience (the ease and rapport between speaker and audience was a constant surprise and delight; indeed whoever was in the chair didn't sit in a chair, but rather leaned against one, thus becoming a chairleaningperson). What were the budget limitations at the Center? Very stringent; the library has only a few hundred dollars to work with. Is there any chance of a full-time Women's Studies program at UC Davis? No way. What can be done about microfilming periodical articles and newspaper clippings? The experience of the Women's History Research Center with Bell and Howell was discussed, as a warning: they are now doing their own.

Sybil Fielding, an older woman from Scripps Library, was invited to discuss the status of women's studies at Scripps College (courses, no major), and the Ida Rust MacPherson Collection. This special group of 2000 books was launched in 1938 by interested donors; it includes works on women in the Western tradition, suffrage, domestic employment, education, and humanism.

The collection is being constantly weeded and developed. May Sarton, poet and novelist, has donated some manuscript material; Norman H. Strouse, noted book collector, is the recent donor of a valuable collection on autographed letters, manuscripts, and first editions of the Victorian writer Marie Corelli. Another related collection is the Addison Metcalf collection on Gertrude Stein. In the fall of 1974, an agreement was made with Research Publications, Inc. of Connecticut, whereby selected holdings from the MacPherson Collection will be microfilmed to supplement those holdings on the history of women which are being microfilmed at Radcliffe, Smith and other selected libraries.

Other women reported on the status of libraries and studies at their campuses: the California State Universities and Colleges at San Diego, San Jose, Chico, etc. At the University of California at Irvine, Judith Stanley reported an interest in structuralist and linguistic approaches. At San Jose State, a Federal grant of $4000 has a bizarre limitation: no books about women as teachers or librarians! (Evidently this is intended to get away from the thinking of women as confined to these roles, but it doesn't do much for the women who *are* teachers and librarians, and who are trying to find a new status for themselves in these professions.) Fay Blake at the University of California School of Librarianship at Berkeley teaches an apparently unique course in schools of that type, on the status of women in librarianship.

Ms. Remick resumed with a further discussion of the UC Davis experience. Much of the impetus for the growth of the Center derived from the appointment of a Chancellor's Committee on the Status of Women at UCD. Apparently some of the most conservative women on campus were appointed to this committee, but the effect was the reverse of what you might have expected. The loyal "Old Guard" were radicalized by their experience! Alike the facts which they uncovered while conscientiously doing their job, and the uproar with which the report was received, turned them all into "Young Turks." Ms. Remick's own experience in the Department of Psychology (when a second woman was appointed there, a male colleague told her, "Now you'll have someone to talk to,") led her to a discussion of the emphasis on male psychology; apparently large amounts of the published research in psychology journals, which purports to describe human psychology in terms of reactions to tests, early experience and the like, is done on the students of Ivy League schools, where most of the students are men. Hence the statements about human psychology that get into the textbooks, with learned authors' names in the footnotes, really only apply to men, and college men at that. To this day, well over 50% of psychological research is done on predominantly male populations (or on rats; apparently it's men and rats first). This bias led into a discussion of subject headings in the library catalog; the audience seemed well aware of Sanford Berman's work in this field *(Sipapu,* v. 3, no. 2), were inclined to brush aside any technical difficulties, and to demand a "truth-in-packaging" concept from subject catalogers. Ultimately, for Ms. Remick, at least, individual differences were more important than sex differences in academic study and research.

Lunch was served in the club library (again, there was no "head table"), and afterwards there were announcements of coming events and an exchange of bibliographies. The International Women's Year will be celebrated by a world meeting in Mexico City in June 1975, and at the end of that month, there will be a pre-conference on the status of women in the profession at ALA in San Francisco. Several women in the field described their own bibliographies, while the function of newsletters (like *KNOW NEWS*), and the sharing of microfilm resources among various schools, was discussed. Essentially the problem boils down to avoiding duplication and coordinating efforts without over-centralization and the reliance of all on one or two individuals who would almost certainly have other responsibilities (not one of the women there said that they were allowed to concentrate full-time on feminist studies or activities). It is also unwise to rely on commercial microfilm services; Microcard Editions, for example, apparently prints less than they say they do, and Bell and Howell have acquired a bad name on several counts. In the end, Ms. Biblarz wisely declined to found a newsletter on the subject, and agreed instead, *just once,* to collect bibliographies and papers, one from each of the participants, plus a dollar, and redistribute them to the other members in packets (the dollar is for postage). What is needed, some felt, is a sort of "Feminist Notes and Queries," a larger version of the "Grapevine" section (edited by Valerie Wheat) in *Booklegger Magazine.*

The meeting broke up around 3:30, with some going off to dinner and others leaving by car or plane. We noticed some remarkable differences between this feminist conference and some other, more mixed library workshops and small groups (dealing with various themes) that we have attended. First, of course, was the ease and informality of the whole setting, and the mutual rapport, between speaker and audience. Second was the warmth and good humor flying around; there were virtually no heavy trips, no revolts or putdowns, and the men present were allowed to speak in their turn, without any sense of rivalry or resentment. Finally, there was no haste or desperation. The women present were riding the crest of a wave that is propelling all of us into new roles as citizens and human beings. — NOEL PEATTIE.

WILL PUDGE *EVER* GET LAID? In this interview, *Sipapu* takes you to the Berkeley apartment of Lee Marrs, one of the leading women artists of underground comics, and the author of *Pudge, Girl Blimp,* former member of the Normal Community Marching Band of Normal, Illinois. But—perhaps you have never encountered Pudge, so that we will have to explain who she is.

Pudge is a fat seventeen-year-old virgin, who runs away from a stifling and loveless home in the Midwest to seek enlightenment, dope, and sex in San Francisco. Her ignorance of life is only matched by her appetite for it; indeed, her appetite at the table all these years has kept her ignorant of the double bed. As the author points out in one of the earliest panels: "Being fat in America means one thing: you are a guaranteed teenage failure." Obviously, she is a comic character with great potential, and by arriving in San Francisco, she is in the best position to encounter not only sex but dope, busts, and older, more liberated sisters. She has the evergreen power of growth, and Lee Marrs, her creatrix, a slender Southern woman with light brown hair, has found that Pudge has a life of her own:

SIPAPU: Where do you come from, and how did you get your start as a cartoonist?

MARRS: I was born in Montgomery, Alabama, the cradle of the Confederacy, and my family lived all over the South and in France. I graduated from American University in Washington, D.C., and having drawn cartoons all my life, I wanted to become a political cartoonist. Although I'd never met him, Herblock (Herbert Block), renowned cartoonist for the Washington *Post,* saw my college newspaper editorial cartoons, and told the editor to send me over for aid/advice when I graduated. I appeared in his office to hear the words that echo down my entire career—"But, you're a GIRL!"

His comments were accurate, if discouraging: syndication of the star editorial cartoonists made it difficult for *any* local talent, and there were *no* women editorial cartoonists. But, if I really wanted to, I should go back to my home town and try. There was no way that liberal me was gonna get anywhere on an Alabama newspaper. I spent a summer avoiding jobs at NASA, NIH, and other dead-end illustration fields to land The Perfect Job—doing editorial cartoons and illustrations for WTOP-TV, the *Post-Newsweek* station in Washington.

SIPAPU: But we didn't know they used artists on television.

MARRS: Sure they do! Slides, news, graphics, weather maps, sets for shows, sketching at trials, documentaries: all of these things you see on TV are created by full-time artists. I really enjoyed working there and would probably still be a TV artist if an administrative changeover hadn't dumped half the employees on the street. I free-lanced quite successfully for a while in and out of NY and DC. But my life fell apart, so I moved to San Francisco. I heard they were doing colorful stuff there in TV. Unfortunately, the recession hit and I did the odd-job route—surveying, fitting-room, checker, etc. Finally I got into display art with Macy's, did slide shows for Standard Oil—allatime saving money to paint whatever I wanted, draw whatever I felt. For a while I ran a graphics and feature story service for community and underground newspapers with two other guys. Alternative Features Services *was* a dream come true in a lotta ways for a lotta people. But not financially.

We sent stuff about the counter-culture, investigative reporting, cartoons and graphics to subscribers all over the world. We still see some of the work appear—although it's been dead for quite a while.

SIPAPU: How did you get into underground comix?

MARRS: I was walking down Mission Street one night, when a slathering beast leapt from the shadows, whispering, "Hey, sister, wanna draw some feelthy pictures?" Next thing I knew, I was chained to a drawing board in an opium den wallpapered in *Playboy* foldouts.

SIPAPU: Yes? Yes! *(feverishly scribbling)* (My God, what copy!)

MARRS: I can see you won't believe the *truth*. *(Wearily)* O.K. I saw underground comix for the first time after moving to San Francisco. I'd checked out the overground NY comics scene years before and there was obviously only nervous breakdowns and frustration to be found in their factory system of operation. But, in the undergrounds, one person could write, pencil and ink the whole comic! It seemed an ideal medium for all the things I liked to do—be funny, write stories, make social commentary, sleep late and draw. There was only one catch—you couldn't do undergrounds and *eat*, too. They paid only $25 a page on publication. It was—and still is to a large extent—like working for free. So I had to wait until I had enough money to *afford* to do underground comix.

SIPAPU: And when was that?

MARRS: In 1972 several women artists in the Bay area got together to start an all-women's-work comic. They had been trying for years to get into the already existing books, but had met the same sort of sexism and exclusivity that was rampant in the straight world. I had not been able to get anywhere, either, in the much shorter period I'd been trying. Being more or less locked out of closed shops, we started and are maintaining to this day, our own book: *Wimmen's Comix*. The fifth issue will be out this month.

Out of that book comes quite a bit of work for some of us. Other books done by the members include: *Manhunt* #1 and #2, *Net Profit, El Perfecto, Facts o' Life Funnies*. And it served as a springboard not only for *Pudge*, but for the work I've been doing in the lately more open overgrounds: *PLOP!, Weird Mystery Tales, Viva*, and *CRAZY*. Currently I'm doing a continuing series for *CRAZY* about growing up female, called "CRAZY LADY."

SIPAPU: So you're a very experienced cartoonist, that's obvious. OK, now what about Pudge? How did she get her start?

MARRS: Pudge came around 1970. I saw how other cartoonists had locked themselves into a character, without much opportunity for growth. I saw in her a chance to express some of the personal things women go through, comment on the times, and deal with things in my own life. But I soon found out that Pudge wanted to do things HER own way. I wanted her to be from the South, like me, and to be very much more aware of what was going on: intelligent, a critic. But she refused to be this. She said she came from Normal, Illinois, and had never, ever been laid.

SIPAPU: But you know there really is a Normal, Illinois — have you ever been there? It's no mean city, either; it's the home of Illinois State University and its famous fighting Redbirds.

MARRS: I only drove through there after I met Pudge. I have a friend who used to belong to the Normal Community Marching Band, and had a sweatshirt, as does Pudge, that testifies to the fact. A local paper there once mentioned Pudge. Anyway, I had trouble placing her with a comix publisher; she isn't beautiful or sexy, there's no violence angle or horror twist. The women's comix collective was interested, but the first sequence was too long for *Wimmen's Comix*, so it was another year before Pudge could come out on her own. *(The Further Fattening Adventures of Pudge, Girl Blimp*, no. 1, 1973.)

SIPAPU: We like Pudge because we can identify with her: some of us used to be skinny boys; a skinny boy is at the same disadvantage as a fat girl. What about the readers?

MARRS: Well, although you can never tell about readers, the ones who seem most enthusiastic are thirteen-year-old boys.

SIPAPU: This is a wonderful possibility for mutual liberation, if they can make a leap of the imagination like that.

MARRS: It's deeper than that. People think Pudge is truly real. I've been threatened with death or worse, if I don't make Pudge do this or that, and especially if I don't do another *Pudge*. (Number 2 is coming out this summer.) Women come up to me and say, "I didn't know you knew my sister Alice, or my cousin Joanie," — or whoever. (It's always a cousin, never they themselves.) Lately, women have been more up front: "That's how *I* felt at my first C.-R. group," and so on. More women write to me about Pudge, saying they had got turned on to comics through the book — never having been interested in superheroes, etc. The fans are quite varied — oldest lady I know of was an 85-year-old mystery writer. (I was a freckled marshmallow myself, and....) The most bizarre fan incident happened at the Underground Comics Festival in Berkeley, April, 1974.

SIPAPU: We were there, too: see our v. 5, no. 2.

MARRS: Anyway, there I was, sitting at a table, with these copies of *Pudge* in front of me, when a boy of about thirteen and a younger boy walk up to me, and the younger one asks me, "Is Pudge going to be here this afternoon?" I explain that no, she can't be, she's only in the comic book. The younger one refuses to believe me, although the older one understands; and as he drags his kid brother away, I hear him say sadly, "Naw, there isn't any Pudge, there's only that old lady!"

SIPAPU: It's obvious that you've got a character here who has taken on a life of her own, as did Sherlock Holmes, and you have a responsibility for her. What about the sources for her adventures?

MARRS: Everything that happens to Pudge is something that *really* happened to somebody else, although, originally, it might not have been so funny. Some of the real stories were sad, and given the right twist, they would have been the same for Pudge. Her adventures are directly distilled from my friends' lives and mine.

SIPAPU: We noticed a similarity between Pudge and certain other young women who come to a never-never-land from a conventional one, and have adventures while remaining straight: Alice of Cambridge falls down a rabbit-hole into Wonderland, and Dorothy is blown by a tornado out of Kansas into Oz, but they both remain essentially right-minded girls while dealing with the weird figures they encounter. Was anything of this tradition in your mind with Pudge?

MARRS: No, experience counts for more here than literary convention. Alice and Dorothy are aware little girls, but Pudge insisted on being naive. Her character determined which adventures *she* would get into. Some tales I have had in mind for her have ended up in other books instead—*she* wasn't interested. However, Pudge isn't totally passive, either. After all, she took the trouble to run away to San Francisco and get an apartment, and make her own way. There are some things she won't put up with; she loses her temper. In the next issue, when she has to get a job to pay the rent, she tries the easy way out, as all of us do. But she's got enough gumption to persevere when things get rough. She's changing—gaining *some* confidence in herself.

SIPAPU: One thing we note is your extremely detailed style; a single frame can have as many features going on in it as an eighteenth-century cartoon, although a deal more legibly. For example, a scene in the clinic where Pudge goes has: a young woman floating up by the ceiling, two bears cuddling in a swinging lamp, a young man with his chest full of arrows, gamblers, zombies, a dog and its owner ("Courage, Igor, the doc'll make you all better"), and a posted list of cancer signals: "vague pains, runny nose, lumps and bumps, haemophilia, hangnails, cramps and aches," plus Pudge herself protesting, "I'm not pregnant!"—and all in a frame less than $4'' \times 4''$.

MARRS: But that isn't my only style. Mei-Lin is done more simply, and with larger figures. I draw to fit the subject-matter.

SIPAPU: Mei-lin, the aerial infant, the six-months'-old Chinese girlchild who smashes sinister conspiracies flying through the air—"after I've had my nap!" We love her. It may be unrealistic, since there is nothing more helpless than a baby, but the idea that *any* baby could grow into a person who could change the world for the better, is a wonderful, liberating idea, beautiful as spring and explosive as a supernova.

MARRS: Glad you like her; not many people have said so. Yet there really is a Mei-Lin, this time, although she has yet to defeat a vile macho attempt to hook the female population on heroin by putting it in cans of Floradora female hygiene spray. The real Mei-Lin is the daughter of an Alabama friend of mine who went to live in Honolulu and married a Hawaiian Chinese. The kid liked being whirled through the air in her sleepy suit while making airplane noises, and so I used her real name and her love of being an "aerial infant." She flies by spreading and extending her ears, and bombs people when she drops her diapers. At her moment of triumph she emerges from her radio-equipped pram to utter Asian aphorisms like "Effective psychology is the key to success."

SIPAPU: We look forward to seeing more of her adventures. By the way, we notice you have several copies of Estren's *History of Underground Comics,* there on the shelf. We reviewed it in our v. 5, no. 2. How did you like it?

MARRS: Actually, it didn't go over too well with the underground comics community. Estren started it as a college thesis back around 1965. It's outdated, and full of inaccuracies. He was forced to update it with some additional sections, including one on the women cartoonists. These are good, but a lot of the artists are only represented in some of their more obscure moods, and some are given only token representation; Dan O'Neill is confined to two frames on p. 163, and others are largely slighted. Maybe the book was encouraging for sales, but how much better it could have been!

SIPAPU: And it has no index.—But to return to Pudge. What is her future? Will she ever get laid? Or shouldn't we ask?

MARRS: Pudge is young, she's only seventeen, she's going to go through a lot of changes. She'll be growing; she has to, and she'll get her head together more. And perhaps someday—

SIPAPU: —some gentle boy, who loves her for her courage and her struggle with herself and the world—

MARRS: —who knows? As in real life, you often go trotting out after your own particular holy grail to discover that the things you find on the journey are more important than the grail.

****The Further Fattening Adventures of Pudge, Girl Blimp,* nos. 1 and 2, are available from Starreach Productions, Box 385, Hayward, CA 94543. *Pudge*

#1 (32 p.) costs $1, *Pudge* #2 (48 p.) $1.25. Postage and handling are included in these prices; volume discounts are offered.***

Usually most documents on the underground comics place the male artists up front and add the women as footnotes, but we feel entirely justified in reversing this procedure. Pudge is far more of a real character than the Freak Brothers and Mr. Natural, those creations of Gilbert Shelton and R. Crumb. They invented freaks in a land of other freaks; Pudge reaches back to our common, normal experience. However, there are some artists who are less familiar than these two. Dennis Kitchen, of Kitchen Sink Enterprises, a division of Krupp Comic Works, Inc., P.O. Box 5699, Milwaukee, WI 53211, draws with a sharp line and a neat clean satire; he is at his most typical in a series called "Ramshackle and Slumlord, Realty." Trina is also a cartoonist with a practical working-class outlook; her "Rosie the Riveter" is an excellent role model for women at work. Finally, there is an artist who is only now becoming familiar: Jay Kinney, a scratchboard artist whose wordless and serious strip, "Midnight," appears in *Arcade, the Comics Revue*, no. 1 (The Print Mint, 830 Folger Avenue, Berkeley, CA 94710). "Midnight," done almost wholly in tall $5'' \times 3''$ frames, is perhaps the most beautiful strip we have ever seen, and represents another new direction for the radical cartoonist's art.

FROM THE CONFERENCES: The COSMEP (Committee of Small Magazine/press Editors and Publishers) met coincidentally with the New York Book Fair and the American Library Association in New York, July 1974. Much of what passed there is now ancient history, but we remember running around in muggy heat wishing we had never come to New York, at least not at that season. The COSMEP conference was held in Columbia University, which was largely NOT air-conditioned, while most of its poetry readings were held in the Huntington Hartford Museum, twenty minutes away by subway. Among its resolutions were one establishing a Definitions Committee, to outline the tasks and positions of the Coordinator and Board of Directors; one committing money to a series of booklets for members on design and production (most of these have now seen the light of day); one censuring the Coordinating Council of Literary Magazines for lack of an open and fair election procedure; and one recommending the University of California, Davis, as the site for the 1975 conference. The Board subsequently confirmed this, and the conference of 1975 will be held there, 4-8 July 1975, as this issue comes out.

The Book Fair was in the worst possible building and the best possible spirits. There we all were, crowded into tiny little booths on the fifth, sixth and eight floors of a corner art gallery, with only a jammed elevator to get us up and down; if there had been a fire, it would have been a major disaster, but anyway the people of New York, beckoned by posters, trooped in to see us. When a sign was put up charging admission, Jackie Eubanks, coordinator of the Fair, blocked the sign from view with her person. Although not all of us sold all we wanted, the Fair was generally considered a success, and there will be two more in 1975; one in New York, in the old Customs House, and another in San Francisco, coincident with ALA 1975, in the Veterans' Memorial Auditorium.

The only panel at ALA New York 1975 that we haven't seen widely discussed deserves to be remembered, however belatedly. It was the Social Responsibilities Round Table's Task Force on Ethnic Studies, and this time it gave a stage for America's white ethnics to walk on. There were mostly Polish Jews—Irving Levine, Michael Novak, Milton Meltzer, Preston David—but some other East Europeans and Italians spoke, or spoke from the audience. Michael Novak, in particular, began by pointing out that many of the people of Eastern Europe were serfs at the same time that Blacks were slaves; that they did not all come here voluntarily, but were forced out, and one out of four went back. Commenting on the incident when Senator Muskie broke down and wept, he remarked, "A good Slav should get mad three times a day, man or woman," and added later, "If you're born Polish you can get angry for free; otherwise you have to go to Esalen and work it out of you at seventy dollars a year," a remark which brought the house down. Finally, he eliminated the "Anglo-Saxon" problem by pointing out that only a minority of citizens are Anglo-Saxon by descent (whatever that means), and claimed that the Puritan work ethic is a misnomer, because almost everyone in this country has to work, not just the descendants of Puritans. (As a matter of fact, the countries sending the most people to the USA in the nineteenth century were (in order): Germany, Britain, Italy, Ireland, and Austria-Hungary. How many Millers in your phone book were originally Muellers, how many Smiths were Schmidts?)

MY LOVE GAVE ME A TURTLE TAG: The third announcement comes from the Island Resources Foundation, Lagoon Marina, Red Hook, St. Thomas, VI 00801. Seems that the Caribbean green sea turtle *(Chelonia mydas)*, is nearing extinction. A food staple in the area for years, it is overfished and preyed upon by poachers. An expedition is being planned this summer to Masefield's "pleasant isle of Aves" in the mid-Caribbean (Colombian territory), to tag the turtles after they nest, "give them a loving pat" and send them back to sea. To defray the cost of this expedition, the Foundation is asking $25, for which you can have your name (or that of your dear one) inscribed on a turtle tag, send you a photo of a nesting turtle and report to you if the turtle is ever recovered. (It isn't clear if you get the tag back.) Anyway, if you "give a turtle your good name" you will be participating in the most original ecological expedition we've heard of in years.

TELL ME NOT HERE, IT NEEDS NOT SAYING: Ernest Callenbach's *Ecotopia* (Berkeley, Banyan Tree Books, distributed by Book People, 2940 7th Street, Berkeley, CA 94710) is likely to be the underground classic of a generation. We find ourselves affirming and contradicting this book in almost every paragraph, because unlike most utopian (or dystopian) fiction it demonstrates that the author can quicken this ancient literary form and catch a thousand ideas that are circulating in our own time.

The scene takes place in the year 1999. The Pacific Northwest—Washington, Oregon, northern California—has taken advantage of an assumed breakdown of American society (the Indochinese war is assumed to have continued to 1980), and a presumed incompetence on the part of the Federal Government, to put an end to the population and attendant disruption by seceding from the Union. The military side of the local revolution is taken care of by the local militia, plus the threat (or rumor) of atomic mines in Eastern cities. The American forces thus paralyzed, the liberated zone is taken over by an alliance of socialists and ecology-minded citizens, who establish a separate republic under the name of Ecotopia. After 19 years of "Chinese-like" (!) isolation, a reporter from an American newspaper is admitted to Ecotopia, to describe for its readers the conditions of life in the "Stone Age" republic. He finds a country totally devoted to the ecological stable-state, whose inhabitants are eager to live as much as possible like Indians, in harmony with the land; who practice drastically revised sexual customs, recycling, a collective society, and something near to tree-worship. The capital of Ecotopia is San Francisco, its Market Street a tree-filled mall, and the countryside is the scene of ritual war games and semi-religious lumber camps.

Obviously, a work like this depends for its success on the author's ability to provoke controversy while suspending disbelief, and in this tightrope-like task, Ernest Callenbach has succeeded beyond our wildest expectations. Varying his reports for the "Times-Post" with a personal diary, he has carried out all the didactic expectations we have of such a work, and at the same time provided the reader with a passionate and deeply erotic love story. The Ecotopian woman, Marissa, is a strong and challenging figure. Most sexual scenes in today's fiction we find silly, cruel, or clinical and boring, but Callenbach has restored delight, challenge, and bewilderment to the over-plowed fields of love. In order to achieve the suspension of disbelief, the author must also make his utopia familiar by echoing sounds and calling up scenes already familiar to us, and this he has done by projecting elements of our life today into the future. The "Wild West" or near–Dickensian costumes; the bold stares of the women; the love of wood, of the sea and of inland waters; the direct approach of everyone to you, demanding personal contact and involvement; all these we recognize as part of the lifestyle of a segment of young people today. For this reason alone libraries should buy it.

The author also has the task of winding up today's problems into a neat or at least plausible solution. Agriculture, transportation, housing, race relations, education, culture, even the keeping of pets, is described. Some kind of answer must be provided the reader, who is inevitably going to be drawn into the devil's advocate position, or at least be watching each chapter to see where he blows it. Here we must report that Callenbach only partly succeeds. He is on firmest ground when he describes the ecological or recycling side of Ecotopia; the watermill suspended on a cable between two banks of a small stream, that provides power for an isolated farmhouse; the plastic bowls that decay on contact with soil micro-organisms; the shoes without composition soles; the public Provo bicycles; the books read, but passed on to friends; all are credible and some of them are operant today among some aware people. On the other hand, Callenbach tends to slide over the areas where even Ecotopian life demands modern industrial technology. Paint is abhorred, because it is based on lead or rubber; wood surfaces are allowed to weather and thus look beautiful, but what this does to the life of a farm building is not so clear. Electric trains are described, but whether you can run an electric railroad without a vast investment in energy—such as stored water power behind a mammoth concrete dam—is not really faced. Whether the thermal sea-power station at Punta Gorda could be made to work without the backing of a large industrial economy is also an open question; turbines do not grow on trees, and certainly the Amerindians—whom the Ecotopians emulate—could not have assembled the parts and the equipment for a mammoth energy-producing structure like the "mad duke's castle" Callenbach envisions. The author seems to fail in his deductive reasoning. Just as the alignment of a pyramid presupposes that its builders had some idea of geometry, so the presence of a television set (the Ecotopians still have them) presupposes the industrial base to make cathode-ray tubes, and a class of engineers, workers and repairmen to make and repair them.

It is in his social structure that Ernest Callenbach is weakest. The Ecotopian universities no longer cultivate psychology and political science; these subjects are no longer considered "scientific," and books are produced on them only for "popular" consumption. What this attitudes does to the ability of the Ecotopian government to monitor and adapt to the changes of public opinion which take place in any society which is not an utter dictatorship, is not spelled out. The Ecotopian revolution is also not clear; at one point we are told that only a very few wealthy capitalists and their families were refugees, at another point we are told that there was a folding of businesses "reminiscent of the closing of Japanese-American businesses during World War II." The unfortunate comparison is not ours, but Callenbach's. The people evidently accepted the massive (and indeed intentional) unemployment and attendant social disruption, in the name of independence and ecology, although the hero does make contact with a villainous reactionary underground whose spokesmen sound like unreconstructed Birchers. (He drops the contact, significantly enough, when the government lets him know he is being *watched.*) Furthermore, he discovers, no one in Ecotopia can simply set up a business, hire and fire workers, and pocket the profits; the workers are partners, and they reserve the right to pick and choose, and to set up conditions. Whether anyone would embark on a small business under these conditions, remains to be seen. Agriculture, too, has been nationalized; the Ecotopians seem as eager to dismiss or destroy the family farm as is Tenneco. Finally, not all the ecological decisions themselves seem wise; in order to eliminate feedlots for cattle and sheep, the animals are driven to the mountains to feed on summer meadows, despite what John Muir told us in *The Mountains of California* (1894) about the disastrous ecological effects of such a practice.

We naturally turned with interest to the racial scene, which is as important in California and the Pacific Northwest as elsewhere. The author rightly perceives that most Third World people in the U.S. (and therefore in Ecotopia) are urbanized. It seems that Blacks, Indians and Asian-Americans participated in Ecotopia) are urbanized. It seems that Blacks, Indians and Asian-Americans participated in Ecotopia's revolution, and afterwards were allowed to form autonomous city-states, with their own police, currency, and postage, but without foreign relations. Whether they would be content with such dependency, parallel to that of San Marino, Liechtenstein, and Andorra, is not clear; the large Irish and Italian populations of San Francisco, and the Scandinavian population of Portland and Seattle, should have the same rights, but do not seem to have demanded them in Ecotopia. Whether such demands would be permitted or discouraged, the author does not say.

The real hollow in the heart of the Ecotopian scheme is, however, the problem of the "Middle Americans" whose present addresses place them within Ecotopia's presumed boundaries. We invite our readers in the region to take a long day's drive between two Oregon cities: Eugene and Klamath Falls. Eugene already looks like an important provincial capital in Ecotopia: the city is full of old houses, the Saturday Market is a thriving institution full of pots and spoon rings and wandering minstrels, everyone has plants in the window, and the whole town swims with ecology and love (except when you get a whiff from the Weyerhauser paper mill). On the other side of the Cascades, Klamath Falls is the town where even the schoolboys wear ties, and which boasts the largest post of the Veterans of Foreign Wars in the whole State of Oregon. Would Klamath Falls accept a life-style based on that of

Eugene? By no means. They'd fight it with every weapon at their command. What is the difference between the two cities? Eugene is the home of the University of Oregon, where students read books like *Ecotopia.* Klamath Falls, on the other hand, is a lumber town, not a college town, where they watch TV. Ecotopians! What are you going to do about the VFW in Klamath Falls?

Then there's the matter of the military. The gentlemen in the Presidio of San Francisco, and in Fort Lewis, Washington, aren't about to be overawed by local populist militia. We seem to recall that a similar refusal to surrender Federal forts led to that nasty little brouhaha in 1861-65. Didn't work out too well for the secessionists, either. In addition, planting atomic mines in other peoples' cities seems a poor way to fight pollution of the environment.

Ecotopia, in short, is an important book alike for its strengths and its weaknesses. The vision of an ecologically responsible world is compelling and imperative; the need to replace sexism and exploitation with freely chosen and *human* love is equally attractive and holds our admiration and allegiance. However, the book suffers from the two crippling misconceptions of our age. One is "Berkeleyism," the belief that everyone (except a few bad capitalists in black top hats) shares the values and standards of the people you find along Telegraph Avenue in Berkeley (or Union Street in San Francisco, or in a commune in the Sierras, or wherever). The other is the "Jericho syndrome," whose sufferers believe that all they have to do is march around the walls of the beleaguered city, blowing trumpets, and the walls will come tumbling down. Neither, alas, is true. They really *like* capitalism in Klamath Falls, at least their own kind of it, — and the government of the United States is not run by doddering pious old fools like Nicholas II, but by very clever gentlemen, who will make every effort to see to it that power doesn't get into the hands of people like Ernest Callenbach. Finally, most revolutions have been made in favor of modernization and technology, not against it.

Actually, not even the Ecotopians of today are that Ecotopian. Entertainment is to be banned from Ecotopian television, but we know plenty of dedicated radicals and gentle doe-eyed plant freaks right now, who watch "Streets of San Francisco" and love it. You can't expect people to be consistent, can you? Betcha even Mr. Callenbach watches entertainment — sometimes. The only person who never watches television, to our personal knowledge, is the poet Gary Snyder, and what is his reward for concentrating on poetry and the ecologically balanced life? A prize, — and swarms of reporters seeking interviews. You can't win!

Indeed, there is a deeper level at which the book's premise is questionable. The quote on the half-title, from Barry Commoner, "In nature, no organic substance is synthesized unless there is provision for its degradation: recycling is enforced," struck us as a half-truth; we can think of several organic substances that resist degradation or at least oblivion for hundreds of years: bone, horn, shell, chiton. Indeed, if degradation worked perfectly, the science of paleontology would be impossible. You could read the whole history of life as the struggle *not* to be recycled, not to sink back into the primordial ooze or to be eaten by the bigger fish.

Human beings, whose brains arose in the course of nature, have continued this struggle against nature with the weapons of consciousness, the "unexpected universe" that developed in their heads: culture, kinship, religion. This did not happen only in Europe. The Hopi have their story of a struggle to the upper world through the *sipapu,* and there were other Amerind civilizations — notably the Incas — who were interested in road-building and developed a strong central government. We sentimentalize and betray Indians when we turn them all into dancing shamans or Mother-earth worshippers. If they want land and the control of their own lives, it is that they may continue on their own development. What if they had independently discovered the compass, built ocean-going vessels and navigated the Gulf Stream, long before Columbus?

The urge to travel and conquer, to leave a name and fame, by founding a family or a religion, building a brass monument or writing a book of poems to outlast a brass monument, is an old and enduring urge. It is older than the wrath of Achilles, old, perhaps, as the cave-paintings of Lascaux. It is usually frustrated, but it turns up in all societies, whether they count stars or count coups. The attempt to suppress it, to recycle everyone back to the daisies or make everyone

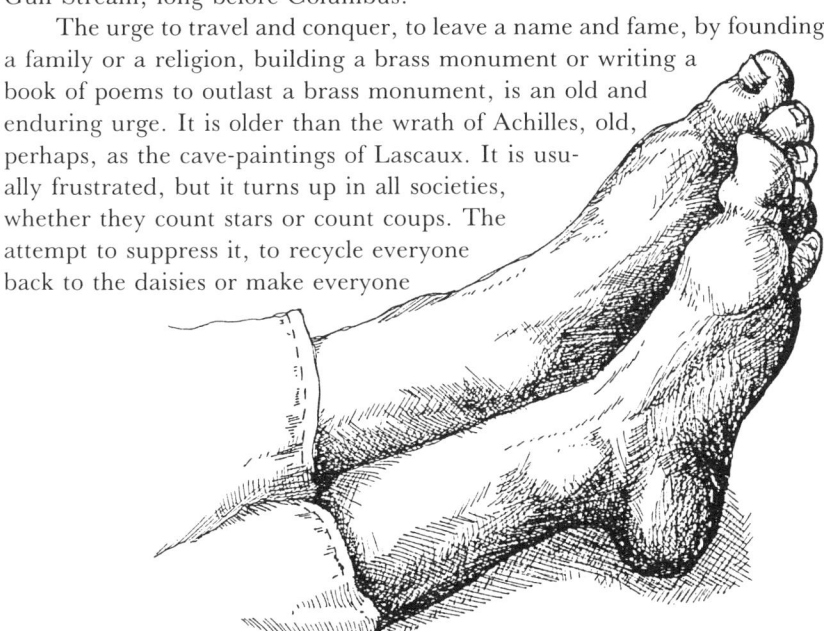

join a sea of collective life, are like the attempts to suppress the sexual instinct, or to crush the survivals of primitive religion. These latter problems the Ecotopians have solved fairly well; by admitting the presence of these urges, they have avoided their perversions: sexual cruelty or superstition. But if the individual's quest for glory, which the French philosopher Vauvenargues saw as central to human endeavor, is suppressed, it is also likely to come out a generation later in cruel and bizarre forms: a cult of the Leader, the plots of the assassins. For we cannot either lash nature to work until it dies, nor be like the worshippers in the drawing on the cover of *Ecotopia*, naked and ashamed, merging with the trees. There is no way back to the pre-technological past, no way back even to the pre-human past, and no way to make people feel guilty for being human. Over the door of Callenbach's utopia, as over the doors of all the other "perfect" societies, is the old French proverb written: "Qui veut faire l'ange, fait la bête"— "who would play the angel, plays the beast."

Flawed as it is, we delight in honoring *Ecotopia*, by Ernest Callenbach, as *Sipapu's* BOOK OF THE YEAR. We urge librarians and teachers to buy it, read it, use it in classes and discussion groups. If we can never have an Ecotopia, we can have a vision of a less exploitative society. And without this vision the people will perish.

7 : 1

This issue is self-explanatory for the most part. Lurie's wife subsequently died (I believe, of cancer). I chaired the Davis COSMEP conference, and after all that preparation, found myself running away from it much of the time it was there. At the same time, it was so hot, I kept my shirt open to the waist: early phase of burnout? Anyway, I'll never do a three-day conference again. The headline is from T.S. Eliot.

THE NIGHTINGALES ARE SINGING NEAR: The Convent of the Sacred Heart, in San Francisco, maintains a school, and thither we wandered, led to the elegant basement theatre of the old Flood mansion, on a windy clear day. There we found some three dozen fidgety eighth-graders, and later some sixty seventh-graders, listening to a gentleman of middle years, who was leading them in a poetry workshop. He asked one student's name, — Yoshio, and broke the name down: into the powerful Y, as in Yes, the long Oo, the soft Ssh, the high sound of I, and the Oo again, and released them into — not poetry as it is commonly taught in schools ("Listen my children and you shall hear") — but into the basic building blocks of poetry, the way Paul Klee released young artists into the secret worlds of art via his *Pedagogical Sketchbook*. To pay him, the Sacred Heart Schools had matched a grant from the National Endowment for the Arts (rather easily done), and he and a young assistant named Robin, an apprentice in the local Poetry in the Schools program, were doing what few such programs in the nation were attempting to do: to make the scholars the artists.

Before we get into this issue's interview, we should emphasize that Mr. Tobie Lurie, a former hotel executive who wrote his first poem at the age of forty, has not confined his workshops to private schools boasting coffered ceilings and huge mirrors at the ends of grand staircases, but has also taught in Kettleman City and Avenal, towns in the driest part of the San Joaquin valley (Kings County), where the children are the kids of migrant laborers and construction workers, half of whom know very little English (Lurie's command of Spanish is strictly limited). But they wanted him in Kings County, the way

SIPAPU

they wanted him in Sacred Heart, even though the prejudice against verses + beards is a heavy one for many school districts to overcome. However, he came, and won over the young people.

As for these young people, we'd scarcely realized how beautiful human beings can be between eleven and fifteen: no illness, no disappointments, a clear-eyed sense of life before them and all of it theirs. Nor how restless, how easily bored they are: don't think you could do this off the tops of your heads; even the guest teacher has to maintain discipline and never forget fairness. When it came to reading the students' poems, he had to make it clear that not all of the poems could be read. Then, with exceptional daring, he and Robin took two poems, by different students, and read them aloud by alternating phrases from each, to produce a combined play for two voices that had the restless pre-teens riveted on the bench and roused them to a heavy applause at the end.

Indeed, Lurie's poems are generally written for several voices; he loves the multiple play of voice against voice, the interpolation of found poem against found poem, and in his published poetry—for to be published, for Lurie, a 5'10½", 155-lb. gentleman with a gray beard, is to be publicly available in print and *on records*—almost all his work is written, and in some cases scored, for multiple voices. As Chopin wrote mostly for the piano, and Palestrina wrote mostly works for singers, so Lurie, a former musician (his wife Jan is a dancer and potter), has specialized in taking the surface features of poetry and has mined it for the depths of *sound* and music within. Yy—Oooh—Sssh—Iii—Oooh— —We turn you over, now, to Toby Lurie:

SIPAPU: What did you do before you got into the poetry stream?
LURIE: Well, I owned two hotels in Santa Barbara: El Mirasol and El Encanto; the first 1954–61, the second 1955–63. After that I was involved in a sea-food drive-in chain, and after that in real estate. But I was always tired of the hassles of management, and wanted to lead a creative life. I wrote my brothers, who were my partners, a letter saying that I wanted out, away out

of their enterprises, because I disapproved of the way they conducted their business affairs. Shortly afterwards I met a Zen master who urged me to seek poverty for my own good; he was just another push in the direction I wanted to move. He told me, "Listen to the small voice at your center. It is authentic. Act upon it." My voice was not small, but loud and strong, and it told me to become myself.

SIPAPU: How did your family take that?

LURIE: I said that for me to do what I wanted to do, they would have to get used to a lower standard of living. I'd been travelling around a lot—at one time I was chairing a corporation called Twilighter Hotels, with branches up and down the coast—and the children all said, "We want a father!" And my wife wanted a husband. So I quit, and wrote my first poems, and got launched on a new career.

SIPAPU: Most people would say that around forty, you're finished. You've made your career, and now all you can do is stick with it, and become, in your time, a second-rate hotel executive.

LURIE: I think the juices of the poet flow as long as his blood does, or hers. I admit I was concerned before I knew, but now I know that there is a time for everyone and my time was held in abeyance until I arrived to take it. I gave free readings for about a year to get a feeling for my work and for audiences. Finally I went to UC Santa Barbara and offered to read some poems, this time for a little bread. The English Department referred me to the Associated Students, who listened to me as I read some poems, liked what I was doing and then asked me what my fee would be. I was thinking: fifteen, twenty, maybe twenty-five dollars; they came up with an offer of $150. I remember, Jan was sitting in the car waiting to hear the news: I came back, said "A hundred fifty!" And we burst out crying with the news, because then we knew we'd make it. You see, we were broke at the time.

SIPAPU: And so now you're on records.

LURIE: Yes. *Word Music* is distributed by CMS Records, and *Mirror Images* by Accent Records.

We paused and listened to some of these, accompanied by texts from Lurie's books, and they turned out to be really impressive: full of contrapuntal and cinematic effects. Some of the poems on the records are in the books (*Mirror Images,* Celestial Arts, 1974, and *New Forms, New Spaces,* San Francisco, Journeys into Language [576 Liberty Street], 1971). The voices on the records were sometimes his (on two tracks), sometimes his, Jan's and a third person's. The result was certainly reminiscent of a whole crowd of innovators: Gertrude Stein, John Cage, even Beckett or Robbe-Grillet. Lurie, however, is not the simple follower of a trend in modern letters. Nor is he a polemicist, nor a writer of scornful manifestoes. He is simply an innovative American, talkative, fond of play and discovery and has come to his style through an independent process of evolution.

In reading aloud some of the poems with Toby and Jan, we recalled how Toby and Robin had spontaneously taken two poems provided by two students at Sacred Heart, and woven them together, providing a new and miraculous poem, stronger than either of the originals. Or how he had taken a poem submitted by an eighth-grader, beginning "I am the Greatest," and turned its schoolboy boasting into a marvelous speech, "in King Cambyses' vein," of which the bombast had the whole school convulsed with sympathetic laughter. Finally, Toby demonstrated the spaced-out quality of the "Hallelujah poem." (This is not the chorus from Handel's *Messiah*, by the way.) You take a drone note, low in pitch, and hum it, "hmmmmmmm," while above and below he weaves the sound, "hallelujah, hallelujah:" and you come in when you can: "HALLELUjah. HALLELUjah." We could readily believe that after ten minutes of this powerful chant, that HALLELUJAH (Praise God), could show itself a word of immense power. — We then returned to the interview:

SIPAPU: Some of your poems seem to have a Zen influence; and others are strongly political.

LURIE: Yes, there's one, called "The W.G. Caper," drawn from the text of the Watergate hearings, mixed with another poem about former Attorney General Mitchell:

1 Mr. Mitchell   I'm sitting
2   I just want to make one thing clear

1   in the sand today   under a windy sun
2 very clear   perfectly clear.

1   feeling   clean and righteous.
2 But I really have   no recollection.

(If you begin with two people, reading line upon line aloud, you begin to see what Lurie is doing.)

SIPAPU: So you got started doing these things, so now how did you break into the schools? We all know that school districts are often afraid to undertake new and controversial projects.

LURIE: I gave a reading at a small college in southern California. There was a public school teacher there who invited me to a teachers' conference in Ojai, and from there I was invited to a major conference of the California Association of Teachers of English in San Francisco, and from this point onwards teachers started inviting me into their schools. In 1969, I decided I would like to expand my activities to the East Coast. So I went to New York and arranged, in some cases by telephone, for readings at various colleges and universities, and since that time, I've been returning East twice a year. This is the first year I've missed, because schools are starting to run out of funds. Everywhere I go, I spend my time in making arrangements to meet with students and young people somewhere else. That's how I make my living.

SIPAPU: So how many hours do you work?

LURIE: About a week a month. And I make enough to keep myself; my wife originally worked as a cocktail waitress during the first year I was getting started, but she doesn't have to do that now. My three children are grown and live outside the home.

SIPAPU: Not so bad! a week a month!

LURIE: But you forget the time I have to spend lining up contacts, and generally making my input into the school systems.

SIPAPU: And, of course, you have to have time to be by yourself and to write your own poems.

LURIE: Yes.

SIPAPU: We noticed what you did with the name Yoshio: how you broke it into its constituent parts.

LURIE: Of course, when it comes to handling words, we've only scratched the surface. Language is a natural resource; we have to break up normal syntax in order to explore its depths. The ordinary sentence is good enough for straightforward communication, but for poetry, we need to explore the sounds within the poem, or the word, and we haven't begun to do that yet. In order to be fully creative we have to free ourselves from the rigidity of the sentence and the word. We are locked in.

SIPAPU: How do the English Departments at schools and colleges see your work?

LURIE: On a public school level (and this is where I now spend most of my time) I am not supported by student funds, but by funds from various sources, including English Departments; sometimes I teach a poetry workshop, sometimes I come as a language consultant. I am now a regular with the University of California, as I am invited to teach through extension courses at the campuses at Los Angeles, Santa Barbara, and Santa Cruz.

SIPAPU: Meanwhile there are the successful appearances you've had with the students in Kettleman City, and Avenal, and...

LURIE: ...and mid-city Los Angeles, Black communities in Chicago, plus over 400 public schools throughout the country, mostly in California.

Lurie here excused himself and we turned our attention to Janice Lurie, an interesting woman in her own right:

SIPAPU: We understand you're into theatre work. There must be a lot of opportunities in San Francisco.

J. LURIE: Actually, I haven't made many contacts since I've been here; I used to do some work in pottery, but mostly since I've come here I've been into modern dance, and also into journal writing. There are groups forming, which study the sharing of written journals and diaries. I've found them very useful.

SIPAPU: Yes, of course, there has been a renewed attention to journal writing; sparked, no doubt, by the continued publication of the *Diaries* of Anais Nin. How did you get into the journal workshop situation?

J. LURIE: Primarily as a therapy device; however, it has become a thing with a life of its own.

— The Luries were then obliged to go out. We found them a remarkably young and close pair; it was with astonishment that we heard that they had just celebrated their twenty-fifth wedding anniversary. Toby Lurie is fifty, but looks no older than forty, and Jan looks no older than thirty-five or thereabouts; the point of mentioning all this is that the change of lifestyle which they have made, from the hotel executive to the poet, and wife, have taken years off their ages. Again, of the many literary figures we know, even those in the small press scene, Lurie and his wife seem to be almost unique in that they are supremely happy people. Here they are, living in a little studio apartment just south of Market in San Francisco, exactly as if they were young marrieds starting out for the first time; there is a complex mobile, made out of cut tin, in the window, and hanging plants; and yet these people are our contemporaries — indeed Toby Lurie was in the Navy in World War II. And their children seem to be happy with them; there are no hang-ups. How is it done? How did they avoid getting trapped in the rich end of suburbia, worrying about who's going to steal their color TV? By correspondence, Lurie answers:

LURIE: The discovery of poetry and the sounds that make it up had nothing to do with the decision to make the break. We knew that it was essential for our survival as human beings to make some dynamic and dramatic changes. We knew it was important for us to lead a creative life. We learned that there is no equation that includes money, genuine satisfaction and happiness in the same formula. We knew that our life must become an adventure. We wanted to grow.

SIPAPU: How do you see your teaching function? Do you feel that you are giving the young people an insight into the structure of poetry that is not to be had by reading it, or by reading masterpieces, however excellent?

LURIE: My teaching function is not to teach at all, but to share with the kids an excitement that doesn't spring at them from the printed page. I've discovered that most kids are turned off by most poetry. I want to broaden the parameters of language and poetry so that young students can explore and recreate themselves through the poetic experience.

SIPAPU: How do you see your relation to contemporary letters? You say that you haven't had much contact with contemporary poets since you came up to San Francisco. But what about some of the extremely experimental writers? Surely people like Michael McClure, with his "beast language," and some of the S.F. Dadaists, like Anna Banana, would have something to exchange with you? Outside your own books and records, have you attempted to publish anywhere (e.g., in little magazines)?

LURIE: I think you might answer this question better than I. Publications are springing up like wildfire. They are often the children of young poets seeking print and they are open to new, creative, innovative voices. Being an oral poet I believe that some of the greatest poems of all will never find the printed page but be born in the ear. You are a librarian—one who covets the eternal record, but I also know that you give credence to the concept that the poem can disappear in the moment that it is discovered. I feel that most poems are born in the guts and only find the printed pages as a matter of habit and routine. We equate importance with what we can see, touch, taste, immortalize. The most beautiful and perfect poems of all mankind occur when the poem is destroyed and reality remains. And that's no bullshit.

SIPAPU: You certainly have broken through to people who never had much experience with poetry before (the children in Kings County) or who have been exposed only to genteel poetry (the students at Sacred Heart). Do you see a future in the production of poetry by women, prisoners, Third World people? Will it be largely oral-based? What's going to happen to American letters when a rising tide of people become known figures and published writers without having gone through the print-oriented and classical schooling that we, and doubtless others, have gone through? Do you feel, in short, that you're the "point man" in the real "revolution of the word?" Or is this all just pretentious bullshit?

LURIE: I'm trying to swim through a lot of garbage and pretense. I don't like the word "poem" because it is so restrictive. I believe in the writings of the prisoners and the Third World people because their poetry has courage. It's direct and honest and utilitarian and that's what I think poetry is all about. I'm interested in non-verbal poetry (= sound poems) because I think language is so damn confusing, and I think we should be trained to listen to the dynamics of sound to feel meanings more accurately. As to whether or not this is all pretentious bullshit I must honestly admit I'm not altogether certain. I do believe deeply in what I am doing at this time.

SIPAPU would like to add that we believe in what Lurie is doing, too. So much pother is made in the small press world, about problems of distribution and grants in aid publication, that it is refreshing to see someone get out and really bring poetry to young people, without having to set up a bureaucracy to do it with.

COSMEPOLOGISTS OF THE WORLD, UNITE!: We also chaired, right after the ALA Conference, the 8th annual conference of the Committee of Small Magazine Editors and Publishers (COSMEP). Reporting on a conference that one has chaired oneself is like introducing one's proposed spouse to a skeptical family. ("Whaddya mean you don't like her pantsuits? She's the most beautiful woman in the world!") Anyhow, this conference, which had been a year in the making, included Elliot Gilbert, of *California Quarterly,* plus Kate Cifra and Don Kunitz, Putah Creek Press, together with Alan Elms, Ulmus Press; most of the participants in the conference committee—all of those named above—were from UC Davis, but there were also Len Fulton and Ellen Ferber *(dustbooks)* who came down from Paradise, California (see our v. 3, no. 2, consecutive issue no. 6, July 1972, for an interview with Len Fulton). In general, this conference seems to have been just right for many conferees, who liked the tight snappy organization we had, and too heavy for others, who found it too bizarre, too political, or just too organized. Certainly it had the university stamp on it, as we relied heavily on the work of Carolyn Norlyn and Sandy Prairie, of the University's Conference Center; some felt our UCD dorms were sterile (a word applied to women, the Moon, or medical equipment). However, no doubt about it, the local food service broke down; not only did the dorms shut down almost entirely for the Fourth of July weekend, leaving us only table scraps at high prices, but most of the good local restaurants took the weekend off, leaving the conferences to deal with Sambo's. This, of course, we had never anticipated.

However, at least three panels rose above the ordinary, two of them spectacularly so. The first, and least spectacular, occurred on 5 July, when a panel of librarians, led off by William A. Gosling, of the Library of Congress's Cataloging-in-Publication program (CIP), discussed what libraries could do for small presses, and vice versa. Other panelists were William R. Eshelman, *Wilson Library Bulletin,* Alfred A. Maupin, Sacramento City-County Libraries, and Cliff Wood, CSU/Sacramento Library, both responsible for small-press publishing in their institutions; and finally Nancy Kellum-Rose, of San Francisco, chair of SRRT, who was suffering from a heavy cold, but who made a good presentation of the needs and hopes of alternative publications in the library field.

The Library Associates sponsored a wine-party, in the Special Collections Department of the UC Davis Shields Library, and the English Department a picnic with chicken, in the patio of the same library, that afternoon; this was our answer to the parties at homes, that previous conferences have enjoyed. (This time, too many peoples' homes were too remote or too small for the kind of hosting we have seen elsewhere.) The next day, 6 July, there were panels on printing (Budd Westreich, *Press of Arden Park,* Sacramento), on binding (Theodore Kahle, Capricorn Bindery, Berkeley), and papermaking (Sidney Berger, UCD English Department). The real explosion that day, and probably the high point of the conference, was the panel on prison writers and publishers, chaired by Ben Hiatt of Sacramento. Hitherto such panels have been decorous affairs, with an account of work done the previous year, and a plea for more support. This time Hiatt leaned back and told his panel of former prisoners and workers in the field, "OK, let 'em have it." A poet who had worked with prisoners made a passionate plea for the prisoner as person, admitting that he himself needed to learn how to proceed from distrust to trust; but the high point was a former female prisoner of many years' experience, Norma Vane, whose love and long memories made one of the great experiences we have heard from one who has been inside. The panel drove way on overtime, but we didn't lift a finger to stop it. We'd have soon cut off an angel in mid-trumpet-blast.

The great sessions of the next day included a Third World panel that we had insisted upon; here, among other speakers, most notable was Prof. Robert Yoshioka (Asian-American Studies Division, UCD), who made a brilliant statement of the rights of Third World people to control their own destiny as writers and publishers. The well-known Black poet Eugene Redmond of CSU/Sacramento was also present, and made an eloquent statement on the history of Black writers, but it was good to hear the dominant remarks made by an Asian-American; for far too long we have heard the phrase "Blacks and women" bandied about as if other groups were supposed to sink decorously into the sand. (If we can't give you the full flavor of these remarks, it's because we had to be dashing about, fixing things behind the scenes; among other things, UCD had elected to turn off the air-conditioning in Roessler Hall that weekend, to save energy. We had to go up to almost the highest campus authorities to have it turned on again. That's what it's like to chair a conference.) Beyond Baroque Foundation is transcribing the Yoshioka speech with a view to ultimate publication; for further information, contact them at 1639 West Washington Boulevard, Venice, CA 90291.

There was indeed a women's panel at this conference, although it was less dramatic than in previous years; partly because some of the leading spirits have dropped out, or were unable to attend; and although there were a few interruptions, the panel caused fewer raised eyebrows than in previous years, and the women at the conference seemed more secure. In addition, their presence melded well with a new panel, on non-literary publishers in COSMEP, an organization founded, and long almost dominated, by white male poetry editors. Anne Pride of KNOW, Inc. (based in Pittsburgh; they send four delegates), chaired both panels, and in the latter, we made a plea for the educative value of Third World, feminist and other writers as having something to teach those of us whose interests are purely aesthetic.

Two bizarre political events marked, if not marred, the conference. One was a showing of the Zapruder film of the assassination of President Kennedy, which was introduced at a panel on distribution by the chair of the panel, with the partial, if majority, consent of the COSMEP Board of Directors, who paid Penn Jones some $200 to bring the film from Texas and explain it. Few events in COSMEP's history have caused as much dustup as this one; most people resented the idea of showing such a film, even those who didn't attend the conference and only heard about it later! We would have preferred that a political panel would have been more directly traced to publication problems, — for example, the harassment (under the Nixon Administration) of the Socialist Workers' Party, whose offices were raided, and who were themselves taken into custody on trumped-up charges.

The other bizarre event, which is hard for us to understand, is that the newly-elected chair of COSMEP, John Bennett, of *Vagabond* (Ellensburg, Washington), having chaired several quick Board sessions, resigned, left the conference, and hitchhiked back to that town, apparently feeling that the pressures of the conference were too much for him. This resulted in some delay and confusion until Judy Hogan *(Hyperion,* Chapel Hill, NC) was finally made first temporary, then fully elected, chair of the organization. Nobody promised her a rose garden, either, although she is handling her job with tact and skill. The next conference of COSMEP is in Austin, Texas; although the new drive of COSMEP toward regionalization will produce a COSMEP West conference in the Bay Area in February.

CLAVERING IN YOUR LUG: Attending conferences used to be a surprise to us, until we'd attended a few. Nowadays, we find that most of the big library conferences in San Francisco take place in the San Francisco Hilton, where they haven't changed the design of the carpet and walls for years (we could draw the designs of both from memory). The People's Librarian Task Force of ALA/SRRT had a program on "Job sharing and work restructuring" (also titled "Unnatural acts"); most of the people had dropped out of the regular work scene altogether, some to live a life of semi-retirement combined with verbal outlawry *(Black Bart),* others to move into the capitalist scene. (Information Unlimited, a group started by two unemployed female librarians, who now have employees in several cities, filling the several requests a day for information that come from business people. Their logo is the three whirling legs also seen on the shield of the Isle of Man.) The best feature of the program was the cutoff device used by two young women at the side of the auditorium. Evidently they had been piqued by our report that an earlier session, some years back, of the People's Librarian Task Force ran on too long; so they limited all speakers to five minutes, and when the speaker ran on perilously near the time, they interrupted the chrysostom with a blast from a New Year's Eve noisemaker, usually right in the midst of the pompous individual's most portentous peroration. We suggest this method of cutting off debates to all meetings. They claim that they couldn't find a bell, but we suspect that they encountered the noisemakers in Chinatown, and never looked back for a minute. Well, we wouldn't either!

On Tuesday, 2 December, we attended a Women Library Workers program. This group, led by Carole Leita, of *Booklegger* (San Francisco), was jammed into a room far too small for its size (apparently by miscalculation). She told of the survey questionnaire that had brought women, whether librarians or library assistants, together, and having described the enthusiasm with which the survey was received, disassembled the meeting into regional groups. By decree of the grass roots, men and institutions are admitted only as non-voting members. Also there has been quite a split over unions; some women saw them as a positive force, others as male-dominated and male-oriented. There will be a $3-$10 dues schedule; contact Carole Leita, 555 29th Street, San Francisco, CA 94131.

The first midwinter conference of COSMEP's Board of Directors took place the weekend of 17 January 1976, in Durham, North Carolina; among other work, they declared 1976 to be the "Year of the Small Press."—The first time that an ALA-SRRT meeting has taken place at ALA Midwinter occurred 19 January, when David Cohen chaired a meeting of the Task Force on Ethnic Studies. A report has not yet come to hand, but they were to discuss library service to Vietnamese refugees, plans for a newsletter, and for a permanent information center at Queens College. Cohen (68-71 Bell Boulevard, Bayside, NY 11634) also distributes a 1975 *Directory of Minority-Third World Publishers and Dealers,* of which we reprinted an earlier edition. There have been quite a number of changes, so that you will want to have this as a ready-reference on your acquisitions shelf.

7 : 2

This issue, consecutive number 14, was a "black-on-blue" issue, and shorter than most of them. In order to save "face," I double-spaced much of it. Jackie Eubanks, one of Libraryland's most controversial figures, is still at Brooklyn College Library.

RISE UP SO EARLY IN THE MORN: Jackie Eubanks is a librarian at Brooklyn City College (a part of the system of the City University of New York), a leader in the Social Responsibilities Round Table of ALA, and now a director of the Committee of Small Magazine Editors and Publishers (COSMEP). Her name, however, is most familiar as an organizer of the highly successful New York Book Fairs, the first (July 1974), described in our July 1975 issue, she led herself. Ms. Eubanks, a tall sturdy woman in her late thirties, with a friendly face, is proud of her working-class background, which she combines with a gift of laughter.

SIPAPU: We'll start with the usual: birth and education?

EUBANKS: I was born in Chicago, the child of a long line of Lithuanian butchers. My grandfather and grandmother came to the Chicago stockyards directly from Lithuania, to work in "The Jungle." After some time they purchased a little butcher shop, and grandpa greeted the customers and sold the meat, while grandma did the meat-cutting. My grandma was a big role model for me: she was a woman butcher before the union; the union made it far more "man's work." Her sons, including my dad, of course became Amalgamated Union men. Back in the old country, of course, peasantry had no sex—so to speak—and what was valued was strength in women and men.

My mom went down and signed me up for a social security card when I was 13, so I could get a job, and I did. I've been at work since, even through school, or better, I've been at work since, with school added as a treat. I left home to attend college—in Chicago. My grandma was the only one who didn't object to my going to the University of Chicago, for no other reason than

this: when the University held the mortgage on her and grandpa's butcher shop, they didn't foreclose. I got a B.A. in 1959, and an M.A. in 1963; during college I worked at the Chicago Public and the University of Chicago libraries, after being an Information Operator for four years with the phone company. My first "pro" job was working for the Army in Germany, and I actually enjoyed it; I learned a lot of administration in a heavily hierarchical society. If the whole Army system had not been directed to wrong ends, I would probably still be there; it was a lot of fun, I worked hard, and had a certain amount of freedom. Afterwards I worked for a year in the American Association of Advertising Agencies, and saw the belly of the beast
at close hand. I decided to put my administrative skills in the service of changing, not keeping, the whole system. I got a job as a reference librarian at Brooklyn College, where I've been ever since. I was lucky, getting a chance to go to college; most of the kids I went to school with didn't get that chance.

SIPAPU: What kind of work do you do?

EUBANKS: In reference, the way I look at it, I work very closely with the people who are paying to support me: the poor folk of the city. Like my own folks. They're the ones who have my loyalty, and not the rich of New York who spend a lot of money in order *not* to pay their taxes and my salary. I've worked as an Education librarian (I picked up a degree in education from Teachers' College, Columbia, in 1969), and now I'm a "history bibliographer" which has meant, in the past couple of years, deciding what to cut back in history at Brooklyn College Library. I also have worked with the Liberation Library, a student-run operation (in abeyance now, as student spirit is confronted with tuition and competition for space). The students have been as pivotal to my education here, as my instructors. In library school I had accepted many of the generally received ideas of the profession, but a big step in my education came when I finally learned to *hear and respect* the real questions put to me, as a reference librarian. A student came to me with a proposed paper on the welfare system. He wanted to know what welfare had done to people; he wanted to see the system from below. Well, of course research isn't funded to those below, it's "welfare" from the middle and upper classes—so we found a lot of research on what "they" are like—the welfare recipients, but nothing on how welfare feels and what it does to you. Another time, an angry student asked me sharply what a subsidy was. I answered innocently that it was a supplementary aid to people. Bull, he said, subsidy is paid to business or to landlords or to food sellers so that they can stay in business. Hmmm, I thought. — This kind of experience has taught me the real nature of my job, and I began rejecting the line that I was some kind of highly-paid civil servant, and became an advocate. I began to notice that librarians (including me) are trained to buy largely from big business publishers, not from groups like (for example) the National Welfare Rights Organization. We all spend tax money (or tax-deductible money) and it's important that we put some money into the hands of those who mean to effect some changes in the system, so that libraries remain relevant to the people they serve. That was one of the motives in starting *Alternatives in Print (AIP)*.

SIPAPU: How did *AIP* get started?

EUBANKS: It arose partly out of the ALA conference in Detroit in 1969, after a New University Conference in Ann Arbor that year. I and a few other librarians formed a Librarians' Caucus in the NUC, and it occurred to us that there was not nearly enough information about which small groups working for social change were publishing what. We promised to have a list out in six months (actually it took eight), but through ALA-SRRT we got support for publishing it from Ohio State University. Later editions, including the forthcoming fifth edition, are being published by Glide Publications, 330 Ellis Street, San Francisco, CA 94102. In producing it, we had no idea how much information there was to catalog; but we did perceive that the "Movement heavies" were heavy just because they had so much information, because they got around the country and kept in touch with so many people. Anyway, it was a first step in our objective: getting funds into the hands of people who want social change. That includes funds being spent by librarians!

SIPAPU: In this pursuit of your goal of social change, do you consider yourself a socialist?

EUBANKS: Yes, but I'm not affiliated with any party now. I'm an activist, and support many change agents that I'm not able nor willing to emulate. Communications, in my mind, are the vanguard of any system. Under out present capitalist system, our libraries are among the very few socialist institutions that serve the people; they are, however, very hierarchical and rigid. As we progress, in order to preserve the freedom necessary to work in a socialist system, libraries and communications in general will have to be committed to anarchism, and libraries will have to be loosened up a lot more. That's not the way some socialists see it, of course, but then I've never been one of those who interpreted socialism as a new sort of totalitarianism. On the contrary, it's our present system that is more and more totalitarian, with its attacks on the First Amendment: the country is heading, with business, to the Right, — with prey-as-you-pay librarians and "information science" for a fee. I'm living right now in a city run by a bunch of un-elected bankers in a country run by an un-elected president.

SIPAPU: That's one I can agree on. Now, let's get to the Book Fair.

EUBANKS: The New York Book Fair grew out of the San Francisco one. I met Ruth Gottstein, organizer of the San Francisco Book Fair, at ALA in 1972; I went up to her in the Palmer House lobby and asked her if she were Doris Lessing. She was flattered, I was surprised, and we became friends. Magic! Luck! I attended the San Francisco fair in June 1973 (and flew to the COSMEP conference in Tulane University, New Orleans that same weekend), and I came back to New York full of enthusiasm, contacted people through the *Alternatives in Print* address list; and so we organized the first New York Book Fair, to be held coincident with the ALA and COSMEP meetings in that city. Many literary people were involved, and many movement groups—it was my aim to bring the two together, for they stand together in benign neglect, out of libraries and bookstores.

SIPAPU: We well remember that Book Fair. There we were, jammed into the two floors of a tall narrow building, with no room to turn around and no way to escape had there been a fire, and when the Museum people wanted to charge admission in the middle of the Fair, and put up a sign, you blocked the sign with your person.

EUBANKS: That's the kind of thing I learned from the Yippies. They taught me that it's always important to see the total absurdity of a situation, not to get hung up on tiny points that won't matter in ten years or even in ten months. If you don't get an inch you won't think of a foot. The child-like attitude is a big thing in my life; my motto is "Struggle and giggle!" I'm proud to be "immature."

SIPAPU: Some people would rewrite that "struggles and giggles," which is not quite the same thing—

(Giggles took over completely at this point. When order was restored)—

SIPAPU: What about your future work in alternative publishing? Or what lies beyond *AIP?*

EUBANKS: It isn't accepted yet, but I'm going to work toward a Ph.D. on "The political economy of publishing." Whether it's in the form of tapes or of a book, or whatever, will be decided by me and the people I'm working with at the Institute for Policy Studies in Washington, D.C. The present system of publishing and distribution is slowly breaking down as the publishing firms are being managed by financial holding companies like ITT, and Gulf + Western (whose main business is forestry). Even the elite Association of American Publishers is worried about profit-making on *every* title; they're currently following models of reprint houses for marketing small-run publications. Their process? Well, first you identify completely (including names and addresses) the 400–4000 libraries and others who will feel obliged to buy, regardless of cost; then you price for high (20%–40%) profit on those "set" sales. Anything sold over the original, identified market is pure gravy. And little effort or feeling is expended on concern for wide distribution of information. Meanwhile, most of us librarians go right on making purchases in a fog, not having the slightest idea of the political economy of the system we're operating in, and only the commitment (but not the cash) to effect dissemination of information. Most librarians don't actually *know* why the cost of the books they're purchasing keeps going up and up at a geometric rate.

SIPAPU: "Political economy" is an old seventeenth-century term, isn't it?

EUBANKS: And an old Marxist one. Anyway, there are no courses in library schools on publishing and the book trade; the acquisitions courses are often concentrated entirely on the "freedom-to-read" issue, seen entirely from a civil libertarian standpoint. That book battle in Kanawha County, West Virginia, was far more a class issue than a civil liberties issue—

SIPAPU: We'd have said rural vs. urban—

EUBANKS: —it was a class issue, and yet the library periodicals didn't bring that out at all. Librarians have been "protected" from that kind of awareness, and especially in the publishing and acquisitions field.

SIPAPU: You have your work cut out for you, in short. What do you intend to do as a member of the Board of Directors of COSMEP?

EUBANKS: As another step in promoting the small press, I intend to

take a survey of the COSMEP membership: their source of funds, their organization and work patterns, their knowledge of and cooperation with other small presses in their local area and in their publishing field. You see, in our society now all the models of organization are commercial and the cooperation and community of the non-commercial, small, independent, "free" press has to be documented and *broadcast*. I see the independent press as primarily concerned with people, not profits, and therefore I encourage small press people to meet with *librarians,* not just to "sell to libraries." We in COSMEP aren't like the Association of American Publishers, which is willing to lobby for prison libraries, but will not dirty its hands to relate to prisoners. COSMEP is working, in *its* prison project, to encourage prisoners to write and to be in touch with small press people, personally receiving their publications. Librarians can take a lesson and do the same, perhaps, beginning with more personal contact with independent press people.

SIPAPU: Then you'd agree with our "object all sublime, which we'll achieve in time": TO HAVE EVERY LIBRARIAN KNOW A POET, AND EVERY POET KNOW A LIBRARIAN.

EUBANKS: It's wonderful! And don't forget the publishers for social change—they need the money too.

8 : 1

Beyond Baroque *is still alive and well; they subsequently moved into the old Venice City Hall (the town of Venice merged with Los Angeles back in the thirties and the quaint little building was unoccupied). Alexandra Garrett is business manager to their publications; I understand that George Drury Smith has retired.*

I rarely demolish a book in Sipapu, *but Alex Jack's* New Age Dictionary *required it. I started going through it and noting errors on the endpapers of my review copy, which list became so extensive that I thought it just as well to warn people, especially purchasing librarians.*

As for Morning Star Ranch: generalities about the passing of this or that era are often premature, but if there's one phenomenon that's gone, it's the hippie commune. I don't know anyone who'd be caught dead in one now.

BEYOND BAROQUE ART IN VENICE: This isn't an essay in art history, and then again, maybe it is. Anyway, the Venice we're talking about has no Doge (though it does have a poodle named Dijon), and the amount of real baroque in this Venice is a good deal less than you'd expect to find in La Salute. We're talking about Venice, California, and the Beyond Baroque we're at such pains to describe is the name of a literary magazine and nonprofit foundation at the intersection of Venice and Washington Boulevards (1639 West Washington Boulevard, Venice, CA 90291), in a city which has long been absorbed (by its own fatal wish) into Los Angeles.

The standard *(not* toy) poodle named Dijon belongs to our heroine, Alexandra Garrett, the librarian at the Beyond Baroque Foundation, who lives with her husband in Santa Monica Canyon, fifteen minutes from the headquarters of Beyond Baroque. We take you now to a fine house near the sea, into the presence of a stocky lady of middle years, with silver-gray hair, known to her friends as Sandy. She comes to the alternative press via a long apprenticeship:

How to get Beyond Baroque

SIPAPU: How long have you been with *Beyond Baroque?*
GARRETT: Since 1973 — three years and one year before that only as a Board member. Before that I was with *Trace,* the little magazine that chronicled other littles, for six years, and with *Coastlines* for five years; for the last two years I was *Coastlines'* co-editor (with Barding Dahl).
SIPAPU: Your education?
GARRETT: I went to an elementary school in Bryn Mawr, Pennsylvania, where I lived; published a terrible poem in the school paper, starred in a fifth-grade drama called *The Dyspeptic Ogre.* Thence through boarding school — we produced a far-out yearbook — and so to Bennington College in 1944. The famous experimental college in Vermont was then in what many remember as its Golden Age. Stanley Kunitz was there, Francis Ferguson (author of *The Idea of a Theatre),* Erich Fromm, Theodore Roethke, even W.H. Auden for a time. When I entered I wanted to be an actress and take nothing but drama courses, but I was forced to take literature, in which I got turned on to Faulkner; and as I was having trouble learning lines, I switched to

literature. Fromm, Roethke, Auden became my teachers, and I became editor of Bennington's literary magazine, *The Silo*. This was my real start in little magazines; I graduated with Stanley Kunitz as my tutor and a book of poems as my thesis. All the time I was going down to New York and picking up remaindered first editions of Faulkner and Fitzgerald in Fourth Avenue bookstores (most of these books we subsequently lost in a 1955 fire). I spent seven months in Europe, published some poems, wrote an article on job-hunting in Paris which was published in *Mademoiselle* (it almost landed me a job in Paris!); instead I came back to Southern California and married Peter Garrett, an engineer. (We have two grown sons.) It was then that I was introduced to *Coastlines*.

SIPAPU: And *Coastlines* was what?

GARRETT: *Coastlines* and *Trace* were probably the only two literary magazines in southern California in 1955. Both were printed with Villiers, a British outfit of which James Boyer May, managing editor of *Trace,* was the U.S. representative. Consequently, Villiers could move the debts of *Coastlines* along as necessary. However, *Coastlines* was not edited by May, but by Mel Weisburd, who had previously been an editor of *California Quarterly,* — no relation to the UC Davis publication of the same name, but instead an early Fifties literary publication in which a few of the Hollywood Ten were published; they did one issue with the complete screenplay of *Salt of the Earth,* the famous film about a Mexican miners' strike.

SIPAPU: What did you do at *Coastlines?* Read manuscripts?

GARRETT: Never was allowed to read a manuscript, until I inherited the magazine along with Barding Dahl. Instead I gave parties.

SIPAPU: Parties? Surely they didn't keep you around just for that. You mean the kind where they say on the invitation: "Come, even if you are baroque?"

GARRETT: Essentially, yes. Tom McGrath, the guiding spirit of *Coastlines,* ran a poetry workshop in his house. It had taken me eight years to find a poetry workshop in the Los Angeles area. Poets were still not considered teachers here in the mid-fifties, and as far as I could determine, not only were there no poetry workshops in the universities and colleges (or anywhere else in the area for that matter), but no poets teaching here. McGrath's workshop consisted of the editors of *Coastlines* (all men), and myself, finally. It turned out that *Coastlines* had given a party to raise money for the magazine, but had made the mistake of providing excellent snacks. They ended up sixty dollars in the hole. I said yes, only if I could have a free hand in running it. They were

The god Thoth interviewing: from a *Beyond Baroque* folder

delighted: *Coastlines* provided live music (one of the editors had a small band), we charged a dollar and it was BYOL. I provided popcorn, ice, and cups, period. We made a hundred dollars half-way through the evening. It was a marvelous shot in the arm for *Coastlines*. Money problems continued, however, and a few years later the editors gave Barding Dahl and myself a choice: they'd fold the magazine and pay off the $500 printer's bill as soon as possible, or Bard and I could have *Coastlines* and the debt. We chose the magazine and the debt. Weisburd went to Illinois on a job, Gene Frumkin and Alvaro Cardona-Hine became widely published poets, and in addition ended up making a living by literature, — an impossible thought in the old days. Bard and I started by selling backfiles to libraries and we made four hundred dollars that way, but the financial troubles continued, and after another two issues and almost two years of fund-raising efforts, we folded for good — in 1964, nine years and twenty-two issues after *Coastlines* started.

SIPAPU: That's a longer run than many periodicals have, certainly more than we've had (seven years and fifteen issues). Still, let's ask this question: you're a good editor: why did you and Dahl not make a go of *Coastlines?*

GARRETT: Well, first of all we decided to raise $2500 in advance, so that we would not go into debt again. We raised $2000, couldn't make the last $500. No grants for small presses existed then. So we refunded the money, and put out a final issue with revenue from the parties. I got dozens of phone calls. Nobody cared about the magazine: it was always "Whaddya mean, no more parties?" Also, I came to feel that *Coastlines* had served its original purpose: to launch its friends and founders into the literary scene. In doing this it developed a personality. This personality, however, was not transferable. We did fold gracefully, however, with our debts paid and our old subscriptions taken over by *Trace*. And we had a splendid final party, announced as a wake, at which Art Kunkin handed out a prospectus of his forthcoming paper, *The Los Angeles Free Press*. And I went over to *Trace* along with the old subscriptions.

SIPAPU: What was *Trace* like?

GARRETT: *Trace* was really a one-man operation, although Helen Luster, Milton Van Sickle, and I worked there, along with others. There in the basement of his house, James Boyer May sat surrounded by hundreds of manuscripts, producing a complete typescript for each issue, and worrying himself into high blood pressure about the magazine's funds. Sankey of Villiers, Ltd., was the publisher and kept carrying the debt, but May worried anyway. Despite the worries, *Trace* continued to pay its authors and published fine prose and poetry. *Trace* listed little magazines, carried their news and notes of births and deaths, and the guide to little magazines was a conspicuous feature of each issue. Others published similar guides, and as these came in, most of them far less complete than the listings in *Trace,* Len Fulton's

Directory gradually became established in May's mind as one of the better ones. But Fulton did not meet anyone from *Trace* until the first conference of the Committee of Small Magazine Editors and Publishers, at U.C. Berkeley, in the summer of 1968.

SIPAPU: You were at the first COSMEP conference? Tell us about it!

GARRETT: I arrived in white hat and gloves—

SIPAPU: Incredible! Anyone arriving in white hat and gloves to a COSMEP conference! You'd never do that now!

GARRETT: Bull! Next conference I get to I will! You don't know me! Anyway, Helen Luster and I were representing *Trace* there, and I'd never been to Berkeley before, and this was at the height of the radical movement there. At the first meeting, and for two days thereafter, the Berkeley radical poets shouted down every attempt to hold a meeting; Carolyn Herron of the Coordinating Council of Literary Magazines (CCLM) was shouted into silence, but the people who had organized the conference waited for two days until the shouters went away, and then only on the last day was it possible to organize COSMEP. Among the principal organizers were Hugh Fox, Jerry Burns, Len Fulton, Richard Morris, Doug Blazek, and D.R. Wagner. At the poetry reading, one poet stood up and slowly removed his clothes in time to the poem he was reading; I was enormously impressed until someone said afterwards, "Oh, Andy Clausen always does that." He had, of course, nothing to do for an encore except put his clothes back on. Anyway, that was the time that Len Fulton was discovered in person by *Trace,* and the job of record-keeping in the little magazine field was subsequently transferred from May to Fulton.

SIPAPU: And now, at last, to *Beyond Baroque.*

GARRETT: Well, the first time *Trace* ever heard of *Beyond Baroque* was when we were invited to a party opening the magazine. There stood George Drury Smith in a Nehru jacket, and a large sheet cake inscribed "Beyond Baroque," and everybody came; but the magazine didn't pay as he had hoped, and Smith has his expensive printing and typesetting equipment repossessed, and it was some time before he could pick up the pieces and start again. I started actively working for Beyond Baroque in 1973; I had been on the Board of Directors since the Foundation was incorporated the previous year. (They put me on because I had experience in the literary magazine field.) George Smith had already decided to start the Beyond Baroque library of small press publications, and put me in charge because I had a lengthier background in small presses than anyone else on the staff. I had now been involved with one small press or another for the best part of thirty years, still unpaid, still crazy. George had done a wonderful promotion in order to stock the library. He sent a flyer to six hundred magazines offering our magazine in exchange and a backfile in exchange for theirs if they had one. Three hundred magazines replied with their exchanges, including a number of backfiles. (Most have stayed on our exchange list, and defunct presses are replaced with new ones constantly.) When I arrived I found a closet packed from floor to ceiling with uncataloged, unshelved publications. My dreams of reading manuscripts and sending searing, searching rejection slips went out the window. My first catalog cards were in pencil (fortunately I print neatly) with only the most rudimentary information, but they were adequate. I have performed many other tasks at Beyond Baroque since then—including cleaning the bathroom, which we all do—but I am still in charge of the library. Ah, yes. And in 1974 I began giving fund-raising parties for Beyond Baroque. The parties haven't changed. They are still good, and the money still helps in a pinch. It's still BYOL and popcorn, live music and dancing, but admission is now two dollars.

AT THIS POINT we adjourned to the headquarters of Beyond Baroque Foundation. Those who expect to see a sleek small office building on Washington Boulevard, or even a portico of Corinthian columns, are bound to be disappointed. Beyond Baroque Foundation is housed in two buildings, each owned by Smith (and the bank); one, in front, is a very unimpressive two-story shopfront, part of which is leased out to a doll factory; the real hub of the BBF is a building in the back, red with a Chinese roof, which Sandy says used to be a railway station. When we walked in we saw several young people, busily at work behind piles of papers and boxes; in one small room was an electronic typesetting machine, with cautions and directions respecting its use; an electronic stencil was tracing a notice which it subsequently printed; on one wall someone had left a map of Middle-Earth with all its names in Elvish; on the ceiling was tacked the 1964 cover of *Beyond Baroque,* which never went to press. It was done in an abstract-expressionist style. There was a sink with coffee cups, and if C. Northcote Parkinson was right when he said that only a living organization has inadequate quarters, then Beyond Baroque Foundation is alive and kicking! Across the small "Pavilion Courtyard" was the back end of the front building; here was the small room used for poetry readings (this visit was 1 November 1976, and their readings are booked up to 1 January 1977). And *there* was the library, arranged around three walls of the room. Not overwhelming in terms of space, but remember that most little magazines are *little*. They don't take much room.

SIPAPU (looking around): So we know how this library got started, you formed it from three hundred exchanges; here's the stage for the poetry readings, and the library runs around three walls. You've got poetry books at one end, and magazines at the other. Where's the catalog?

GARRETT: Over here, in four drawers; it has a cataloging manual; it shows the holdings of every mag we have, as well as the entries for books, all interfiled. Everything we have is donated, including the backfiles; we don't have a penny to build this library. We also list, in *Beyond Baroque's New*, the names and addresses of incoming periodicals:—but things have changed since there were only two or three poetry publications in Southern California: now we list only new SoCal publications!

LUNCH! With us, lunch isn't a simple meal, it's a philosophical principle! We went diagonally across the street to a sandwich place, and there met George Drury Smith. Smith is a tall man with a serious countenance, now embraced by a short beard. A former high school teacher, with a wide knowledge of languages and literatures, Smith began to tell us about the origins of his periodical:

SIPAPU: You're the only one who can tell us: how did you come by that weird title for the magazine?

SMITH: In the middle of the night, of course, in 1963.

SIPAPU: Very illuminating! But what's *wrong* with baroque?

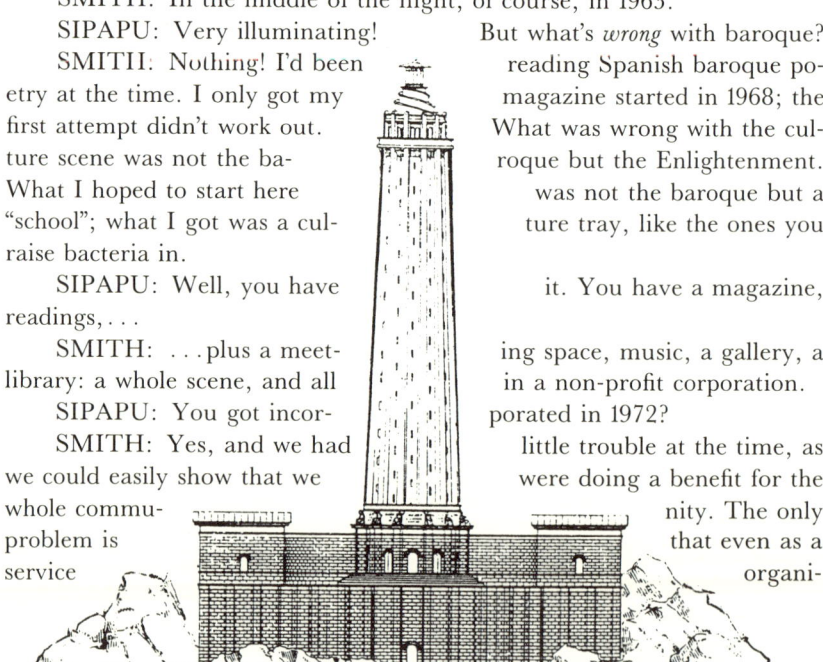

SMITH: Nothing! I'd been reading Spanish baroque poetry at the time. I only got my magazine started in 1968; the first attempt didn't work out. What was wrong with the culture scene was not the baroque but the Enlightenment. What I hoped to start here was not the baroque but a "school"; what I got was a culture tray, like the ones you raise bacteria in.

SIPAPU: Well, you have readings,... it. You have a magazine,

SMITH: ...plus a meeting space, music, a gallery, a library: a whole scene, and all in a non-profit corporation.

SIPAPU: You got incorporated in 1972?

SMITH: Yes, and we had little trouble at the time, as we could easily show that we were doing a benefit for the whole community. The only problem is that even as a service organization we've had increasing problems with the U.S. Postal Service; the charges are rising every year.

SIPAPU: But why did you start *Beyond Baroque* in the first place?

SMITH: Simply, that I wanted to get into the literary scene. I've been doing *Beyond Baroque* for eight years, averaged four issues a year....

SIPAPU: But by your numbering, it looks as if you've published seven hundred issues. How do you account for that?

SMITH: Don't worry. We started with issue number 691, which simply means: this is issue number 1 of 1969.

SIPAPU: O(h).

SMITH: And while there was a thirteen-month gap in 1970, we've also had *Newletters,* and its successor, *New Magazine,* both contribution work plus news notes of what's happening here and in southern California generally.

SIPAPU: Now, what about your newest creation, Literary Publishers of Southern California?

SMITH: It isn't our creation at all; it has no connection with us, save that their first meeting was here, and that we function as a mail drop and answering service. (They also have a desk here.) At the first organizing meeting we had thirty members; we will cooperate with COSMEP's Western Region as much as necessary.

AFTER LUNCH we took leave of our hosts and wandered around Venice. Most of the famous canals are filled in, but the community is a curious territory of broad but quiet streets running roughly east-west, parallel to the seashore, with short connecting streets between. It being Monday, most of the shops were closed; craftspeople tend to be open Saturday and Sunday, and they take Monday (and sometimes Tuesday) off. There were bookstores, bars, a pottery factory called Kilnjoy, and (inevitably) a store called The Merchant of Venice — this one sold furniture. Down on the Boardwalk, a police car moved along at five miles an hour, allowing a girl in a bikini and a slow dog to move in front of it; a half-naked boy with a beard whom we'd seen at lunch was down there with his girlfriend. The lone and level sands stretched far away to the sea: there was no dreamy Adriatic, no promise of a Lido, out there, but only a few sails on the rim of the world. We'd come to the place that the South African novelist Dan Jacobsen describes in his book *No Further West.* Surely, beyond the calm November ocean the planet ended. Japan, and even Hawaii, were inconceivable. Posters urging the election of Communist Party candidate Gus Hall were everywhere, but the presence of posters on walls and telephone poles doesn't mean that much, as every visitor to Europe knows; it only means that there have been some busy volunteers. Old houses, painted in Italian pastels, seemed waiting for the sand to bleach their colors still further. Not a dynamic community, in terms of Houston, or Berkeley, even, but still vulnerably alive.

The time came to return to our Foundation headquarters and to ask the last few questions, one to our hostess, one to our host:

SIPAPU: You have a pretty ambitious set of projects going on here.

GARRETT: Don't say ambitious! We're not ambitious at all. We know our limits, and we'd like to get rid of some of the things we're doing. We'd like to keep our readings, but we'd like to stop arranging readings for poets elsewhere, which we do now whenever we can. (This is our "Poets' Bureau.") We'd like to stop offering the place for meetings and make this purely a place for publications, poetry readings, music, and literary workshops, — plus the library. We have enough to handle — and more!

SIPAPU: And you, Sir, tell us, surrounded by all these machines, this office, this library: — tell us, where it will all end? Will you fail, will you triumph, will you go mad?

SMITH: Maybe it's already happened!

SAN FRANCISCO FAIR: More than two hundred independent presses gathered to exhibit their work at the fourth San Francisco International Book Fair: a large increase from the sixty exhibitors who displayed their books and magazines at the 1971 San Francisco Book Fair at the Hall of Flowers in Golden Gate Park. This year's opening day was greeted by warm sunshine and local musicians. The opening day crowd was not especially large, but the spirit was there: the spirit that small presses have displayed everywhere from New York to Germany, which has kept small press literature alive in America. A wide range of material from fine printed books, offset books and magazines, newsletters, mimeo publications, radical and social awareness books was in evidence, with a large amount of handout material (mostly poetry broadsides). The organizers of the fair were Deborah Johansen, a consultant in marketing and production, associated with Glide

Publications, and Claire Peterson, a small press publisher himself. However, the fair was marred by two incidents: on Friday, 8 October, U.S. Park Service police (the fair was located on Government property and its use was approved and secured by contract) decided that they had let themselves in for more than they had expected. Mumbling something about how some of the exhibitors were bad for the Government's image, they at first tried to tell the fair organizers that they couldn't sell food at the concession stand, only to find that the organizers had already secured a permit; they then proceeded to check out the book exhibitors and found two objectionable comics on display. Obviously upset over *Tits and Clits* and *Color My Cunt* they demanded that the covers be covered up. (Both of these titles are being promoted and sold by feminist organizations.) This request was turned down by the Fair's organizers, who argued their case on the principles of a free speech and a free press; and for nearly five hours, discussions of court orders and threats to close down the fair were held between the organizers and the police, as an ever-increasing army of cops gathered with walkie-talkies in their hands.  Cars were made to move from parking places previously okayed by the police themselves, although in fairness let it be said, that many of them were blocking fire lanes when there was other space previously available. Lawyers representing the fair were called in as the harassment continued into the closing hours of the first day's activities. Finally, a compromise was worked out, in an apparent concession to the Park police to save face: the police agreed to cease further harassment in return for a committment from the fair people to cancel all amplified music scheduled over a three-day period. The planning committee, on the advice of their attorneys, reluctantly agreed to cancel the entertainment, paying off the musicians involved. It was either this or cancel the fair entirely, since the contract did not specify that amplified music could be played on Government property. Apparently satisfied with their semi-victory, the Park police were seldom seen during the rest of the fair. (Some fair organizers also objected to the amplified music noise, and in truth the huge barn-like steel structure would have been hard to work in if there had been a continuous barrage of sound.)

The final day of the fair witnessed a more damaging event. A stainless steel statue with mosaic facing and a hammered bronze head, the work of the late Benjamino Bufano, landed flat on its face in the parking lot of Fort Mason, in the late afternoon of 10 October. The statue, approximately twelve feet tall, and closely resembling the Madonna, had been secured by fragile steel cables at the end of a parking lot stall. Apparently the victim of a careless driver, the statue fell at about 5:45 p.m. John Bryan, former editor of the late

San Francisco Phoenix, an alternative tabloid, witnessed the event and jotted down the car's license number, remarking afterwards, "The placing of a valuable piece of art in a parking lot is absurd. This is a perfect example of the lack of concern we have for the work of San Francisco's greatest sculptor." The statue is apparently seriously damaged.

U.S. Park Service police say that they are continuing an investigation into the matter. We hope that they will continue it with as much vigor and concern as they placed on such issues as whether or not a magazine is obscene. But don't count on it. San Francisco's homicide and rape rate remain staggering while the city's finest rack up court statistics with the arrest of drunks and prostitutes.

Despite the problems of the opening day and the tragedy of the closing day, the fair was a success. It is obvious that alternative presses are a force to be reckoned with. As if to prove this, many of the fair people closed out the last evening at a party in a warehouse, drinking beer, "smoking," and enjoying the music of Robert Crumb and his Zoot Suit Serenaders. — A.D. WINANS.

We can only add that during the two days we were there, the fair was in its best quarters ever; the huge building, from which thousands of GI's had embarked over the years to Pacific destinations, rang with at least some music and even a Dada show on the balcony. There was space, air, and seagulls flashing past the windows on the water. And yes, the people came. And yes, we lived off tuna sandwiches and Acme beer. It was a good scene, in spite of the hassles, and we're hoping it can be there next year. As for Crumb, he lives in our valley now, and the great cartoonist, creator of "Mr. Natural," turns out to be a tall quiet man with a bandleader's thin mustache and a big Adam's apple, who wears pinstripe suits and a fedora, neither drinks nor smokes, and is perfectly competent on the guitar and banjo.

ALA RESOLUTE? We didn't go to ALA's 100th in Chicago, since our appetite for centennials and similar festivals usually cools after the third or fourth announcement of the upcoming event; so we missed the one occasion there that had any awareness of what is happening, viz., the resolution on sexism and racism, introduced by the Council on Interracial Books for Children, 1841 Broadway, New York, NY 10023. (They publish a *Bulletin,* to which all, without exception, should subscribe.) The Council, long a critic of ALA's "hands-off" liberalism, pushed through a resolution, now binding upon ALA, that we believe will far transcend in importance the mere centennial observance that hosted it. The text of the resolution (passed by a sweeping majority) promised that ALA would demand racism and sexism awareness training in library schools; that ALA's Administration Section would develop a model in-service program of the same kind of training for library personnel; that a cluster of named ALA divisions would develop programs to awaken library users to the problems of racism and sexism; and that the

Resources and Technical Services Division would develop a plan for the reform of cataloging practices that now perpetuate racism and sexism. (The full text of the resolution is available from the CIBC at the above address.)

Immediately the CIBC ran full tilt into opposition from the ALA's Intellectual Freedom Committee, and from conservative librarians, who maintained that ideas, even harmful ones, must be protected in the name of intellectual freedom, and (in the case of the conservatives) in the name of "the American way of life." The CIBC carried its point, however, even over the cynicism of those who believe that this was one more "do-gooder" resolution without any teeth in it, and now the ALA is committed, on paper at least, to erasing racism and sexism among librarians by a concerted program of good old-fashioned consciousness-raising.

The CIBC quotes both sides of the debate in its v. 7, no. 4; analyzes and disputes the IFC correspondence; provides a wealth of illustrative materials; and finally offers us all a book, *Human and Anti-Human Values in Children's Books, a Content-Rating Instrument for Educators and Concerned Parents,* CIBC, September 1976. *Sipapu* will try to deal with these issues as they come up.

The gist of the CIBC's argument is unarguable: books which demean the racial and sexual status of children—status which is unchangeable, as they are born with it—works great harm on them. A book which describes people as less than fully human, less than capable of fulfilling their potential, because of sex or race, or a book that prettifies their condition so as to make it seem cute or quaint, while avoiding their real struggles toward freedom and equality, at best sets up the wrong role models, at worst exposes them to taunts on the playground where real race and sex encounters occur. This much seems true. The counter-argument seems to be that these ideas are merely ideas, and that if we start censoring books by refusing to buy them, or through censoring by selection, we are still censoring, pure and simple, and demanding "balance by censorship." The CIBC rebuts, and rejects any attempt to "balance by censorship": they admit that to achieve balance would require "eliminating all but a handful of books in any library collection," but they say that they are not asking for any such holocaust, only asking for the recognition of the covert white-male censorship that already exists.

"Balancing," according to the CIBC, has another built-in flaw: the flow of books that are implicitly, at least, racist and sexist, far outnumbers the trickle of books that are the other way round. This (asserts the CIBC) results from the control of publishing houses by white males. In addition, the idea that "all ideas are equal to others" result in a situation of "do nothing" in an inherently unequal society. "Indeed," they tell us, "the American public library cannot but reflect the true nature of the American system—and that system is a tyranny of race, sex, and class." (Class is introduced here.) If the American system and hence the American publishing industry were totally

equal and just, then there would be no problem; as it is, Libraryland's "hands-off" liberalism amounts to condoning racism and sexism. "Silence gives consent," says the CIBC. The IFC's answer to this was extremely cautious; while not denying the importance of minority viewpoints, they "do not support any efforts to suppress works that do not meet the non-sexist and non-racist criteria established by various groups, including the Council for Interracial Books for Children."

The meeting must have been tense, at least as described by the CIBC. (The IFC has not yet produced its own version of the event, so far as we know.) One librarian, defending the CIBC resolution, cried, "If this is freedom, I for one want less of it," while others insisted that even freedom to be racist was still freedom. As we were not present at this debate, we can only recommend the preface to *Human and Anti-Human Values* as a thorough challenge to the intellectual-freedom position. The book deserves a review.

The preface to *Human and Anti-Human Values* discusses, in detail: racism, sexism, ageism, conformity, escapism and individualism, as all being destructive to their victims, and points out the necessity of a personal and collective effort to overcome inequality and injustice. It also dismisses the defenses of "good intentions" and "literary value" as cop-outs for ignorance and prejudice, and defends the collective of its authors from the charges of "nit-picking" by insisting that they want to expose and remove "every vestige" of harm done by racism and sexism. "It should be obvious by now," they add, "that we frankly seek to impose our values on children's books" (p. 22).

The text of *Human and Anti-Human Values,* available from the CIBC at $5.95, takes each book to be reviewed; provides basic information; reviews the book (reviews are unsigned, but we are assured that the reviews are done by a member of the group most affected); points out not only its overt acts of oppression but also probes for subtly conformist messages such as "You can make it: others have," or, "The white folks will help you out," or even "Go your own way; don't support those militants." After each review, a standard form appears, with spaces to check off: these are (for example) "anti-racist," "non-racist," "racist (by commission/omission)," etc. with spaces for evaluating art and literary text; there are spaces for "Builds negative/positive images of minorities/females"; and spaces for overall judgment of art and text. Rarely checked is a space in the lower left corner of each form: "Inspires action vs. oppression." An examination of the work shows, interestingly enough, that the criticism of the work, as exemplified in the review, is often stronger than the checks in the forms would suggest. Art work is often considered superior to text, and many books which are anti-sexist and anti-racist end up being judged as ageist. On the other hand, if these works are at all what the reviewers say they are, then it is incredible how many insensitive books there are floating around on the market. In most cases, it would seem, the authors of the books reviewed never did their homework (this is especially applicable in histories and biographies) and relied entirely on out-of-date secondary sources (borrowed, we'll bet you, from the you-guessed-it-here-it-comes-folks, Local Public Library. If this is true, the authors do indeed stand convicted; but if their sources were equally racist and sexist, where do the adult collections stand?) Still, not to care, not to dig deep, not to examine "received truths" in the light of new evidence is always damnable, whatever the subject and whatever the nature of our society. And yet, there are surely cases in which the reviewers in *Human and Anti-Human Values* have read a message into the author's work which the author never intended, and they are perhaps unfair and certainly merciless in their exposure. Even Chairman Mao admitted that there were "degrees of guilt," but these reviewers seem to echo the Psalmist: "They are corrupt, they have done abominable works, there is none that doeth good" (Ps. 14:1).

Yet an author, no matter how sensitive, nor how well-read, may quail at the approach of these Beckmessers, with their checked-off forms and their vigilant determination. One solution to their challenge is to turn over all manuscripts to the CIBC for approval before publication, thus avoiding a negative review in a future book or in the CIBC *Bulletin*. Shall we opt, then, for making the CIBC our guardians, letting them "impose their values on children's books?" Shall we ask them to assign their own seal of approval on dust-jackets and to present anti-racist and anti-sexist writers with gold medals? The CIBC has made no such offers, and would authors accept them in this role? Surely, the hard-pressed CIBC staff would be working overtime!

Indeed, are they competent to undertake such a major critical task? Many times the reviews mention class discrimination, but this factor is not clearly brought out in the preface and not at all in the forms. Nor is there any provision against anti-gay, anti-handicapped, or anti–Christian values. After all, a child has no more choice about being born poor or handicapped than about being born black or female; gayness does not appear to be a matter of conscious choice but of development; and to grow up in a predominantly Christian country and not be Christian is to be exposed to all sorts of pressures, covert and open, as those who have been harassed by self-appointed evangelists well know. Finally, although capitalism is often mentioned in the reviews in *Human and Anti-Human Values,* as the source or ally of racism and sexism, "anti-capitalist" is not identified as a positive value to be checked off in those forms. Some would call this a cop-out, others would call it prudence. Where does the CIBC stand?

The debate on class struggle vs. race/sex liberation has not been settled on the Left, and perhaps the CIBC is wise to stay out of it. However, it cuts across the other debate, the one of intellectual freedom vs. social responsibility, the one between the IFC and the CIBC: to which we now return.

There seem to be four major problems concealed within this debate. The first is, that by identifying the librarian as a person to be trusted, by making the trustworthy librarian the socially conscious librarian, the CIBC moves, however unconsciously and imperceptibly, toward a "test" for the "real" librarian: a move which leads in the direction of certification in some way, shape or form: what happens, then, when the certification forces, which some believe to be racist, meet the CIBC coming round the mountain? If most minorities are to be found in non–ALA-accredited schools, and the CIBC asks ALA to insist in race and sex awareness training in its schools, will the two join hands, or collide? Will this amount to an ideological test for admission to the profession? A second thought is that the CIBC and IFC may have taken up positions which are ultimately irreconcilable. Either you believe that everyone has the right to make her/his own mistakes, even if the mistakes inadvertently end up hurting other people; or you do not. The debate becomes that which W.H. Auden described (in his introduction to Henry James's *American Scene),* as that between those who believe that everyone should *do right,* and should be compelled to do right, — some by persuasion, others by force, — and those who believe that everyone should *be free,* for without freedom to choose, even doing right has no moral value. To have to choose between these, in short, is to have to choose between virtue and freedom. A third point (we're going too fast, but we know philosophy takes time) is that in challenging the entire system of racism, sexism, etc. the CIBC is taking on a whole society, a society which has shown itself stubbornly resistant to change, especially when this change is demanded by the intellectuals. The recent Kanawha County, West Virginia, disputes will be remembered by all. In this regard, the high praise given in *Human and Anti-Human Values* to Eloise Greenfield's *Paul Robeson* will be noted by those librarians most of whose patrons will be willing to call themselves anti–Communist. Fourthly and lastly, if it comes to a debate between First Amendment freedoms and

Fourteenth Amendment rights, which are taken up in v. 7, no. 4 of the CIBC *Bulletin,* the ultimate resolution lies not with the CIBC, the IFC, or any individual debater. The issue can only be settled in the Federal courts.

The CIBC's efforts to stem the racist tide deserve all praise. The ALA resolution, particularly where it mentions eliminating racism and sexism from Library of Congress subject headings, is highly commendable. Yet we wonder if the CIBC has not taken on a task too vast for its powers. Will changing children's books change society? Is anything less than a total effort to change people's thinking—including weeding adult collections—not just a cop-out? And will 214 million Americans go along with a re-education program, via books supplied to their children? Will the law insist on it? Will authors respond to the CIBC's reviews of their work? Will the CIBC ultimately help reform society, or will they divide over class vs. race/sex? It's too early to tell. Meanwhile, we suggest that the egalitarian, anti-racist, and cooperative values espoused by the CIBC may have won over the ALA, and certainly have the moral edge, but they are a long way from winning the important battle: the battle for grass-roots, street level American public opinion.

POSTSCRIPT ON SEXISM: A most revealing insight into the whole question of role models for young children was discovered by Stephanie Waxman, a former pre-school teacher and author of *What Is a Girl? What Is a Boy?* (Peace Press, 3828 Willat Avenue, Culver City, CA 90230, $3.95). She discovered that encouraging girls to play ball and boys to sew, and showering them with non-sexist, non-racist books, did nothing at all to change their sexist behavior ("Only girls can be in the playhouse!" "Only boys can be Batman!"). One day, a boy cornered her on the playground and asked her, with much trepidation, "Teacher, will I always be a boy?" The question astounded Ms. Waxman, who assumed that *everyone knows* that you always (well, nowadays, it's almost always) stay the same sex you are when you're born. But what *everyone knows,* of course, is not necessarily obvious to the kids, who in this case had got sex *roles* mixed up with sex *identity.* Sex identity is absolutely necessary as a part of growing up, but it is based on anatomy, and consequently Ms. Waxman devised a set of pictures that straightened things out at once. In order to show the differences between the sexes, she had to show pictures of both sexes, clothed and naked, long hair and short hair, in all roles, and both child and adult. The result, she told us, was an instant change in playground activity; as soon as the children discovered that the differences between them were anatomical and that no one was in any danger of turning into anyone else, the sexist behavior stopped immediately. Anyone could come into the playhouse, and everyone got a turn at being Batman. Of course, this highly recommended book carries its own dangers: many conservative communities are incensed at the idea of showing children bare bodies. This uncovers one possible center of sexism: fear of nakedness, and ignorance of bodily structure. As long as this is maintained, it becomes possible to

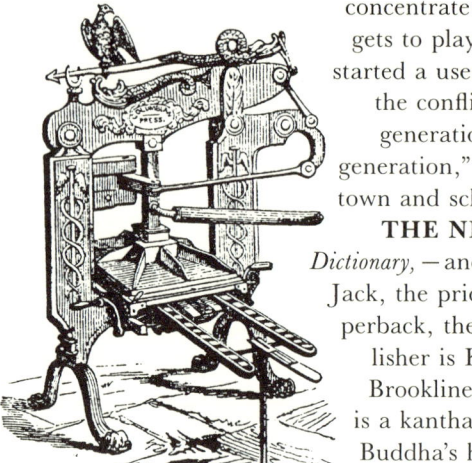

concentrate on who has long hair and who gets to play ball. Ms. Waxman's book has started a useful cure, but still there remains the conflict between the alert and aware generation and the pre-1950 "command generation," who make the rules in many a town and school district.

THE NEW AGE requires *The New Age Dictionary,* — and here it is! The author is Alex Jack, the price is $10 hardbound and $5 paperback, the name and address of the publisher is Kanthaka Press, P.O. Box 696, Brookline Village, MA 02147. And what is a kanthaka? Kanthaka was the name of Buddha's horse, which carried him out of his palace and on to the road that eventually led him to enlightenment, — when he was still Prince Siddhartha Gautama. This dictionary, therefore, is a list of terms drawn mostly from the "spiritual disciplines," the "heads" rather than the "fists" of the new age in which we are now living. As such it includes terms drawn from Amerind, Buddhist, Chinese, Christian, Hindu, Islamic, Japanese ... etc. sources of myths, religions, mystical and contemplative practices; there are also entries for celebrated figures past and present, modern authors, rock stars; and some drug terms in common use. Except for Chairman Mao Tse-tung, there are no political leaders, and political terms are excluded. Derivations are given in some cases; cultural origins in most, or the language origin. Etymology appears rarely; pronunciation is limited to a key in the introduction. The book, although it lacks illustrations, abounds in most excellent tables and lists: look under *chakras, Sufism, sacred books* and *sacred islands* for concise lists simply not to be found elsewhere. There are also tables of synonyms in various languages for *God, love* and *peace.* If a dictionary had a virtuoso cadenza, it would be this one: it has nine different definitions of the word *meditation.* The author, Alex Jack, has studied philosophy at Benares Hindu University, and has been active in the peace movement.

Our first reaction on opening this attractive blue cover and its typeface by Zapf, was to succumb to the demon of envy for not having thought of the idea ourselves. There is no question that a lot of definitions are here that will not appear in Webster's for a long time to come. And having been consulted, and listed as a consultant, and indeed appearing in the text itself, is indeed flattering. However, flattery could not blind us to the fact that some probing of the text suggested the presence of errors, as well as omissions and misleading statements.

The excellence of many entries in this dictionary, including explanations not seen elsewhere (see under *aargh, Necronomicon, quark, Shambhala, Zen Patriarchs,* and a thousand other entries), plus its huge number of terms from theosophy and various "revealed" volumes (some of which we never heard of, like *Beauty Unknown),* cannot blind us to the need for caution in using this work as a reference guide. In what we question, we urge not a wholesale condemnation but a revision before a second edition is planned.

Thus, in a book which has nine different definitions of *meditation,* it is strange to find none of *enlightenment.* Also, while there is a definition of *reincarnation,* there is none of *rebirth* or *resurrection.* The reason for this may lie in the author's definition of *anatta,* which is given as "non-ego"; in fact it is the Buddhist doctrine that there is no soul or *Atman,* and therefore rebirth is possible while reincarnation is not, for a Buddhist.

Jack also seems to have a more blinkered view of the Judeo-Christian tradition than of the religions of the East. For example, although he concentrates on Christian mysticism only, the mysticism of Christianity is so tied up with its doctrines that there is no reason to omit *Bible, testament, eschatology, apocalypse, charisma, millennium, sin,* and *hell.* Similarly while there are entries for *Kabbalah* and *Zohar* there is none for *Talmud.*

Even with the occult and Eastern religion there are some curious omissions. In a book purporting to treat of alchemy there is no mention of *bain-marie, crucible, cucurbit,* or *distillation.* Cross-references lead us to the *Eightfold Path* but there is nothing there: the real entry is under *Noble Eightfold Path* (the adjective is not common); there, admittedly, you can find the steps named in both Pali and English. However, the author has a further confusion in geometry: under *tetrahedron* you find "a pyramid with three sides," while the definition under *pyramid* suggests that the author has trouble visualizing the side opposite the apex as anything more than a mere base. Also, in a book which treats of pyramids it is unusual to find no entry under *Gizeh,* or *obelisk;* just as in a book exalting theosophy (see the introduction) it is surprising to find no mention of *Ojai. Lee, Ann,* is here, but not *Noyes, John Humphrey; Frodo* and *Bilbo* are here but no definition of *hobbit* (Tolkien is given without his death-date, while Bilbo is relegated to *The Lord of the Rings,* in which he appears as a minor figure; *elf* and *orc* are also absent). *Korzybski* is here but not his disciple Sen. S.I. *Hayakawa; Khotan* is here but not its chief work, the *Book of Zambasta;* Krishna is here but not the *Hare Krishna movement;* Waley, Arthur, but not *Needham, Joseph.*

Of misleading entries there are unpardonably many. *Japanese* is not unrelated to other languages; *shaman* is not a Siberian word; *pagodas* do not always contain relics; *Pahlavi* is more than an alphabet; the genus *Sequoia* does not belong to the pine family, although it is a conifer; *Mars* is not the god of health, nor *Saturn* the god of time; *Pelagius* is not described by saying "his name signifies the doctrine" that "one could initiate action toward his own salvation"; the *Mandaeans* are not a Christian sect; lines have been dropped from the definition of *moha,* rendering it unintelligible. The definition of *llama,* a "high being of the Andes," is interesting in view of the definition of *high;* we do not normally associate the *Tylopoda* with bliss; also, while the ninth definition of *meditation* is "The Tao of cats," we looked in vain for their *mantra* under *purr.* On the other hand, we are told that the *cross* is the symbol of Christianity without being told why; the entry under *Holy Spirit* is hopelessly confused; the entry under *Blackfeet* ("people of Montana and Alberta who speak Blackfoot") might as well not have been made at all. The author's opinions of the etiology of *cancer* and the reality of *Holmes, Sherlock* should have been given with at least a hint of the notion that others, sometimes, think otherwise on these subjects. Ursula *LeGuin,* Jonathan *Kozol* and Simone *Weil* all have their names misspelled. (The last is particularly self-defeating, as the reader might suppose that "Simeon" Weil was a *man.*) *Odysseus* would not know what was meant by calling him a draft-dodger, while Oscar *Wilde* might not know what a gay activist was. (Few tendencies are more dangerous than anachronistic projection.) Finally, *Harlequin* is not the "invisible sprite of pantomime"; you can see him all summer long in Copenhagen's Tivoli; and his hand, we fear, is on this madcap dictionary.

For the sake of its precision in other matters—names of the *Kent State* victims and the *Fort Hood Three,* its elucidations of Sri Aurobindo, Alice Bailey, Edgar Cayce, etc., we cannot condemn this book entirely. But we would have forgiven everything if there had been a bibliography at the end. But when we turn to the last pages, there is only a picture of the author and his "spouseperson" on the beach. They look like nice young people, but that is not enough. Whoever wants to delve into these subjects should refer to Hasting's *Encyclopaedia of Religion and Ethics,* Wissowa's *Realencyclopaedie der Altertumswissenschaft,* Robert Graves's *Greek Myths* and Roger Vaillant's *The Aztecs* . . . to begin with. —Enough. The second edition will doubtless be better.

AND ALL THE MORNING STARS SHOUTED FOR JOY!: *The Morning Star Scrapbook,* by Unohoo, Coyote, Rick, and The Mighty Avengers, published by Morning Star Distributing, P.O. Box 134, Occidental, CA 95465, for $3.95,—takes us back to an early encounter we had with Morning Star, Lou Gottlieb's famous "hippie ranch" in that haven of utopianism, Sonoma County, California. One late summer day in 1967 we went to

Morning Star, brought a melon in time for dessert, fed the people (or some of them), and were welcomed and shown around. Shortly after this the locals made a judge shut down the ranch with a decision that is still in effect, nine years later. This scrapbook is the record of the life and (not death, but suspended animation) of Morning Star. The folk-singer's place was the inspiration for thousands of communes around the country, in Canada and Europe, dying and rebirthing. Unlike Morning Star, most of the other communes have survived, not by nudity and dope, but by hard work and learning to work with the neighbors. The homework is not to be neglected, but the original inspiration isn't to be forgotten either. The book in question is derived from carefully-preserved photographs by the hippies themselves, plus extensive blow-by-blow accounts derived from newspaper clippings: the newspaper from which many of the clippings were made, burned down, and so many of its archives are charred and so reproduced. Gottlieb, formerly of The Limelighters, went to jail rather than abandon his belief that the original sin was the private ownership of land. Tolstoyans and Diggers will understand what he meant. The pictures in the book are full of lovely young people with no clothes on, but what we saw, coming at the end of summer, was a group of people properly dressed for our cold fall nights, but living in tepees, a stone structure and even a well-lit packing box. Inadequate shelter, yes, but the welcome was generous and genuine. No checking out at gates! And where else can you find a picture of a baby suckling from its mother while the mother is standing on her head? You still don't get it? Well, STAND ON YOUR HEAD!

8 : 2

SIPAPU

I drew this masthead myself. It was borrowed from the flyer I did after issuing three issues free.

Women Library Workers is still going, but Booklegger Press is now the sole property of Celeste West. The periodical has not appeared for some time and I have not seen her for some years, which is a pity, since at once we were friendly colleagues and she still commands great respect. So far as I know, the book mentioned on p. 168 never appeared.

I am unable to identify the Prof. Slaby of Stanford.

QUIET, PLEASE, WE'RE DOING A REVOLUTION: The scene is an old house in Berkeley, home of Carole Leita (rhymes with Rita), coordinator of Women Library Workers, and of Nancy Schimmel, storyteller, daughter of singer Malvina Reynolds (who lives downstairs). There are extremely comfortable couches; posters; an immaculate small sunny kitchen, books and boxes of literature, but no cat. Light beer and tortillas with cheese and salad have just been served. The whole atmosphere is one of comfort and industry. Carole Leita is a solid young woman, jeans and white embroidered top, very curly dark hair with several white threads, very alert eyes and a serious, quiet voice. She's been in this house six months; with WLW two years.

SIPAPU: ... thank you for an excellent lunch. (Lunch is, with us, a *consuming* interest.) We'll start with the usual: birth and education?

LEITA: I was born in Waco, Texas; spent time in Japan, Colorado, the Philippines—in short, wherever my father went; he was a master sergeant in the Air Force. When I was sixteen and through with high school, I found myself at Kinchloe AFB in the Upper Peninsula of Michigan, so I went to Michigan State University where I was Carole Smith (Leita was originally my middle name), plus a registration number. I dropped out of MSU, and got a job at a Mexican restaurant in Cheyenne, Wyoming. Coming to work one day, I found the place padlocked by the IRS; the man who owned it had failed to pay his taxes, and skipped town, so I couldn't collect my week's wages. I came back to Michigan and waited on tables again, and then moved to Minot, North Dakota, where my father had retired. There I got my first job as assistant librarian at a local public library, re-entered college (Minot State), got a B.A. and married. My second library job was at the local college, as periodicals and documents librarian, although without the M.L.S. When it came time to find a new chief, — a man from Taiwan (who was really crazy; he used to go through people's wastebaskets) was jumped over three women librarians, who had more background and experience than he. We asked why, and were bluntly told, "He's a man, and you're only women. Shut up and go back to work." That was Lesson One—or at least one lesson.

SIPAPU: But you must have a master's degree from somewhere...?

LEITA: Yes, my contract was not renewed, ostensibly because I didn't have a master's, so I came to Minneapolis, got my library degree at the University of Minnesota, and went to work there in the Reference Department. There we received *Synergy*.

SIPAPU *(aside to the audience):* You *cognoscenti* are doubtless aware that *Synergy* was the predecessor of *Booklegger Magazine;* that it was federally funded and published out of the California State Library, and edited by Celeste West, then of San Francisco Public Library. It ceased publication in 1973, when funds were cut off.

LEITA: I was conference program planner for the Minnesota Library Association in 1972, and invited Celeste West to speak at the conference. She did, and soon afterwards I divorced, came to California, and joined the *Booklegger* staff. Since I didn't want to return to my maiden name of Smith nor keep my married name of Hanson, which is just as common as Smith in Minnesota, I wrote the aunt I was named after, and asked her if she could let me use her name, and she said yes.

SIPAPU: What aunt wouldn't be flattered? So now your name is Leita.

LEITA: It's a German name, although a search of directories has turned up no clue as to its origin.

SIPAPU: But you still haven't got to Women Library Workers!

LEITA: The 1974 conference of the American Library Association was the beginning: you'll remember it was preceded by a pre-conference on women, out of which came SHARE (Sisters Have Resources Everywhere) and its *Directory,* which is still available (2d edition, 1976, $2 prepaid, $2.50 invoice, from WLW, 555 29th Street, San Francisco, CA 94131). Out of this conference, and out of the conference at San Francisco in 1975, came Women Library Workers, which was born 1 July 1975. We realized that women working in libraries suffer a double discrimination; first, as workers in a sex-typed occupation they've been exploited as a source of cheap labor; second, within the occupation itself they've been paid less than men and are still excluded from the status jobs and power positions. Women Library Workers was formed to change this state of affairs. To quote a phrase made popular by a recent movie: "We're mad as hell and we aren't going to take it any more."

SIPAPU *(aside to the audience):* Don't think that the lady on page 167 is typical of WLW. But on the other hand, don't be surprised if you find her in their ranks! (Innocent, yes; ignorant, NO!)

LEITA: We're tackling the problem on a grass-roots level. In the past two years, over 500 people have joined WLW and have set up chapters in fifteen states. They're using their knowledge, skills and energy to work on a local level for enforcement of affirmative action in hiring and promotion, equity in wages and benefits, continuing education, career lattices (horizontal and vertical opportunities), and permanent part-time employment with benefits. I recommend that people who want to know more about what people are doing to make changes, read an article in *School Library Journal,* January 1977: "Beyond Awareness: Women in Libraries Organize for Change." Anyway, WLW sent out a pre-issue of its *Newsletter,* in the form of a questionnaire, in September 1975, and the first real issue of the *Newsletter* appeared in February 1976, with Helen Josephine as editor.

(Helen Josephine, though married, is another woman who has chosen a public name that was originally a middle name. She is with us now, a slender woman with glasses and long brown hair.)

LEITA: *Women Library Workers* (the name of the periodical is the same as that of the organization), comes out 6 times a year, has a circulation of seven hundred, costs $5.00 for institutions, dues $3.00 and up according to income (average seems to be $10) and gives jobbers 10%. Renewals, however, have been fantastic; some renewals have been (spontaneously) as much as $50; from one member who is actively involved outside WLW we got a renewal of $100. Everyone does what he or she can.

SIPAPU: But you pay yourselves?

LEITA: Of course. Our new bylaws, just ratified by membership, provide a structure whereby WLW will be governed by a Council made up of representatives elected by Chapters. The Council will have the prerogative of hiring a new staff, if they want to, but whether it's me and Helen, or others, they'd be paid for their work. We don't believe in volunteerism.

SIPAPU: Neither do we? (Except for the editor.)

LEITA: Helen edits the *Newsletter,* getting $50 an issue, and I'm office manager, doing accounts, records and mailing, at $200 a month up to the end of this year. After that, I've decided to travel. We love travelling, with Nancy, as storytellers, and we'll be telling stories to adults and children alike, in schools, libraries, coffee houses, bookstores and festivals—wherever we can get a gig.

(At this point Nancy Schimmel thought she heard a band outside, playing the *Internationale,* so we all hurried down to the street and found that it was a Berkeley band that turns out for public events to play old Left songs,—the specific occasion being a city election that involved propositions which concerned the welfare of tenants. When we all got ourselves together again, we resumed):

SIPAPU: What do you see as the first need?

LEITA: Libraries need to be revolutionized, but just as that's not going to happen right now to society at large, so it's not in the current cards for libraries either. (By revolution, I mean a drastic change in the way things are run.) Our way of working to change the structure is through the majority who do the work in libraries—the women. Women make up more than 85% of the work force but the people who have the power and control—the bosses—

are overwhelmingly men. It's in most women's self-interest to work to change the way libraries are run. Our purpose is not to perpetuate the hierarchical bureaucracy, but to work toward recognition — real recognition, in terms of pay and status — of people who do the front-line work and not just the paper-pushers in the back offices. WLW's members are activists, but they're also individuals who see the problem and its solution from many viewpoints. As a result, we have several goals from which members and chapters can choose. That way, one chapter can put its energies into working for continuing education for all library workers, while another chapter focuses on salary equity. We're clear on what our goals are, but within that, we leave lots of room for the members to choose issues and tactics.

SIPAPU: So, obviously, library workers can only participate as far as local conditions and their private feeling allow them.

LEITA: That's it. There are degrees of belonging: some are totally involved, some send money instead of working on issues. We have no requirements for membership other than agreement with our purpose. We cross class lines — that's one thing we agreed on early — the organization is for all library workers. Only a few people have refused to join us because we don't make the MLS a criterion for membership.

SIPAPU: Are any of your members on the ALA Council? The Social Responsibilities Round Table of ALA cares a lot about such figures as regards their own group.

LEITA: Yes, ten or so. We also have members active in NOW, the NWPC, unions and many other organizations. This year eight more members are running for ALA Council.

SIPAPU: How do you reconcile your forward-looking views with the fact that society in this country is conservative, and even that librarians as a whole are conservative types?

LEITA: Libraries as a whole have been in advance of society. They promoted education, books and literacy long before a substantial part of the society was literate. In the past, the public library was seen as the "people's university." The current freedom of access issue is "ahead of society."

SIPAPU: What is your position with regard to unions? Last time we checked, WLW and the unions were moving on parallel, but not necessarily intersecting, tracks.

LEITA: WLW will never be a union, and I don't believe there will ever be one national union for library workers. There just isn't the strike potential. Library workers need to know what union or other alternatives are available to them in their work place for them to be able to make decisions as to what's best for them. WLW is trying to make that information available to its members. In general, library workers affiliate with whatever union is organized in their locality. In academic and school libraries these tend to be teachers' unions, and in public libraries the public employees' unions. Some states don't yet permit public employees to unionize—which might become another issue for us.

SIPAPU: We usually conclude these interviews with a "where are you going, what's the future"-type question. But you seem to have ancitipated all that!

LEITA: As I said, I'll be going on the road next year as a storyteller, not as an organizer, and that will enable me to walk away from the organization and look at it from the outside. Then I'll be able to see how it works.

SIPAPU: We also try to get in the information that is available about methods of production. You look a lot like *Booklegger!*

LEITA: Why?

SIPAPU: Well, because of the graphics.

LEITA: That's because we started out using the *Booklegger* graphics and part of the equipment. Remember, I'm part of *Booklegger,* and *Booklegger* is a part of WLW, in that all the Bookleggers are WLW members. We still share the Booklegger mailing address, though we've moved the files and equipment to a larger space. Our content, though, is quite different. The main purpose of the newsletter is communication between members. We need to get word to each other about what works and what doesn't, and why, and we need a forum for discussion of issues. And the newsletter is the main link to members who live where there is no chapter, but want to know what's going on. We also try to include information on publications, meetings of other groups, — whatever may be of interest to our readers.

At this point we adjourned to the drive-

way of the Berkeley house, where we found a large white van drawn up and ready to go, to take three young women, plus their books and good words, across the U.S. Entering, we found beds in the back, and places for food and books, and learned that the name of this White Whale of a vehicle was MOBY JANE (the name has probably been painted on the side, by now). It seemed a safe and commodious transport, and whether its occupants tell stories or sell books, or both, we can only urge you to await its arrival in your home town. If you wish to see it, or just wish to join Women Library Workers, write Carole Leita at 555 29th Street, San Francisco, CA 94131. Men can also join with full voting rights, and we joined post-haste at the news.

BOOKLEGGER PRESS OUT OF DANGER: Booklegger Press, publisher of radical librarians' *Booklegger Magazine* and of feminist books, survived financial crisis by going to their readers for support. An announcement in *Booklegger* #16, regarding temporary suspension of the magazine, due to debt and lack of cash flow, brought in thousands of dollars of contributions. "The wine auction at California Library Association's December 1976 annual conference, plus a nationwide lottery for a selection of feminist books, from Women in Distribution, also helped pay our debts—with seed money left to begin again," said editor Celeste West. "This time we'll build on rock. But in this game, we'll always keep in mind Gertrude Stein's words, 'If a thing can be done, why do it?'"

Future plans for *Booklegger* include the fall publication of the book *Revolting Librarians Rides Again,* edited by Valerie Wheat and Celeste West. Manuscripts for this anthology are still being accepted (write Booklegger Press, 555 29th Street, San Francisco, CA 94131, for details). The new cycle of the magazine will begin in 1978. It will be a combination of *Booklegger Magazine* and *Feminist Review of Books,* and is being partially funded by a grant from the literature program of the National Endowment for the Arts.

FROM THE CONFERENCES: Aren't you glad that you have us to cover all sorts of conferences that librarians never got to? Anyone can manage to come to their local or state library association meetings, and some to ALA, but your subscription money gets you, via us, to gatherings that exist on the perimeters of your consciousnesses. Here are several:

WELL, WHAT TECHNOLOGY IS APPROPRIATE?: Our campus was part of the grand tour of Dr. E.F. Schumacher, author of *Small Is Beautiful* (Anchor, 1973), a book which, along with its author, has attained cult status in the past few years. Schumacher, a scholar from the London School of Economics, tall, bulky, sixtyish, graying, with a faint middle-European accent, appeared several times during the conference, and lunched with a select group (we weren't one of them) at the University of California at Davis Faculty Club. In general, Schumacher teaches that large institutions and corporations do more harm than good, not only driving out small farmers here and in the Third World, and displacing farm workers, but also lowering the quality of food and the quality of life for all citizens. This corporate advance into basic industries also wastes energy and expends effort into unnecessary and destructive technologies; the tractor replaces the mule when the mule could have done a better job at less ecological and social cost. The contemporary suburban middle-class style of living in this country is wasteful and doomed anyway.

Opposed to this viewpoint is the belief, proclaimed by a group called the U.S. Labor Party, that all this is simply a trick by capitalists to take away the workers' standard of living, which could really be attainable to all if the capitalists could be overthrown. The USLP, which blames everything on the Rockefellers, was held by some U.S. leftists to be itself a shadow opposition funded by the Rockefellers. Actually it was backed by Lyndon LaRouche. It was noteworthy that no left party appeared at the conference, and none of them have joined in the attack on Schumacher and his ideas, despite the traditional Marxist position that "there's enough to go around." The conference, therefore, sometimes became a one-sided heckling scene in which the Schumacher forces loftily ignored the USLP. Exhibits outside UC Davis's Freeborn Hall overwhelmingly emphasized the new ecological and scarcity-minded forces, in which Zero Population Growth, The Farallones Institute, and various small outfits offering ecological toilets and solar power collectors were much in evidence.

The conference lasted three exhausting days: both the book and the conference were a poor illustration of the idea that "small is beautiful," as both go on to inordinate lengths. Before the end the *Sipapu* forces retreated, beaten by an apparently inexhaustible torrent of words. From the long hours on the hard seats in Freeborn a few highlights may be chosen:

Sim Van der Ryn, director of California's Office of Appropriate Technology, described his 8-person office as being involved in consciousness-raising and demonstration projects. The city, dependent on the country, must be aware of the support system that upholds it. The more people who are aware of the problem, the more possibility of change. For Van der Ryn, a world of no-waste coherence, of diversity and simplicity, appeared to be the answer. After his introduction, a panel on agriculture and intermediate technology was moderated by Richard Rominger, a Winters farmer, the fourth generation on his land, who was later named California's Director of Food and Agriculture. Rominger, a taciturn if friendly man, wasted no words in introducing his panel. The liveliest of these proved to be Roger Garrett, UCD, apparently a spokesman for the opposition, who saw mechanization as a response to the lack of an adequate labor supply, and who disagreed with the idea that a labor-intensive agriculture could adequately feed the nation. Other speakers, however, emphasized the disillusion and the ecological waste of mechanized agriculture, some pointing to Japan, some to old East Europe, some to the American Midwest, as examples of an era in which small was indeed considered beautiful. In particular, Phillip LeVeen, of UC Berkeley, pointed out the role of large landholdings in California as a cheap-labor-based method of agriculture.

The ethical basis of intermediate technology was explored in the afternoon, particularly by John Coleman of the Graduate Theological Union, who criticized Schumacher for ignoring economic rights and personal freedoms. Schumacher himself entered the discussion for the first time here, criticizing rich corporations whose needs are attended to first. Always skimming the edge of socialism, Schumacher never comes close to a Marxist formulation, which is why he appeals to liberal groups and not to radical ones. To the USPL criticism that upper levels of capitalist societies are never changed, he can only offer that plants should be locally controlled. How we get from here to there is apparently beyond or beneath his attention.

Schumacher's role in this conference appeared to be that of a solo piano in a very diffident concerto: he appears late, sounds and recapitulates the main theme, is granted his cadenza, and finally leaves the development to the orchestra.

Intermediate technology and the Third World were explored principally by Lyman Van Slyke, of Stanford, who reported on the success of small industries in the People's Republic of China; large-scale development is not ruled out, but meanwhile, in an intensely political environment, local dams, chemical industries, backyard iron and steel, machinery and its repair are the "small fives" still carried out there. A local industrial system relieves the center of much planning, and a weak national transportation system relieves it of much excess work. Is this a virtue of purely temporary necessity? P.K. Mehta, of UC Berkeley, showed slides from India, illustrating its poverty as the result of industrial investments, not the lack of them. The production of textiles for export to the West has resulted, according to Mehta, in the widespread unemployment seen in his slides from Calcutta. Garrett Hardin, of UC Santa Barbara, very properly inverted the question: supposing we wished to harm poor people, how would we do it? Cure their illnesses and feed them, but give them no work. Result: revolution! It was plain that we had, over the years, been going the wrong way (Mehta).

Hardin also suggested that a thirty-hour week, and a six-hour day, were normal for human beings: forced to work an eight-hour day, we spend the last two hours faking it. Cheers from the back: "Tell that to the Regents!" In point of fact, those who work for themselves, not for institutions, put in twelve-hour days much like the independent farmers who were the heroes of this conference (ask Richard Rominger).

Schumacher's evening cadenza disappointed many who had not heard the orchestra during the day. His generalities, as some saw them, began with an insistence on the real economic value of human freedom, not simply the freedom to sleep under the bridges crossing the Thames; meanwhile the fuel crisis is something to live with from now on, and a personal commitment toward the saving of a dwindling energy supply will be insufficient unless it is combined with a missionary spirit. We must, in short, stop rearranging the deck chairs on the *Titanic*.

Questions directed toward Schumacher brought out the hesitancy in his view between the necessity of changing everything, now, and the possibility of survival through backyard personal commitment. Probed by feminists, he admitted that he would not now have written that passage in his book in which he suggests that women ought properly to be raising children, as it is ultimately more important than other kinds of work; however, some women were still not satisfied, pointing out that virtually all the speakers were men. Schumacher's final pitch to the audience was that of many another reformer, namely, get the message, join us and get to work.

As if to reflect the critics of the "small is beautiful" theory, Friday's program was led off by John D. Kemper, dean of the College of Engineering at UC Davis, who pointed out that small is not always beautiful; what is needed is not necessarily small technology but appropriate technology. Examples of inappropriate technology include the SST, space exploration, and large solar-power collectors — roof-size collectors are better. Tom Bender of *Rain*, the Portland, Oregon magazine of alternative technologies, talked the audience into turning off the overhead light, and opening a few doors, thus giving everyone fresh air. For Bender, dreams were more important than skills, and the right dreams only — he was for eliminating advertising, franchising, outside businesses; for him, values formed the framework for economics — a viewpoint the reverse of the classical Marxist one.

Professor Herman Koenig, of the Department of Electrical Engineering, Michigan State University, gave a classic doomsday speech concerning the availability of energy and raw materials. We're running out of iron, down to taconite, fossil fuels will start disappearing before the end of the century, even nuclear fuels are not inexhaustible; the fossil fuel era will only be a blip in the earth's human history. Americans will have to give up their mobility, change their lifestyles, adjust their values. Solar collectors can't run on solar collectors; work put into these is greater than the work generated. We'll have to move everybody back to a decentralized agriculture. Wild applause followed these remarks. After him, Louis Lundborg, retired chairman of the Bank of America, stressed the need for keeping up pension funds not, as before, solely by using performance stocks, but by emphasizing service industries and investing in prestige projects, such as paramedical services.

Schumacher re-entered, this time to insist on labor's need for planning from management, and for the need for a new job pattern, such as planting trees; since it requires no great skill, and trees can be planted almost anywhere, Schumacher saw a vast tree-planting project as the answer to the labor problem.

Sim Van der Ryn, Office of Appropriate Technology, described the celebrated Dunsmuir Leather Works case, in which the only industry of a small Northern California town was closed down because the women who did the work, making leather clothing, did it at home. To urban unions this meant *sweatshop*, and they saw to it that the business was stopped. To rural women, accustomed to doing their work at home anyway, it was a valuable source of income, and the work could be done in humane surroundings, not in a factory. Legislation to correct this inequity was fought by the unions. In general, official hassling seems to be endless: "It always costs too much and there's a rule against it anyway." In part, this reluctance to accept small-scale lifestyles is that large based on the fact that large units like to deal with large units, viz., large unions with large corporations, large bureaucracies with large bureaucracies: their lawyers speak the same language. In part it arises from the tendency of almost everyone to sue everyone else: trying to indemnify everyone becomes impossible. Result: no one will take a risk on anything new; for example, you can't get insurance for innovative playgrounds. Building codes also strangle new lifestyles, and there is the effect of the Occupational Health and Safety Act (OSHA), which forbids, it appears, almost everyone to do anything.

At lunch we joined a workgroup which was setting up a Land Institute, whose members proposed to wait out doomsday, the collapse of civilization, somewhere back in the foothills. We ventured to point out that if there is a collapse of everything, the last available fuel would be seized by the military, and land trusts and communes would be gasless too; but this left the pioneers in some confusion, so we slipped up to the auditorium again.

The last session we had the patience to sit through was on questions of scale, and was moderated by Paul Craig, director of the UC Energy and Resources Council. Kenneth Watt, professor of sociology at UCD, explained that, contrary to popular opinion, rising wages cause energy use to go down, or rise very slowly, per capita; high-energy technologies however, have mass unemployment and an immense growth of export trade — "We're now exporting everything that isn't nailed down." The growth of microchip communications is likely to produce still more unemployment.

Substituting for Wilson Clark, of the Governor's office, was Professor Slaby, of Stanford University, who with a cry of "Vengeance! Darkness is coming!" gave a fine classic socialist speech. The crisis is in values, not oil, he said, and waste makes our system work, mostly waste in the military, which has spent $1.7 trillion since 1945. Tinkering is not enough, the people who have power will not give it up without a struggle, government will infiltrate and co-opt. His speech, like Prof. Koenig's, received a standing ovation. After him, Emiliano Varanini sounded almost pedestrian, as he explained that we get what we deserve; and where he works, at the California State Energy Resources and Development Commission, we do what we know we can do.

Beyond this it was not possible to survive. Three days of speeches are more than anyone should have to take, and we beat a retreat. In the light of this conference, and in the light of President Carter's energy proposals, delivered to Congress and the nation late in April, we might humbly offer a few thoughts:

The people concerned with energy conservation and small-scale technology are going to have to fish or cut bait. Either there is no time, as Professor Koenig suggested, and we must stop rearranging the deck chairs on the *Titanic,* or there is time, as President Carter subsequently told us, to make changes that are gradual and fair, although some sacrifices will be necessary. If the first is true, then we should all break into a chorus of "Abide with Me," because it's too late to change our ways overnight. You're just not going to get a California woman to walk ten blocks through eighty-degree heat, with three small children trailing after her, to get to the market if she can use her station wagon. And you're not going to get people in central Pennsylvania to live through a winter like the last one without any heat at all.

The British poet, W.H. Auden, immigrating here, described "the excesses of the climate, which is either much too hot or much too cold or much too wet or much too dry, or even, in the case of the California coast, much too mild, a sort of meteorological Back Bay. And then, — oh, dear! — the *insects,* and the *snakes,* and the *poison ivy*.... The truth is, Nature never intended human beings to live here." If this is the case, it will be difficult for us human beings to keep alive in the United States, even if we eliminate everything that puts people out of work or runs on nuclear power. As for time, nobody seemed to notice that it is the only non-renewable natural resource out of which we are doomed to run out not only collectively but individually; it appears that there is a Sheik, darker than any in OPEC, who waits with uplifted scimitar to deprive every one of us of this resource, and he won't negotiate, not with prince or president or scholar. (Even we editors must meet his deadline.)

If, however, we can change from our present system of life to a more ecologically and socially responsible one gradually, so that people have time to get adjusted to new things and do not suddenly find themselves reduced to the peasantry, and if the President can lead us to this new way of living, we at *Sipapu* will be glad to cooperate. You understand, Mr. President, that we will have to keep our electric typewriter, however; it cost us $250, and besides, Doug Galbraith can't prepare camera-ready copy from a nylon ribbon. Meanwhile, persons interested in pursuing the Schumacher way of life can subscribe to his newsletter, *Intermediate Technology*, 556 Santa Cruz Avenue, Menlo Park, CA 94025.

THE TENTH ANNUAL COSMEP CONFERENCE met in some disarray at Holliston Junior College, Lenox, Massachusetts, 23–26 June 1977, in the heart of the Berkshires, a few miles from Tanglewood and from Alice's Restaurant (now moved to an estate named Avaloch). (We're late getting this issue to you because we wanted to report this conference.) This was the second conference held in a rural area, but it was less successful than it might have been, seeing that the beds were military, the dorms noisy, the woods breeding-grounds for mosquitoes, and most of the poetry abominable. The conference staff mistakenly supposed that this was the ninth, not the tenth, annual conference, and the Board showed conflict in its politics; Judy Hogan of North Carolina *(Hyperion, Carolina Wren Press)* was elected to a third term as chair, over the opposition of Jackie Eubanks *(SRRT Newsletter,* New York) and Ruth Gottstein *(New Glide Publications,* California) who first entered the lists as potential co-chairs. No provision for this arrangement was made in the charter and by-laws, and after vehement objections were made by Virginia Scott *(Sunbury,* New York), Ruth Gottstein withdrew and the Board elected Judy Hogan the chair, by a narrow margin. The Midwestern representative to the Board did not even attend the conference at all.

The Board meetings took place in a small red building near the main estate house, outside which was parked a huge bookmobile from the Dakota County Library System in Minnesota, which COSMEP intends to drive around the East and South bringing small press books to the people. We have a permanent memory of this immense empty vehicle (to which COSMEP does not even have the title: it belongs to the National Endowment for the Arts) guarding the entrance to the "little red schoolhouse" wherein sat a more than usually contentious Board. (People would wander in, murmur "They're at it again!" and wander out.)

The program of the conference, held inside the main building, or out on lawns and terraces (one had the feeling that this ought to be Dumbarton Oaks, but it was somewhat less consequential), included repeated concurrent workshops, some of which were only filled with panelists at the last minute; among the best were groups on editorial skills, accounting and business practicalities (we wandered among these, much as we would do if covering an ALA conference). A particularly fine workshop was conducted by Mr. Robson of Pennsylvania, an amateur astronomer of many years' experience, who outlined and demonstrated the application of scientific concepts to the creation of poetry and prose. His system of phonograms, which indicate on specially ruled paper the level and pitch of words to be spoken, would have been useful to the many poets who read at the long poetry reading on Friday night. There those who had signed up found that their names were to be chosen by lot, and not in order of signing-up; in addition, five poets who arrived at the last minute from Pittsfield persuaded the person chairing the reading to let them go first irrespective of the lot of the others. Most of the people reading spoke either in a monotone, or imitated Dylan Thomas without that master's understanding of the limits and possibilities of the human voice; an exception was Luis Rivera, a New York Puerto Rican with a fine sense of music. A second poetry reading was organized in the "little red schoolhouse" the next day, but it conflicted with a book fair, and while the book people got and spent, the poets, lacking a sufficient audience, laid waste their powers (and these were among the better people). Sad to say, only one or two of the members of the Board of Directors attended either of these readings.

The principal issue facing COSMEP at this tenth conference seems to be its immediate future. A.D. Winans *(Second Coming,* California) carried a motion to make the Board (with a referral to the membership) provide some plan to make COSMEP self-sustaining in the next five years, but the talk of the corridors was that the growing strength of the regions, particularly the East and West (the South is organized, the Midwest just getting there) would lead them eventually to break away from the parent organization. The Board agreed to raise the membership dues from $20 to $25, with $2.50 of every such contribution to go to the regions, in addition to what the regions charge on their own (it costs $10 to join COSMEP West, for example). Jackie Eubanks and Ruth Gottstein opposed this motion, on the ground that COSMEP National still needed support. However, the East seems ready to carry out its own tax revolt, while the West seems ready to merge with Literary Publishers of Southern California to form a new, independent group, to be called Western Independent Publishers. The existence of WIP will depend on the will of the membership of COSMEP West, to be debated at its regional meetings in this coming year; but the West is financially secure and some of the oldest members of COSMEP living in the West (it was founded in Berkeley in 1968) are apparently ready to go it alone in a new organization. Presumably, then, COSMEP National would end up as an umbrella organization, with only regional officers and national Board attending the annual meeting. Already the Board has decided, on another motion by Winans, to renounce the use of membership dues to finance midterm meetings.

In other innovations, there were panels on gay literature, Third World (at which, again, the star was Luis Rivera), and feminism. However, the overall impression was that COSMEP had come to a parting of the ways. The organization seems to be levelling off at 1200 members — the coordinator, Richard Morris, circulated a group of letters from non-renewing members —

and the future of this organization seems to be in regional groups and low-cost systems of distribution. The next conference seems to be headed to Chicago, summer of 1978. That's ten years after the Democrats and the Yippies met there — what next?

THE NATIONAL WOMEN'S STUDIES ASSOCIATION met in convention in San Francisco, 13–16 January 1977, and here is an impression of that event by Nancy Seale Osborne, a graduate student at the school of Information Studies, Syracuse University:

"There are more antecedents to the founding convention for people interested in and involved with women's studies across the nation than one person can mention. Several that I can think of occurred in Cincinnati, April 1976 ('Women in the Third Century'), and Bryn Mawr's spring conference, 'Women in History.' At these places the women began the groundwork for selection of delegates to represent regional areas. The delegates subsequently chosen represent a broad spectrum of academic, community, and non-traditional constituencies. They were chosen by lot, and efforts were made to raise money for those delegates who could not afford the trip, or whose constituencies could not afford to send them.

"Twenty-five delegates were chosen for each of twelve regions; in addition, each program within a region was entitled to delegate representation. Thus a total of nearly 500 voting delegates attended the three-day convention. Held at the University of San Francisco, it was sponsored by San Jose University and the Santa Clara Commission on the Status of Women. The original aim of the founding convention was to 'provide and encourage non-sexist, non-racist, feminist education in traditional and non-traditional areas.' Among the workshops held were 'Action programs to combat math avoidance,' 'Grantsmanship' (grantswomanship?), 'American women in media and the arts,' 'Lesbian resources,' 'Working with women in prison,' and significantly enough, 'Moral and legal assistance to members in danger of losing their jobs.'

"Concurrently with the workshops, charter subcommittees met on the details of the constitution, which were then hammered out in plenary sessions. The plenary sessions were arranged to give any one of the delegates a chance to speak: not only were floor microphones monitored to permit two-minute speeches, but floor monitors at the sides of the auditorium carried 'stop action' signs, which the chair honored to permit discussions of parliamentary procedure. Two recorders took minutes, and the careful control of the debate, and the great care taken to preserve each person's right to be heard resulted in a constitutional document truly representative of the issues of women's studies. It will be printed by the Feminist Women's Studies *Newsletter* this spring.

"Harrison and Tyler, comediennes, were at the conference one night, and another night saw a conference by Meg Christen, Margi Adam and Holly Near. The conference was given a great high by this concert; even afterwards, a plenary session continued until two in the morning. For those of us who travelled on a charter flight from the East's bitter winter, we are convinced that the sunshine and flowers that welcomed us helped to create an exciting scenario for social growth and change."—NANCY OSBORNE.

"YOU JUST LOVE CONFERENCES, DON'T YOU?" asked a poet friend. Yes, we do; they're a splendid addiction, and we arrive at them with *éclat,* attend with *savoir-faire,* exit with *panache,* and report with *sangfroid.* For example, when the California Library Association held a series of forums on "Publishers and libraries," we hastened to attend the northernmost, held at CSU Chico, 14 May 1977. The morning was largely devoted to a meeting of the North State Chapter of CLA, in the library of this beautiful campus; Ethel Crockett, California State Librarian, reported the progress of legislation devoted to setting up a California networking system, and Stefan B. Moses, Executive Director of CLA, described that organization's daily work and progress. The afternoon session was the one more to our interest: the panel (moderated by Don Johanns, director of the Butte County Library) included Ellen Ferber, of *Dustbooks,* Paradise, California (her particular interest is the Small Press Book Club, now owned by the Dustbooks organization); Grace Gilman, of Shasta County Library, and Joyce Scroggs, of Plumas County Library (a big library system and a small one); and Frank Goodall, of McGraw-Hill, which has a regional office in the area.

The librarians had a number of problems of acquisitions and binding to discuss, and Ms. Ferber acquitted herself nobly in describing the small press publishers as enduring a whole way of life; claims and correspondence arrive between meals, discussions of the next issue are hashed out over breakfast coffee, and the devoted life of the small press publisher, like that of any true artist, ends only with sleep and finally death. None of this would change this existence for a king's, and yet we find that there are many who see the life of publishing as more like that of a wealthy speculator.

Such a man, surely, is Frank Goodall. Describing the financial constraints of large publishers, the tightrope of popular taste that they must always walk, the uncertainty of the business, he nevertheless displayed his own certainty by being in the forefront of *every* discussion. When questions came from the panel to the audience, lo! Frank Goodall's voice led all the rest.

He answered every question, whether it was directed at him or not, and turned aside all criticism with an appeal to the financial realities. Example: when we ventured to criticize the habit of perfect-binding, and then slapping between hard covers, important works (Auden's last *Collected Poems,* done by Oxford University Press, comes to mind), and added that we thought this a bad practice, suggesting that such bindings only be applied to cookbooks and travel guides easily superseded, — Mr. Goodall genially described the stringencies of "packaging" a book, and the problems of setting up a final cost within which all work, including binding, would have to be done. That some books are worthy of a more craftsmanlike treatment, even at higher cost, was not a notion he chose to discuss. He also denied that the invasion of large corporations had done much harm to books; indeed, he insisted that most of the "Big Board" companies that had entered publishing were now getting out (an entirely credible statement, as far as it went, but what had they done while they were there?).

We drove home by country roads from Chico, more than ever convinced that whatever may be the case with energy supplies, in book publishing, small is indeed beautiful. We have yet to see a small press publisher who would prepare a major poet's *Ausgabe letzter Hand* with a binding designed to fall apart in six months of average use.

WE WEREN'T AT DETROIT (they missed that *panache*), but the ALA SRRT Ethnic Materials Information Exchange Task Force sent us the minutes of its meeting of 20 June, 1977, via Donald Cohen of Queens College; it appears that the racism and sexism awareness resolution of the last ALA conference was not rescinded (it would have been political and moral suicide to rescind it); the meeting also emphasized the importance of Portuguese- and Hawaiian-Americans, as well as the need for librarians to use Alex Haley's *Roots* as a basis for local building of ethnic collections in all communities. A merger with the Disadvantaged Minority Concerns Subcommittee was also discussed. At the ALA membership meeting on 22 June, a resolution transmitting their concern with ethnic minorities at the forthcoming White House Conference on Libraries was also overwhelmingly approved. That same afternoon, the racism and sexism awareness resolution was extended to include creed and national origin; this includes all white ethnic groups as well, although lifestyle and geographical differences are still not taken care of, and class distinctions are not confronted. On the other hand, *The Speaker* seen by many as a civil-liberties attack on anti-racists, was not withdrawn, despite protests, from ALA's endorsement; this film, describing the efforts of a group which wants to protect the right to speak of a racist visitor to a college campus, has been widely criticized as showing the Black and other protestors, who object to the speaker, as simply wild-eyed militants without a serious case. ALA's first voyage into the area of public film seems thus to have backfired, and SRRT groups are apparently seeing it as a betrayal, as it seems to pit the anti-racists against the intellectual freedom champions. More of this kind of division we do not need. We haven't seen the film, but it seems regrettable that the ALA starts from this position. To have to choose between justice and freedom, in short order and on insufficient evidence, is always wrong.

THE FIELD OF UNDERGROUND COMIX moves ahead at a startling pace. We find these counter-cultural nifties far more lively than most of the standard poets; they have completely escaped any kind of co-optation, and their fantasies are too solemn for the radicals, as well as for the fastidious straights. Not for the squeamish, the best of these artist-writers do a far better job of describing the world as it is than the sociologists, novelists, Party workers and academics.

Lee Marrs, whom we interviewed in our v. 6, no. 2, July 1975, has apparently brought her *Pudge* series to a close with the third issue. Pudge does indeed get laid, is disappointed at the initial sensation, but has already had experiences with another woman, and is now set free of her hang-ups to enter any number of possible roles, — president, astronaut, star, ditch-digger—*after a li'l ol' snack.* What she is unlikely to do is to go back to Normal, Illinois, and be an ordinary wife and mother (actually, Pudge would never be ordinary in any role). The last volume is particularly good on details; a small child is wearing a "Save the porpoises" button; the fight for Proposition T, which gave local constituencies to the San Francisco Board of Supervisors (upheld by the defeat of Props. A and B, 3 Aug. 1977), is continuing in the halls where Pudge works; there is a small boy Pudge looks after, named Nary ("the Virgin Nary"). It's a companionable book. However, the fate of Mei-lin, the Aerial Infant, who saves the world from inside her pram, is less fortunate. She is sent off into outer space by an older woman who tells her that the revolution is now succeeding and that her superhuman assistance is now merely interfering and paternalistic: "Listen, Mei-lin; we are finally taking responsibility for ourselves. Equality for real! We're asking you to retire!" And off she goes. The idea that she might be given a gold safety pin, after a testimonial dinner of pablum — that some consideration, after all, a little tact, might be shown her, — does not occur to our relentless author. Well indeed might Mei-lin say (though she doesn't), — "The revolution devours its own *children!*"

The comix magazine *Arcade* continues to be an exciting showcase of witty disrespect and vulgar fantasy; in its no. 3, Fall 1975, there is a short story by Charles Bukowski, "Bop, bop, against that curtain," illustrated by Robert Crumb. Crumb is the perfect illustrator for Bukowski. He has the exact feeling of growing up in Depression California, — the macho bars, the fights and the strippers, the desolation alleys. The same issue contains a marvelous comic-strip life of H.P. Lovecraft (1890–1937), the famous writer of horror stories and creator of the Cthulhu mythos. As a gigantic tentacled creature bursts into his hospital room in Providence, Lovecraft is shown still shouting: "My stories have been adapted for the motion picture screen and starred such talents as Debra Paget and Sandra Dee!" Nor must we forget Gilbert Shelton, whose "Advanced Motoring Tips" have the most improbable information on driving to be found outside *Popular Mechanics*. *Arcade* is available from The Print Mint, 830 Folger Avenue, Berkeley, CA 94710.

Shelton's own *Fabulous Furry Freak Brothers* are now in their fifth book of adventures, in which they move to rural America. Boondock County appears to be a savage mountain region of rattlesnakes, river sharks and rednecks, but Phineas T. Freakears runs for sheriff and actually wins! Fat Freddy's cat manages to follow them in all their adventures. 75 cents from Rip Off Press, Box 14158, San Francisco, CA 94114.

The above press now has its own periodical, *Rip Off Comix*. This features more of the Freak Bros., as well as Wonder Wart-Hog, the world's most repulsive super-hero, plus the work of Ted Richards, and also Bill Griffith, a particularly zany artist whose work suggests a Hollywood background; he writes from the "Griffith Observatory," and his characters are often concerned with making it in showbiz or living it up around the purlieus of something that looks like the environs of Hearst Castle. His pinhead character Zippy, when interviewed in *Arcade*, comes up with answers that might have come from one of the Three Stooges; his character Mr. Toad is a cynical has-been hoofer and stand-up comic.

Without any question the most successful of these satiric comix has got to be *Occult Laff Parade,* a magnificent attack on one cult after another; satanism, voodoo, shamanism, and retired–Florida Star-Trek-Christianity ("Bud Tuttle and Commander Jesus"). Perhaps the most succinctly treated is the cult of sheer fear, given hilarious treatment in the one-page "Teddy meets the Kootcha Bug." Here everybody's deepest fear — that he will turn into the unknown enemy himself — is finally exposed and flaunted. The literacy of these artists is considerable; when in Jay Kinney's "Death Is Love," the two young people are finally expelled from the cult headquarters, they are made to resemble Masaccio's *Expulsion of Adam and Eve* in the church of the Carmine in Florence. Kinney is himself an excellent craftsman, and his women are hauntingly beautiful. *Occult Laff Parade* no. 1 came out in 1973 from the Print Mint; we haven't seen another issue since.

OUR CONCLUDING ITEM is neither contemporary, relevant, revolutionary, nor efficient; it has nothing to say to anyone except librarians, and only to those librarians who love wit and beauty (a Tiny Minority, we're coming to believe). It hasn't even been picked up by *Wilson Library Bulletin*'s

"Booktrucker," as far as we know. It is by Margrete Baur-Heinhold, and is called *Schoene alte Bibliotheken* (Munich, Callwey, 2. Aufl., 1974 [Kulturgeschichte in Einzeldarstellungen]). You don't have to possess an extensive command of German to enjoy these pictures of beautiful old libraries, including not only the Bodleian, All Souls, and antique chained libraries of the remote past, but also the marvelous rococo libraries of 18th-century Germany and Austria, located in cloisters and palaces (the urban ones were all destroyed in World War II), and most of them almost unknown except to connoisseurs of this most fantastic of architectures (like the late Cyril Connolly, who mentioned them in his last book, *Previous Convictions* [Harper and Row, 1963]). Here "the atmosphere is deeply religious although no detail can offend the delicate susceptibilities of an unbeliever." Here are fine volumes on intricately carven bookcases; the room looks like a sea-shell, a porcelain pepperpot or an ink-well; there are statues of virtues and vices, wind-swept atlantides holding up vaulted ceilings showing St. Jerome translating the Vulgate, or the whole of the Council of Trent in full procession, or even angels topped by arch-angels disappearing in little clouds of glory. Nowhere is there a rest room, a readers' advisory desk, a check-out counter, a catalog department or an acquisitions department; there is no need for any of these things, as obviously nothing is ever added or taken away, and should you mention such words as BALLOTS, OCLC, or LIBS-100, you would probably be stricken from behind by a little grotesque fiend armed with an ivory dart. There are large decorative cartouches in one of these libraries, marked "K," "L," "M," "N," but you can bet your bottom *thaler* that these have nothing necessarily to do with Law, Education, Music, or Fine Arts. This book is, in short, a vast relief for all those who are feeling dehydrated by too much of the efficient and the practical, and who long instead for loveliness, whimsy, and peace—a touchstone for those, the happy few, who are OUR READERS.

9 : 1

I did this cover myself, in imitation of the rock concert posters of the previous decade. My former philosophy professor, Frederick Sontag of Pomona College, did a book on the Unification Church which got a couple of negative reviews in this issue (not included because of length and lack of relevance for today). I don't think he was very happy when I sent the issue to him.

The young people who lived in the other house on this ranch (we called it "The Funny Farm") were equally unhappy when they saw the cover: they thought that I was inviting everybody in the world to a party, and where were they going to park all the cars?

Joe Bruchac is still running the Greenfield Center outfit, but he has ceased publication of Greenfield review *(he once accepted a poem of mine) and he was unable to get further funding for his Prison Project. Bruchac and his wife are now continuing to teach and their publication list is monographs with a strong emphasis on Third World writers and poets. Joe is a very fine man and I hear from him occasionally. He was later chair of COSMEP during one of its more divisive eras and kept his head through the whole difficult year.*

My position on the ALA film The Speaker *and my association with a group that was protesting it brought me extremely insulting and angry letters from Vision Films, Inc., who had produced it. These I ignored. This was the first time I had seen the film, and it left me so angry I had to walk around the block to cool off. My understanding is that after a flurry of orders, librarians' demand for* The Speaker *dropped off, and the film is not now in print.*

NOEL PEATTIE PRESENTS IN WINTERS

SIPAPU

v. 9, no. 1: consecutive issue no. 17...

JOE BRUCHAC AND THE CHAINED PEOPLE
FRED SONTAG AND THE MOONIES
GRATEFUL READERS
LIGHTS BY LOVE LIGHTS
THE FUNNY FARM, JAN. 1978
ROUTE 1, BOX 216, WINTERS, CA 95694 USA
TICKETS $4.00 AT DOOR OR FROM EBSCO'S,
FAXON'S, MAC GREGOR'S, MOORE-COTTRELL'S,
POPULAR SUBSCRIPTION SERVICE, ETC.
FREE TO EXCHANGE PAPERS, LIBRARY SCHOOL
STUDENTS, AND PRISONERS. ISSN 0037-5837.
MEMBER COSMEP, APS.. COPYRIGHT © 1978 BY NOEL PEATTIE

JOSEPH BRUCHAC III is a tall, slender, quiet man with dark brown eyes and a soft walk, who is occasionally seen at conferences of the Committee of Small Magazine Editors and Publishers (COSMEP); but who is most of the time at home in Greenfield Center, New York, a small town on the fringes of the Adirondacks. He has his own periodical and publishing outfit, both named after his town, and is well known as a poet and publisher, of a very unusual kind. We take you now to his home:

SIPAPU: *Contemporary Authors* makes your birth and education a public record: born 1942 in Saratoga Springs, NY; successive degrees from Cornell, Syracuse, State University of New York at Albany, with a dissertation *(The Linguist's Staff)* on the novel in West Africa. Yet while well-known in the small press scene, you're not a conspicuous public figure. Greenfield Center is a small place northwest of Saratoga Springs — had to get an old map to find it — and there's a rumor out that you're the fourth generation on that land, and that you're part Indian. Which tribe, please? Which parentage? And what brought your people there, in a remote corner of the historic southeastern Adirondacks?

BRUCHAC: To begin with, I'd like to mention the fact that the information on me in *Contemporary Authors* hasn't been updated in quite a while. (I just sent in a corrected update a few months back.) I never did that dissertation at SUNY-Albany, but dropped out of the Ph.D. program there, and eventually got my doctorate at the Union Graduate School, in a non-traditional Ph.D. program. I was able to do a "creative thesis" — a collection of translations and original poems, titled *Border Crossings,* and I was privileged to have Chinua Achebe, one of Africa's foremost writers, agree to be on my committee. I should explain, perhaps, why I dropped out of the SUNY program and never wrote that thesis. My major reason was that I was being pushed into writing a book *about* African writing, rather than doing something creative of my own. That seemed doubly wrong for me. Too many things have been written *about* Africans, black Americans, and other ethnic groups by people who have only superficial knowledge of them. The field of African literary criticism is overflowing with "Western critics" who make the kinds of mistakes that the anthropologists used to make, and still make, in describing the customs and beliefs of American Indian people. I have a deep and abiding interest in African writing and close friendships with many African writers, but I realized it would be wrong for *me* to write the kind of book Robert Bone wrote about "The Negro novel in America." I'm not saying that I'll never write anything about African writers — I had an essay in *New Letters* on Achebe's poetry two years ago. What I am saying is that certain projects should be, and will be, better done by African writers themselves.

To answer the other questions — on one side of my family (my father's) I'm pure Slovak. His father and mother both came to the U.S. just before World War I from the Czechoslovakian village of Turnava, 70 miles east of

Vienna. My Slovak grandfather (whose name, like mine and my father's was Joseph Bruchac) left there to avoid the war which everyone in Europe knew was impending. Greenfield Center had (and still has, in the second and third generations) a sizeable Slovak community, and so they eventually settled there. On the other side, my mother's, things are a bit more complicated. Her mother was a Dunham and could trace her lineage back to the *Mayflower*. Daniel Webster was a distant relation. (The house I live in was built by my mother's father on the foundation of the Dunham homestead in Greenfield Center, a house which was burned down in a feud in the early 1920's.) The Dunhams were well-off people and owned a great deal of the land in Greenfield, as well as a couple of mills—one for lumber, one for cider. My mother's grandfather, whose name was Jesse Bowman, is the person who influenced me most during my childhood. His father's people had come to Greenfield Center and the Saratoga area during the late 1800's from Canada. Although I have no direct records of it, I am pretty sure that their tribal affiliation was with the St. Francis Abnakis (a Maine Indian people who were forced to emigrate to Canada during the violent Indian wars of the 1600's). He and his people worked in the woods, and his father made ash wood baskets, which he used to sell to tourists in Saratoga. (There was, traditionally, an Indian encampment in Saratoga Springs in the 1800's and early 1900's, and Indians from Canada used to come to the area to sell things in Saratoga during the summers. Some, like my grandfather's people, stayed on and were "assimilated.") My grandfather never liked to talk about being Indian, even though he was very dark-skinned. Being Indian in those days meant that you would be treated badly, sometimes very badly. When a child he used to get in fights at school with people who called him a "dirty Indian"—until he jumped out of the schoolhouse window in the fourth grade and never came back. It was a real scandal when he married my grandmother, who was a graduate of Skidmore College and Albany Law School. He had been working for her father and when they got interested in each other, her father tried to break it up. He didn't succeed—luckily for me!

SIPAPU: No one would deny that there is an Indian presence in your poetry: *The Manobozho Poems (Blue Cloud Quarterly,* 1974) and *Indian Mountain and Other Poems* (Ithaca House, 1971) are a clear proof of it. The presence is not assumed, it is innate. Yet at the ninth annual conference of COSMEP (University of Texas at Austin, 1976) you came right out and said you didn't use the terms "Native Americans" or "Native People" (used, among others, by *Akwesasne Notes* and the American Indian Movement). Although Amerindian, you don't take a radical political stance; although a member of COSMEP, you don't engage yourself in its politics. Reasons why?

BRUCHAC: From my background, I think you can see why I don't call myself an American Indian or Native American. I prefer not to use those kinds of labels, for one. For another, I know what I am and what I believe.

If, from my writing and my ethnic background, I am classified as an American Indian or Native American writer, I'm not upset. But it is not a claim I make for myself. I could just as easily be called a Slovak-American writer. I prefer to try to do a good job of being a human being.

I have no quarrel with the term "Native People" and I'm not violently opposed to the use of the term "Native American." I think that "American Indian" is just as good, if not better, than "Native American," for a number of reasons. First, "American Indian" has been used for a long time, and a lot of people are as comfortable with it as with anything short of their *real names*. Secondly, "Native American" is a problem, because it still makes use of a name derived from an Italian sailor...

SIPAPU: ...who may never have got here, and anyway, the late Samuel Eliot Morison *(The Northern Voyages,* 1976) gives a different origin for the name *America*...

BRUCHAC: ...Thirdly, the word "native" has been used in the pejorative sense just as the word "tribe" has been. Lastly, and most importantly, rather than talking about "Native Americans" or "American Indians" I would like to see people begin to recognize that there were, and still are, many widely diverse *nations* of people on this continent. We lump them all together as "Indians," and then, by coining the new phrase, "Native Americans," we feel we have made things right—while we still remain blind. And when we do refer to separate nations of people on this continent, we continue to mess them up by calling them by other than their real names. It is *amazing* how many of the various peoples of this continent are known to the American public by names which they never—until *forced to*—called themselves. The Dine People found themselves called Navahos (which means "enemy people" in the Pueblo language); the Hodiosawnee found themselves called "Iroquois" (which means "Snake people" in Abnaki), the Lakota (or Dakota) found themselves called "Sioux" (which infers "enemies" in a non-Lakota tongue). Actually, the fact that we know most "American Indian" or "Native American" people by the names their enemies called them, is a lesson in history, and in American attitudes toward them. Anyhow, when I object to words like "Native American"—which I may even use myself, at times,—it is an objection which should really lead into this kind of explanation. And an objection which relates to the dislike of the misuse of language. I try, as far as humanly possible, to write and speak with clarity.

SIPAPU: And the political stance?

BRUCHAC: If one defines political activity on the part of, or for, American Indian people as taking up a gun and shooting white people, *no,* I have not been political. And if one defines taking a part in the politics of COSMEP as involving myself in all of the many issues which come up in COSMEP, and involving myself in a vocal way, then, once again, I am not political. However, I don't agree with either of those definitions.

What I have done, which I feel is an intensely political, even a "radically" political stance, is to focus my life and my activities, writing included, on walking in balance and respecting the Earth. There are some other American writers whom I feel have this approach and are pretty well known — Wendell Berry and Gary Snyder, for example. It is not that I feel, taking COSMEP as an example, that some of the issues people are deeply involved in, are meaningless. It is rather that I feel that they are issues which I will gladly give an opinion on or cast a vote about, perhaps, but not issues which I can spend a lot of time on. I believe in focusing energy. I have most modest aims and I try to remain true to them. I was on the COSMEP Board once. My main interests were to start the Prison Project, and to try to involve more Third World people in COSMEP. I did not run for office again when my term ended. Instead, I remained with those things. Indeed, I am still with them, just as I am still living in the house which I grew up in, the house which my grandfather Jesse Bowman built. — Getting back to American Indian people ... some of the most radical people are the true conservatives. The old men and women who still know the old ways and the languages, who see the Earth as a Mother and all living things as our relatives. One of the reasons I am good friends with the people at *Akwesasne Notes,* a newspaper which I admire and have read for years, is that they seem to remain true to those old people and still are able to speak to an extremely wide audience. I think that the Hopi, the people of peace, have the right idea. They also say very frightening and very radical things — which I believe in — in their prophecies. There are, I should add, many ways to be true to your beliefs. I feel that many of the people in AIM (maybe even the FBI agents) are being true to theirs and are doing important things for Indian people. I also believe that I am the kind of person who can be most effective when he speaks carefully and quietly.

SIPAPU: While in college you were active in Civil Rights work, and in the anti-war movement; in 1966-69, you were a teacher of English and literature at Keta Secondary School in Ghana. Yet your work does not seem to be overtly political in the obvious fashion many might expect from such a writer. How do you handle the expectations that surely your students at Skidmore College, and possibly your colleagues in writing and publishing, have of a writer so *engagé?*

BRUCHAC: Here again there may be a problem of definition. What is "overtly political?" Or maybe the problem is, that in asking the question, you aren't familiar with some of the things I have written. That shouldn't be surprising, because I don't think of myself as a particularly well-known writer, though I have faith in my own work. I have a novel which was published two years ago by Thorp Springs Press, called *The Road to Black Mountain,* which contains some overtly political situations and statements. And my new novel, *The Dreams of Jesse Brown,* which Cold Mountain Press is about to publish, deals with the massacres at Wounded Knee and Sand Creek, the

Custer Fight, and a vision of the destruction of the United States of America. As a writer I've been influenced by Pablo Neruda and Nicolas Guillen (the poet laureate of Cuba), and I've had my co-translations of both writers published in various magazines *(Seneca Review, Paintbrush)*. I was also influenced by Robert Bly's stance on political poetry in the sixties and early seventies. Equally deep influences, though, have been the works of the ancient Chinese, especially the T'ang poets, and the oral traditions, myths and folk tales of the various American Indian nations. I think that those influences show most clearly in *Flow*, and in *This Earth Is a Drum*. I've been told that there is a quiet tone to those poems; and I like to think that it is a quietness which contains strength. I've studied the martial arts for five years now (I have a brown belt in Pentjak-silat, the little-known Indonesian martial art which is closely allied to Kung-Fu Wu-Su) and I think that you find that same kind of quietness there. I believe that a person who has truly studied any of the martial arts is usually one who walks quietly, but with strength. Let me quote the title poem from *This Earth Is a Drum:*

> Near the mountains
> Footsteps on the ground
> sound hollow.
>
> This is to remind you
> this Earth is a drum.
> We must watch our steps closely
> to play the right tune.

I firmly believe that a poem, a story, an essay, or an interview is a "political" act. I am very much in agreement with something Chinua Achebe said: "Art for art's sake is just another piece of deodorized dogshit." That can be found in a superb essay of his called "Africa and Her Writers" in his collected essays, *Morning Yet on Creation Day*. I highly recommend it—and not just to students of African writing. His piece, "Publishing in Africa," should be of interest to small press people everywhere. In that essay, he says, "I believe that a spiritual bond exists between the true artist and the community." I believe that also. A great many writers whom I admire have that kind of sense and sensibility. I mentioned some earlier. I'd also like to recommend the work of Leslie Silko; her first novel, *Ceremony* (Richard Seaver Books) was published in 1977, and hasn't received anything like the kind of response it should have gotten; and also Simon Ortiz. Simon has two recent books of poetry that I like very much. The first is *Going for a Rain* (Doubleday) and the second is *A Good Journey* (Turtle Island Foundation). Simon and Leslie are two of the best Native American writers we have.

SIPAPU: Prison is a tough nut to crack from the outside, as well as the inside. You've started a successful prison writing project at Comstock; you've also started the COSMEP Prison Project (whereby COSMEP members send free copies of their output to you, to be directed to various prisoners). Now then: How have you avoided the hassles that closed the Folsom, California, Writers' Workshop in early 1977? Or are you just lucky? A prisoner wrote us from Oregon that he wanted to know how such a project could get started in Salem. Can he do it, or does it take someone from the outside—and well, frankly, what's the magic word? Also, some of us who are friends of the Prison Project are secretly worried. How many copies of our publications should we send? What gets tossed out by prison officials (and what gets tossed out by bored prisoners)? In a word, how do you speak to people who are in a living hell, while you are unwounded and free?

BRUCHAC: There are no easy formulas or simple answers as far as prisons go. I think any writer who works in a prison would do well to realize that he is working in a system which is para-military, highly conservative, runs by *RULES*. If you can find out what the written rules and the *unwritten* rules for any given prison are (and they vary from joint to joint) you'll stand a lot better chance of getting something going and keeping it in motion. Without compromising my own integrity—and never *forgetting* that I am dealing with a system which through its very nature is more destructive than constructive—I have always tried to abide by the rules of any prison I have done a workshop in. Yes, the prisons (correctional facilities, as they're now called) *don't* work, yes, we should work hard for meaningful alternatives, but when we are doing a writing workshop inside a prison, we have to remember that *is* where we are. And being there may make the difference for one of your inmate students between surviving or dying (literally, as well as spiritually). I have seen dozens—no, more than that, *hundreds,* of people in prisons find a new life through a writing workshop or through creative writing. Perhaps it is only a temporary thing and the doors will still be closed to them when they get out, but I hope not. And the self-knowledge you can gain in a writing course in a prison, the freedom it gives you, is just as important as being a published writer.

Workshops can, in some prisons, be started by inmates. It depends on the prison, or the month, or who wants to start the workshop. The best bet is to get a State Arts Council behind you. If they initiate or back a workshop, you have a good chance of getting one off the ground. That is how my workshop at Great Meadow (Comstock) got started—through New York State Arts Council money, channeled through the America the Beautiful Foundation. That is how the workshop at Arizona State Prison got going— through an inmate (Charley Green, now dead) who had an idea, and started writing to the Arizona State Arts Council about it. One thing I'm now doing is surveying both people inside and COSMEP members: do they know of a workshop in existence, would they like to teach one? When I get all that info together, we can help to start making links. Donna Dorian and Carol Muske of Free Space/Art without Walls are doing similar things by linking writers outside with writers inside. They've done some amazing work with the women's prison in Bedford Hills in New York, and put out a videotape and a small poetry collection called *Songs from a Free Space.*

I think if anyone could read through the thousands of letters we have on file from people in prison who have received material from the COSMEP Prison Project, they would lose their secret worries. The responses are so moving, at times, that you feel like crying . . . and I know for a fact that the magazines or books we send one person usually get passed around to many others. As a rule of thumb, I would suggest that anywhere from 50 to 100 copies of a book or magazine should be the most anyone should send us. If that book or magazine has a limited focus or audience (by *limited,* I mean in terms of the people we send things to) then considerably less than fifty copies would be fine. We don't, for example, send "gay" material to people unless they request it. Books of poetry or literary mags, we send to anyone. We also try, as far as possible, to send people things we think they'd like. (I shouldn't say *we,* Carol Bruchac does all that work and does it very well.) On the other hand, even one or two copies of a book or magazine are certainly welcome; I'm just trying to indicate an upper limit (which can be stretched — we made great use of the more than 500 books Unicorn Press sent us, and the more than 1000 books and magazines from The Smith).

Prison officials don't throw the stuff out. The envelopes are addressed directly to the inmates. They either get them or they are returned to us. (We get about 10% returned each time.) We only continue sending things to people if they write back to us and say "send more." So I think that very few, if any, of the things we send get tossed out by bored prisoners. (And that is largely because we have been sent such fine publications, too! By "fine" I don't mean just "good-looking." Inexpensively done literary magazines are just as closely read as the hardbound volumes from Unicorn Press. I doubt that there has ever been a better overall audience for COSMEP publications, than the people behind bars.)

And how do you speak to people in prison? You speak to them as human beings. Whether caged or free, you have that in common with them.

SIPAPU: Besides your success with prisoners' workshops, you've got another, less publicized secret. The 1976 catalog of Greenfield Review Press lists no less than twenty-four published, or forthcoming, poetry titles, some of them already out of print. When COSMEP is putting a huge van on the road, to sell their material, while other, smaller publishers are struggling to get every inch of publicity they can to distribute their unsold paperbacks, how can you finance and distribute such a large publishing program? You wouldn't publish that many if you had thousands of copies sitting in the attic or the cellar or the back porch. Or maybe you do, and you're just hoping for the Good Luck Fairy to come along?

BRUCHAC: That is another big question. Let me deal with the financing first. Leslie Silko once told me that she thinks of her writing as a "gift to the Earth." A way of saying thank you for all the good things we have been given. I think of publishing and writing both in the same way. Publishing may be a somewhat purer gift because there is less of myself in it. I think that someone reading a fine book of poems by Leslie Silko or Kofi Awonoor or Jimmy Lewisohn or Mei-Mei Bersenbrugge does *not* automatically connect those books with someone named Joe Bruchac—except in a very removed and even abstract way. I also don't publish to "make my name" (as someone once suggested). If anything, the time I spend on publishing takes away from the time I could spend in that pursuit. I also publish because I enjoy it. I love to be able to see a book become real from a manuscript I've read and responded to, to be part of that process. (It is also quite painful to have the inevitable delays by layout people and printers, and the gremlin mistakes that creep in, appear in a finished book.) I do not publish to make money—just as I don't write to make money. I make money so that I can publish and write. (But, if I *do* make money from my publishing and writing, I don't complain.)

I started publishing with the money Carol and I had in our bank accounts when we came back from Africa in 1969. I continued publishing by spending money on bringing out a magazine and books which other people might have used to buy a color TV, and vacation in Bermuda. (We lead a pretty simple life—at least by middle-class American standards. In the growing season we live off our gardens, in the winters we heat mostly by wood.) We began also getting support from grant money—CCLM grants for the magazine and NEA grants for the press. We have received two NEA grants in the past three years, of $5000 each. Most of the money from those went into the press. All of the money I earn from poetry readings, writing workshops, and what little I get paid for my poetry,—that also goes into the account for the press.

The other financial source, which has been more and more important in recent years, is sales. The first few years our sales were pretty slow. Only one of the first four books we published had sold out by that time. But the virtue of a small press is that you can live with slow steady sales. We have now reached the point where virtually every book we publish eventually at least pays for itself. That makes it possible to do more books.

Well, we *do* have a few thousand books in our house, and stored in what used to be Grandfather's general store and gas station. Some of the books we've published just haven't sold. But I think they will, eventually, and we have storage space—and faith. Distribution?—there are a couple of things that have been great for us. One has been the use of flyers. We make one up for each new book and send it out to libraries and to a list of possible buyers made up in large part by the author. A second thing has been personal sales by the author. In addition to a 10% royalty, we now give all our authors a big discount on books they buy outright or take on consignment to sell. In addition to those two things, we do a catalog every year, and have a few distributors that buy regularly from us. Like all small presses, though, we are always looking for new ways of distributing our books. The COSMEP van is a great idea. I also think that more small press people should consider starting bookstores of their own, for small press publications. I have found out that ordinary people will buy small press books gladly—once they exist. But you can't get the Dustbooks *Directory* in the local supermarket.

SIPAPU (aside to audience: He means, of course, Len Fulton and Ellen Ferber's *International Directory of Little Magazines and Small Presses,* 13th edition, 1977-78, Dustbooks, P.O. Box 1056, Paradise, CA 95969, $8.95. We know most of you know about it, it's in Winchell and Sheehy, but there's always someone out there reading about it for the first time): Here you are, an administrator at Skidmore; correspondent and friend of prisoners all over the country, publisher and poet, and yet the hardest thing to do in this maze is to find time "to stand and stare." What's your defense? How do you thrust away the great time-wasters of this planet? Perhaps by declining all interviews—except this one?

BRUCHAC: I think that it is possible to say that the more you do, the more you have to do. I'm busy, but not frantic. I'm also not alone. Carol handles the details of the COSMEP Prison Project and the financial affairs of our publishing. And I have good friends, not all of them human beings, who help keep my strength. I find time to be alone and think, too. I run a college program at Great Meadow for Skidmore College now. The prison is fifty miles away. So, three nights every week, I have that hour's drive up and the hour's drive back to be alone and think, driving through the Adirondacks which I love. I got a pair of snowshoes for Christmas and there is 90 acres of woods on my father's land just a quarter-mile away. I've spent quite a bit of time the past two weeks in those woods, following the tracks of gray foxes and deer, or just standing and listening. We also have a canoe, and in the summer and fall, I can get out on the many little lakes and the streams. Working in the garden, cutting wood for our stoves—these, too, are times for thinking, or not-thinking. The eight to ten hours a week I spend on Pentjak-silat help me find some of that inner solitude, also.

Although we have a TV we keep it in a back room and my two sons seem to regard being told to watch it as some kind of punishment. Aside from an

NFL game now and then, and things like *I, Claudius* on ETV, I don't get into the boob tube. I learned something in my years in Africa, and it has to do with time. Too many people in this country are slaves of time. They're used by it. African people know how to use time, and they have a different time sense. So, too, do American Indian people. Instead of flowing with it, accepting it and using it, Americans try to keep ahead of time, to fight it. They talk too fast and they don't listen. They eat too fast and they eat too much. They also think that once they're past the age of 30—or 20! they're over the hill. But in other cultures a person isn't even looked upon as a full man or woman until they've been a grandparent! I'm 35 years old now and I'm just beginning to learn a few things and do a few things. If I'm lucky and can manage to keep walking in balance, one day I'll be an old man. I'm looking forward to that.

(*The Greenfield Review*, P.O. Box 80, Greenfield Center, NY 12833, publishes two double issues a year, subscription price $4, has a circulation of 750 and was founded in 1968. A short bibliography of Bruchac follows):

BOOKS: Poetry: *Indian Mountain and Other Poems,* Ithaca House, Ithaca, NY, 1971; *The Buffalo in the Syracuse Zoo,* Greenfield Review Press, 1972; *Great Meadow: Words of Hearsay and Heresy,* Dustbooks, Paradise, CA, 1973; *The Manabozho Poems,* Blue Cloud Quarterly, Marvin, SD, 1974; *Flow,* Cold Mountain Press, Austin, TX, 1975; *This Earth Is a Drum,* Cold Mountain Press, 1976; *Entering Onondaga,* Cold Mountain Press, 1978. Forthcoming works: *The Good Message of Handsome Lake,* Unicorn Press, Greensboro, NC, 1978; *There Are No Trees in the Prison,* Blackberry Press, Brunswick, ME, 1978. Fiction: *The Road to Black Mountain,* Thorp Springs Press, Berkeley, CA, 1976; *The Dreams of Jesse Brown,* Cold Mountain Press, 1978 (forthcoming); *Turkey Brother and Other Iroquois Folk Stories,* The Crossing Press, Trumansburg, NY, 1975; *Stone Giants and Flying Heads: More Iroquois Folk Stories,* The Crossing Press, 1978 (forthcoming).—Non-fiction: *The Poetry of Pop,* Dustbooks, 1973.

Editor of: *Words from the House of the Dead: Prison Writings from Soledad,* ed. with Wm. Witherup, The Crossing Press, 1974; *The Last Stop: Prison Writings from Comstock Prison,* Greenfield Review Press, 1973; *Aftermath, An Anthology of Poetry in English from Africa, Asia, and the Caribbean,* ed. with Roger Weaver, Greenfield Review Press, 1977; *The Next World, An Anthology of Young American 3rd World Poets,* The Crossing Press (forthcoming in 1978).

Bruchac also has a wide list of critical articles and translations, and poetry and short stories published in over a hundred different magazines.

THE PERENNIAL CONFERENCE of the California Library Association met in the San Francisco Hilton, 10-14 December 1977. *Sipapu* was born at one of these conferences—in a bar, naturally—and we keep drifting back to them, year after year. The first day opened with a full-day program, put on by an Ad Hoc Committee of Periodicals and Serials Librarians, on "Periodical De-selection in Academic Libraries." No question, of course, that the need is urgent. No question that John B. Wood, CSU/Los Angeles, and Lynn M. Coppel, CSU/Fullerton, put on a good program, although some of us who have been through the experience of a de-selection program were already aware of the problems and solutions. Nevertheless, we couldn't help feeling that we had been invited to our own funeral, and then had been asked to admire the flowers, the music, the lighting, the sermon, and the baked meats afterwards. There were eleven other speakers, far too many to comment on, but among the outstanding ones was Lawrence Marshburn, of the University of Redlands, who described how that library reduced its list of periodical titles from 1600 to 500, and relied on borrowing from a periodicals bank (Center for Research Libraries) for photocopying items; as it happens, however, Redlands is a purely undergraduate library and the faculty are given to understand that they must do their research elsewhere. Sheila T. Dowd, Assistant University Librarian for Collection Development at the University of California, Berkeley, beginning her talk with a quote from Jane Austen (the passage "Can we retrench?" from the first chapter of *Persuasion*)— described how the budget for serial subscriptions had risen to 68% of the total budget, and how it was reduced by cancelling at least 5% of the number of titles. The effect on the Moffett Undergraduate Library was heavy, but room for new titles was made. The plan is to institute a regular review, and check the method every five years.

Barbara Case, Head of the Cataloging Section of CSU/LA, described a nearly catastrophic project, in which the Kennedy Library there did a secret study of periodical use by re-shelving patterns (periodicals, once bound, do not circulate). They revealed their candidates for de-selection to the faculty, recommending an overall 25% of titles for cancellation, and received an overwhelmingly hostile reception. The faculty, who were discomfited by the secrecy in which the project had been carried out, responded with the most vituperative attacks on the library's staff and its head, Morris Polan. The general view of the faculty was that the librarians were fussbudgets, anti-intellectuals, who were going beyond their prerogatives in telling the faculty what they should read, and Mr. Polan was grilled remorselessly at faculty meetings. He stood his ground, however, proved that many of the supposedly most-valued periodicals were never cracked open, and a substantial portion of the recommended list was actually cancelled. The wounds, however, were slow to heal.

In the afternoon, Bruce Golden, professor of English at CSC/San Bernardino, described a much happier outcome, in which the faculty were spoken to frankly at the outset and involved every step of the way; Doris Banks, of CSU/Fullerton, described fears that accreditation would be lost by de-selection as unwarranted, claiming that "accreditation is an idea whose time has passed"; while Margaret Ellis, of UC Riverside, gave a practical how-to-it talk on handling de-selected titles.

Some problems arose for us in the course of this long day; in our experience, the periodical titles least used are apt to be the ones most heavily dependent on library subscriptions for support. While no library exists just to keep journal publishers in business, and everyone can point out some "unnecessary" periodicals, often the periodicals of limited use and circulation — small literary magazines and scholarly journals of restricted scope — are the very ones that young scholars and writers find open to them. The larger, more established periodicals already have their stable of favored contributors, and in some cases you have to pay to get in them; the contributor defrays the cost of publication, at least to some extent. Finally, a number of these titles are themselves published by academic institutions, so that in a sense, the periodical you de-select may be your own. In any case, when libraries can no longer afford to handle the rising costs of periodicals in their budgets, and when publishers desperately need library subscriptions, and young writers and scholars need to be published, in order to make a name for themselves, get that grant or promotion, — then clearly something is bound to strain or break. Will the whole enterprise have to be sustained by government? Or will a survival of the fittest (or the luckiest, or those with connections) order these matters to finality? Don't ask us; ask the Dodo who had none of these advantages.

Unfortunately, also, this program coincided with another, hosted by the Palomar Chapter of CLA, entitled "Sex and salary," which concerned itself with equal pay among comparable professions. The members of the Palomar Chapter, which includes San Diego and Imperial Counties, described in detail their battles to get the San Diego Public Library's employees paid as much as other city employees with comparable education and training. Their argument is that librarians are underpaid because librarianship is a women's profession, and the statistics certainly seem to bear them out; the salary of a librarian there, required to have a college degree and a master's (or 24 semester hours of library education), is roughly $150 a month less than the salaries of many other jobs, such as personnel analyst or community development specialist I, which don't require the master's. Faced with a demand for a 17.5% salary increase over two years, applicable only to librarians, the city authorities proved recalcitrant, and at last report (if we understood the situation correctly), the matter was unresolved, apparently because the inequality is built into the system and it would cause too much of an outcry to try to change it now, or at least in such a short time. We raised the question with one of the panelists afterwards, of why the important job of providing information to the public had become, over the years, considered "women's work" and therefore underpaid; she suggested that it was partly the way the information was provided—in books, rather than in machine-readable tapes or lab reports. Whatever the cause, the San Diego case represents a difficult case to crack; the battles and runarounds go on. An extensive bibliography and other information in a "workshop packet" can be obtained from Anna M. Martinez, Senior Librarian, San Diego Public Library.

The next day, the Collections Development Chapter devoted 'nother whole day to a program with the alarming title of "Microforms . . . they're upon us *now!*" The meeting was originated by Eric MacDonald, of the University of California, Irvine, and the morning session was a series of lectures, while the afternoon session was devoted to panel reactions and questions. The brightest spot in the whole day, however, was the luncheon speaker (the lunch itself wasn't much), Allen B. Veaner, head of the UC Santa Barbara Library, and author of several books on micropublications. He successfully deflated the exaggerated claims and hopes of many people who had expected miracles from microforms, — pointing out the problems of expense, the lack of any but expensive and bulky readers, and the problems of theft and mutilation.

The CLA opening general session began with tributes to State Senator John Dunlap (D-Yolo-Napa-Solano-Sacramento-Sonoma), who had pushed a comprehensive Library Services Act through the Legislature; the Senator was plaque'd and clapped by hundreds of soulfully grateful librarians, and he certainly deserves his applause. After this followed a bizarre contrast; a director of Warner Brothers, Jack Schaefer, was introduced, and showed us slides of his new color film, Ibsen's *Enemy of the People:* how this was relevant to library work was unclear, but it appears that Steve McQueen is getting the big role because he thought he'd like to play the elderly, bourgeois Dr. Stockmann, though in the film he looks more like a gentle San Francisco hippie. The director in his remarks told us that he saw Ibsen's drama solely as a conflict between two brothers, and did not mention the obvious conflict between private greed and public responsibility. It seemed to us that Jack Schaefer was exactly the kind of person whom Ibsen would have detested, but we kept the thought to ourselves for the moment.

We fled the conference on Sunday afternoon to attend a publication party and poetry reading, held in a bookshop on Geary near Cornwall, where Blythe Ayne, poet of Nebraska, read aloud from her book *Love Bath* (published by The Fault, 33513 6th Street, Union City, CA 94587, $2). See what you get by subscribing to this journal? A nice view of a young poet, reading her work in a bookshop hardly large enough to turn around in; the poems are all about love and lovers, past and present, and the scene a rainy night in San Francisco. Sounds like what people pay a large sum of money to get to Paris to find—and they won't find it there. And her poems are good; one of many fine small press publications coming out of the greater Bay country. Thank you, Blythe, for the love and hard work in the poems—and both are important. Now, back to the sad variety of CLA:

The next morning we presided over a business meeting of the Collections Development Chapter. The decision was taken, after some discussion, to present a coordinated program on collection development policies. The Northern California coordinator is Vernon Lust, Shields Library, University of California, Davis; the Southern California coordinator, Eric MacDonald, UC Irvine. We welcome the names of interested persons, as well as copies of policies of various libraries; they should be sent to the Editor of this magazine.

Governor Jerry Brown, late 45 minutes to a meeting of the California Society for Librarians, delivered an address expressing thanks to the librarians for thanking him for signing State Senator Dunlap's bill (and he got a plaque, too). He then launched into a defense of libraries, but as he went on and on his discourse had less and less to do with librarianship and more and more to do with space travel; he began with satellite-based information centers, and launched into the space age, mentioning libraries only occasionally.

The evening was devoted to the California Library Association's private showing of the controversial film, *The Speaker* (see *Sipapu,* v. 8, no. 2, July 1977, p. 178, and the library press generally). The film, as by this time everyone knows, concerns a high school history teacher, advisor to a student committee, which invites a speaker named Boyd, who is known to maintain the inferiority of black people, to speak at a racially integrated high school. The teacher, named Victoria Dunne, on the verge of retirement, takes a strictly neutral civil-libertarian position, and makes little effort to counsel the students. After pressure from the school board and protests by black students, the invitation is withdrawn, and the film ends with Ms. Dunne's farewell to her class and a quotation of the First Amendment.

Part of the trouble with this film was that everyone in it, in the school or in the community, who opposed inviting Boyd, the Schockley-like speaker, was made to seem either oppressive or hysterical. The black students were seen as disruptive (the more disruptive, the bigger Afro), and the school board were seen as heavy-handed. (As a black member of the audience later pointed out, school boards which are largely white do not usually defend the views of black people, but here there was only a concern for the businesses of white store owners if a riot should ensue. The patronizing attitude was obvious—at least to blacks.) In addition, however, Victoria Dunne (how *did* they get that name—"Victorian and done with?"—it's worthy of Amanda McKittrick Ros!), although a history teacher, displayed the most incredible ignorance of history; she literally "did not know" whether Boyd was a scientist or only a racist (later on she called him a scientist), and she did not correct a boy who said that the inferiority of black people has "yet to be disproven," although it is over a hundred years since Alfred Russell Wallace, who had travelled among native peoples in Indonesia, pointed out that the mental capacities of people in food-gathering and hunting societies are as good as those of people in industrial societies, — and all modern anthropology has been founded on this fact. Finally, this teacher, who is winding up thirty years of respected service at this school, tells her students that "there are no absolute standards of right and wrong." However libertarian her viewpoint, this statement, coming from one in her position, is simply incredible. True that no group can dictate its standards to any other, still, no teacher, so completely spaced out from reality and her job, so unable to advise the students she is supposed to be advising, so completely unable to respond with anything but stubbornness to the counsel of her principal or the school board, would be retained for thirty days, let alone for thirty years. We have known lots of teachers, black and white, male and female, official and self-appointed, and all of them certainly did know right from wrong, if they didn't put it in the context of a particular group; certainly none of them put racism in the context of "no absolute standards." A film which hews to a completely neutral view of racial tension, which makes anybody who stands for freedom and dignity look ridiculous, which spreads pseudo-science, half-truths, and lies as part of being "objective," and in which the heroine can't (for all practical purposes) tell right from wrong, —is an immoral and stupid film, and its perpetrators are guilty of a wicked act. Readers of H.C. Andersen's *Snow Queen* will know what we mean, or, for that matter, of Ibsen's *Enemy of the People*. (What the Master of Skien would have thought of all this, surpasses our vocabulary, indeed our imagination.)

At any rate, we objurgated the film, publicly, largely because no one but black people (at that point) were objecting to it, — and then had to leave the room to cool down. When we got back, R. Dean Galloway, of CSC/Stanislaus at Turlock, was also attacking the film, insisting that ALA had never given permission for its name to be placed on the film—the filmmakers had just "leaped to conclusions" and put it there.

WE WENT HOME AND TOOK CARE OF BUSINESS on Tuesday, and therefore we skip to Wednesday ("'I skip forty years,' cried the Baker, in tears"), when we heard a wind-up of the certification dispute (see *Sipapu*, v. 8, no. 1, January 1977). The promised mail survey had been taken, and the results were now in: Regina Minudri told us that 44% were generally in favor of certification, registration or licensing (carefully distinguished); 67% generally opposed; and 46% had other comments, neither directly opposed nor in favor, but generally relevant to the whole problem. Obviously, these figures result from the filling out of a complex questionnaire, and the analysis of written comments. There was a high percentage of people (11%) who thought that C/R/L should be limited to M.L.S. holders; 13% thought that the M.L.S. is all a librarian needs, so no need for C/R/L; 11% thought that an M.L.S. equivalency test should be established for those without the degree. (A full breakdown of the responses can be obtained from Regina Minudri, then of Alameda County, now of Berkeley Public Library. It's well worth study, even if it only runs for four pages.) The committee, convinced that it would be impossible to get certification through such a divided body, and that it would be impossible to convince a reluctant California State Legislature, under the circumstances of such division, that certification was necessary,—recommended to dissolve itself—with the permission of the President of CLA (which permission was granted later at a general Membership Meeting).

After that we wandered into a meeting of the Chinese Librarians' Association (whose chop was printed on its side in the printed program) with the Asian-American Librarians' Caucus. Here again there were lessons in racism awareness, as Connie Young Yu not only took apart the stereotype of Asians in Kurt Wiese's *Five Chinese Brothers* (a story which the Council for Interracial Books for Children has described as the vulgarization of a real and powerful Chinese tale of resistance to oppression) but also analyzed the stereotypes in textbooks, where there is now legal protection against their use.

From there we went to a meeting sponsored by the Bay Area Social Responsibilities Round Table, on "The Information Poor in America." The principal speaker was Thomas Childers, author of a book of that title (Scarecrow, 1975), and he described the survey on which his book was based; defined information (as apart from education), and defined "need." From his remarks, a composite portrait of the information-poor emerged as the portrait of a Poor Slob, who lives in a culturally-deprived area, gets his information largely from newspapers and non-print media, lives on myth, rumor, and folklore, and suffers neglect or run-arounds from agencies. The panelists responded variously: Pat Turian took exception to the lack of information in Chicanos found in Childers's survey; Catherine Saxton described the burnout of librarians attempting to deal with the problem; Jane Irby protested the lack of clear goals, in the reference work of libraries; after all, she said, most people ask their friends and neighbors about the things they're most interested in, and only come to the library as a last resort. This last seemed particularly relevant: the previous speakers' remarks had sometimes reminded us of the famous scene in E.M. Forster's *Howard's End,* in which a group of Edwardian ladies interested in "uplift" sit around discussing how to spend poor Leonard Bast's money for him, supposing they had been willing to give him any. Fay

Blake pointed out that social conditions which deny people information also need to be changed, which seemed even more to the point; and yet, at the same time, there was little recognition that there are a large number of bits of information which are vital to some people, but which cannot be found, or found quickly, in every library. The score of the Saturday afternoon game, for example; the decision of the jury in the county courthouse, the excellence (or execrability) of the singer's performance—these things may eventually turn up in the library's files, but if you want the information *now,* you will want to watch the game, attend the trial, hear the concert.

In addition, it occurred to us that there are a large number of people who are actually misinformed, regardless of their education: nobody mentioned, as they might have, *The Speaker,* in which a number of people, including a history teacher, who ought to be rich in information, is all ready to give credence to a pseudo-scientific lie. "Alone, and palely wandering," we came to the conclusion that a monstrous fraud lies over the whole of librarianship, viz.: librarians actually know everything, whereas (the truth will out!) they only know where to look it up. Perhaps this is the reason why the profession of knowledge has been cynically "left to women" (and so ill-paid), and why the California Legislature does not care to certify us. Perhaps, over the doors of your new library, should be carved the words of Will Rogers: "We're none of us completely ignorant: only just ignorant of different things."

That evening, we moved into the last membership meeting, which, after the usual list of committee reports, three resolutions were proposed and passed; one in favor of equal pay for comparable work, growing out of the San Diego Public librarians' struggle, and directly including support for the same; one arising out of a question propounded to Governor Brown by Ann Mitchell of UCLA, giving high priority to the development of a proposal for alternatives to direct user fees in publicly funded libraries; and a third, relative to *The Speaker,* proposed by Rita J. Jones of the California Librarians' Black Caucus, the text of which follows:

> WHEREAS: the film *The Speaker* purports to deal with the issue of the First Amendment in a contemporary setting, and is designed to serve as a major resource for public broadcasting and programming in various settings; and WHEREAS, The method of production was questionable; and WHEREAS, This film is purported to represent ALA's position on intellectual freedom; and WHEREAS, In actuality this film does not do justice to either the First Amendment or intellectual freedom; and WHEREAS, *The Speaker* is condescending, simplistic, and insulting to blacks, women, librarians, educators, and students; and WHEREAS, *The Speaker* violated the Library Bill of Rights by failing to provide a mechanism for the discussion of both sides of a controversial issue; now therefore be it RESOLVED, that CLA express disapproval of the film, *The Speaker,* and CLA urge ALA to withdraw its endorsement and promotion of the film.

An interesting by-play followed. Norman Tanis, of CSU/Northridge, chair of the Intellectual Freedom Committee, proposed a substitute motion, which acknowledged the anguish of minority librarians who had seen the film, and urged that ALA make an effort to provide a constructive solution to the problems of racism in our society. We suggested, in due course at the microphone, that the substitute resolution, as such, made no recommendation as to what was to be done with the film itself, whereupon Rita J. Jones had a "lightbulb." Quick as a wink, she was up on her feet, and behind the microphone, saying that the substitute motion had a great deal to recommend it, and that she would like to add the whole of its text and its "RESOLVED" to her own proposed resolution. This move was viewed with mingled consternation and delight. Mr. Tanis asked if his motion (proposed and seconded) might not be voted on first, but the chair, skillfully guided by the parliamentarian (who admitted that shortcuts, not technically legal, were being taken, while someone called from the audience, "We're getting deep into Roberts'!") allowed that the amended motion would have to be voted on first, before a vote on the substitute motion was taken. In answer to a question from Tanis, the chair ruled (no doubt, correctly), that once a motion was moved and seconded, its fate depended on the House, and not on its movers; and that the only way to rescue the substitute motion in its purity was to withdraw it—after which it could only be voted on *after* the main motion, as amended (by a preliminary vote), was voted on.

After this, the Intellectual Freedom forces had no choice but to see their motion co-opted into the main motion, and they were obliged, therefore, to vote for the amendment, and ultimately for the main motion, in one of the fastest end-runs we have seen in many years (well, several) on the parliamentary gridiron. A few librarians held out, doubtless because they felt the motion was carried by fancy footwork, but at least the California Library Association fared better than the Library Associations of Minnesota (where a substitute motion, much milder, was provided as a fallback and finally won), and Pennsylvania (where a strongly worded motion, without a substitute motion, went down to decisive defeat). We're not sure if that tactic would work in other states, but it might be useful to get the texts of substitute motions, wherever possible, whenever the film comes up for debate, and at least be prepared to meet them. Meanwhile, in spite of its show of strength, ALA continues to distribute the film with its name, however obtained, and "the debate that nobody won" continues from state to state. Those with information on the debates in other states are urged to send them to this office for summary. And why can't ALA begin to admit, that just conceivably, just this once, it might *(horribile dictu),* maybe it's just barely within the realm of conceivable possibility, be *wrong?*

MEANWHILE, IN COSMEP (Committee of Small Magazine Editors and Publishers), an organization with many library ties, a similar battle erupted. This time it was over the inclusion of a book (Dick Whitson's *How to Meet and Bed Girls,* from Programmed Studies, Inc., Box 113, Stow, MA 01775, $29.95), in a travelling van, run by COSMEP, and owned by the National Endowment for the Arts. The feminist presses in COSMEP were naturally offended by this book (which included some sado-masochism) and threatened to walk out of COSMEP's tenth annual conference in Lenox, Massachusetts, July 1977, if this book were not withdrawn from the van. The van made a brief foray into South Carolina and Georgia this winter before mechanical problems forced it to come back to North Carolina; it carries largely poetry and other non-commercial titles, and many objecting to the book were also objecting to the intrusion of a clearly commercial item.

The 2½ hour debate at the COSMEP conference was finally settled by making a decision that while COSMEP does not support censorship, if any materials submitted by a member press to the van promoted racism or sexism (which are not in the interests of anyone's civil rights) the Van Project would not be obliged to accept them. Decisions on possibly offensive materials were to be made by the elected Board of Directors of COSMEP. The Board also committed itself to seeking legal counsel to protect prople working on the van.

At press time, Whitson had withdrawn his controversial book (which would have been expensive to carry, and actually consisted of only a few pages of pasted-up material), and replaced it with one on auto repair, at which he is possibly more proficient. Meanwhile, however, a battle crupted in the col- umns of the COSMEP *Newsletter*—which is worth read- ing on its own account; if you're not a pub- lisher, you can get it for $25 a year from Richard Morris, its Editor, P.O. Box 703, San Fran- cisco, CA 94101. The pages of COSMEP's *Newsletter* have for years functioned as a sort of Middle-Earth, in which Elves, Men, Dwarves, and Orcs battle each other with fell pens, and in which there are mighty bards and dark counsels hard to unriddle. In this particular battle, the banner of free speech at any price was supported by Madge Reinhart, A.D. Winans, Joe Flaherty, and others, and the foes of sexism were Anne Pride, Arlene Stone, Jackie Eubanks, and others. The free speech group compared the Board's action to that of Soviet officials when these removed American translations of the works of Russian dissident publishers from the Moscow Book Fair in 1977. The social responsibilities party demanded consideration for the feelings of women who in the past have been exploited by men and even killed by them, and are still being exploited and killed. The principle of free speech vs. social responsibility, therefore, is still not settled in the minds of COSMEP members, even as it is not settled in the minds of ALA members. The more hopeful contend that the two principles are inseparable, and that these rights are mutually reinforced, and best considered together in a free society, rather than isolated from each other or falsely thrown in opposition to each other. Others, perhaps more anarchist in tendency, see any demand for "responsibility" as oppression, and contend that the camel's nose is well under the tent when any material that some consider offensive is excluded from any particular vehicle of expression — such as a book van. The whole debate is, of course, an extension of the "Berninghausen debate" carried on in the pages of *Library Journal* some years ago, and now sharpened by concrete instances of offensive material ("that film" and "that book").

Our commentary must be brief. While there are many subjects of wide dispute, such as foreign and domestic policy, the right way to raise and educate children, and the right way to spend taxpayers' money, and it is important that all sides be heard on these questions, — there are facts which have obtained such general consensus that they are no longer unproven hypotheses, nor even "theories," but facts indeed. Among these are the real humanity of women and non-white peoples, and consequently their right to life in freedom from oppression. Science and experience have established these facts; they have been defended in political and military struggles; and the law has confirmed them. Few members of ALA or COSMEP would deny them, even now.

Should unlimited protection, then, be given to those who deny these facts, or who advocate methods of oppressing people? Surely they are entitled to stand on the street corner and pass out their handbills, but does this mean that they can invade any organization, enter any school, and claim the equal protection of the laws? Need COSMEP accept "that book" simply because the publisher has put his money down, and is it total censorship to deny him just one van in which to sell his wares? Is it censorship for ALA to withdraw its name from "that film," and halt its distribution thereof? Have these private organizations, which have a reputation to protect, no right to protect it? In the case of the school district (fictional) mentioned in *The Speaker,* is Mr. Boyd denied every chance to express himself, simply because he cannot speak at one point? The answer to all these questions, surely, is NO.

However, it might have been better if ALA and COSMEP had provided against such intrusions by carefully-worded statute or contract language. If ALA had placed an escape clause in its contract with the makers of "that film," and if the COSMEP Board had enacted its resolution before the appearance of "that book," and again placed an escape clause in its contract with the publishers who are submitting books to the van, and if the fictional school board in *The Speaker* had adopted a written policy regarding racist speakers on school property, then the people who teach the inferiority of black people, and the people who try to make you believe that the way to please a woman is to stick a broom handle into her, — would have been duly warned. They could have read the fine print in the regulations or contracts, signed them and followed instructions, — or exercised their God-given rights to take their poison elsewhere.

No member of an organization should be required to tolerate that organization's official sponsorship of doctrines, demonstrably false and contrary to law and public policy, which have in the past and can be expected in the future to redound to his or her own hurt, — providing that the restrictions on the organization, derived from such objection, apply only to the scope and activities of that particular private organization, and that the restrictions are spelled out in statute or contract. To say that such a person, objecting to the sponsorship of doctrines by his or her own organization which work him or her harm, is guilty of censorship, — seems to us insensitive and hypocritical, and stretches the notion of censorship beyond reasonable limits. However, whether *all* such expressions of false and malicious doctrines should be at *all* times forbidden to *all* people, is another thing entirely; and the courts have not yet imposed such sweeping bans, nor does public opinion seem ready to require them.

Intellectual freedom and social responsibility are not really opposed, if only because a society in which human dignity is respected is likely to be freer than one in which it is derided. If respect for the rights of some means a greater dignity for all, then by all means let us support the groups most likely to lead us to that goal, however remote it may be.

TURTLE TIME AGAIN: You've been through a lot of heavy stuff the past few pages, and so we want to take you back to the Caribbean, where there is hope for the green sea turtle, *Chelonia mydas*. Since 1972, over a thousand turtles nesting at Aves Island (see *Sipapu*, v. 6, no. 2, July 1975, p. 118) have been tagged, and undoubtedly many of them bear the names of our readers and their dear ones. Now the Island Resources Foundation (P.O. Box 4187, St. Thomas, VI 00801), asks you to join them for $25, marking the check "SEA TURTLE," and you will thereby aid in a preservation and conservation program, and also get a pre-cast pewter turtle pin. It's nice, and we have one. Certainly the whole experience tortoise something.

WE PASS ON (OR RATHER PASS OUT) to other political concerns. *Cover-up Lowdown,* no. 1, by Jay Kinney and Paul Mavrides, published by the Rip-Off Press (P.O. Box 14158, San Francisco, CA 94114), takes a good if offbeat look at the Kennedy assassination conspiracy theories. It consists of two comic books, back to back, and a removable centerfold. Part of one side is devoted to a series of one-page frames illustrating various unexplained facts about the assassination, footnoted by various authors; this periodical takes no stand on the question and cannot verify the assertions made; we doubt that any independent investigation is likely to lead to the truth at this point; too many witnesses have disappeared and too much evidence is missing or sequestered. However, Kinney and Mavrides take off from there; they go on to Wounded Knee and wiretapping, and finally produce a page showing conclusively that "YOU KILLED KENNEDY! AND HERE'S THE PROOF." A questionnaire for scoring ("Why was your library card in Oswald's wallet?") proves surely no more absurd than many "serious" explanations of the tragedy (we recently saw an article purporting to show that Aristotle Onassis did it, and that Jesus didn't die on the cross). There is also a story about a private Eye (one big Eye in a trenchcoat) named Eye Yi Yi, who uncovers a plot to turn the whole state of Indiana into a shopping center. "We're a group of decent, responsible Christian men, devoted to our families & our flag — who just happen to represent a consortium of big banks, oil companies, developers and politicians. IT'S A POWER GRAB, YI YI, AND YOU CAN'T STOP US!" The centerfold, however, is the real center-piece: you're supposed to remove it carefully, cut and paste according to instructions, and behold! you have a huge pseudo-organizational chart in the form of a Moebius strip, linking Everything to Everything Else, an endless universe of allegations for all the cranks that ever there was, they'll all be there because, because ... the FEDERAL RESERVE controls THE PRESIDENT which connects with COCA-COLA which leads to COCAINE which controls YOUR CHILD'S BRAIN. We would like, nay we *implore,* Rip Off Press to publish this strip separately, in color, and on a much larger scale; it's hard to read, and harder to share with others. Alternatively, it might be used as the basis of a short film, to be shown at those "Cinema Nightcaps" the audio-visual people cheer us with at state and national library conferences. All they'd have to do would be to film the slowly moving strip, to the background music of "Teddy Bears' Picnic." PLEASE, please, do it, Mr. Fred Todd! (The cost of this item is 75 cents, and it's worth a lot more than many $17.50 tomes we see nowadays.) (Incidentally, the meeting of the capitalists of Cornutopia interrupted by Eye Yi Yi briefly resembles Rembrandt's *Syndics of the Drapers' Guild* [Rijks Museum, Amsterdam.])

From the same publisher comes Bill Griffith's *Zippy Stories* (95 cents). We think it is time that the savants who study this highly specialized periodical became aware of Griffith and Zippy. Zippy is a pinheaded creature in a clown suit, with a dada mind and picaresque adventures; he likes to invade territory, wealthy homes or carny shows, and cavort around disturbing everybody. When he campaigns for national office he tells the people at the railroad station in Omaha, "I'm glad to be back in Peoria!" He also turns out to be the man at the top of the Transamerica Building in San Francisco who switches the red light on and off with his head. There are also a few scenes from the life of Alfred Jarry, and some strips of Griffith's other characters, Mr. Toad and the Toadettes. None of this is as important as you think it is, only different. Griffith himself appears in his strips as a thin man with a hairdo that stands up like a Plains Indian's crown of feathers; he spies on people with a monstrous telescope sticking out of the "Griffith Observatory."

A further step into the land of the disturbing is Paul Fericano's *Stoogism Anthology* (Scarecrow Books, 1050 Magnolia, #2, Millbrae, CA 94030), which contains an introduction by the author, a filmography of the Three Stooges by Leonard Maltin (an amazing 190 items!) and stills from the Stooges' films. There is poetry by Blythe Ayne, John Bennett, Jane Conant-Bissell, and other small press poetry heavies, by no means confined to the West Coast.

In the last issue but one (that's v. 8, no. 1, now out of print) we reviewed Alex Jack's *New Age Dictionary* (Kanthaka Press, Brookline Village, Mass.), and found a fault or two therein. Now Mr. Jack, an editor of the *East-West Journal*, reappears as a poet. Jack, who covered the Vietnam Conflict for a group of newspapers, now puts the conflict into poetic perspective: *Dragon Brood* (Kanthaka Press, P.O. Box 696, Brookline Village, MA 02147, $3.50) opens:

> In the Western Heaven in some future aeon
> Where iron cars succumbed to thick dry heat
> and surest paths were flown by bees and birds,
> where firmness brought great statesmen sound defeat,
> and yielding way to strength, the weak conquered."

Mr. Jack's poetic ear is, in short, not much better than his dictionary-making ability; the language of all characters seems to be jammed into Shakespearian meters:

> Damnation, Lan, for helping Xuan escape.
> —His abdication we may still prevent.

We managed to get through the heroic language of the *Silmarillion*, as it contained the clue to the other works of Tolkien, but this hangs on nothing but the protest, as old as *Twelfth Night*, "But I've rehearsed it! *and 'tis poetical!*" We cannot recommend this text; 'twere better left unspoken, nay, unwrit, And so to bed.

E.F. SCHUMACHER: We gave an extraordinary amount of space to the conference under the leadership of Dr. E.F. Schumacher, "Small is beautiful," at U.C. Davis, February 1977, in our last issue. This coverage may have been of historic importance, because on 8 September 1977, Dr. Schumacher died. He had been asked to leave his friends' home in Geneva to talk to a group in Zürich; he boarded a Swiss train, but as soon as the train entered the canton of Fribourg, he became ill, and being taken off at Romont, died on the way to the hospital, of unknown causes. He was 66. Dr. Schumacher, trained in Germany, and interned as an enemy alien in Britain when the war broke out, was an economist of the University of London. A quiet, gentle man, he came to stand for more than he might have expected, and his idea, although it will be twisted, denied, or defended, stands as part of our world. Meanwhile, a small, but surely beautiful, publication pays him homage.

9 : 2

The illustrations for v. 9, no. 2, were done by Jane Barrett, who lives in Southern California. Judyl Mudfoot and Sasha Newborn are divorced; she now does business as "J. Mudfoot, Printer." Futz the cat died in a heat wave.

In the wake of Proposition 13, we did indeed lose Californian subscribers; also in Massachusetts and Michigan, which enacted similar statures by initiative and or referendum. Shasta County (California) closed all its libraries this year, failing a tax referendum. Part of the problem is that small rural counties with no big tax base are mandated by law to support programs they have no money for.

The answer to my question, "Who, if anyone, gave permission to Vision Films to use the ALA seal and statement of sponsorship on the film?" (The Speaker) turns out to be simple: ALA Council did it. Apparently some protestors resigned after a fiery debate.

I quote here some of the text that reached those of us who opposed the film. The issue eventually dropped out of public discussion, but was not forgotten. Ten years later the Black Caucus of ALA and the Social Responsibilities Round Table declined to endorse for ALA president a black woman librarian who had supported the film.

WE MEET AGAIN in the shade of California's Proposition 13, the so-called Jarvis-Gann Amendment to the constitution of that state, which we anticipate will have heavy effects right here in this farmhouse-office: obviously a large number of our library subscribers—about ¼—are from California, and faced with drastically reduced revenues, some of them may reduce their expenditures by cutting us off. We devoutly hope that this will not happen; we also hope that other states will come in to help us. If not, we may be forced to raise our prices or to cease publication entirely (perish the thought)! Although the work in putting this rag out is considerable, we'd rather do this than just about anything. So keep us up! Love (and $4) is all you need!

POET AS PRINTER AS POET: This interview begins in an old house in Santa Barbara, far from the great estates of Montecito or Hope Ranch,

off the fashionable shops of State Street, down in a quiet part of town where there are still old houses, gardens; with a tall self-determined woman in her thirties named Judyl Mudfoot, who has a partner named Sasha Newborn; and they, in turn, have a Kluge printing press and a tomcat named Futz. The partnership does business as Mudborn Press, publishes two magazines (*Rockbottom*, and *The Village Idiot*), produces other poetry and prose titles, and Judyl herself is the secretary and treasurer of Western Independent Publishers. Judyl's hands show that she has learned a trade, and learned it well.

SIPAPU: We'll start with the usual: birth, parentage, education?

MUDFOOT: I was born in Boston in 1943 of English stock, to parents born in California and Kentucky. When I was young we moved back and forth across the country, — lived a couple of years in northern Italy. I went to public schools, got a B.A. from Stanford, an M.A. from U.C. Santa Barbara, — both in English literature. At UCSB I was a teaching assistant. I've been in Santa Barbara about 4½ years since I moved back.

SIPAPU: We'll, you're certainly not in English literature now. Sounds as if you might have had a break — a revolution, so to speak.

MUDFOOT: I'm not in a university, but I'm more in literature than I ever was before — contemporary American. There was a break, summer of 1968; I got a divorce, left school, moved to New York City on a bus. There I got a job in editorial production at Holt, Rinehart and Winston — college textbooks; they're interesting to produce because they're usually complicated (drawings, tables, photos, headings, etc.). But what I was "really" doing was pottery. I feel very lucky I don't have to make that distinction any more, between what I do 40 hours a week and what I "really" do. Anyway, I made lots of pots, useful teapots. I got competent, but not really good at it, which showed, when I tried sculptural pieces, — they came out of me, so I loved them; but I knew they didn't work. I tried to continue making pots in the trip out here, digging what felt like clay and firing them in campsite grills, bricked up sort-of like kilns (I carried the bricks with me). None of the pots turned out well, but that wasn't the point — I had something to do, to hold onto, some continuity. I was pretty miserable and unsettled — even though I was with Sasha, whom I love, living outdoors, eating well, with no responsibilities.

SIPAPU: Perhaps you wanted to move on to something more verbal.

MUDFOOT: I was moving on, but then I didn't know where, let alone to what. I'd done some writing, even sent poems out to magazines (all rightly rejected), but poetry and then printing came later. It started when I was in the right place at the right time: at the Bluebird Cafe here in Santa Barbara when Robert Jackson was organizing the first reading there. I was writing in a notebook; he said "Are you a poet?" I said yes, and read at that reading, under my real name, the one I use now—it'd been sort-of a secret name until then.

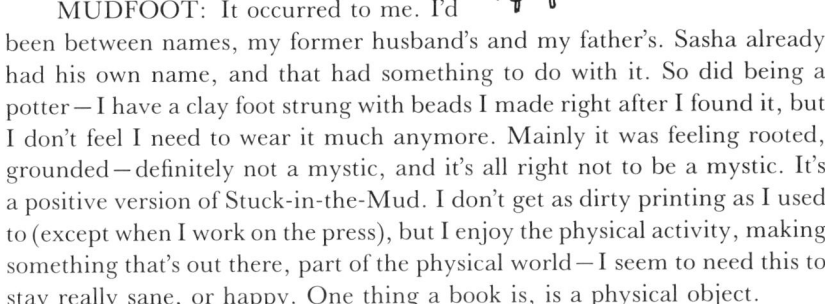

SIPAPU: About the name: where did that come from?

MUDFOOT: It occurred to me. I'd been between names, my former husband's and my father's. Sasha already had his own name, and that had something to do with it. So did being a potter—I have a clay foot strung with beads I made right after I found it, but I don't feel I need to wear it much anymore. Mainly it was feeling rooted, grounded—definitely not a mystic, and it's all right not to be a mystic. It's a positive version of Stuck-in-the-Mud. I don't get as dirty printing as I used to (except when I work on the press), but I enjoy the physical activity, making something that's out there, part of the physical world—I seem to need this to stay really sane, or happy. One thing a book is, is a physical object.

SIPAPU: But it has a verbal side.

MUDFOOT: Yes, so I don't have to give up anything, including all that verbal training.

SIPAPU: OK, so you got started in printing. Who taught you? How long have you been doing it?

MUDFOOT: I've been doing letterpress a little over two years. If I'd started much younger, school might have worked, or an apprenticeship, but printing didn't occur to me then. Recently, I do much better on my own—with help, of course! Graham Mackintosh has been wonderful; also Alice Karle and Peter Katoff (of Doggeral Press)—I bought my first press, the Kelsey, from Alice, and now share shop space with Doggeral. I did two books on the Kelsey—not something I'd recommend, unless that's what you want to do and that's what you have, as it was for me. Often I feel I'm starting all over again now I've got a full-scale automatic press. I'm doing books now (some for some other small press publishers), and we publish prose books ("fiction"—though we don't especially like that word), but these we have printed by other people. You can't do everything yourself—or at least we can't! And there are the magazines, *Rockbottom* and *The Village Idiot*. I read some MSS. for the *Idiot,* do proofreading, but that one's really Sasha's.

—Sasha Newborn, a short, stout fellow with a cheerful beard fringe, enters—he brings the first existing six issues of *The Village Idiot*, a short (8 pp.) magazine of original, unpublishable, wholly publishable material; everything in it seems fresh, defiant, readable: the quintessence of the small press movement.

SIPAPU: But are you still continuing these magazines?

MUDFOOT: Yes, *Rockbottom* no. 6 is coming up, and *Village Idiot* no. 7.

SIPAPU: We're interested always in where our contributors get their money: how do they survive, is it possible to make one's living in the small press field?

MUDFOOT: We're staking what we've got betting that it is. We started on very little—a few hundred; it's amazing how little it takes; we were both working part-time then,—Sasha did typesetting, I did technical editing, mostly data processing texts. Now we have some capital, which I inherited from my parents, and we're putting it into equipment and supplies. I can always go back to editing—though I'm getting spoiled, working only for Mudborn—and I've done bookkeeping too.

SIPAPU: But it's getting harder now, what with inflation: we've found that rising postal costs forced us to raise our prices. How do you propose to survive in the face of inflation?

MUDFOOT: One answer: we're getting equipment now, before the price goes higher. We don't want to price the books high, so we've got to do longer print runs (700, a thousand,—500 just won't work) to ever make a living. And postal increases hurt. If your costs go up, you've got to raise prices to support yourself and keep going. Don't underestimate the value of your own labor; too many small publishers and printers do. Making it as a small—*really* small—business is difficult enough.

SIPAPU: Oh, you do job printing?

MUDFOOT: Yes, I'm doing a book now for Cold Mountain, in Texas,—which I'd recommend, not because of the printing, but because the poems are fine; it's by Stephen Leggett. I'd like to spend maybe a quarter of my time printing for other literary publishers—it'd cover my overhead. But I can't take on anything for a while; I've got four, five Mudborn manuscripts that've been waiting for me to get the press going. We expanded Mudborn, bringing in Kerry Tomlinson as art consultant. Sasha and I remain as partners, but we're not good at everything. Kerry's finding art for *Rockbottom*, designing covers for it and for the *Nearbooks*. She did this one, for some poems by Stephen Kessler.

SIPAPU: We're confused. You have *Rockbottom*, *The Village Idiot*, and now *Nearbooks*....

MUDFOOT: Look at *Rockbottom* no. 5. This issue has two nearbooks bound in, the Kessler poems and a prose piece by Millie Mae Wicklund. We do an overrun on those pages (the divider/cover is heavier paper), and staple them as separate booklets.

SIPAPU: Very convenient. But what's this ... something called *Readings*, and then a *December Book* ... more books out of magazines out of books?
MUDFOOT: *Readings* goes back to the beginning, before we were Mudborn, or considered ourselves publishers. Those are pamphlets we put together for the Bluebird Cafe readings, one poem each of the

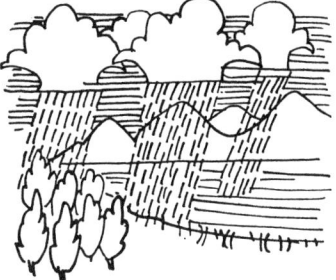

poets who read each month. *December Book* is an anniversary volume, with the regulars from the readings after the first year (it's the first Mudborn production; I've got a couple of poems in it).
SIPAPU: OK, now here's the central question: how does being your own publisher and printer affect your work as a poet?
MUDFOOT: Being my own printer makes me sweat — I did it for my first book, *Presents*, because I'd started printing I knew exactly what I wanted, and I could do it. I'm trying to do that for other poets, particularly for first books — working with the author on design, paper, colors, etc., to make it really their book, because the first book is terribly important, how it feels, how it turns out. It's certainly less complicated emotionally when it's somebody else's work — and I've been more a printer/publisher than a poet these days. Printing/publishing is the next step after writing; it's a continuation of the same process, the process of communication. Because until a work's published — or read publicly — the communication hasn't been made. If it's published, then there's still the problem of distribution, and I'm optimistic about WIP's (Western Independent Publishers') warehouse and other distribution projects — as a group, we can reach a wider audience than any of us could as independent publishers. For me, there's also the incredible joy of printing — watching a blank sheet go in and a printed page come out was magic the first time I did it, and it's still magic — after all the work, the magic, and that's the joy. When I was younger, I never considered a trade; I was going to be a theoretical physicist; then I wanted to be a humanist scholar, like the ones in the Middle Ages. I found the joy in doing something with my hands in pottery, but that wasn't right for me, required something I'm not and didn't use all I am. Printing feels right — I work impossible hours and get nowhere and not get discouraged. And I feel strong: my other partner is a 2300-pound machine, and we work together.
SIPAPU: But of course, not all writers/editors/publishers can also be printers; the huge mass of small press material available since about 1960 has appeared because of the development of offset printing, which made inexpensive poetry magazines possible.
MUDFOOT: Nobody should be a printer who doesn't want to be one. We can print more because I love printing; we're not paying for somebody

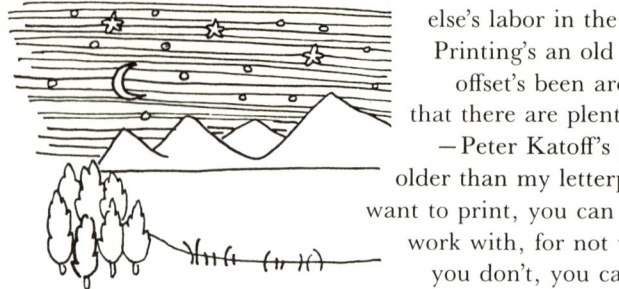

else's labor in the letterpress books. Printing's an old technology—even offset's been around long enough that there are plenty of old machines—Peter Katoff's got an offset press older than my letterpress. So if you *do* want to print, you can find something to work with, for not very much; and if you don't, you can afford having it printed—I had 200 copies of a poem printed for the price of a medium-cheap meal out. Books cost more, so most small publishers have to work at something else, but if you're determined, it's possible.

I've got nothing against offset—we use it where we think it's appropriate. But not many use offset with the flexibility the process makes possible—artwork without buying engravings, photos, not having to position the text straight on the page. The possibilities don't get exploited enough. I still consider myself apprentice-without-master as a printer, but I wouldn't attempt text angled across a page now, let alone scattered type—Alastair Johnston (Poltroon) has done some beautiful things with this sort of letterpress. But I can't imagine David Arnold's *Chain of Letters* (Trike) letterpress—even offset he needed a printer with good equipment to lay down that much black ink.

The house in which we have been talking is small, scarcely more than a bed-sitting room, kitchen, two small studies (one serving as a warehouse for what used to be Literary Publishers of Southern California, and is now the southern California area of Western Independent Publishers). (Judyl Mudfoot is the secretary-treasurer of this outfit.) The first thing you notice about the house is that it is decorated with broadsides: poetry on every wall, designed by Mudborn Press or their friends; in the back a typewriter is going full blast, which there as here is like the sound of a living heartbeat. The place is full of paperbacks and posters, but it is the broadsides that attract the most attention.

SIPAPU: Here's one of yours....

MUDFOOT: Yes, that's from when a group of poets ran for the County Democratic Central Committee here. I printed up broadsides as part of the campaign. No, none of us got in. That was in the 1976 primary.

SIPAPU: And then there are some postcards....

MUDFOOT: Yes, they're fun and easy to do. I printed one for each reader for a series that a group we're part of sponsored (the Contemporary Literature Center of Santa Barbara). They're also great to hand out, at bookfairs (I printed them on-the-spot at Garden Theatre last year), particularly since I don't seem to get around to doing business cards.

The Kluge press is out in a mechanic's stall next door—it's a huge heavy thing, over a ton of machinery on a great cement floor (it would break through any house floor). Several pages of a new book are in its chase now; it has a huge flywheel just waiting to revolve cosmically.

SIPAPU: Well, now we see that you've got plenty of work ahead of you; and yes, it all does fit together. We've got only one question: that phrase in Old English on every issue of *Rockbottom, Mæg ic be mē sylfum sōagied wrecan:* what's it mean, what's the source? Maybe that's your secret.

MUDFOOT:
May I by my self truesong make
(opening line, *The Seafarer*).

OUR LAST TWO ISSUES have devoted considerable time and attention to *The Speaker,* the controversial film on the right of a racist speaker to address a racially mixed school, which bears the imprint of ALA. The debate continues in *Library Journal, American Libraries,* and elsewhere. Some papers that have not apparently been published, have emerged from an "Ad Hoc *Speaker* Committee," chaired by Sanford Berman of Hennepin County Library, Minneapolis, MN, and from Vision Associates, New York, the makers of the film.

The ad hoc committee (of 65 librarians, including us) signed a statement that runs as follows (Berman's celebrated short paragraphs are here condensed to save space):

WE ARE ASHAMED. AND DISGUSTED. The American Library Association has produced a film, *The Speaker,* that purports to deal with intellectual freedom and the First Amendment. It does not. Instead, it distorts and confounds the First Amendment. But even worse than this intellectual dishonesty is the film's wanton assault upon black people. In effect it says: "Blacks are irrational. Blacks are unprincipled. Blacks must be 'protected' by whites. And blacks may indeed be less than fully human." As librarians and citizens, we reject this film. It does *not* speak for the whole profession. We are ashamed that it was ever made. And disgusted that A.L.A. continues to support it [20 April 1978].

Vision Associates (665 5th Avenue, New York, NY 10022) used the list of signatories to send two replies. One, dated 22 May 1978, runs in part:

Shame and disgust are not the sole prerogatives of your group. I, too, have felt the same emotions, but obviously for different reasons.... Our mail is running 50 to 1 in favor of the film from audiences who are using it.... The nation's leading authorities, including Prof. Thomas Emerson whose book *The System of Freedom of Expression* is considered one of the most important works on the subject of the First Amendment ever written, has praised the film unreservedly for being a superb exposition of the First Amendment. Representative Barbara Jordan, a legislator and lawyer of some distinction, and a leader of the black community, praised the film unreservedly and stated that she saw nothing racist or offensive with it ... the continued efforts of the Ad Hoc Committee to enforce the will of a small, but vocal group on the rest of the country seems to give a lie to your professed dedication to our free institutions....

A second communiqué, dated 1 June (both were signed by Lee R. Bobker), quotes Professor Emerson, "the outstanding authority in the world on questions regarding the First Amendment" (but surely it's an Amendment to the Constitution of the United States, not the world) as saying,

> It was superbly done. It presented, in the context of a concrete situation, many of the problems which revolve around the theory and application of the First Amendment in a democratic society. In doing so, it successfully achieved one of the fundamental objectives of the First Amendment, which is to make us think about difficult issues and make up our own minds about them. The purpose and significance of the First Amendment have to be learned anew by each generation, and this film makes a notable contribution toward that end.

If this paper may dare to disagree with a planetary authority, — surely the only fundamental objective of the First Amendment is to prevent Congress from making any law "abridging the freedom of speech, or of the press"; as for "thinking about difficult issues, and making up our own minds about them," that is neither enjoined nor prohibited in our copy of the Constitution, any more than voting is; we can refuse to vote, nay, even to think, and watch television instead. However, be that as it may, a flock of other documents have descended on this office, and more shall doubtless appear. A Committee to Defend Intellectual Honesty, apparently based at the Library School of the University of Maryland at College Park, issued a statement saying, "The poor taste, skillfully racist format, and clouded interpretation of the First Amendment in *The Speaker* destroy the integrity of the Association and should be soundly denounced." An SRRT Task Force on Consciousness-raising, headed by Donnarae McCann, said,

> What throws some viewers off the track is that the film makes a virtuous point: "Let's try to make courageous decisions." But to devise a dramatic situation in which courage was needed, the script writers had to come up with a threat, and this threat was presented in the film as black Americans.... Everyone who is supposedly siding with the black majority and trying to have the speaker's invitation revoked speaks either out of fear of blacks ... or in terms of unprincipled compromise.... The black community is portrayed as not knowing the difference between what is constitutional and unconstitutional, between right and wrong.... The ALA Black Caucus has stated that it does not oppose the discussion of any subject, including the belief that blacks are inherently inferior to whites. But the OIF has not permitted blacks in this film to explain that the genetic inferiority theory is not only racist—it is also a belief which cannot be lumped together with ideas we arrange in an intellectual spectrum; it is unique in that it denies the basic humanhood of a group of people.... OIF's failure to consult blacks on the script or on the production of the film implies that blacks are considered inferior and unable to understand the First Amendment. This

attitude was again expressed when the debate of *The Speaker* was rigidly curtailed by the ALA Council at the midwinter meeting, when the arguments of the Black Caucus (outlined in its statement) were scheduled only after being rendered powerless—after all votes on the film's future were completed. What a travesty on the true principles of intellectual freedom!

This appeal, like others, requests the withdrawal of ALA's sponsorship and distribution of the film. At this point, it seems useless to request the withdrawal of distribution; over 100 libraries have ordered copies, and the ALA seal appears irrevocably on all of them. Those of us who don't like the film are beginning to feel like sand-castles undermined by a rising tide; and yet, even as our bases melt, there are some questions that refuse to wash away. One is, who, if anyone, gave permission to Vision Films to use the ALA seal and statement of sponsorship on the film? We have seen no letter of approval, nor any defense by any high ALA official. A distinguished colleague has correctly pointed out that a statement or letter, post-dated, could be concocted at this point; and we believe it. Nevertheless, any such letter would have to be signed. The signer could then be quizzed, and with what consequences! More disturbing yet, there recently came into our hands a book, *Human Variation: The Biopsychology of Age, Race, and Sex,* edited by R. Travis Osborne, Clyde E. Noble, and Nathaniel Weyl (New York, Academic Press, 1978), which is surely the most formidable racist volume to appear for some time. This book frankly divides the human species into several subspecies ("Negroid" and "Caucasoid" among them), and goes to great lengths to prove the relative superiority of Europeans and to a lesser extent of the peoples of East Asia, in matters of intelligence. It urges, after a dazzling display of charts and graphs, and a witty set of "definitions," that the European peoples, acknowledging their sometime oppression of others, undertake the responsibility of taking care of the unfortunate others. Skimming is, of course, inadequate as a treatment of this book and we challenge any learned reader (that's ALL of you, surely), to obtain a copy and systematically demolish it. After that, the reader can then address the problem of why so many black and other Third World people still regard academics with apprehension. A touch of sun, perhaps? Or is paranoia "only a heightened form of awareness?"

We weren't able to follow all the aftereffects of the debate at the 1978 ALA conference in Chicago, but apparently substantial progress has been made in getting the charge of the Intellectual Freedom Committee changed to reflect social responsibility; the debate at the time seemed to us singularly sterile, and we hastened off to the meeting of the SRRT Task Force on Peace (a feisty group, the SRRT has long needed one) headed by Elizabeth Morrisett. Two speakers from Jonah House, a peace community in Baltimore, Esther Cassidy and Joan Burds, talked about their work in simple living and protests against nuclear facilities. Their periodical, *Year One*, is obtainable from Jonah House, 1933 Park Avenue, Baltimore, MD 21217 (no price given, but you know what to do about that). It includes statements by Phil Berrigan, Liz Roiley, etc.

We have to apologize for the skimpy coverage of both the ALA and COSMEP conferences, but both of these have been covered in such detail in previous issues of this and other publications that the umpteenth description of another conference on management (for those who can't manage) or distribution (for those who can't distribute) is beginning to seem to us, at all events, like the umpteenth omelet in the hotel coffee shop. We were glad to take the opportunity, however long delayed by storms, to board a KLM flight to Amsterdam, where we discovered that the ancient Dutch tradition of independent publishing is in full sway; there exists, far more vigorously than in Britain, and in a far smaller compass, a small press organization, Stichting "Drukwerk in de Marge" (= Printing in the Margin Foundation), with several dozen members printing mostly in Dutch, some in Dutch and English, with lots of poetry books in the bookstores (we saw them ourselves). The officers of this org are changing, so that we cannot give you the right address to write to, but a leading member, Ric Blok, Futile Press, P.O. Box 812, Rotterdam 3000, Netherlands, is not only a good point of contact but is also interested in American writers; we saw a translation of Whitman made and published by him, and although Whitman in any other language but English seems incredible — rather like seeing your best friend with a paper bag over his head — Blok's oral command of English is enough for us to give him the very best recommendation to those of our creative readers who would like to publish in Dutch and English (parallel text and translation, or maybe just translation). Like any editor/publisher, Blok of course may choose among his manuscripts; however, he does have contacts among other publishers in what appears to have replaced Paris and London as the avant-garde and expatriates' city for the Seventies. Incidentally, an attempt by a feminist-lesbian party, popularly known as "Sophie," to establish itself in the States-General failed recently owing to a lack of sufficient signers to a petition; however, the attempt was conspicuous, if not successful, and we are aware of no similar attempt in other countries. (The name "Sophie" appeared on the steps of the Post Office; supporters wrote "Sophie er warm," derisive antagonists wrote

"Sophie er dood.") We should not be surprised to see her revive in the near future.

T-SHIRTS! T-SHIRTS! CRAZY ABOUT T-SHIRTS! You are? Well, the people in the white coats will be here in just a minute, but before they arrive, we want you to array yourselves in T-shirts of the best: for example, if you live in California, you can get a T-shirt protesting cuts in California library service. Elizabeth Talbot, 4008 Loma Vista Avenue, Oakland, CA 94619, explains, "Unlike police, firefighters, and medical staff, we have no professional uniform and thus are invisible and unidentifiable in a crowd." She was alluding to the hasty decision taken to close all Alameda County libraries and lay off all but a handful of core personnel; as one Supervisor said, "Let's take the library next . . . the library will go a little quicker." The material of the T-shirts is 100% cotton, pre-shrunk, and the colors are light blue and light yellow. The graphic shows a monster emerging from a garbage can, and the text says, "CALIFORNIA LIBRARIES JARVIS-CANNED." Sizes available for SM, MED, LG, and XLG. Cost is $7.00. We've just heard that funding has been restored to San Francisco City-&-County Libraries, but not to Alameda County.

The turtle people (Island Resources Foundation—see *Sipapu,* v. 6, no. 2, and v. 9, no. 1) are also doing T-shirts for $5; contact Kathy Finnerty, P.O. Box 4187, St. Thomas, VI 00801. Our own pewter turtle pin has occasioned much comment and we are sure that the T-shirt will look well when worn with a terra-pin.

Incidentally, those of you who tried meditation—Transcendental Meditation, founded by Maharishi Mahesh Yogi, the one where you get a mantra to repeat to yourself, at some cost—if you've forgotten to repeat it lately or haven't kept up with the SIMS people, not enrolled in their classes and vaguely wondered where your money went—you may be astounded when you hear what's been happening while you've been away. There came into our hands a most astonishing combination of periodical and brochure, *World Government News,* April 1978, issue no. 4, lavish in color and lots of gold, and there on the cover sat His Holiness the Maharishi on a dais surrounded by flowers and flags, like a smiling bearded Undead Person, a great-great-grandfather who popped out of a coffin with a vision of the Great Beyond. Clapping international figures flank him on either side. It turns out that the Maharishi has acquired a large hotel in Seelisberg, Switzerland (canton of Uri) and has inaugurated the World Government of the Age of Enlightenment. The several ministries of this government (as of Natural Law and Order, of All Possibilities, of Health and Immortality) all seem to be chaired by very young people; the Minister of Celebrations and Fulfillment and his wife look to be about in their twenties; the Minister of All Possibilities is surely in his teens. We're rather doubtful about the role of a Dutch lieutenant-colonel named Cramwinckel, who is Chairman of the

218   A Passage for Dissent

Supreme Military Council; the text talks about "making the nation invincible," and there are pages on the role of retired people, agriculture, etc. in making the nation invincible. The "physics of invincibility" are demonstrated on the back cover showing a young person levitating in the lotus position. There are many courses and videotaped lectures; if they are not all pretty much the same (as we suspect) there must have been a lot of videotaping going on in preparation for the big meet 12–14 July 1978. In a sense this periodical is really a call to interested persons (presumably middle cadres) to attend. We detect a certain resemblance to Moral Re-Armament: the Swiss hotel headquarters, the central charismatic figure, the top people whom one has somehow never quite heard of before, the indoctrination of a lot of young people. How did it all happen? How did an apparently simple thing get that way? Was there always too much money involved?

At the extreme opposite view of human consciousness, we have a game. It's called *Class Struggle* and a company has been formed to sell it: Class Struggle, Inc., 487 Broadway, New York, NY 10013. It's a board game with a general pattern of Monopoly, and some elements of Parcheesi or Snakes and Ladders; the rules are largely based on simplified Marxist (not liberal) insights, and the square spiral ends up at No. 84 (1984), REVOLUTION. Two major classes — into one of which you are born, via the toss of a marked die — Workers and Capitalists, take steps along this spiral with the aid of numbered dice; along the way there are chance cards, as in Monopoly. Four other players may be represented by small businessmen, farmers, professionals and students — none of which can win on their own, but they can volunteer to join alliances with one of the Major Classes, on their way to Revolution or Nuclear War. Nuclear War, by the way, is square No. 81; if the Capitalists land here it brings an automatic end to the game. Landing on certain squares enables you to organize trade unions and a workers' political party, while others give either capitalists or workers, debits or assets, sometimes both, depending on what is happening to them. The first of our friends who took this on, played the Workers, and even though she had all the Minor classes with her, she failed to organize trade unions or a workers' party, and so lost: very instructive. The Capitalists are deliberately given some unfair advantages, notably in having the right to cast the first die and to determine the direction around the table, in which the players get their turns; this is also part of the instructional nature of this game.

No one will be surprised that this is the work of a teacher, Bertell Ollman (Oxford), who is an Associate Professor in the Department of Politics at NYU, chairman of their Center for Marxist Studies, co-editor of *Studies in Socialist Pedagogy*. No one will be surprised that it took him seven years to devise this delight, and no one will be surprised that there has been some little difficulty about his position as chairman of the Department of Politics at NYU. He himself admits that the Capitalists frequently win, but insists that it works out at about 50-50.

Our own impression of *Class Struggle* is that it is undoubtedly a lot of fun, but that even the advanced and tournament rules thoughtfully provided by the author fail to allow for some possibilities along the way. For example, right now there is a three-cornered struggle going on between "revisionists" (CP), Maoists and Trotskyites for the development of a workers' party. Which one the author favors is not clear; inter-party struggle on the Left is not brought out clearly. Again, the role of the Minor Classes is not perhaps sufficiently elucidated. For example, no one supposes that they could win a revolution by themselves, but is it entirely obvious that should they ally themselves with the Workers and together win the Revolution, that they would still have non-worker interests which would require attention? The Farmers, for example; is it clear to them, as a CHANCE CARD insists, that Revolution in the U.S. would not resemble the Revolutions in Russia or China? Again, there are a large number of people whose consciousness simply isn't headed in this direction. For example, the game teaches that religion and spectator sports are opiates of the people, without also pointing out that they engage the attention of millions of people who really are more interested in these things than in games like *Class Struggle*. That some churches, at least, have a sense of social responsibility, and that sports may bring the competence of minorities into public view on the TV screen, is not mentioned.

A great big hole, indeed, in the game is the role of group consciousness other than class: ethnic, sexual, etc. Once again, the question, "Class or Race ... or what?" is dodged or at least set aside for the moment. In addition, we have all the people who are living off the land or are on an environment ecology trip; pollution gets in here, but not as an area of human consciousness. And there are the artists and intellectuals, and the cult followers—some of these are mentioned in chance cards but they don't really impinge on the outcome of the game except momentarily.

We submit that the real reason this game is ultimately less than satisfactory as a teaching tool is that the United States is a great deal more complex than any other country. This idea is ignored, for example, in the square which says that "the works of Marx and Engels, in paperback (100 volumes) sweep the country." It strikes us as incredible that 100 volumes of political theory, history and economics, no matter how brilliant, would ever sweep this country. In short, once again, like so many brilliant forecasts, from Hal Lindsey to Ernest Callenbach, it's true if you come prepared to believe it. If not, it remains, well . . . a game.

And a footnote: a short step along the way is labelled "Pornography." For most of us pornography is no longer necessary: kicks are too easily available, few spend much of their time looking at *Playboy*. Love, on the other hand, is nowhere mentioned, and most of us have some kind of preoccupation with love, with spouses and families. If this is an obstacle to social justice, let's have it out straight. But if that's the case, how many lovers will buy Professor Ollman's box of tricks? They're a lot less fun than someone to love.

10 : 1

The cover shown here was done by Walt Stevens to my general order: I wanted a fancy baroque cover with a slightly erotic tinge. The artist put the editor peeking out from behind a nymph — I only found that later!

Elliott Shore is now working for the Institute of Advanced Studies in Princeton. His book, Talkin' Socialism, *has just been issued by the University Press of Kansas.*

SIPAPU

Vol. 10 No. 1 — JAN. 1979

A newsletter for librarians, collectors, and others interested in the alternative press, which includes small presses, "underground" papers, Third World and feminist work, and dissent literature in general. Price: $4.00 for two issues a year (new price effective 1/1/78). Free to exchange papers, library school students and prisoners; but library schools and prisons themselves pay the full amount. Canadian subscribers, please remit in US funds. Californian subscribers please add 5% tax (applicable on periodicals coming out less than 4 times a year). No stamps! Editor & Publisher: Noel Peattie, Route 1, Box 216, Winters, CA 95694; ⓒ Noel Peattie. Also: Peter J. Shields

CONSECUTIVE ISSUE NO. 19

BEGINNING OUR TENTH YEAR: Conceived at a California Library Association conference in December 1969, when a small group met in the Happy Valley Bar in the Sheraton-Palace, San Francisco, and born in January 1970, *Sipapu* has viewed the seventies without forgetting its conception in the sixties. The poor old sixties kept dying so often (the latest: Winterland in San Francisco closed on New Year's Eve) that it's hard to believe they're dead. But certain things *are* dead: the belief in gurus who want all your money, the belief in tripping as a way of life, or a way to Godhead, the belief that Mars and Venus are habitable, and even the belief that if we all support Richard Nixon we can win in Vietnam. Others, including some we no doubt hold today, will perish in their turn.

Meanwhile, it appears that the U.S. military have translated "sipapu" as "sacred fire" and applied it to the name of a defense missile. We protest against this, not because the name is ours—it belongs to the Hopi—but because they have mistranslated the name and applied it to a weapon. The day after it appeared on "60 Minutes" half a dozen people had to stop us to tell us about it. "And how'd you break *your* leg?" Thanks, but no thanks. Everyone ready for the eighties?

A GENTLE WORD FROM PHILADELPHIA: Elliott Shore, curator of the Contemporary Culture Collection at Temple University's Samuel Paley Library here, is a Philadelphian born and bred, who is now running an Office of Education grant called the "Alternative Acquisitions Project." Shore, a quiet, smiling, dark-haired man in his twenties, just got married over the holidays, to a lady named Kathryn:

SIPAPU: We'll start with the usual: birth and education?

SHORE: I was born on 24 February 1951 at Hahnemann Hospital in Philadelphia. I have lived in Philly all but one of my 27 years. (That year I spent in London.) There is really very much similarity between the two cities, so I felt very much at home. I went to the oldest public high school in the country—Central High School—which won the highest number of awards for merit scholarships the year that I graduated—and I didn't get one. I was pretty smart but I didn't get into the school I wanted: The University of Pennsylvania. That year marked the height of minority recruitment, so I went to Temple. I was an honors student in European History, and went on to the London School of Economics and Political Science for an M.A. in International History. It was harder to get in than to get out, so I spent a lot of time traveling and going to shows and movies. When I came back, I had to get a job. The Sixties were over. I started working at Temple University's Paley Library which has an alternative press collection.

SIPAPU: What was it like growing up in Philadelphia's Jewish community at the time? How is it different from Boston or New York? Did you really (as you once told us) collect bubble gum cards?

SHORE: All right, I'll stop there and tell you more about my childhood. Yes I do, — did, — collect baseball cards, although if any of your readers would like to buy them, I'm willing to consider reasonable offers. I also drive a 1954 De Soto for which I need the trim on the passenger side, and a radio. I was on a championship baseball team when I was taller. I bat right and throw right and live in a neighborhood which has fantastic bakeries and butcher shops. That's enough!

Anyway, Philadelphia has been in decline since the Erie Canal was built but it boasts the largest per capita consumption of ice cream in the country, and the largest park in any city in the world! For you library fans, Temple houses the manuscript copy of the Declaration of Independence in Jefferson's hand with Franklin's corrections, and the manuscript of *Ulysses*. It also has the Contemporary Culture Collection (CCC) to which I earlier alluded. I started to work there as an assistant to put together some newspapers in order for microfilming by Bell and Howell. The filming was never done for B&H, but the library decided to do it for our own archives. The curator of the CCC left in 1974 and I got the job.

SIPAPU: Temple University: its background? How is it appropriate for such a collection?

SHORE: Because it characterizes itself as a "People's University." It is a large, urban school located in an old and deteriorating section of the city. Its tuition is relatively low and its student population more or less reflects the diversity of Philadelphia from which many of the students come. Its position as a "state-related" institution, although precarious whenever the State Legislature gets truculent (or lazy), is relatively strong when compared to many private institutions. (Temple University, chartered 1888, was founded by Russell Conwell, a Baptist minister, but is now non-sectarian. It popped up in the news when it honored China's Prime Minister Teng with a degree during his visit in January 1979.)

SIPAPU: What's the origin of the CCC — how's it staffed, financed?

SHORE: The CCC was started in 1969 by some English Dept. faculty and a committed librarian. We were getting some free copies of papers that the librarian didn't want to throw out, and the English faculty wanted to see the purchase of some small literary press items. So the collection became a general one in terms of subjects, with the unifying factor being the nature of the publishers. So we have a library in miniature, representing virtually every subject from points of view of small, independent, or alternative presses. Most of our material is in the form of periodicals, about 1500 titles, of which about 300 are current subscriptions. We have a small but growing collection of fully cataloged pamphlets and a moderate-sized collection of small literary monographs.

SIPAPU: What's its function in the life of Temple? Is it used by teachers and students? What's its scope and destiny?

SHORE: The collection has moved three times in the almost ten years of its existence, which should reflect its growing importance. Now that it is located in a permanent place in the building, use has tripled. It is primarily used by undergraduates doing papers for courses in almost all of the disciplines. Few instructors use it, although those who do, use it frequently. The collection is primarily seen as a research archive, and we are attempting to collect manuscripts relating to all segments of the alternative press. Two of our largest collections are the papers of COSMEP (Committee of Small Magazine Editors and Publishers) and those of Youth Liberation. Although we have increased current use, our feeling is that we will ultimately be a research collection. We are currently rethinking our acquisitions policies in order to preserve the alternative press of this period. For example, we are speculating on cutting back on subscribing to newsprint periodicals and getting them in microform. The fact that we are a marginal part of the library — one full-time staff person (me) plus ½ of 1% of the library acquisitions budget, — severely limits our options. Many of the special collections that were set up in the boom period of the sixties are facing limitations imposed by falling budgets. It will be interesting to see what our fate will be.

SIPAPU: What are its, and your, connections with Collectors' Network, founded by Russell Benedict (see *Sipapu,* vo. 3, no. 2, July 1972)? What's happening with the Network and its newsletter? How do you see the future of the Network?

SHORE: We were one of the earliest members of the Network when Benedict started it in 1969. We even have a full run of his priceless newsletter, *Top Secret.* The Network has now grown to forty members, and we have tried to take over the redistribution of duplicates which Benedict did so well. Jim Danky, of the State Historical Society of Wisconsin, is editing *Collectors' Network News.* A new issue is planned soon. The future? I don't know; I would like to see alternative press materials integrated into general collections, but I certainly see a need for our special collections.

SIPAPU: Describe, *ad libitum* but not *ad nauseam,* the Alternative Acquisitions Project.

SHORE: The Alternative Acquisitions Project is an attempt to expand the number and kind of libraries that collect some alternative press materials. The project is one of the Office of Education, Office of Library and Learning Resources, Library Research and Demonstration Projects. The project is based at the Contemporary Culture Collection, and has an advisory Board of librarians and publishers: James Danky, State Historical Society of Wisconsin; Sandy Berman, Hennepin County (MN) Library; Noel Peattie, President, WIP; Patricia Glass Schuman, Neal-Schuman Publishers; Judy Hogan, Carolina Wren Press; Jawenza Kunjufu, Third World Press; and Luis Rivera, Shamal Books. Daniel Tsang, editor and publisher of *The Gay Insurgent,* is the research librarian for the project. An innovative part of the project is the use of COSMEP members and librarians, taking model, fully cataloged collections of alternative press books, pamphlets and periodicals directly to small college libraries. There are 485 colleges in our sample; thirty have responded to our questionnaires. They're four-year undergraduate institutions across the country. We plan to visit up to fifty of the institutions. Those that we are unable to get to, will receive a sample of twenty or so small press titles. So far, we have made arrangements to combine several visits into "small press days" at libraries in Wisconsin and in North Carolina. We are in the process of surveying the alternative press with a questionnaire which will complement the one sent to the librarians. From the two, we hope to come up with guides to help both groups work together. The guides and further visits will be completed if we receive a second year of funding.

SIPAPU: What present connections does Temple have with *Alternatives in Print?*

SHORE: *Alternatives in Print: International Catalog of Social Change Publications* is being compiled this year at the CCC with the help of a grant from the National Endowment for the Humanities. It will be the sixth edition and will be published by Neal-Schuman Publishers. It is compiled by a task force of the ALA's Social Responsibilities Round Table; Mimi Penchansky and Jackie Eubanks are co-editors, and Judy Koroljow is the compiler. It will be greatly expanded to include full author and title indexes. The number of presses included will almost double, to about 3000.

SIPAPU: How do you see trends in purchasing of small and alternative publications by libraries in the next five years? What can publishers expect embattled librarians on short budgets to ask for in the immediate future?

SHORE: From preliminary findings of our survey, and please bear in mind that it is smaller academic institutions that make it up, — we are discovering that very few are actively seeking the alternative press. However, it appears that there is great interest in finding out more about it. One thing that gives me hope about its possible future in libraries with diminishing budgets is the low price of most alternative press publications. If librarians ever get over the belief that price is a necessary indication of quality, we may see more of alternative literature in libraries.

If your library wants to be part of this scene (advises *Sipapu*), and if you have not received any material from the project, write Elliott Shore, Contemporary Culture Collection, Samuel Paley Library, Temple University, Philadelphia, PA 19122. The project is directed toward college libraries, but to be part of the Collectors' Network, or to learn more about alternative publications, is possible for any library.

INDEPENDENT NO MORE: Deck Hazen, of the Progressive Writers' Guild, has been a free-lance journalist with City on a Hill Press, in Santa Cruz, California, for three years. He is currently working on his first book, *The Next Student Rebellion.* Here he reports on the transformation of the *Santa Cruz Independent:*

"Everyone who has worked with a collective decision-making process knows that it can be a big headache at times. The *Santa Cruz Independent* seemed to have more than its share and many of its loyal readers were aware of those headaches, but few people were prepared for the announcement, in August 1978, that the *Indy* had been sold to Gilroy publisher Jerry Fuchs.

"Santa Cruz is a beach town which became the site of one of the University of California's postwar campuses in 1965. Thereafter it became the site of many campus and community political struggles, from the actions against UC investments in South Africa to a local initiative to limit rent hikes.

"The *Independent* was born in 1976, in this leftist milieu. It reorganized several people who had been recently dispersed, following the demise of its predecessor *Sundaz* (which folded for lack of money that same year). Pulling together $20,000 in borrowed funds, the *Independent* published its first issue in July 1976. It appeared every week since then, gaining a great deal of community support for its coverage of city and county political events, and offering an alternative to the Santa Cruz *Sentinel* — a conservative daily paper, long established in the business community, and reflecting a predominantly noncritical attitude towards land development and abuses of social justice — as the *Independent* was to see them.

"The initial structure of the *Independent* was designed for collective decision-making; however, the paper was legally owned by Richard Cole and Tim Egan. The tensions arising from these two forms of management — classical entrepreneurship and collective participation — caused a severe strain on the staff, and an abnormally high turnover rate. In 1977, Egan sold his share of the paper to Cole, but as Cole's influence over the paper increased, so did the problems; although Cole was a competent editor and writer, he had few skills at business management. The greatest problem was the outstanding debt, due September 1978. Cole had no provision to pay off the several thousand dollars owed.

"In April 1978, Jerry Fuchs, publisher of the Gilroy *Dispatch,* offered Cole $75,000 for the *Independent* and a way out of his dilemma. Cole was interested in the deal, but the staff, still locked into the tradition of collective decision-making, was divided. While a few supported the sale, many others, fearing a loss of collective control, and the changes the sale would cause in the style and content of the paper, opposed it. Several staffers left in the next week, while the deal fell through. Others tried to raise community money to purchase the paper, but this attempt, too, failed. It was not until July 1978 that the final transaction went through, between Cole and Fuchs's agent, Charles Ledden. There are conflicting reports on this deal; Fuchs contends that Cole knew of Ledden's connections before the deal went through, and suggests that Cole might have withheld the information to secure staff approval. But Bob Johnson, longtime *Indy* staffer and one of the two full-time paid editors, claims that no one, not even Cole, knew of Ledden's connections with Fuchs until after the papers were signed. Johnson stated that everyone thought Ledden was an independent purchaser; according to Johnson, Ledden was prepared to mortgage his mother's house to come up with the money.

"The change of ownership brought with it another round of staff defections. In October, Johnson; the editor, Kelly Garrett; the other full-time paid writer, Tim O'Neil, all left; bringing the total number of quitters to fifteen since the Fuchs takeover. In an interview with the Santa Cruz student newspaper *City on a Hill,* the three major staffers cited poor pay, low morale, and a lack of common purpose among *Indy* staffers, as their reasons for leaving. Privately, ex-staffers suggest other, more political reasons. The change of ownership—not just the change in personnel, but the change in format as well—raises important questions for the community journalists, and their readership everywhere. Can a newspaper be considered truly alternative if it is privately owned, run in the traditional 'top-down' editorial fashion, and funded by commercial interests—even if it reflects a liberal or progressive perspective?

"For example: although the new *Independent* shows only modest revisions in content, Jerry Fuchs asserts that the paper will still be an 'alternative'—at least, to the *Sentinel*. There have been a few changes in the paper's design—more advertising, particularly in the first few pages; a new slant on political endorsements, reflecting a fairly left-Democratic party orientation. Nor has the paper shifted to the right, nor has it become more like the Santa Cruz *Goodtimes* (a commercial entertainment weekly). However, ex-staffers and community people close to the old *Indy* are convinced that the new paper will slowly become less progressive and more commercial. While no one is predicting the paper's sudden death, Bob Johnson and others suggest that the paper will become more irrelevant to what they see as community concerns.

"The student paper, *City on a Hill,* has meanwhile expanded its coverage into higher circulation, and increased its sales downtown. A small-town feud has erupted between the two papers, and in the meanwhile, Johnson, Egan and other old *Indy* staffers are assembling a new paper, the *Phoenix,* with the aid of community people. According to Johnson, the *Phoenix* will begin with fortnightly production and move to weekly as soon as conditions permit; it is hoped that this will come about as soon as six months. The paper will be collectively run and will pay particular attention to bookkeeping. Whether or not Santa Cruz can support three weekly papers and a daily is less problematic (given advertising revenues) than the question of the role of three

competing weekly papers. The *Phoenix* will have added competition; the bureaucracy of the new *Independent* may lead it to increased conservatism; while *City on a Hill,* because of its volunteer staff, may be unable to compete in quality and in-depth reporting—driving it back to the UC Santa Cruz campus. Fuchs contends that the demise of the old *Independent* was as much a product of its collective anarchy as of its financial troubles. Thus the journalistic developments in this small California town in the coming months are as much a question of organization as they are of the battle for readers."—DECK HAZEN.

BOOKS: First of all we want to

recommend Malcolm Margolin's *The Ohlone Way,* illustrated by Michael Harney; it's about Indian life in the San Francisco and Monterey Bay areas, and is published by Heyday Books, Box 9145, Berkeley, CA 94709. Ohlone is a name given to a group of Native Americans whose combined territories ran roughly from Big Sur to the Carquinez Straits; of differing, but similar languages, they were never unified into one empire but kept their own chieftaincies and their own customs, although there was some intermarriage and a great deal of trade. The Ohlones were hunters and fishers, and their way of life has been reconstructed with the most careful patience by Margolis, who ended up loving a people whose last full-blooded member died in 1935. Plain in his narrative is that the civilization that the Ohlones had, vanished though it is, was nevertheless a beautiful one, and though the last sweat-house is down and their descendants are humble citizens of a State they never asked for, still the voices of the past are powerful in memory. Dull anthropological reports are here transmuted into purest gold. No area of Ohlone life is omitted from birth to death; the shaman and the chief; war and secret societies; womenfolk and wildlife; are all alike celebrated with a clear vision that spares no limitation and makes the best of a culture radically different from our own. The impact of the Franciscan missionaries is also recounted without anger but with a thorough understanding of why this mission could only end in the destruction of the people it sought to convert. (Even the missionaries perished; we had not known that the priest at Nuestra Senora de la Soledad literally died of starvation at his own altar.) Meanwhile, we are therefore glad to salute this book with its fine illustrations as our Book of the Year 1979.

EELS' REEL: Persons distracted by sensational revelations regarding Presidential assassinations and UFOs may not have noticed that the venerable small press publisher, Swallow, has published a book that at least starts to close the books on the Loch Ness problem: Roy P. Mackal's *The Monsters of Loch Ness* (1976). Mackal, an American biologist, came across the amateurs who have been lurking around Castle Urquhart with cameras for years, and came to the conclusion that their enthusiasm, though commendable, lacked a theoretical and research basis. Quickly attaching himself to their work, he investigated not only the reported sightings and extensive literature, but also took charge of deepwater photography and eventually brought round a part of the scientific community to his side. His conclusion: yes, there are creatures in Loch Ness; his best guess: large eels, living off salmon. Bolstering his view: eels are among the few creatures able to live in both salt and fresh water; eels don't just die, they disintegrate, body and bones alike. (*Sipapu*'s own expedition to the area in 1976, although it resulted in no sightings, prompted the reflection that since Scotland was covered with an icecap in the Pleistocene, anything in Loch Ness *now* was probably out in the sea before that, and therefore is still out there today.) He sets Halliday's

"Great Orm" aside, and considers the possibility of a surviving plesiosaur as a good runner-up. Photographs of a flipper look flipper-like, without being indicative of any one kind of species. There are extensive limnological studies, and the whole work has a definite severity and precision not matched in such researchers of late. Meanwhile, there remain Morag, and a curious painting of a lake creature on a textile from Central Asia, and all manner of sailors' tales, and the works of Bernard Heuvelmans (you thought this was an underground paper? it's underwater, too!) and there still is this Beast in Loch Ness, who has made a' the Sassenachs confess, that howe'er they might ogle for a keek at that Bogle, their search brought them mickle success.

10 : 2

This is consecutive issue number 20, and this interviewee, too, has changed jobs: Jack Shoemaker got out of the approval plan business in order to devote more time to North Point Press. North Point now has an impressive variety of titles and is one of the most distinguished imprints in the West.

THE BOOKDEALER AS SCHOLAR, PRINTER, POET: Jack Shoemaker is a quiet man with a dark beard, who owns Sand Dollar, a bookshop at 1222 Solano Avenue, Albany, 94706. Both of us have been so busy that this interview was conducted by mail.

SIPAPU: As usual: birth and education?

SHOEMAKER: I am a native of Alta, California, born in 1946. My father was a Marine, hospitalized and discharged after the war, 2000 miles from home (Statesville, North Carolina) with recurring attacks of malaria and battle fatigue. My mother worked in the same hospital as an aide. I rather think my father always intended to return to the south, but the upheaval of the war and the responsibility of a family kept him here in search of work. He became (eventually) a project engineer for satellite launch crews; and like so many families we moved around a lot, living in towns that were previously small towns until they were targeted for expansion by NASA: Lancaster, California; Huntsville, Alabama; Santa Maria, California. I was lucky enough to have settled in central California for a continuous high school experience.

To uproot children so continuously perhaps deprives them of a sense of continuity and permanence, but it can also give them a sense of adaptability and adventure. I have never felt especially deprived. But I have a strong desire to sink roots here, and have lived around Berkeley for over eleven years.

My family on both sides were Baptists, and I was raised as a Southern Baptist, essentially in newer western churches that were slightly more liberal than their southern counterparts. But it was a fundamentalist background.

I was a licensed minister at the age of fourteen, and fully expected to spend my life in some sort of pastoral context. Several of my uncles are ministers or deacons, and a good part of my family is faithful to the church unto this day. I regis-

tered in college (in Santa Barbara) as a Homiletics and Pastoral Theology major, but I had entered school drawn toward a major in Seventeenth-Century Literature, and switched rather quickly. I was rather typical, I think, in discovering in the mid-sixties Zen Buddhism, war resistance, Allan Ginsberg, and all the other foundations of the so-called counter-culture. These discoveries were well-timed with my "crisis of faith" and my conversion was complete. My own crisis was one of belief: in the vocabulary, background and with the fundamental requirement of the literal interpretation of the Bible. It was not with the essential morality nor with the mystery, and I feel quite comfortable considering myself a Zen Christian agnostic.

I was quite fortunate in having a number of very fine teachers, almost invariably members of the English department. One introduced me to Ezra Pound, another to Carl Jung, a third to Gary Snyder. My course was set. Encouraged by several of these teachers, I left the formal academic setting, and, convinced I could be more focussed and directed on my own, began my own independent reading, which continues.

I married in 1965. My wife, Victoria, and I have two sons. Our oldest is about to enter high school. I have nearly always done exactly what I wished. The support of my young family is a joy, and the structure a relief.

SIPAPU: Your life before the store—publications, friends and associates?

SHOEMAKER: My life is of a piece, and I have always been a bookman, whether as a reader or a writer, a bookseller, a publisher, an organizer of poetry readings, an advisor, archivist or bibliographer. I have been very lucky in my profession. I have nearly always been able to work only with books I liked. I have only once worked in a general trade bookshop. The rest of the time I have been able to work in contexts specialized within my interests. I have worked for and with some great booksellers. My own specialty has been modern American poetry, with a few related areas of interest. Poetry seems obvious. And yet I'm hard-pressed to explain why, exactly. I had been fascinated by the Transcendentalists, and native American philosophy. I had decided that I had to learn to be native, to be American, in the context perhaps of Charles Olson's work, and I was looking for continuity. There was no escaping the serious moral, spiritual and political questions of the mid-sixties. Had there been a viable group of young American philosophers working at that time I might have been drawn toward philosophy. But they were nearly all thinly disguised sociologists. Poetry could embrace nearly all those concerns, and did. (This is not an insight unique to me: Lyndon Johnson was afraid of poets and writers, so much so that the literature budget of the N.E.A. was not quite 2% of the N.E.A.s annual budget for the arts, and this was not a mistake.) If religion was the opiate of the masses, then sociology was the alcohol and politics the caffeine. Poetry involved curiosity and the spirit, dilemma and decision, history and respect. There were others involved in the same questions. (I have never liked the idea of poets as shamans—rather I appreciate their being fellow-travellers.)

And so in 1965 I married and left college. Through a set of remarkable circumstances I found myself in a coffee shop just off Highway 101 late one evening describing to a wealthy young man my idea of a "perfect" book shop. This was to be an "activist" book shop, but the primary activity was to gather together in one shop the "right" books, to have a series of poetry readings, and to believe that this would affect our community. I like to think it did. In 1968 we started the Unicorn Bookshop, in Isla Vista, just outside Santa Barbara. On reflection it was an odd place for this shop. Isla Vista is the living community that surrounds the University of California at Santa Barbara—14,000 people, mean age 19.3 years, not a family in sight except my own. It was a student ghetto. And it was Santa Barbara, where it is always 70° F. and clear. We opened a book shop for poets, and though I have travelled a good deal since then, I have never seen a shop with the stock we had in that tiny shop. Fifty percent cloth, specializing in poetry, the classics, good fiction, selected political books; we had on our shelves (and I still have a shelf list) the complete Bollingen series, the complete Loeb Library and Oxford catalogs, every book published by New Directions, etc. We had every small press and every little magazine we could locate. It was an incredible stock. We then organized a reading series, and over 50 poets read there in the next eighteen months. The shop was owned and backed by Ken Maytag, and for a young bookman it was like a dream. Alan Brilliant joined us and directed the Unicorn Press. For a brief time The Unicorn existed as a kind of ideal book shop in a most unlikely place. The Unicorn survived for quite a while, but I left in 1968, and retired to the mountains behind Santa Barbara. I had, by that time, gotten very close to a poet from San Francisco, David Meltzer, and we decided to begin a small press. (One might remember that in 1967 small presses were rather uncommon and quite precious. The arrival of a small press book in our shop was evidence of certain investment, was unusual, and cause for celebration; unlike today...)

SIPAPU: Your association with Peter Howard and Serendipity Books?

SHOEMAKER: In 1968 we moved to Oakland, settling near Lake Merritt. David Meltzer and I began publishing books and broadsides under the imprint of Maya. Clifford Burke took on our commission, and over the next two years we issued thirteen books and three broadsides, publishing quartos of poems by Jack Hirschman, Jon Brandi, Clayton Eshleman, David Meltzer, Gary Snyder, Asa Benveniste, Robert Duncan, Cid Corman, Harvey Bialy, Lew Welch, Philip Whalen, Bill Bathurst and Theodore Enslin. The Maya quartos stand as testimony to Clifford Burke's enormous talent and resourcefulness. David and I had decided at the beginning that we would do exactly three broadsides and thirteen quartos and then suspect the operation. However, we were forced to consider one more book, Mayakovsky's *Electric Iron,* translated by Jack Hirschman and Victor Ehrlich, and once we finished that book we separated, David continuing his interest through Tree Books and Journal. My wife and I then began to publish books under the Sand Dollar imprint, which continues.

Once settled here I took a position with Serendipity Books, working with Peter Howard. Serendipity Books is a shop specializing in Modern First Editions, modern literature and literary magazines. Peter Howard is a great bookman and a demanding teacher, and it was under his guidance that I began to learn the subtleties of bibliography. Whatever I've accomplished as a cataloger, bibliographer or archivist I owe to him. In working with him I matured as a bookman, and my various debts to him, both personal and professional, are enormous. Pete provided the exposure and means, and freedom with restraint, to develop. We began to distribute selected small press books to the trade with six small presses working in a cooperative manner. This became Serendipity Books Distribution, the first such attempt singled out by the National Endowment for the Arts as a pilot project for distribution, and eventually became SBD, managed for nearly ten years now by Jeanetta Jones Miller, who expanded its scope and abilities far beyond our initial expectations. We also began to supply small press books and magazines to libraries on an Approval Plan basis, with buying profiles tailored to the needs of each library. And we began to handle archives of poets, cataloging, appraising and offering for sale the papers of young American poets. Beside my normal activities within the shop, these were the three activities that absorbed me there. It was, altogether, an exciting, invigorating, stimulating place to work.

I remained with Serendipity for about six years. In July, 1974, I left it, with Peter Howard's blessing and help, to begin Sand Dollar Books with my wife, Victoria. Our shop, in many ways, is a continuation of what I've been doing in the book business from the beginning. For a variety of reasons (one being that I had grown tired of "the street," the continuous vulnerability of being always "on" and accessible, etc.), we began the shop as a mail order business in the basement of our home, seeing customers by appointment but primarily doing business by mail. For another set of reasons, two years later we rented a shop. (One of the reasons was simple: we had outgrown our basement and the shop threatened the rest of our family space. Another was the growing number of visitors and their intrusion on family life — it became rather difficult to separate our home life from our business, difficult especially for my wife who was literally torn between two full-time jobs: our small business and being a wife and mother to two growing sons.) Even though we had a shop front, something over 75% of our business remains mail order. We specialize in poetry and in books on the dance and ballet, our two shared interests. We have managed to accumulate what I believe to be the largest standing stock of poetry, nearly 10,000 titles, in the country, and that is our vision: to have at hand a complete stock, from Chaucer to d a levy, whether published by the small, commercial, or university presses. We've made some progress but there's still a long way to go. One day I would like to see it all, on a wall (or set of walls). We handle approval purchase plans for several university and college libraries, supplying poetry and some fiction; we catalog and appraise literary archives; we issue monthly "New titles lists" offering newly published books of poetry, literary magazines, and books in various fields of use and interest; and we issue occasional Modern First Edition catalogs of out-of-print materials. And we continue to publish books under the Sand Dollar imprint, having accomplished 28 titles since 1970.

Ours is a very particular *kind* of book shop, working within several restraints to articulate a specific, some might say, eccentric, — aesthetic. I like to think our kind of bookselling, and bookshops in general, serve an educational function. We handle only poetry, and books on the dance, and books in various other fields (ranging from philosophy, through ecology, to art, science, orientalia, theology, etc.) that we or certain of our customers like. We are by no means general, in any sense. We can then give the books we carry a kind of attention impossible in the general trade. We do not lose faith in a title simply because it is six months old, but stock and restock books particular to our interest. We've been known to list titles 25 years old simply because they seemed important to the moment of our reading. We are a bookshop for readers, and customers on our mailing lists begin after a while to see our limitations, and even appreciate us for them. Finally, we are a very small enterprise, surviving on about 500 faithful readers and 50 or so libraries, and this allows us to pay a kind of attention to our customers that may be rather uncommon in the marketplace. I enjoy knowing what people are reading, working out from correspondence the fabric of their study; it is rather common for us to know when ordering a new title for stock which of our customers will buy it. Knowing the books and the customer gives a sense of wholeness to our effort. There is a great deal of paperwork and drudgery in the book business, and ours is coupled with the paperwork, taxation, and anxiety suffered by any small retail

business in America. Somehow this is, for us now, offset by the pleasure of doing exactly what we wish, selling books we like, dealing with readers we know and enjoy. And somehow we have, without government grants, survived five years, — scrambling often, sure, but relatively intact. (I have always thought that poetry and small press publishing in general should survive in the marketplace, and would, if given the context. That's where we are, right in the middle of the marketplace, and it gives me real pleasure to have survived. Not all small press books will sell, nor should they, but if they do not, perhaps the publisher should re-examine his motives. I like the marketplace and the audience to be seen as a sorting mechanism, similar to the passage of time. But all this is a different question)...

SIPAPU: What should libraries expect of your Standing Order Approval Plan?

SHOEMAKER: The Standing Order Approval Plan is quite simple. In this time of budget cuts and limited staff I am surprised libraries are not using such a plan for new book acquisition in all fields. I know several collection development librarians and bibliographers carrying the impossible burden of a subject too wide, say, "Literature, English and American," responsible for both retrospective buying and new acquisition. In America this year there will be published over 40,000 titles. The need is for a variety of qualitative selection methods, and an Approval Plan can be one. It can save time both in selection, and in accounting. The librarian must have faith in the taste and constancy of his dealer, and the profile must be monitored regularly by both the librarian and the dealer. The library will have a single invoice to deal with, instead of several dozen invoices.

SIPAPU: How did yours begin?

SHOEMAKER: Our approval plan began more by accident than by design. A librarian friendly with our shop found her weekly visits curtailed by other burdens, and asked if we might set books aside for her less frequent visits. She was pleased with what we had chosen on her behalf, and we began talking about her collection and its needs, attempting to articulate a "buying profile." Soon after we began mailing our monthly selections to her with an invoice "on approval." She was then able to spend more time with retrospective buying, searching, and organizing want lists. The need was apparent for such a program in small press publishing which even then (1969) was showing signs of its eventual explosive growth, and we realized that our system could be adapted and tailored to the needs and systems of other libraries.

The last few years dozens of new book dealers and "distributors" have sprung up, and the book trade is now rank with amateurs, many of whom know neither the vocabulary nor the ethics of the business. First, a Standing Order is a contract, and a contract is necessary for both sides to operate well and effectively. We promise not to cancel any Standing Order without six months' notice to the library, and we perform our service in full right up to the day of any such cancellation, giving the library as much time as possible to set up alternative methods of acquisition. This insures them against any gaps in their collection. Next, we expect the same in return, to enable us to adjust our standing orders with the individual presses as necessary. Finally, a Standing Order Approval Plan is just that. The librarian has the right to reject any item sent and to return it to the dealer for *full credit*. This differs from the Blanket Order system, for instance, where the library is bound to keep everything sent, and yet I know of dealers offering an "Approval Plan" and either refusing to accept returns at all or crediting those returns in a punitive manner at less than the full original billed price.

SIPAPU: How does it work?

SHOEMAKER: It works, I think, very well. We long ago decided that with our present operation we could handle about fifteen such programs efficiently — we have no desire to become a large computerized library supplier, and the approval plan is only a small part of our operation. (By the way, this is not only a small press plan, but more accurately a poetry plan. We supply to several of our schools, poetry published by the commercial and university presses in addition to that published by the small presses. In addition to our approval plans we issue monthly "New titles" lists of recently published books. Many libraries find it more to their liking to order from these. And we also handle retrospective requests, want lists, author lists, etc. Our current standing stock includes more than 10,000 titles of modern poetry, ranging from rare editions to new and used.) Our procedure is straightforward. We do not solicit new accounts; but when approached by a librarian we begin by trying to learn their collection, how it is used, its scope and present holdings. In my experience it is best to work with a single librarian. We work out a buying profile tailored to the collection. This profile must not only deal with which authors or presses are to be collected, but which edition, cloth or paper, is desired, whether the library wishes to collect broadsides, recordings, magazines, etc. The profile is the entire key to success or failure. Once the profile is established we begin selecting and gathering the appropriate books. Every six weeks or so we organize the lot and ship it to the library under a single invoice. We expect the library to receive the books and immediately process the invoice for payment. After that is done the librarian can then examine the books sent and make his/her selection. Any books rejected should then be returned to us and we issue an immediate credit memo to be used against a future invoice. From our standpoint there are three keys to any given approval plan being a success. The first I've already mentioned. The buying profile must be one in which everyone has confidence, and it must be constantly adjusted and examined. Last year, with seven plans in operation, our returns averaged less than 5%. Secondly, we must expect the library to process the invoice and issue the check with all speed. If this is to work for us, we must balance the cash flow. Each year we deal with over 600 small presses, each billing us for their publications on a 30-day basis. Many invoices become due and payable even while the books sit on our shelves, being gathered for our next shipment to a library. We agree to issue credit memos in full which can be used against a future invoice, so the library incurs no risk in processing the invoice even before their own selection process begins. Finally, we must demand that the library wrap its return as well as we wrap our shipment, so that no damage occurs in the post. We cannot issue credit on books damaged in transit.

We do not give discounts in our program, but at the same time we charge no handling fee or book fee—each book is billed at its retail price and our postage charges are those charged by the post office. I remember seeing invoices from a well-known book jobber, wherein he purported to give libraries a "discount." He would bill a book retailing at $2.00 at $1.40, a 30% discount. But his bill would include a per book fee, in this case $1.00, and a "handling post" fee amounting to about 25¢ per title, so that the library actually paid $2.65 for the $2.00 book.

SIPAPU: What's all this about publishing yourself?

SHOEMAKER: My continuing interest in the art of the book has led my wife and I to continue publishing books under the Sand Dollar imprint. We've published 28 books and broadsides, work by Harvey Bialy, Robert Duncan, Jeanetta Jones, Michael Palmer, Romulus Linney, Ronald Johnson, Leslie Scalapino, Michael Davidson, Theodore Enslin, Howard McCord, Gus Blaisdell, Peter Whigham, Charles Stein, and Jonathan Greene. I have also had the opportunity to produce and/or design books for other publishers, ranging from fine press editions (*Oracles* by Reynolds Price, published by The Friends of Duke University Library and *Kora and Ka* by H.D., published by Bios) to trade books produced by offset (*The Good News According to Mark*, a new translation by Reynolds Price and published by him, and *The One-Straw*

Revolution, an Introduction to Natural Farming, by Masanobu Fukuoka, published by Rodale Press.)

Like many people watching publishing in this country develop over the past fifteen years, I have some grave concerns. There has been a tremendous growth in the number of small presses during the seventies, but they remain extremely vulnerable in the marketplace and many could not survive without federal funding. The readership remains extremely limited and distribution remains a critical problem. The average print run of small press poetry books remains today what it was in 1970, about 1000 copies, and the books remain in print for an average of three years. It would benefit the small press community to recall Robert Creeley's Divers Press. In the fifties Divers Press was issuing about 300 copies of their titles, books by Charles Olson, Creeley, and others, and they were remaining available for about three years, some longer. Creeley was meeting his market. Today a 1000-copy edition meets the demand and often exceeds it. It is also interesting to note that in a country of 215 million people 40% admit to not reading a book at all last year, and sales of 35,000 hardcover copies can land a piece of fiction on the *New York Times* best seller list. The statistics are all very discouraging, but they evidence deeper problems than the worry that a first book of poems may gain for its author 200 readers, half of whom he knows on a first name basis.

On the other hand we've all watched while New York commercial publishers have absorbed one another and finally found themselves absorbed by huge conglomerates. "Bottom-line" accounting coupled with other computer-based depersonalizing vocabularies and effects have changed New York publishing drastically. A huge machine has been slowly created that can, when it wants, do a very fine job of producing, distributing, and selling tens of thousands of certain select titles. But one cannot plug a book of limited appeal into this same machine and expect it to function efficiently. What I fear is the tyranny of the mass audience, something similar to what has plagued television from its inception. Unless a title can sell at least 14,000

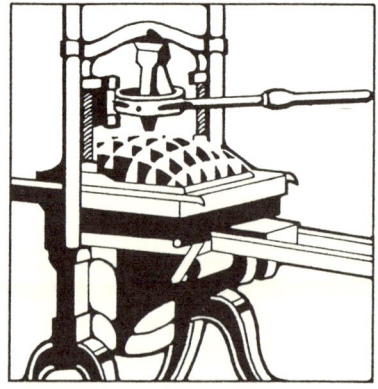

copies (Doubleday's figures in 1977, given at a conference held at The Library of Congress, called "The crisis in publishing") it will not be published—the machine cannot handle smaller numbers. Marginal books, which include not only poetry and fiction but books of importance in all disciplines, are falling through the crack. There is a readership too large for the commercial houses. It is my feeling that the only hope is the rebirth of the medium-size publishing house, one which does not wish to become large but sees its role clearly in the entire spectrum of book publishing and which remains at all costs independent, both from the large conglomerates and from crippling dependency on exterior funding agents.

I am currently involved in just such a press. North Point Press is a partnership between William Turnbull and myself. We will begin publishing, ten titles a year, in the spring of 1980. We will issue finely made books for the trade, publishing poetry, fiction, essays, anthropology, translations, anthologies, etc. We intend to demonstrate that well-made books need not automatically be more expensive in the marketplace. A lesson learned from the small press movement is that it is this care that makes the difference, not whether one has huge budgets or staff. One person paying constant attention to each title throughout the production process is the key. Promotion and advertising, also, are not just a matter of money, but one of finding each book's place in the marketplace and paying appropriate attention to that title in all phases of promotion. Handling a few titles with such care will enable us to pay particular attention to each one.

None of this is experimental at all — it is simply commonsensical. And we intend to sell the books. It is absolute folly to publish books no one buys or reads. Our efforts will prove themselves or fail in the marketplace. I see no ethical problem whatsoever in expecting to make part of my living publishing books in which I believe. Like so many small press publishers I have worked for years and given hundreds of hours to the editing and publishing of books without any recompense whatsoever except for a tax claim on income tax. I'm beginning to think that this normal small press process distorts publishing. If small press publishers expected something more from their work than membership in some association or having their egos rubbed by grateful authors, they would exercise greater restraint in what they chose to publish and would follow through more completely in distributing and selling their books. Many small press publishers lose interest in a book when the first box arrives from the binders', and no one, least of all the author, is well served.

Too many serious questions are involved here to deal with briefly, but the time seems long overdue for some examination. There are over 600 active small press publishers, over 500 active little magazines. Commercial and university presses will issue 40,000 titles this year. It seems that almost no one reads. I think it's time for anyone contemplating writing or publishing yet another title to examine his efforts, motives, and expectations. If he cannot convince himself of the validity of what he's up to, the imperative to take a risk and plunge ahead, then how can he expect to appeal to the "ideal reader" already buried beneath the mass of what's already available? In my life books are serious business, and I've always remembered Lew Welch's definition of Aesthetics: "Not very many people do it very well. No one knows why."

SIPAPU: To switch back to your other hat: how do you see the role of the bookdealer in the small press scene?

SHOEMAKER: The role of the bookdealer in the small press scene is rather obvious, it seems. Booksellers make available to readers the efforts of publishers. Book shops can be the most efficient way of exposing books to an audience larger than the friends and relatives of the poet and publisher. In the seventies small press publishers have occasionally looked upon the bookseller as some sort of enemy or stumbling block. Booksellers are, yes, selective, but not nearly so much as any given one of their customers. No publishers, small or large, has any "right" whatsoever to any space in any book shop if the book shop does not feel its customers will buy it. (This distrust often arises when an amateur, ill-made product attempts to crash through into a professional environment.) It is a rare bookshop indeed that would refuse to stock a book it felt would sell—in fact we are one of those rarities.

Small press publishers, for the most part, are hobbyists, publishing books not for the profit to be made from them but for other reasons. I have heard small press publishers badmouth booksellers, apparently jealous of the shop's 40% mark-up, questioning why the shop should make that much profit, saying that a bookseller "does nothing" for his money. That is absurd, and only evidence of the publisher's ignorance. A bookseller must have space, and anyone can quickly ascertain how expensive that is throughout the country. He must exist as a small business, with the insurance and taxes and other requirements, state, federal and local. He must pay the necessary employees, for to do a good job one must have good help, and good help is rightly expensive. And he must handle books from hundreds of presses, thousands of individual titles, whatever his specialty. We once figured that in our shop, an efficient one we think, we handle the average book six times between receipt and delivery, each book, whatever its retail cost. From an honest cost-efficient bottom line we cannot handle a book retailing for $1.50 without taking an absolute loss. But in our context we cannot not afford to handle it, however many times we must.

SIPAPU: Sage advice to publishers?

SHOEMAKER: My advice, I guess, would be for the small press publisher to understand that it is no easier to run a small bookshop than it is to run a small press. Quite the contrary in most cases. A small bookshop survives without access to government grants, for one (and I think it should). Unlike federally funded distributors, most book shops buy their stock outright, without the consignment billing procedure which allows a distributor to stock a title and only pay for what sells as it sells. (At least this is our procedure.)

Perhaps I should be very specific here to illustrate one point. Sand Dollar depends for a great part of its gross on sales to libraries. Since we pay post to most publishers our average mark-up is 35%. For our approval plan libraries, which account for over 35% of our gross, we gather titles over a six-week period and then ship them on approval to the libraries. The library must then receive the books, handle its own selection procedure, process the return, handle the accounting, and send the invoice into the bowels of its own accounting department whence the bookseller can expect his check. Most publishers bill us at net due 30 days. This means that a great part of the six-week shipment will already have come due before the shipment is made. Libraries average 90 days to pay. This is a very strict problem of cash flow. If we were independently wealthy we could pay every bill on receipt and not worry when we were paid, but we are not. So on occasion we have been a slow-pay account. I only want small presses to know that this is not malevolent, nor is it evidence of bad faith. It is a problem slow to correct itself, and must be understood.

My only other piece of advice to small publishers (from a bookseller's point of view) is to pay at least as much attention to the production of the book, from its design and binding to the size of the print-run and the price, as the poet did in writing the poems, as much care as they expect of the eventual reader. And to deal with the bookseller in some civilized, concrete, reasonably professional manner—I cannot count the number of invoices I've received that *lack* the publisher's name and address—and to consider *our* problems before they quibble about discounts.

SIPAPU: Do you want to touch on your experience with the NEA?

SHOEMAKER: I served as a member of the Literature Panel of the National Endowment for the Arts for four years, serving as the chairman of that panel for the last year of my service.

It was an invigorating challenge. I was stunned by the overview and scope of a "literature program." To be called upon to exercise and defend one's aesthetic so constantly is an education in itself. I have always loved books because the experience one has with a book is solitary and private. In the context of a democratic panel making judgments, this privacy is violated, sometimes violently. Like anyone there I sometimes felt good at what was done by the panel, and sometimes concerned. Like everyone there I lost some old friends and found new relationships distorted. The process of trying to make qualitative decisions in a populist democratic process is nearly impossible. Art by committee is (aside from film) doomed to ultimate failure, I fear, and so is the judgment of what "art" is. Like many who have served the NEA I have grave doubts about the nature of federal funding for the arts, its impact and success. But those are questions beyond the scope of this interview.

CONFERENCE ON CONFERENCES: We didn't go to the COSMEP conference this year—it was held in Port Townsend, Washington (the first time in the Pacific Northwest), and seemed to have been taken over by a group of people who saw it as a Krzy Kosmep Konference, announcing their intentions in a flourish of Ks. (An attender told us that at least two of those Ks belonged to Ken Kesey, whom we regret not having seen.) Frankly, we always believed that what COSMEP needed was to sober up, not go wild, especially since the failure of their van project; so we settled down to our troubles at home.

Necessity of one sort or another, however, took us to the ALA conference at Dallas, for a day or two, and gladly we quit the city of heat and sad memories. Our principal reason for being there was to attend a workshop for newsletter editors, and if there is the slightest improvement in our appearance, you can set it down to the extremely well-organized work of Robert L. Baker (Venture Publications, Chicago), and Ed Howard, director of the Vigo County (Indiana) Public Library.

The meetings were held in a small room in the Dallas Hilton, and after an introduction and overview (Friday night, 22 June), by Ed Howard, Robert Baker selected the "elite eleven" from the fifty or so newsletters sent the judges beforehand (ours among them). The prize-giving had more than a touch of Rotary in it, and it was obvious that the standards of the judges were rather more conventional than would permit our own success, but there was nevertheless an important lesson being driven home with each award: front-page immediacy, name-plate, two-page spreads, feature plays, leads, columns, etc. The Brooklyn Public Library *Bulletin* won in four of these categories, but the Oklahoma Department of Libraries' *Source* won the "best overall" prize. Examples of runners-up were given, particular newsletters exhibited on slides for favorable comment (we got that far), and the criteria fairly and justly explained. The company then adjourned to the room downstairs, where there was a display of newsletters (some seemed to have got left out), and conversation with wine and cheese.

The best part of the whole session came next morning, when Howard P. Hudson, who purchased the *Newsletter on Newsletters* in 1968, and who lives in Rhinebeck on the Hudson, spoke on the art of newsletter writing. He described the German merchants as the originators of newsletters, and cited the *Boston News-Letter* as an early American newspaper of the time. For Hudson, newsletter-publishing was "narrowcasting," in that your audience was always specialized. He emphasized the importance of being in control of your own newsletter (a survey showed that only 45% of newsletters surveyed gave the full editorial control to the editor); for him, a model letter is the *Kiplinger*. (Of course, *Sipapu* makes no attempt to conform to this model.) He also mentioned the necessity of a distinctive title; there are three newsletters all named *Impact*.

Edgar Frank, Director of Production at Year Book Medical Publishers, in Chicago, spoke on the use of newsletter art; some of his presentation was well known to the more experienced in the graphic arts but in any case it is difficult to illustrate graphic techniques with only a slide show and an hour's time. In the afternoon he spoke on the mechanics of production (typesetting on Compugraphic, offset, paste-up, etc.). In the afternoon Kimberly Whitman, who does newsletter work for the American Heart Association, spoke on circulation (change of name, mailing lists, postal regulations), and finally Donald Stewart, summarized the workshop by correctly describing the newsletter as an art form.

Along with the program of the newsletter workshop was published the results of a survey taken among participants (remember: these are all library newsletters). Without reproducing all their tables, it was interesting how far the results of the surveys departed from the "bell curve." For example, 45% of editors had been in service only one year, and 34% between two and four years; 20% between five and ten years—this suggests "burnout" followed by rotation. Again, 90% had a circulation of less than 4000; the largest percentage is the one we fall into: 24% between 501 and 1000. The editor's job is full-time for only 5%; 45% have full editorial control (43% don't, 10% "other"); 36% have an editorial policy, 44% don't, 20% other; fortunately only 15% have to suffer the indignity of an editorial board; and the amount the editor writes varies strangely: 23% of editors said that they only wrote 5-10% of their newsletters, 19% said that they wrote nearly 100% of their stuff. Similar irregular curves were described by editors estimating their time; we suspect that some work is scammed, deadlines drive the amount up, and a certain amount of floor-pacing goes on (try and estimate that, if you please).

Our impression of this workshop was that it was tightly organized and well worth attending. If anything, it tended to emphasize the handsomely conventional in newsletters. A beige paper, a broad gray stripe, an artist's rendering of the new building, a photograph of the new Assistant Director, these marked the businesslike newsletter. However, the quality of so many newsletters (including our own) and (by extension) that of so many other small press periodicals, is so much in need of improvement, — that we judge this workshop as having been well worthwhile.

On Sunday, 24 June, Donnarae McCann, who has been active in the fight against racism in children's books (author of *The Child's First Books*), chaired a meeting of the Social Responsibilities Round Table's Task Force on Consciousness-raising. We attended with some hesitation, as we expected a roomful of shouters, but it appeared that this was the second annual meeting of this task force, and that Donnarae McCann was somewhat disappointed that last year's group was so diminished this year. She introduced Fredrick Woodard, of the University of Iowa, who gave a very fine talk, one of the best we've heard in years, on "Patterns of racism in today's media centers"; Woodard gave accounts of subliminal racist messages in an antidrug film (that it's the blacks who are bringing this stuff in here). His message: the white middle class must give up prospects of endless growth (some of them have, at least a few) and that minorities must give up blaming whites for everything. He then launched into a close historical analysis of the Americanization movement started among immigrants over half a century ago, emphasizing its relevance to black self-help today. Our only point of disagreement with him was when he appeared to advocate color-coding of books; this (unless we grossly misinterpret him) seems to us to be prejudging or prejudicing books in a way that might have unexpectedly unfortunate consequences.

The audience was almost entirely black or female, and the room was nearly empty. Both of these facts seemed unfortunate to us. One woman was wearing a T-shirt that said: "If you liked the Sixties, you'll love the Eighties," explaining to an inquiring neighbor that it was the revival of the revolutionary impulse to which her slogan alluded. We regretted the premature nostalgia....

On Monday, the last day we were there in Dallas, there was a meeting jointly sponsored by the Association of American Publishers and the Resources and Technical Services Division of ALA, on "Libraries and Small/Alternative Publishing: Book Selection and Acquisition," to which we went, to see the troops drawn up as usual and blaze away at each other with predictable musketry. We came in at the end of Elliott Shore's speech on the mutual misconceptions of the alternative press and libraries, and heard a list of sources from the a/p (including us); James Danky described the Alternative Acquisitions Project, and gave a lack of librarian control as a reason librarians don't buy any of this explosive stuff. More to the point, even, than that, was that (in the words of one librarian interviewed by Danky during his tours of American libraries): "The Sixties Never Arrived Here." In our opinion, this is more true than many intellectuals ever comprehend; large areas of the United States could be marked "TSNAH." "If you liked the Sixties?" Here the seventies are about to expire, and some of us still don't understand. We did not linger, therefore, for the panel discussion, knowing that such sound-offs are frequently disappointing, bound as all participants are by middle-class rules against blowing the whole thing open with a firecracker. Also the futility—learned during the sixties—of attempting to do any such thing.

11 : 1

This Sipapu *is shorter than other issues and consequently was double-spaced. Interviewee Dan Poynter now calls his outfit Para Publishing, perhaps to emphasize the fact that his list contains books on how to publish, as well as books on sky sports. Perhaps since "para" can begin both para*chute *and para*graph *— but this is pure speculation on my part. You'll have to ask him!*

My views on censorship and freedom of information change over the years; I might today write differently about Time Bomb. *One reader was horrified that I hadn't condemned the thing entirely. Actually, getting hold of a pound or so of plutonium isn't all that easy. And it's poisonous; you wouldn't want the cat or the baby to lick it. "Wash your hands, children..."*

SIPAPU 1980: JAN.–JUN.: V. 11, NO. 1. = Q.I. NO. 21.

AS WE FINISHED OUR LAST ISSUE, we considered the possibility of closing down this publication. Besides the fact that costs rise while our subscription list remains stable or slowly declines, we have found that as the years go on, we were becoming victims of our own modest success. In the early seventies it was the Third World in America that was calling for attention; librarians were begging for awareness-lists and information on Afro-Americans, Chicanos, etc.; while feminism emerged as a leading topic later in the decade. In the later seventies the small press took fire, COSMEP became well-known, and book fairs and panels impressed the importance of small press activities on librarians. In all of these stages of consciousness-raising, *Sipapu* had a tiny part to play. Now, all our readers know about the Third World and the counter-culture; feminism is widely discussed; and there is an annual review of small press publications in *Library Journal*. In our race against obsolescence, we needed a new theme. Ecology? Radicalism? Fine printing? all very interesting themes, and not to be neglected, but already well voiced and to some extent the domain of professional writers and publishers in the field.

At length it occurred to us that there is one theme which is familiar to all, and superficially very popular, but which when actually discussed seriously, raises the hackles of many citizens otherwise outwardly peaceful. That theme is peace. The events of the last few months have alerted us, in common with others, to the fact that another world war could indeed break out, and that it would cast other concerns, group or private, into permanent irrelevance. The literature of peace is still scattered, books and periodicals urging disarmament are not well known, and at peace rallies the people seeking peace are apt to be surrounded by other special-interest groups with their own particular axes to grind. In addition, there are large areas of the country in which a public stand for peace is still considered equivalent to appeasement or simply "unpatriotic," i.e., in bad taste. These facts suggest that, without losing contact with our friends of the past, and while continuing to welcome ethnic and small-press publications for review, we should try to round up and present to you serious works on the peace movement in America today. We're less interested in leaflets or rally announcements than in bibliographies and substantial reference works, as well as periodicals and series on the subject.

OUR OWN SMALL PRESS, the Cannonade Press, may seem ill-titled to any who have read the above remarks, but actually this Kelsey 6 × 10 is so styled because it *fires off broadsides* — poetry broadsides, obviously; harmless verse (if you can believe there is such a thing). You can get our "Green poem" for free, along with other broadsides from Konocti Books, while they last, just by checking the appropriate space on the inside back cover. Also catalogs from Western Independent Publishers; the catalog is still available as regards publishers, even if the warehouse is no longer in operation.

¡PARACAIDISMO! is this the name of a revolutionary movement in Paraguay? The name of a theological tendency among the worker-priests of Brazil? Not at all; it is simply the Spanish title of a book on parachuting, or skydiving, the subject-matter and sport of what is certainly the most unusual of small-press publishers. For every thousand poets, and every hundred genealogists, there can be only ten who have something to give the world, in the small press scene, that is more than a reflection of themselves; and this most courteous gentleman with a fringe of gray beard, whose very house above Goleta, California, invites a skyey leap as far as Santa Rosa Island, —

turns out to be neither a dreaming poet not a self-sustaining hobbyist, but a businessman with a head hard as nails and a considerable willingness to share his time and talents with others; his book, in the original English, is the bible of every skydiver. We introduce you to Dan Poynter, publisher, and member of the COSMEP (Committee of Small Magazine Editors and Publishers) Board of Directors:

SIPAPU: Birth and education?

POYNTER: 17 September 1938; grew up in San Francisco, moved east for 11 years, got smart and moved to Santa Barbara five years ago. I studied economics in college (University of the Pacific, Stockton) and spent the next two years in law school. Spent the next 15 years in marketing and became a hardened businessman. As a parachute user, designer and salesman, I came to understand all sides of the picture. Now I am applying what I have learned to publishing. The competition in this field is easy, since most of the people in publishing are not marketing-oriented. They publish what appeals to them, not what might appeal to the consumer. Instead of promoting a book once they have published it, they go on to the production of a new book.

SIPAPU: Your occupation, before skydiving and parachuting?

POYNTER: After school, I worked for or ran parachuting companies in Oakland, CA, Flemington, NJ, Orange, MA, Manchester, CT, Boston, and New York City. I began publishing my own books part time, and later graduated to full time.

SIPAPU: But how did you get into skydiving—through military service or civilian life?

POYNTER: My skydiving began in civilian life. I was studying for finals in law school when a friend suggested that we drive up to the Napa Valley for a jump. It seemed like a good idea at the time.

SIPAPU: Skysports of all sorts: hang gliding, parachuting, ballooning, all of them—how many are you into? How many licenses do you hold?

POYNTER: I hold all the licenses/ratings in parachuting: Gold Wings (= 1000 jumps), Master Parachute Rigger, Instructor/Examiner, Past Chairman of the USPA, etc. Is this interview about publishing or skydiving?

SIPAPU: You have us overwhelmed. How did you get into publishing?

POYNTER: I fell into publishing. I began by submitting articles to *Parachutist Magazine* in 1963. While they didn't pay, the articles helped me to develop my writing ability, established me as an expert on the subject, and provided me with a reservoir of material which could later be strung together for a book. I worked eight years compiling the information for *The Parachute Manual*, a 500-page technical treatise, $8\frac{1}{2} \times 11$, which I decided to publish myself after talking with two friends who had published. One had gone with Prentice-Hall; the other was self-published. I decided I knew the market better than any publisher, and am still convinced I was right. Today my $30 tome has become an industry standard, and can be found in every parachute loft, military and civilian, in the world.

SIPAPU: Where do you get all your information?

POYNTER: Everything you could want to know is in your local library. I write off for information and do as much of the research as I can here at home (I have a rather extensive technical aviation library here). Sometimes I take a trip to a larger city or to a specialized library. Then it's more letters and usually a second trip or two to fill in the holes.

SIPAPU: We note that you operate your publishing business out of a very nice home on a hill overlooking the Pacific, just up the coast from Santa Barbara. Just how successful has your publishing business been?

POYNTER: One bestseller is in its ninth revised edition with over 125,000 copies in print, and I have several books which sell at a steady rate of ten to twelve thousand copies per year — year after year. The titles with a low volume (1000 per year) carry a higher relative price ($9.95). So far, I've moved over a quarter million books for more than 1 ½ million dollars in sales. Annually, the business grosses in the low six figures and last year I shipped 66,000 books.

SIPAPU: A tad more than most COSMEP members are making these days. Yet here you are on the COSMEP Board. What have you learned there, and what have you taught?

POYNTER: In serving on the COSMEP Board, I have learned about a side of publishing that is new to me — the literary side. It has been a privilege and a pleasure to serve with the present Board. While I understand that some past Boards did not function in complete harmony, this one is cooperative and hard-working. Without exception, they have enthusiastically accepted every program I have offered for their consideration. I have served on numerous other Boards for many years, and it has been a great challenge to propose the better programs for COSMEP.

SIPAPU: What do you see as the future for self-publishing?

POYNTER: Very positive. In fact, it will be the only way to get a manuscript into print. 300,000 book-length manuscripts go unpublished every year. Now that the big soap and oil companies are buying up New York publishers, they are concentrating on the hot sellers. Unless you have published successfully before, or are a political or Hollywood personality, your chances of even having your manuscript read are close to zero — and decreasing all the time. Therefore, the only alternative is self-publishing. Self-published books will double in the next six months, quadruple in the next year and a half. This is the hottest growth segment in the publishing industry.

SIPAPU: If all these unpublished manuscripts are either unread or unpublished — and if there is a glut of small publishers on the market, as we see it — how is one to achieve distribution? Through organizations, or what?

POYNTER: The most *efficient* method of distribution, considering the time and money invested, is to let the major distributors (Ingram, and Baker & Taylor) handle the bookstore/library trade for you. Concentrate your efforts on the non-book outlets who usually buy in larger quantities, pay promptly, are happy to get 40% (only) off and who have never heard of returns. For example: if your book is about scuba diving, approach dive shops, scuba catalog houses, specialized travel agencies, etc. Use your imagination: where would you look for information on a subject that interests you if you weren't bookstore/library oriented?

SIPAPU: One can only fall from heaven in so many ways. Where do you go from here?

POYNTER: I come from a long line of literary people, Kathleen and Frank Norris, Stephen Vincent and William Rose Benet, but I doubt that I am a publisher for any hereditary reasons. Consequently, I don't know what my next book will be, and I don't talk about my work until it is on the press anyway. Most of my books are out in thirty to sixty days. I just see a need, make a decision, and *go*.

Dan is the author/publisher of *The Self-Publishing Manual*, a treatise on book writing and marketing which will be useful to publishers of all sizes. The revised second edition is $9.95 postpaid (Californians add 60 cents sales tax) from Parachuting Publications, P.O. Box 4232, Santa Barbara, CA 93103.

THE WHOLE PROBLEM OF PEACE is that it now has to be defended as a losing cause, as against war, or that it has to be seen as preferable to war, providing certain conditions are admitted. The terms of the debate are set by those who are preparing for war, and on a strategical basis, this puts the peacemakers at a disadvantage. In a sense, anyone who stands for peace today has the burden of proof put on her/him to prove that (s)he is not Neville Chamberlain. The situation has changed greatly since Hiroshima, and meanwhile a periodical called *The Progressive* has been putting it all down in a series of articles.  Under the title *Time Bomb: A Nuclear Reader from "The Progressive,"* edited by James Rowen, The Progressive Foundation (315 Gorham Street, Madison, WI 53703) published this year for $3.50, a selection of articles from its columns on nuclear war, nuclear power, and above all their famous debate on publishing the "secret" of the hydrogen bomb. The articles — we do not usually approve of books made out of a periodical, but then we may do the same one day, while there is always the possibility that some libraries do not subscribe to the lesser-known weeklies—begin with the "atoms for peace" program, and gradually move in to military applications of the atom to the famous article, temporarily forbidden publication for a while by the Federal Government—on how the H-bomb works (not "How to build an H-bomb," which is a different bag of cats entirely; many can explain how a car works, without having the resources to start a new automobile company). It turns out that obtaining the plutonium is only the beginning: a reflecting shield is also necessary; but the magazine's case for freedom of the press is overshadowed by the larger concern that a secret of this magnitude does more to hinder the public's understanding of the issues than would the publication of the "recipe" for creating trouble on a large scale. (To their credit, the editors include at least one cartoon expressing an opposite point of view.) Although there are sufficient articles of a familiarly scary variety here ("The Day the Bomb Went Off"), we felt concerned right from the start by the article on the repressions necessary to preserve the plutonium society ("Nuclear Big Brother"). In fact, this book has alike the strengths and weaknesses of a parade of witnesses—i.e. it is apt to be seen as a parade, or indeed a vaudeville—as each writer comes out and does a star turn to defend or attack some part of the theme in question. When it comes to the question of suppressing the famous "how-to" article (which was nothing of the kind), they come close to a question which neither our society, nor any other, has satisfactorily answered: to what extent can we tolerate publication of

material which governing authorities deem unacceptable? Their answer is good as far as it goes, but it almost begs the question by denying that the temporarily-suppressed article is really a cookbook. Their principle is fair; the application thereof could nevertheless have unfortunate repercussions. However, if there is any matter deemed totally impossible for publication, or inadmissable, is there any matter which is not ultimately subject to this standard? We end up at the point at which any thought may lead up to the "dangerous thought." And then we are in for full totalitarian thought control. It's worth noting, at this point, that almost all civilizations until the end of the eighteenth century would have said, "Of course there are dangerous thoughts, which may not be published or even hinted at." To this day, millions, perhaps even a majority, of Americans, would say the same. While many earlier defenders of First Amendment freedoms urged *The Progressive* not to persevere, and while *Sipapu* doesn't print recipes for vegetarian beef stew, let alone hydrogen bombs, we'll take their side. This week, the problem is not with the publishers, it's with the Pentagon and the President.

11 : 2

John Wilcock asked to be interviewed for this issue of Sipapu; *I believe he sent me a sample of what it would be like and I took him on. We've never met.* Other Scenes *apparently ceased publication in 1974.*

Winds of Change *published an article of mine and a poem or two, but folded a year or so after this article. Crumb had ceased his association with the paper some time before that. I won't forget the time one of the editors — there were several over the years — called me up and asked me for a thousand dollars. I said I would consider a loan, but what this chap wanted was what Robert Frost, in another context, called "The Gift Outright." I could barely keep a straight face, because one of the few meetings of the staff I had been to, showed them to be a bunch of happily disorganized young people, but not those you just hand out a thousand dollars to.*

Crumb still lives in Winters; he still does cartooning, but is also much involved with his dance band, the Rural Sophisticates.

SOME FOLKS READ hastily, and thought we were shutting down as of our last issue; in fact, we were merely reorganizing our efforts to include and indeed emphasize the peace movement, while not losing sight of, nor rejecting review copies of, periodicals and monographs from other social concerns and from the literary small press. Our only object is to keep going by changing fronts of attack. Peace, justice, and literature are almost all one situation, to be dealt with together. You ask in samhill how? Then we refer you to v. 2, no. 4 of the *New Orleans Review* (Loyola University, New Orleans, LA 70118), where you may read John Morressy's story "The Detour," which is the best allegorical account of the final abyss we have seen anywhere. If they are out of copies, ask them to do an offprint. Read that story and you'll never forget it — or the increasingly strong probability which awaits us all.

"IS THERE ANYBODY THERE?" SAID THE TRAVELLER: Few independent publishers have a reputation in more than one field. They may be known as poets, publishers, makers of directories, arts organizers, or commentators on the passing scene, but at best their work emphasizes one field at the expense of others. Yet, John Wilcock, over fifty, clean-shaven, looking like one of a million vaguely Bohemian New Yorkers, is one guide to those who have read his books on Mexico, Europe, Greece on $5–$10 a day, and another to those who have read his protean-anarchist publication, *Other Scenes*—which changes titles and addresses, metamorphosizes and comments on everything he notices. He has co-founded underground papers and written a gossip column in the Bahamas. We take you now to 43rd St., NY, NY:

SIPAPU: Sheffield, England, claims your birth. Can you tell us about your education?

WILCOCK: I went away to boarding school on the moors between Yorkshire and Lancashire but didn't learn much there. Failed Latin, Greek, French, mathematics, barely passed out of school at sixteen, went straight to work for a daily newspaper in my hometown: Sheffield, a steel town something like Pittsburgh but not as big.

SIPAPU: You got right into reporting for the Sheffield *Telegraph*. Would it be as easy (or indeed was it as easy then) to get into journalism, either in England or America, now?

WILCOCK: In those days, as I still suppose, everybody wanted to be a big London Fleet Street reporter, which meant working for one of the national dailies. In the meantime you took your enthusiasm and your shorthand skills—no reporter could get a job without shorthand—and grabbed any job you could get. This was the late forties. Anyway, I learned to type by taking newscopy over the phone from impatient district stringers, imprecations coming over the earphones every time you fumbled a word, and I covered crownings of May Queens and collected the names of mourners at important funerals.

SIPAPU: You're well known as a founder of the *Village Voice*. Its foundation must be legendary now, to any young reader. Who got together with whom, on what hot Manhattan night, and who came up with what hot ideas?

WILCOCK: The *Voice*! Its first issue was 26 October 1955, but a year before, on my first arrival in New York, I'd gone into a jewelry store on Eighth Street—after my first two days in town from Toronto, where I'd been living since I left England—and asked the owner why Greenwich Village didn't have some famous artists' and writers' paper. "Why don't you start one?" he asked, and so I put a notice in a bookstore window on Sheridan Square and held a few meetings, but nobody had any money. Next year (1955), I met two of the people who'd attended those premature meetings, Ed Fancher and Dan Wolf. They said they had some money and were going to start a Village paper. Did I want to help? The title came from Norman Mailer who was a school friend of Danny's girlfriend Rhoda, whom he later married. Mailer was a stockholder and also wrote some early columns, very controversial. People used to argue over literary matters in those days; you've no idea how civilized it was.

SIPAPU: Since you also wrote for the *East Village Other,* did the *Other* grow out of the other, was there a revolt, a transfer of allegiance, a cheerful straddling of fences?

WILCOCK: After ten years of doing a weekly column I was getting letters from readers who objected to my implications that America's current leaders (it was Johnson time) were murderers by waging a war in Vietnam. From *Voice* readers! It was time to get out and I started writing a column for the *East Village Other,* which was started mainly by Walter Bowart, an artist who had this idea of using offset to do what in effect was a collage newspaper. It had never been done before and was truly a historic breakthrough. There were some offset papers but none that were out of the traditional linear mainstream. The *Voice,* which had been paying $25 a week for the column lately (after years of paying me $5), asked me to quit writing for *EVO* or leave the *Voice.* So I went over and edited *EVO,* which is where we began the Underground Press Syndicate (now Alternative Press Syndicate), whose founder members were: *Berkeley Barb, Los Angeles Free Press, The Paper* from Lansing, Michigan, and the *San Francisco Oracle.*

SIPAPU: Origin of *Other Scenes?* How did you choose the name, and how did you get started on it? Is it still being published, and what does it do for you and its readers?

WILCOCK: The first column I sent Bowart, while I was still at the *Voice,* was headed "ART AND OTHER SCENES," and dealt with the absolute necessity, all through history, of forgery's place in the art scene. Bowart chopped off the "ART AND" thereby giving me a title, that was first a column, then (after I left *EVO*) a newsletter, mailed to subscribers from Los Angeles, Hong Kong, Athens, and London, where I produced issues in 1967 and 1968. In March 1968 *Other Scenes* appeared as a monthly tabloid; it went to fortnightly a year later; became a national magazine for two issues (being dropped by the distributor for "offensive" sexual and political content—e.g., Nixon wearing a swastika armband, a cover with Teddy Kennedy's picture on a poster reading "Wanted for Murder or President"). Meanwhile, *Other Scenes* has continued to be my umbrella publishing company title for publications ever since. These have included: *In the Cannes* (daily gossip and scandal newsletter distributed free during Cannes Film Festival in 1973 and 1974); *Soho Confidential; Soho Saturday; Nomad; Far Out News; Collage; John Wilcock's Secret Diary;* and latterly *The Yellow Journal.* Most of these newsletters, or mini-mags as I prefer to call them, are designed to be given away to five hundred interesting, significant and sensible people whom either I know in various parts of the world, admire for some reason, run across in my travels, or who request a copy (with or without payment). I like to think that I began with five million readers (one of my earliest employers was the London *Daily Mirror*) and I now have five hundred readers. I prefer the five hundred, and can probably claim to be one of the few publishers who knows exactly who his readers are.

SIPAPU: But do you give it free to everyone you meet?

WILCOCK: Only to the people I pick out at certain places: museum and gallery openings, publishing parties, movie screenings — anywhere one can assume that those present are intelligent and creative. Incidentally, my definition of an intellectual is anybody who reads and thinks. Those are the people I like as readers. I like to record the nitty gritty of everyday life, people's conversations, what's on their minds, hints of new fads or trends, reporting at a very basic level, eschewing big names and stars but paying attention to really talented people whose concepts and imaginations have not yet been noticed by the world at large.

SIPAPU: Why don't you do this as a columnist for some larger publication? Wouldn't it be more rewarding and reach a larger audience?

WILCOCK: I'd love to, but no existing publication seems to want it. For me, publishing is the only way I can unload some of the enormous input of information and ideas which I have. For the first ten years of the *Village Voice* I wrote a weekly column on just those lines, as I said above, but having left to do underground papers I seem to have phased myself out of commercial journalism. Because I can't seem to write what magazines want — as opposed to what I want to write — of necessity I have to publish my own writings.

SIPAPU: To go back: you say you "pay attention to really talented people whose concepts and ideas have not been noticed by the world at large." (*Sipapu* tries to do the same.) Can you name some of these people?

WILCOCK: I found myself having Lenny Bruce stay in my Perry Street apartment when he first opened up at the nearby Village Vanguard. And I went off to psychodrama with Woody Allen when he started his first stand-up comic stint at the Bitter End, so we could do a column together, which would be a departure from the usual plug/interview. Woody was calling himslf Walter Allen at the time, but nobody recognized him the night we were at psychodrama. I found myself hanging around Andy Warhol all through the late sixties (and Timothy Leary around the early sixties), because I felt somehow these were heavies and I couldn't understand why some people were able to dismiss them so easily. These days I still hang around the art scene which is full of creative, inquiring, offbeat (even anarchistic) minds and I'm always admiring "stars" whom nobody else has heard of, but who I, having known them for years, feel have fantastic talent which will break through one of these days. I could name a dozen people at any time but I'm not going to because most people wouldn't have heard of them — yet.

SIPAPU: Most of us have only *heard* of Beautiful People. So how did you get in contact with Andy Warhol? and start *Inter/VIEW?* Are you still connected with it? Is this a sideline to your story, or is it still central?

WILCOCK: I could say, confidently, indeed defiantly — that I don't know any Beautiful People. I knew Andy well from hanging out at the factory all through the late sixties, going to parties with him, to visits at various

colleges or other institutions, watching him make innumerable movies and seeing him three or four times a week at some periods. One day he was complaining that he didn't have the Hollywood money that he kept hoping to get to make a big-scale movie, and I said to him, "All my friends have papers, Andy. Why don't you start a paper?" Four days later he phoned me up — maybe the *only* time he *phoned* me up — and asked "What kind of a paper?" I said obviously a film paper and said that we *(Other Scenes)* would provide the typesetting if he would pay for the printing, and thus it came about. He said he wanted it "Black and white like *Rolling Stone*," which came as a shock; because everybody imagined he'd want something far out. He provided the editorial staff, focus, and also the title: *Inter/VIEW*. One year later, my business in ruins, as all the new alternative papers for which we had been doing the typesetting had gotten their own equipment — my paper not much in demand, my marriage beginning to break up — the "Movement" collapsing, I decided to sell out my 50% of *Inter/VIEW* to Andy for $6000 (twelve months' typesetting bills at $500 per month) and left the country. He gave me $5000 in cash and two Warhol flower paintings (which any dealer will give you $500 apiece for); they had just come back from an exhibition at the Tate Gallery, London. I still have them, but I rarely see Andy any more, although I think he's one of the most important artists of this century. This includes Picasso, Magritte, and Marcel Duchamp, who are his nearest predecessors.

SIPAPU: Now for the other half. How did you get into travel writing? How much of your life does it take up, what part of your income does it provide?

WILCOCK: I was working as an assistant editor on the *New York Times* travel section (don't forget that I had lots of serious journalism experience on London papers, Canadian magazines, UPI, etc.), about 1960 when I met Arthur Frommer, who had done two books, *Europe on $5 a Day* and *New York on $5 a Day*. He was seeking a writer for a book on Mexico, and I'd been there, so I left the *Times* and took $1000 to Mexico, travelling on chicken-filled buses and sleeping in fleabags, and eleven weeks later I came back with the manuscript of *Mexico on $5 a Day*. I later did books for him on California, Las Vegas, Japan, Hong Kong, Yugoslavia, India and Greece. At the moment the only title I still possess any rights to is a combined book on Greece and Yugoslavia (now on $15 and $20 a day), which I revise every two years. It sells 40,000 to 50,000 copies on each printing. I get a small (7½%) royalty, cheap. But I also pay most of the expenses of being in Greece, revising it, usually with any helpers I can find. (I'll be going in spring 1981, so I can always use assistance if I don't have to pay anybody's fare.)

SIPAPU: That's a lot of work. What part of your income does it provide?

WILCOCK: Travel writing is a lousy way to make a living and even though I live economically, about $1000 a month (all-inclusive), it still provides less than half my income. I've been blackballed twice for membership in the Society of American Travel Writers. I don't know why, but it may be because I have an abrasive image, gleaned, perhaps, from my years as a radical publisher. I regard myself as much more radical-cultural and radical-sociological than radical-political. My current political philosophies can be summarized in one sentence: Politicians are crooks. There are, however, a very few statesmen and stateswomen.

SIPAPU: If there is any label to pin on you at all, we'd have to call you a "free-floating, -wheeling journalist." Do you have any comments on contemporary journalism/small-press/alternative-papers/:publishing?

WILCOCK: As for contemporary publishing I think we're nearing the glorious time when every man or woman can be his or her own publisher. It's healthy for people to publish, either their own or other people's stuff, if it has nothing to say. Most poetry says nothing to the vast majority of the population, including myself. Bad poetry (i.e., anything that would be more banal as prose; lacking vision or intelligence) should be kept to one's self or given only to friends. Most (bad) poets use poetry as a copout; they know if they said this stuff to people they'd be laughed out of intelligent society. But to me, the more it is wrapped up, decked out in finery and regarded with awe, the more ridiculous and superfluous it seems. I am not saying that there is no good (i.e., meaningful, clever) poetry around, but I am saying that you don't see much of it.

In my opinion people who publish should do it because they want to do it, not because they want to make money out of it. It's unrealistic and arrogant to believe that people are just dying to get hold of the boring garbage that appears in most "little magazines" and are willing to pay for the privilege. To an aspiring "little publisher" I'd say: expect to lose money. How much can you afford to lose on your magazine every month or every year? Write it off. If you get any money back, regard it as gravy. Another of my pet peeves in this direction is the whole business of grants—especially when it applies to academics who are satisfying their own vanity and ego by publishing at the public expense. And often getting paid for it too! I guess my heroes are people who are dedicated and and are willing to pay in some manner for their dedication.

(Wilcock's publications may be obtained from 4137 Grand Central Station, New York, NY 10017. For $2 he will send you a package of whatever seems appropriate, or available from his recent publishing.)

BLACK HILLS ALLIANCE GATHERING: From Janet Mercurio and Isao Fujimoto, of the University of California, Davis, we bring this account of a manifestation against the attempt to use the Black Hills of South Dakota as a "sacrifice area" for the exploitation of its mineral resources:

"For one week in mid-July 1980 we attended the Black Hills International Survival Gathering near Rapid City, South Dakota, sponsored by the Black Hills Alliance. The Alliance, one of many groups in the Northern Plains region dedicated to responsible stewardship of the land, organized the conference to address the issue of the Black Hills' designation as a 'National Sacrifice Area.' Such a designation means that an area rich in minerals should be sacrificed for energy development at the expense of human habitation and agriculture. The assumption made for this is that America's need for non-renewable energy sources outweighs the consequences, which include the depletion of all the area's water supplies as well as the contamination of the surrounding soil, air, spent water, and life forms, including humans. Especially, in the case of uranium mining, the environment becomes polluted with the mobilized atomic particles; the Alliance has already been documenting cases of environmental and human contamination from regional uranium mining. The question—whose responsibility is it to clean up or to try to compensate for these crimes—is still open. The Gathering addressed itself to these and other questions in order to discover which powers have allowed these decisions to be made, and these situations to take place—and to determine more appropriate courses of action regarding the use of the land.

"Besides ecological and ethical reasons for protesting governmental action in the Black Hills, the Alliance is also reasoning on historical and legal grounds. The Fort Laramie Treaty of 1868, signed after the Powder River War between the U.S. and the Sioux Nation, stipulated that a designated area west of the Missouri River, including the Black Hills, be established as a reservation, 'for the absolute and undisturbed use and occupation of the Sioux.' But as soon as gold was discovered in the Hills, this treaty was ignored. The need for other valuable minerals today has created a similar disregard for the Treaty of 1868. As compensation, the U.S. government has granted a minuscule sum (the value of the land in 1868, plus interest) as a token retribution for the taking of the land — as if such a monetary value could be assigned to it! (One of the Alliance's battle cries is, 'The Black Hills are not for sale!')

"The wide assortment of speeches, discussions, workshops, practical demonstrations, ceremonies, and entertainment that comprised the Gathering's program were held on the barren rolling hills of the vast Great Plains. The Black Hills range — known as the sacred 'Paha Sapa' to the Lakotas — was barely visible in the distance. When we arrived at the site, we joined the others in hand-carrying our gear to the assigned sleeping area already dotted with multi-colored tents and tepees. One ridge was used as the primary meeting area and was lined with makeshift, yet sturdy, structures of pine boughs, logs, and tarps. These shelters served their purpose well during the ten-day conference by providing us with protection from the changing, extreme weather — which included strong, dry winds, electrical storms, and scorching hot sun. A few water towers, some portable outhouses, a food co-op, and cafeteria area were the only other items brought for the comfort of visitors to this endless cattle range. 'Survival' indeed was an appropriate adjective for this Gathering.

"The only other evidence of human habitation on these plains came from the territory beyond the neighboring ridge: Ellsworth Air Force Base. Its B-52's, KC-135 refueling planes and fighter jets continually took off and landed directly over our heads, rudely interrupting the serenity of the natural environment. As the world's largest concentration of land-based nuclear strength, it provided a fitting contrast to the Gathering and its views: nuclear warheads vs. opposition to uranium mining; military strength vs. decentralization of power; high consumption of fossil fuels vs. conservation of natural resources.

"The gathering brought together activists from all over the nation and from many parts of the world, concerned not only with environmental and anti-nuclear issues, but also with women's issues, holistic health, alternative energies, appropriate technologies, politics, sustainable agriculture, minority rights, etc. The topics addressed at the Gathering were therefore varied and sophisticated — all participants realizing that their single-issue organizations face similar obstacles and opposition as do other groups. The Black Hills Alliance is itself a coalition of local farmers, native Americans, miners, and local citizens who want more citizen participation in the decision-making process affecting their lives.

"One of the major components of the program was the Citizens' Review Commission on Energy-Developing Corporations, which is designed to target the multinational corporations that are exploiting the resources of the Black Hills. The other major focus was on the Forum on Indian Genocide and the Planned Extinction of the Family Farm, a program which drew attention to the common problems of Indians and farmers: the pollution and expropriation of their lands.

"Opening ceremonies were led by John Trudell, a Cherokee activist who welcomed the gatherers with the wish that we might gain a feeling of the power of the sun, wind, rain and earth during our stay on the plains, as native Americans have done throughout history. In contrast to such natural power, the concept of military power he thought a misnomer, because the military only provides terrorism and that true power comes only when it is generated by the people. In an inspiring and emotional manner, reminiscent of the late Rev. Martin Luther King, Jr., he insisted that we, the people, can be as powerful as earthquakes and volcanoes in combating the political and economic forces which are aimed at keeping us oppressed. He claimed that these forces intend to keep groups of people fighting each other instead of thereby preventing them from recognizing and opposing their actual common enemies. He therefore asked us to develop what he calls 'resistance consciousness,' which does not allow individual egos to get in the way of building meaningful coalitions. He also observed that native Americans feel oppressed but not powerless while it is the other way around for middle-class white Americans; that we need less pride, John Wayne style, and more humility; and that our recent social reforms have lacked a key ingredient: land reform. He concluded with the reminder that because people are what generate good energy and power, we should all take good care of ourselves in order to provide good energy. As did King, Trudell promoted non-violent action by suggesting that people should be motivated not out of hatred, as a reactionary would, but rather, positively, out of love for the Earth.

"Russell Means, the A.I.M. (American Indian Movement) spokesman involved in Wounded Knee II, 1967—wearing a headband, a sleeveless vest revealing healthy muscles, and taking a determined stance—presented a powerful address, the address of a warrior. Preferring the term American Indian, rather than native American, to describe his people, Means explained that Columbus called the people he encountered 'En Dios,' not 'Indios,' because they were 'in God'; he did not think he was in India, Means explained, because at that date India was called Hindustan and the name India came much later. As a member of the Black Hills Alliance, he considers the 'sacrifice area' designation murder, not only to his own Lakota tribes, but also to the other Indian people in similar situations: the Navajos, Hopis,

Northern Cheyenne, and Crow. He asserts that, 'We *are* resisting being turned into a national sacrifice area, a national sacrifice people!' He went on to reject Marxism, capitalism, and Christianity by saying that European culture will eventually destroy itself. He feels strongly that the Chinese, the Vietnamese, and the acting leader of the Navajos, Peter MacDonald (whom he called 'Peter MacDollar'), have begun to incorporate the nuclear age into their cultures, rather than rejecting it as other Third World cultures have done. He is waiting for the prophecy of his people, of the Hopis, and of others—that Mother Earth will retaliate, and the abusers of the land will be eliminated. That is the revolution he is awaiting. Until then, he wants to remain not a leader, but just himself—an Oglala Lakota patriot.

"Winona La Duke, a member of Women of All Red Nations (WARN), who has attended Harvard-Radcliffe, and who has done extensive research into the power structure of energy development on reservations, spoke next. Her publication, 'The Council of Energy Resource Tribes: An Outsider's View In,' available for a small donation to WARN, P.O. Box 2508, Rapid City, SD 57709), describes CERT as the governing body that authorizes energy-related development on Indian lands. It is supposed to represent 25 tribes which own a large share of the West's energy resources, but Winona La Duke claims that it only represents the 25 individuals comprising the council because they have no accountability to the people in their tribes. Agreeing with the opinions of Russell Means, she considers Peter MacDonald, CERT chairman, a traitor to his people for agreeing to the terms for uranium, oil, geothermal, natural gas, and coal development in conjunction with the U.S. government and with private industry. Winona La Duke also suggested that LaDonna Harris, candidate for Vice President of the Citizens' Party, was not acting in the best interests of Indians when she, too, dealt with CERT. (LaDonna Harris was not present at the Gathering, however, to respond.) Finally, Winona La Duke concluded her well-documented speech by advocating direct action to prevent, or retard, the many detrimental, imperialistic enterprises conducted on Indian lands. She enthusiastically advised people to stand in front of mining operations if necessary, citing the many Navajo occupations, which set back mining projects for years, as examples of effective resistance.

"Many other articulate people shared their stories, ideas, and spirit with the Gathering. These special guests helped it to become clear that the good work done in the past had required constant struggle, and that future good work will require more of the same. We left the Gathering knowing that there was much work to be done, but that there were many allies all over the world working towards the same basic set of goals: a healthy, equitable ecosystem."

(For further info: Black Hills Alliance, Box 2508, Rapid City, SD 57709). — JANET MERCURIO AND ISAO FUJIMOTO, UC Davis.

A BREATH OF FRESH AIR: Some time ago we vaguely considered putting out a local community paper, to be called *The Yolo Tomato* — "Splats you in the Eye with the News of the Day." The only person who could have possibly done us a masthead, we reflected, would have been Robert Crumb, the celebrated creator of Mr. Natural, Flakey Foont, Shuman the Human, and other sleazy characters of a latter-day urban Bohemia. It was just as well that this consideration remained as vague as it did, because not only did we have neither capital nor connections, but we did not personally know Robert Crumb. Now, however, there is a Yolo County paper, and it does have Crumb as the director of its artwork, and the creator of its masthead. From a conversation with Martin Barnes of Capay, in his office at Davis, we gleaned the following facts about the county paper that lives in the country, yet gets much of its support from people who work and live around the University of California, Davis: *Winds of Change.*

Winds of Change started off with a government grant from the National Center for Appropriate Technology, which (thanks to Senator Mike Mansfield, D-MT), was located in Butte, Montana. It was cut off from Federal funds after its first issue, apparently for being too controversial. The staff huddled, and decided to switch (at least partially) from a/t to local coverage, and since then they have had a modest success with monthly tabloids of eight pages each. Its organization is democratic, as you might expect; most alternative papers have learned from the formerly monolithic regimes of the *Berkeley Barb* and the *Los Angeles Free Press* — at least one of these now dead as the result of trying to replace one-man empires with democratic procedures (as well as of other causes). Decision at *Winds of Change* is by consensus; Barnes is the only salaried coordinator; otherwise the staff switches around writing and layout tasks, although some staffers have semi-permanent assignments as regards areas to be covered. Thus, a column named "Yolo Gardens" carries advice from a peculiar character signing himself "early human" (as in "early lettuce"). Its typesetting is done at cost by the UC Davis *California Aggie,* it rents space in the Cal Aggie Christian Association's house, and the staff proof the typesetting themselves.

Distribution of the paper is through pledges (subscriptions or time commitments), and by lads who trot the paper all around town. Outside contributions are welcomed, but full participation is through Monday night meetings, when projects are reviewed and discussed. In addition, the paper is trying to root itself in the community through an emphasis on Yolo County material, particularly as regards experimental agriculture. Its ideology is agrarian-populist. (The only other Yolo County monthly paper, Woodland's *California Farm Observer,* published by F. Hal Higgins until his death some years ago, concentrated on agbiz concerns.)

Winds of Change has not been without its share of controversy and opposition, however. Even in a small town, we'd say particularly there, passions run high; and when *Winds of Change* challenged the location and style of the Winters Community Center at Main Street and Railroad Avenue, winds blew with equal force and in the opposite direction. This town, our own home, was divided over the wisdom of locating the community center right in the modest back yards of a mini-community of ex-railroad cars, turned into homes for poor folk. These cars were regularly decorated with Christmas lights in the holidays, and Crumb himself had dwelt in one with his wife. The cars are now blocked from view by a conventional building (a local firm, Living Systems, had asked that the center be designed with solar heating), and at least one of the cars was relocated. Some demanded why the center was being attacked by those who had taken up no part of the building costs; others wrote in to say that they missed the Christmas lights, and that this complaint was something that had needed to be said, and that for many years. Most folks agree that the center was badly needed, and even *Winds of Change* agreed that it represented a tremendous effort on the part of the people of Winters, but at least some wish that it had been located in a different place—perhaps where the radio telescope, serving as a satellite communications center now stands: namely, opposite the brick City Hall (built 1912, after the earthquake of 1892). Perhaps this last sentence describes our own position.

Winters, founded in 1875 with the coming of the railroad, has a population of 2580—just above the description of the Bureau of the Census, of a small town as having a population of 2500 or under. There is no longer any railroad. The address of *Winds of Change:* P.O. Box 1004, Winters, CA 95964. The cost of a subscription: $10 per annum. We recommend that at least Sacramento Valley libraries subscribe.

12 : 1

A.D. Winans has not read, so far as I know, with bottle in hand since that poetry reading. Todd Lawson died last year of complications resulting from AIDS. Tom Clark got a lot of flak for his exposé of the Naropa Institute, as he later did for his attack on the language poets in Poetry Flash; *I salute him for his courage.*

ALA WEST: When the American Library Association comes to San Francisco, there's no excuse, short of anthrax, for failing to report to you. We found ourselves commuting from the Great Central Valley to the City, to save money, but it was hard on the little car too, as we later learned. Once we got tangled up in a double Iranian protest (= one set of Iranians protesting against the Iranian government, plus the other set of Iranians protesting against the attempts of the first set of Iranians to support an attempt to overthrow the Iranian government, while both blamed the United States for the present condition of Iran and its government); another time we managed to find a parking space in spite of the attractions of a huge Gay Parade, which used the space outside the conference center as their staging ground, drawing around 100,000 people in the cool windy air. The rest of the time, it was simply the normal day in San Francisco, which is wacky enough for anyone.

Probably the single most memorable event of the conference was held in the Civic Auditorium, Saturday, 27 June, from nine to twelve. The ALA Intellectual Freedom Committee and related groups sponsored a meeting called "Intellectual Freedom in the 1980's: The impact of conservativism," and the keynote speaker, whom we came in to hear just after he got going, was Michael Farris, Executive Director and General Legal Counsel, of the Washington State chapter of Moral Majority. Mr. Farris was courteous. He briefly quoted Sam Adams, to the effect that virtue is the foundation of republics. From there he went on to describe his cause as one which is unappreciated; while Helen Bannerman's *Little Black Sambo* was banned from libraries for its racism, he observed no comparable sensitivity to parents wishing to protect their children from public displays of nudity, or otherwise offensive material; and charged us all with a double standard. Tackling the ALA Freedom to Read guidelines on how to handle a patron who finds material objectionable, he pointed out that the procedures call for stalling tactics, making the patron fill out forms instead of getting immediate attention to his or her problem. Finding in the guidelines an allusion to "Big Brother, the censor," he reminded his audience that Big Brother, in Orwell's *1984,* was a government official, not a private citizen demanding his rights. Mr. Farris then took on a sex education book which he believed was intended for young children, or for the young people's section of a library. According to him—for he was holding up a book which most of us could not see, as the hall was vast and totally filled—it described, he told us, self-stimulation, and sex without love; and showed naked couples making love. This book, he insisted, should be on a protected shelf, not available to any child just wandering through the library in search of something to read. He explained that he had given his own daughter, aged six, some sort of sex education, but she had not been allowed to just "look at anything"; and concluded by asking for cooperation from librarians in recognizing the sensitivity of conservative people, as they had learned to recognize the sensitivities of blacks and women. He pointed out that the Moral Majority was the largest non-union organization in the State of Washington, and that they had, or would have, the power to withhold taxes from libraries that ignored them. (A young man in the audience said, "That's just the trouble! You're threatening us!" To which Mr. Farris answered, "Come now, there's no need for this outburst.")

In general, Michael Farris's position was that of the balanced, but conservative lawyer. He did not deny any group's right to speak, but discouraged their right to be visible (for example, he deplored pro–ERA buttons on librarians, which he saw around the conference, as a breach of objectivity). It was in answering questions that he began to betray the weakness of his position. When someone asked him whether he would give equal protection to anti-draft literature as an example of freedom of the individual, he suggested that both pro-draft and anti-draft literature should be shelved away from general casual use, as being too controversial. When someone asked him about sex and violence in the Bible, he refused to dignify this question with an answer—although there is, allegedly, a town in Texas that has put the Bible on the restricted shelf for just that reason, and there is also a position on sex and violence which Scripture enunciates clearly (see, in a Christian context, John 8:11, and Matthew 26:52). The meeting then took a break, with both sides (no doubt) feeling some relief.

The second main speaker, although much more in line with the liberals who doubtless made up most of his audience, was (curiously enough) less interesting. Dr. Charles Park, Professor of Education, University of Wisconsin at Whitewater, gave a Menckenesque speech recounting the follies of censorship from the Puritans to the present, recounting the absurdities of small-

town councillors and local preachers with which a certain kind of history is full. His speech was weakened for us by his inability to see that a new force has entered American life, one which is determined to suppress popular discussion even as it ignores the tendencies leading toward nuclear war. We skipped much of his speech and all the later panels—including a little room in which you could meet Mr. Farris himself, rather like the Wizard of Oz be-
hind the curtain; we went off the the exhibits, and ended up interviewing Elizabeth Morrisett at a nifty Basque restaurant around the corner (nowhere but here and in New Orleans could one find a continental restaurant just around the corner at low prices: we have no pleasant memories of eating in Dallas). Naturally, she recognized the Basque flag crossed with our own over the bar.

We ended up helping staff the COSMEP booth, partly to make conversation with Celeste West and Todd Lawson, but also because we felt the urge to contribute our time to help. Most exhibitors don't know how to catch the public attention—we've learned to bring along a soap-bubble bottle, blow bubbles, and then stuff people's bags with freebies. You can't get involved with talking with people, including your own staff, and you can't be found eating—exhibitors don't eat, they photosynthesize by artificial light.

Because we were commuting, we missed a chance to see Sanford Berman (who has often been mentioned in these pages) being given the Margaret Mann Citation for his reform of subject cataloging; we might have missed it anyway, since it was given at eight in the morning on Sunday. As Berman explained to us, "There's a certain amount of ambiguity in the hour selected," going on to explain that the original plan was for an award ceremony at a Resources and Technical Services Division luncheon. What happened to the lunch? Well, there ain't no free lunch. What he finally managed to say, we missed, and if it was anything other than "Thank you," which he says very well, you'll have to write him for it at the Hennepin County Library, Edina, MN. When we finally got there, driving around the Gay Parade, it was time for the Social Responsibilities Round Table's Ethnic Materials Information Exchange Task Force, a group that's been chaired by, or at least inspired by, David Cohen, of Queens College, for many years. The program was on multilingual education, and it included far more speakers than we had the inclination to hear; Delia Martinez, who chairs a Committee on Implementation of WHCLIS Resolutions, gave a general report on the work of the Task Force, with emphasis on participation and networking, and (in answer to one question from the floor) took a position against the attempt of Senator Hayakawa (R-CA), to establish, by constitutional amendment, English as the official language of the United States. (We also oppose this amendment.) We commuted home before going on to the Canadian and American panels on multi-lingualism, and also missed Sen. Hayakawa's speech to the first ALA membership meeting that evening. Commuting does have its handicaps, but you don't get overloaded with conference input, either.

We didn't get back until Monday afternoon, and then we attended part of the SRRT program, their major public program, on the Ku Klux Klan. The principal speaker was Lucas Daumont, spokesman for the National Anti-Klan Network, who gave a vigorous statement on the activities of the Klan as of 1981. He described it as a sophisticated political organization with middle-class members; indicated that the largest Klan outside the South is in California; described the Klan training camps, with their social and cultural activities for families; and added that this paramilitary group now admits Catholics, in order to assist anti-busing groups in South Boston and elsewhere. Daumont also described the "sympathetic ally" method whereby the Klan infiltrates conservative protest groups, offering them the Klan's mailing lists and phone network, and the way that the Klan invades high schools by isolating "wannabees" (whites who appear sympathetic to Third World people, as in, "I wannabee one of them"), before attacking the Third World people themselves. The speech was convincing, and we had to duck out of the Jack Tar Hotel and out on an errand, before we could hear the other speakers.

A friend told us that the other speakers included Ann Ginger, an attorney from the Meiklejohn Civil Liberties Institute in Oakland, who emphasized the importance of showing both sides of the question—as, presumably, they do at Meiklejohn; and a Mr. McGee of CalTrans, the California Department of Transportation, who urged research of the literature, and pointed out the need for subject headings to cover all forms of religious as well as racial violence. When we got back we found questions and answers in full swing, including a Maoist speaker from Liberation Distributors, whose question was more in the nature of a plug. The answers to several questions pointed up the influence of the Klan in the military, as well as among retired military personnel; described the incident in which a North Carolina library was obliged (or felt itself obliged) to admit a Klan meeting to its conference rooms; and emphasized the necessity of self-defense and of mass confrontations, in which a huge number of people would say to any proposed Klan meeting, "No way!" This mass-based multi-racial protest was alleged to have worked in the sixties, and is for many the only sure defense now.

A short business meeting followed, with only a score of people in attendance, in which a long-debated new constitution was passed for the SRRT.

In addition, the group agreed that the draft agreement between ALA and its divisions, must be printed in full in the ALA *Bulletin* with both pros and cons, as the Round Tables are not content with the agreement as presently drafted.

The next morning (Tuesday, 30 June) we dropped in on the SRRT Action Council, where a budget of over $15,000 was approved. The SRRT newsletter was to be put out from the ALA headquarters, and there was a discussion of the leadership of the newsletter. While we were there, an anti-Klan resolution was to be issued as Membership Document No. 10, while action protesting Sen. Hayakawa's presence at ALA was deferred. The Council also discussed the ALA Office of Intellectual Freedom Newsletter, with questions regarding its effectiveness in discussing SRRT concerns, and decided to defer any action regarding it, as it was wisely agreed that the OIF performs a function which, while sometimes at odds with SRRT activism, nevertheless has a value in and of itself.

In the afternoon, the SRRT Tools for Consciousness-raising Task Force held a meeting on the "Impact of multi-nationals on children's book publishing," presided over by Bradford Chambers, head of the Council on Interracial Books for Children; the keynote speaker was Kirsten Stjedarn of Sweden, who demonstrated the invention and triumph of the multi-national book, in which the pictures are all the same and the text can be anything that sells: Swedish, English, Japanese or Hausa; the figures become blank, rather like the faces you see in airports, and the resulting cost-effective co-publishing represents the world publication of slick picture books, spreading international mediocrity and a conventional view of life. National production, especially in Third World countries, of local authors is thereby inhibited, and the slides (which oddly enough did not include the work of Dick Bruna, who was criticized a while back in the London *Times Literary Supplement* for almost this very reason) amply documented Fru Stjedarn's statements. Most impressive was the reaction of the children as she reported it; as soon as the children were made aware of the deception practiced on them, by being shown the same book in various languages, they turned against the characters depicted in the books: "They must be Norwegians, they're doing such stupid things," etc. Sheila Harty, author of *Hucksters in the Classroom,* began a speech describing the legal side of the problem . . . but again we headed for home, and this wound up our ALA conference-going. So soon? Why? The answer appears in the next section: we had *another* conference to go to.

COSMEP, the Committee of Small Magazine Editors and Publishers, held its first meeting on the West Coast since 1978 and its first meeting in California since 1975 (see our v. 7, no. 1, January 1976). This meeting was held in San Francisco's Fort Mason, the old Army post whence thousands of GIs sailed for the Pacific Theatre and later Korea. Some of them saw their last of America right here; for us, while we're glad that Fort Mason is now a cultural center (the home of Greenpeace and similar organizations), the place will always be full of ghosts. In reality, however, the room upstairs in Building E was full of hard chairs and gentle people, and the tone of the meeting had changed greatly from the earlier conferences. The non-literary presses (see right) predominated overwhelmingly; the vast majority of the persons present (according to the statistics taken by Joseph Bruchac of *Greenfield Review* at an opening session) represented the small publishers of how-to

books—legal books, pet books, genealogy publications, etc. The poets and writers of earlier days had disappeared—whither? That was the question of the conference.

A COSMEP conference is now almost entirely a how-to-do-it nonstop workshop, as it was before; the writers' conferences run by Bill Wilkins of *Nitty-Gritty* have been discontinued. To come from a librarians' conference to a COSMEP conference is to move from the First World to the Third, from rich buyers to poor sellers, from vast halls and busy booths to small rooms and little tables of eccentric literature, put there by hopeful people. In general, however, personal battles and institutional politics aside, we'd rather be at a COSMEP conference than an ALA conference, if only because you get to know people faster.

We chaired an opening meeting on how to sell to libraries, with Judy McDermott of the Cataloging in Publication (CIP) program at the Library of Congress, John C. Frantz of the San Francisco Public Library, and Loris Essary of *Interstate* (Austin, Texas; Essary is the present chair of COSMEP). McDermott explained carefully and well the resources of LC available to small press publishers, Frantz emphasized an upcoming Book Festival at SFPL (16-19 April 1982), and Loris Essary, who worked for some years as a library assistant at the University of Texas, summed things up from the underside position. We explained the ways by which small publishers can attract the favorable attention of academic librarians. In a later session that afternoon, 3 July, Richard Cleland of the Association of American Publishers described its work in the intellectual freedom arena (while we helped fetch some wine for a tasting session later), and when we came back, Dan Poynter of Para Publications, Santa Barbara (see our v. 11, no. 1), was describing work with direct mail, Diane Leahy of the San Francisco *Chronicle* described the book review gig, and Nan Hohenstein described book publicists and what they do—we had a clear impression that they are for the very wealthiest presses only, those who have a sure-fire (usually non-literary) title to sell.

The wine tasting fortunately followed the dinner, else we would have been too *besoffen* (after an excellent seafood dinner at Scott's with a carafe of white wine) to perform at the poetry reading. As it was, there were some seventeen different poets reading, all taped for a Channel 25 series by Todd S.J. Lawson, of San Francisco Arts and Letters Foundation, who has developed a program called "Lawson and Arts" to videotape such readings and interviews as come his way. Joseph Bruchac and Susan Bright were among the best performers, but the star of the show was A.D. Winans who read aloud, at some length, with bottle in hand—Courvoisier, apparently, the brandy of Napoleon.

We stayed overnight (at great expense) to attend the meetings which kept right on through the Fourth of July (business as usual for this crowd!). Denise Kastan, of the distribution service Small Press Traffic, described her work: attention to bookstores, reading series, foundation support. She handles only literary books, at 40% consignment, six copies at a time. Terry Nemeth, of Bookpeople, described that distributor's involvement with 600 presses plus 230 trade houses, and invited us to understand the problems of a distributor, methods of packaging and the personal approach. Susan Bright, of Texas Circuit, described her work with distribution in Texas; this outfit is apparently also including some out-of-state presses. She was the one who raised, and endeavoured to answer, the question: where have all the authors gone? Meaning, of course, the literary presses and their authors, who founded COSMEP and at one time dominated it. Her answer tallied with our experience: into audio-video on the one hand, and into fine printing on the other. Lawson's program of last night is an example of the one, and our own experience with a Kelsey press the other. The most likely explanation—ours, not hers—is that publishing in magazines and books is so chancy, given the lack of support for publication, and the huge number of competing entrants, that many authors have gone back to self-publication, some by the newest of media, some by the oldest.

A meeting on book fairs followed, with Karen Gottstein and Leigh Davidson of International Periodicals Service, on exhibits; Joseph Bruchac on the principal virtue of author's self-promotion (= start small); and Loris Essary, on economy of scale, together with an account of his experiences in a COSMEP booth. All agreed that we are, in the words of a report from the Coordinating Council of Literary Magazines, "more than a gathering of dreamers." Our own experience staffing the booth at ALA made it plain that how-to books and literary books sat uneasily together in the same booth, and certainly in the same catalog; librarians taking home such a catalog end up being nonplussed as to what to look for first. Some sort of division has to occur; if only to make it plain that there are two different kinds of publishers.

The last panel we had patience for was one on money, which resolved itself into a panel on how to find such financial breaks as might still be available from the Federal government. Ruth Gottstein of New Glide Publications (soon to change its name to Volcano Press) spoke on the restriction of small business loans, still denied to "opinion molders," including publishers. Phyllis Ball of the Association of American Publishers told far too little about the fate of the National Endowment for the Arts, whose budget for 1981-82 is to be cut from $150 million down to $80 million. The NEA, target of much controversy, will have even less to assign to publications under the Reagan administration. The legislation arising out of the Thor Power Tool Co. case, S.578, introduced on 26 February by Sen. Moynihan (D-NY) to relieve taxes affecting publishers and other businesses arising out of unsold inventory, did not win her confidence. As for postal rates, she reported that the library subsidy was being phased out, and she of course assumed a rise in the first-class rate. In addition, education and library funds were to be cut out of the Federal budget entirely, a deep cut in CETA funds was to be expected; block grants to states were to be given to replace these, in which it might be expected that competition for funds in the governments of the several states would result in the arts budgets being eliminated entirely in each state. Her mottoes for the eighties: keep your overhead low, mind your cash flow, share information, and continue to work with libraries.

Yet another wine tasting seemed in the offing; but we hurried home, sober if disappointed, in order to be in one piece, in order to give you this report. On our last drive down from the Great Central Valley to the cool blowy city of San Francisco, we found that we had carried a passenger, whose departure we celebrated as follows:

The moth,
having lived
under the folding back seat of the car,
all the way to San Francisco,

when the back seat was opened,
flew out.

My! Is this the other world?
Why is the air different?
O paradise! O dazzling light!
O! San Francisco!

REVIEWING small press publications is not too far from novel-reviewing, of which the late Cyril Connolly said, "it's like building bridges in an impossible tropical climate." In this case, you can go out and cope with the creepers, the vines of poems and manifestoes; or you can regard the small press publications themselves as the machetes and 'dozers, and see the climate which breeds commercial creepers as the source of what you're trying to cut through. No way, either way: words are being used to cut through words.

David Armstrong's book, *A Trumpet to Arms: Alternative Media in America* (Tarcher/Houghton Mifflin, 1981, $15) is a natural to send to us, as we have been discussing the alternative media, their rise and fall, for ten years ago. And it's a natural for Armstrong, who was editor of the *Berkeley Barb,* now editor of the *Syracuse New Times.* His column, "The American Journal," we quoted in our last issue as an epitaph for the *Barb.* Now he blows his trumpet, the title of which is a verse from the pen of Tom Paine, and unfortunately, it's all too short, while still delightful to hear—like many trumpet-calls. The 384 pages can barely give an overview of the founding of the *L.A. Free Press* (1964, first distributed at the Renaissance Faire there) to the present; seventeen years are a short epoch in the world's history, even in America's history; but whole dynasties of Babylonia can be reduced to a paragraph, while this period is absolutely jam-packed with fascinating and peculiar personalities. Weirds—articulate, intelligent, revolutionary, offset-press-wielding kooks—filled the period, and he thinks he can get them all into 384 pages? HAH! Anyway, Armstrong's survey is so briskly written, so full of personalities and anecdotes, that it belongs on the reference shelf of any inquiring librarian interested in the nation's publishing history. Like Estren's *History of Underground Comics* (see our v. 5, no. 2), it's a subject that everyone has been aware of, but that no one has done thoroughly before. We wish that we were in it, and more importantly, we wish that Armstrong had devoted more space to COSMEP, and more space to the radical or alternative papers in the professions, such as our own; but in any case, Armstrong had to finish his book, leave out huge areas of consciousness (the music, the posters) and get it done before he suffered the fate of the learned tortoise who was going to write a bio-bibliography of Achilles. Armstrong's work, in short, will be the standard work on alternative papers for some time to come. If we had to commend any part of it particularly, it would be the pages on the rivalry of the *Berkeley Barb* with the *Tribe.* As we followed it, the *Tribe* was hopelessly out of contact with reality, and he shows just how they drifted away. (By the way, we seem to remember Art Kunkin selling the first copies of the *L.A. Free Press* that day at the Renaissance Faire. It was August—and hot—and there was this weird little man—we steered clear of him—.)

The other major book of the season is Sanford Berman's long-awaited summary manifesto of manifestoes, *The Joy of Cataloging: Essays, Reviews and Other Explosions* (Oryx Press, 1981). This is a book for dipping into, not steady reading. Why not for steady reading? It's a sharp and tingling brew, that's why. Berman is a lifelong crusader against stupid insensitive cataloging, as he sees it, and this includes racially insensitive subject headings; and many of his chapters read like memos from the head cataloger—indeed, he starts many of the chapters just that way: "On (date), the head cataloger wrote N.N...." and then you know that N.N. is going to get it, double strength. For opening at random, however, Berman's new book is enlightening, well-documented, even funny. Turn to the list of subject headings for "Juvenilia," for example, and you will be refreshed at once by the brisk, common-sense-Americanese of Berman's selected subject headings. There, you may applaud Berman's SHOW-AND-TELL PRESENTATIONS, his USEFULNESS, even his SIZE AND SHAPE; or you may dislike his NOSINESS, OVER-ENTHUSIASM, BOASTS AND PRAISES, even his TEMPER TANTRUMS. But you have to admire his UNDERSTANDING (PERSONAL QUALITY), his DIGGING, and above all, his CLEVERNESS—which won him the Margaret Mann Citation mentioned above, thus putting him in the ranks of his most formidable critics. In the adult sphere, his article on "Cataloging Castaneda" is particularly fine, in pointing out that Castaneda's works should be classified under scheduled works for "paranormal/occult" (133.4 or BF 1563-1584), rather than under the numbers for Yaqui ethnography—on the ground that they are considered fiction by most anthropologists. (The following exchange of memos was recently reported in a large academic library: "I'm tired of Carlos Castaneda—I wish people would stop Yaquing about him." "Shaman you!") Berman's spoof of library research literature, "Megasucrose Levels and Manual Bibliographic Searching," is a delight for anyone who has fallen asleep over one of those papers in *Library Resources and Technical Services*.

The real test of Berman's book, however, is not sampling pages for teasers and outrages, but putting his principles to work in a real library, preferably a tiny library in which you have to do all the work. Special libraries of all kinds—storefront, church, non-profit organization libraries, are a great test for this, as you will find, working in any one of these, that the entire burden of acquisition, cataloging, and reference falls on you, an unpaid volunteer, without the benefit of OCLC, Mansell's pre-'56 whatchamacallit, or even a student to pester. Desert-island cataloging, then, will force you to simplify; your friends will expect you to work on principles they can understand; and you may have to abandon both Dewey and LC in order to develop a simple reader's classification that suits the situation and doesn't cost $40 or more to buy (reader's classifications are not discussed in this book). You will then be far better off if you have read Berman's books and articles and absorbed his lessons for librarians, than if you come into the situation with a lot of preconceived ideas from library schools or earlier experience in a more traditional library. You'll have to substitute DRAFT for CONSCRIPTION, invent a form subdivision—DEMONSTRATIONS, PROTESTS, RALLIES, ETC., to follow the name of the outrage being protested (*sa* VIGILS), and learn that the number of subject headings necessary to assign to a booklet should not be dependent on the length of the work in hand. (On the other hand, if you're typing every card, you may not feel free to make as many subject headings as Berman does with his on-line system at Hennepin County Library.) You'll prefer title entries where these seem the likeliest route of inquiry; where a corporate entry is the real author, you may wish to actually prefer title and make added entry for corporate. And finally, you won't be interested in the height of the book in cm.—unless you have an "Oversize" shelf—not likely; you won't have enough shelving as it is. This, then, is the perfect situation in which to study Berman's book; which is not to say that it hasn't wider applications. The Citation is proof enough of that.

These two books can be recommended without hesitation as central to that audience which we always imagined, here at *Sipapu,* was peculiarly ours: the socially aware, progressive librarian. A deeper probe by (perhaps) a different reader is necessary with Tom Clark's book, *The Great Naropa Poetry Wars* (Cadmus Editions, P.O. Box 4725, Santa Barbara, CA 93103, $5). We referred in our v. 11, no. 1, to Clark's short story, *The Master;* now this is the real story on which *The Master* was based, the public physical humiliation of the poet W.S. Merwin and his friend Dana at the Naropa Institute in Colorado, where Merwin was one of the teachers in a poetry workshop administered by a Tibetan Buddhist lama—who had surrounded himself with guards. The origin of the Tibetan Buddhist group is here related; its transfer to America, the rise of the group in Colorado, and its entry into the poetry scene; here Clark, a poet with several books to his credit, speaks not as an anti-Buddhist but rather as an historian of culture and power. When he comes to the incident involving Merwin and his companion, he is as objective as his outrage permits him to be. He describes the raid on the couple's bedroom, the guards, the forced undressing, the insults, the physical abuse, the watching lama, the passive audience; no one has contradicted him as to the veracity of his story, nor has anyone explained, any better than he can, why Merwin and Dana stayed at the place for three weeks afterwards, nor what the ultimate effects on them were. Obviously the couple aren't talking. What amazes us is that when Clark published an early account of the whole business and called for a poets' boycott of the whole Naropa Institute, all poets with any Buddhist connections—according to Clark—and admittedly we have only his side of the story—hesitated to comply with the boycott or sent him some kind of demur, while all poets from the Third World peoples in America immediately endorsed the boycott—perhaps because they had some previous acquaintance with public humiliation and violence. In any case, there ensued one of those acrimonious debates of the intelligentsia that remind one of the debates over Count Libri's thefts, or the Moscow trials. The question still remains, why did Merwin and Dana not leave immediately and give the local district attorney an account of the incident. For us, we would gladly boycott any such place; the idea of guards in a Buddhist poetry workshop is self-contradictory. But then many things among intellectuals are self-contradictory.

POETRY BOOKS: The major poetry event of the season was the reappearance of Bob Kaufman, whose small book, *The Ancient Rain,* was published by New Directions in 1981 ($4.95). It includes poems from 1956 to 1978, and the dates are significant, because Kaufman, one of the original Beat poets whose work excited admiration in the fifties in San Francisco, left that city for New York in 1960. According to the preface by Raymond Foye, "the New York years were filled with poverty, addiction, and imprisonment," although he did publish *Solitudes Crowded with Loneliness* (New Directions, 1965). In the meanwhile, however, Kaufman, in part prompted by the assassination of President Kennedy, took a vow of silence which lasted nearly ten years. This silence nevertheless did more for the author of *The Abomunist Manifesto* than the dozens of books that Beat and post-Beat poets published since, did for their authors. Out of the silence and the imprisonment Kaufman fashioned the one thing absolutely essential to poets, which few of them ever achieve: a voice. It is less strong in such poems as "Small memorial to myself" and "Lone Eagle," but strongest in "The American Sun" and *The Ancient Rain.* "Ancient Rain" is a concept of importance for Kaufman: it seems to signify divine justice, truth which acts in its own good time and exposes chauvinism and racism (Kaufman, born in New Orleans, is of mixed black and Jewish parentage). Kaufman sees the Ancient Rain falling on American history, on Presidential assassinations and on Crispus Attucks, punishing the Confederacy and judging the United Nations. Most political poems that drop historical notes and accuse personal enemies become unbearable—the capital letters of proper nouns litter the poem like fake broken columns in an old cemetery, but Kaufman is sufficiently distant from his subject so that *The Ancient Rain* does not just seem like the voice of one eccentric poet with an axe to grind—which is sometimes the case with Ginsberg and even Blake—but seems simply right: history's eventual judgment, as right as rain. Practically nothing has been heard about this book, even in the small press review media. We came upon it only by chance.

We missed National Nude Days, July 11-12, perhaps because we were too busy skinny-dipping ourselves to get this paper out on time. In any case, Jan Smith, of The Naturists, P.O. Box 132, Oshkosh, WI 54902, tells us that "mixed-sex skinny-dipping is as American as apple pie." Why this message is even necessary is a mystery only to those who live in rural America; the rest of you may find it necessary to take a long ride to Cape Cod to really enjoy yourselves. The headquarters of our own vast publishing empire are arcana, but if you want to know why we planted a 4-meter-high hedge of Arizona cypress, then you want to know more than is good for you. The Oshkosh group also publishes a new journal, entitled *Clothed with the Sun*. Be sure and ask for it before five p.m. local time, which is when the mosquitoes come out.

Finally, we're completely buffaloed by the arrival of some advertising for Three Mile Island Creamy Mushroom Dressing. You see, we have got on the list of the commercial organic food movement, although when we retire from this job we will probably open a goy delicatessen. On the other hand, we can't be sure whether this is a joke very expensive to the manufacturers, since they have come up with a real mushroom salad dressing, or simply an easy way to make bucks. Is this the Eastern equivalent of medfly jokes? Find out more by writing The Catalyst Company, 393 N. Euclid, Suite 203, St. Louis, MO 63108. And remember folks...

S P R E A D   T H E   W O R D !

12 : 2

The cover here, was adapted from a Christmas number of The Argonaut, *dated sometime back in the 1880s. You'll notice that the Indian maiden, who evidently represents the spirit of California, is looking out the Golden Gate and wondering, "Wait, what the hell happened to the goddam bridge?"*

The Argonaut, *whose masthead boasted that it was "read and quoted throughout the world," was still barely alive when I came to San Francisco in the late fifties. By that time the paper from which Ambrose Bierce, who had been the editor, had banned the phrase "honest miner," because there was (in his view) no such person, had become fearfully dull. Indeed, the issue I borrowed to have the cover copied was thoroughly bourgeois and conservative, although the vista of a leafy, dreamy, California of a hundred years ago seems paradise now. That was when Oakland was noted for its great groves of liveoaks. Really.*

I have omitted Ellen Ferber's interview from the anthology because she has radically changed her life: she was Len Fulton's assistant editor at Dustbooks and has left him to continue her teaching at Chico State University.

I subsequently got on the Librarians and Publishers Committee (now the Librarians', Publishers', and Vendors' Committee); and Frank Goodall got off. The LPV is now very much concerned with getting librarians to visit the exhibits.

SIPAPU

v. 12, no. 2

a passage between two worlds

consecutive issue number twenty-four

a newsletter for librarians.

MEMBER
COSMEP
COMMITTEE OF SMALL MAGAZINE
EDITORS AND PUBLISHERS
BOX 703 SAN FRANCISCO CA 94101

THE CALIFORNIA LIBRARY ASSOCIATION went back to the San Francisco Hilton in December 1981, back to the Continental Parlors and Continental Ballroom, and at least they had changed the carpets: instead of the shield-boss in red and blue they had a swirled acanthus pattern in brown and gold. The Librarians and Publishers Committee, meeting on Monday, 14 December 1981, had us staring at the new carpet pattern in some distress, however; the moderator, Frank Goodall, discussed ex-

pansions with glee, dismissed the small publisher as dead, and then made room for William F. Adams, manager of western book sales for the Lakeside Press, R.R. Donnelly and Sons, Chicago. His presentation was a set of slides on the Donnelly operations; it was the kind of show that might be given to a newcomer to the firm. (The Lakeside Press was one of the fine old imprints of the late nineteenth and early twentieth century.) Those who lingered for questions told us that the answers were more interesting than the presentation itself, but we felt that showing company literature in audio-visual form was not what we had expected from a lecture entitled, "The book planning process — production from manuscript to the finished product." At all events, the lack of small press representation on the CLA Committee for Librarians and Publishers is a grave omission, more embarrassing with every passing year.

The committee on which we have the honor to serve, Intellectual Freedom, discussed coalitions for this cause; after a slide show from public television, Fontayne Holmes of Los Angeles, outgoing chair, gave a state-of-the-art review, and a number of speakers described coalition-building among interested groups (such as the ACLU) and others, in their areas, to serve the cause of intellectual freedom. The Coalition for the Right to Know, a Northern California group, was described by Lynn Smith and Esther Helfand; the former has connections with the Unitarians. Ray Nelson, of El Cerrito, president of the California Writers' Club (founded by Jack London; their logo is Columbus's ship), was among the more interesting speakers. The general theme was the necessity of finding friends in a hostile environment, drawing around the wagons and protecting liberty.

This, basically, was our encounter with CLA. As time passes, we get less and less interested in speeches and motions; our resolution wilts as the number of resolutions rises, and on leaving the precincts of the Hilton, we soon forget the political arguments in its chambers. The Continental Parlors are now doubtless occupied by toothbrush salesmen, but the white herons are still out there in the estuary of the Napa River, to be seen on the way home.

Through the kindness of Sanford Berman of Hennepin County Library, Edina Minnesota, we were provided with the documents and reports of the **MID-CONTINENT FORUM FOR THE FUTURE OF LITERATURE,** held 3–5 October at the University of Minnesota, Minneapolis. The theme was "Paper is free," which is not exactly true if you are a printer, but then even this group, sponsored by a number of small press distributors plus the Coordinating Council of Literary Magazines and some local cultural institutions, is part of our consumer society. The idea for this conference arose out of a Great Midwestern Bookshow, and it was principally concerned with government and private funding for literature, budget cuts, and the market for intelligent reading material.

A general compendium of statements resulted from individual conferences, but most of the task forces were there to defend the small press and the "Redskins" against the establishment publishers and the "Palefaces" in American literature. Some of the reports were vital, some too familiar, and others reminded one of the fellow who proposed to march through the Pearly Gates bearing the device: "Head of 57 Committees." Among the best were: Mark Vinz, retiring editor of *Dacotah Territory,* who spoke on "The business of poetry" ("There comes a point in the life of any editor when he's reading *careers,* not poems.") Much of the librarians' forum, though overly long, gained from the work of Sanford Berman, who here, as elsewhere, bolstered his remarks and accusations with footnotes. This paper was reproduced in the educators' section, where we also found Charles Alexander, writing on "Publishing some light, or notes in the silence," in which academic poetry and the tradition of Eliot and Auden is given its come-uppance in favor of Blake, Whitman, Zukofsky, Pound, and Stein. This rather predictable assault (after all, if the Redskins have experiences, the Palefaces have ideas) was followed by the Service Organizations' corner, in which Susan Grieger described "The Loft," a bookstore serving literature and the arts, plus Grady Hillman's projection of a mid-continent circuit for poetry performance. The Publishers spoke up through Paul Feroe, of Ally Press, "Refusing government support for publishing," in which Feroe took a long-needed swipe at the great grant mystique, and Arnold Perrin, of Wings Press, echoed him: "I say, let the government grants dry up! It's time for editors to bring the marketplace of ideas to the marketplace." C.W. Truesdale, of New Rivers Press took a different view: "On being in the minor leagues for fourteen years," protesting, "What the writer-as-publisher learns very quickly is that he must function in a world in which his values and interests are ridiculous if not insane." Diane Kruchkow, of *Zahir* and *Stony Hills,* now living in Maine, pointed out the dangers of government censorship in "The literary anti-establishment, rising."

But by far and away the best contribution, at least in its applicability to librarians, was by Joseph Richardson, of Plains Distribution Service, which has now closed its operations. Signing himself "not a writer, editor, or publisher," Richardson offered in "Notes on Plains Distribution Service, funding for literary activities, and promotion," some home truths about libraries and about distribution through arts agencies, college campuses, etc. His account of the sad reception that Plains poetry books had at the state conferences of the Library Associations of North and South Dakota is sad enough, but what is one to make of the librarian at ALA Detroit who asked if "it wouldn't be wonderful if all the writing in the world could be placed in one book?" From here on the Coast, we can't imagine what she meant, but "of course," says Richardson, "she never thought that if her dream came true she would be out of a job." The situation at Grand Rapids, Minnesota, was even more disgraceful: "For two days, the Plains Bookbus was sitting outside the Grand Rapids Public Library—tied by a power cord into the building. On the first day, shortly after arriving, I introduced myself to the Director of the library and invited her to tour the bus. She told me that she would try to make it out to the bus later. She would also advise other members of her staff to visit the bus. For two days the poet and author we had sponsored gave workshops in the library. For two days the only librarian we saw in the bus was the children's librarian. Other than a couple of children's poetry books, we were unable to sell books to the library."

Richardson also gives examples of comments received at ALA Detroit and state conferences:

"Oh, I see you have poetry. Well, we don't have too much call for that sort of thing." "It costs too much to keep these little books. We have to catalog them, send them off to the bindery, and they are always getting stolen. They don't fit our shelves, they are just too fragile."

(Editor's *obiter dictum:* if there's no call for them, why is that they are always getting stolen? But to pursue):

"Oh, there are just so many of these titles. It is too difficult to discover which are the good ones—no one on our staff reads poetry." Adds Richardson: "Who on their staff, selects history, biography, romance, and westerns?"

Editor again: We have on our own account and with the assistance of COSMEP West—Western Independent Publishers, distributed poetry broadsides to roughly 700 high school libraries and public libraries, in rural communities—*free*. The answer seems to be that librarians will pick up poetry if it is free, but they'll be damned before they'll pay a dollar for it.

To return: "We are applying for a grant to buy this sort of thing. If we receive the grant, we'll keep you in mind." As Richardson rightly observes,

"The dependency on the grant program relieves them of the responsibility of buying their own."

To get away from this mess, Richardson has a number of suggestions: a state-level review of small presses; poets on the platforms of state library conferences; literary round tables at conferences also; poetry readings in the libraries ("have a dinner for the guest poet before the reading and invite local dignitaries"—by all means, yes; did you expect that poets can recite on a cup of instant coffee?); and, waive the table fee for small presses wishing to exhibit at state, regional, and national conferences. As Richardson observes, with well-directed tartness, "We simply do not have the money to bribe those attending library conventions with suites filled with shrimp, wine, and famous personalities."

Discouraged with public libraries, Richardson tried the schools: "At high schools, we were used as a twenty minute circus act for every class imaginable. We would give a short talk and then the class would come through the bus in a horde. Those who really wished to spend time in the bus were few and seldom granted the opportunity because of scheduling or 'campus regulations.' Rarely were we able to sell books to high school students."

So on to the universities and state colleges: "Almost a cliché at 'institutions of higher learning' is the fact that only two or three members of a twenty-member department will show up at poetry readings . . . There we were, parked on the Moorhead State University campus (western Minnesota, just across the Red River from Fargo, ND–Ed.) for a full day. Notices of our being on campus had been placed in every English department mail box. One old soldier from the department showed up—Mark Vinz, co-founder and President of Plains. The same happened at Bismarck, Hibbing, Bimidji, Cedar Rapids, and many more places."

After giving several possible explanations—professional jealousy from failed writers in the departments, packaging and place of imprint ("The myth that perfect-bound and printed in New York must be better than saddle-stitched in Minneapolis is alive") and a hostility to the new and difficult

("Poetry is of little use and difficult to teach"), — Richardson goes on to his one glorious triumph, — an old college of mines founded in 1885 on the Keewenaw Peninsula:

"The all time great campus was Michigan Technological University at Houghton. They have a very small English department stuck away between the campus nuclear reactor and one of the country's best metallurgical laboratories. Many of their students are card carrying members of scientific societies by the time they reach their senior year. An author's reputation means little to them. Robert Bly read for three hours to an audience of 300 students and teachers. William Kloefkorn read for an hour to 600. Mark Vinz almost died and went to heaven on the spot when he read to an absolutely packed room of around 350 people. MTU at Houghton is absolutely the most receptive campus Plains ever set foot, or tire, on. So many in the audience even remember poems — two years later!" Richardson gives a number of possible reasons for this amazing acceptance, of which the one we most find convincing, is that "their intensive scientific studies leave a vacuum which is filled, in part, by poetry." However, bureaucracy always has the last word. "When we tried to obtain financial backing from the Michigan Arts Council to work more in the Upper Peninsula, they referred us to the person in charge of high school programs for the state." Exit the Plains Bookbus.

The whole of Richardson's fascinating report goes on for 23 pages, but we have excerpted only that portion of it which deals with libraries. Without having driven a bus ourselves, our own comment must be limited to a general impression that when culture becomes professionalized, the professionals lose interest in culture. That is to say: when there are large English departments, or tightly controlled libraries, they tend to exclude potentially threatening figures like poets; when, however, poetry is rarely met with and the culture vulture is a *rara avis*, the art of verse is better appreciated. If this sweeping generality is at all true, then it would be advisable not to overdo it at Houghton. But then all sweeping generalities sweep too broadly, anyway.

13 : 1

For this 25th consecutive issue of Sipapu, *we were actually bidden to go to the Conference on the San Francisco Renaissance by our boss, the late (and lamented) Nelson Piper. We remember the pouring rain and the excellent seafood restaurants of San Diego. A later result of the trip was a visit to the Davis campus of Michael McClure, a most charming person, whose poetry became easier to understand once he read it. McClure is, of course, a master at reading. He has a soft, expressive voice.*

Michael Davidson transferred to the UCSD English Department, and his successor, Stephen Rodefer, a "language poet" (if we can be forgiven for labelling poets), left the campus somewhat abruptly after two years there. The present curator of the Archive for New Poetry is John Granger.

Dennis Brutus has finally been allowed to stay in this country. The peace movement at Winters is presently inactive.

WE'RE STARTING OUT WITH A CONFERENCE this time, because it leads directly into our interview. The CONFERENCE ON THE SAN FRANCISCO RENAISSANCE took place not in San Francisco, but at the University of California, San Diego, and the reason for this was that the Archive for New Poetry (of which more later) had just bought the files of the late Lew Welch, a poet who died (presumably) in 1971, and was a close friend of the San Francisco poets who appeared at the conference — Gary Snyder, Michael McClure, and others. To San Diego, therefore, we hastened, nay, flew, at the insistence and with the assistance of the Library at UC Davis, missing the first flight but coming in for most of the day's session.

Finding where the conference was turned out to be something of a problem. The UCSD campus sprawls over several hills, and there were no signs to guide us in the rain. The UCSD Library helped us locate the building, which was in the Center for Music Experiment. Once we were parked and settled, we found a very unconventional atmosphere. In the first place, when this site was a military base, long ago, this building had been a bowling alley. With the coming of the University, the space was converted into a Center for

Music Experiment, which obliged it to become a music studio. Two rooms at the back held the tapes, while in front of these rooms, but behind the panelists' table, was a fascinating collection of musical instruments old and new, of which the most interesting—to us—was a Chinese drum, about a foot wide and four inches thick, which gave a low D, with several overtones, every time it was struck. Curiously enough, the speakers, many of whom claimed an interest in jazz and Eastern art, never touched these instruments during the conference (except Gary Snyder, who showed us how to make a rattling percussion noise with a stick and the studs on the rim of the drum).

The panel that we missed included Marjorie Perloff, from UCLA, Albert Gelpi, Ron Loewinsohn and James Breslin, and was chaired by David Antin, author of *Code of Flag Behavior,* a professor of Visual Arts at UCSD. Evidently this was the panel not to miss, as Marjorie Perloff, having done only part of her homework, allegedly declared that the San Francisco Renaissance poets were a bunch of self-indulgent beatniks who had never read Milton. Allusions to this dispute crackled through the rainy afternoon air and continued throughout the conference.

The afternoon panel included Robert Duncan, Michael McClure, and David Meltzer, and was introduced by Michael Davidson. Davidson is the curator of the Archive for New Poetry at UCSD. The subject of this panel was "The various arts of the S.F. Renaissance," and it was plain that all of these people had been involved with some art besides poetry; Meltzer had read poetry to jazz (nearly everyone in the S.F. Renaissance was an early student of jazz); he remarked that Kenneth Rexroth's readings to jazz were not of poems written for this purpose, and so these did not harmonize with the jazz, while Meltzer's poems were designed to fit the music. Michael McClure had been involved in assemblage painting, and indeed started out as a painter when he arrived in San Francisco in 1956. Robert Duncan was involved with the theatre, and assisted at the first production of George Hitchcock's *Faust* (subsequently published as *The Devil Comes to Wittenberg;* cf. *Sipapu,* v. 11, no. 2). Duncan proved to be a non-stop maker of epigrams ("You don't believe in God? Then what kind of a God don't you believe in?") and reminiscences of anyone and everyone in the poetry scene, which he could well express, since he was born in 1919.

The evening readings were by Duncan and William Everson (Brother Antoninus). Everson, whose seventieth birthday is this September, is now almost unrecognizable to those who knew him in earlier years, as he now has long white locks and a spreading white beard, which gives him the appearance of a tree-spirit; the man's mortal nature, however, was shown by the almost incessant trembling of one hand and side, which he himself attributed to Parkinson's disease. Nevertheless, although Everson had to stop sometimes when overcome by emotion or searching for the right thought, he showed that his mind was as keen as ever. We were glad that we had the foresight to give him a ride back to his hotel—otherwise he and his friend would have had to spend the night on the UCSD hilltop!

The morning panel on 10 February was devoted to Lew Welch, whose papers have just been acquired by the Archive for New Poetry. In celebration of this event, the present conference was originally designed to be a Lew Welch Conference, but expanded as it went on. Dan McLeod, of CSU/San Diego, chaired this panel, which included Gary Snyder, David Meltzer, and Michael McClure. McLeod gave a short life of Lew Welch, from his birth in Phoenix, Arizona, 16 August 1926, to his disappearance from the vicinity of Gary Snyder's home in Nevada County in 1971. Gary Snyder described Welch's work as a teacher and student, emphasizing his linguistic studies and his "creative hedonism," by which Snyder apparently meant the open and relaxed approach Welch had to writing; what Snyder called his "shamelessness." McClure read passages from Gertrude Stein and Lew Welch and demonstrated their relationship, while also attributing some of Welch's style to his friend and poet Kirby Doyle. Meltzer also described Welch as teacher, stressing his purity and devotion to the art of poetry. For Welch, as for Meltzer, writing consisted of two things: listening to the tribe, and having something to talk about. He read passages from Welch's book, *Ring of Bone,* and explained them.

The afternoon panel was devoted to "California—place and proposition" and was introduced by Donald Wesling (UCSD). Robert Duncan described his own fourth-generation California background; his family had lived in northern California (Modoc County) for many years, but he was born in Oakland. The Duncans had also become involved with the theosophist movement (one of his poems is called "Ominous in Ojai"). William Everson described how hard it is to talk about California when you're in it, as it would be hard to get a fish to describe water; mentioned his own association with Robinson Jeffers; and finished by describing the west as the home of creativity and the east as the home of recognition.

Gary Snyder compared early to late Chinese nature poetry; the first was by local poets writing about simple things, the later by bureaucrats writing about majestic landscapes. He described the California we have lost, the vast waterfowl marshes of the Great Central Valley, by way of example. Snyder's emphasis was on bio-regions as a foundation for poetry.

Todd Gitlin described his origins in the Jewish radical tradition in California, and his early involvement with radical labor activity. Donald Wesling, UCSD, concluded the panel by describing various myths current about California.

The poetry reading that evening was by David Meltzer and Gary Snyder. It was a pleasure, here as elsewhere, to be in the hands of poets who knew whereof they spoke, and in addition, knew how to speak. Subjected (as we have been) to rantings and ravings, the soft, eloquent, instructed voice has our total allegiance.

The morning panel on 11 February was on "Postwar politics and community." Jerome Rothenburg (UCSD) gave his recollections of the fifties; Michael McClure described the anarchist circles in 1954–1960 which formed the earliest audiences of Beat poets. He alluded to the earliest reading of Ginsberg's "Howl" in December 1955 to these young workers (there seems to be some dispute as to the actual date of this incident). He read from his poem, "Listen, Lawrence," a reply to Ferlinghetti's "Populist manifesto," — announcing "Politics is dead, biology is here." He also read from his new book of essays, *Scratching the Beat Surface.*

Todd Gitlin, UCSD, described the present as a rumor of the past, and the sixties as having been subject, too, to the same rumor; i.e., much of what happened culturally to people during the sixties, was based on what young people had heard about the San Francisco Scene in the late fifties. He described the continuing tension between individualism and community in American life and letters, pointing out that communities were based on exclusion as well as inclusion.

William Everson described his days in the conscientious objectors' camp at Waldport, Oregon, where he had some contacts with anarchists; there was a noticeable difference between the old atheistic anarchists and the new religious ones. He told an amusing story of his break with Kenneth Rexroth over his first wife; also he described the visit of the British critic Cyril Connolly to San Francisco. (For Connolly's all-too-brief summary of his visit to Beat California, see his last book, *Previous Convictions*.) Everson emphasized that the first major publication of the S.F. Renaissance writers, *Evergreen Review,* issue no. 2, pointed to a community that did not have in fact, the validity that it appeared to possess.

Bennett Berger, a sociologist formerly at UCD and now at UCSD, described his Berkeley years as a graduate student during the period under discussion. He denied that his was the "silent generation," stated his position within the Jewish radical tradition, and denounced the kind of history written to suit radical stereotypes devised by the media. He differenced cultural radicalism from political radicalism, suggesting that they rarely come together; but, when they do, the result is something like the San Francisco Renaissance.

The afternoon panel tried to place the S.F. Renaissance in American literary history; the speakers, this time, were all critics. Roy Harvey Pearce (UCSD) described the role of the academy as conservator, but also described his own life when Jack Spicer was one of his students: a fascinating eccentric Spicer turned out to be. Fred Moramarco described the problems faced by those who come after a generation of great writers; in this case, the writers are still living. Quoting Philip Whalen's description of San Francisco at that time: "O noble and yummy beast!"—he alluded to the first reading of "Howl" (giving it the date of 13 October 1955). And finally he described the writers which the San Francisco poets rejected and revolted against: John Crowe Ransom, the poets around the *Kenyon Review.*

Ron Loewinsohn described the role of marginality in American literature, the writer's role in giving the solitary reader freedom from the loony bin or the jail. He also described the difference in poetry readings; before Allen Ginsberg, the audience was passive, as at a classical music concert; now the audience is participant, as in jazz. Marjorie Perloff described the movement in terms of its primitivism, its projective verse (projective as a jazz performer projects outwards with his instrument, leaning into it and toward the audience), along with its interest in what she styled the pre-Raphaelite and occult. She made the point that in spite of what Duncan himself had said, there were serious differences between the two approaches of Pound and Duncan to poetry (Duncan had by that time left the conference).

James E. Breslin described three generations of American poets: the earlier modernists (Pound, Eliot), the middle generation, and the San Francisco Renaissance group. He also described very vividly the situation young poets found in the fifties: with Pound, Eliot, Williams, Frost, and some others it appeared that there was no more work to do; these titans loomed over every writer's shoulder. The middle generation (Roethke, Lowell, Merwin, Snodgrass) offered no clear model to oppose to the modernists, and so poetry became a model of academic experiments. Scrupulosity and perfectionism inhibited the writers of the period. Now the S.F. poets, who revolted against that, are themselves the successful revolutionaries, just as the moderns first were; although William Carlos Williams wrote an introduction to "Howl," he was never really comfortable with Ginsberg and his contemporaries.

Albert Gelpi was fated to sum-up this summing-up; the last in a panel of critics. For him the S.F. Renaissance poem points to a world which is more than the sum of its parts. He made a distinction, originally Pound's, between perceptual and conceptual artists: the S.F. poets were perceptual and Pound, who had started out conceptual came to his perceptual period at last, while William Carlos Williams remained modernist and conceptual. Both kinds of artists are still with us.

Gelpi also repeated Denise Levertov's distinction between organic form vs. aesthetic form, in poetry, as apart from free verse; the S.F. poets had a form, but not just free verse.

The last evening's reading of poetry consisted of: Ron Loewinsohn and Michael McClure; but we were obliged to catch the last flight that night back to Sacramento. This reading, like all the day sessions, took place in the Center for Music Experiment.

THE ARCHIVE FOR NEW POETRY at the University of California, San Diego, represents an attempt to collect all poetry written in the English language since World War II. Located in the Central University Library's Mandeville Department of Special Collections, the archive has developed extensive holdings in rare and limited edition monographs, little magazines, broadsides, phono-tapes, records and ephemera. In addition to these materials, the archive has collected seven single-author files: the Marianne Moore Collection, the Paul Blackburn Archive, the Clayton Eshleman—Cesar Vallejo file, the Lew Welch Archive, and the Joanne Kyger correspondence file; and most recently, the Charles Reznikoff Archive.

The originator of this project is Roy Harvey Pearce, a professor in the UCSD Literature Dept., who began working with the Library's Acquisitions Dept. ten years ago, collecting little magazines, small and fine edition monographs, poetry broadsides, etc. from the postwar era. His scholarship increased as the collection expanded, and he is now an important scholar in the field of 20th century American poetry, while the Archive is one of the largest such collections in the country.

The Archive's main function is to collect the publications of small presses throughout the English-speaking world. The emphasis seems to be on American presses, as among the ones named are Black Sparrow, Capra, Cranium, Oyez, Shameless Hussy; there are some English ones as well. Serials are well represented: the Archive claims complete sets of *Black Mountain Review, Caterpillar, The Fifties, Floating Bear, Open Space,* and (we believe) *Sipapu.* (If they don't have it, they can buy the first eight volumes on microfilm, and so can you, dear reader; drop us a line.)

The archival quality of the Archive, however, rests in its unique collections of a single author, including correspondence, published works with corrections and emendations in the poet's hand, newspaper cutouts, posters, drawings, notebooks, and memorabilia. Authors represented include Marianne Moore (published material only, but with corrections); Ken Friedman, artist and poet, chronicling the "Fluxus" movement; Paul Blackburn, major poet, tape-recorder of the works of others—with his tapes; Eshleman's translations of Cesar Vallejo, manuscripts and books; and the files of Lew Welch. Welch, around whom this conference was originally planned, disappeared from the hill country near Gary Snyder's house, leaving a note which ended "gone Southwest." He has not been seen since 1971, and is presumed dead, to the extent that poets die at all. Welch figures as a major character in Jack Kerouac's novel, *Big Sur,* and was a friend of Gary Snyder, Charles Olson, Marianne Moore, Kirby Doyle, and others. The *Selected Letters* are being brought out by Grey Fox Press; his collection of poems appeared under the title *Ring of Bone;* his essays and criticism as *How I Work as a Poet.*

Other recent archives include those of Joanne Kyger, former wife of Gary Snyder, and Charles Reznikoff, the Jewish lawyer-poet who was associated with the Objectivist movement. Donald Allen, publisher of the Grey Fox Press, published under an earlier imprint (Four Seasons) many of the San Francisco Renaissance figures for the first time; his correspondence, manuscripts, corrected proofs and reviews are here in the Archive.

A major portion of the Archive's activities is the poetry reading series on Wednesday afternoons in the Revelle Formal Lounge. During the past years, the series has featured John Ashbery, Robert Creeley, Adrienne Rich, David Antin, and others. Of course the readings are taped and the tapes preserved for re-hearing, and of course the readings are free and anyone can use the tapes in the Library. The Archive also publishes a quarterly *Archive Newsletter,* which includes news of events around town, a calendar of readings, art activities, etc.

Anyone interested in the Archive for New Poetry should contact its curator, John Granger, Special Collections Dept., Central University Library, UCSD, La Jolla, CA 92093.

The Poet and the Muses

MICHAEL DAVIDSON, HIMSELF, curator or director of the Archive for New Poetry, editor of its *Newsletter,* also of *Documents for New Poetry* (a pamphlet series—see p. 294), and Associate Professor of Literature at UCSD, is a tall slender man with blond hair and blue eyes, very quick on his feet and soft-spoken. Born in Oakland, CA, in 1944, he got a B.A. in English from San Francisco State University, a Ph.D. from State University of New York, Buffalo, and was a post-doctoral fellow at UCSD until 1975, when he accepted his current appointment. He has seven poetry books out, a flock of papers, and is also co-editor of *Credences* (SUNY Buffalo). All this we gleaned by doing out homework, chiefly in the reference book *Contemporary Poets.* Now we talk to the poet himself:

SIPAPU: The question now arises: when did you first perceive your calling as one of the poets of the English language? Or did you start (metaphorically speaking) from some other place and come "here"?

DAVIDSON: I have trouble locating exactly where or when it became clear that poetry was to be a life form for me, although I do remember an occasion in high school when I showed a poem to a local creative writing teacher (the poet B. Jo Kinnick, in fact) and she said "yes," it was, in fact, a poem. Having that permission (for what must have been a ghastly piece) was about as good a place as any to begin. But I think that I had always felt that I would be involved in the arts—early on it had been music (my mother's influence); and poetry came to be the focal point during my student years at S.F. State. There I worked in Creative Writing (though that process and that program dis-educated me more than it gave me any actual information about writing). I gained my firmest sense of the direction in poetry that I had to follow when I worked in the Library at S.F. State as a student assistant, and worked under Robin Blaser, who, as a major San Francisco poet in his own right, showed me my first "experimental" poems—those of Jack Spicer, Robert Duncan, Charles Olson, and others with whom he had worked. From that time on (say, 1965) I knew that one had to "dig in" with a poetics—that there wasn't one "poetry" but many poetries, and that among them there was often internecine warfare. I stuck to the Black Mountain-San Francisco nexus pretty much from then on, at least until I completed graduate school. Blaser kept hearing me talk about Dylan Thomas, W.H. Auden and the more civilized modern masters and promptly gave me copies of the Donald Allen anthology, Jack Spicer's poems, and the Kelly/Leary anthology; and that was the beginning.

SIPAPU: Roy Harvey Pearce founded this collection out of his interest in modern and post-modern writing (so say your Archive press releases): how did you meet him, how does he figure in your professional career, and what is his relation (official or otherwise) to the collection now?

DAVIDSON: I always admired Pearce's book, *The Continuity of American Poetry,* and had used it extensively in my graduate work. I came to San Diego to teach at the State College here (now San Diego State University) but didn't make contact with Pearce until the Archive job opened up here at UCSD. Prior to that, i.e. before 1975, a graduate student, Kathleen Woodward (now at the University of Wisconsin at Milwaukee) had run the Archive for New Poetry on a part-time teaching assistantship. I was the first regular "curator," and Roy Pearce has always been the "angel" of the collection, providing advice and support.

SIPAPU: What is the future of the Archive: its budget and collecting scope: and how do you see its role in the UC system?

DAVIDSON: I would have to say that we are continuing to grow. We just bought Jerome Rothenburg's papers and these interface nicely with our Blackburn and Reznikoff collections. I would like to do more publishing through the Archive. *Documents for New Poetry* is a monographic series presenting interviews, unpublished essays, transcripts of lectures, correspondence, and other documentary materials from various of the Archive's single-author collections. We have published a long interview with Edward Dorn, a checklist of Paul Blackburn's published work and a collection of documents from the Objectivist group. This year we published *The Five Songs,* by Robert Duncan, in a handsome, hand-designed, holograph-reproduced edition, sponsored by the Friends of the Library. I would like to do other such books, but it depends on our ever-fragile funding source with the Friends. We have no trouble buying books since our budget is the same as that for the regular English/American Literature fund. This means that we can literally buy anything published recently, and practically anything retrospectively. Where we are somewhat constrained is in the purchasing of single-author collections, but the Friends have been very supportive so far.

SIPAPU: The *Contemporary Poets* essay on you suggests that you see the world of fact and language as *The Mutabilities* (to borrow a title of one of your own books), that you see language as constantly changing, etc. To what extent is this a fair picture of "where you're at," today (as apart from then)? And since the changing implies the changeless, otherwise change could not be estimated, is there a big "constant factor" in your life and thought that the aforesaid essay took little heed of?

DAVIDSON: I don't have a copy of *Contemporary Poets* handy, so I can't say whether or not it's accurate. Basically I would say that the "constant factor" in my work (this is your phrase) is the notion that art is a dynamic fact in life — it is not a reflection, imitation, or projection of some prior, already constituted reality. Therefore I try to work, as Duncan might say, in the largest field of events happening in writing — to include as much of what's going on as can be incorporated. I think we have gone far beyond the expressive paradigm by which the poem exists solely at the behest of intimate, personal feelings, and by which language is "used" to transform, work-up, heighten, or otherwise "contain" those feelings. "Language is a prime of the matter,"

Olson said, meaning that it is productive rather than re-productive of meaning. And meaning is made in language, even though that language is no less produced by a social complex lying beyond it. That social complex is a profoundly linguistic fact itself and probably could not exist without its relation to the linguistic base (any more than it could without its economic base). In this sense, I like to think of my work as being political in that it interrogates the linguistic contingencies between that social complex and my own experience.

SIPAPU: Finally—what about your relation to the poets (Everson, Duncan, Snyder, McClure) in this S.F. Renaissance conference? Obviously you're much younger than they are (McClure, the youngest, was born in 1932). How do you see your work as relating to theirs? Are you more inclined to affirm you identity with them, or to state your differences?

DAVIDSON: Well, I did my dissertation (SUNY Buffalo) on Robert Duncan and am now writing a book for Cambridge University Press on those poets, so my commitment is pretty strong, at least to one aspect of the scene. I know most of them personally, although I relate to younger poets who live there—Michael Palmer, David Bromige, Ron Silliman, Ron Loewinsohn, Leslie Scalapino, Bob Perelman and others. Duncan continues to be the grand master, although I don't think I take after him stylistically. "The Beats" were never much of an influence—I distrust the bardic, vatic position, the poetics of unmediated participation, the two-dimensional populist stance. But I admire their energy, their public iconoclasm, their humor and satire.

BRUTUS VS. CAESAR IN SOUTH AFRICA. Writes Judith Getts: "Dennis Brutus, South African poet and political activist, has been shot once, imprisoned, banned from teaching or writing in South Africa; yet years later his life in the U.S. remains one long, unrelenting cry against a government he cannot believe in, within a country thousands of miles away.

"An exiled South African, Brutus, after 12 years of teaching at universities in the United States, may again be a man without a country. This winter (1981-82) The Office of Immigration and Naturalization, Chicago, refused to extend or renew the poet's visa. Despite demands of the OIN that Brutus leave the country immediately, he is still residing in Chicago as he attempts to negotiate a change in visa status from temporary residency to the permanent residency normally accorded distinguished scholars.

"African writers are frequently found between a rock and a hard place; i.e., between their homeland and a foreign country. Brutus is no exception. Both his political activities and his writing place him in troublesome positions, no matter where he turns.

"In 1963 Dennis Brutus was arrested by South African police for attending a meeting of the South African Non-Racial Olympic Committee (SAN-ROC), an organization protesting discrimination within the Olympics. He escaped, only to be recaptured and to escape again. While attempting to reach the Olympic Committee in Baden-Baden, Germany, that same year, he was captured at the Mozambique border, handed over to South African police and taken to Johannesburg. While attempting to escape again, he was shot. After 18 months of hard labor in the prison on Robben Island, he was released, placed under house arrest, then exiled from South Africa.

"In South Africa, these events have apparently given Brutus the stature of a martyr who proved flameproof at the stake, and who therefore was exiled in order that he might not be useful to dissidents. But in America he is best known for his political poetry:

Saffron and orange and blood
like this
seeped into the sky on other dawns
riding the army truck to prison
looking through bars at the island's day

"While much of his poetry circulates through South African ghettoes and in communist countries under false names, internationally he is known equally as a major African poet and as president of SAN-ROC and as chairman of the International Campaign Against Racism in Sport.

"As head of SAN-ROC Brutus has, since 1964, been able to convince other countries to bar South Africa from the Olympic Games, and in recent years, Zimbabwe as well, because of these countries' racial discrimination in sports, which constitutes a violation of the Olympic Charter's first article.

"The impact of this action on South Africa's view of itself in world politics has not been minimal, for, as Brutus says, little can compare with the disappointment of British colonists when they are prevented from challenging Englishmen in football. As South Africa assures its populace that their nation cannot be cut off from international competition, here is proof that South Africa can indeed be benched at the Olympics.

"Last year, Brutus and SAN-ROC attempted to bar Britain from the winter Olympics for supporting (as they claimed) apartheid in sports. The United States also came under fire for politicization of the Games before it boycotted the 1980 Games. Campaigns like this one have earned Brutus sharp criticism from outside South Africa, as well. *Sports Illustrated* said of him, 'every tawdry political distraction to international sport now enters through the door that Brutus and SAN-ROC first cracked open in the name of justice. In Montreal there was very great concern that sport and its youthful pawns were being damaged a great deal more than South Africa.'

"Yet Brutus does not at all appear to be the sharp-tongued 'dark genius of dissent' he is said to be. As professor of English at Northwestern the contrast between academic and political poet-dissident is distinct. There are the poetry readings in the campus library's sunken garden; and there are the readings at Marion Prison. There are classes on the English Romantic poets, and those on African literature and politics. In one of these classes, he talked about the time he had read poetry with Ted Hughes in London. Hughes wore a voluminous black cape and a black hat; Brutus described him as 'so sinister, so menacing, but such an impostor!'

"For fourteen years before he was exiled, Brutus was known as a school teacher in South Africa. Born in Salisbury, Zimbabwe (Rhodesia at that time) in 1924, of South African parents teaching there, Brutus grew up in South Africa. As a child he spent many hours sitting around the wasteland which separated the black ghetto from the white townships. 'Among the rubble and litter,' he writes, 'wild tendrils of purple convolvulus curled in and out, showing up brilliantly against the white builders' sand in the morning sunlight.' There he escaped into literature and fantasy; he described himself in those days as 'a boy who could be so abstracted that he could pause with a cup held to his lips and go on daydreaming until the cup fell and broke; or could be so attracted to the sound of a name that he could sit on a pile of soiled linen, chanting "Angelo" endlessly to his own made-up tune until he fell asleep.'

"Brutus's parents reared him on Tennyson, Wordsworth and Browning, and sent him to a school where English nuns encouraged black youth to feel equal to whites. The State eventually took over the school, claiming that such teaching would create frustrated blacks who would start demanding equal education, jobs and pay. He went on to Fort Hare University and Witwatersrand University: two other private schools which promoted racial equality, until taken over by the State shortly after Brutus graduated.

"After Brutus has taught high school for fourteen years, he was declared ineligible to teach in South Africa. He therefore enrolled as a law student at the University of Witwatersrand, Johannesburg, making his living writing short stories and poetry and by taking a job as a 'tea boy,' i.e. doing office errands and making tea in a university department. Shortly after this, he was forbidden to write, and no paper was permitted to publish his work.

"His early collection of poems, 'Sirens, Knuckles, Boots,' and 'Letters to Martha,' gave Brutus his initial popularity in the West. These works describe the horrors of prison as a symbol of society's evils inflicted upon, and corrupting, the helpless, innately good, human being. They carry more weight than some later writings: anger at injustice meets anger's control. Part of Brutus' views at this point is his refusal to believe that human nature is essentially evil. His determination to meet life's harshest circumstances head-on, is a pervasive theme of these and later works.

"After his release from Robben Island, he was exiled and in 1966, Brutus and his family went to Britain. For five years he worked for the International Defense and Aid Fund of the United Nations, working to free South African political prisoners. From Britain he came to the United States in 1969, when the University of Denver offered him a visiting professor's job. Afro-American studies were in the air, and African literary figures and dissidents were in demand as teachers. But one of the reasons given by the U.S. Office of Immigration and Naturalization, for their refusal to renew Brutus's visa, is that such programs no longer required Africans as teachers.

"Where is Brutus now? Latest information suggests that he is still a tenured professor at Northwestern. A spacious room in a remodeled Victorian house in Evanston serves as his university office. Outside there is a view of Lake Michigan; inside colorful posters, and leaflets advertising human rights campaigns are tacked all over the walls. Papers haphazardly cover his executive desk and tumble to the floor, where open cardboard boxes of books await them. But somehow Brutus can always locate, in this turbulence, what he's looking for. While he is looking for some paper, an overseas phone call may interrupt him; and when he hurries off to class, whether the course is devoted to African literature or politics, he will explain that African art is created for the community. The personal identity of the artist or his subject is unimportant; only the message to the community matters.

"Thus he has defied the bans on his poetry by publishing under the pseudonym 'C. Ensor' and by publishing works abroad. But yet, for Brutus, 'revolutions aren't made with words.' When Brutus speaks of black poetry in the United States, he says, 'so many of them deceive themselves, that there is a kind of verbal magic; if you say the thing, you are going to conjure it into existence.'

"Brutus, poet, is against all predictions, a romantic. 'There recur in my poetry certain images from the language of chivalry — the troubadour in particular. The notion of a stubborn, even foolish knight-errantry on a quest in the service of someone loved; this is an image which I use in my work, because it seems a true kind of shorthand for something which is part of my life and my pursuit of justice in menacing South Africa.'

"Like a knight in Tennyson's *Idylls of the King,* a work which has influenced him since childhood, Brutus is a romantic. Even his descriptions of a landscape become sensuous. In 'Nightsong: Country' he writes:

> All of this undulant earth
> heaves up to me:

> soft curves in the dark distend
> voluptuous-submissively;
> primal and rank

"Gessler Moses NKondo, literature instructor at Yale and author of a dissertation on Brutus's poetry, explains that sexual experiences are used as a symbol of union and connection with one's love, with South Africa, with humanity. This sexuality is elevated to a myth with Brutus as 'the troubadour always yearning for the distant lady, and the lady is so distant it's difficult for him to consummate his love. For Brutus the distant lady becomes South Africa,' says NKondo.

"Brutus never comments on how he feels about teaching in the U.S., but he writes:

> but see the corpses of students
> in the streets of Soweto
> who died for profits
> for the students
> of the good ol' U.S.A.
> see the corpses bleeding
> in the streets of Soweto.

"At Northwestern few whites take courses in African literature; not all English majors there know who he is, although in the past graduate students have come to Northwestern to study African literature with Brutus. On campus he is generally viewed as a folk hero or madman, but at times it is apparent that he relishes being seen in both perspectives. Those who do not like him think him caustic and short-tempered, which he certainly is when his politics are under fire; but in day-to-day life he is calm and soft-spoken, with a languorous voice.

"One poem closes: 'But somehow tenderness survives.' Brutus has twelve sons and daughters of his own, some attending universities, some beginning families of their own and the youngest living with his wife in England where Brutus spends the summer. In 'For My Sons and Daughters' he writes:

> my loneliness; my failures; my amalgam wish to serve:
> my continental sense of sorrow drove me to work
> and at times I hoped to shape your better world.

"Backed by Northwestern faculty, writers and supporters nation-wide, Brutus continues his appeal to remain in this country. The Dennis Brutus Defense Committee, which handles additional information on his case, pay legal fees and asks supporters to write to the Office of Immigration and Naturalization on his behalf, can be reached at 2730 Hampton Parkway, B2, Evanston, IL 60201, phone (312) 328-5935."—JUDITH GETTS.

WINTERS JOINS THE PEACE MOVEMENT: Our home town finally became active in the public concern over the nuclear arms race, and we can't claim any credit for it; the claim must go to several young family people, including Lorie Hammond and Mary Oak, who with Al Vallecillo and Denise Cottrell organized a potluck in the city park on 26 June 1982, once the heat had cooled down. There were paper cranes to fold, sign-up sheets for further work, and a mass release of helium-filled blue and white balloons, about fifty of them, which all took off in a SSW wind at sundown. This breeze carried them in the general direction of Yuba City, Oroville, Paradise, and Mount Lassen. Subscribers lying along this historic path are urged to send us any shreds of balloons with "SUPPORT THE NUCLEAR FREEZE" or similar sentiments written on the tags attached to them. Experience has shown that a really *peaceful* balloon can travel as far as 80 or 100 km. Nuclear radiation can spread even farther and faster, which is the point of the balloons.

It would seem that a potluck with lots of babies and puppies isn't very impressive, but as William Faulkner once said, "If you want to get something done in a town, get the women and children in on it. The men don't have the time." Faulkner knew his small towns. Of course a freeze is only the beginning, and must ultimately be joined with larger issues, but we have to start somewhere.

THE BEAR IS THE PROSECUTOR, THE TAIGA IS THE LAW: The taiga, of course, is the Siberian sub–Arctic forest, and this is the motto of every prisoner sent to one of the numerous prisons and concentration camps of the Soviet Union. Avraham Shifrin, now living in Israel, has published the second edition of *The First Guidebook to Prisons and Concentration Camps of the Soviet Union,* available from Bantam in paperback for $6.95. A fold-out map shows an astonishing number of dots, most of them in the eastern part of the country, but some situation in such geographically remote places as Wrangel Island, north of the eastern tip of Siberia. Most of the "factories" and "colonies," some of which make "folk art" for sale to tourists, and others of which make defense weapons systems (thus relieving the Soviet Union of a large part of their defense budget), allow Soviets to claim that they spend a large amount of money on human services needs. The map shows locations of downtown prisons, with exact addresses plus a few photographs of prisoners, plus names of camp commandants. "How to get there" is amply described—for places accessible to tourists and camps that the author and his collaborators know about. Obviously, especially in eastern Siberia, there are large areas in which there may be many more camps than anyone knows anything about; the same holds true of desert central Asia, and along the uninhabitable but still inhabited shores of the Caspian Sea. One map from this area is drawn entirely from the recollections of a single prisoner.

Of particular interest in this book are coverages of Gary Powers, the U-2 pilot shot down over the USSR when Eisenhower was President here; of Raoul Wallenberg, the Swede who rescued hundreds of Jews in Nazi Eastern Europe, only to be arrested by the Red Army (he seems to be one of those who got as far as Wrangel Island, and this book suggests that he might still be alive). In addition, there is some coverage of the food riots in Novocherkassk near Rostov, in 1962, a subject ill covered in the world press. Many accounts are given of camp revolts which required outside military power to subdue; and many prisoners are there because they are religious (Christian, Jewish or Moslem) or because they sought autonomy for their particular region (Ukraine, Latvia).

A reading of this important reference publication casts a long shadow over many struggles here in the U.S. The struggle for the control of the Black Hills, for example, is as important as the struggle for the independence of Latvia, but the response is somewhat different—after all, Russell Means is still alive. Hunger is widespread in these prisons and camps, and the author makes some play with a strike in an American prison which occurred when the prisoners had been served chicken day after day after day. "They demanded beef, and they got it," he says, after having described a Soviet prisoner who was (he alleges) observed cooking a piece of his own leg over a fire.

Whether or not this last story is true, it seems obvious that not only the number of prisons, but the condition of prisoners, is worse in the Soviet Union than in the United States—a statement which many of us will find difficulty in admitting. There are, however, many people in our own country who would like to lock up truants, loiterers, all those who cannot give a good account of themselves, especially if they aren't white and well-off. Shifrin tells us that the Soviet threat is posed against "leftists" and capitulators to the Communists: "The camps are coming closer and closer." But they could equally well start here, under a right-wing regime. After all, we had them here, erected for Japanese-Americans, in World War II. And some Japanese died in them (we knew one). Our conclusion? The struggle for freedom takes place on all fronts and in all directions.

13: 2

This issue (consecutive issue number 26) was difficult to do because of the insistence of Bradford Chambers on getting everything right, including my introduction. He took things hard. Brad died in 1984, sincerely mourned by the progressive wing of the library community, including myself.

Diane Callum has subsequently travelled to Nicaragua and gives poetry readings. She is the only person who can wear a black silk jacket with "POET" in red on the back, and get away with it. We have read together in Davis and Berkeley.

THERE ARE THREE KINDS OF PEOPLE when it comes to liberty vs. censorship in book selection. One is the liberal type, which holds to the view that America is a wide spectrum of opinion, from infra-Red to ultraviolet Right, and that the library must include every range of the spectrum and favor none in particular. A second, which in contradistinction to the first, has little favor with most librarians, holds that America is a country in a covenant with God, or at least subject to standards of decency, and that words and books which offend the same, must be purged. A third type, the socially conscious, is the subject of our interview.

Children's literature, long viewed by adults as an instructive confection, was once outside these controversies. But now, young adult "problem" novels, the naked lad in Sendak's *In the Night Kitchen,* and other challenging children's books offend the Moral Majority; while, on the other hand, feminists, people of color, disabled people and others have charged that children's books often contain racism, sexism, and other forms of bias. These activists are opposed by those who see children's literature solely as "art," and by those who regard *any* criticism of content as censorship. Among those who have been taking a critical look at the content of children's books is Bradford Chambers, editor of the *Interracial Books for Children Bulletin.* Agree with him or not, let him speak for himself:

SIPAPU: Let's start with birth and education, cultural background?

CHAMBERS: The education I received did nothing to promote an

understanding of racism and sexism. Far from it: my formal education was designed to show the son of a white, relatively well-to-do family his proper place in the world. The texts I read at school (both here and in England) suggested that I, being white, was superior to people of
color. I am lucky that the dinner table discussions at home contradicted most of this. I am also lucky that my father provided an antidote to the messages in the textbooks. He was a biologist, and before I had read any books on the subject, he had firmly debunked the myth of white superiority.

My mother had hoped to go to college, but in her day young women of her class went on the "grand tour" of Europe instead. Although my mother had ambitions to write, she ended up meeting societal expectations, managing a large household (four sons, I the youngest) and considerable entertaining of scientists (male, of course) and their wives. Then came a serious injury from an automobile accident, and my mother's hopes and ambitions were ended.

I began school in England, because my father was invited to conduct research at laboratories there. I first attended an all-boys boarding school in Cambridge, where Latin was a required subject from the first grade. Every Sunday we all marched in a column two by two, dressed in top hats, long pants, and Eton jackets, and made faces at the women we passed on our way to King's Choir Chapel. When I first transferred to a day school, there was a fellow American in my class. Our classmates nicknamed him Al Capone, and me, Scarface. He and I were forced to become enemies, for at recess our teachers divided the class into two groups for combat, and it was simply taken for granted that the two American "gangsters" would be the leaders in that type of activity. When my father went on a world lecture tour, my brothers and I were sent to school in Lausanne, Switzerland. The only school that had an opening for me was an all-girls school, and here I unlearned some of the male chauvinism of the English schools.

Back in this country, I attended boarding schools before going to Amherst College. There I gained the hostility of the Dean's office by organizing a four-college conference to consider how, in post–World War II years, we might build a more just society. In those days there was intense rivalry between the four colleges—Amherst, Mt. Holyoke, Smith and the University of Massachusetts. While the administration could do little about inter-college dating, they went out of their way to discourage academic cooperation; even inter-collegiate sports were dimly viewed (it is very different today).

After considerable conflict over the conference, it was decided that I should take a year's leave of absence from Amherst. I transferred to New York University, attracted by the department of sociology—then a relatively new field, virtually unknown at Amherst. One of my professors had published a classic study of gangs in Chicago. He had found that the gangs were primarily a product of urban communities whose ethnic or racial populations were in transition. When I was at NYU, teenage gang warfare was becoming an extremely serious problem in New York. While there were gangs in the Lower East Side and elsewhere, the fighting gangs were situated along the environs of Harlem. Harlem, with some of the most congested areas in the world, had long been hemmed in by the surrounding Irish and Italian neighborhoods, but was then attempting to expand. Although the New York press blamed the Black gangs for the conflicts, there was abundant evidence that the gangs were actually a white problem. The white kids in the area, encouraged by their parents, formed "rumbling clubs" to contain the blacks, and the blacks responded by organizing gangs for defense. The black gangs, in other words, with their war counselors, guerrilla captains, deb and sub-deb divisions for the "girls" and even groups for the "tiny tots," were responding to white racism. For my M.A. thesis I decided to write about this phenomenon. While I was dong the research, 12 teenagers were killed in gang wars in New York City.

After graduating, I continued my involvement with the gangs in a largely white area next to Harlem dubbed "Mousetown," but instead of studying the gangs, I worked to develop positive programs. In those days settlement houses were the recognized agencies to deal with juvenile delinquency, but teenage gangs were treated as "bad apples" to be kept away lest they contaminate the "good apples" the settlement houses were able to attract. The gangs were left to roam the streets. My work was to meet the gangs in their own haunts and try—to use an expression that became quite popular—"to channel their activities into constructive outlets." Now all that seems quite old-fashioned, but at the time it seemed radical social work. To support the work I received a fellowship from the American Philosophical Society. I was fortunate, also, to have the support of Saul Alinsky, whose *Reveille for Radicals* was for long my bible. I wrote about my work with the gangs in magazines like the *Survey Graphic, American Mercury, New York Times Magazine,* and *Reader's Digest.* After that, I did free-lance writing and editing, editorial work for some children's periodicals, etc.

SIPAPU: Your political development: how your consciousness got raised?

CHAMBERS: A major turning point for me came when I was collecting documents for a young people's book on the civil rights movement, then taking place. The media reported on the *events* of the struggle, but did little to explain why they were taking place, and school textbooks were (and still are) equally deficient in putting these events in context, and relating them to the history of struggles against oppression. To help fill the void I compiled *Chronicles of Black Protest,* which brought together historical documents of the struggle of blacks for social justice. The book was quite successful. It received the 1969 Brotherhood Book award of the National Conference of Christians and Jews, and so it got into a great many schools.

While researching *Chronicles of Black Protest,* I became more and more committed to racial struggles for equality. It was then that I first learned about the Council on Interracial Books for Children (CIBC). Two of my children were attending Downtown Community School (DCS) in New York City. I had volunteered to organize a project to bring children's authors, and editors, to speak with the students about issues connected with children's book publishing and I was also helping with the DCS annual award for children's books that promoted human rights. DCS Principal Norman Studer, a highly innovative educator, had started the award, and the contest had become a high point of the school year. (It was in connection with this award that Norman Studer, along with a number of librarians, editors and authors, had helped found CIBC in 1965.) One particularly hectic day in 1967 — in the midst of demands from conservative parents to curtail the school's scholarship program for minorities — Norman Studer asked if I would take his place that evening at a CIBC meeting. I have been with CIBC ever since.

When I joined, CIBC was judging the manuscripts submitted to its first Annual Contest for Unpublished Children's Books by Negro Writers. (In those days "Negro" was still used.) The contest was one way CIBC hoped to change what was then referred to as the "all-white world of children's books" by encouraging the publication of black authors. CIBC felt that publishers would be more likely to pick up a manuscript if it had won an award. And it was true that Third World authors who had unsuccessfully made the rounds of publishers' offices got their manuscripts published after they had won a CIBC award. Mildred Taylor's manuscript, *Song of the Trees,* was rejected so many times that she nearly gave up. Once CIBC had given it an award in 1975, the book was published by Dial. The sequel, *Roll of Thunder, Hear My Cry,* won the Newberry Medal. For some blacks, the CIBC contest was the gateway to a new career: writing for children. Walter Dean Myers, now a well-recognized author, was working in the Brooklyn Post Office when he heard about the contest. He tried writing, submitted a manuscript, won the first CIBC award, and this led to a job as book editor in a major publishing house.

Over the years, contest guidelines were developed to make sure that books were both anti-racist and anti-sexist, and the contest was expanded to include Asian-Americans, Chicanos, native Americans and Puerto Ricans. Prizes were awarded in each category. That the contest resulted in a number of beautifully written, highly acclaimed books would seem to contradict the charge from some quarters that CIBC guidelines inhibit a writer's creative powers. (The illustration at right is from a famous book of the past — *Ed.*)

In addition to Mildred Taylor's Newberry winner, several CIBC books have been runner-ups; the illustrations for another CIBC contest winner, Margaret Musgrove's *From Ashanti to Zulu* (Dial) won the 1977 Caldecott Medal.

Despite its achievements, the CIBC contest was always one of the best-kept secrets of the library world. The *New York Times* frequently reported the contest winners, the annual supplements of at least one encyclopedia and the Children's Book Council's *Awards and Prizes* regularly noted it, but the major library journals were silent about the contest throughout its ten-year existence. The contest continued until 1978, when we were no longer in a financial position to keep it going. The outlook for resuming it in the near future is dim, since publishers have become less and less interested in books by minority writers.

SIPAPU: CIBC: how it arose, how you got involved with it?

CHAMBERS: CIBC grew out of the Civil Rights movement of the 1960s. A teacher at one of the Mississippi Freedom Schools (begun as part of the voter registration drive and attended by many black children) sent an SOS to his mother in New York, asking for print materials that black children could identify with. His mother, the children's book author Lilian Moore, searched for such materials but found none. This search spurred her to bring together, in 1965, a group of editors, writers, and librarians, concerned about the lack of good children's materials about blacks. This group became CIBC. Author Franklin B. Folsom was the first chairman, and civil rights lawyer Stanley Faulkner, the first treasurer.

The contest I mentioned earlier was one of the group's first efforts to encourage the publication of books by and about minorities. Another was the publication of the CIBC *Bulletin,* which began in 1966 with a first issue of 8 stapled pages. The *Bulletin* has certainly grown; now going into its 15th year, it is now a magazine running as many as 48 pages and published eight times a year. The *Bulletin* is often controversial but consciousness-raising. Its objective is to provide librarians and other educators with the perspectives of those our society have long oppressed—minorities, feminists, older people, disabled people, etc. Book reviews are written by members of the groups depicted, for we have found that the surest, most effective, way to uncover bias and stereotypes, is to ask for criticism from those who are struggling against their oppression. Who would have more sensitivity to bias and be more concerned about accurate, non-stereotypical presentations than members of the group portrayed? In addition to ethnic background, the reviewers we seek are activists working for social justice. Our approach caused not a little eyebrow-raising in the early years, but today the reviews are generally accepted as an extra and valid dimension of literary criticism. *Bulletin* reviews are now regularly selected for inclusion in the two review annuals *Children's Literature Review* and *Contemporary Criticism*. H.W. Wilson's *Education Index* has been indexing *Bulletin* articles for several years, and the *Bulletin* and other CIBC activities are regularly noted in the ALA *Yearbook*. A *Bulletin* article, "Whitewashing white racists; *Junior Scholastic* and the KKK," was selected as one of the "best contributions to library literature" by *Library Lit. II, The Best of 1980* (Scarecrow Press, 1981).

Bulletin reviews are indeed critical, but there is much to criticize about our society, and once you start to recognize that children's books reflect the biases of society, no detail is too small to ignore. Moreover, people are not always in agreement on what constitutes a "small detail." A dressmaking detail—a bow or a sash—while not an essential piece of clothing, may often alter the total effect. A small detail, indeed, may hold the key to a physician's diagnosis. With this in mind, it is a critic's responsibility when reviewing a book, not to overlook what may be regarded by some as a "small detail," but which may linger in some memories long after much of the book has been forgotten. This applies especially to children's books portraying different cultures, where attention to accuracy and authenticity is crucial.

The *Bulletin* is by no means all negative. Our reviewers find quite a few books to praise. This may come as a surprise to some, but the books that the *Bulletin* has recommended in recent years number into the hundreds.

We have also found that biased books make marvelous tools to teach children about bias, and rather than advocating the removal of such books, we urge that they be used in that manner. Once children gain insights into the nature and function of stereotypes, they are quite able on their own to spot stereotypes in books, on TV and wherever bias occurs. Providing children with the skills to identify bias gives them a sort of defense, an antidote against the worst effects of bias. After all, we are not asking that children's books remove women from the kitchen, but that they not limit women to that role. We are not asking that people of color be shown as saints, but rather that they not be restricted to subservient and stereotyped roles.

Eight years ago CIBC set up a resource center to assist educators in countering racism and sexism in school and society. Since then we have developed a large number of print and AV materials toward this objective. We publish, besides the *Bulletin,* books and teaching manuals, we create filmstrips and slide shows, develop lesson plans and school curricula — all with a conciousness-raising thrust. Some of these materials are being used by librarians, teachers, parents, church and community leaders, in their localities or in workshops. Each item comes with a training manual and discussion guide.

A growing number of our materials are for use directly with students. We are particularly proud of "Violence, the Ku Klux Klan and the struggle for equality," the first informational and instructional kit of its kind for use in junior and senior high schools. For its work in developing this material,

CIBC just received the 1982 Human and Civil Rights Award of the National Education Association. But we have found that it is not just older students who can deal with the issues of social justice. Among our most enthusiastic supporters are fifth and sixth graders whose teachers have introduced them to the CIBC "Winning 'justice for all'" curriculum. At ten and eleven, children are particularly concerned with what is "fair" and "unfair," and they become very much concerned about bias and discrimination. This six-week curriculum gives children insights into the institutional practices of discrimination, and the inequities that result from these practices. It has been very successful in 44 states and 5 foreign countries. We are just completing an AV resource which deals with issues of equity and social justice for first and second graders. And we are about to work on one for kindergarten! A free catalog of our CIBC materials comes from 1841 Broadway, New York, NY 10023.

SIPAPU: Your own outlook, on children's books primarily; how important is it that books about minority groups, or books about scenes likely to involve minority groups (urban settings, certain rural areas) be written, or revised before publication, by members of the appropriate groups? Should an "Establishment" (white, male, etc.) writer ask for revision, or just stay away from the subject entirely?

CHAMBERS: There is no question that *any* author has the right to write on *any* subject. However, when white writers choose to write children's books about other cultures, especially those of people of color, they generally shortchange their young readers. There is a reason for this. Almost all whites grow up in a white cultural milieu and have only superficial experiences with people of color. They are also inundated with stereotypes and misinformation about minority groups in literature, textbooks, radio, TV. Then, too, there is no question that whites and people of color experience different realities, and that they perceive things differently. Therefore, it is very unlikely that white writers will adequately and *accurately* portray the cultural experiences and responses to minority groups. It is cultural arrogance to think otherwise. So, given a choice, then yes, it is preferable that books about minority groups be written by members of the group depicted. Writers from minority cultures can offer young white insights that they would otherwise not get, and offer young minority readers a validation of their lives that is so often missing from material by white writers. Let's also recognize that while people of color in the U.S. must live in two cultures (the dominant white culture and their own), they generally remain as uninformed as whites, about Third World cultures other than their own. Ours is a *very* ethnocentric society.

This is not to say that white or majority writers cannot write about minority cultures. They can make very important contributions by examining, for example, the dynamics of white racism. It is simply that what they write will not be coming from the same perspective as a minority person. In a pluralistic society, where differences are respected, then, yes, intracultural writing would be much more effective; but it would not be easy; in such a society writers would be more likely to appreciate the difficulties.

You ask if an "establishment" author should request "revisions" from members of minority groups. I think writers should do their own revisions. On the other hand, I would certainly hope that *any* children's book author who chooses to write of cultures other than his/her own, would seek input from members of the groups depicted. That is legitimate and necessary research. No one without intimate knowledge of a sport, or of a particular science, would write about these subjects without getting some expert advice. Similarly, no editor would publish such children's books without checking the content with an "expert."

The way in which racial groups are depicted in children's books is a major contributor to the way that white children think about other races, and to the way that minority children form their own self-image. Surely some "expert" input in this area would be all to the good. The same principle applies to the preparation of bibliographies. It does no good to merely put together lists of children's books about a particular minority. Chances are better than even that those lists will contain not a few biased books. CIBC has urged libraries to develop a process to assure some minority input in the preparation of such bibliographies. For white librarians to invite minority input for the book selection process will not assure total accuracy, but it will cut down on a lot of unnecessary heartaches. Such a model book selection plan was featured in the CIBC *Bulletin* back in 1976 ("The Iowa plan—a due process for handling book challenges," v. 7, no. 7). The plan incorporates racism and sexism awareness training for librarians and outlines ways to bring minority input to communities of different populations.

SIPAPU: Should we actually launch a program of affirmative action in culture—i.e., publish more work by oppressed or disadvantaged people, or about them, and let the middle-class white males wait in the wings, so to speak? Or should we expand the pie to include opportunities for everyone?

CHAMBERS: About 20% of U.S. children are children of minorities, but of the 2000 children's books published annually, roughly 1% are about these children. This denies minority children positive role-models and a literature relevant to their lives. It is also a loss to white children who, as a consequence, grow up ignorant and disrespectful of other people's values and beliefs. That is why CIBC has long advocated affirmative action to seek out and publish talented Afro-American, Latino, native American and Asian-American writers and artists.

Yes, we should definitely work to expand the pie so that greater opportunities will be available for everyone, so that there will be more diversity and so that no groups will be excluded. But enlarging the pie without altering the proportional share of its slices will be inequitable also. The reality is that white writers are—and always will be—favored over minority writers. This does not mean that they have any inherent "right" to be published at the expense of non-white writers. I suggest that it is more pertinent to look at the "right to publish" that is currently being denied to minority writers. They are disproportionately *under-represented,* and children's literature is the poorer for it—as we are all.

SIPAPU: If we should get more money to minority publishers, emphasize the disadvantaged to the disadvantage of more favored groups, how do we deal with the charge of the "Moral Majority" types that claim *they* are the insulted and injured, that *their* values are flouted, and *they* demand as much consideration as anyone else?

CHAMBERS: I assume you are talking about textbooks rather than children's trade books, since these are what Mel and Norma Gabler of Texas, and other so-called Moral Majority (MM) types are complaining about. Phyllis Schlafly, incidentally, has called on the right to make school textbooks one of its top four priorities.

As many research studies show, minorities, women and numerous other groups have long been stereotyped in textbooks. Their history and perspectives have been distorted or omitted, their concerns have been ignored or ridiculed. Serious scholarship, as well as a concern for social justice, necessitates that efforts be made to provide more accurate, more inclusive textbooks. It is not a question of emphasizing one group to the disadvantage of others. Instead, it is a question of representing a diversity of viewpoints, particularly the viewpoints of groups who have been discriminated against and whose voices have not generally been heard. The Moral Majority seeks to make books even more exclusive, as regards alternative viewpoints, than they are today. Groups like CIBC, on the other hand, seek to make them more inclusive. We don't mind including the Moral Majority view—as long as other viewpoints are there also. In that respect the Moral Majority people have no cause to feel "insulted and injured."

The Moral Majority is not really calling for equal space but for total space. They insist that U.S. policies and leaders not be criticized. And their demands have already had an alarming impact on the adoption requirements of Texas, a key state today in determining textbook content. For example, the 1980 Texas criteria require that textbooks "present positive aspects of

America and its heritage ... shall not contain material which services to undermine authority ... shall not encourage lifestyles deviating from generally accepted standards of society." The Moral Majority is also demanding that all students, not just their own children, be taught absolute standards of right and wrong. They are pressuring for textbooks that permit but one right answer to questions and that disallow critical thinking and value judgments. Therefore, it is totally impossible to make the Moral Majority types happy, and, at the same time, educate a responsible citizenry. Should the colonists have worried because King George felt "insulted and injured"?

A small digression here, concerning school textbooks: These books carry the official sanction of the educational establishment and are required reading by law. A case could be made that textbooks that omit or distort the histories of women and minorities violate the equal protection guarantees of the 14th Amendment.

SIPAPU: To what extent does the quest for fairness impair not only general freedom, including the freedom of the wrong, but (when pursued by librarians) expose them to the charge of no longer being "neutral"?

CHAMBERS: Far from impeding freedom, the quest for fairness enhances it. What better way do librarians have to achieve intellectual freedom than by offering perspectives that have traditionally been left out? Almost all books that are published—and therefore the overwhelming number of books in library collections—are written from a middle- and upper-class white perspective, and they generally reflect the sexist values of our society no matter what the author's gender. On issues of racism and sexism there is no conceivable way to achieve a neutral collection, since the collections are so imbalanced to begin with, and anti-racist, anti-sexist books are so terribly limited in number. In view of this, the charge that a quest for fairness will somehow interfere with the librarians' position of neutrality is a false charge.

Many librarians seriously question the concept of neutrality in book selection. To begin with, let's recognize that the existing book selection process— which begins with what gets published— is not truly neutral. One apparently innocuous example: the romance books for pre-teenagers in which young girls devote themselves to finding and getting Mr. Right. It's no accident that books like these (they have been called training bras for the Harlequins) were the rage of the 1950s, that time of general conformism and raging sexism. (And it is interesting that they are being published and popularized again now, when there is a backlash to the feminist movement.) Publishers who churn these books out, and the few librarians who endorse them, are not making a neutral choice: they are endorsing some very specific messages.

For children's librarians to become aware of the messages contained in books and to carefully consider the worth of books that endorse and perpetuate racism, sexism and other anti-human values, is simply a way to clarify the selection process, not de-neutralize it. Put another way, the act of selection involves judgment about what is valuable and vital, and sensitization to minority and feminist concerns is one way, among many, of informing that judgment. I do wish that more schools of library science would show an interest in message content and introduce sensitizing courses that will enable children's librarians of the future to analyze content as well as literary values. We are encouraged, however, that children's literature professors, and reading and language arts instructors, at colleges and universities are definitely showing more concern.

SIPAPU: What is the largest currently-ignored group which you see as needing adequate favorable treatment in children's books?

CHAMBERS: Many groups are still omitted from children's books, but it would be unfair to single out one group most in need of "adequate" representation. Some believe that book publishers met their responsibility to minorities by responding to the pressures of the Civil Rights Movement and publishing books on black themes. In the late 1960s and early 1970s children's book publishers did come out with quite a few such books, some good, many more far from adequate. Publishers were reacting to the Federal funds that enabled libraries to purchase such books as much as they were to pressures from the Civil Rights Movement. "Black is gold," they used to say.

Once the Federal funds stopped, books on black themes became fewer and fewer. As for other minorities, the situation is bleaker still. We are just completing a ten-year update of a special 1972 *Bulletin* on children's books about Puerto Ricans. The high point for these books was 1972, when a grand total of 18 children's books on Puerto Rican themes was published. A graph which will appear in the next *Bulletin* tells what happened subsequently. By 1974, there was a precipitous drop to 3 books, then a slight increase over the next couple of years to 7 books in 1977, followed by a steadily downward trend to zero books in 1980.

The group that is most represented is, ironically, the one most consistently *mis*represented. There are more children's books about native Americans than about all other minority groups put together, but, with a

handful of notable exceptions, these books reinforce traditional stereotypes. Despite all the new awareness of the oppression of native Americans, the average children's book continues to depict them as painted, whooping "savages," or as "exotics," not as people living and continuing to be oppressed in today's world. That is why Mary Gloyne Byler, a native American critic of children's literature, has said, "There are too many children's books about American Indians."

SIPAPU: Bilingualism: help to smaller children, or handicap in adjusting to an inevitably English-speaking society?

CHAMBERS: There really is no substance to the charge that non-English-speaking children will be at a disadvantage unless they stop using their native language at home and start speaking only English. Numerous studies now show that bilingual children who develop proficiency in both their native language and a second language, have intellectual and academic advantages over monolingual children. The important thing is that children learn the cognitive skills in the language that is spoken at home, whatever language that is. Once they develop cognitive skills, around grade 3, they can readily transfer those skills to English. In what is known as transitional bilingual education, children are taught reading and other cognitive skills in their native language, while studying English as a second language. Sometime between the third and the sixth grades, the native language is dropped and the medium of instruction becomes English. In maintenance bilingual education, the medium of instruction is divided about equally, once the cognitive skills are learned. Some subjects are taught in English, others in the native language.

An outstanding model of maintenance bilingual education is the Rock Point (Navajo) School, in Chinle, Arizona. Before the program was introduced in 1971, there had been intensive efforts to begin teaching Navajo children English in kindergarten, but by the sixth grade they were two years behind U.S. norms in reading skills. A bilingual program introduced Navajo as the medium of instruction from kindergarten through sixth grade and for about 50% of the time thereafter. Instruction in English was introduced in the middle of the second grade. By the end of the sixth grade the children were performing somewhat *above* U.S. grade norms in English reading.

A big problem in our society is that any language other than English is considered somehow inferior. The opposite holds true in some other countries, where different languages are shown equal respect. There are those who believe that proficiency in more than one language improves the speaker's ability to reason and to consider alternatives. A lot of confusion surrounds bilingual education, and I would like to recommend to *Sipapu* readers a toll-free number they can use to obtain factual information about it: 800-336-4560 is the number of the National Clearinghouse for Bilingual Education in Rosslyn, Virginia.

SIPAPU: To what extent are we in the mess we are in, because, while "majority rules" in this country, the minority has few, if any, rights other than what the majority is willing to grant the minority?

CHAMBERS: I believe the mess we are in goes well beyond majority vs. minority, whites vs. people of color. It is the value system of our society — with values like acquisitiveness, competitiveness, aggressiveness — that are at the root of the mess. These anti-human values must be changed before we can hope to attain race and sex equity and social justice. This explains why, for example,  the CIBC *Bulletin* has broadened the scope of its concerns to consider the societal values reflected in children's books and other learning materials. We believe that in reflecting the values of society, children's learning materials perpetuate them, and we want to see those values changed. I agree with the conclusion of an article you wrote about CIBC, which appeared in *Sipapu* some years ago (v. 8, no. 1, consecutive issue no. 15, January 1977; pp. 152–157) that children's books cannot change society (our p. 156). That would be expecting far too much. But children's books can provide content that questions traditional assumptions and role models, and so help achieve a more equitable, just society.

Now, to return to your question about an oppressive majority. Your question implies that we have majority rule in this country. I disagree with that. Political and economic power is concentrated in the hands of a relatively few well-to-do white men, and they benefit very materially from this society's value system. Even though all white people benefit, in some degree, from white skin privilege in a racist society, the majority of white people are actually harmed by the present system's values. Unfortunately, few whites recognize this.

In my view, those oppressed by the present white male establishment constitute the majority of people in this country. When you consider the number of women of all colors, male minorities, poor white males, disabled people, gay men and lesbians, older people, working people—that's a huge majority indeed. When these groups come to see the interrelatedness of their particular oppressions, and work together toward common goals—whites seriously confronting racism, males seriously confronting sexism—social change will assuredly follow. Of course, that is what consciousness-raising is all about.

SIPAPU: Where do we go from here? Is the outlook bleakly totalitarian, or are we raising more consciousnesses than ever before?

CHAMBERS: Globally and nationally it is possible to see both hopeful and terrifying trends. I recall reading about a panel of historians and philosophers—Toynbee, Sartre, Russell among them—who were brought together in the 1960s to consider the state of the world. They observed that Western nations were becoming increasingly militaristic with ever-mounting military budgets, and they concluded that by the year 2000 Western society would be essentially totalitarian. However, between then and today, political consciousness has been rising at an accelerated pace. Blacks sparked the process with the Civil Rights Movement of the 1960s. All kinds of movements

since then have broadened people's consciousness, and many more people are becoming aware of the essentially oppressive structure of our society. The struggle that these movements provoke is, of course, the important thing. As Frederick Douglass said, "If there is no struggle, there is no progress." It is when these struggling movements begin to understand each other's issues and form coalitions, that there will be a possibility for turning around the thrust toward totalitarianism. I think the special issue of the CIBC *Bulletin* which we have just published is pertinent to this discussion. It reports on militarism and education and draws links between issues of racism and sexism and our society's strongly militaristic bent. We hope to reach people active in a range of equity struggles and to help make connections between their particular struggles and the antinuclear/disarmament movement. The patriarchal, racist militarists have the power, but they are not invincible if the rest of us manage to get ourselves together.

(Address of the Council on Interracial Books for Children, and of the *Interracial Books for Children Bulletin,* or CIBC *Bulletin,* as described on the preceding page: 1841 Broadway, New York, NY 10023; $15 for institutions, eight issues a year.)

AND NOW, A TREAT.—*Sipapu* has never done a travelogue, other than conference-going, but when Diane Callum of Winters gave us this description of her train trip through central South America, we jumped at the chance. "The Train of the Dead," they call it in sophisticated São Paulo, Brazil, but Diane took it, with her family, and loved it, and lived to tell the tale:

"O TREM DOS MORTOS: 'The train of the dead' they called it, and rightly so, because after seventy-five hours on this mediaeval wrack, you were beyond beat, more than pooped; you were literally *morto,* dead! Forget the nostalgic old-world luxury of the Orient Express, or even the new world practicality of the Amtrack Metroliner. A hard-topped covered wagon with straight-backed wooden chairs, and reject horseshoes for wheels is the picture of the *Trem dos Mortos* that plods its way from São Paulo, Brazil, to Santa Cruz, Bolivia.

"But for all the hardships, there's nothing like the pure joy of having survived this three-day trek through mountains and jungle. The pattern of adjustment of the passengers followed an arc from vertical sobriety and propriety to horizontal rolling in the aisles.

"Even the first-class passengers preferred rolling in the aisles. Geraldo, for example, was a high Bolivian official who spent the entire trip 'high'—on *puro:* Bolivian firewater; the equivalent of Wild Turkey mixed with diesel fuel. Geraldo could always be found in 'steerage' in a floating crap game that floated throughout the train. It didn't matter if Geraldo won or lost because he was the only one who could afford the game and the endless rounds of drinks. He made the rules—he and a few other slumming officials. It wasn't really slumming, either, because the sheer exhilaration of the macho adventure went beyond class distinctions, with jokes, and toasts, and belly laughter that could ripple water. But no matter how slurred the speech became, or how total the camaraderie, the officials were always addressed as *senhor*. So Geraldo would drink and gamble with the *canpesinos* until he could barely see. Then came the true test or propriety: to see if he could amble back to his first-class sleeper, through twelve lurching cars at three a.m. Two out of three times he ambled short—but always into a compliant lap.

"*Puro* was the universal solvent that merged the diverse social strata and languages into a common babble of intimacy. *Puro* sent the tall, blond American with 'eyes like the blue sky' into the octopus arms of four Bolivian peasant women; *puro* even let nursing babies sleep in strangers' arms. But the real bond of friendship was the trip itself—rubbing elbows with others and sharing this experience into limbo.

"On the first day everyone had his own neat basket of food: strangers politely shared or refused what their neighbors offered. As the baskets became depleted, strangers became first cousins—part of an extended family that extended the entire length of the car. A greasy chicken leg was devoured by two children who had never met before. A farmer from São Paulo courted a widow from Campo Grande with a basket of mangoes. The train itself made frequent stops: milk stops in the morning by a complacent Brahmin who would let herself be milked and then outdistance the train a few miles. Sometimes a barrage of women carrying trays of exotic-smelling empanados on their heads would come through, or men from the countryside would slit open green coconuts with their machetes. And the street-wise children were everywhere—selling, buying, or begging. There was only one stop no one ever could figure out: a full stop by a swamp in the Mato Grosso. No one—nothing around for miles—except a figure in white gesticulating madly. It was the cook fishing in a jungle pond for the evening meal: He was catching piranhas, hundreds of the deadly delicacies, for a surprise. The whole train had a numbers pool going, betting on how many he could manage to catch in 10 minutes.

"Sleeping arrangements were based on lottery too. The first night was a sequence in high camp: head falling on neighbor's shoulder, followed by profuse mutual apologies, then nodding out again, falling fast asleep on the same neighbor's machete. The second night a few nocturnal leaders emerged to organize the fray: women and children into the aisles on top of the luggage, lying prone; men in semi-prone positions on the seats. By the third day, however, there was a raucous free-for-all.

"By the time the train crossed the border at Corumba, incest had run rampant in the extended family. The tall blond American never did extricate himself from the four Bolivian women; for all anyone knows, he's still in a *ménage à cinq* somewhere in the foothills of the Andes. Geraldo, sober and in a spotless uniform, was hardly recognizable except for the pleasure-loving twinkle in his eyes. As for the rest, they knew they had really been something. An entire life cycle had run its course in those few days on 'The Train of the Dead.'"—DIANE CALLUM.

14 : 1

I selected Karl Kempton as the "farthest out" of poets writing today—and found a friend. I subsequently published a small poetry book of his, in a more conventional style, The Light We Are.

HOW IT IS WITH US: We are raising our subscription price from $4.00 per year to $8.00 per year, a 100% price increase. No other library periodical, including those surveyed by *Library Journal,* can make this claim. (*Library Journal* does not list us in their annual surveys of periodical prices.)

TWO DRIFTS IN POETRY have flowed in our time: one is the tendency to what John Ciardi has called the "American voice-box," the increased sound of vernacular, demotic speech, heard from whites, blacks, Chicanos, women: a democratization of language first heard from in Allen Ginsberg's "Howl" (1956). The other has been an increased emphasis on experiment, particularly in visual poetry and concrete poetry, less acclaimed, but still significant as one of the few really experimental forms left in our time. The late *West Coast Poetry Review* had some examples of concrete or visual poetry, and so did a periodical called *Typewriter;* but most librarians are unaware of it.

And what is visual/concrete poetry, you may ask? Simply, any poetry that has an appeal to the seeing eye as well as to the reasoning sense and to the hearing ear. With concrete, or completely visual, poetry, the visual aspect takes place over all other forms of expression, seizes the reins of the chariot of Apollo, and takes off wherever it pleases. Arion Press, San Francisco, under the direction of Andrew Hoyem, recently published a large folio collection of visual poetry, from pre-Socratic Greece to the present (i.e., a poem by Hoyem himself). These were all shaped poems, with the exception of a few of Apollinaire's *Calligrammes.* Even those, including the shaped poems we have issued from Konocti Books *(Sun Poem* and *Moon Poem),* are timid beside Karl Kempton's *typoglifs.* What follows is an interview with a major figure in

the extreme avant-garde of visual/shaped poetry, a gentle chap with an extraordinary sense of beauty, once you learn to tune your fiddle to his key:

SIPAPU: We'll start out with the usual: your birth and education: since you're not as easily researched as some writers; you're not in *Contemporary Authors, Contemporary Poets, International Who's Who in Poetry*, etc. How did you get launched?

KEMPTON: before answering your first question i want to thank u for providing this opportunity to discuss my poetry and publication with u, and thru u, with your readers. from my rap sheet i've created a translation of my birth stats: — i was born in the year of the steel penny, a fiscal nu year baby in the windy city, which iz to say, july 1, 1943, chicago. my father was a service metallurgist for u.s. steel, and his father had workt his way to the top management level of u.s. steel, and so, within this frame, i was guided from junior high school in downey, a suburb of l.a., to become a technocrat. i graduated from the university of utah, with a b.s. in economics, with minors in mathematics and history. in the summer of '71 i returned to the 'u' for graduate work in economic history and middle eastern studies / — only to drop out in the spring of '73 to devote my energies to poetry.

rather interesting your use of the word "launch," considering i live 40 air miles north of space-port west, vandenburg, and from where i see, if conditions are rite, on a missile exhaust stem a five-petal bloom as the second stage roars into space. from within the belly of the beast came my first poems — i was drafted into the army in '65 while working as a statistician in cost analysis for douglas aircraft on the apollo project. i had dropt out of school and returned to southern california from utah. what i wrote was barf on the page to keep me sane. while stationed in germany, i came across kerouac's work which tot me that there iz only one rule in writing and that iz to communicate.

out of the army, and changing my major to economics, i completed college in a year, staying away from english and writing classes, in order to develop my own style. while in graduate school or during that time, i encountered three forces which stand out at this moment, that make the tripod supporting my launch. the movie *orpheus* by jean cocteau. it was not only the majik he worked but most important to me, the way that orpheus received poetry—dictated to him over the car radio. (this came to me just the other day.) secondly, there was the discovery of concrete poetry, which once again illustrated nu possibilities, tho here, instead of rapture there was 'i can do better than that,' a statement taking years of work to justify. it took me a couple of years just to find the grid i waz to compose with, the weaver's grid. the third leg waz meeting and becoming fast friends with charles potts. he brot several vektorz into play, into my awareness: — contemporary amerikan poetry, small press publishing az an act, and semi-foenetik spelling, which i used in association with my vizualization of language. of the host of poets charlie potts pointed out, i'd have to say that charles olson has had the most profound influence by knocking down my horizons with one hand and with the other hand clearing the surface of the page upon which i was now free to compose nu possibilities.

SIPAPU: Like anyone else, you started out simple and became complex; i.e., you weren't doing typoglifs in first grade, you had to discover them. There must have been steps from "there" to "here and now."

KEMPTON: my first glif using the x-y grid was completed in november of '73. it waz about a square-inch diamond pattern stroked out by the plus sign (+). it seems az tho a dam waz blown up along my stream of expression, bekuz since that moment i've been most fortunate to be az a vessel thru which there iz a constant flow. what i had to do then, az i did with poetry, waz teach myself art. for u see, i'm self tot in both these forms of expression. so i tot myself by way of looking thru art books, at collections of art from around the world, from the most ancient forms, cave paintings, rock paintings and glif work, etc., to contemporary works. the resulting first typoglifs were illustrations accompanying my poems, but soon the vizual aspect eclipsed the written. and during this year i moved from the city of salt to sacramento; in fact, a block away from wally depew, a concrete poet, who within a month moved away leaving me to continue the neighborhood tradition of vizual poetry. also, during this time frame the works of victor vasarely and m.c. escher cot my attention.

the reading of *White Goddess* by robert graves in the fall of '74 shifted my focus from that of wanderer thru world art to that of looking into my genetic background. it took olson's advice to dig deep in one place. this is how and why keltik knotwork came into my focus; out of which evolved the first RUNE book. at the same time: my interest in knots brought my attention to found objects that were knotted—wires and strings—which i would either sketch on the spot or take home on my walks around sacramento. out of this came the first section of LOST ALPHABET FOUND. when i moved to this area, the pismo beach area of san luis obispo county, i was captivated by the

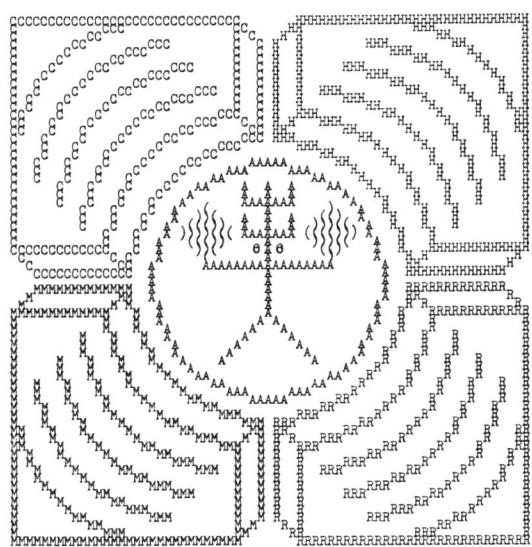

Karl Kempton: *Charm*

knot tying of the mother's tung, the ocean tying of sea grasses and kelp. the book grew from its 27 conceptual letters to 111 after a year's work.

my interests and influences cover a wide spectrum which has enabled me to compose on and around a variety of forms. RUNE took over two years to compose. RUNE 2 took me less than a month. RUNE 3: SHIFT took five years, with considerable research into the geometry of illusion, and during '78 my interests in north amerikan indian art, micro electronic az design, found objects and geometry all came together in a 4 section manuscript which has been publisht in part in its sections, and has just been accepted by xerox sutra editions. RUNE 4: KRITERZ AND FABLEZ OFF THE MOTHER TUNG is based on foam patterns from the surf. i'm now typing RUNE 5: BODY LANGUAGE based on diagrams of anatomy. RUNE 6, tentatively titled, FIGURATIVELY SPEEKING is also in process. RUNE 4 thru 6 are gestures towards the origins of writing such as LOST ALFABET waz. RUNE 7: INDIAN WEDDING will be a bringing together of eastern indian and amerikan indian patterns and language, which at the moment, iz a concept with considerable labor ahead of me.

SIPAPU: The casting of the KALDRON: circumstances of its founding, origin of the name, etc.?

KEMPTON: KALDRON iz a continuation of the rainbow resin publications i started in '72 in the city of salt. i founded KALDRON in '76 to continue publishing a poetic focus which developed while in sacramento: both the vizual and the majikal lyric poems. i pickt the tabloid format for two

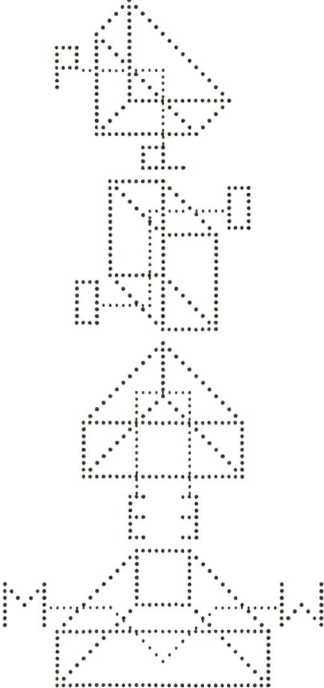

Karl Kempton: *Poem* (#2)

reasons, page size and economy, which was important since this waz going to be an example of free enterprise, a free publication. it waz more difficult to find a name. after two weeks of searching i gave up and consulted the chinese orakl, the *I Ching*. i tossed a non-changing line hexagram 50, the caldron, only one of two man-made objects given a hexagram. i changed the spelling to illustrate the newness of this vessel whose mythical, inspirational and nourishing powers r rooted world wide.

in '77 i decided to create an international visual poetry and language-art show at cal poly in san luis obispo, and i asked two friends, david and patty arnold, to aid and abet. i called it visualog. this show changed the direction of KALDRON from one of poetry and some visual poetry to that of a journal of vizual poetry and language-art publishing historical and contemporary work from around the world. nobody else was providing this service on a 'regular' basis and the work i knew that waz available in quality did not match what i saw being publisht. i wanted to end the prejudice surrounding visual poetry which i believe grew out of publications from the east coast. KALDRON haz evolved to a position of being a vital link in the global network of vizual poetry and langwij art: it iz the only publication of its kind in the country: and the only larj format magazine of its kind in the world devoted to the vizualization of langwij.

[From Fulton and Ferber's *International Directory of Little Magazines and Small Presses:* "A visual poem or language art work is a wedding of literature and art composed for the eye (sometimes for the ear as well). The sum of the images is the poem or work."]

SIPAPU: We really like the visual splendor of *Rune 2: 26 Voices* (*Typewriter*, #10). (Especially because the typoglifs done with A's do not spell out a big "A," etc.) They have the power of 19th-century ornamented typefaces (cf. the book of that title by Nicolete Gray). By contrast, your preference for lower-case text and spelling simplification has almost a clipped, dramatic effect to it. Do you see this as contrast, or is it all part of one way of looking at things? Is this a move toward demotic script and democracy, or a new way of seeing (and seeing into) the world?

KEMPTON: thanx for your favorable response to RUNE 2: 26 VOICES which iz a homage to the letters we use in the written form of our language. each letter waz given a pattern which iz a mandala, a vizual tool for meditation, or the pattern can b looked upon az either an amulet or a charm shaped by or from the resonance of the letter thru a chant.

these 26 letters in various combinations create a very ruf semblence of the spoken aspect of our tung, a tung which is amerikan, not english, az our schools attempt to maintain, pretend to teach; and it iz within theez schools we've all learned how out of integrity our spelling iz with the way our tung wags. i am deeling with a material objekt, a ritten word, and its vibraashun, itz sound.

i'm also working at eroding the conceptual agreement we have surrounding definition, because our langwij to a larj degree shapes the way we think; shapes the way we see; and the way we respond; which in turn echoez back into/onto our language making for many complex ripplez. Our tung is set up like the old patriarchal world-view, one thing following another in a line of cause-effekt; a machined universe. but our sciences and our metaphysiks and our mysticizms have shown us otherwise. our tung iz out of faze here az well. my poems address this concern by adding az many dimensions az i can onto a word, letter or abstraction (which by the way can b lookt upon as thot, coming into being). hence, my use of optical art to create after-images suggesting the energy, or an ora surrounding an objekt; and my use of illusion pointing to the fakt that what we assume to see, is not the actual action kot. for exampl, this page iz condensed lite, not what we've kum to accept without thinking in this day of matter-manipulation.

my spelling has generated eether positiv or negativ reakshun with very litl komment of gray-zoned indifference; the main komplaint seemz to b that i make our langwij look like german! an akt i'm not responsible for. our roots are teutonic, anglo-saxon. i'm merely ironing out the french and latin folds

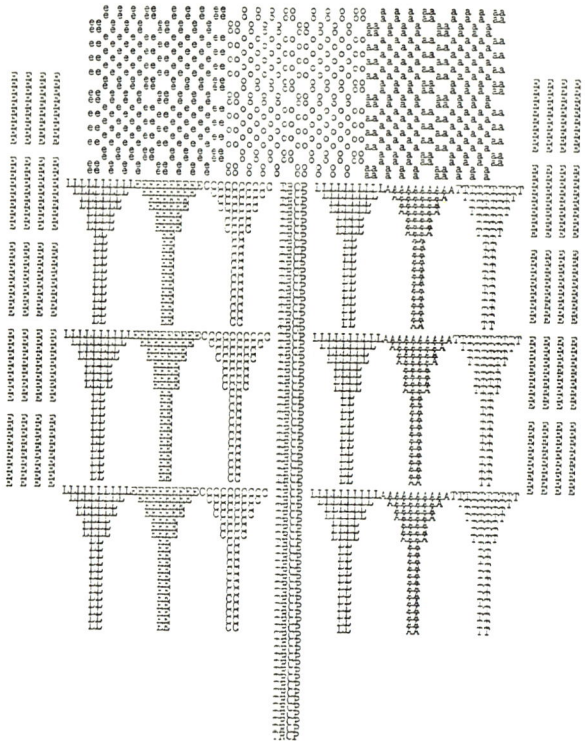

Karl Kempton. *Electroplate*

kreest into our tung. also, this spelling brings my verbal sense to the reader—konsider what a texan's spelling would du: many words with longer vowels.

SIPAPU: Now then: Visual, shaped, or concrete poetry has a long ancestry. What parts of this tradition most attract you, or do you see it as not all that relevant to your work? (We're thinking of Venantius Fortunatus, George Herbert, &c.) (Also cabbalistic and sufic diagrams, mediaeval Christian texts in the shape of a fish, &c.)

KEMPTON: konkreet poetree was a short lived phase of vizual poetry, a poetree of fragmenting language into its parts and sub-parts for examination. vizual poetry haz roots az deep az one wants to take the vizual expression of language. my interest in knots led me to the uncovering of the following which i have found very intriguing. the word *amulet* in several languages iz related to the word *knot*. when magical knots were tied, spells were chanted thru the tying. when the spoken became written, amulets became patterned with spells, prayers and the like. this iz the root of vizual poetry az i have come to understand it—to this point. so here i am, looking over my shoulder at the first vizual poems i composed based on knot work—i waz working with the source of my art without any conscious awareness.

within the concrete tradition the only 'school' which attracted my attention was the japanese, seechii niikunii in particular. he died a few years ago and hiz wife publisht a collection of hiz work, a beautiful book, the historikal work which attracts my attention the most, outside the illuminated BOOK OF KELLS, iz the islamic tradition. on the whole, the historical work which pulls me in iz usually directly or indirectly related to the sacred in which i alwayz find clear sharp lines, a balance and radiating hight vibrations.

SIPAPU: Visual poetry is like love: you start with holding hands and go on to kisses, and then on to bigger and better things. So readers familiar with acrostics may go on to discover poems shaped like a cross or the sun, and presently you arrive at Apollinaire's *Calligrammes,* or Karl Kempton's typoglifs and typestracts. At which point does this material become really interesting to you? Another way of putting this is, where's the frontier, what can we put aside as already explored, what remains to be explored in this field?

KEMPTON: first i'd like to clear out the use of *typestract* to label my work. william fox came up with this description when he publisht my first glifs in WEST COAST POETRY REVIEW. when he approached me with this label there waz an immediate negative response. it felt too restrictive, too tied to modern art, tied to a particular time frame and contrary to my skope which haz always been world wide, from the vastness of the past to the vastness of the future. so, i coined the term *typoglif* wedding the term glif from the terms describing the most ancient vizual expressions of language to a typewriter or typemachine. typestract waz like a line while typoglif to me iz a vibration penetrating a wide spectrum of possibilities.

a vizual poem becomes interesting to me when excitement iz brot forth by it but how this excitement is triggered i am unsure of. all i can say iz that it is beyond the verbal element which iz why vizual poetry exists. i have developed a particular sense of what i want to express and how i want to project the expression on the page and of course this spills over into how i take in other work tho in my editorial process i drop my personal views for that of the visual poetry and language art community at large.

the shaped poem i'd say is, if not fully explored, like the sonnet, nearly exhausted. but this is just an opinion. dick higgins could answer this question of regarding the shaped poem better, in that he has a collection of 700 or so such poems. like anything else, the frontier iz the horizon line we draw by being closed to new possibilities. there is no field closed to exploration but exploring is one thing, and the result of that effort is what counts, what determines a work to be of lasting value or not, or of any value at all, other than the process the particular individual enjoyed during the making.

SIPAPU: Describe the show you recently took around the country with

Loris Essary and Dan Raphael. What did you do? How did audiences react?

KEMPTON: "tung behind the i" waza multi-media performance series which loris, dan and i blended into two 15 minute sets of each of our individual expressions. a performance would begin with an overture sound track accompanied by slides of essary's vizual poems overlaid with slides of stained-glass windows. loris's sets consisted of a one man play, some performance art and poetry. dan would pick his two sets of poetry delivery from four sets he carried within his head. my sets were made up of poetic delivery accompanied with sound track and slides, again overlays, from RUNE 2, and from RUNE 3 a series of 6 slide presentations with voiced sound tracks.

it took us a year to put the tour together, the bookings and the scheduling, of finding spaces willing to pay us. march 15 i flew to austin where loris and i put our ⅔ of the series together and on april 1 we flew into portland where dan's sets were added. from april 6 to may 4 we gave 21 performances in 27 days along the west coast and thru the southwest: vancouver, canada; portland and ashland, oregon; sacramento, santa cruz, and san francisco, arroyo grande and san luis obispo, all in california; scottsdale, tempe, and phoenix, arizona; las cruces, santa fe, and albuquerque, new mexico; and el paso and austin, texas.

i feel that were were extremely well received. of course the audience response was different from place to place, and by the way, most of the spaces in which we performed were galleries, so that the audiences were not just poetry oriented. and tho we bookt ourselves as avant-garde, we feel az tho such a term is outdated for what we provided, that what we gave the audiences is something nu, unique, given the multi-media approach of our performance, and to carry with us, to sell, laughing bear press publisht TO TASTE, a collection of some of the works presented on the tour.

SIPAPU: The *Gamut* competition: for what kind of work was first prize awarded: a group of works, or one single item?

KEMPTON: i have been honored by the judges of THE GAMUT concrete poetry contest. i am a co-winner along with scott hemles. 290 poets and artists from england, canada and the u.s. entered. i submitted two poems from RUNE 3. one was five pages long and the other 10. tho each poem is a series, individual poems can be lookt upon az poems in themselves.

SIPAPU: "Concrete" vs. "visual" poetry: the Library of Congress now has a related-reference under "visual poetry" to "concrete poetry." To us there are differences: "touch" one, "see" the other; and also, in visual poetry, there is still some concession made to text, in concrete poetry text is fully subordinated to visual appearance, whether or not a clearly organized pattern is distinguishable therein. A difference to us: is it a difference to you?

KEMPTON: concrete poetry iz a post world war 2 development and expression within the long tradition of vizual poetry, az to when it actually

Karl Kempton. From *Indian Wedding*

began and who can b considered among these poets or this poetry is a matter of opinion. concrete poetry does seem to be the first international poetry movement. this poetry is a poetry of fragmentation, a fission process examining the parts and stuff of language, of extracting energy thru pulling apart. its roots r traceable to the futurist and dadaist movements earlier in this century. on the other hand, visual poetry is a fusion process, of creating energy by bringing together parts. today's vizual poetry is more than ever a wedding of the vizual arts with poetry, a poetry and literature wedded to collage, sculpture, drawing, fotografy, painting, xerography, etc.

SIPAPU: Describe, preferably in visual poetry, that we may all see: (a) yourself; (b) your bride.

KEMPTON: (See above) this will either be the cover or the title page of RUNE 7: INDIAN WEDDING. our marriage ceremony is a hindu fire ceremony so what u c here is the word or seed, OM, floating above us kneeling on a design which iz a chumash pattern. our home iz on an old vilij site and we r getting married at home. the concept for RUNE 7 came about before meeting my spiritual teacher and before ruth and i had any thots of marriage. in fact we were just getting to know each other when this came to me, the title for RUNE 7.

This ends the interview with Karl Kempton. Some further facts about Kempton and his work follow:

Kaldron, P.O. Box 541, Halcyon, CA 93420, founded in 1976, $3.00 for each copy, expecting 2 issues a year. Donations accepted. Circulation 1000. (This is a new address—supersedes earlier ones.)

Kempton submitted to us a bibliography plus a list of periodical appearances, without numbers or issues; we list only part of the first page, plus a few notes of our own on concrete/visual poetry:

Books:
   LOST ALPHABET FOUND, West Coast Poetry Review Press, Reno, NV, 1979
   RUNE, Bern Porter Books, Belfast, ME, 1980
   RUNE 2: 26 VOICES, Typewriter, Iowa City, IA, 1980
   EON PULSE, Editions Brian Lane, London, England, 1981
   FILM STRIP LOJIK, Curved H&Z, Toronto, Canada, 1983
   BLACK STROKES WHITE SPACES, Xerox Sutra Editions, Madison, 1983

Co-author:
   VENERATIONS/precincts of the 5th apocalypse, with Michael Hannon, rainbow resin press, Grover City, CA, 1981
   constellations/REASONS AND METHODS, with Kirk Robertson, Duck Down, Falon, NV and rainbow resin press, Grover City, CA, 1981
   KO with Loris Essary, Noumenon Press, Austin, TX (forthcoming 1983)

Other titles:
   Four posters published by PANOPLY, 1977 (Venice, CA): RUNE, CARPET, BOXES, and NASCA PLANE 3 (now distributed by Kempton)
   FILM SKRIPT, rainbow resin press, Grover City, CA 1982
   THE LETTERZ U ALWAYS WANTED TO RECEEVE, rainbow resin press, Grover City, CA, 1982
   POEM, curved H&Z, Toronto, Canada, 1982

Anthologies and catalogs:
   SOUTHWEST: A CONTEMPORARY ANTHOLOGY, A CRITICAL ASSEMBLING, OGGI POESIA DOMANI (Italy), CITTA E POESIA (Italy), JAPAN AU (Japan): Seoul, Korea: International Mail-Art Exhibition of Visual Message '82; NRG Anthology (Portland, Oregon), 1983

Periodicals:
   10-5155-20: see p. 37 of this issue of Sipapu.
   Editor and Publisher: KALDRON, an international journal of visual poetry and language art.
   Co-editor: CAFE SOLO, Series 2, nos. 1/2 and 3/4.

Co-editor: OPEN RING.
Guest editor *10-5155-20,* no. 5.
West Coast Poetry Review, no. 12.
West Coast Poetry Review, nos. 17, 18, and 19, corresponding to its volume 5, nos. 1, 2, and 3.

No. 19, which is the same as v. 5, no. 3, is also an issue, and a triple issue at that, of *Precisely,* nos. 3, 4, and 5. That is, *Precisely,* nos. 3-4-5, is the same as *WCPR,* no. 19, which is the same as *WCPR,* v. 5, no. 3.

You might expect that the triple issue of *West Coast Poetry Review* is just the same as the triple issue of *Precisely.* That may be true, but it is not our impression. We have handled this set, and we are convinced that the triple issue of *Precisely* only corresponds to *West Coast Poetry Review,* v. 5, no. 3, which is consecutive issue, no. 19.

Both *West Coast Poetry Review* and *Precisely* are (at this point, and to our knowledge), no longer being published. First serials librarian to cheer leaves the room!

Anyway, if you have, or can get, *WCPR/Precisely* for their last joint issues, you will have all you need to know about concrete poetry—unless you want to read a work by Dick Higgins, *George Herbert's Pattern Poems* (Unpublished Editions, P.O. Box 73, Canal Street, New York, NY 10013). On p. 12 we mentioned *To Taste,* —published by Laughing Bear Press, P.O. Box 23478, San Jose, CA 95153; it contains a number of shaped poems and typoglifs by Kempton; also Loris Essary's play, "The Death and Life of Elmer Fudd," which is worth reading; cost $4.00.

Finally, if you get *Rune 2,* from P.O. Box 409, Iowa City, IA 52244, and hold each page up to the light, you will discover something quite beautiful!

AS IS WELL KNOWN, librarians (*our* kind) don't go to conferences just to listen to lectures and chair committees. They go to party and they go to *plot.* This document is one that emerged from our semi-secret meetings at ALA. It is a response to the recent unfair criticism, as we see it, directed at Bradford Chambers, editor of the *Interracial Books for Children Bulletin,* and at the Council on Interracial Books for Children, New York. Such attacks have taken place in the American Federation of Teachers' organ, *American Educator,* April 1983, where the CIBC was paired with Lyndon LaRouche's organization, U.S. Caucus of Labor Committees, as an example of left vs. right in propaganda. Other misunderstandings have been demonstrated by top ALA figures.

The following statement has been revised and also some few changes have been made by Chambers and his editor. Essentially, however, it remains the statement signed by several of us in Los Angeles, 27 June 1983:

"REVISED STATEMENT of the AD HOC COMMITTEE to SUPPORT THE COUNCIL ON INTERRACIAL BOOKS FOR CHILDREN

"The culturally pluralistic press performs an important role in librarianship, unifying and educating the profession around the themes of racial, sexual, and personal diversity, including choices of politics, religion, and lifestyle. It points the profession toward a direction not always considered seriously.

"Publications such as *Interracial Books for Children Bulletin,* the organ of the Council on Interracial Books for Children (CIBC), and many others, provide diversity of voice and access, and encourage cultural pluralism. Yet we hear voices which would discourage these tendencies.

"We hold that the CIBC has, since 1966, been doing what teachers and librarians should have been doing for many years — namely, reaffirming the freedom, dignity, and equality of the individual citizen, on which our democratic government is based. While exposing the hidden biases against racial groups, women, people who are 'different,' as seen in books for children, CIBC has enlarged its scope to include discussions of militarism and homophobia, and has sponsored writers from targeted groups. In addition, CIBC has provided extremely useful bibliographies and guidelines for librarians interested in the positive aspects of peoples outside the American mainstream.

"We have learned, each in our own way, that discrimination pervades mainstream American culture, and that our institutions (including libraries), reflect this fact. We are not content with this discrimination, however, and call on librarians to examine their own preconceptions in these matters. Some of us have moved away from a position of bewilderment and anger at CIBC, through a self-criticism, followed by a better understanding of the critical position taken by the Third World, feminist, gay, and disability rights activist contributors to the *Bulletin*'s page. As librarians, editors, writers, we have known the temptation to believe we were intellectually 'pure.' But unlike Galileo's contemporaries who could not believe there could be spots on the 'pure' Sun, and therefore blamed the dirt in his telescope — we believe that even an uncomfortable truth is worth listening to.

"If it were clearly understood that criticism that makes the hearer uncomfortable is not censorship, — we might help, as librarians, to reduce the strangeness of Americans to each other, while giving each group its best chance to express their 'right to be different' — to borrow a phrase of Lillian Smith.

"We call attention to positive discussions of the CIBC and *Bulletin* editor Bradford Chambers, in recent issues of *Technicalities,* the *SRRT Newsletter,* and *Sipapu,* and invite librarians to read these documents.

"Above all, we resent the implication, wherever expressed, that criticism by the oppressed is simply another form of censorship. While many of us are 'mainstream Americans,' all of us have learned from criticism of this sort. We therefore call for a transformation of public values.

"As practicing librarians committed alike to intellectual freedom and to social responsibility, we denounce all smear attacks against CIBC. We express our support for its continuing efforts to sensitize teachers, librarians, writers, and publishers to racism, sexism, and other anti-human biases in children's media; to promote truly multi-cultural children's literature; and to produce resources on vital but widely neglected topics like militarism, the Ku Klux Klan, homophobia, and Central American oppression. No other organization has done these things so well as the Council on Interracial Books for Children.

"We invite the profession to give them support."

(A large number of signers, 8 or 9 if that's large, have signed the original. If you wish your name attached to this document as co-signer, pray contact the editor.)

UNDERGROUND PUBLICATIONS IN PUERTO RICO: Borinquén, "land of the proud lord," is for many the preferred native name of Puerto Rico. Luisín Lares Medina, of Lares, PR, takes us on a tour of the present *situación puertorriqueño:*

If we want to talk about Puerto Rico's underground publications, we have to first define what Puerto Rico is, and how it is "underground." For many people Puerto Rico is an integral part of the United States of America. They believe that sooner or later Puerto Rico will become a State of the Union. Some of these people believe that Puerto Rico is a colony of the United States, solely because it doesn't have full statehood. Others hold that Puerto Rico is destined to relinquish its position as "Estado libre asociado" (Free associated nation), or Commonwealth of the U.S.A., and become independent as Borinquén, "land of the brave and proud lord." Puerto Rico has an area less than 10,000 sq. km. but 3.5 million inhabitants; about 2.5 million Puerto Ricans live out of the island, largely in the U.S.

Has Puerto Rico an underground—political or literary? Not as the United States, or the United Kingdom. The main thing to remember is that Puerto Rico is still a colony of the U.S.: political, economic, military. If a particular Puerto Rican municipality wants to build a sidewalk, Federal money will be used, and Washington will tell them what materials to use, and how to build that sidewalk. Consequently underground figures are political, but not with the sense of freedom that many self-styled underground figures are in the U.S. For example, Juan Antonio Corretjer is respected by all segments of Puerto Rican society—but politically he has less than 200 followers. He participated in the brief Puerto Rican war against the U.S.: 30 October 1950. Jailed, he became a Marxist-Leninist; urges citizens to carry guns, illegal or not; talks openly in favor of urban guerrillas; advocates the overthrow of, by force and violence, the imperialist, capitalist, colonialist U.S. administration in Puerto Rico.

Sr. Corretjer doesn't care a damn about the Establishment, right? So why is he respected? How does he reach all those other puertorriqueños? He gets paid for writing a column in *El Nuevo Dia,* owned by the Ferre family, who are reputedly as rich as Rockefeller. Here then, is the paradox of an underground movement, which takes place in an island which has been a foreign colony since 1493, and which is now too small and too crowded for a real underground. And under the extended-family system, dozens of relatives and friends entrap the most determined rebel in a web of accommodation, which protects the individual as well as suppressing his bid for freedom. The result is a part-time underground movement, if the phrase makes any sense.

René Marqués, one of Puerto Rico's best writers, remarked in an essay that underground writers often arose at the peak of a nation's development. Before 1940 Puerto Rico was one of the poorest nations in Latin America, its economy entirely based on agriculture. The first elected governor of Puerto Rico, Luís Múñoz-Marín, started "Operation Bootstrap," which with help from Washington, began to turn this situation around. The resulting roads, factories, schools, agricultural production, made headlines in the U.S. and elsewhere—but what happened to the writers? According to Marquez, those most qualified to be in the underground joined the reformist movement for social justice. They used their writing skills to support the peaceful revolution. Two sources of optimism encouraged them: Marxist-Leninist (at that time acceptable), and capitalist. Opposed though these were, both systems denied fatalistic views of life, maintaining that humanity could take control of its own destiny. For René Marqués, influential writer and editor (1919-1979), Puerto Rican literature was pessimistic as long as the government was optimistic. During the 1950s, a new aggressive spirit occurred. As the population moved from the villages to San Juan, and many others from the island to New York and other big continental cities, living largely in slums, more of them came into the life of the new American empire which had succeeded that of Spain. Puertorriqueños found themselves drafted into the U.S. Armed Forces, and sent to Korea, with the outbreak of the Korean Conflict on 24 June 1950. On 30 October 1950 the Puerto Rican Nationalist Party declared war on the United States of America. The following day, 1 November, two Puerto Ricans attempted to assassinate President Harry S Truman, then residing in Blair House. Both were stopped: Griselio Torresola was killed, and Oscar Collazo was captured after killing Pvt. Leslie Coffelt. On the Island, thousands of protestors were jailed by the U.S. Armed Forces. The Revolution lasted only 24 hours.

Today, Puerto Rico is the home of writers, who, in the words of the patriot José de Diego, are "inside the Establishment, but against it." In a country where 87% of the population votes, political activity is high—but is forced to work within the system. Puerto Ricans have more than 120 radio stations, close to 35 cable TV stations—a higher concentration per square mile than in most English-speaking countries. Consequently, access to mass media is easier than in the U.S., Canada or U.K. Still, those who can afford the biggest ads are the biggest companies, the same ones that threaten the delicate Island environment.

Misión Industriál, a public advocate for ecological issues, has until recently been publishing two small periodicals, *Canaselle,* and *Correo Ambientál;* but because of funding problems these two may have ceased publication. In Adjuntas, a small town in the central range, a group called "Arte y cultura," lacking a publication of their own, have printed some papers on the dangers of land exploitation by a copper mine. Although big companies back the mine, the Establishment papers have given the ecologists a big coverage. Without big game to hunt, some hunters have got permission to hunt one of the wild pigeons (perhaps the white-crowned, *Columba leucocephala,* which is very common on the eastern end of the Island). While the government prepares regulations, several groups are organizing to protest any kind of hunting in Puerto Rico. Without a publication of their own, they are using the straight press to present their views to the people.

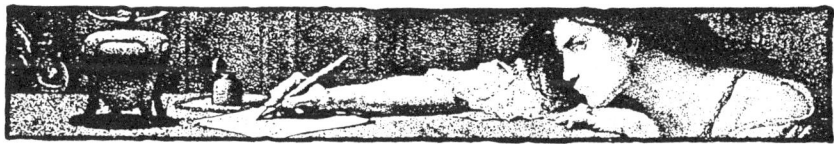

When it comes to gay/lesbian/feminist concerns, the only gay/lesbian publication is *La Verdad,* a tabloid of Marxist-Leninist outlook, of good technical quality printed on an irregular basis. In much of Puerto Rican society, gay/lesbian attitudes are accepted; on most TV comedies, someone is presented as gay, so that there is an Establishment acceptance, at least on the surface, of this point of view. As for feminism, nearly 50% of students attending PR universities are women; perhaps North American women will come to describe their Puerto Rican sisters as conservatives.

Religious freedom in Puerto Rico is total, as in the U.S.A. However, most churches established in the U.S.A., although still "Establishment" in outlook in the Island, once they get abroad become independent of their American origins, as far as extensive Puerto Rican followers are concerned. Those with mostly Anglo followers maintain their continental ties.

With regard to organized labor: the Puerto Rican government has reiterated to foreign and continental investors, that only 18% of workers are unionized. Consequently, Puerto Rican unions are a part-time underground: although labor unions on the Island are more conservative than other protesting groups, while radical leaders are rejected politically, they have a better chance to reach top union positions. *La Voz del Obrero* is printed in magazine format, and is based in Ponce and Peñuelas by oil workers. *Linéa Viva* is a highly technical publication by electrical workers, and *La Denúncia* is a half-tabloid belonging to the Union of Social Services Workers. FMPR (Puerto Rican Teachers' Union) publishes *La Verdad* (same name as the gay/lesbian/feminist periodical), and "radical" in contrast to the AMPR (Puerto Rican Teachers' Association), which publishes two monthly tabloids, *Asoma* and *El Vocero Informativo,* as well as a monthly magazine, *El Sol.* Other unions lack a voice, although the Instituto Laborál de Educación Sindicál, started in San Juan and now with branches in Ponce, Mayaguez and Arecibo, teaches non-credit courses in organization, labor relations, &c.

Here we must apologize for using the term "the Island" to refer to Puerto Rico, as the country includes several smaller islands, inhabited however sparsely, and included in the Spanish cession of 1898. Among these are Culebra and Vieques. One of the hottest struggles of Puerto Rican issues in the endeavour to push the U.S. Navy out of their installations in the island-municipality of Vieques or Isla Nena (Baby Island) as the local fisherfolk call it. Although there have been no local publications exclusively concerned with Vieques, Establishment as well as mainland periodicals, including radical ones, have printed protests against the Navy's use of the island as a bombing range. The issue is important to a score of Puerto Rican newspapers, however. And a series of booklets, consisting of newspaper articles and explanatory matter, on every nation of Latin America, including PR and Vieques, has been published by Movimiento Ecumenico Nacional, under the title of *La Cruz de los Pueblos.* The National Ecumenical Movement consists of ministers and layfolk from Methodist, United Presbyterian, Disciples of Christ, and Catholic backgrounds.

Intercámbio was initially published as

a periodical but has not been seen for over a year. It was dedicated to Vieques and to the peace of the Caribbean, and was published by the Proyecto Carìbeño pro Justícia y Paz, funded and supported by the American Friends Service Committee.

El Comite Nacional pro Defensa de Vieques is one of the biggest organizations sponsoring the struggle for control of Vieques. Once in a while they do a broadside. But most of the material available on Vieques is printed in the establishment press and in political publications.

In the field of International solidarity, Puerto Rico has two well-organized groups in support of the Central American nations of Nicaragua and El Salvador. They print single sheets and issue solidarity bonds—these last being the only such activity in Puerto Rico sponsored by the underground. These two groups operate mostly in the Lawyers' Palace, showing movies and holding conferences.

PRISA, the working arm of the Movimiento Ecuménico Nacional, publishes a monthly newsletter of 8 pages known as *Resumén de Notícias*. The subjects include unions, consumer affairs, ecology, Vieques, struggles against oppression in the Caribbean, Latin America, and Africa.

In the colonial but pluralistic democracy of Puerto Rico, going underground is a part-time activity—if the phrase be allowed—and there are few underground publications as North Americans understand the term. The best underground publication in Puerto Rico is the same old Establishment press.—LUISÍN LARES MEDINA

Of great importance is a book by **PEACE PILGRIM,** d. 1981: *Peace Pilgrim: Her Life and Work in Her Own Words; Compiled by Some of Her Friends.* Santa Fe, NM, An Ocean Tree Book, 1983 (P.O. Box 1295, Santa Fe, NM 87501). This 198-page book is free, although the compilers are charging $6 to bookstores, discount on orders of 5 + ; this suggests a donation to carry on with the work of publishing her message, and for this purpose an appropriate address is Friends of Peace Pilgrim, 43480 Cedar Avenue, Hernet, CA 92343. Seekers of detailed information may wish to contact the Peace Pilgrim Collection of the Swarthmore College Peace Library.

And who was Peace Pilgrim? Well, we seem to have been the last to find out, for she was killed while riding in a car by a head-on collision, near Knox, Indiana, 7 July 1981. But she was born around the very beginning of the century, and by her own account came from a poor family, had little education, dedicated herself to a life of service, never married, worked with the American Friends Service Committee, never took alcohol or tobacco, gave up meat. Such a background might be admirable, if not particularly interesting. But toward the end of 1952 she felt called toward a further step. Against the advice of all her friends, she abandoned her home, her possessions, her identity. With the help of a lady in California she contrived a stout tunic with the lettering PEACE PILGRIM on the front, and WALKING

25,000 MILES FOR PEACE on the back (this last phrase changed over the years), and without scrip or staff, stepped in front of the Rose Parade on 1 January 1953. She refused to identify herself as anything but Peace Pilgrim, to officers and clowns, rich and poor alike, as she wandered all over the fifty states, ten provinces of Canada and parts of Mexico. Everywhere she spread her message: war is unnecessary; the cause of war is immaturity; the only light is the Light of Christ within. She borrowed her phrases from the Quakers, but did not adhere to any religion, and Bible quotations are not extensive in this book.

And what did she accomplish? Well, she talked to thousands of people, warded off evil and escaped danger by fantastic good luck, corresponded with thousands through a P.O. address in Cologne, New Jersey; accepted speaking engagements, rest, food, when offered; lived without money; led tours in Alaska and Hawaii; survived blizzards and sandstorms, and depended all the while on the trust of strangers. Evil she met with non-resistance and non-animosity and won. Food was hers a-plenty: from a sharecropper's cabin to the dining-room of the Waldorf-Astoria (where a friend took her: we'd have given anything to see her in her "PEACE PILGRIM" tunic in the Waldorf-Astoria!). And everywhere her message was: "There will be no universal peace until there is universal inner peace."

And now to the book. It contains a rambling account of her pilgrimage, complete with incidents (some of which are very near to miracles); "Thoughts to ponder," simple sayings and teachings; her poems; newspaper articles and an interview given just before her death. On the basis of this book, it would be perfectly correct to think of her as a saint in the style of holy Francis; but not more than that. For she readily denied the role of Messiah, or some sort of secret-holding boddhisattva or guru. She speaks (we haven't heard her voice, but tapes are available from the Whittier address given above) in a completely simple American voice, not that of a salesman or a politician but that of a profoundly decent neighbor, "in whom there is no guile." The poems are not works of art; they are simple meditative verses, but as she was free of vulgarity or egotism, so the poems are beyond questions of taste. It is this overwhelming clarity, honesty, and simplicity that impresses one about the Peace Pilgrim, in contrast to the L. Ron Hubbards and the Jim Joneses who have complicated "answers" that can cost you your money or your life.

Of course, there are many people who have taken to a life of simplicity; many who have wandered; there are even those who have abandoned their past and taken different names. But these last, at least, are in nunneries and monasteries. What Peace Pilgrim uniquely did, was abandon her identity and then cast herself on the world, sustained only by the presence of God. Her rewards were infinite. Never once was she frightened, never once was she ill. Instead she slept on a bench in a railroad station, and heard a voice saying to her "Thou art my beloved daughter, and in thee I am well pleased."

She refused disciples; those who tried to keep up with her fell back exhausted. (She had prepared for the journey by hiking the Appalachian Trail.) She founded no church, established no order, spent all money given her on printing and postage—for when she stopped to rest, she had a pile of unanswered mail. Friends sheltered her; police released her in despair; truck drivers protected her; professors pleaded with her to come to classes. She helped everybody; drunks stopped drinking; a neurotic lady stopped being afraid of cats when she gave her a kitten; a crazy boy gave up trying to hit her. These are some of the things that Peace Pilgrim did, and there are also many other things which she did, the which, if they should be written every one, we suppose that even the world itself could not contain the books that should be written.

The introduction concludes with a simple verse, too light to be an epitaph:

Free of earth, as free of air,
Now you wander everywhere.

14 : 2

Arthur and Kit Knight were another couple who were interviewees very desirous of being interviewed. They came west for the COSMEP conference and came to my house. They're a very charming couple.

Booker's Small Press *has impressed me as somewhat less pompous than when I first saw it. It has changed publishers and now does crisp book reviews.*

"Akabar del Piombo" was not really Girodias, but it was the name chosen by Girodias for a collage artist from New York named Rubenstein. I think I have a complete set of his books. There are four titles. This is specialized collecting at its best.

Diane di Prima's Memoirs of a Beatnik *is the best Olympia Press title I know. It is magnificently erotic, also very funny, and is a wonderful portrait of the New York scene in the fifties.*

DISCIPLES OF THE BEAT ANGELS: Arthur and Kit Knight have been publishing since 1971 (but see below) a curious periodical with a strange address: *The Unspeakable Visions of the Individual,* P.O. Box 439, California, PA 15419. This annual publication costs $10; per copy/sample is $3.00, but rates vary, as some back issues are more expensive; v. 1 (all three issues) listed at $75, v. 2 (all 3 issues) at $50, &c.

And now what is *The Unspeakable* about? Kerouac and friends: the Beat generation. This publication belongs to the select group of reviews that celebrate and explore the literary dimensions of a particular author (e.g., James Joyce) or a group of authors (the Romantic poets). In this case, it's the Beats who get the attention. We take them up here, in *Sipapu,* because theirs is a less well-known field than that of William Shakespeare (for whom, incidentally, we have the highest respect). Arthur Knight is a tall, clean-shaven, professional type; Kit Knight, his wife, is a lovely short-haired blonde, and they came to see us here in the summer of 1983:

SIPAPU: You're a nice-looking couple: how did you get into all this Beat stuff? Did you meet and marry at City Lights? Reception at Vesuvio's? And then how did you get to California, PA?

ARTHUR: My earlier wife, Glee, and I founded *The Unspeakable Visions of the Individual* in 1971; three issues came out that year, three in 1972, two in 1973; v. 4, "The Beat book," was a one-issue volume; with that, we went annual. However, "The Beat book" got a big reception on its appearance in 1974; there were favorable reviews in the *Village Voice, New Republic,* &c. — Glee died in 1975 after a long illness, and meanwhile I had got to know my student, Kit. One evening I knocked on her door — and hence, this remarriage.

SIPAPU: The intent of the periodical: origin of its name; its history?

ARTHUR: It started out as a mimeo, like many scholarly publications; moved to offset. The origin of the name? That's a phrase in Kerouac's *Visions of Cody.* The free-wheeling style of the magazine is derived from Kerouac's own rules. (The typeface is a neat sans-serif).

I was too young to be a beatnik during the critical years of 1958–1962, when I was in San Francisco. I was a student in my junior and senior years at S.F. State (now California State University, San Francisco). I knew Lawrence Ferlinghetti and Kenneth Rexroth, attended the latter's salon, but was not interested in "the scene." Only after I got a teaching appointment in California, Pennsylvania (south of Pittsburgh in an old mining district, later the site of the COSMEP conference of 1980), did I get more interested in the Beats. I read a lot of their work in 1967–1969 — and decided that Kerouac was a first-class prose poet. I hosted the COSMEP conference here at California, PA, and invited Allen Ginsberg; he came and was remarkably open to everyone, approachable at almost any hour, warm and free. That was the first time I met him.

SIPAPU: But how did you get to Appalachia? South of Pittsburgh isn't exactly where your budding Am. Lit. prof. wants to end up. What *are* your origins?

ARTHUR: I worked for a periodical in Napa County, California, called the *Redwood Rancher;* it was originally farm-oriented, but became more regional. Eventually I became publicity director for the Sonoma-Marin Fair, and lived above a barn in Calistoga. Moving from this, into college, graduate work, publication was all a matter of time. Also, I'd worked in a junior college in Michigan, and spent the year 1966 in Pennsylvania.

SIPAPU: What's the difference between you and any other periodical that publishes Beat or post–Beat literature?

ARTHUR: We're archivists! We use primary material only — letters,

confessions, interviews; no critical stuff or new poetry. So far as we know, we're the only such archival magazine devoted to the Beats. We justify our title of archivists by keeping an immense file on Beat poets and Beat literature of all kinds.

SIPAPU: The Files! The Files! What is in those files?

ARTHUR: We've been keeping them since 1954, or at least collecting back to there. I did a lot of photographing of writers, especially Western ones, back in those days; I was always collecting portraits. Consequently, I have photos and correspondence of, and with, Henry Miller, Tom Blackburn, Irving Shulman, Ray Bradbury, and other writers who came to Hollywood as screenwriters. Now a ton of files helps fill an eight-room house in California, Pennsylvania. The rest of the space is for me, Kit, and Tiffany, who arrived in 1977.

SIPAPU: The future of your magazine? Plans of your own besides it or beyond it?

ARTHUR: We're always moving to new possibilities, and what with my teaching and our publication, we're busy all the time. Both of us are writing poetry: I'm doing dramatic monologs and she's doing her own work, and we've just come back from California, where we collected material on a new book on the California literary scene and sensibility. If something happened to me, Kit would continue the mag., and we will continue it as we have continued to fund it in the past, without subsidies; selling off other small press mags., received for the money and to save space.

SIPAPU: Now then, Kit! Other people in the book business (publishers, writers, &c.) who know the two of you have often expressed the feeling that Kit is the tough one. Why?

KIT: Not so much tough as blunt. I've been told I was blunt, even devastatingly blunt, more times than I can count. And I'm sure that that feeling goes back to being hit by a car when I was seventeen. A person who spends nine weeks in a coma, then close to a year relearning easy things like how to walk and talk — probably isn't going to have a lot of patience with chit-chat or small things. If you're going to do a job, do it. If you want to say something, say it. The year of 1970 came and went — everybody else got a year older, and I learned what mattered.

SIPAPU: What's your background, Kit?

KIT: My father was a career Navy man. I was born in Rhode Island because he happened to be stationed there. I have no sisters, but one older brother, and he was born in Pennsylvania because my father happened to be stationed in Pittsburgh at the time. I attended 13 different schools before I graduated. My dad retired from the Navy after 21 years, six months, and three days in January, 1965. At that time I was 13 years old and we were living in Long Beach, California. And I was awfully sorry to be leaving the Navy life; I liked the frequent moves. My brother didn't like the life. My parents decided to move back to Pittsburgh because all of my mother's family still lived there. Between my 13th and 17th years, I just went to school. I was one of the editors of my high school yearbook, which won an award that year. I had made tentative plans to go to Temple University in Philadelphia and major in journalism. Dreams of "Brenda Starr, girl reporter."

Then I was seventeen and in the middle of my senior year of high school. I had been asked to the prom the night before during a "couples only" skate at the ice skating rink. It gets dark early in January and a light rain had been falling. The car wasn't using its headlights and I couldn't see him and he couldn't see me. That car threw me 42 feet before I landed. Both of my knees were crushed, I had seven pelvic fractures and a skull concussion. The left side of my face was ripped off by the asphalt as I slid on the road. Plastic surgery repaired that.

SIPAPU: We never would have known. You look just fine.

KIT: I know. You're not supposed to know by looking. That's the idea of plastic surgery.

I woke up nine weeks later in the hospital. Then I started the recovery. Eighteen months later I was, more or less, back to where I had been before the car hit me, except I moved a lot more slowly. I still walk slowly. It annoys my six-year-old daughter on occasion. She bounces along and there's poor old mom, have to wait for her!

The skull concussion was the worst of it. It gave me a cerebral hemorrhage which resulted in a stroke. The left side of your brain controls the right side of your body. I was right-handed before the stroke, but then I could no longer control my right hand. (She holds her right hand up in front of her face, and we can see it quiver.) I did learn how to stop my right hand from making large erratic movements, but I was never able to gain enough control for those fine motor movements necessary for writing. Even brushing my teeth with my right hand is awkward. It would take me a long time to eat a meal using a fork in my right hand.

Because I was so frail, even 18 months after the accident, my doctors decided Temple University, which was 350 miles from my parents' home, was too far for me to go away to school. So I decided to attend California State College, which was about an hour away. That was in 1971, September. I had met the man who would become my first husband a scant six months after the accident; it was already assumed I would marry him. I was home for the weekend from the rehabilitation hospital, still in the wheelchair (I was just learning to use my legs again) and I hadn't had the plastic surgery yet. To say that it was an extremely vulnerable time in my life would be an understatement. I wasn't even 18 yet.

I broke my left leg again two weeks after we were married. The knee was weak from the first break and when I fell off the bicycle, a plain old two-wheeler, my left knee was trapped between the bike and the road. That breaking of the leg was the symbol for the break-up of the marriage. A two-week marriage has to be one of the shortest on record (although we lasted, officially, for three years). I learned that one does not base a marriage on gratitude.

ARTHUR: Kit wrote a few stories about Mark in my creative writing class and I remember going home to my wife at that time, Glee, and telling her, "That marriage will never work."

KIT: Marriages break for all sorts of reasons. I wasn't in love with Arthur, then; I simply outgrew Mark. By 1975 I was graduating from college and ready to get a divorce. It came through in August, 1976, and Arthur and I got married three days later.

I liked Arthur when I was his student. We never dated until after Glee died. When another student told me that Glee had died, although I had never met her, I felt bad for Mr. Knight. He was the only professor I ever had who talked about his wife as if he actually liked her. The rest of them either pretended they didn't have wives, which meant they were on the make, or they talked about their wives disparagingly, i.e., "the old battle-axe," or "the old ball and chain." But Arthur spoke well of all three of his wives, even though the first two marriages had ended badly: the first in annulment, the second in divorce, and now this third one in death. I sent him a

sympathy note and he came over to my apartment to thank me for it and that's how we started to date.

SIPAPU: Quite a background. What are your specific duties with *The Unspeakable Visions of the Individual?*

KIT: I'm the basic keeper of books and records. I do all that. We keep records on who bought what, when, and how much they paid for it. I keep the records up-to-date. I answer letters from subscribers, crank or fan, and Arthur and I together come up with editorial judgment of what to print. I do some of the soliciting for new material; Arthur does the bulk of that, though. Our duties to the magazine aren't clearly divided; I do some things and Arthur does some things. Exactly who does what depends a lot on our personal inclination and/or the amount of time required. I do 90% of the annual billing. Arthur does 60% of the typing, or more, for each issue, because he's a better typist. He does 100 words a minute. I can only do 60.

SIPAPU: Why did you decide to publish a magazine, and why did you settle on a strictly Beat content?

ARTHUR: I wanted to publish a magazine since about 1963, when I worked for a little regional publication in northern California called *The Redwood Rancher,* which was a magazine for farmers. Then someone in Los Angeles bought it—a relatively young guy in his thirties who had worked in advertising for Hunts Foods—and wanted to change it into a general-interest regional publication. I went to work for him after I got out of San Francisco State College and returned from a trip to Europe. I liked the work, but I didn't make any money doing it, and it took a lot of my time.

So then I went into teaching. For a year I taught English at Anderson Union High School near Redding; then I moved to Riverside, where I taught journalism for a year at Riverside City College. I'd never taken a journalism course, but I'd had practical experience, and I was a good photographer. After Riverside, I taught English for a year at a junior college in Michigan, then moved to California State College (now California University) in California, Pennsylvania. People like to kid me about that: from California to California. And they wonder about how I happened to move to northern Appalachia, which is where we're located. I got there the same way you get anywhere: there was a job available, and I took it.

Why the Beats? Well, the title of our magazine comes from Kerouac, so there was obviously an initial interest in them. I became interested in Kerouac the second year I lived in Pennsylvania, which was 1967. The magazine was started in 1971. Actually, we've published Beats all along. In the first three issues—we did three a year—we published Kerouac, Ginsberg and Ferlinghetti. So there was an interest in them. It became exclusively Beat, the magazine, in 1974. We wanted to do an issue devoted to Herbert Huncke in 1973, but only half the issue dealt with Huncke; the other half had work by miscellaneous writers.

We were annoyed because we hadn't done what we wanted to do. So we thought we'd put together a real issue dealing with the Beats, and we did *The Beat Book,* Glee and I. We figured we were going to throw away our money, because we didn't know how the book would be accepted, and it would cost $6000 to publish it. We hadn't left town, literally, in about two years, because Glee had rheumatoid arthritis and could barely walk. So the magazine was something we were committed to. And we liked the work of the people. We wanted to do a successful issue, although the Huncke issue did get more favorable attention than anything we'd done prior to that, and it was the seventh issue we'd published. It *seemed* popular, although we weren't quite sure, because we spent almost $1,000 on the issue, gave most of the copies away, and it did *not* break even. So there was no real reason for us to spend $6,000 to do the one we wanted to do. But we thought, what the hell, people buy new cars for that much and five years later they're rusted pieces of junk. So we'd have $6,000 worth of Beat books under our bed. A lot of people have a dream that they never try to achieve, and I think that's sad. We had half of the necessary money to produce the book because we hadn't gone anywhere, and we got a loan for the rest.

The Beat issue turned out to be the first thing we did that went into the black, although not immediately because we made no effort to market it. It came out very late in 1974. By October of 1975 Glee was dead. So then I didn't make an effort to market it because I was just trying to survive. I was 37 and an unwilling bachelor again.

Kit and I began to push the book some, by the time we'd decided to stay together, but it was about two years old then. It did all right, though, because we got favorable attention in *The Village Voice, The Los Angeles Times, The New Republic, American Poetry Review,* etc. They all gave our address, and that did generate sales. Even without pushing it, orders came in. It seemed like a good focus, and no one else was doing it. No other magazine is, even today.

SIPAPU: You've met most of the major figures in the Beat movement: Snyder, Ginsberg, Corso, etc. Some of them have been to your home. Do you have a favorite?

KIT: Burroughs. Superbly bored. The man has been there and seen it all and is back to tell you there isn't anything new, really. And absolutely no one is going to tell him white is red. He knows. He gives the phrase "laid-back" new meaning. No, he's never been to my home, sadly.

SIPAPU: Have you ever talked to him?

KIT: Yes. But I get more of a kick out of just watching him deal with other people. I've heard him read on two occasions and he really is a fine reader. Does amazing things with his voice. Throws it. I wish he would come to our house; I'd love to have him as a houseguest for a weekend, observe him up close.

SIPAPU: Why is it that the Beats are only now being recognized as writers of some stature?

ARTHUR: Well, 25 years after the fact I think people can view them nostalgically, and with more perspective. They can treat them seriously, if they deserve serious treatment. At the time, it was difficult to treat them seriously because they were media people in a sense, beatniks. And how do you treat a beatnik seriously, or a rock star? It takes time. But they've endured, and they've done important work. I would think that Ginsberg is one of our best candidates for a Nobel prize. He's not only been enormously successful aesthetically, he's also been popular, influencing an incredible number of people—if not as a poet, then as a guru. He's been in the forefront of our culture for 25 years.

SIPAPU: Does Beat writing have some sort of persona? For example, with the existentialists, it's the outsider; and with the Greeks, it's the tragic hero.

ARTHUR: I think they share certain concerns. Ecology would certainly be one of them. Ginsberg is very concerned about the environment. And more than 20 years ago Gary Snyder was talking about ecology and people polluting the environment. Virtually no one talked about it then. I think they share a concern about a pure kind of life, and a concern with genuine feeling.

They presented an alternative lifestyle; they asked, "Why do we have to have a car, or two cars? Why do we have to surround ourselves with people; what's wrong with being alone?" Also, their work tended to spring out of their own set of experiences, as opposed to writers prior to that who were writing about things that had very little to do with their own set of experiences, like Eliot writing "The Waste Land." I'm sure that didn't come out of an autobiographical impulse. "Howl" is much like "The Waste Land" in that both make big statements about society. But Ginsberg's comes from an autobiographical stance, and Eliot's didn't. Ginsberg uses the language real people use in everyday life. The diction prior to the mid-1950s tended to be very artificial, with the exception of William Carlos Williams. Whitman's diction was the diction of the streets, the diction of the common person. The Beats examined society in the sense that they examined themselves, and they were part of society.

I think that's why their work is so real and will endure. A lot of poetry is not very convincing. The work seems made up. At the end of *A Portrait of the Artist as a Young Man,* Stephen Dedalus is leaving Ireland and going to Europe, and the last thing he says is, "I go to encounter ... the reality of experience and to forge in the smithy of my soul the uncreated conscience of my race." And that's what the Beats do. In defining themselves, they define all men and women. From the smithy of their souls they forge a collective soul.

SIPAPU: Talk about your writing some. When do you write? How much? What kind?

KIT: Poetry from our daily experience. I don't rhyme when I write poetry. I write like I talk and I don't talk in rhyme. Arthur and I are both more interested in people than landscape or philosophy. My favorite writing time is late morning and early afternoon and I keep going until it's time to knock off to fix dinner. How much? Not as much as I should. Right now I seem to be more interested in doing short stories than poems. I tend to ramble too much, and that style is better suited for short stories than for poetry. Also, my stories don't tend to have plots; they just sort of begin and end. Actually, my stories are like 15-page letters. But I've heard some good things about them from editors.

SIPAPU: Do you print them in your own magazine?

KIT & ARTHUR (simultaneously): No!

KIT: I have bad dreams about self-publishers. Part of the writing process is finding your own market and if you print your own story or poem in your own magazine then you aren't doing part of your job. Some other editor has to have enough faith in your work to put his or her own money into its publication. If your work doesn't get published, maybe that's a clue. Now there have been some fine writers who were their own publishers: Whitman, of course, and more recently James Drought, who wrote *The Gypsy Moths.* But most people shouldn't self-publish.

Obviously, with the interview with Arthur and Kit Knight, which began this issue, we would be remiss in not describing, however briefly, three sample issues of *The Unspeakable Visions of the Individual.* The ones in question are no. 10, 1980; no. 8, 1978 ("The Beat Journey"); and no. 5 (= v. 5?) ("The Beat Diary"). Each has interviews, poems, letters, miscellaneous *inedita.* For example, in "The Beat Diary," there is an interview with William Burroughs; in "The Beat Journey," one with McClure, and in no. 10, one with Imaru Baraka; correspondence between John Clellon Holmes and Allen Ginsberg (the one still unknown, the other already famous, etc.) However, the text, even though printed in a cool unpretentious sans-serif, pales into significance beside the photographs. Arthur Knight prefers to take photographs of people when they are not noticing; the apostle of the candid camera, he catches astounding pictures of virtually the entire Beat scene when they are at the beach, dancing out of ecstasy, typing, talking to each other (in person, or on the phone), hugging—there isn't one of a pair of them making love, but we dare say it's only a question of time. To look at these shots is to see, and *feel*, literary history being made. (Would that the Knights, and the camera, had been around in 1820; we might have seen Shelley plain!) The climax of all of these, however, is a photograph accompanying an interview with Gary Snyder ("Moving the world a millionth of an inch"); it shows Gary Snyder in the improbable location of a New York subway late at night. For those of us for whom that location is danger's very name, and especially late at night, the sight of Gary Snyder, sitting as calmly in this unlikely environment as if he were on a stump upon his own beloved San Juan Ridge, — is as heartening as it is funny. This annual can be recommended wherever interest in the Beats is found.

There are fewer strictly literary periodicals this time we wish to review, but Richard Peabody's *Gargoyle,* issue 22/23, has interviews with Jaimy Gordon, Paul Metcalf, and others, and a good selection of poetry and short fiction. However, this is one of the few literary mags that really does a conscientious and objective job of small press reviewing; those who wish to review small-press publications as they come out, and get news and opinion, should subscribe ($8/3 issues to libraries). For us the high point was the interview with Maurice Girodias, the French publisher of Editions Obelisk and Olympia Press, son of Jack Kahane, who published Henry Miller in his Black Sun house. Girodias has been tossed out of France, and apparently does not have a publishing house of his own, although he is publishing his autobiography, *The Frog Prince,* with Crown. He denies having written many of the notorious Olympia Press titles himself under strange pseudonyms; but we wonder. Olympia Press published, early in the sixties, a number of works by one Akbar del Piombo, including collage-novels (*Fuzz Against Junk,* 1960) and nonsense-erotica (*The Double-Bellied Companion,* 1967?). WHO IS AKBAR DEL PIOMBO? If it's not Girodias *lui-même,* can he tell us?

Everybody has been waiting for the first issue of **SMALL PRESS,** the R.R. Bowker entry in the field of small press critical periodicals. Diane Kruchkow of *Small Press News* had a disconcerting encounter with the man in the Bowker booth at a major convention; the letters section in this issue included one from a writer (Grant Burns of *New Pages*) who was skeptical, given Bowker's history of ignoring the small press scene, of their ability to do it properly; and the ads we saw, which suggested that there were no other periodicals in the field, struck us as a slap in the face. What have *Small Press Review, Small Press News,* and the rest of us been doing all these years?

Well, the first issue (to be mailed in September, but delivered in October as "September October 1983"), is out, and it lays many fears to rest. Bowker's entry is not designed to compete with others in the field. It calls itself "the magazine of independent book publishing," so presumably it doesn't tell you how to get your newsletter out. And it doesn't do book reviews (in contrast to another letter-writer, we're glad, as the folks at Bowker are not literary as such, still less counter-culture or radical types). It does do some interviews, but so far it has stayed away from small-press politics and conferences. What it does do, is show the new aspirant to fine-small book publishing how to produce a product that will appeal to the discriminating. This is different from the grubby details described by Merritt Clifton's "Help!" or the legal tangles handled by COSMEP Newsletter's "Dear Deborah." Instead, the right note is struck by the cover, on which Barry Moser has depicted the apparatus of composing stick, chase, furniture, and rising among them like a great topical flower, — a full, rich glass of California claret. The sorts in the stick have begun to spell out Salut ... but it is obvious that the master of the Black Art has begun to taste success even before he has started work.

And success is indeed, the keynote of this journal. Allan Kornblum of Toothpaste Press has a masterly article on book design. Ed Hogan, comparing notes with others, tells you how to shop for paper. An article on Ten Speed is subtitled: "the color of success." The ads are for book printers, printers, and a few smaller ones for publishers like Sierra Club Books. Last p. but one shows a page from the *Hypneroto-machia Poliphili,* 1499, printer Aldus Manutius, which you might emulate this afternoon (once you've downed that glass of claret).

Of course, we have nothing against teaching people how to publish fine books for the discriminating and succeed at it. We have a letterpress book in progress now, as explained on p. 1 of this issue. And we don't believe that unless a poem is printed in mimeo by a "street poet," it isn't any good. However, small press people should be warned, that this is the scene viewed from mid-town Manhattan (Bowker just moved to 205 East 42nd Street, New York, NY 10017, which may account for the delay in publication). And that means the point of view of those who have money, and aspire to make it. Those of you in the small press scene who are looking for the cheapest typesetter in town, will not find the answer here. And librarians will find more of use to students of design than students of literature. The subscription price is $15 through 31 December 1983.

(Incidentally, three of the periodicals closest to the small press scene, and commenting on it, are located not in big cities but in small towns: *Small Press Review,* Paradise, California; *Small Press News,* New Sharon, Maine; and our own activity seven miles north of Winters, California. And we don't believe the small town is dying. We listen to "Prairie Home Companion" every Saturday night.)

Finally, of course, what is not mentioned here is that the small press started up in the 1960s as an alternative vision, not only to big-time publishing but to success-oriented America. If not revolutionary, it was rebellious; if not anti-capitalist, it wasn't hip capitalist either. But Bowker's periodical doesn't have that funky alternative vision. In *Small Press,* you can learn how to print and publish — with wine.

15 : 1

This issue of Sipapu *contains the longest interview ever, with Zoia Horn of the Data Center. Zoia remains one of our best and dearest friends. She gets a chance to tell her whole story here.*

Dutch publishing deserves a better history than I give it in this issue. Martinus Nijhoff produced a collection of clandestine publications under the German occupation, but the whole story of printing and publication in the Netherlands, from Coster to "Drukwerk in de Marge," has yet to appear — to my knowledge.

THE DATA CENTER, 464 19th St., Oakland, CA 94612, (415) 835-4692, was one of the tour points from the California Library Association's annual conference, in Oakland, Dec. 1983 (see below). We made a special point of going there, because this old office building is the workplace of Zoia Horn, our present interviewee — and of many other hard workers. It was a pleasant stroll from the Hyatt Regency where the conference was held, — and there was a good restaurant on the way back.

The Data Center (there seems to be something wrong with the date in the illustration; perhaps the "9" in the date should be a "5"?) is an outgrowth of the North American Congress on Latin America (NACLA), a progressive research organization opposed to U.S. imperialism in the region. The Data Center, however, is its own organization, and is principally concerned with maintaining its own clipping files. Yes, we're back with the filekeepers again, and file cases, Princeton files, pam boxes meet the eye in every one of the large rooms upstairs, along with banners, posters, a coffee room, and an offset press. There's a cheerful staff, children run in and out, and meanwhile, what's in those files?

Corporations, corporate issues, foreign investments, industries (agbiz, banking, communications, energy, health services, labor, manufacturing, mining ... you name it). There are general world files, countries alphabetically arranged, special files on U.S., California, Bay Area.

Other clipping files include: criminal justice, intelligence, military, non-

governmental organizations, and personalities. Special files include: the right to know, the New Right, environment, and women. These topics are presented in local, State, and Federal reports, corporate reports, official foreign publications and U.N. papers, together with a large number of clippings from a great variety of newspapers and periodicals, across the political spectrum. There is also a library, but the library is really ancillary to the files, rather than (as in most libraries) the other way around; keeping up the files, and making them available to scholars and organizers, is the heart of the Center's work.

The Center also sells the results of its clipping activities. "Press profiles" are velo-bound sets of clippings from mainstream, labor, business, political, and religious periodicals. The material here covers the New Right: "Updates," 3 v., $25 each; "Fundamentalists and financiers," $6.50; "Toxic nightmare," 3 v., 478 pp. $50, &c. There are also special coverages for Central America, plant shutdowns, &c. all available on a yearly basis from $30 to $330; corporate profiles, geared to a specific company; clipping and search services. Annual individual memberships in the Data Center are $20 (regular), $35 (professional), $50 (supporting); institutional—please inquire.

DATA BEYOND THE CENTER: An active worker in the Data Center is Zoia Horn, a quiet librarian of middle years, whose gentility conceals a romantic, even a victorious past:

SIPAPU: Your birth and education?

HORN: I was born in Odessa, a southern city on the Black Sea, in the Soviet Union. In winter it was cold enough for an igloo of packed snow to remain for weeks as a special playhouse for children. In summer, the heat was often intense, and damp from the sea. It was a lovely city with broad avenues lined with trees. The steps going down to the harbor were made famous by Eisenstein in the film *Potemkin*. There was a massive Opera House where the interior glittered and sparkled with chandeliers, dark red plush, and gold.

My memories included those mental pictures as well as parks, a kindergarten where I played the triangle and formed boats with three stacks made of plastocene, a ride in a sleigh drawn by horses through the streets, piano lessons, and being excruciatingly embarrassed while performing in the annual children's concert, because my mother had shaved my head as a health measure during those typhus-ridden years. There was also the play "Uncle Tom's Cabin" performed by actors with blackened faces on a local library stage.

Still another memory picture is of the pervasive sadness of the people gathered in the streets after Lenin died. Even the sky seemed to be sympathetic. The pink clouds seemed to mirror the red flags carried by the mournful marchers. To this day, Chopin's "Funeral March" brings back memories of that heavily sad occasion.

I learned to read before being enrolled in a private school when I was 7½ years old. (Children started school at 8.) We wore uniforms, carried our backs in rucksacks (leather backpacks), sat on long, dark bench-desk arrangements that rose like theatre seats. This was during the N.E.P. period (= New Economic Policy), during which the government permitted a return to limited "free enterprise" in order to get the economic wheels running. My father's family were shopkeepers and small businessmen. Most of them had emigrated to the United States before World War I. They prospered; one brother had become a physician, another a pharmacist; a sister was married to a successful insurance broker. They persuaded him to join them in this country where the streets were reputed to be "paved with gold."

Mother's family was less affluent. They had moved from a small town to Odessa, and there they had set up a small boarding house. But despite the lack of money, they had surprisingly supported her in her desire to go to the local "gymnasium" (= high school). (Few "girls" attended school, let alone High School, during Tsarist times.)

It is strange that there are no stories in our family of the Revolution. What has been reported as a cataclysmic occurrence, as "Ten" (or Forty) "Days that Shook the World," stirred no memories. Incredible as it seems, it obviously was possible to go about one's personal business while a society was being turned upside down.

We left the Soviet Union in 1926. I celebrated my eighth birthday on the ship that was bringing us to America.

SIPAPU: Introduction to the world of culture through libraries? Your personal discovery of America?

HORN: As soon as I mastered the English language I began to read voraciously. An aunt sent me a box of books she bought at one of the famous Macy sales. My mother and I made a monthly subway pilgrimage from Brooklyn to Seward Park Branch, New York Public Library, in Manhattan, where Mother had (somehow) found that here were Russian books. I was first sent to the children's room, but soon the librarian gave me a special pass to the adult section. I read, in English, the Russian writers my mother knew: Tolstoy, Turgenev, Chekhov and Dostoevsky. Heavy fare, but comforting in a way. One day, as I was browsing in the stacks, I felt a firm hand on my shoulder. Above me stood the librarian (I blush at the stereotypical image, but there it was). She was tall, slender, hair pulled back in a tight bun, dark skirt and white blouse, a pair of gleaming glasses. She said, firmly, "Come."

I followed her, in fear and some concern. Had I done something wrong, I wondered? It was so difficult—little things tripped me up. She stopped at a group of shelves, looked for a minute, and then pulled out one book, then another. "Here," she said, "try these. They are about people your age. I think you will like them." She handed me Louisa May Alcott's *Little Women,* and Mark Twain's *Tom Sawyer.* I was to read *Little Women* many times. The March family became for me the model of a good American family. Many years later my daughters laughed at the 19th-century lady-like manners that I had adopted and internalized. Although I had at that time been in the U.S. three years, it was this librarian who helped me set my feet firmly in this country. She was to lead me from Alcott and Clemens to Jack London, and much later, to Thoreau. She introduced me to the best values that characterize this country. I have been grateful to her, and determined to do the same for others.

This was the same librarian, who remarked casually one day, that there was a piano in the basement that needed playing. It hadn't been used for a long time. "Perhaps I would care to try some of the music in the case beside it, while I was waiting for my mother to finish selecting some of her books." This librarian cared; she had eyes in the back of her head. She knew what people needed, and shared her knowledge and expertise. She was cool, and seemingly impersonal, but she was a real strong catalyst for strengthening the individual in this particular society.

It is no wonder that I chose to become a librarian.

"The premise of democracy is that a people can govern themselves. The condition for this assumption is that the people will have the information they need to make wise political decisions." Perhaps it is because I was an immigrant, that I take so seriously the ideals of democracy which were introduced to me by the librarian in the Seward Park Branch of the New York Public Library; by the principal of my first elementary school, who took me under her wing; by a number of sensitive, dedicated teachers in high school; and by some brilliant and inspiring teachers in Brooklyn College. I was imbued with the idea that change for the better was possible, and that, in a democratic country, individuals could make a difference. By reading and learning, voting and lobbying, joining with others in associations, by speaking out and making known their demands to their government, a responsible government could be maintained, that was accountable for its actions.

I have found no reason to want to change these beliefs.

SIPAPU: The celebrated imprisonment of librarian Zoia Horn (there's a bunch of librarians out there who were wearing saddle shoes with candy-cane laces when it happened, so please, tell us again).

HORN: My particular contribution is to present an experience of intellectual freedom that has been a long time developing; but one which synthesized suddenly during an extraordinary series of events.

They started early one Monday morning in January of 1971.

I was standing at the kitchen sink, finishing my orange juice, looking out to the bridge over the broad Susquehanna River. It was peaceful, ordinary, quite typical of Lewisburg; a small town in the center of Pennsylvania.

Suddenly I saw two men walking in the street. They were dressed in dark formal business clothes, so unlike the casual academic types familiar to me. There was a strangeness. People were rarely seen on that street at eight in the morning. Most people were in cars, going to work. At the rate these men were walking they would pass my door in six seconds. I waited. In three, there was a ring at the door. I ran downstairs and opened the door to two F.B.I. agents, who showed their identifications and asked to speak to me. That is how the Kafkaesque nightmare began.

I invited them into the apartment, asked them to sit down. They said they wanted to ask me some questions. But, first they read a statement telling me of my right not to answer. I asked, "What is this all about?" They said I would soon know, when I started answering the questions.

It was getting late. I excused myself to phone the home of the assistant reference librarian, Pat Rom, to tell her I would be a little late because I had two visitors. There was a short silence. Then, in pure Oklahoman, "Funny thing; I have two visitors too."

Back to the living room. Would I answer some questions? Well, what is this all about? We played these lines, with variations, several times. Finally, I said, "No thank you, I prefer not to answer." Would I like to see some photographs? Well, I like photographs. But these, I was sure, were not for my pleasure. And so, I said no, I preferred not to. By that time I had discovered that one of my visitors had come all the way from Florida; the other was a local agent. Before departing they presented me with a subpoena. It requested me to appear as a witness before a Federal Grand Jury in the U.S. Court in Harrisburg, the very next morning. The case was "United States vs. John Doe."

Later, at the library, I learned that four of us had each been visited by two F.B.I. agents at exactly the same time. Two students, and two librarians!

The synchronized visits, the serving of subpoenas by F.B.I. agents (rather than by the usual local deputies) and the complete secrecy of a John Doe case, was unnerving even to the American Civil Liberties Union lawyer whom we met for guidance an hour before reporting to the Federal Court. Inside the Federal Building, we were directed to the seventh floor, thence to a small room where we were soon joined by other witnesses, as ignorant as we. A few young nuns in street dress, a feisty maintenance man from Washington, D.C., and his very tense, taut-nerved sister.

It was not until late evening of that first day that we learned that we were involved in a "conspiracy case." The charge: Fr. Philip Berrigan, Sister Elizabeth McAllister, several priests, a Pakistani scholar, and still other people as co-conspirators had planned to kidnap Henry Kissinger and blow up heating tunnels in Washington, D.C. The news had broken while we were driving home to Lewisburg. A very good friend in California whom I had informed, the previous day, about the very strange F.B.I. visit, had picked it up and called me.

"I complain of you."

The days now combined the amorphous doubts and fears of Kafka's *Trial,* and the incredible absurdities of Dodgson's *Alice Through the Looking Glass,* with, perhaps, more than a generous dash of Orwell's *1984.* We were to believe that the same priests who stood quietly in communal prayer at Catonsville waiting to be arrested for burning draft records were violent, lawless men. This, while U.S. troops were at that very time on "pacification," napalm, and defoliation missions in Vietnam. We were to disbelieve our minds and senses when we observed the warm camaraderie that developed among the witnesses waiting their turn, and compared it to the rigid, cold, humorless behavior of the F.B.I. agents who guarded the halls.

"The beauty of a conspiracy charge, from the government's point of view, is that not very much needs to be proved. It need not be shown that the defendants did the things they talked about . . . all that need be shown is that there was some kind of agreement to commit an unlawful act, and that at least one 'overt' act was committed in the process of moving toward that end . . . Phone calls and letters were the chief examples of the 'overt acts' in this case." (Cf. Raines, John C., *Conspiracy: The Implications of the Harrisburg Trial for the Democratic Tradition;* Harper/Row, 1974, p. 18).

When the conspiracy indictment came out, a meeting at 43 North Water Street, Lewisburg, PA was listed as one of the "overt acts." I lived at that address.

After considerable sparring on our behalf by our lawyer, to obtain total immunity from prosecution (for what, I didn't know), I waited to testify before the Grand Jury. In a conspiracy case, one doesn't know how a perfectly innocent act may somehow be fitted into a spider web that enmeshes you and transforms the witness into a defendant.

I now waited with others in the little, aseptic room, high above the court becoming familiar with the roofs and enchanting architectural details that, in former times, were gayly placed sometimes far beyond the view of pedestrians below. Within, we coalesced into an understanding, loving, and supportive group. We felt the agony of each one as he or she was called to the Grand Jury room. Our common bond was our anti-Vietnam War stand and our indignation at the arrogant power used by our government to suppress criticism.

My turn came. A Grand Jury in its English origins was established to determine whether there was real cause for a legal case, or whether malice had created a situation that the local community had to ameliorate. An indictment was issued if there was cause; and the judicial system then took over. In this present period, however, Grand Juries were being used all over the United States to intimidate people who were speaking out against the Vietnam War. They were empowered to demand responses to all questions. In that process they threw out huge nets to catch the names of all who dared to seriously, publicly question. My turn came.

Our lawyer walked me to the door and I went in. I sat behind a long table with two prosecuting attorneys, one of whom was Guy Goodwin who specialized in these anti-dissident inquiries. On the other side was a stenotypist. Before us were the 21 men and women of the Grand Jury. The questions began: What happened at this place, at that time? Who was there, what was said, who said it? What else was being discussed? Who was discussing

it? Whom do you recognize in this photograph? What are their names? Where did you meet them? What occasion was this? What occasion was it when you met?

I felt nasty, ugly, and alone as I responded, watching myself being turned into an informer on neighbors and friends as surely as those who cooperated in Nazi Germany. No matter that I could describe only a party here and luncheon there where people ate and drank and talked, sometimes seriously, sometimes not, never of kidnapping, never of violence. Most of the people in the photographs I had met for the first time in the Federal Building and witness room. But in this sinister jigsaw puzzle the consequence of perfectly innocent things that you say are not known to you. A simple remark could have far-reaching effects, could endanger friends and others. I was questioned for only two hours.

Perhaps this is a good place for a brief explanation. I had met Fr. Berrigan once at a friend's house one evening after a night stint at the library. The friend knew I would enjoy meeting Father Phil whom I had admired for his stalwart leadership in the anti-war movement, and phoned me to come.

I was against U.S. intervention in Vietnam as far back as 1963 when we sent military advisors to South Vietnam. I participated in anti-war marches and demonstrations, wrote letters, contributed money, stood on vigils, refused to pay the federal telephone war tax. At Bucknell University, in the town of Lewisburg, Pa., I was easily identified as part of the anti–Vietnam War group. But the other big institution in Lewisburg was the Federal Penitentiary.

Boyd Douglas, a prisoner there, came daily to Bucknell on a work-study release program. He had a part-time job pasting labels on library books. He seems to have sought me out (I was then head of the Reference Department). I was aware that he had other friends in the anti-war community. He needed other people to talk to, he needed acceptance, approbation. Fr. Berrigan was by then his neighbor in the penitentiary in a part of the prison reserved for trusted inmates. He glowed in the importance that his growing new friendship with Father Phil provided. He offered to take a note to Phil, if I wanted, but since I barely knew him, I never took advantage of this offer. He arranged for me to meet an inmate who was an artist and photographer when I decided to have a display of books and materials on prisons and prisoners, in the library.

Later Boyd Douglas asked if I would have Sister Elizabeth and others at my apartment for students and faculty to meet. I was delighted. Two sisters and two priests came after a visit with Fr. Berrigan, and there was much coming and going, much eating and drinking. At ten that evening I fell asleep on the carpet. The two nuns slept overnight and left the next day. Another time, Boyd Douglas asked me to serve lunch for Fathers Joe and Neil and others. A friend and I prepared pots of chili, but only Boyd and the two priests came. At no time was there ever any discussion that was more than that of concerned people searching for democratic ways to effect change. I didn't like Boyd Douglas particularly, though feeling his great need for friendship.

Boyd Douglas, it turned out, was an informer and *agent provocateur* for the Federal Bureau of Investigation. He smuggled and transcribed letters to Father Phil Berrigan; and attempted to institute acts of violence.

To use a prisoner as a spy is an obscenity. A prisoner is a powerless person. For those with authority to use a prisoner as a spy is equivalent to an adult's molesting a child. Neither prisoner nor child has any real option: resistance is foredoomed. Now . . . back to my story.

The Grand Jury continued its questionings. I went back to my reference work at Bucknell. I was married that spring and moved to California to be with my husband, Dean Galloway. On the flight to Dallas, where ALA was having its annual conference at Dallas that year, I realized that I had to alert other librarians to the dangers to our constitutional freedoms and to the policies we espouse in the Library Bill of Rights. My whole experience had been too reminiscent of Nazi Germany where a Reichstag fire was used to create hysteria against dissidents and neighbor was set to spy against neighbor, and where many academics acceded to the new regime, by silence, thus contributing to the destruction that followed.

I presented the resolution on Government Intimidation to the Membership meeting. And, after some discussion, it passed overwhelmingly. It was presented by Page Ackerman (UCLA) to Council, and after an attempt to shunt it to a committee, it was adopted. In essence, it *recognized* the danger to intellectual freedom by the presence of governmental spies in libraries; *went on record* against the use of grand juries to intimidate anti–Vietnam War activities; *deplored* the use of conspiracy trials as a weapon against critics; and *asserted* the confidentiality of the professional relationship of librarians to the people they serve by defending their right not to divulge information on users' reading habits, or on circulation records.

I settled into a new life and a new job.

In December, I was phoned by a friend close to the case, who told me that I could expect to be called as a government witness at the trial, which was set for January, 1972. And indeed, in early January, I received a phone call, then a visit from a sheriff from Sacramento with a subpoena to appear in Harrisburg, Pennsylvania. During that past year the letters between

Father Phil and Sister Liz had been leaked to the press by the government prosecutors, and were prominently featured in *Life* (or *Look*, I forget which). The first indictment had been rewritten and the accusations of kidnapping and of blowing up of heating tunnels, were now joined by charges of raids on draft offices, some of which were admitted! The new indictment had the effect of "defus(ing) and even negat(ing) the earlier bombing and kidnapping charges since in order to prove conspiracy the government needed only to show that one of the three acts had been contemplated"

DR. CROPROT

(Raines, *Conspiracy,* p. 10). The conspiracy case diverted the energies that would have gone to the continued struggle to end the Vietnam War, to raising money and preparing for the legal defense. It was obvious that whether the government won or lost the case, it had siphoned off energies and sowed disunity and doubt among the anti-war groups.

I flew to Harrisburg. There was a warm reunion, joined by our very young, brilliant, empathetic lawyer, Alan Black. We talked hard and long. We talked of the trial, of what had been revealed in the press that we had not known; we talked of the continuing horror of the war in Southeast Asia; we talked of testifying and of refusing to testify. We needed to free ourselves and each other to do what each had to do without being compelled by the thoughts, beliefs, or actions of the others.

When it was her turn, Jane Hoover went into that green courtroom that Tony Scoblick, one of the defendants, correctly described as being inside a green olive, and testified. Her testimony and her manner had a devastating effect on the government's case (we later learned that this case was built on the accusations of a paid informer, F.B.I. agents, and the personal letters of a man and a woman). All four of us had been subpoenaed as government witnesses, ostensibly to substantiate some of the testimony that the informer would subsequently give. Whether they thought that four women who had befriended Boyd, would be easily cowed by the imper-

sonal manipulation of a court procedure to provide the needed base of credibility for their star witness, I will never know. But, I'm sure they rued the day. Pat Rom, the other librarian, testified with similar effect. Betsy Sandel had steeled herself to refuse to testify in protest. But two minutes before she was to take the stand, she was persuaded by someone from the defense to reconsider. It was soon to be my turn. I had discussed the alternatives with Alan. I had left my options open to the end. He laid out the possible consequences. I had asked and found out how testifying or not testifying would affect the people on trial. I felt free to take the opportunity to protest the attacks being made by my government on the freedoms which were basic to my life as a citizen and to my work as a librarian. I sat and scribbled my statement on a piece of yellow paper. When Betsy finished I told Alan what I had decided and showed him my statement. At the bench the judge suggested that I think over my decision because there are dire consequences. He gave me several days to decide. I stayed with old friends in Lewisburg. When we returned, I had decided to stick to my decision. The jury was sent out before I came in to prevent "prejudice to the case." I asked permission to read my statement and it was granted. I read:

> Your Honor, it is because I respect the function of this court to protect the rights of the individual, that I must refuse to testify. I cannot in my conscience lend myself to this black charade. I love and respect this country too much to see a farce made of the tenets upon which it stands. To me it stands on:
>
> *freedom of thought:* but government spying in homes, in libraries, and universities, inhibits and destroys this freedom.
>
> *freedom of association:* yet, in this case, gatherings of friends, picnics, parties, have been given sinister implications, made suspect.
>
> *freedom of speech:* yet general discussions have been interpreted by the government as advocating conspiracy.
>
> The realities of overt killings in Vietnam have been obscured by the unrealities that I have encountered here.

The judge, angry at the reference to a "charade," shouted, "Take her away," despite the defense lawyer's efforts to keep me out of jail. I was handcuffed to a chain around my waist and taken to the local county jail. An encouraging editorial appeared in the *New York Times* the day of my appeal, but it was to no avail. I returned to jail the day the trial ended, in 16 days, surprisingly. The defense had decided not to plead their case, but to stand on their actions, reputations, and way of life. I was watching TV in the noisy, crowded dayroom in jail when the news came. It blew my mind. They were saying, in effect, "This is your case, gentlemen, and you're stuck with it." The jury eventually eked out a verdict of guilty on the count of letter-smuggling, but after many days of deliberation returned to announce a deadlock. Since then, all charges have been dismissed.

I was free again.

It would be heartening to say that ALA sprang to my support, that the Intellectual Freedom Committee used the opportunity to discuss, in print, the intellectual freedom relationship of this issue to the Library Bill of Rights, and to government intimidation. But that didn't happen. As a matter of fact, quite the opposite occurred. ALA Executive Board issued a statement saying it could not support my action because I had defied a legally constituted court of law, and the LeRoy Merritt Foundation had to reverse itself before it offered $500 in aid. I was in jail when I read the ALA statement. Not a comforting experience, but made particularly onerous because I had not asked for their support. They may have been reacting to pressure from the Social Responsibilities Round Table to mount a campaign for disseminating information and fund-raising. SRRT put on their own campaign and I was flooded with wonderful letters in jail and badly needed funds.

That summer Dean and I flew to Chicago for the ALA Annual Conference, hoping to clarify the issues. It took five hours of being questioned before the Intellectual Freedom Committee, until Mr. North, ALA's attorney, was able to agree in front of that committee that my refusal to testify as a protest against the governmental attack on our Bill of Rights was indeed related to our Library Bill of Rights and to the Government Intimidation Resolution. ALA Executive Board on the recommendation of ALA's Intellectual Freedom Committee reversed their previous statement and came out in support of my stand.

An eloquent new Government Intimidation Statement was written, accepted, and now stands among our basic intellectual freedom documents. To me, library work is a daily act of faith. It implies a belief in rationality, in the possibility of change based on information, knowledge and judgment. It implies respect for people and their individuality and it encompasses a sense of wonder at the beauty and ugliness, the courage and strength that are part of all our daily lives. I would like to see the new members of the library profession imbued with a passionate commitment to serve people in their need to know and I would like to see active commitment to our basic freedoms that make it possible to learn and to create changes toward a gentler, fuller, and kinder way of life.

SIPAPU: Your position with Data Center—when you began, what you do.

HORN: I came to Data Center in 1977 as a volunteer. A journalist friend had suggested that I could be helpful there, and they were "such nice people." I was "between jobs," had just moved into a small apartment in Berkeley after having exhausted job possibilities around Turlock, where we lived, and where Dean Galloway, my husband, was director of the library at California State College, Stanislaus. Data Center turned out to be an extraordinary library and a continually exciting experience. For a traditional reference librarian (which I am), one of the most satisfying experiences is to provide information that answers the question and is useful. If in the process, there is also a teaching of the strategies of searching and a sharing of the fun in the quest, then the day seems brighter and the feet stop hurting! And at Data Center, there is still another satisfaction. The information, when found, will be used, most often for the purpose of helping to create changes that would improve life for people.

The information gathered, organized and provided was needed by investigative reporters, environmentalists, activists of all kinds, and just ordinary people concerned about being powerless in this complex society. This was indeed, I discovered, a socially responsible library! Here were people who clipped articles from hundreds of newspapers and magazines, sorted, filed, prepared hundreds of clippings on specific subjects like plant shutdowns, a profile of Bechtel Corporation — stuff like that. Thus, two days after  the invasion of Grenada, there was a neat packet of perspectives on that event from the columns of the New York *Times, In These Times,* and many others. For a traditional reference librarian, it was agony (at first) to be dependent on walking heads. There were, of course, no indexes, not even a list of contents of the file drawers. If Fred was out, there was no way to find anything in the Banking and Finance file, and if John was at home, the Labor files became an arcane mystery, &c. Over the years, the files have been organized by a growing people who joined the staff, and by a continuous flow of volunteers, some of whom came to do research and stayed to help. All show commitment to providing information that is not readily available about corporations, investments, Reagan administration, labor, Latin America, and my own special interest file, the Right to Know. For a librarian there is excitement in knowing that the knowledge gathered was going to be used for improvement of life for people somewhere. I learned as I never had before how interconnected the world's people are. An iron manufacturing plant built by G.E. in Singapore in 1978 resulted in the closing of an iron manufacturing plant in Ontario, California, with its accompaniment of unemployment and community depression. Connections like these need to be made and the information disseminated.

I went from a volunteer to a member of the staff. I'm now a kind of resident librarian consultant, available to help, but with my own very special

Right to Know file. When I first came, I rapidly shifted from a compulsive, cataloging of books which I discovered were comparatively little used, to the organizing of the clippings in the Labor file. It still stands as the best organized file, and the most accessible. It was to be the prototype for other files, with a full index. But the dream of indexing this flowing, changing mass of clippings on ever-changing developments and urgencies in all fields has long been discarded. The patterns for organizing the files were created, a numbering system was developed. Outlines of the files provide some general access and the walking heads have increased in number and share their knowledge.

Working at Data Center has been a rare experience. It is a non-profit, public interest organization. Foundations have contributed, membership subscriptions help, users who aren't subscribers drop money into the box for the Center's maintenance. There is now a research service that brings in money, and there are products like ISLA, and packets of clippings on important current concerns, e.g. "Ethical investing," corporation profiles, "New Right."

The organization is democratic and egalitarian. Everyone on the staff gets paid equally. Decisions are arrived at through discussions and consensus. But beyond even this is the atmosphere of an extended family. There was an infant in a playpen when I first came. I became a surrogate grandmother as the others were surrogate aunts and uncles. We stopped to play, or pick him up, occasionally even diapered him. It was sad when he graduated to play school. There are picnics, wonderful birthday celebrations and even a staff softball team.

SIPAPU: Your concern with Right to Know. Horn vs. government suppression of information. What does the Right to Know concept fully imply?

HORN: The First Amendment was created to protect the governed from the governors. In a democratic society the citizens need to have free access to all kinds of information because they must participate in decision-making. When governments withhold information the country is in deep trouble. There has been an increasing growth of secrecy and suppression of information by the U.S. government which has accelerated to an alarming degree during the Reagan administration. Open censorship was attempted (unsuccessfully) when the "Pentagon Papers" were to be published by the New York *Times* and the Washington *Post* (1971). The revelations uncovered the untruths and the disinformation that was fed to the public about the Vietnam War. But, of course, it was after the fact. Open censorship was applied by the government to former C.I.A. agents who felt that the people should know about the agency's activities. Ostensibly, the reason for the regulation was to protect agents' lives and "national security." Most frequently these rules have been perceived as an attempt to avoid embarrassment for the illegal, ugly actions which the C.I.A. initiated and in which it participated. Thanks to the

Freedom of Information Act (FOIA) (now endangered by the Reagan administration), the C.I.A.'s role in experimenting with mind-altering drugs on unsuspecting people, its role in trying to prevent the election of Salvador Allende in Chile, and then its disruptive and undermining activities in bringing down that government are now known.

UNCLE PENNY

There was open censorship of news during the U.S. invasion of Grenada (1983). By not permitting news reporters onto Grenadian soil while the invasion was occurring, the government was able to tailor the news and thus influence public opinion without interference. By the time reporters were able to examine and report on some misinformation, the "action" was over, and the press was pushed into the distasteful role of yapping dogs criticizing a "successful rescue" of American citizens.

Censorship by a government interferes with the right of people to know what their government is doing. It's a way of avoiding and of stifling criticism. Both criticism and dissent, however, are the healthy correctives that keep a government honest and responsive to the needs of its people. But, while overt censorship is at least visible and can be fought, far more dangerous is the hidden censorship of which we are not aware unless some incident reveals a pattern of manipulation and suppression of information. Such discoveries can sap faith in the government, and in social institutions, and make us adversaries instead of the participants we want to be. When 50,000 copies of a Department of Energy magazine are withdrawn and placed in a storeroom because several articles therein deal with the unsolved problem of dangerous nuclear waste, the once reliable source of accurate and disinterested information is endangered. Ignorance is perpetuated and people become powerless to control their fate. That action, however, reflected the administration's pro-nuclear position.

Budget economies also reduced the gathering, organizing and publishing of important statistics dealing with people's welfare. This resulted in confusion and inability to check on the efficacy of programs. This policy had to be reversed. Access to census material had to be reduced. Numerous government documents were dropped without adequate consultation as to need and usefulness. Price increases on many government documents used in library reference departments have resulted in cancellations of the orders. The already reduced Federal support so curbed the book budget that important documents could not be purchased. While public services, from baby care to barn construction, have been limited in U.S. government documentation by the current administration, increased "secrecy" classification has been encouraged; while an attempt has been made to muzzle some 100,000 former governmental employees, through an Executive Order dated 11 March 1983. Congressional action delayed implementation of this order, but in the meanwhile, telephones have been tapped, organizations have been infiltrated, undermined, thrown on the defensive by legal action. A blacklist of prominent citizens was created by the head of the United States Information Agency, which had the fiscal effect of denying them funds to travel and speak in foreign countries, because they had been critical of various administration policies. Even scientific conferences have been affected: papers to be read at a conference in San Diego were withdrawn in 1982.

What happens if the press is controlled, or owned by fewer and fewer conglomerates, and the information is colored by that control? The questions that must be raised deal with the usurpation of power. In a democracy, power resides in the people as citizens, voters and taxpayers. Information, of itself, is not power. But what is undeniable, is that without information, people are powerless. Those who are in a position to control, manipulate, or suppress information can also create false information. The projections of Huxley and Orwell are no longer just fictional horror stories; they depict societies in which information is so controlled that truth and reality are what those in control say it is, and criticism and dissent are wiped out.

SIPAPU: First vs. Fourteenth Amendment: how does Right to Know affirm social responsibility?

HORN: If you have the right to speak freely, you have the right to have information to speak intelligently. We support having all kinds of books in our school and public libraries because we are supporting the students' or other persons' right to know, to be informed and enlightened by a vast variety of facts and opinions. The Gablers (Mel and Norma) in Texas, the Moral Majority and others have been very active in attempting to limit this variety. Fortunately, organizations have sprung up to battle these attempted incursions on our right to know. People for the American Way has been battling textbook censorship, the National Organization against Censorship keeps many organizations informed, the ACLU is ready to do battle in many censorship cases. The most heartening development is the Coalition for the Right to Know, in California's Bay Area, an umbrella organization which includes the Data Center among others. This local coalition can use the many talents of its members to write and deliver messages to media, as can the more traditional outfits of the American Library Association and the Freedom to Read Foundation.

For myself, I have always considered publicly-supported libraries to be

open to everybody; everyone has the right to use and to borrow books and other materials, the right to get help in finding information, the right to use the meeting rooms. The collections are supposed to represent the widest and deepest range of ideas, facts, opinions, as well as cultural and recreational expressions. The library epitomized the nation's faith in knowledge and in people.

Libraries, therefore, embody for me, the practical application of freedom and equality: freedom to choose among a myriad of ideas, opinions, forms of expression: and equality of every individual to this feast. But, I have also understood that there is a constant dynamic tension operating between freedom and equality. In libraries, as in the society of which they are a part, there have been periods in history when the word "free" incised in stone on the front of public library buildings meant "free" only to white people. It was only when public pressures directed at making the services equally available succeeded in that aim, that there was library freedom for everyone. Now when some libraries charge fees for interlibrary loans and fees for finding information by searching data bases, the alleged freedom, in my view, becomes spurious. The ability to pay becomes the prerequisite for service. It is then, the presence of equality that gives freedom its reality. But equality becomes just a concept until great public pressures demand equality in practice. Just such pressures secured the freeing of the slaves; just such pressures produced women's suffrage. Just such pressures continue to produce a better treatment, through civil rights and women's liberation, for people of color and for women.

Today, however, government's stress is on freedom — defined as freedom for enterprise, and freedom from governmental regulation. Equality, along with ecology, is little mentioned.

Many libraries have a rich history of helping immigrants become citizens. Naturalization procedures required knowledge of our Constitution, and also the democratic principles underlying our society. Libraries helped develop literacy, and started the children off on the road to good citizenship. In this, the public libraries of New York City and Cleveland were outstanding.

When the sixties came along, this kind of service was rediscovered as "social responsibility." Librarians realized that not only immigrants needed special services. Many groups of people who lived, worked, and paid taxes were simply ignored, when it came to planning library services. It was so logical, we now saw, so fair, and so right, to identify these groups, and to start to learn to serve them. Here was another thrust for equality, where freedom alone had failed. The ALA conferences of 1969, 1970, and onwards were vibrant with discussions and battles on "consciousness raising": racism, sexism, homophobia, and other prejudices that affected people's access to libraries and the information they stored. This thrust for equality disturbed many established librarians who were comfortable with serving those who already used the library, the white middle class. Conscientiously, collections had been built to reflect those values, and satisfy those people. What was now being asked of librarians was that they should reach out into the unknown: to people whose information needs were not known, whose language patterns were strange, if not indeed foreign, and whose lifestyles were certainly different.

Combined with this push for "outreach" came the need to develop greater sensibilities toward the people who were to be better served. This led to the critical study of words in the language of the majority, examining these for evidence of racism and sexism. Books began to be examined critically for slurs and stereotypes, as new criteria for book selection. Greater awareness made it possible to step into other people's shoes, to see how it felt to live in an atmosphere of denigration. Staff and public were made aware of the many unconsciously accepted expressions and behaviors that reduced some folk to second-class citizenship. A "Racism and sexism awareness" resolution became, after considerable discussion, ALA's policy in promoting greater sensitivity in this area. (The name was later changed to "Resolution on prejudice, stereotyping and discrimination.")

However, this move toward equality was attacked as being in conflict with the Library Bill of Rights. Some librarians assumed that books would be removed or labelled, and that the "awareness" program would compromise the "neutrality" of libraries. As a member of the ALA Intellectual Freedom Committee, later as its chair, I was appalled by the arguments presented against the resolution, and amazed by those who presented them. A clarification was eventually arrived at, after public meetings permitted expressions of many voices, presenting broader concerns than those heard in the IFC or the Office for Intellectual Freedom. However, the head of the OIF dismissed our use of the phrase "libraries as institutions for democratic living" as "boiler plate," and the identification of libraries as "educational institutions" was questioned by a committee member because education implied teaching. As a result of this conflict, it is not to be wondered that, the 1980 version of the Library Bill of Rights no longer mentions democracy or education. The division between the concept of intellectual freedom, and the concept of its applicability to everyone, became a division between the First Amendment and the Fourteenth. The Fourteenth Amendment states that the rights of citizens (including black people) cannot be abridged by the States. These rights include all those covered in the Constitution itself, plus the previous thirteen amendments, and naturally including the First. The Fourteenth Amendment, therefore, extends the effect of the First Amendment to the citizens of all the States, equally.

Apparently what disturbs some librarians is the pressure for positive action in support of democratic principles. The first Intellectual Freedom Committee was intended to "safeguard the rights of library users to freedom of inquiry" (1938). The first Library Bill of Rights (1938) spoke of "growing intolerance, suppression of free speech, and censorship, affecting the rights of minorities..." It was followed by the first official ALA Library Bill of Rights in 1939, which referred to the "library as an institution to educate for democratic living." There was, then, obviously a clear commitment to democracy and to safeguarding the right to information needed for the furtherance of that democracy. With each revision of the Library Bill of Rights, the commitment to active participation in educating for democracy and protecting the people's access to information has eroded, at least in the official statements of this major organization of librarians.

I think it is fair to say that many librarians are indeed, socially responsible. They have extended library services to jails, to home-bound, and into rural areas; they have, indeed, established other language collections, created Information & Referral Services, hired more minority librarians, and have done all of the above, with developed sensitivity to the many racial and ethnic groups in our society. That social responsibility must now be harnessed to the formation of local coalitions with other groups for the preservation of the lifeblood of democracy, the free and equal access to information, the right to know.

We have been in touch with the Dutch small press association, Stichting **"DRUKWERK IN DE MARGE"** (= Printing in the Margin Foundation), a group of non-professional and non-commercial printers and publishers, whose current secretary is Jan Keiser, Leidse Slootweg 4, 2481 KH, Woubrugge, Zuid-Holland, Netherlands. There is also a P.O. B. for addresses: Postbus 16477, Amsterdam Z. O. The purpose of describing this almost entirely Dutch association (their only 3 foreign members are in Belgium, Germany, and Thailand, the latter almost certainly a diplomatic post) is that

first of all, given the long historical connection between Britain (and other English-speaking countries) and the Netherlands, there is some interest, as evinced by their bibliographies, in English-language publication; and secondly, to a degree far greater than is true of any American small-press group, they are interested in printing and publication history, and maintain a library in Dutch and English on typography, composition, printing and bookbinding. Those interested in these fields in this country might wish to contact them. The Foundation was started in May 1975, some seven years later than our COSMEP, but already has a long list of printers. Besides a *Bulletin,* which comes out once or twice a year, they also publish a *Bibliografie* (text in Dutch, explanations in Dutch, English and German), which is a comprehensive listing of all members' publications (in contrast to our COSMEP catalog, which is a catalog and not exhaustive). The latest of these 3 bibliographies costs 30 Dutch guilders (ca. $15), and an inspection of it shows that the publications are almost entirely literary, many of them letterpress, the vast majority in Dutch but some English and French titles and some translations. Authors wishing to see their work appear in Holland, or in Dutch, might apply here; still more appropriate would be the decision of an American small-press publisher to do the work of some Dutch author in English. Since most Dutch students routinely learn English in school, finding translators should be no problem. It is possible that there might be grant support for such activity. Curiously enough, the only Netherlands-based publisher listed in Fulton and Ferber's *International Directory of Little Magazines and Small Presses,* 19th ed.,—Ins & Outs Press, P.O. Box 3759, Amsterdam,—is not listed in the membership list of Stichting "Drukwerk in de Marge."

15 : 2

Since her appearance as interviewee in this, 30th consecutive issue of Sipapu, *Theresa Vinciguerra has retired from* The Poet Tree, Inc., *to devote more time to writing.*

The Poet Tree has changed its name to the Sacramento Poetry Center and its address to 1727 I Street; poetry readings are held at Hannibal's Cafe. The director is Mary Moore and the editors of Poet News *are Patrick Grizzell, Luke Breit and Mary Zeppa. They have published an anthology of Sacramento poets under the title of* Landing Signals.

LAND WITHOUT BANNERS: The new regionalism in American poetry and thought stands on a different footing from the regionalism of the turn of the century. That was preoccupied with naturalism, dialect stories, and historical novels; this arises out of an ecological concept of region as a territory within a state or crossing the boundaries of one or more states,— each having its own biota and hence its own semi-mystical relationship to the land, its creatures and native peoples. The poet, modern intruder though he may be, marries the region and becomes its bard, while other people in the area develop, with and through him, the same bio-regional consciousness and begin to interact with each other and with the land in ways that disregard conventional state and international boundaries and capitals. This kind of thinking is currently being developed by local community papers, the periodical *Rain* in the Pacific Northwest, by the Planet Drum Foundation, and by such poets as Gary Snyder in the foothills of the Sierra Nevada.

A parallel, although not necessarily derivative, pattern emerged in American poetry with the publication of *A Geography of Poets, an Anthology of the New Poetry,* edited by Edward Field (New York, Bantam, 1979). Earlier anthologies had been based on the work of one school, one magazine, or even one state or region; or had emphasized ethnic background, sex, sexual orientation. This book, however, though it took in poets from across the nation,— arranged them not alphabetically, nor by birthdate, nor by the poem's title, but by regions: Northwest, San Francisco and Northern California, Southern

California, The Great Plains, &c. (Again, how refreshing: Field did not begin with New England or New York). Field's purpose was to show that you don't have to go to New York for poetry any more, but beyond that, he wanted  to show the enormous variety that is going on in American poetry today.

An outgrowth of this regionalism is the "poetry center," a place where poets and writers read, where festivals are held and books are collected. We've already covered one such: Beyond Baroque in Venice, California. (They've moved into the old Venice City Hall since we covered them in our v. 8, no. 1, consecutive issue no. 17, January 1977; mailing address: P.O. Box 806, Venice, CA 90291.) The allegiance of the Beyond Baroque people, in our view — *if not theirs* — seems as much to the avant-garde as to the Los Angeles scene, although admittedly hundreds of Southern California poets have read there.

We come now to a regional literary center in an area not celebrated in American literary history, nor part of a major metropolis. The Poet Tree, Inc., at 2791 24th Street, #8, Sacramento, CA 95818 is so close to our own turf, that we invited its founder and Executive Director, Theresa Vinciguerra, to lunch:

SIPAPU: Your birth and education?

VINCIGUERRA: Coney Island! in a Sicilian and Jewish neighborhood, and born of Sicilian descent. Although we were not rich I went to parochial schools, there and in Southern California. Immaculate Heart High was caught up, while I was there, in the liberal Catholic movement. Sister Corita had taught there, and presently the Sisters of the Immaculate Heart of Mary abandoned their habits and drew closer to the community. James Cardinal McIntyre, then Archbishop of Los Angeles, barred them from Communion, and the Sisters and some lay Catholics began meeting as an underground church in private homes, with Masses sung in English. When someone informed Cardinal McIntyre about this, he closed the underground churches; I left the Church then and never went back; but the artistic temperament, the idea that we are here on earth to *create,* and the sense that the individual is responsible to his or to her community — these things I learned at IHHS — have always stayed with me.

Then, I attended California State University at Los Angeles from 1969 to 1971, working at the Music Center in Los Angeles (all those free admissions!). I took English courses, travelled in Europe in the summer of 1971, but didn't have any clear ideas about writing until I came here to the University of California, Davis, and took courses from Karl Shapiro, the poet.

SIPAPU: How did you find him? He's not everyone's cup of tea.

VINCIGUERRA: Very encouraging, a great teacher, but in a quiet, non-demonstrative way. I first began to write good poems for him, but when I married William Sullivan, we moved to Irvine, where I went to the University of California at Irvine. I hated Irvine, but my husband was willing to leave his job and go back with me to Davis to get my teaching credentials; all I could think of doing with English was teaching it. I taught a continuation school at Holmes Junior High in Davis: poetry, drama, Italian; quit to have my son; returned later to teaching at Dixon High — but then finally decided I'd had it (at least, at the secondary level) with teaching at the end of that year.

SIPAPU: So far, a familiar pattern.

VINCIGUERRA: Not from here on out. I lost my next child: a stillbirth at seven months. The event changed my life. I started to write again after a four-year lull. We moved from Bryte to Sacramento, where I found a job at a psychiatric facility for children as a staffing reports writer — but I didn't last long there for two reasons: it was too depressing to read those case reports — and — I got pregnant again. I was paranoid all the time that I would lose it. I was fortunate this time, she was a healthy girl, but my marriage broke up in the process. Then a new life began.

SIPAPU: And that was the poetry center.

VINCIGUERRA: Yes, I'd always — since at least Davis and Shapiro — dreamed of a place where writers and artists could get together, a poetry organization. I placed a little ad in the *Sacramento Bee,* with my telephone number, around May 1979. About ten people answered and we met in a pizza parlor. By July 1979, we were incorporated as Poet Tree, Inc. We started readings in galleries and pubs, as we had no headquarters of our own, and in October 1979 we held a reading of six major poets in the area — and raised five hundred dollars. This led to the first issues of *Poet News,* our newsletter, and *Quercus* (Latin for oak, alluding to the California Valley Oak, *Quercus lobata* — Ed.) — our bi-annual magazine. Pat Grizzell, our art director, attracted attention with his posters and publicity. In 1981 the old abandoned Sierra School in Sacramento, just south of the freeway, became the focus of a community renovation project as an arts and community center. We agreed to renovate room #8 and sign a one-year lease. We've been there ever since. The room houses our office—two desks, a file, a small press library and enough space for about 40 people to attend our readings. For the readings with larger draws—such as the Bly one with 300 people, we rent the 24th Street Theatre, which is right down the hall.

SIPAPU: Present activities and future plans?

VINCIGUERRA: We have a Board of eleven Directors, who set the major policies and goals of the organization. Mary Zeppa is our current President. *Poet News,* edited by Pat Grizzell, Mary Zeppa and Luke Breit, is our forum for local activities, interviews and reviews, along with some poetry, and *Quercus,* which I edit, is our poetry magazine. If you are published in *Quercus* you automatically get a reading at The Poet Tree, but you don't have to publish there in order to get to read there; Victoria Dalkey is our Program Director; she heads our reading series. *Quercus,* since it only accepts poets from the Sacramento Valley area, is not eligible for grants from the National Endowment for the Arts, although it has received support locally from the County of Sacramento's Cultural Awards Program. The California Arts Council has given *Poet News* grant support, but for the most part they're reluctant to fund periodicals because of the problem of continuing liens; they'd rather fund books and reading series, so we will apply next year for a more expanded reading series. By the way, we average three readings a month, and we do have an ongoing poetry craft workshop every week headed by Jane Blue.

Day-to-day decisions are made by our largely volunteer (that's a euphemism for grossly underpaid) staff, over which I have responsibility as Executive Director. Most of us have other jobs on the outside. I do free-lance ad writing to support my children and myself, which cuts into my own writing; when I was working on my Master's at California State University at Sacramento, with Dennis Schmitz, over the last three years, I was able to write fairly consistently. I've come close to quitting as Executive Director many times, because of the extensive commitment it involves. But it would be like abandoning a child. We've only begun to give Sacramento poets the attention they deserve. Sacramento isn't as familiar a place for poets as San Francisco, and some of us here have felt lonely, detached. I think Poet Tree has been able to change that.

SIPAPU: What are the advantages of living in Sacramento rather than in the Bay Area? What does Sacramento do to your head?

VINCIGUERRA: "Sacto" as a location is not perfect, but I'm determined to keep trying here. In contrast to the Bay Area it's quieter: less socializing, so there's less distraction. Keeping up the focus on Sacramento as a vital community of poets is important to me. The autumns are beautiful;

I get most writing done in the fall. Summer is impossible! With the temperature rising into the 100s (F.) (= 39°C.), I can't write at all.

SIPAPU: The future of regional writing as you see it, from experiences with your contributors and how the area has shaped them?

VINCIGUERRA: As I see it, our future is on a precarious axis, — we could take off spinning or plunge. Survival gets harder as money — everywhere — gets tighter and the printer's bill keeps going up. But local writers continue to band together and support each other through groups like ours, and if they do, there's hope. For example, we are sponsors of a project called *Landing Signals.* Initially many local artists donated pieces for a benefit auction for the project, and we made a generous sum of seed money. So people do come out and help.

SIPAPU: Any further thoughts on Great Central Valley / politicians / tomatoes / growers / "Aggies" / pickup trucks / winter fog / summer heat?

VINCIGUERRA: A sense of place is central to poets: and I'm talking about both exterior and interior place. The external world in which you exist — that *place* — cannot help but make an impression on the internal world, and it is from there that the poet begins to write.

We conclude with a poem by Theresa Vinciguerra, first published in *Divergent Lines,* a Sacramento regional magazine:

NONNA:

The eyes of codfish were her delicacy.
Grandpa would save his for her,
sever carefully the heads from the scaled bodies
and slide them onto her plate.

Mangia gli occhi! She coaxed me to share
her feast. But at seven I grimaced
and shut from their stare my own eyes.

Of what visions did she taste?
The shores of her Catania,
The smell of that unforgettable Sea,
a salt-fresh antidote to the odors of garbage

that flooded through the alley windows
during those long, Brooklyn nights in summer?

Ten o'clock, everyone still up,
some in the house, some lounging
outside on the stoop, she went
into the kitchen—her short
stout frame rocking from side to side as it moved
across the worn blue linoleum—stopped
in front of the stove, speard the one
fish-head left-over from supper, then
turned to me, who followed her
like a calf: *Venga, bimba,*
mangia bene.

And I wonder, if this, her last
eye is still on me
because now I will look straight and long.
I will eat of the delicate feast
that she has brought me.

16 : 1

I'm completely out of copies of volume 16, number 1, perhaps because it was my famous erotica issue with Lily Pond. Lily granted me an interview with a tape recorder and then edited the transcript, which was entirely appropriate, since in this context a woman might well wish to edit what she had said into an interior mike. (You can have the original tape if you will send me a million dollars.) Yellow Silk *remains one of my favorite magazines and issue no. 26, just out (fall 1988), is better than ever.*
Later pages describe one of our earliest tackles with the McCalden case.
Denise Dee is no longer doing the Closest Penguins and has moved.

PUBLISHING AS A TOTAL EROTIC EXPERIENCE: Lily Pond, editor of *Yellow Silk,* a journal of erotic arts, has, in the midst of a new era of repression and fear, when pleasure is suspect to Left as well as Right, created a new, happy, whole-hearted approach to writing and publishing about love and sexuality. Her magazine, founded in 1981 and now approaching its fifteenth issue, features stories, poems, essays (by Mary Mackey and others), fine arts, and even cartoons! As soon as you touch on such a subject, you find that what turns some on turns others off, and Lily Pond has had her share of rejections and misunderstandings. But she has seen more erotic literature in the past four years than practically anyone on Mother Earth, and her one standard of publication, beyond the quality of the work, is "ALL PERSUASIONS; NO BRUTALITY." We take you now to a small apartment in the Bay Area where she works and lives with her cat, The Pooh, surrounded by plants, art books, drawings of lilies—an atmosphere of light, love, and work. (Address: verygraphics, P.O. Box 6374, Albany, CA 94706.)

(Readers may or may not be aware that all but the first of our previous interviews were conducted with pad and pencil, and then written up at home; one with a typewriter; some were even done by mail, without a meeting with the person interviewed, and one was conducted by a contributor. In this case, we had recently bought an Aiwa tape recorder, and it proved to be the perfect interviewing device for Lily Pond, who loves spontaneity in (nearly) all things:

SIPAPU: We are at the home of Lily Pond, editor of *Yellow Silk,* the Journal of Erotic Arts, — and we have some questions for her.

LILY: (watching the scrambling): Once we find them.

SIPAPU: The usual: your birth, parentage, education?

LILY: O, there goes the teakettle! (as it spills on the questions. Teakettle music-box tinkly sounds; the teakettle has a music box in its base which plays "Anniversary Waltz" whenever the teakettle is lifted.) — I was born in 1947, September 30th, Detroit, Michigan; my father was a doctor; my mother is, and has been over the years, a photographer, play director, mother, embroiderer — a creative volunteer-type person from suburbia.

SIPAPU: But those are good things to be. An artistic background, in short.

LILY: Yes, there were a lot of books, records, and everything in the house; my father always played the piano, and was real musical, and also randy — I mean, he was good-spirited. My mom always felt no challenge was too high, that it couldn't be met; which could be a pressure but was also a positive effect, and she always tried to find, within the somewhat limited realms that her time lent her, creative solutions to — what to do with the back yard; I mean, she would do cement blocks for a patio with marbles for designs in them down the basement. I mean, this is the kind of thing that she would do, that you might find in *Woman's day* — but they were creative uses to solve her problems.

SIPAPU: Sure! Sure!

LILY: And then, when my dad died, five years ago, she suddenly started doing photography and now is showing everywhere and winning prizes. And so now that she's released from the roles she was brought up to follow, this means that she is released to the full use of her creative talent. And it's been wonderful, watching her blossom.

SIPAPU: But it's marvelous! What a wonderful releasing background! You know, so many people are uptight, and they're fighting their parents, and —

LILY: O, my God, I fought my parents horribly. I was a beatnik when I was twelve. They didn't understand me, and they eventually kicked me out of the house for being too strange.

SIPAPU: Then it's really not that simple, is it?

LILY: No, not at all, I went to the Haight-Ashbury in 1968, and—

SIPAPU: Then we must have seen you! We would go down there and wander around—

LILY: Then I was one of the people who waved at you!

SIPAPU: OK, it's marvelous, it's so great!

LILY: When I was a kid I was given lessons in anything I wanted: art lessons, singing lessons, piano lessons—all the things a nice upper-middle-class Jewish girl could ask for, you know—and it gave me a real art-historical cultural background.

SIPAPU: So we see. (We're looking at art nouveau, *The Sacred Spring* by Nicholas Powell, a record collection with everything from Motown to Dial-a-Poem Poets, Diego Rivera painting of lilies)—

LILY: My mother took that photograph (pointing to a picture of a lily pond, sitting on the piano)—all my pictures are of either flowers, birds, or sex.

SIPAPU: The flowers, the birds, the bees—well, we certainly see, Lily, why you wanted this to be spontaneous, because the next question we were going to ask was not the question we were going to ask, but leads off from it; and that is—the Haight-Ashbury, and what it did for you?

LILY: Well, for some reason the negative side occurs to me first, which is, it made me scared about my own power in the world. It made me feel that anything could evaporate any moment; that nothing was hold-on-to-able. The positive side: well, they're totally interwoven; while many people were getting their degrees, I got mine ten years later, at thirty-one—while they were learning the structures and strictures of life, I was learning the color and madness and despair, the passion and the pain in life's extremities! So while others were learning the discipline, and I was learning the love part, I had the advantage—I couldn't be doing the magazine without that street stuff in me!

SIPAPU: Now a question that derives from the periodical itself. Whatever happened to Tom Nos and Jim Roby, mentioned as missing in *Yellow Silk* #1?

LILY: These are guys I went to high school with and still dream about; not so much about Jim Roby, now I know that he's in government service, or something like that, the last time I heard about him, so I don't dream about him so much any more; no one knows about Tom Nos; I dream about him so often, that when I see him, I say, "Oh, it's Tom! I must be dreaming!" We were never that close, we never dated, we were just "sympatico," as they say — but he did a drawing, of two lovers kissing, a man and a woman kissing. It touched me so much! If anybody knows where Tom Nos is, please let me know. (I've tried calling in all the phone directories of this country, plus our alumni secretary.)

SIPAPU: I think this is going down with some of the great mysteries of the sixties — like Roger Calkins —

LILY: Like Mrs. Calabash.

SIPAPU: Mrs. Calabash? Was she married to Judge Crater?

LILY: No, don't you remember, "Good night, Mrs. Calabash, wherever you are"?

SIPAPU: Yes, of course. Now, this is a big one: how you got started with *Yellow Silk*.

LILY: Just thought it up one night, started it the next day. I didn't know what I was doing . . . just (snap of fingers) okay!

SIPAPU: Indeed, we would suggest that one does not usually know what one is doing when one starts a magazine or one wouldn't do it.

LILY: But that's true of anything.

SIPAPU: Possibly.

LILY: How do you know what you're getting into when you're getting into it? How could you possibly know? (more music-box teapot music)

SIPAPU: That's the teapot, folks (music). So you just got started: you thought it up one night, you were going to do a magazine of erotica . . .

LILY: No, actually the first night I was going to do a magazine of the kind of writing I most liked (including the kind of writing I did), since you never find it all in one place or on a regular basis. Next night I was going around thinking, you know, any time anyone reads my stuff, or looks at the pictures on my walls, they say, "That's pretty graphic, that's pretty erotic." If I called it an erotic magazine I was more likely to get the kind of stuff I most liked, and this would distinguish it from all the other poetry magazines. And it turned out I was right, way more than I ever knew, because not only has its erotic content brought me for four years now, submissions that remain exciting to read and publish, but I can't imagine reading ten thousand poems a year on any other subject without getting completely bored!

Even when they're bad, they're about love and sexuality, you know, so how can you ... well, it's not too horrible! And also, it's such an intuitive position that I'm finding out what it means to me, I'm finding out about all the connections it makes in my life, and all the choices I make, and how that choice was representative of what distinguishes me from other people in ways that I wasn't conscious of. It's also connected me with people like Mary Mackey or Gary Epting (the artist) who have the same effort in some of their work which tends toward the same direction as *Yellow Silk*. So that's very exciting.

SIPAPU: Indeed. The title came to you in the same ball-of-lightning fashion, we take it.

LILY: Actually, I thought it was too long, I figured you needed *two* syllables. And so, *Yellow Silk,* which was inspired by reading this book: *The Life of an Amorous Woman,* by Ihara Saikaku, written in 1686, published now by New Directions, originally a dissertation with a million footnotes; I always felt that the entire footnote that this book put out was one of yellow silk — it's the life of a courtesan from youth to old age; and I wanted my magazine to have the same feeling — and so I came up with the name; I can't remember when I came up with that either; it's the real important moments of life I tend to forget! But I did go around asking people if they could come up with a name for the magazine which had two syllables, and this guy I knew at KQED came up with the idea of SPANDEX, which I didn't think was quite right!

SIPAPU: No! which reminds us, for many years, the old *Illustrated London News,* which used to carry only ads on its cover, would have at the top of the cover, "Fit Triplex, and be safe." We used to think that Triplex was something rather intimate, but when we asked a respectable English lady, it turned out that Triplex was automobile windshield glass. Now, we love the name *Yellow Silk*...

LILY: Thank you!

SIPAPU: We love the name, because what it has, is smoothness about it, and a sense of luxury — "Luxe, calme, et volupté" — exactly right.

LILY: What does that mean?

SIPAPU: O, that is a phrase from Baudelaire: "luxe, calme et volupté:" Luxury, calm and pleasure.

LILY: O, I see! (Summoning cat). You want her to be part of the interview?

SIPAPU: Of course, cats are always part of interviews. I check for people's cats. Now, other than the cat, who are the keepers of the flame: the assistants, the coordinators, the editors, the people whom you work with...

LILY: I don't work with anybody!

SIPAPU: But you have a whole list of them, on the masthead!

LILY: I know, they call up and say, "I know a great bookstore for you to try, in Peoria," and so I put their names on there, because they helped. I'm being grateful to everyone as far as possible.

SIPAPU: It's perfectly marvelous! But it does give a rather misleading impression.

LILY: But I do this less and less. There are people who help with proofreading and mailing.

SIPAPU: We see. We thought you had coordinators and that you had gathered a team.

LILY: Not at all. I do it all myself.

SIPAPU: And therefore the Albany office will be just a small office...

LILY: No, it's just a P.O. Box...

SIPAPU: Just a P.O. Box?

LILY: It's just this place!

SIPAPU: Then it's just like ours! . . . but you do have benefits to sell magazines.

LILY: Yeah, I had a benefit on Superbowl Sunday, not to sell magazines, as much as to meet the poets, hear the poems read out loud that had been in the magazine, and bring the *YS* readers together.

SIPAPU: Could you tell us more about the benefits; we couldn't get to one, was that the one you're talking about? Everybody reads; did you collect some money?

LILY: Very little. It was very poorly attended, for a *Yellow Silk* benefit; although well attended for a poetry reading, because of the Super Bowl. All material was from *Yellow Silk,* and each set opened with an erotic folk singer.

SIPAPU: And you're going to do some more.

LILY: O, they average one a year in the Bay Area, and one a year in New York, but this one was a year and a half later, because I just didn't have the energy.

SIPAPU: You may be aware that my previous interviewee, Theresa Vinciguerra, of Poet Tree, holds an annual erotic poetry reading in Sacramento.

LILY: Yes, but we didn't get invited this time. Either they have already heard all our poetry twice, or they didn't want to hear our poetry again!

SIPAPU: Of course, we know from personal experience, that they move things around and try to give people a chance...

LILY: Yes, that's good. And, to push the local scene...

SIPAPU: ...is absolutely central, and surely we're all agreed on that.

LILY: I want to say, coming back to staff, that I'm looking for the first permanent staff member besides myself. (Found! as of April 1985: a subscription manager.)

SIPAPU: Ah, what is your subscription list?

LILY: Let's put it this way: I printed 3500 last time, and I'm selling out, so I think I'm going to print 4500 this time. What's your circulation?

SIPAPU: One tenth of that. And a lot of that is simply exchange copies. But let's face it, maybe both of us will benefit from this!

LILY: Most certainly!

SIPAPU: Now: your motto is "All persuasions: no brutality." But in our heads, this leads to a non-violent stance, and ultimately to a certain kind of political position. We wonder if you had given that any kind of thought?

LILY: I figure *Yellow Silk* is my politics. During the middle seventies I was very heavily feminist, even to the point of being separatist, but I just withdrew from the whole thing, 'cause it seemed like you were supposed to be angry all the time, and negative about so many things, and whether it's pornography, or "intrasexual persuasion disharmony,"—the whole Left is so divided that you can never keep track of whom you're supposed to be mad at! And so giving a positive image of the ways we all love, and feel about love, *that* represents my politics—the kind of politics I understand. All that energy, political, spiritual, sexual, —to give a positive image of that, to do this is itself a political act.

SIPAPU: We sympathize very strongly. In an era of propaganda, radical and establishment, to draw a picture of lovers or to write a poem about them, rather than to take a photograph of destruction, —is to take a stand. We know there are people who disagree with us, but—to hell with them.

LILY: However, I want to make something clear. I don't have a non-brutality policy for the sake of a theory of non-violence. I have it because seeing brutality, or reading about brutality, physical or emotional, sexual or otherwise, —makes me sick!

SIPAPU: All right!

LILY: So my objection to brutality, where something sexual is concerned, or anything else is concerned, is not from any theory—

SIPAPU: It's just a gut reaction!

LILY: Just a gut reaction! Now, this policy has been challenged by some people, so I did some reading about it and some thinking about it, and, to the extent that you can understand the minds of other people, —my feelings were simply reinforced.

SIPAPU: Of course, we think they are with all decent people.

LILY: I don't say that — I don't think that. It's my suspicion that people who are involved with the more abrasive forms of sexuality are there because they can't feel enough in the less abrasive ones. I would wish they feel more, but I can't enlist thousands of people into therapy, because I don't have the right to feel that! So I'm not going to say that they're indecent; I'm just going to say that they're not where I'm at; and my magazine's at where I'm at!

SIPAPU: We were extremely interested to read your issue no. 13, — now $10.00, — with illustrations by Eric Gill. Seems to us that you brought out something that gets neglected, viz., the belief that religion and sex can't have a common focus or a common point of arrival. We found this immensely cheering; we don't know if you want to expand on that subject.

LILY: As I said a couple of answers ago, I believe that the spiritual, the erotic, and the creative force within us is the same force. Certain religions have bound themselves to see it otherwise; but I think that worship of that force is the supreme religious act! Which isn't to say that you worship sex over spirit or over creativity: but I think that to separate that out is to be suffering under an illusion. Apparently being raised Jewish ... I used to have a joke that Catholics felt sexual guilt and Jews felt guilt about everything else. Anyway, being raised Jewish, I wasn't given a sexually oppressive upbringing, and also, my dad was comfortable with his sexuality and communicated that on a regular basis — frisky he was! Jewish law says that a woman must be satisfied, sexually, by her husband.

SIPAPU: Far out!

LILY: And it also says that were

sexual "knowing" not an important thing, it wouldn't be called "knowing"—or words to that effect. There's a quote like that in Issue #13, the issue that you're talking about. Anyway, that's what I had in mind when I came to put Issue #13 together, but instead there was a lot in there that just talked about religion and sexuality from a more antagonistic basis, or less than a "high" standpoint, which made me realize that the view of most people on this matter was different. Is that a cohesive answer?

SIPAPU: Yes, it's a cohesive answer; it's just that our suggestion is that you should go ahead and get some more contributors on the project, and maybe you'll get where you want.

LILY: I could do that, but I don't announce my themes in advance, because I don't know what they are ahead of time.

SIPAPU: What, aside from brutality, do you reject, and what do you look for?

LILY: I look for brilliant writing: I reject poor writing. You see, I'm in a radically unique position in this world, I think, having read some ten thousand erotic poems a year, for four years. I think I know how people say things, over and over and over, so I'm looking for the person who says it differently: who has dealt with that area of life, and with language, to such a degree that they can say it in their own way, and not in the way that anyone else has or can say it. For some reason the same phrases and words repeat themselves ... "rainbows" ... "juicy"...

SIPAPU: Yes, of course.

LILY: I can't tell you how many men have sent me the story of the whore in Southeast Asia or somewhere who was really a wonderful person. Variations on that story, and variations on the story of the man who follows a strange woman in the street who turns out to be his wife, but you don't find that till the end, variations on the story of the blue-eyed chick on the bar stool who suggested—any number of things; variations on the story of the group who popped into the car to go to the beach-house—and what "developed" ... I look for originality, craft, passion. I consider this an *erotic literary* magazine. If it's erotic and not literary, it doesn't make it; if it's strongly literary and not erotic, it doesn't make it.

SIPAPU: We want to give you our impression of the distinguishing characteristic of *Yellow Silk*...

LILY: Oh-oh.

SIPAPU: ...and let you comment on it. The thing that distinguishes this mag above all others, and from what someone else might have done with it, is that the editor likes ... *wit*. She has a sense of humor.

LILY: Oh, you mean the poem about "only a Supreme Mind/could create a creature with one body and two behinds"? (Issue 13, p. 16) Did you read that poem?

SIPAPU: Yes, that is typical.

LILY: ...it's an interesting use of language.

SIPAPU: Yes, but in addition, the thing that strikes us as keeping the interest going, is that the editor seems to have made a discovery, which is not original with her, but has got lost in the male ruck, the heavy stuff, which is so depressing to read—

LILY: You mean, all the literary stories have death in the first paragraph?

SIPAPU: We're not speaking of that, so much, as the fact that in antiquity the thing that distinguished writing about sex was that it was considered somewhat funny. After all, here are supposedly sane adults going about their business and then all of a sudden they can't stand it any more and they take off their clothes and make love, and that's funny!

LILY: Unless all the rest of it is, and that's the only part that isn't? The fact that people put on their clothes to go sit at desks—that's funny—that's absurd!

SIPAPU: All right! Since there is, you'll admit, at least some humor in the mag, my questions are—and in a sense you've already answered them,— Is sex funny? When is it and when isn't it?

LILY: I rarely think sex is funny; I take it very seriously. That's a real interesting question. Perhaps passion is the only feeling that involves every corpuscle. And that's not a laughing matter.

SIPAPU: No, at that point it isn't. And that's why we said—when is it and when isn't it. There is a point at which it becomes very serious.

LILY: Now I think what I'm looking for in the magazine: sure, there are plenty of poems that are just delightful or stories or situations, like adolescents' traumas that if handled well are funny, because we're all stumbling through. I think that profundity is another thread of the magazine; I

don't mean leaden pro- found, I mean as
the circulation in your body is profound.
I can't be held and it can't be defined in a
shape, but without it there's no life. And I
feel that's the same thing in my heart or my
or my core, whatever it is, that I feel must
resonate, when I read a piece, in order for
it to make it in. On the other hand, when
it's funny, it's because the awkwardness or
the situation sur- rounding it are

funny, really. And stepping outside and viewing it from the outside can be funny, and the messiness can be funny. And delight can be funny its own way.

SIPAPU: Of course, yes. (More music-teapot.) I notice you list a legal person on the masthead of your contributors' list.

LILY: I just call him up and ask him copyright questions, etc. He has nothing to do with the nature of the magazine.

SIPAPU: Aaaah!! We thought you had this individual in case somebody said, "Good heavens,"...

LILY: You're the second person in the last week who's asked me that, so I bet a lot of people think that.

SIPAPU: We just have been doing some research on censorship—all the major cases of the late fifties and sixties—

LILY: I did a paper on that once. All the Supreme Court decisions.

SIPAPU: Oh really? We're supposed to be doing that now. You're probably aware that questions of pornography and censorship have in recent years, turned around, and feminists are now posing questions in this area that many men are unprepared to handle. Have you been reading this, or followed it at all?

LILY: Oh, yes, some. I've also been following the discussion in *Harper's*. Have you seen it?

SIPAPU: No, but we've seen position papers in the library field, and of course librarians are extremely exercised about this. What position, if any do you take?

LILY: Anybody who censors anything will censor *Yellow Silk,* which is why I'm against any kind of censorship of sexual pornography. And I said it before and I'll say it again: the only way to combat it is to create a strong, healthy alternative, —which is what I'm doing. There was a letter in response to the pornography forum in *Harper's,* the recent issue, which said, "We can get around it by just never showing anybody fucking,"—i.e., you can describe it, talk about it, so D.H. Lawrence and Henry Miller would escape, but you can't show it in pictures and send it across state lines. I'm saying: what do you want? Words are weaker than pictures? Or words are more artistic than pictures? I'm publishing "fuck art," with the emphasis on art; I mean this is part of everybody's life, why shouldn't it be part of the culture? There's been a lot of discussion in *Yellow Silk,* Mary Mackey and myself especially, on what's the difference between erotica and pornography? And one of the major things was, why was it created? Did Eric Gill (cf. unpublished drawings of Eric Gill, issue #13) do these things just to make money, or did he do it to sell a lot of copies? No. He did it because it was beautiful to him, and this is what arose from his erotic/spiritual/creative center. Or take Diego Rivera, showing a woman embracing, with great sanctity, a large bundle of calla lilies (picture on wall) — why if he had shown her embracing a large body of a man instead of a large bundle of lilies — why shouldn't it be seen as coming from the same place? within the artist's heart. If this is the catalyst for the creation of a piece of work, simply because it's sexual doesn't mean it's pornographic. If he'd done it just to get somebody off, or just to make money (or frequently both) — it's different; it's just a different category of creation.

SIPAPU: Besides, your *Harper's* correspondent would have to dismiss Alex Comfort's *Joy of Sex;* that shows people making love.

LILY: But even that's different. It has a different purpose ... it's not exactly art...

SIPAPU: No, basically the book is didactic, how to do it.

LILY: Yes.

SIPAPU: Now that that has been settled, we notice your reactions to all this are about the sanest we can think of. They're feeling reactions; you haven't intellectualized the subject to death.

LILY: Perhaps that's due to my limited intellectual capabilities!

SIPAPU: No, but we think that's a large part of the success of the magazine, and what it means to its thousands of readers. Here is somebody who is not either talking the subject to death, or condemning it.

LILY: That's very nice. That's just what Patrick said. Here is *Presumptions,* published by Patrick Miller, another periodical, a two-pages-every-three weeks periodical; read what he said in the bottom corner: (1442a Walnut St., #58, Berkeley CA 94709; 3 free issues).

SIPAPU: (reads) "These poems have appeared in issues of *Yellow Silk,* a journal of erotic art, published quarterly for several years now by Lily Pond; issue 13 is the best yet. Lily stole the hearts of typographers everywhere by printing a number of stunning and previously unpublished drawings by one of our heroes, Eric Gill. *YS* intelligently avoids both cheap heartless titillation and dull academic ahemming over what is erotica, by plowing the rich and unpredictable ground between those extremes. (A sexual remark right there!)

LILY: I never thought of that!

SIPAPU: (reads) "My only criticism of Lily's discretion is that she often publishes too much in her quest for a sensual language encompassing 'all persuasions, no brutality.' But even in the shallows of *Yellow Silk* one finds some exploration of human desire that runs truer and softer than the daffing lopsided adolescence of *Playboy,* whose perspective still seems to dominate the erotic sensibilities of American publishing, film and television. To me Lily's endeavor is noble, in the friendliest sense of the word, for nobility that lacks a distinct and warm-bodied sensuality is just plain insufferable... A sample copy is three dollars, a subscription is ten dollars through forty, a sliding scale—pay what you can—from *verygraphics,* P.O. Box 6374, Albany, CA 94706."—Which brings us to—library subscriptions! Our subscribers are almost entirely libraries; since you don't bill, what is it that they should be expected to do?

LILY: Oh, I have to bill libraries; yearly; I've gotten used to that reality of life.

SIPAPU: Do you have any library subscribers?

LILY: (consulting file) Ames, Iowa; Madison, Wisconsin; Albany, California; SUNY Buffalo; Temple University, Philadelphia...

SIPAPU: That's our old friend Patricia Case, when she was working there. Or her predecessor, Elliott Shore (interviewed in *Sipapu,* no. 19).

LILY: Yeah! and University of Wisconsin at Milwaukee, and UC San Diego at La Jolla; Washington State University, Pullman, that's about it.

SIPAPU: That's a pattern we might expect. From the enormous number of magazines available, libraries must choose. What will the charge be to libraries?

LILY: Minimum of fifteen dollars a year. They can pay more if they can afford it! And a sample copy is three dollars; I just can't afford to ship sample copies for free.

SIPAPU: Indeed. Meanwhile, we see you as approaching the whole thing of erotic publishing with an instinctive rather than a calculating approach; which makes all the difference in the world. For example, the calculating or manipulative person is not someone you want to trust in bed—

LILY: Ahh, I've made some mistakes!

SIPAPU: We've made some mistakes too!

LILY: Remind me to give you something—it's from a center spread—don't have to look at it now. [This is "State of the Union," a dialogue between Lily Pond and Richard Russo. Too long to reprint here, it's on pp. 6-7 of the Summer 1974 issue of *Métier,* published by the Berkeley Art Center Association, 2124 Kittredge Street, Box 104, Berkeley, CA 94704. Copies available from them or from *YS.* The dialogue is about surrender and traditional roles, and much of the issue is devoted to sensuous art.]

SIPAPU: So, I assume, the future of the magazine could be the same! While love, and men's bodies and women's bodies remain the same, the course of the magazine could be like that of a sailboat on San Francisco Bay: you have to keep changing your point, if you want to keep sailing upwind on the same bearing with regard to the wind. This can happen in the course of a magazine, and we wonder if you've seen it happen with *Yellow Silk,* or if you foresee such a thing.

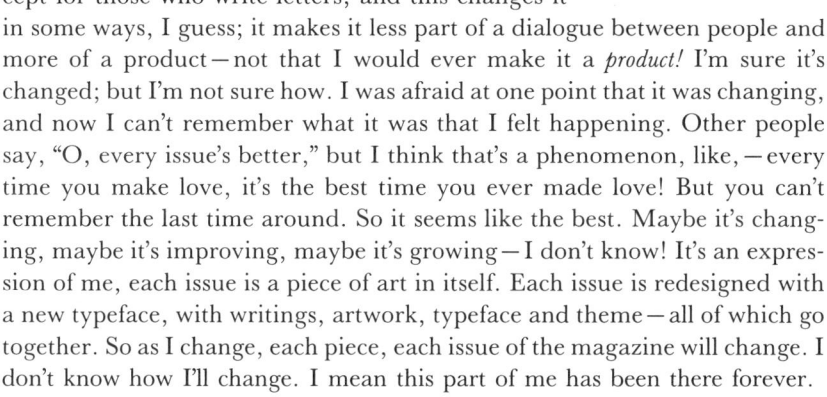

LILY: Well, I've seen it come from the point where I had all the subscribers' names and addresses memorized, to the point where I don't know most of them, and if I get a subscription manager I'll know even less, and it seems to me it'll make it less personal on a certain level, except for those who write letters, and this changes it in some ways, I guess; it makes it less part of a dialogue between people and more of a product — not that I would ever make it a *product!* I'm sure it's changed; but I'm not sure how. I was afraid at one point that it was changing, and now I can't remember what it was that I felt happening. Other people say, "O, every issue's better," but I think that's a phenomenon, like, — every time you make love, it's the best time you ever made love! But you can't remember the last time around. So it seems like the best. Maybe it's changing, maybe it's improving, maybe it's growing — I don't know! It's an expression of me, each issue is a piece of art in itself. Each issue is redesigned with a new typeface, with writings, artwork, typeface and theme — all of which go together. So as I change, each piece, each issue of the magazine will change. I don't know how I'll change. I mean this part of me has been there forever.

SIPAPU: It always will be.

LILY: I really don't feel I have the ability to predict...

SIPAPU: It's a little like trying to predict the next important person who will come into your life!

LILY: Who would have predicted the magazine three days before it started? I was never interested in doing a magazine; never would have occurred to me!

SIPAPU: You never worked on somebody else's magazine?

LILY: No!

SIPAPU: Spontaneity! We love spontaneity! Well, basically that's what we have to ask: maybe you want to free-associate or ask "why didn't you ask this," or ask something else.

LILY: There is one thing I'll say, and that's that I just got finished typing up the letters-to-the-editor section for this coming issue, and there's this one guy who wrote how he was lying on a beach in the Bahamas, with the bougainvillea and the hibiscus and the emerald and turquoise water — and Issue #12 of *Yellow Silk* and it was enough! With all those young bods wandering the beach he wasn't even tempted; and it wasn't even a moral decision, it was an aesthetic one. He said that those experiences which we fence off from others as being erotic are severely limited in this culture; and for me, reading the material and doing the magazine are very erotic experiences. I once said in an interview that *Yellow Silk* touches the part of you and me that making love touches. People write in saying, "O, it doesn't get me hard...."

SIPAPU: O, yes, that's ridiculous; we remember reading those letters.

LILY: Reading the material and doing the magazine touches the part that making love touches. It seems to me that that's what pornography is trying to do; touch that part of our experience, but it doesn't really, so people stay unsatisfied. And it's not just doing it that gets touched; it's the erotic experience of an involvement with the real world in a very unique way, — doing this magazine. So it's not just that the final product that is an erotic experience; but working on it, the whole process is.

SIPAPU: Publishing as an erotic experience: we like that.

LILY: It would be very sad to think that anybody doing publishing wasn't having an erotic experience, although I suppose that's the rule.

SIPAPU: It should also be anxious, and hassling; but one should have the creator's joy, indeed. You should be able to say, — This will really tickle people where they need to be tickled.

LILY: I don't know why they shouldn't be tickled on more than one level!

SIPAPU: Yes, more than one level and more than one place. Well, thank you very much; and in conclusion, would you like to say anything about your personal appearance?

LILY: Lily Pond is devastatingly gorgeous, although she is not tall, thin, with long black hair!

CONFERENCES BRIEFLY TACKLED: Due to the death of the editor's eldest brother, Malcolm R. Peattie (31 March 1985) this issue has been considerably delayed, and as a consequence our reports on conferences are so overdue that they require only a summary. The CALIFORNIA LIBRARY ASSOCIATION met in early December 1984 in the Bonaventure Hotel in Los Angeles, a bizarre location which resembles one of Piranesi's prisons with Muzak. The account you read by former IFRT chair Sue

Kamm, as published in *American Libraries,* was (as we see it) substantially correct, short though it was. Californian subscribers probably got the account published in the California Library Association *Newsletter,* v. 27, no. 1, January 1985. Our slight but significant amendment was to Stefan B. Moses's account, as part of his "Truth Missions Chronology," that the Intellectual Freedom Committee "okayed" an exhibit mailing to Truth Missions. Both we and the chair, Peter Mollema, wish to go on record as saying that there was no vote taken on this issue; we merely said nothing much as Moses indicated that he intended to mail the literature out to Truth Missions, in the hope that he—Moses—would pick up the pieces as they came along.

For those who have been hiding in a broom closet, Truth Missions is apparently the creation of David McCalden, a libertarian Ulsterman whose activities have prompted a number of organizations in the United Kingdom and the United States to break off relations with him, expel him, and after he had made his impression on them, to try to devise ways by which such a person could be excluded in future, *a fortiori.* Due to the Anglo-American system of free speech, as well as the loose networking prevailing in our societies, news of McCalden's approach travelled slowly if at all. Journalistic, environmental, and other organizations have had encounters with McCalden, and the California Library Association had been drawn into the conflict some months before the beginning of the chronology detailed in the CLA *Newsletter.* The Intellectual Freedom Committee had been trying to resolve a dispute between McCalden and the Torrance Public Library, which declined to add to a "BANNED BOOKS WEEK" exhibit, certain books published by or approved by McCalden which suggested that the Holocaust of six million Jews in World War II either did not happen or did not happen on that scale. Our guess is that McCalden, a libertarian, opposes U.S. military action in the Middle East; opposes it because it's the likeliest reason that the U.S. would be drawn into war; opposes war as an infringement of liberty; and therefore concludes that such intervention would be taken, most probably, in defense of Israel, and that the Holocaust, often  given as Israel's reason for being, never took place on the scale that its apologists suggest. If this is a caricature of McCalden's position, we apologize; certain it is that he has broadly attacked the Simon Wiesenthal Foundation of Los Angeles, an institution devoted among other things, to proving that the Holocaust did indeed take place, on the scale popularly attributed to it, if not larger.

The chronology of the events given in the CLA *Newsletter* is correct (subject to the foregoing trifling correction). The California Library Association did indeed offer a table to McCalden, and therefore he could by custom claim a meeting space; did indeed take this offer back under pressure, then re-offer it under threat of suit; and then take it back a second time, when the Los Angeles Police Department told CLA "severe security problems exist ... cannot guarantee safety." The situation might have remained purely internal had the American Jewish Committee not been tipped off to what was happening, had not the Los Angeles *Times* not carried extensive and (in our view) objective coverage of the situation as it developed, and had not the Los Angeles City Council and the Library Commission promptly threatened to sever relationships with CLA. In addition pickets by concentration camp survivors were to be set up, apparently, at the hotel entrances, and some librarians would have had trouble crossing that picket line.

Not surprisingly, opinions were divided at CLA. Some librarians blamed the librarian who tipped off the American Jewish Committee. Others blamed the L.A. City Council for attempting to prevent free speech by breaking off relations with CLA, and the Library Commission for following suit (which means, kids, if you're a librarian and work for L.A. Public, you don't get time off to do things related to CLA). One of our oldest and most respected friends in the profession subsequently suggested that CLA should have spoken "truth to power," and a resolution was put together, not without reluctance on our part, by the CLA Information Committee that read thus:

"WHEREAS, a body of professionals, such as the California Library Association, has the right to determine its own policies, directions and philosophy; and WHEREAS, such a body of professionals has a right to be heard in the facts of a case concerning its policies, directions, and philosophy; and WHEREAS, a political body, elected by the people, such as the Los Angeles City Council, has the responsibility to hear all the facts of the case before taking action; THEREFORE, be it resolved that, the California Library Association, deplores the coercion by the Los Angeles City Council in the intent of its resolution of November 16th, 1984.

Somewhere in the next few hours, however, senior members of the CLA, including two former presidents, brought to the attention of CLA's Council the interesting fact that a body elected by the people, and responsible for preparing budgets, is not lightly to be lectured to. Since we weren't at that Council meeting—it may have been a special one—we can't present the arguments, but it's interesting that the following was *unanimously* passed on 4 December:

(RESOLVED) THAT the Council of the California Library Association is cognizant of the strong feelings of Membership in regard to the statements of certain local and state governmental officials pertaining to the Association's involvement with Truth Missions; THAT Council also recognizes the right of these officials and agencies to speak on issues of public policy; FINALLY, Council has a sense that the matter is largely an internal one, to be dealt with by the appropriate mechanisms of the Association. Council, therefore, wishes to go on record as urging Membership to withhold any actions or statements directed toward individuals and agencies outside this organization.

The second membership meeting adopted this resolution with few dissenting votes that afternoon, after which we left. It seems that afterwards McCalden identified himself and asked to speak, but he had omitted the precaution of taking out membership in CLA (as we recall, you don't have to be a librarian to join); and as no one could be found to sponsor him, he was denied the right to speak, and left.

As we said above, it appears that other organizations have had problems with McCalden, and like them, CLA has now taken steps to prevent a recurrence of this kind of embarrassment, or if you prefer, has suddenly discovered censorship, or, if you want to put it that way, has locked the stable door after the horse has been stolen. The 1985 CLA president, Linda M. Wood, in the January 1985 (v. 27, no. 1) issue of the CLA *Newsletter,* repeated her oral statement at the conference that "A better policy and procedure is needed regarding vendor-sponsored programs at conference," and went on to ask for unity and speedier decision-making procedures at the highest level of CLA when emergencies arrive. The April and May issue (v. 27, nos. 4 & 5, p. 4) carried the following press release, "issued . . . to the prominent library publications" (we didn't get one; tsk, tsk!) apparently as a result of a Council meeting of 22 February 1985:

> Following the cancellation of the Truth Missions program which had been scheduled for our December 1984 conference in Los Angeles, the California Library Association Council acted upon recommendations of the Conference Program Planning Committee to clarify the Association's policies affecting the admissibility and inclusion of programs on sessions to be presented as part of the CLA conference progam. — At the time of the 1984 conference, a policy restricting commercial vendors or outside unaffiliated groups from requsting meeting space did not exist. Meeting room accommodations were provided on a space-available basis, to such vendors or groups upon payment to CLA of a nominal room charge for commercial vendors to have contracted for exhibit space in order to be eligible to request meeting room space. — Following the recommendation made by the 1985 Conference Program Planning Committee, the Council of the California Library Association amplified the above conditions with the

following policy: *that all conference programs must be sponsored by an association chapter, committee, or constituent organization* (i.e., California Institute of Libraries—CIL, California Library Employees Association—CLEA, or California Society of Librarians—CSL). As before, the Conference Program Planning Committee must approve all proposed programs. —Stefan B. Moses, Executive Director.

Our own impression of this is that the machinery is in place, but there is no sure-fire method of making it work—probably could never be. For example, a controversial figure might persuade the members of the CLA Intellectual Freedom Committee, and also the Conference Program Planning Committee, that in the name of justice, fairness, balance, etc. (s)he ought to be heard; and then the whole freedom-vs.-responsibility/sensitivity issue would surface again, although probably there would be more time to review the whole procedure. Or, the personality might actually join the Association, and then, gathering a few supporters, demand some sort of platform as a member.

This is exactly what happened in COSMEP, the Committee of Small Magazine Editors and Publishers, when McCalden joined it with his Truth Missions organization. COSMEP was putting out a catalog of its members' publications; McCalden inserted his ad, following the usual procedures, and paying the usual fee; and the COSMEP Board, after consulting their attorney, were obliged to conclude that there was nothing obscene or libelous in the ad and that refusal to include the ad of a member in good standing would expose them to a lawsuit. The catalog therefore appeared with the ad, and in the ensuing controversy, which divided COSMEP about fifty-fifty (as we seem to recall), John Crawford, of West End Press (Minneapolis) resigned as treasurer and member of the Board in protest over what he perceived as the insensitivity of the organization's leadership. There were also protests that the COSMEP *Newsletter* did not give as much space to letters of comment from members on this issue as they should have.

For some the moral of these stories will be that in a supposedly open, tolerant, democratic society there are subjects that are taboo, because they offend the liberal leadership. For us, who do not agree with McCalden, the fact remains that there is no way to prevent a person from getting into an open society or one of its organizations and using it for his own advantage. On Wall Street, this is called a takeover. In politics, this is capturing the party. Intellectuals—librarians and publishers—are more protected and less prepared for such activity. A political or financial "litmus test" for entry into either CLA or COSMEP is unthinkable (which is why the Simon Wiesenthal Center perhaps uses the wrong word in its promotional literature when it says that McCalden was "accepted" for membership into COSMEP; this implies some sort of scrutiny or screening, while on the contrary COSMEP is open to any publisher "of limited circulation" (as we recall the bylaws), without description or qualifications. Short of reorganizing these organizations and indeed all society on strictly authoritarian lines, wherein troublemakers would be clapped into dungeons with toads, there seems to be little that can be done about this (the literati would be the first to object to this clapping, and therefore the first to be so clapped).

It might have been possible for Stefan B. Moses to have said nothing to McCalden, but under the rules then applying, as long as he purchased a table at the conference, he could put on a program (the table itself would have been enough to start trouble). The attitudes of COSMEP's leadership are beyond our comment — we weren't at their Board meetings; but they have no way of excluding anyone from membership who is self-defined as "small press." COSMEP may also be considering "guidelines" to prevent appearing to sponsor racist or sexist materials, but this latter issue has surfaced before with the sexist material on their book bus (see *Sipapu,* vol. 9, no. 1 = consecutive issue no. 17, early 1978; pp. 201-204. Our position on the feasibility of guidelines is less sanguine than it was seven years ago). In any case the leaders of both organizations were unprepared to deal with such a person as McCalden, though they might have studied what happens to a culture when it becomes infected with anti-semitism. For not doing their homework they may be faulted, although patterns of intellectual responsibility in an open society lacking consensus are not always clear and may well remain so for some time to come. (COSMEP's leadership may be more at fault than CLA's; they'd "been there before" with the "bus incident.")

For the rest of CLA, the most interesting programs were those of the Intellectual Freedom Committee, at which Angus Mackenzie, author of *Sabotaging the Dissident Press* (see our last issue) spoke on government subversion of dissent papers, and E.J. Josey's address to the first General Membership meeting, at which he gave his usual eloquent pitch for coalition-building.

The emotional weather at ALA Midwinter (Washington, DC) was much more pleasant. This is E.J. Josey's year, and he will "rejoice and be glad in it." He and his staff set in motion the plans for a President's Program, "forging Coalitions for the Public Good," which will be held at the Annual Conference in Chicago in June. This is to be a participation program, with facilitators and poster sessions, if we understand it correctly. For those of us who have seen libraries isolated and librarians frequently treated as slightly amusing, this idea seems our last, best, hope. The other issue that is reaching action stage is that of ALA's Strategic Long-Range Planning (SLRP, universally described as "Slurp"). This general review of ALA's activities is supposed to clarify the Association's mission and that of its units, improve their services, "work in a more coordinated and cooperative manner, and use available resources more effectively," respond to changes in the society that affect ALA, and develop strategies for further planning and evaluation. For some this seems a $70,000 boondoggle. Our attitude is that it may well be, but

it might work like the medicine applied to senates in Swift's *Academy of Lagado:* "beget unanimity, shorten debates, open a few mouths which are now closed, and close many more which are now open; curb the petulancy of the young, and correct the positiveness of the old; rouse the stupid, and damp the pert."

We bade farewell to our service on the Executive Board of the Intellectual Freedom Round Table (I-fart to its scoffers) by obtaining the approval of that body, together with the approval of ALA's Intellectual Freedom Committee, of a refusal to support the bill of Sen. Bob Packwood (R–Ore.) to deregulate the broadcasting media and abolish the Fairness Doctrine. This bill of Sen. Packwood's meanwhile died, but is expected to be revived. The chair of the Federal Communications Commission says that he can make this change unilaterally, according to a statement made in the committee room. Meanwhile, the IFRT and the rest of the intellectual freedom community in ALA is dealing with the problems of labelling pop music records, which the Congress of American Parents and Teachers find are too heavy for them, and also with the problems of alleged Israeli Government censorship of West Bank problems, which latter cause, like much in the Middle East, remains unclear and unresolved by this publication's press time.

The Social Responsibilities Round Table's Task Force on Alternatives in Print sponsored a panel on the "New World Information Order" from a Third World perspective; unfortunately, we arrived too late to hear this, and can only refer you to their latest publication, *Field Guide to Alternative Media.* "A directory to directories, bibliographies, indexes, review media, and bookstore and distributor catalogs, the *Field Guide* lists and annotates 164 resources ... copies are on sale from the ALA Office of Library Outreach Services for $6."

For us, however, the cutting edge of progress at this particular moment in ALA history rests not with SRRT but with GODORT, the Government Documents Round Table, and its affiliates, which have been fighting a desperate battle against the U.S. Government's current "privatization of information." For those of you who are uncertain of the meaning of this new phrase, it refers to governmental cancellation of monographs and serials of interest to many consumers and small business; attempts to circumvent the Freedom of Information Act; attempts to censor or prohibit the publication or wide dissemination of scientific papers, including those not "classified" by the Department of Defense; and the contracting out of publication and dissemination of material now issued by the government, including material presently received by partial or total Federal depository libraries. In short, we are not dealing with a single problem, but with a mass of them. Implicit in the plans of the current Administration, which has initiated this tendency, are two ideas not entirely without merit: the reduction of government publication and paperwork—every agency wants to have its own newsletter to justify its existence—and the recognition, not entirely absent from even radical thinkers, that there are some things that private enterprise can do "better" than the state (after all, underground newspapers are a form of "private enterprise," too). However, when all the unwanted and self-serving newsletters from the Department of Redundancy Department are eliminated, we still find the government has gone out of its way to cut a lot of material that is valuable not only to consumers but also to industries which they might be expected to protect—the fisheries industry, for example.

We got there late, to the Dupont Plaza; difficulty of finding a hotel off the beaten track or two or three in Washington, only to find it was SRO in the one meeting we would have to applaud above all others. The Paperwork Reduction Act is responsible for some of the cuts, but others have resulted from the decrees of the Office of Management and Budget (part of the Executive Branch). We were referred to Donna A. Demac's *Keeping America Uninformed* (Pilgrim Press, $8.95), while at the same time cautioned against taking government publications too seriously—budget cuts mean more sloppy editing. The result now means the elimination of waste in printing little wanted material, and the rise of on-demand printing. On the other hand, this Administration has seen the rise of a Federal Publishers' Committee, of which the aim is to simplify costs by privatizing existing federal publications, cutting others out of the budget entirely, and slashing funds for the rest. The remaining agencies have discovered the difference between access and mere dissemination, between real info and junk-news + department puffery. Since budgeting allows no opportunity for editing or rewriting, there is no possibility of good quality publications.

As far as we're concerned, the long-range implications of this change are even more important than the erotica/pornography debate or the sexism/racism of children's books, both of which we have treated. Granted, these two are important issues, but they do not have official status. Somehow, we can manage to allow for the venality of commercial publishers; or at least refuse to buy their products. But we (naively, perhaps) expect the U.S. Government to be neutral or at the very least *decent*. After all they're taking the taxes of Americans of a wide spectrum of opinions. When they appear to be suppresing information or selling it off to a private buyer, we wonder why we seem to be buying that information collected with our tax money, and presumably available to us at the cost of distribution. The people who paid have a right to know.

Meanwhile, we escaped from the conference ratrace to join Richard Peabody and Gretchen Johnsen, editors of *Gargoyle*/Paycock Press, one of the small but valiant band of magazine/small press publishers in Washington, DC, for dinner and an expedition. We all quickly agreed that Washington is the country's least appreciated city, confirmed that survival lay in avoiding Federal officialdom, and after dinner headed out to suburban Maryland to view The Writers' Center (P.O. Box 606, Glen Echo, MD 20812-0606, phone [301] 229-0930; the Washington subway doesn't go that far yet, you take the N-4 or the N-5 bus out Massachusetts Avenue to Sangamore Road). Allan Lefcowitz, chairman of the board, was on hand that night to show us around a complex of facilities far larger than we remember having seen on the West Coast: photography workshops, print shops, and a gallery, plus a larger poetry library than we had seen for some time outside West Coast bookshops. When it comes to wide open spaces for inspiration, give us the West; when it comes to facilities, the East Coast still has it, particularly here, where there is a full list of courses available (writing workshops, production

workshops, &c.), a Book Gallery, typesetting and design rooms, press and darkroom, word processing room and library, plus two multipurpose rooms, one of which can seat up to 280 people. There is also a newsletter, *Carousel*, well produced and providing not only announcements but also book reviews, and finally a 96-page volume, *Center Pieces* which is subtitled "selections from workshops at the Writers' Center, 1977 to 1980." There are poems and short stories, but we found the graphic art most fresh and unusual (foldouts, see-throughs, &c.). The book is copyrighted 1981 and may no longer be available. At all events the Center is worth support by local area libraries (at least!) and its publications should be subscribed to.

The Writers' Center is located in the Waldorf School; the Poet Tree (last issue) is also located in an old school. Here's one idea about what to do with old schools; although it occurs to us that a library planning new space might provide for the inclusion of just such a center, if the librarians wanted to get some local support and make the library a center of creativity and culture, not just an "information center." Too far out? Hmmm.

To return to the two young people who introduced us to this Center we're enjoying *Fiction/84,* a double issue of *Gargoyle* (25/26) built like a hefty paperback (419 pages; $7.95). Their address is P.O. Box 3567, Washington DC 20007. Gretchen Johnsen's *Journal* is a special issue of *Cumberland Journal* (no. 15; $2.00; Box 2468, Harrisburg, PA 17105); wry literary jottings from August 1978 to August 1981.

THE NEW UNDERGROUNDS: Some time ago, after we had reviewed *OP* magazine (v. 14, no. 2, page 15), and exchanged copies with them, we received an issue, the first, of a magazine called *Sound Choice,* from the Audio Evolution Network (P.O. Box 1251, Ojai, CA 93023). They claim to be a successor, or one of the successors, to *OP,* and in their first issue they reviewed a number of magazines, including fanzines and music 'zines, but also (having, evidently, access to *OP*'s files) *Sipapu.* The review was brisk, but worth quoting in part. After quoting our masthead statement which ends with "...all forms of alternative publishing in general," the reviewer continues:

A lofty goal but I get the feeling that editor Peattie has never seen 98% of the publications that constitute the contemporary "underground" press. Either that or he ignores the material that he couldn't imagine being catalogued by a college library. Still, there is something inherently good about this publication (although it seems geared toward librarians and English professors) and I'd recommend other editors and publishers to start inundating Peattie with their alternative press creations.

A fine dash of cold water in the face and we found ourselves welcoming it. We wrote back saying that indeed, the only way to keep up is to try keeping up; that what was underground in the sixties and seventies is no longer around or has been co-opted, and that we indeed wanted to see what was "down below" in the eighties. We certainly haven't got 98% of what's being published, but from the long lists of reviewed items in *Sound Choice,* as well as its own pages, plus the small number of titles that have come our way, we can indeed make a few generalities:

One, the new undergrounds are less crafted, more anarchic; they are as far beyond the *San Francisco Oracle* as that paper was beyond the *San Francisco Chronicle;* the drawing is as different from the old underground comics as those were from "Pogo." Two, they are all, nearly, involved with or referential to, music. These writers and editors live on sound, and are as contentious about it in the letters section of *Sound Choice,* as earlier generations were about words and graphics. And three, yes, it's hard to imagine their periodicals being cataloged by a college library. But then, we're out to change college (and public) libraries. That's the whole point of *Sipapu!*

Sound Choice itself features the same "letter" plan that OP did, and this apparently turns many of their readers off. By this we mean that in the "A" issue they describe bands whose names begin with "A," as well as the music scene in places like Alabama, Arizona, and Albany. Besides this method—which strikes us as merely eccentric; have they read Dr. Seuss's *On Beyond Zebra?*— they have record reviews, an interview with one of *OP*'s editors, and a long strip by R. Crumb. The "B" issue has interviews with Mykel Board and Chet Baker, as well as music from Belgium and Burundi (illustrated with stamps. If we're ever asked to start a small tropical republic we'll fund it all on beautiful coins and stamps). The price of *Sound Choice* is six issues for $12, and we think it's what its name says for libraries. We can easily imagine cataloging it—and here's an advantage of the "letter plan"; it provides nearly automatic indexing, even if *Sound Choice* isn't yet indexed elsewhere. So for librarians, it isn't merely eccentric, after all.

Factsheet Five is also a general counter-cultural review periodical with reviews of magazines, 'zines, music, etc. It calls itself "the zine of crosscurrents and cross-pollination," and is available from Mike Gunderloy, 6 Arizona Avenue, Rensselaer, NY 12144; quarterly for $8.00, and at that price, it's a bargain. Less fun to read than *Sound Choice,* and with definitely smaller print, it is nevertheless a necessity for keeping up with records and periodicals you just wouldn't find anywhere else. In short, no, it isn't all in *Ulrich's,* and much of it isn't even in *Fulton's.* Bibliographies of new creative arts periodicals are the greatest need in library collecting today, and *Factsheet Five* is making an important contribution towards filling that need. Of course, Mike isn't writing for librarians, but librarians ought to write him. There is (in our perception, at least) a strong libertarian slant to his cuts and quotes, and some parts are just wacko ("why is there pubic hair?" he asks, and we answer, though we weren't asked, "because somebody left off the 'l' in the sign directing people to the public library.").

Among the periodicals that these biblio'zines mention we come first to a periodical, now defunct, called *Lobster Tendencies,* which published 12 times between November 1982 and June 1984. We never saw it, but it probably resembled its two successors, *Lobster Tendencies East* (c/o Michael Kaniecki, 141 Ridge Street, #8, New York, NY 10002) and *The Closest Penguins* (625A Natoma Street, San Francisco, CA 94103; when penguins want to go swimming the back row of penguins push the front row in to test the waters; if they don't get eaten by orcas, everyone jumps in). The prices of these mags seem to be measured in stamps, but pricing and invoicing are not where they're at. Denise Dee, editor of *The Closest Penguins,* explains it all in her handwriting (most of the texts of the mags are handwritten with felt-tip pens, but fortunately the handwriting is quite legible): "I wanted to hear people singing songs that could make me cry or feel something listening to them not just aimless no solutions anger or the anti system who cares or phony poetry songs w/words and imagery like stuff from bad literary magazines I mean personal songs like someone was saving a seat at their table for you" (*The Closest Penguins* #4). In short, what we're seeing here are stories that don't "work" in the conventional sense, accounts that relieve you and make you stop feeling weird. What is called for is the personal, the sensitive as apart from the consciously literary: the mag as experience and epistle, rather than as the carefully managed showcase for rising young talents: "this is a place where people can admit what they feel without being laughed at or ostracized ... You'll probably never be the 'next big thing' in one of their magazines but you can be a part of something special in ours. . . ." (#5). We think it important to quote from Denise Dee's editorial because we think it important to remember that these are not litmags for English lit. people to aspire to but rather documents from those who have been hurt or at least stigmatized. (*Lobster Tendencies East* is more confident: "Q. Six years ago you founded a movement and chopped off your hair so why are you wearing bangs? A. I've abandoned the forehead as incurably optimistic.") In any case they represent a new frontier of creative publishing, beyond beat, hippie, street writing, and the love letters they get (apparently) shows that their work means a lot to many people (most of them, naturally, young). We certainly think the San Francisco one, at least, deserves support from local libraries; and you can write Denise Dee at that address for two books from Lobster Tendencies Press: *Sadness (Down the River of Dreams)* and *The Best of Lobster Tendencies*. We haven't seen these books.

The Duplex Planet is another magazine that starts from a curious and compassionate background. David Greenberger (P.O. Box 1230, Saratoga Springs, NY 12866) has evidently been in contact with the forty-six old-timers who live at the Duplex Nursing Home in Jamaica Plain, New York, and over the years he has published their remarks and poems, especially answers to questions, in *The Duplex Planet*. To the question, "Who are the Beatles?" one senior citizen replied, "I don't know anything about the Beatles. I never worked for them and they never worked for me." "If you could travel through time, where would you go?" "Japan." "What's wrong with artists?" "Errors." (The nation's art press please copy.) And quotations, "I have no use for a crook." (Francis McElroy.) (Send a copy of this to Richard Nixon.) "Goldfish grow to the size of horses. They're bit-trained in Brazil." — Wm. Ferguson. (You must not *carp* at that remark.) In short, *The Duplex Planet* is a marvelous collection of voices from the other side of seventy, working-class admonitions from the folks who've damn well earned their retirement. Greenberger, however, is not simply concerned with providing an escape, a showcase, a litmag for nursing home residents; he is interested in reaching out to the world beyond nursing homes, to all of us, for he is convinced that these seniors have something to say, that they are at least as important as some Cabinet officer of three or four administrations back. And certainly Ernest Boyes Brookings's verses (he started at age 82) are more readable than any memoirs. "Do apes have picnics?" he was asked. "I don't know, my dictionary's too small." Price of this little gem is $12 a year. We're sharing all our copies.

Other mags in this group include *Real Fun,* Box 14253, Philadelphia, PA 19125—comix, cartoons, radical snippets; 6 issues/$5; the best here is "Zippy's Oath of Office": "I solemnly swear that I will confuse, befuddle and

perplex the receptionist in the outer office of the President of the United States and will, to the best of my knowledge, send out for a nuclear freeze and several arbitrary but entertaining amendments to the Constitution of the United States ... Am I slipping in the polls yet?"—Also *Jet Lag* $12 from 8419 Halls Ferry Rd., St. Louis, MO 63147, a music review magazine, and since we're not part of the music scene, we aren't able to comment; *Canadisc,* a catalog from Paul E. Comeau, P.O. Box 142, Saulnierville, Nova Scotia, Canada B0W2Z0, largely devoted to overlooked Canadian popular music of all kinds; *Boys and Girls Grow Up,* a weirdo comic published, at 75 cents per issue, from P.O. Box 5718, Richmond, VA 23220 and finally *The Church of the Sub-Genius,* offering a periodical which was way over our heads. You can get it from P.O. Box 382, Baltimore, MD 21203.

SPECIALTIES: Some times ago we received a review copy of an item we couldn't review. We could do nothing with it because it consisted of a couple of cassette tapes of recorded poetry, and we hadn't any player. Now we do, so last night we sat down with *Black Box Magazine* no. 11 ($37.50 from The Watershed Foundation, P.O. Box 50145, Washington, DC 20004), and were rewarded by the astonishing sound of Otis Brown recording live at "The Dove" in Baltimore, Maryland. If you haven't heard Brown, an Afro-American poet with strong jazz and bop rhythms in his work, sounding away in your very own living room, you haven't heard what oral poetry can do and what the possibilities of recorded poetry are. The cardboard box in which *Black Box* cassettes arrive contain two cassettes, each with two sides ... a dozen poets, two hours' playing time. While we can't agree with their conviction, as quoted in Fulton and Ferber's *International Directory of Little Magazines and Small Presses* (20th ed., 1984–85): "the age of the page is ending (at least where poetry's concerned)," we can certainly recommend this magazine to any persons or libraries who possess a player.

Our only problem with readings of this sort is that by their nature they cannot permit the hearer to skip around and find a poem he likes, at least not as easily as a reader can; also while some of their poems are recorded live in concert, and others are studio productions, the presence of a face and a gesture may just be central to a poetry reading—and these, of course, are lacking here. (On the other hand, since a revolution was recently launched on Iran with the aid of cassette tapes and players, maybe we shouldn't be so cautious.) A backgrounder recently supplied us indicates that The Watershed Foundation is "the world's largest producer of recordings by poets," and Watershed Tapes offers old masters and younger poets, including readings from poets whose work was never recorded when they were alive (these being done in collaboration with the authors' literary executors and heirs, so you won't just get a famous actor doing Shakespeare). "Most Watershed albums are in stereo," according to Executive Producer Alan Austin, "and all use the Dolby (tm) noise-reduction sytem. All producers are themselves poets, who take the trouble to familiarize themselves fully with the poet's work before undertaking a production." There is also a wide selection—multicultural, multiracial—as the Otis Brown tape shows; a priority for women poets, because they have got left out of earlier tape catalogs; and, interestingly enough, distribution to bookstores via the Inland Book Company. The 1985 Pulitzer Prize poet, Carolyn Kizer, was the first poet to make an album for Watershed (1975; the magazine has been going since 1972). She was for many years the president of the Foundation.

It is possible to grow closer to this Foundation by means of its membership auxiliary, Watershed Associates, by donating $25 a year (it's non-profit) to assist in the production of new poetry recordings. This new project enables Associates to vote for their choice among pending Watershed Tapes albums, the winning cassette then being offered to Associates at wholesale price before it is offered to the general public. However, this first time around, the voters tied Stanley Kunitz and Ntozake Shange (two more different poets it is hard for us to imagine), and so both tapes will be issued in the manner described above, together.

The slight attention we've given to the Watershed so far has nevertheless convinced us that they're doing something centrally important. How much you appreciate their work depends on whether you are sound-oriented or print-oriented; we still like the shape of fine letters on a page, as much as we like a well-trained voice (we only began to understand

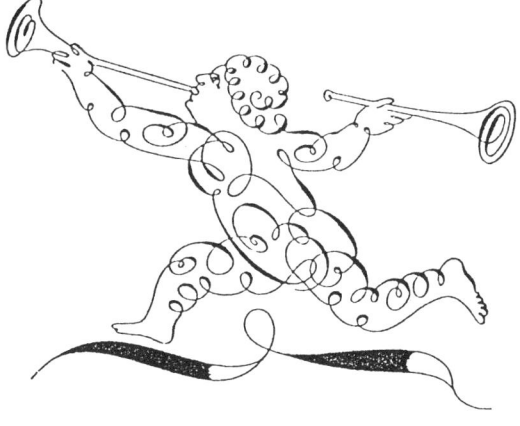

Michael McClure once we heard him read). Finally, of course, there are the poets who, so far from abandoning the page, are expressing their work in visual form, almost to the exclusion of meaning and certainly beyond the capabilities of performance. It would seem that poetry can go the performance route, or the graphic art route, or stay in the middle — and still be interesting. (As a footnote it should be remembered that in antiquity all reading, even solitary reading, was reading aloud; the change came in the Middle Ages when monasteries enforced a rule of silence.)

16 : 2

The "'Truth' and consequences" article involved me in conflict with both libertarian supporters of McCalden's right to speak, as well as a visit from a friend of McCalden. There were also people who thought I should have gone farther in my criticisms. This article represents for me, however, an early effort to think the matter through: intellectual freedom vs. social responsibility. It isn't easy, and I am not done with it yet.

NEWS OF FORMER INTERVIEWEES: Theresa Vinciguerra (v. 15, no. 2) has resigned from the position she held at Poet Tree, Inc., in order to spend more time at her own writing. The Directors of that organization have changed its name to Sacramento Poetry Center. Michael Davidson, curator of the Archive for New Poetry at the University of California, San Diego (see our v. 13, no. 1), has left that position for one on the campus English department.

THE INDEXERS: Those of you who have watched our masthead carefully over the years have noticed that since volume 14, no. 2, consecutive issue no. 28, we have been indexed by "API," that is, the Alternative Press Index, with whom we had been corresponding, off and on, over the years. (We were at one time indexed by CALL, Current Awareness of Library Literature, but have not heard from them for several years. If you have, pray contact us.) At all events, meeting with them in the small upper room that was allotted to small press publishers at ALA Midwinter 1985, we decided to interview them by mail, and came up with the following results:

(The Alternative Press Index has had a long history, taking it from Carleton College in Northfield, Minnesota, to Toronto, and now to Baltimore; the staff has changed over the years to what we believe to be a complete turnover, and therefore there is no person who can recite the whole history of AIP from beginning to end. They published an article in Missouri Library Association's *Show-Me Libraries* — an excellent publication we have had occasion to consult before! — Oct.-Nov. 1982, p. 21-24 which gives an account of their origins. We're blending info from that with their responses to our questions in the hope of producing a coherent article.)

SIPAPU: Your origins: how the collective got started? The educational/radical background of a typical member? Age group?

API: We got started from a 1969 Carleton College–based conference led by Vocations for Social Change, which encouraged people to work at jobs directed toward social change. A small group of students and faculty conceived the idea of creating an index to the publications which amplified the cry for social change and social justice. By the end of the first year, 100 volunteers (including some of *Sipapu*'s old friends, such as Jackie Eubanks, see v. 7, no. 2) were indexing some 72 periodicals, many of them "underground" papers. Frankly admitting they were advocates, not neutral bibliographers, they gave a cold shoulder to the radical Right. The Social Responsibilities Round Table provided them with a list of alternative subject headings, and the index was prepared with the use of Carleton College's computer.

Unfortunately, there were logistical problems. Carleton College had never really supported the Radical Research Center where the operations of the Index were run, and its computer had to be used surreptitiously. In the hope of finding a more supportive environment the collective moved to Rochdale College, Toronto, Ontario, and renamed itself the Alternative Press Centre (October 1971). Unfortunately moving set the Index behind, as volunteers dwindled and the cost of paying workers rose. The price of a yearly four-issue volume rose from $30 to $60, but during the four-year stay at Rochdale only four issues were published.

Peggy D'Adamo adds: We answered an appeal from the Centre, for volunteers, in the spring of 1974. I'd just graduated from the University of Maryland's library school while Chuck D'Adamo, with a background in philosophy and sociology, was interested in working at a social-change-oriented job. Arriving in Toronto, they found three burnt-out people, and the Index 2 ½ years behind. (In the fall of 1974, the D'Adamos brought the Index back to Baltimore.)

I think the "collective aspect" only got started in Toronto and since the move to Baltimore it has been refined and "institutionalized" (so to speak). It is my impression that there wasn't a real collective structure at Carleton College. I guess the educational/political background of the APC collective members hasn't changed much over the years. Most collective members have been in their early 20s, with some college or a B.A. Most are people who are already somewhat politically active but not affiliated with any Left party. We usually don't hire the super-activist types — they do apply but they are always over-committed. Over the years we've had feminists, environmentalists, community activists, gay activists, etc. Our former workers are now lawyers, day care workers, truck drivers, social workers, nurses, graduate students and even a librarian or two.

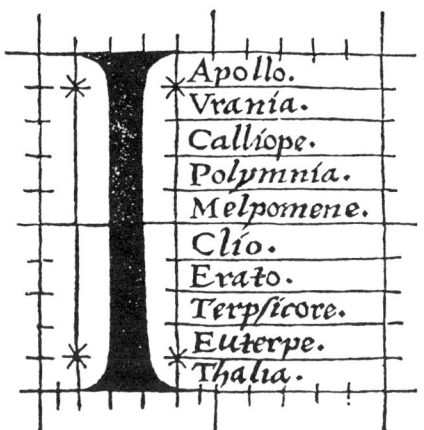 In the meanwhile, of course, the stream of alternative publishing had shifted course; there were fewer underground papers, and more publications of a topical nature: environmental, feminist, devoted to alternative sources of energy, prisoners, and so on. Collective organization was everywhere seen to be more comfortable than hierarchical, while structure came in as specializations developed, training was set up, work shared, and responsibilities rotated. Decisions were made by all paid staff at weekly meetings.

SIPAPU: How did you recruit members? What were your demands on them?

API: At Toronto they recruited through the local radical/alternative community (which was pretty developed in those days in Toronto). Most APC collective members were expatriate U.S. citizens. They also had a communal living situation which was based as much on economic facts as on philosophical principles. Our answer to your question #10 (see below) describes how we recruit new collective members here in Baltimore. In the early days here in Baltimore, there was a period when we lived and worked collectively too. We lived in a row house and also ran the Index out of it. There was no library at that time. We did that until we found the money to rent a small office. It was very intense, spending so much time with the same small group of people. We were all young, with no major commitments (like children, relationships, etc.).

SIPAPU: Your organizational structure? *Who* decides *what* should be indexed by *whom?*

API: Technically, we are a non-profit, tax-exempt corporation (section 501 (c)(3) of the IRS code). We assume the appropriate titles when necessary. In reality, we try to be as collective as possible in our structure. Some work is shared equally (data entry, indexing, office work). Other jobs are rotated regularly (issue coordinator, computer person). Some jobs are held for longer periods by one person (bookkeeping, checkbook balancing, etc.). We meet every week to distribute weekly indexing, data entry, make mundane and serious decisions. We rotate chairing the meeting and taking notes (alphabetical order by last name). The chair of the weekly meeting gets the first turn to pick what he/she will index first and we just go around until all the publications are chosen. That way, we always get to go first some time, and by picking publications one at a time, no one person gets to pick all the "good" ones. Volunteer indexers pick what they like to index. Each of us gets six magazines a week to index. Theoretically the weekly hours break down like this: 12 hours indexing, 2 hours data entry, 6 hours office work. Each of us works one day a week in the office (6 hours) in addition to the collective meeting. We work on a 12-week schedule with weekly deadlines. The issue coordinator's job is to keep everything on that schedule (among other tasks). It's taken us a long time and lots of experimentation to come up with these procedures. It may seem very bureaucratic—it probably is—but it works without creating a lot (hardly any) interpersonal conflicts.

SIPAPU: To go back a bit—Toronto, Rochdale College—what was it like?

API: I was only in Toronto briefly myself. When I took over the APC, there were two other people with me. I stayed in Baltimore, while they spent the summer in Toronto, effecting a smooth change. Both of these people have since quit the APC. Two of the three workers in Toronto were people originally from Carleton. They were living collectively at Rochdale as well as working there. They were living with other people too, who had nothing to do with the APC. They had fallen hopelessly behind in publishing due to a variety of factors: lack of money, delays due to moving to Detroit and then a few months later to Toronto, problems getting the APC legally situated in Canada, problems with their own immigration status, problems with the computer programs (the original programs from Carleton had to be completely rewritten), higher printing costs, etc. By the time we arrived in Toronto, the situation at Rochdale was pretty bad too. Rochdale was a highrise apartment building on Bloor Street which was owned and operated by the tenants. By that time, it had a pretty bad reputation. Rent wasn't collected regularly; the mortgage wasn't paid and the building was put into receivership. We had originally planned to move to Toronto ourselves but with the problems we were having with immigration and the situation at Rochdale, we decided to move the APC to Baltimore instead. Shortly after we left, all the tenants were evicted from Rochdale and it is now a home for senior citizens. Being from Baltimore and being somewhat connected to the radical community here, it made sense to come here.

SIPAPU: Present lifestyle? Collective life, decision-making, gardening, childcare?

API: Pretty varied. There are four collective members. Maybe each should speak for him/herself.

I am Peggy D'Adamo. I am currently working 20 hours a week and have been with the APC the longest. I have two children (both raised at the APC in the early years), a 7-year-old boy (Karl) and a 5-year-old girl (Janine). I am the only collective member who has worked here with small children. Right now I am also active in my community association (being president for the third year). In the past I have worked in the local food co-op, local chapter

DSA, a local socialist-feminist group, day care group, etc. I live in a house with the father of my two kids (he bought it) and have a vegetable/flower garden, etc. I also like to sew a lot, especially quilting.

Elizabeth O'Lexa describes herself as "reclusive" and "eccentric." In addition to working for APC she is a lesbian playwright. When not writing or working, she sleeps with her lover.

Before coming to the APC, Nancy Kennel worked for a gay rights group in Seattle, taught at a women's university (13,000 women and no men) in Korea, and diddled around in graduate school. In the past she has been active in Asian-American theatre but moving to Baltimore put an end to that. She is a semi-published writer and lives with her husband, a graduate student. She doesn't drink, smoke, do drugs, or play loud music. In short, she is pretty dull.

Our newest collective member, Bill Wilson, is not available to comment on himself at this time — probably because he is always so busy with DSA activities.

SIPAPU: How do you apportion work, how do you select periodical titles, or reject them? What about back-indexing, covering lost years:

API: We take six publications for each 20-hour work week. We try to give ourselves a break from indexing in the middle of the quarter, but that's not always possible. Summer tends to have fewer issues published and we sometimes have less work then.  At the end of the quarter if necessary we take extra publications to make sure as many issues as possible appear in the right (chronologically correct) quarter. The biggest problem we have is getting publications in the right issue, due to the publications not being received by us in time, and to their late publishing schedules.

The Index is current in its publication schedule, thanks to hard work and our new computer system. In 1974–1975 the Index was forced to delay publication (due to moving) for so long that the collective decided to skip publishing volumes 4 and 5. When the collective got settled in Baltimore, an additional collective was hired to produce those volumes at the

same time current indexing was being done. This process was completed by 1982, but for a year two collectives were both indexing.

We select new periodicals for indexing once or twice per quarter, depending on how many we recieve and/or solicit. One individual from the collective does a thorough review of the publication, then makes his/her recommendation to the collective (either index, reject, or exchange with for library holdings), and the collective approves or disapproves after examining the publication. We index over 200 periodicals currently, and at this point we're mainly concerned with these selection criteria:

1) Does it duplicate information already indexed?
2) Do we already have too many publications devoted to this issue?
3) Does the publication seem to be financially stable? Will it continue publishing?
4) Is it useful to researchers, activists, or political theorists? Are libraries, college or public, likely to subscribe to it?
5) Who is it affiliated with? Political viewpoints and organizational affiliations are important. Who writes for it, who makes up the organizational staff?
6) Are the majority of the articles substantial and long enough to be indexed? (See "Introduction to Index" for guidelines on what we do NOT index.)
7) Is this publication likely to have a national appeal, or can the principles/situations be extended to apply to areas/organizations outside the local area of coverage?

SIPAPU: The role of the computer? Which one? How do you run it?

API: Our computer is invaluable. All our subscription records are computerized, and a file from which we produce our annual *Directory of Alternative & Radical Publications* is on computer. Needless to say, it would be impossible to produce the Index without it. We have used a number of computer facilities over the years; currently we are using a personal computer and programs designed for and made available to us by the Baltimore Information Co-op (BIC). BIC is an organization devoted to making computers accessible to progressive and non-profit organizations such as APC. BIC also has office space in the Progressive Action Center, where APC is located, — meaning that "our" computer is finally right here in the same building with us.

BIC has markedly simplified and streamlined the long process it used to take to produce the index on the Johns Hopkins computer. We've also just begun using the Workers Action Press in the Progressive Action Center to print the actual Index, so virtually the entire process takes place in the same building. We still transmit the finished index to Johns Hopkins to print because they have a faster laser printer; we take this copy, lay it out, and Workers Action Press reduces it and prints the Index.

Each indexer is responsible for entering about 1,500 articles of data each issue, then correcting the data. (We used to keypunch it, which was an incredible hassle by comparison.) We rotate the job of running the final computer programs to compile the Index. The people who publish *Connexions* magazine in Canada visited us for a day to observe the Center and its operations, as they intend to begin a Canadian version of the API. So they will be modeling their index after the API, and intend to purchase from BIC the computer programs to make it possible.

SIPAPU: Vacations, burnout: how do you handle these?

API: Vacations: we each get one week for each year worked up to 3 years; 4 weeks for 5 years, and 5 weeks after 5 years. Accommodating holidays can be a problem, because if one person takes an office day off then it's only fair that everyone else does too, — which means closing the library for a whole week. We close the library the week between Christmas and New Year, then only days when someone is on vacation or sick. Since most of the work week is indexing, done outside the office, if someone has one week off, that means the library only has to be closed one day.

Burnout: good question. We haven't solved it any more than any other organization. We try to be as flexible as we can by "trading" work with each other if we feel we can't do it—i.e. someone may index 3 publications in exchange for someone else's batch of data entries. And we bitch a lot about indexing at the collective meeting. That helps. To see us pick publications each week you'd never believe you were watching a bunch of politically-committed individuals.

SIPAPU: How can one join the staff or the friends of the Alternative Press Index, and how do you select and train people? What responsibilities are entailed?

API: Our staff consists of 4 paid staff members. We ask for a one-year commitment when we hire. We do "collective job interviews" when hiring, and advertise the position mainly on bulletin boards and hang-outs of progressive organizations in Baltimore.

We interviewed nine people recently for the two open positions. Not many people are willing to commit themselves to a 20-hour-a-week job. We trained the new collective members for about one month, which included teaching them all the office/library duties, computer data entry, and critiquing their indexing, which work they did only after reading the ENTIRE subject heading guide (which is not light reading). Friends are volunteer indexers who volunteer to do specific publications. We have a "manual" on how and what to index which we give them, but all volunteer indexing is carefully checked by a collective member before it is entered as data.

SIPAPU: Your future?

API: 1984 was the first year the APC ever broke even financially, so planning for the future heavily emphasizes advertising for new subscribers so that we can continue to grow. In the beginning of the year we closely examined the Index and eliminated several publications that we felt no longer served our readership, while selecting new publications is an ongoing process. Since we've been using BIC's computer system we've greatly improved the readability of the Index by using bold and regular type, longer title lines (meaning fewer abbreviations), and some punctuation which was not possible with the old system. Also we now use laser-printed copy instead of printing straight from dot-matrix computer printout. So now that the Index looks the way we've wanted it to, we'll continue to expand its content. More subscribers would mean more income, which could mean another collective member and more publications we could index.

As for the library, we've been working on our book collection, which is meager at best, but until this year has not been cataloged and shelved by subject. Someday, in the far-off future, we dream of putting the library periodical collection, which is enormous as well as unique, on microfilm. This, however, is something we're financially unable to do at present.

SIPAPU: Thank you! (Address of the Progressive Action Center: 1443 Gorsuch Avenue, Baltimore, MD 21218—in an old Pratt branch library; includes APC, BIC, Central America Solidarity Committee, Democratic Socialists of America (DSA), Red Wagon Child Center, and Workers Action Press. Mailing address of API: P.O. Box 33109, Baltimore, MD 21218. Frequency of API: quarterly. Price: $100/military/corporates, $100/educational/libraries, $25/schools/individuals. This price may seem high, but the coverage of around 200 periodicals, including gay, environmental, and controversial publications not indexed elsewhere, makes it worth it. We use this with students all the time. We are grateful to API for the extra work they put into this interview.) (Phone: 301-243-2471.)

"TRUTH" AND CONSEQUENCES: Readers will remember from our last issue the problems faced by the California Library Association in its conflict with Truth Missions, headed by David McCalden, the man who says that the Holocaust of European Jews never happened, at least not on that scale. Such readers will recall that CLA's contract with McCalden, for a booth in the exhibits area and a program, was cancelled under social pressure, renewed under threat of suit, and finally cancelled a second time under threat of violence. Our own handling of this difficult subject has subsequently seemed to us, and perhaps to some readers, less than satisfactory; so that when we heard

that Chapter of Academic Research Librarians (CARL) under the direction of Alan Rich (UC Santa Cruz), was going to present a program entitled *"Truth" and Consequences,* we motored over the Sonoma State University at Rohnert Park to hear it. (In California's lovely hill country, one doesn't *drive,* one *motors.*)

Stefan B. Moses, Executive Director of CLA, reviewed the events and decisions which led to the crisis. He laid stress on CLA Council's approving the presence of Truth Missions in the official program of the 1984 conference: pointing out that it was his impression that McCalden and the other panelists on his program were going to confine themselves to the theme of getting unpopular books in libraries; McCalden was not going to defend his own historical thesis, as such, at all. As far as Moses was concerned, when a librarian blew the whistle by going to the American Jewish Committee in Los Angeles, with the news of CLA's relationship with Truth Missions, he made a mistake: he visited AJC, at their invitation, without a lawyer in tow. However, he claims that the AJC told him they would "wipe him out," and therefore he polled the Conference Program Committee by telephone, and they agreed that he should cancel the contract with McCalden. When McCalden threatened litigation, CLA's counsel advised Moses that he would probably lose, so Moses restored the contract.

By this time the news was leaking all over California, so while the CLA office took calls and opened letters (we were perhaps one of the few who did not bother that office), Moses became concerned about security arrangements—as well he should have, since there had been threats of picketing and violence to the conference and its exhibits. The Los Angeles Police Department said that they could guarantee the safety of the conference and exhibit area; and the Hotel Bonaventure was prepared to set up a carefully controlled and monitored territory for the Sunday night program. It was when Moses began receiving death threats, and the LAPD withdrew its guarantee of safety (perhaps because there was a Prince concert in town tonight, and their forces would be spread thin), that Moses's defenses began to crumble. The Los Angeles City Council voted to sever ties with the California Library Association (here Moses played us a tape of part of their proceedings), and the Library Commission of Los Angeles delivered Moses an on-the-spot ultimatum by telephone, obliging Moses and CLA President Bernard Kreissman (UC Davis) to confer and capitulate (16 November 1984). The Simon Wiesenthal Center (9760 West Pico Boulevard, Los Angeles, CA 90035) which keeps alive the memory of the Holocaust—and which McCalden has a running feud with—held a short program in the form of a travelling exhibit—in which, naturally, McCalden's books were featured.

Linda Wood, director of Riverside City and County Library, president of CLA for the calendar year 1985, described CLA's previous record of

outward success and goodwill and internal harmony. The Truth Missions involvement did CLA a lot of damage; many people refused to renew their memberships, many local library boards asked what was going on. Avoiding internal polarization and blame-fixing, Linda Wood took no sides on the issue, and gave up on trying to explain the whole wretched mess to the public. Damage control, followed by reorganization, were her strategies, and she outlined her steps toward this end: 1. Document the whole thing and conceal nothing; 2. Require member or constituent sponsors for all programs (cf. our last issue, p. 395); 3. Provide balance on controversial programs; 4. Set up an Emergency Action Committee, which without being an Executive Board, could nevertheless take action when minutes counted. Her final impression was that the membership wanted to go ahead and forget the whole thing, but that a lot of valuable lessons had been learned, and that the test would come in Oakland, at the next annual CLA conference (November 1985).

Judith Sessions, director of the Meriam Library at California State University, Chico, brought to her account a wide variety of experiences with ALA intellectual freedom groups. She chose to focus on the present activities of ALA in this area: its suit against the National Security Agency over the *Puzzle Palace* papers, the Indianapolis and anti-pornography laws (here they find themselves estranged from the National Organization for Women, but not necessarily from all women), the Lacy Commission report, the gay bookstore issues—and many others too numerous to mention.

There were many questions from the floor. Zoia Horn raised issues of racism and sexism. Another colleague read aloud a letter from Arthur Koestler about someone's professed ignorance of the Holocaust (first published in Cyril Connolly's periodical *Horizon* (London); for the text of the letter, see its anthology, *The Golden Horizon,* London, Weidenfeld and Nicolson, 1953; p. 71). Exact details of the history of the Truth Missions encounter were gone over and straightened out (no, CLA's Intellectual Freedom Committee hadn't voted to admit McCalden, but they hadn't taken a strong stand against it, either); and the meeting adjourned to the Sonoma State University Library, there to drink wine and eat cheese.

This meeting seemed to go very well for the participants, particularly the panel, but our earlier impression remains: that the Association, and the library profession in general, are and were unprepared to meet McCalden or to deal with sensitive people (like Jews) and sensitive issues (the Holocaust). The issue remains unresolved, and bears a strong resemblance to the issue involved in ALA's film, *The Speaker.*

Anyone who has followed this periodical's coverage of intellectual freedom and social responsibility over the past sixteen years has understood that our position on this troubling question has changed and evolved; also that we usually find more questions than we have answers for, even though some of these questions are purely hypothetical. Nevertheless, the dilemmas faced here, like those faced seven years ago, by librarians, may indeed result from a lacuna in the philosophy of the library profession.

Professional librarians concerned with intellectual freedom may encounter (at least) seven forms of expression:

1. Truths (the Earth is round)
2. Opinions (Republicans? Democrats? a third party, Left or Right?)
3. Moral questions (abortion, homosexuality: right or wrong?)
4. Matters of taste (J.S. Bach, or ZZ Top?)
5. Minority theories or opinions, not generally accepted by scholars in the field (Bacon wrote Shakespeare's plays, the Air Force has a flying saucer and its occupants in a refrigerator at Travis AFB, Fairfield, California)
6. Offensive language (four-letter words, racist attitudes and epithets, pornography)
7. Outright lies, false statements knowingly made to frighten or hurt people (Black people are inherently stupid, the Holocaust didn't happen).

Librarians have at one time or another encountered texts (= books, periodicals, other materials) embodying all of these seven. They have met them with the Library Bill of Rights, and with careful selection tools. They have even met them with a new awareness, sometimes, of community concern (the Library of Congress changed at least some of the offensive subject headings). But in general, these defenses, while adequate for the first five, where the profession is understood and supported by the populace in general, — have not fared well with no. 6, and (we submit) failed completely with no. 7.

We won't go into no. 6 here because we've dealt with it in our articles on the Council on Interracial Books for Children (see our issues no. 15 and 26), save to say that not only women and Third World people, Jews and the handicapped, need to be respected, but also conservative country people too. But that is for another issue. At present we see the matter thus: the professional theory of intellectual freedom, which is a libertarian one, takes no account of lies: statements, knowingly false and not intended as works of fiction, which deny a people's heritage and status, with the ultimate object, and possible result, of oppressing and humiliating them.

The passage from the proceedings of the Los Angeles City Council included the voice of one Council member who said that libraries, which ought to be the repositories of truth, should not contain a falsehood. Of course, as Judith Sessions pointed out, libraries contain more than just truths: they contain the different kinds of texts we have listed, and doubtless many more.

Whether they should also collect books embodying lies (Black people are dumb, there was no Holocaust), except in the case of omnivorous research collections (i.e.: the Hoover Institution); or — and this is a separate question — library associations, which are not libraries! should promote or seem to promote such books, their authors and publishers, — is unsettled at this point, as far as the profession is concerned.

Some librarians trained in the present libertarian tradition of intellectual freedom might say, "Buy the book but don't promote it." Others will say, "That's a cop-out. If you don't believe it, why get it?" But no librarian will be found publicly saying, "THIS BOOK TELLS A LIE." To say that, would be considered: close-minded intolerant of new or controversial ideas; rude, offensive — if not to the author, then to an inquiring patron; possibly involving conflict with the little cult around the corner. Consequently, librarians will assign the book to our class 2, or our class 5; possibly to 6. Its presence on our shelves, or your promotion of it, will be defended with some such statement as, "We collect all opinions, no matter how offensive to some, since freedom for what we want implies freedom for the detestable."

Notice: correct grammatical construction would have made us write:

"...freedom for that which we, personally and collectively detest." The quote is never quoted just that way. For, the traditional libertarian position begs the question: detestable to and for whom, and for what reasons? Because some people have trouble facing difficult or embarrassing truths (e.g., alcoholics fool themselves about the amount of their drinking, politicians skim lightly over their errors of judgment). How much is it our business to know? Are the facts of the Holocaust really not yet established? The bibliography is voluminous, the survivors are legion. Are we unsure of this mountain of evidence, or do we want to appear neutral in a difficult hour?

According to the Simon Wiesenthal Center's *Response*, v. 11, August 1985, the Institute for Historical Review, with which McCalden has been (at least until recently) affiliated, was obliged to apologize after having been sued by Auschwitz survivor Mel Mermelstein, where Mermelstein heard of their offer of $50,000 for proof that Jews were gassed at Auschwitz. The suit also named as defendants Willis Carto, "widely identified as the largest contributor to extreme right wing causes in the United States," and David McCalden, "founder of the IHR and currently head of Truth Missions." The apology forced out of them by the court's settlement, reads as follows:

> The Legion for Survival of Freedom, Institute for Historical Review, Noontide Press, Elisabeth Carto, Liberty Lobby and Willis Carto do hereby officially and formally apologize to Mr. Mel Mermelstein, a survivor of Auschwitz-Birkenau and Buchenwald, and all other survivors of Auschwitz for the pain, anguish and suffering he and all other Auschwitz survivors have sustained relating to the $50,000 reward for proof that "Jews were gassed in gas chambers at Auschwitz" [Simon Wiesenthal Center, *Response* v. 11, p. 5].

The *Response* adds,

> An unprecedented public apology (reprinted in part above) was agreed to by those defendants named, as well as David McCalden.... The defendants also agreed to formally acknowledge the October 9, 1981, judicial recognition by Los Angeles Superior Court Judge Thomas T. Johnson that "Jews were gassed to death at Auschwitz concentration camp in Poland during the summer of 1944."

If neutrality in controversy is a part of the professional ethic implicit in the Library Bill of Rights, then some librarians who wanted to be on safe ground might still have to be neutral in this controversy. They would feel obliged to answer a student, who asked for information about the Holocaust, "Here are some books on the (alleged) Holocaust. The court has handed down one opinion. Here are some others that still say it didn't happen. Make up your mind." Of course, we've all been trained to answer reference questions out of books, instead of relying on total recall, but could we really dig out the dates of Adolf Hitler (1889–1945), and then pretend we weren't sure about the event for which his dictatorship is most famous? We're not saying that any librarian has, or would, make that remark to a student; only that nothing in a librarian's code obliges her to make the following distinctions:

1. This book tells the truth.
2. These two books offer honest differences of opinion.
3. This is fringe stuff, rather way out, but maybe there's some fragment of truth in it.
4. This is a &%$#@*# LIE.

We're forbidden to even hint at such a comment. That's LABELLING!

However, the public does, after all, trust us, as the remark of the Los Angeles City Councilman suggests, and pays us accordingly. It requires us to be fair; but also to be honest. It will not tolerate us pretending suddenly that we don't know something, when apparently we know everything else. While it is true that the lie that the Holocaust didn't happen has spread in some communities (which is one alleged reason why *The Diary of Anne Frank* frequently appears on banned book lists), there are too many survivors, plus Allied military personnel and civilian rescue workers, who saw the camps just after they were liberated, — to pretend that the Holocaust is just a myth or a theory.

If this is true, then a crack appears at the very foundations of our beliefs and practices in the intellectual freedom field. We practice information science, yet there are times when we dare not say that the information is inaccurate, bigoted, or even deliberately misleading. Either we know; or we do not know; when it comes to matters of fact, witnessed or suffered by millions. We can, and indeed should, be neutral, on matters of taste or opinion; but not on matters of clearly established fact. Any smarmy remark on the order of, "But, of course, librarians don't really know, do they? they just know where to look it up," can and should be countered and refuted by the thousands of librarians in public, academic, and special libraries who are, to a greater or lesser extent, experts in their fields — and so treated, and so rewarded — who consult each other in the course of a working day, and who trust each other to have the facts as well as the bibliographical references. We *do* know. And we know about the Holocaust. That it happened. Why not face up to it?

What would you think of a doctor, who, being asked, "Does smoking cause cancer?" chose to answer, "Here are two books. Read — smoke — them both. Make up your own mind," adding, *sotto voce,* with a hacking cough, "the tobacco industry is pretty strong in this county ... and they've promised to build us a new clinic..."

At present the library profession is getting along on goodwill, written policies, sound professional attitudes and book selection tools. Most of the time they carry us pretty far. What we're suggesting is that American librarians are to some extent sheltered, that they do not see that when racism and anti-semitism become to some extent acceptable, when lies are admitted under the cloak of "minority opinions" or "strange theories," the intellectual atmosphere is slowly corrupted. The public loses confidence in our honesty, and Jews, and other people with a history of oppression, —begin to mistrust us. The profession, while in technical matters very "state-of-the-art," is in intellectual matters largely, though not entirely, unaware of the twentieth century. As long as we do not know, or let others think we do not know, or care about, its atrocious history, as long as we cannot tell that century's truths from its lies, we will be the victims of the race-baiters, unable to deal with their fables. "'What is truth,' said Pilate, and would not stay for an answer."

We therefore suggest that ALA undertake a thorough study of what racism and anti-semitism do to a culture, and follow this up with a rewriting of the Library Bill of Rights, which should include the responsibilities of librarians in dealing with sensitive areas and people. But this can only be done by a study of the facts, since appeals to sensitivity are likely to be rescinded if admitted (as happened some time ago; the racism and sexism awareness clause was excised from the Library Bill of Rights some years ago).

At one time the National Library Week people put out a poster of which the text ran: KNOW WHAT YOU'RE TALKING ABOUT—READ. We'd like to see them publish it again.

POSTSCRIPT RE: COSMEP: The Committee of Small Magazine Editors and Publishers (COSMEP), which carried McCalden's ad, in its catalog of member-publishers, has also been criticized for its promotion of his work. Executive Director Richard Morris writes, "It was not fear of a lawsuit that prompted us to publish his page. It was simply the belief that refusing to allow a member to participate in an organization project would constitute censorship ... It was only about a year later that it was suggested  that we might have been liable in a lawsuit if we had refused to publish it." Others, including Steve Fankuchen, editor of *Shmate,* have thought differently and said so in no uncertain terms; but granting Morris's account of the motives for the Board's decision, there are differences between the library profession's predicament, as we see it, and the situation COSMEP found itself faced with.

One obvious difference is that McCalden (at this writing) is a member of COSMEP and not of CLA. (Although he could change memberships easily. And one obvious similarity is that he had a contractual relationship with both.) On the other hand, while the library profession is a profession which the public trusts, as we have suggested, and while this trust is extended to its constituent organizations, national and state, —COSMEP is a trade organization, and one without discernible standards. To quote its entry in *National Trade and Professional Associations of the United States* (1985): "Members are 'small' publishers who are concerned with improving the promotion and distribution of their magazines and book titles." Nothing is said about improving the quality of these publications; COSMEP says nothing about whether its members' publications are wonderful or worthless. How could it? Its members include publishers of books of poetry, publishers of books on how to train your dog, publishers of books on funerary hair-styling and publishers of catalogs of toys. Where's the unifying set of beliefs, the political line, the shtik? Nowhere; and nowhere to be sought. Consequently, guidelines which eliminate racist, anti-semitic, or sexist materials would operate under the difficulty that the publisher of such materials would say, "Nobody told me that I had to have a 'correct' political attitude when I joined COSMEP: and as a member in good standing, I demand full participation in all of the organization's programs; even if other people in the program don't like the stuff I put out." On the other hand, anyone who chose to publish in a catalog, or distribute via a COSMEP book bus, would have to take his or her chances, that someone else on the same trip was distributing material he or she might find offensive.

At least some members of the COSMEP board advised against the making of a catalog, perhaps for just these reasons. For ourselves, we prefer to exhibit with New Pages Exhibiting (formerly Alternative Press Exhibiting Service—APES), which is open to "progressive" publishers, and consequently gives a far less heterogeneous impression to the visitor. And we didn't try to get into the COSMEP catalog.

Beyond the libertarian position lies the responsible one. The story goes that there is a proverb: "In the East (= Eastern Europe) nothing goes and everything matters; in the West (= Western Europe and the U.S.) everything goes and everything matters. We don't try to get away with saying that maybe the Holocaust never happened, that maybe it's all a myth anyway, and it's all relative, so so what? And we also hold, that intellectual workers—librarians, writers and publishers of all kinds—have a special responsibility attached to

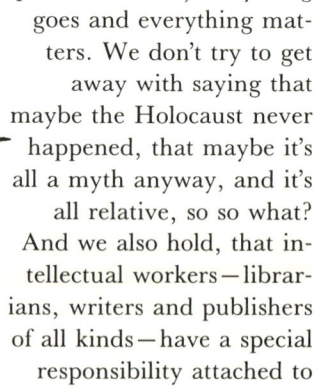

their freedom; to tell the truth, and not to play games. McCalden's presentation before the Canadian Library Association, as reported in *Library Journal*, met with a stony silence. That may have not been enough, but it was certainly better than what we went through, on two fronts, in California.

So much for our understanding of this subject so far.

ALA CHICAGO 1985: We accepted the suggestion of staying at Loyola University's dorms on this trip, to save money, and found that it was merely more of a hassle. One of the dorms lacked air conditioning, and the breakfast facilities resolutely refused to open before the stroke of 7:30 precisely, in spite of the fact that many ALA programs begin at 8:00. And it's too far to walk. Gale buses were infrequent, and—well, never again. On the other hand, there were some fine programs, one sponsored by GODORT/IFRT/SRRT, called "Whose information is it anyway?" which offered the pros and cons of the privatization of Federal information. Robert Willard, of the Information Industry Association, was undisturbed by the directives of the Office of Management and Budget, and the Executive Orders, which have cut down the budgets of Federal departments doing a lot. As far as he was concerned, privatization did no harm, and the title question was trivial, since in his view, we'll all get all the information we'll need anyway (whether supplied by government or private business). Donna Demac, author of *Keeping America Uninformed: Government Secrecy in the 1980's* (Pilgrim Press, 1984), took the opposite view with much vigor, seeing privatization as *the* threat, and perceiving the difference between her and the Administration's spokesmen as a fundamental question of values: supply-side economics vs. democratic spread of information. She questioned the very legality of OMB's actions. For Allen Adler, of the ACLU, it was (predictably) a constitutional and Bill-of-Rights question. The Constitution of 1787 does make provisions for the Federal Government to provide information to its citizens, but what we're seeing under this Administration is the triumph of cost-benefit analysis over these constitutional provisions.

The other program, also concerned with intellectual freedom in a political context, was sponsored by SRRT's Task Force on Alternatives in Print: "The alternative press under the second Reagan régime: thriving under repression?" The phrase "second Reagan régime" reminded us of Napoleon III and the Second Empire, and perhaps there's indeed a touch of Bonapartism there; but we'll let others find the difference if any. This program was excellently chaired by Jackie Eubanks of Brooklyn College Library. Among the speakers were: Haki Mahabudhi (Don L. Lee), a Black publisher from Detroit, who is now a professor of English at Chicago State University. He gave the history of his Third World Press, and his periodical publishing ventures, which are to be revived under the title *Culture, a Black Holistic Journal* (continuing *Black Book Bulletin*). Ellen Sawislak, representing New Society Publishers, described her house as advocating non-violent social change.

This collective, of which the first publication was *Reweaving the Web of Life: Feminism and Nonviolence* (though we remember reviewing their publication, *Tell the American People,* years before that, under the Movement for a New Society imprint; see our v. 15, no. 2, consecutive issue no. 30); does a lot of social self-help books, and works on Central America. They do pay themselves, although they are a tax-exempt non-profit organization. Chip Berlet, editor of *The Public Eye,* a periodical supported by the National Lawyers Guild, and a member of the Alternative Media Syndicate, began by describing the split in APS between the specialized papers such as his, and the weekly or monthly papers with their local issues and entertainment features. The most important part of his talk described the right-wing attack on radical papers by means of harassment libel suits, which use up thousands of dollars of the defendant's money, during the process of getting them dismissed. By this means, such right-wing figures as Lyndon LaRouche and Willis Carto make it impossible to write anything about them (the "libel" need not be really libellous; it's enough that all editors, great and small, be challenged in court and put out of business; and no publisher, however small, is immune from such attack, according to the speaker. Whether the Intellectual Freedom Committee of ALA would touch such a problem — since libraries are not affected as such — remains [as the coroner said] to be seen). According to Chip Berlet, the U.S. Internal Revenue Service is also back in action, questioning the tax-exempt status of controversial magazines such as *Mother Jones.*

Words that Wound: Proceedings of the Conference on Freedom of Expression and Racist Propaganda (Australia. Human Rights Commission. Occasional Papers, no. 3) is available from the Australian Government Publishing Service in Canberra. It caught our eye because this subject is being hotly debated among librarians now (see this and previous issues of *Sipapu*). The experience of most other English-speaking countries in this troublesome area of freedom of expression vs. racism is that their laws descend from the English common law, which permits certain controls on freedom of expression, while the American Constitution, as amended, broadly permits freedom of speech, of the press, and of assembly, no matter who is offended by the results. Australian law has no such proviso (as Canada and New Zealand do) against hate propaganda, but there is a role for the Human Rights Commission to play in receiving complaints of group libel. (When the Racial Discrimination Bill was debated in 1975, there was a prohibition of racial propaganda in it, but this was taken out.) The Hon. A.J. Grassby, former Human Rights Commissioner, was accustomed to working from a position of conciliation and good will, but he thought a strong case could be made in Australia for an anti-racist-propaganda law, and evidence in favor of such a law, or at least evidence of discrimination, was made on the same day by a variety of speakers, — Aboriginal, Jewish, Greek, &c. (Part of the point of that excellent Australian film *Caddie,* that came out a few years ago, that in leaving her middle-class husband, who beats her, and taking a job as a barmaid, Caddie loses class status, but also reinforces that position by taking a Greek lover; Greeks are shunned by "Old Australians" in part because of their numbers.) Mr. Creighton Burns, editor of "The Age," argued against legislation in spite of the possibility of increasing racism on the ground that it would be very difficult to draft legislation that worked, and if prosecutions failed, these failures would only incite racists to flout the law and draw attention to their successes. He proposed community action as the solution. The general feeling among the speakers was that Australia is a very racist country; that there is a lot of public indifference to many serious problems; and that at least some Australians fear that their country is more racist than the United States. We're not sure of the price of this book but it's probably around four or five dollars for ninety-seven pages. Recommended for all who take an interest in this continuing problem.

Another searching inquiry into "state-of-the-struggle" literature is provided by a pamphlet (74 p.) from the A.J. Muste Memorial Institute, 339 Lafayette Street, New York, NY 10012: *Where Do We Go from Here? Tactics and Strategies for the Peace Movement* (the Institute's Discussion series, no. 1). Some thirty-six men and women, many if not all veterans of the Movement in the Sixties and Seventies, answered eight questions: on the inevitability of nuclear war, on the peace movement's attitude to the Soviet Union, civil disobedience, the Democratic Party, counter-culture, separatism, &c.

Some of the names are quite familiar, like Abbie Hoffman and Noam Chomsky; others are known chiefly by co-workers in the Movement, such as Anne Braden and Holly Sklar. What seized us immediately upon reading these valuable essays was the degree to which they had all learned from "Sixties rhetoric": all of them were talking down-home sense. Examples: "the left's weakness is horribly highlighted by the miserably inadequate answers we give when people ask us how we would do things differently? To say that we wouldn't have war, or racism, or sexism, or that we'd have equality, or democracy, convinces no one because it doesn't explain what kinds of institutions would allow these advances." (Michael Alpert) "Has Left political thinking, rooted strongly in Rationalist/Marxist/Materialist ideology, failed to properly assess the role that Religious Belief plays, not only in the personal life of the individual, but in the political life of the group?" (Norma Becker) "In fact, Lenin and Trotsky proceeded immediately to destroy workers organizations and to eliminate any possibility that producers could control the means of production, the minimal condition of socialism..." (Noam

Chomsky) "By arming further, we become a military state, the biggest of the 'banana republics...'" (Ann Morissett Davidson) "The so-called 'Peace Movement' you talk about is a bunch of harpies who care more about correcting each others' vocabulary than reaching millions of Americans. They are the folks who talk of reaching 'the masses' and brag about not watching television, who have never talked to anyone who rode in the SMOKING section of an airplane." (Abbie Hoffman) "Above all, the peace movement must recognize that 95 percent of the American people are to our right politically" (Patrick Lacefield). Obviously, these are sentiments with which we wholly agree, and if the movement begins to understand them, we may indeed see a genuine understanding between this country's Right and Left. After that, we can unite and face the problem together—maybe. On the other hand, war may be set off for the most irrational reasons or non-reasons, and thus involve the American peace movement. Witness the Bert Dodson strip below:

Beg pardon, Bert Dodson, for footnoting one of your strips: "Afterwards it was suggested that he might have lost the ear in the pillory." Our source: *Encyclopaedia Britannica,* 11th edition, 1910, article "Jenkins, Robert."

We owe one to Wendy Rose, who has a better right than we do to call the first part of her book, *The Halfbreed Chronicles, and Other Poems* (West End Press, P.O. Box 291477, Los Angeles, CA 90029; $4.95): "Sipapu." She interprets the Southwestern people's use of the term as "a place of emergence": of the human species from underground; we understand that the Jicarilla Apache interpret it directly as the birth canal; but she has a right to it that we don't, as she is Amerindian and we aren't; we borrow, sans license, but with apology. Meanwhile, even if we did come through a birth canal (so did you, dear reader), we must still defer to this poet who writes ("Nuke devils: the Indian women listen"):

"for my blood runs from the rivermouth
from my bony banks flashfloods bubble.
  ***

I topple the machinery
that rolls into the buffalo mounds,
break from electric trees their tops,

fall completely and forever
into star sand."

We have never seen a better description of how White America looks from the outside, as this, from "Backlash" (concluding verse):

It's not that your songs
are so much stronger
or your feet more deeply
rooted, but that
there are
so many of you
    shouting in a single voice
    like a giant child.

"Loo-wit" is the name by which the Cowlitz People know Mt. St. Helens: "Lady of fire." The eruption of 1982 is the result of intrusion on her flanks, in the poem of that name, — in this book. The Cowlitz People must have seen the eruption of the early nineteenth century.

Since we haven't been down to Nicaragua ourselves, we can only turn to a fellow-citizen of Winters, Diane Callum, who has. Our readers last met her traversing Brazil and Bolivia on the "Train of the Dead" (*Sipapu* no. 26, pp. 317-319). Here we find her returning to...

WHERE POETS FEAR TO TREAD: Returning to San Francisco from Nicaragua last August 13, [says Diane Callum], I was singled out for harassment at airport immigration. Eight of the ten members of our group had gone through U.S. Customs without incident. I was next. The female customs official excused herself for a moment, returned, left again after I was at her cubicle, then came back again. She asked me where I had been — which was obvious from the stamp on my passport: Nicaragua — and the purpose of my trip — which was also obvious from the entry form: pleasure. But actually vocalizing "pleasure" as the purpose of my trip sounded so absurd under the circumstances that I added, "I'm a poet. I went there for the poetry." A sneer eclipsed her taut smile.

"I find it hard to believe...," she began. Her anger was palpable. "I find it hard to believe that there's much poetry in a country like Nicaragua."

"Oh, but there's lots of poetry." I felt like a canary flitting around an alley cat.

"Were you part of any Christian organization?"

"No." I knew she was asking me if I was part of Witness for Peace and if I had been involved in the hostage situation on the Rio San Juan. I also knew from reading a pamphlet on U.S. Customs that she had no right to be asking me that question — nor the following ones. But I was just riveted by her controlled fury. And I was afraid. She could body-search me, and the humiliation of that invasion terrified me more than anything. So I answered her illegal questions.

"Were you a political observer?"

"No." Then she asked the name and location of the travel agent who had booked the tour. Luckily our group had had the foresight to go through Customs on the buddy system. My buddy Cynthia was there with me, supplying answers about the tour because by now I was in a kind of dreamlike paralysis where my mouth could move and make intelligible sounds, but my thoughts were frozen in fear of the implications of those questions. However, when the customs official — the *Migra,* as illegal aliens call the INS officers who terrorize them — asked to see our tickets, I froze. Ironically, I was the only one in our group without a ticket. In Mexico City, I had made a breakneck effort to get the group on a flight that had been wrongly scheduled two hours later, and in the process, I had left my ticket behind. Not that I needed it since I had a boarding pass. *Now,* though, I needed it.

Something unlocked for a moment in my frozen brain: the synapse went to my lips:

"I think my ticket is with one of the others who went ahead . . . in our group," I fumbled. And Cynthia pulled out a mass of paper, saying, "Here's some pieces of tickets."

Her curiosity satisfied about the who and how of our trip, the *Migra* turned to Cynthia and asked her what she did for a living and where she lived.

"I'm a teacher at a two-year college near Davis where I live.."

"Oh, I didn't know there were other universities than the University of California, in Davis." And so it went; the banter was civil. The taut smile was back in place. The pressure was off me for the moment, but I knew it was inevitable that I would be searched.

"The agricultural inspectors will see you now," said the *Migra,* putting our passports in a plastic folder. Following the flickering red lights that marked the way to the inspection station, I felt I was following a chorus line bound for hell.

"Are you okay?" asked the First Inspector.

"Yes."

"Are you sure you're okay?" he asked again. This was it: I knew it: a set-up for a drug search.

"Everything all *right?*" asked the Second Inspector. But suddenly they were waving us on, and they hadn't even opened our bags. I couldn't believe it, and fully expected someone to stop us on the way out. But we were through.

On the other side, I collapsed and wept into my friends' arms. First aid was applied: *Flor de Caña,* the white rum of Nicaragua. The shot of rum was mother's milk compared with the searing indignity I had just experienced. Why had the *Migra* singled me out? Was it because I had said I was a poet?

Was it because I had felt so free to be myself in Nicaragua that I had misjudged freedom of expression back home? Was it who I was — something in my being? For ten days in Nicaragua I had been accepted — even cherished — for who I was in that small, embattled land. That acceptance had animated me. At a night club in Managua, Commandante Bayardo Arce, one of the nine leaders of the FSLN, asked me to dance. Ernesto Cardenal, Minister of Culture, said he would like to publish the poetry I had given him. And this acceptance came to the whole group. We visited schools, hospitals, and farming cooperatives, giving out medical equipment, clothes and school supplies — receiving in turn love and compassion. I barely slept. I hardly ate. I debated hotly: politics, poetry, women's rights. There were people who sought us out to complain about the system, to support the system, — people arguing poetic theory with the same vigor with which they debated politics. I couldn't get enough.

I also couldn't stand the irony — my tax dollars paying for the guns that were killing these people. "What can we do?" we asked them.

"Go back and tell people what you found here," they said. "Then your government will change its mind. Tell your government to let us live." — DIANE CALLUM.

17 : 1

This is number 33. I've never actually met Art Cuelho — indeed, I've never been in Montana. Art has subsequently learned a little Portuguese and returned for a visit to the Azores, publishing the results of his journey in My Island Called Me Home *(the Azorean paper he sent me mentioned* Sipapu*). Art reprinted one of my poems in his anthology,* Breadbasket with the Blues.

I met Bob Kaufman only once, at a bookfair in Fort Mason. A.D. Winans introduced us. Kaufman came around five minutes later and touched me for a dollar. I reported this to Winans who said, "Congratulations! That means he likes you!" By the time I saw Kaufman he was dying on his feet, and of course I would have given my last dollar to a dying poet. Winans's piece appeared less than a year after I first met Kaufman.

MEANWHILE, BACK AT THE RANCH: Art Cuelho, publisher of Seven Buffaloes Press, Box 249, Big Timber, MT 59011, is editor of several serials, some new, some no longer being published, which deal with the life and literature of rural American workers, — ranchers, migrant workers, Western and Appalachian country people. We have noted his work several times before (consecutive issues nos. 28, 31, 32) but now we need to know more about this Azorean-American, one of the most prolific publishers in the West.

SIPAPU: More than with other interviewees, we need to know your parentage, birth, education. Evidence (your publications) suggests you grew up in California's San Joaquin Valley, but your home is now Big Timber, Montana. And you write well. How — in the largest sense — did you get from there to where you are now? How old are you, and how did you manage?

CUELHO: Both my mother and father are first-generation Azorean-Portuguese-American. I grew up hearing both sets of grandparents speak in broken English. Every time I'd stop off to see Grandam Laureano in Hollister she'd talk awhile in English and then right in the middle of a sentence she'd switch to Portuguese. I'd have to remind her that I didn't speak the language.

photo by Tom Dokey

My parents spoke the Azorean tongue when they didn't want us kids to know what they were saying. I think I missed a lot by not knowing the language, because all over the valley in the summer they have Portuguese Celebrations, and our people from the Nine Islands always spoke in their native tongue. My Azorean heritage would have been increased if I could have understood the conversations of my people as they told stories about family and relatives.

I think my Azorean roots account for a big portion of my grassroots philosophy of life. My ancestors, for centuries, were simple farmers and whalers, which gave me a birthright bond with the common man. Because the Azores are located 2000 miles off New York City in the Atlantic Ocean, and 900 miles off the mainland of Portugal—my people's folkways remained unique and sometimes primitive. They farmed primitively too. I recently did a rural painting from a color picture book that the tourist department of Terceira Island sent me of two men plowing. A *man* instead of a *horse* was pulling the plow through the corn furrows.

You see the poorer people in the Azores had the strongest dream to come to America. I think they may have had a more ambitious and adventurous spirit than those who stayed behind. My Grandma Laureano had such a strong desire to leave her hometown of Biscoitos that she snuck out in the early dawn without her mother knowing that she planned a trip to America. She was seventeen, the only girl in the family, and never saw her mother again.

I wrote a true and humorous short story based on my mother's folks called "Papa's Naturalization." Grandpa Laureano had decided to become an

American citizen before my grandmother. He didn't have the patience to wait for her to come with him. They were raising eleven children and my grandmother did not have time to study. She wanted my grandfather to wait until some of the kids were grown. She wanted them to become American citizens together and resented him studying every evening after the cows were milked. The day Grandpa Laureano headed toward the courthouse to get his citizenship papers, my grandmother took his Sunday dress coat and laid it in a puddle of mud outside the rained-over yard in front of their farmhouse. A little smile creased grandpa's lips as he sat down on the porch steps. Grandma Laureano had won that battle. As a writer I drew some of my material from my immediate family. William Saroyan, who is also from Fresno, did the same thing with the Armenian people. Saroyan has inspired a lot of valley writers, including myself. Over one of my work areas in my studio I have a quote from his writing about what an artist should live up to:

> The writer is a spiritual anarchist, as in the depth of his soul every man is. He is discontented with everything and everybody. The writer is everybody's best friend and only true enemy—the good and great enemy. He neither walks with the multitude nor cheers with them. The writer who is a writer is a rebel who never stops. He does not conform for the simple reason that there is nothing yet worth conforming to. When there is something half worth conforming to he will not conform to that, either, or half conform to it. He won't even rest or sleep as other people rest and sleep. When he's dead he'll probably be dead as others are dead, but while he is alive he is alive as no one else is, not even another writer. The writer who is a writer is also a fool. He is the easiest man in the world to belittle, ridicule, dismiss, and scorn: and that also is as it should be. He is also mad, measurably so, but saner than all others, with the best sanity, the only sanity worth bothering about—the living, creative, vulnerable, valorous, unintimidated, and arrogant sanity of a free man. —William Saroyan*

Of course, one of the keys to my ethnic identity has been the result of starting from a background of hard-working farmers and dairymen. In fact where I grew up in the Riverdale community you were not thought very highly of if you did not work like a horse. I started working in the fields with the hired hands when I was eleven. My oldest brother Gene started when he was six. You know you hear about people who used to work from sunup to sundown. I overheard my father telling a Portuguese lady three or four years ago that when he grew up they did not stop working at sundown. If they had a full moon they kept working into the night. One of the driving fores in my father's struggle stemmed from his being poor. He told me about Grandpa Cuelho's shabby harness and that when he tried to plow the worn dry leather

---

*"A Writer's Declaration" from The Whole Voyald and Other Stories, by William Saroyan. Copyright 1950, The Curtis Publishing Co.; copyright 1950, 1951, 1952, 1953, 1954, 1955, 1956, by W. Saroyan.

would snap and go flying through the air. He'd have to borrow harness from the neighbor who kept the leather oiled properly so it would not fray. A large part of my motivation as an artist and publisher comes from my father's example and the workload that he labored with from the time he was a child until he was sixty-five years old when both family farms were sold. One of my father's feats as a young man was what he did with an ax. He corded up five acres of wood at three dollars a day. My father worked in the time when you got 85 cents a day. To give you some idea of how farming was in his blood he once dry-farmed ten thousand acres out on the west side of the valley in Fresno County. Later he farmed three thousand acres of irrigated land for forty years at Wheatville, which is the town where the old stagecoach ran, eventually leading to Coalinga and the Coast Ranges.

But my rural roots were more than just my personal family. Often it was something in the surrounding area that made you aware of the valley's history. Sometimes it was a single tree standing out in a field. Farmers year after year carefully edged around it with their rigs and refused to chop it down to make it easier for them to farm. It marked the spot where the first schoolhouse had been built. The farmers respected remnants of their past. You have to realize that Central California is a vast open flat plain six hundred miles long and 60 to 80 miles wide. Isolation still dominates the landscape here. So you see why a single tree on the horizon can grow in stature beyond its ordinary everyday appearance. It is often the only survivor among the endless waves of barley fields. This remote loneliness out in the West Side area while you are driving a tractor or irrigating makes you very aware of memories — moments out in the hot sun alone. It conjures up your daily thoughts, fantasies — what you will do that weekend, your girlfriend, the drag races on Saturday. You look forward to the small things in life because all week long you have toed the mark. Have been held down. You want to break out of it. The same kind of thing happened to me when I became a writer and a poet. I wanted to break out of the valley into a larger world. Although I would not return to the farm until I was thirty-three years old, from the first time I left that world behind I felt the drama of it much like Sherwood Anderson when he quit his paint company. It's like you choose the road of art instead of money. I never had that wild desire for publishing, at first, that I had for writing. In time it got into my blood too, but mainly it was a means to being my own boss and to work at something that had value to me.

Another important aspect of how I view people stems directly to the Wheatville farm. There was a community of ten different families who lived there on our place. Sometimes during the peak of the barley harvest or the picking of cotton in the fall, my father had as many as twenty men working for him. These families were of every nationality and from every region in America. So I grew up with the minorities: the Blacks; the Mexicans; the Dustbowl immigrant Okies; hoboes and drifters of every description. In short: the salt of the earth. Once I saw this hobo reading *Of Mice and Men* and I thought: that would be my idea of a readership, someday. The simple act of a common man reading me while he is at work tend-heading on a pull-harvester rig while harvesting grain.

I was born in Fresno, California on May 20th, 1943. I lived the first twenty years of my life in the Riverdale area, which is twenty-five miles south of Fresno. I never lived in any town until 1963 when I was twenty years old and left for the Bay Area. I have never gotten used to living in town. Even after twenty-two years of not living out in the country I still long to wake up in the morning with open fields all around me.

I graduated from Coalinga Junior College in 1963. I majored the first year in Agri-Business and the second year in Liberal Arts. I've never taken an advanced English class in my life. My English out of high school was so poor that I took bonehead English in junior college. I am completely self-taught as a writer, poet, and painter. I've never taken a literature course. I've never studied under anyone. I've never given a reading. I've never attended a workshop. The last time I was up in front of an audience was in my speech

class in junior college. I'm not a public person at all. I make no effort at all in this community to let others know I am involved in the arts. I guard my privacy like a hawk. However, some people in town come over, and we talk, and I give them books to take home and read.

How I got from Riverdale to Big Timber (MT) is a novel in itself. Actually, two of my books in print cover my road years. *Road Ghost Lament,* a short novel and short prose. And *Say Shoshoni Winds,* selected road poems (1967-1978). From the time I was twenty to the time I was thirty-three my life was in constant flux from one place to another.

I've lived on McAlister Street and Turk Street in Frisco. Several places in Marin County. I've lived in Grantsville, Utah. Albuquerque, New Mexico. Oak Hill, Texas. Spokane, Washington. Lake Tahoe. The Crow Indian Reservation and three farming communities in Montana. I've spent the last ten years in Big Timber. Owning a house, buying a printing press, and finding the right lady finally made me hang up my rambling shoes. I might add that I've rambled to the East Coast twice: once to New York City, and once to the World's Fair in Montreal, Quebec. I came back through Canada and dropped into the States at Minnesota.

After the road years I tried to get a handle on all that I had created in the thirteen years that had passed at that time. All of my ten novels needed major work, and still do. I still have high hopes of getting my complete work organized into the final stages of book form. It's very difficult to keep track of my writing because of my productivity. I might not write a poem for a couple of months and then turn out thirty in six days as I did recently.

But why all this early drifting, this rootless prodigal son wandering? How do I categorize that restless spirit after my boot heels have cooled? Well, I had a very strong urge to experience life firsthand. Perhaps I had a streak of Jack London in me, but there were no gold fields left in Alaska, no money to make Gauguin's island, the best I could hope for was to go with the natives like Melville. I just read *Typee* this winter, and never heard of Jack Kerouac when I was rambling. It was just some free spirit in me that led me to the Crow Reservation and to dancing in the Sundance in 1973.

The writing of poetry fit better my gypsy lifestyle. I quit writing prose during my early road years and drew my inspiration from the different places I visited. At times I would be in the wilderness, pitch a tent for a day or two. Sometimes I would winter in Texas. Spend a month in Albuquerque. Head for the farm for a while. End up in Frisco. Then Spokane. Make it back to the reservation. And start the cycle over.

SIPAPU: Like many another small-press publisher, you're shelling out your own money to keep Seven Buffaloes Press and its various publications going. (No evidence, there, of grants and benefactors!) How do you survive, day by day? Driving a gravel truck? Any family, and how do they take it?

CUELHO: It's true that I've financed the individual author books, the anthology series, and the periodicals. But I've never lost money on anything I've ever published. On the other hand, I've never given up on any selection either. Linda Hasselstrom of now defunct Lame Johnny Press once asked me if I had any *flops*. No, I haven't. It'll take ten to fifteen years to sell out some of the selections, though. I know better now, how to select titles for print. I stick to a series or author that has strong sales potential and who is willing to hustle his or her book. Except for the brand-new newsletter *The Bread and Butter Chronicles* (Rural American archives) everything is pulling its own weight. *The Azorean Express* is now breaking even after only six months in existence. The reason: past supporters get behind any new publication I launch.

Recently I started a review campaign to circulate early reviews of *Black Jack* and *Valley Grapevine* issues, which are actually anthologies. Both *V.G.* and *B.J.* were literary magazines in name only. The reason for this was the CCLM grants that I received, were for magazines, but they didn't care what kind of format you had. I was never literary-magazine oriented. I wanted hefty volumes to stand the test of time as any good book or work of art must. This is why I had the purist stance of not letting any book reviews, interviews, ads, columns, or advertisements of any kind between the covers of any of my

anthologies where the pages are solely dedicated to poems and stories, art work and photographs. No essays. Essays and lofty criticism have always signified highbrowism for me. They belonged to the realm of scholars and philosophers. One of the things that always pissed me off was Plato: not having any place for poets in his perfect *Republic.* It inspired these lines in my satirical longpoem *Black Garden Follies:* "And Plato, don't forget / through your perfections / I spit. No welcome signs for poets / in your ideal state, / but there's poetry / on every palace gate."

I've never been satisfied with the small press maxim that if you broke even you were some kind of success. You are only a success as a publisher, or at any other occupation in life, if you make a good living for yourself and your family. I've had to work harder at it than most for two reasons: one, nobody else has a rural or working people press: so I can't swap literary ground gained by others in my field. Two, at times my press was the only employment I could find here in Sweetgrass County. There is no industry and very little farming here. Mostly ranching, and most of the land is marginal, except for the creek and river watershed areas. The rest of the topsoil in the county is shallow and full of shale rock. This county has a primitive road system, compared to what I was used to in California. We have 450 miles of gravel shale roads. Just twenty-two miles of paved. Once I had been here awhile, I worked out as a laborer for people who had become my friends, such as the Osens, a carpenter family. And Dale Arlian, who has an excavating business. My reputation as a hard worker is what got me hired for the excavating job. The job came to me. I didn't even have a job application filled out for the county. I thought I was safe in my garage studio. But some must be envious of my freedom because I was sucked out of here as if art was a wild fart in a hurricane.

Although I don't have a benefactor, I now have one friend who is something of a patron. For instance: the last three months he has donated four or five hundred dollars to my distribution and stamp fund. He has instructed me to leave him anonymous, which is hard for me to do, because I like to give credit where it is due. Jim Wayne Miller sent me $50.00 worth of first class stamps today. Stamps are the backbone of my operation because everything is sold by mail and I can easily go through $100 worth of stamps in two or three weeks. One recent book order was taken by Pat Salyer of Kingsport, Tennessee. She took twenty dollars of the money she had budgeted for groceries to buy books. When truth gains importance over what you put in your belly, the highest form of compliment has been paid.

Yes, for the last year and a half I've driven a gravel truck and helped to build and repair the county's bridges. Before that I worked for two years for Ullman Lumber and Hardware store as a clerk and as a driver of their lumber truck. As far as the family goes in one way or another they have helped put the books together. Before Cindy was married she glued the finebound books. Now Vera has taken over that job. My wife Mae helps me with the collating and also develops the printing plates. She still writes occasionally of her Okie past in the valley.

The last thing a poet thinks of is money. When I began to publish the financial end of it loomed like a bear claw over my soul. Actually, it wasn't my family or the job that robbed me of precious time for my own creative endeavors. It was the press. It takes up so much time my art has been sidetracked for the last eight years. But a press has a positive side. You are in control of your own literary destiny. You can make more connections as a publisher than you can as a writer. So my press over the years has secured a readership for my books. Also the press is a potential means of quitting my job. I have a fear of routine employment as some people have a fear of snakes. It sidetracks my visions. It gives my spirit a perpetual bowel movement. Also when you are raised on your own expanse of land you have an independence that you try to regain if you are forced to work for others. I still don't mind working for my friends, but the lumber yard job and the county job often put petty demands on you. It can sour you as a writer if you lose your love and respect for the common people. I suppose I feel like Faulkner when he quit the post office. He wasn't going to be at the beck and call of everybody who wanted a one-cent stamp. That's not saying the county job is completely negative. I've written some road work poetry. One of the poems had to do with the building of a road from start to finish.

SIPAPU: How did you get on this trip? Who were your mentors and/or inspirers? How, in short, did the idea of publishing a rural workers' periodical come to you?

CUELHO: Actually my involvement as a publisher started out very modestly. More than anything else it came as a result of my friendship with Roxy Gordon. I first met Roxy when I was working on a Hysham, Montana farm almost twenty years ago. Roxy had access to a printing press at a very young age. He made his living doing magazine and book layout and design at Cold Type. We had both lived on Indian reservations so we decided to do a *Reservation* issue. Roxy, and his artist-poet wife Judy, had lived on the Assiniboine Reservation to the north of me. They had already published some of my early Indian poems in the *Vista* newsletter that was produced on a mimeograph. The first issue of *Black Jack* was only two 8½ × 11 sheets of paper and was released in 1973. It sold for only a dime and we gave most of

them away in bars and to friends. The second issue was a chapbook on the oldest living Crow Indian, Robert Summers Yellowtail, Sr. It was a historical story on Yellowtail's debate with Senator Walsh* on whether Congress was going to open up the Crow Indian Reservation to white settlement and liquidate the existence of the reservation altogether. These two issues were co-edited by Roxy Gordon. Roxy also designed my book covers and did text illustrations for me. For two or three years the covers were printed in Texas and shipped to Montana.

By the third issue I was doing *Black Jack* by myself and I changed the format. I began taking poetry and prose from outside the State of Montana. *B.J.* #3 was printed in mimeo by Kell Robertson in the Mission District of Frisco. The 125 copies were mailed from there to Billings, Montana. They never got much circulation and I still have two or three dozen of them. They're actually more in demand now because several libraries want complete sets of *Black Jack*. By the fourth issue I had already gone to an eight-page anthology. I also initiated individual titles, for each issue. Number four's title was *Father Me Home, Winds*. *Black Jack* #5 was the first finebound issue and was called *In the People in the Land*. It was also the first issue in which the San Joaquin Valley poets and writers were featured. In 1977 I only knew two writers besides myself and my younger brother Badger Stone (alias Michael Lynn Cuelho). Gerald Haslam, the Oildale Okie writer who had introduced me to Wilma Elizabeth McDaniel the Okie poet and writer from Tulare, was another. At this time, I had barely scratched the surface of the creative activity taking place in California's heartland. To give you some idea on just how fast I can tap a region's literary wealth once I set my mind to it—one year later I founded *Valley Grapevine* and the first issue had twenty valley contributors. Then in 1973 I published the largest anthology of my publishing career to date. It was issues #2–#3 of *V.G.* called *Proud Harvest*: 160 pages long. I followed it with issue #4, *Home Valley*, which featured five valley short story writers. Then came #5, *99 Vintage*, which featured nine valley poets. Issue #6 was *At the Rainbow's End: A Dustbowl Anthology*.

One important thing should be said about my *Valley Grapevine* anthology

---

*Thomas James Walsh, Democrat, represented Montana in the U.S. Senate from 1913 to 1933. He died on the way to President Franklin D. Roosevelt's first inauguration. (Biographical Dictionary of the U.S. Congress)

series, first in Central California: it was supported strongly by libraries, but I got only random coverage from the media. Ron Mahoney, head of Special Collections, at CSU Fresno, still buys everything that comes off my press. Camille Gavin of *The Bakersfield Californian* reviewed almost all the valley books I released. She also did a little piece on myself and my press. Morgan Hewitt of San Joaquin Delta College at Stockton wrote an article about Seven Buffaloes Press too: "Lone publisher keeps valley literature alive." I can't stress enough that my valley connection to poets and writers is a result of my friendship with Gerald Haslam who teaches at Sonoma State. Gerry has a pet project called *Okie Archives.* I published a collection of his valley Okie and Southwest stories in *Hawk Flights: Visions of the West.*

Much of what I've published has not been done according to any master plan or any kind of vision that I had. My compulsiveness is fortunate because when you let practical ideas overcome spontaneity, quite often you kill a brainstorm before it has a chance to shower. There has (of course) been some progressive growth through more traditional channels of hustling the media and picking up on any leads that would give my press some exposure. This often comes too late to a lot of small press publishers. Like them I've had periods when I wanted to give up, but working a mundane job has a way of inspiring you to get your press together in a money-making business sense. I've never done commercial printing so my sales come directly from books alone. One thing that helped me to open up regions was the policy I had for *Black Jack.* It was geared for the exploration of various rural and working people in features from *B.J.* #4 on. I focused on three to five separate categories in each issue. Sometimes it would be a region I zeroed in on; or ⅓ of a road novel like *The Song of Joe Raven* by Jack Steele that I featured in *B.J.* #5. I had even coined a term called *The Spotlight* where poets and writers, themes or regions, would be featured. *B.J.* #6 was the American Hobo issue. *B.J.* #8 had the title of *Okie Faces and Irish Eyes,* and featured the Dustbowl and Oklahoma. *B.J.* #9 had the longest title in the history of my press: *One Day a Hawk Came By, and Frightened, My Horse Spoke to Him, Asking.* It featured 33 pages of the prison poet Gary Allen Kizer. It featured five short story writers, Roxy Gordon; John Moore; Steven C. Levi; Ben L. Hiatt; and Warren C. Miller. It was in *Black Jack* #10, *Hard Row to Hoe,* that I made a major policy change. I began to realize that by featuring several regions, themes, and artists, — that my focus was kind of like a splatter-gun. And my sales weren't all that good. So I initiated one entire *Black Jack* issue on one theme: men and women on the job. This single theme started to pay off so I repeated it with *B.J.* #11: *Family Traditions.* But even though the focus was on one theme, I still broke that theme into more than one heading. For instance the special headings breakdown in #11 were: *The Ozarks; Grandfathers; Okies and Oklahoma; The Dakotas;* and *Family Traditions.* But all of these five sections had a single focus on family traditions. It was in this last number that I decided to feature the

Southern Appalachian Mountain Region. I had observed some poems in *The Laurel Review,* edited by Mark Defoe. I wrote to Mark, and he supplied me with a list of a dozen Southern poets. I had planned a twenty-page feature of this, unknown-to-me, literary region. Little did I realize that the Southern Appalachian Mountain region covered a ten-state area from Ohio in the north to Georgia in the Deep South. Each poet whom I contacted gave me further names and addresses: until in no time I had put their work in an entire issue, which became *B.J.* #12: *Step Around the Mountain.*

The fact that I only came out once a year never allowed me to build up a subscription list, as I would have if I'd had a magazine coming out two or three times a year. A year or two before the CCLM grants dried up I had kept *Black Jack* afloat for ten years. In January 1984 I released the last issue of *Black Jack* #13, a ten-year anniversary issue called *Rural Cream.*

So I never, *per se,* decided to start a rural workers' periodical. My roots were rural, my rambling was mostly in the Western States, and my heart was in the country. I featured this kind of literature because I was simply familiar with it.

In an important way the first *Black Jack* issue and the last were linked by my interest in the American Indian. The *Rural Cream* anthology led out with a 22-page feature on the American Indian. The opening story was "The Iliamna Monster" by Steven C. Levi of Anchorage.

The ironic part of my farm roots was that it took 12 years before I featured the American farmer in *From Seedbed to Harvest.* But this is understandable when you consider that I would not have known enough farmer-poets to feature seven geographical regions in the U.S. and western Canada. Over half the poets in *From Seedbed to Harvest* I never knew until I searched them out a few short months before the anthology appeared. The *Seedbed/Harvest* anthology was the first success I had outside *Hill and Holler: Southern Appalachian Mountains Anthology.* One disturbing fact stuck in my craw. Over fifty percent of the farmer-poets did not bother to buy one copy of this one-of-a-kind tribute. This signalled to me that the lack of support in *Black Jack* and *Valley Grapevine* would continue in this new series. But there was something positive in *From Seedbed to Harvest* that took the bad taste out of my mouth from the contributors' not supporting it strongly. One contributor did buy 60 copies. But this was the first anthology that reached a readership ouside of poets and writers. It was read by people on the farms and ranches. This happened because of the numerous positive reviews and also I think because of the media focus on the plight of the family farm. It must be remembered that my literary tribute came one year before Farm-Aid. I'm obviously not Willie Nelson or a famous rock group so my tribute is still very laid-back in national media eyes.

Some poet-and-writer friends of mine who are lamenting the loss of the traditional family farm way of life in Rural America are telling me over and over that what I am doing is important as a record of how things were in the heyday of the family-operated farm. My own self-observation on this is that I may in some way be doing in poetry and story form what Alan Lomax did with folk songs. Research, and my three newsletter-periodicals dedicated to Rural America, means keeping a record. And with my rural review, *Hard Row to Hoe,* I am aware of a continued growth. More and more rural books keep coming in. To some degree I feel that the Rural Writing Movement has always been there, but no one has ever brought all the various sides together as a group. I don't think all the various factions will unite. The Cowboy Poets will be meeting in Elko, for the second year in a row. A Rural Celebration at Marshall University, Marshall, Minnesota, will take place in May of 1986. The feedback that I get back from all this is like a vacuum cleaner of ears and eyes because my friends keep me informed of everything that comes across my desk, that is rural.

SIPAPU: We librarians have some trouble straightening out the varied publications that come out of your Big Timber P.O. box. If you could tell us what periodicals run from—when—to when—and what (if any) is the difference between periodicals named *Hard Row to Hoe* and monographic publications (= single books) bearing the same name? — we'd be grateful. We'd also like to know what to subscribe to, and what to claim, and what to buy as back issues which were launched before we subscribed.

CUELHO: *Black Jack* anthology series ran from issue #1 in 1973 to issue #13 in 1984. *Valley Grapevine* anthology series ran from #1 in 1978 till #6 in 1982. *Hill and Holler: Southern Appalachian Mountains* anthology series has three volumes in print. Ironically, this anthology series, which has no connection to my rural roots here in the West, is the one that is still active, while *Black Jack* and *Valley Grapevine* have gone the way of fossilized dinosaur toes. But there is hope on the horizon. The success of *From Seedbed to Harvest* has triggered *The American Farmer* series of anthologies, and I am currently collecting for the second volume. I've also started a new series called the *Pan Size* series. The size of the books is 4 × 7 inches. I will focus on poems, both long and short, non-fiction, humor, a collection of *Thirteen Classic Nudes* by Badger Stone. My brother Badger is also a poet, writer, artist and publisher. Last autumn he gave me 5000 sheets of 8½ × 14 paper, plus a copy machine. These two donations of his inspired this *Pan Size* series.

Now we come to the three newsletters. *Hard Row to Hoe: Reviews from Rural America* still has 14 issues in print. *The Azorean Express* has two issues in print. *The Bread and Butter Chronicles, Rural American Archives,* has one issue in print. I have published four books on Okie and Dustbowl writers and poets. They are not a series, but I think of them as one group and their writing reflects Oklahoma, Texas, and Arkansas roots that were grafted onto their lives in Central California. I am speaking of Gerald Haslam's already mentioned *Hawk Flights* (see *Sipapu*, v. 14, no. 2); Wilma Elizabeth McDaniel's *The Fish Hook,* Dorothy Rose's *Dustbowl: Thorns and Roses,* and *Valley Grapevine #6: At the Rainbow's End: Dustbowl Okie Anthology.*

There were certain transitional moves made from *Black Jack* to *Valley Grapevine* and from *B.J.* to *Hill and Holler* that will confuse the librarian. For instance when I did *Black Jack #7* the title of that issue was *Valley Grapevine.* At that time I did not know I was going to start a series of writings on Central California. But when I eventually did start the *Valley Grapevine* series I took the same *B.J.* #7 issue as the first issue in the *Valley Grapevine* series. The same thing happened with *Black Jack #12: Step Around the Mountain,* the Southern Appalachian issue. It became *Hill and Holler #1.* Sometimes the idiosyncrasies of the Crawdad King are hard to decipher.

The first time I used the name *Hard Row to Hoe* was in *Black Jack #10.* And when I started my rural review of books newsletter I still felt I had not milked all the good out of that title. More than any other title that I have coined (and this is a common American colloquialism) it symbolizes the struggle of my press. It's a grassroots expression out of field labor, the backbone to my rural experience. And I think *Black Jack #10, Hard Row to Hoe,* is a forerunner of *From Seedbed to Harvest.* It was the first anthology to have a theme of men and women on the job. To this day I don't know of an American publisher who has done on-the-job anthologies of working class people. My friend in Canada, Tom Wayman, edited *Going for Coffee,* a working-people anthology of Americans and Canadians, but it focuses on industrial jobs. Peter Christensen has a poetry book called *Rig Talk* that takes in the roughneck labor of the Alberta oilfields.

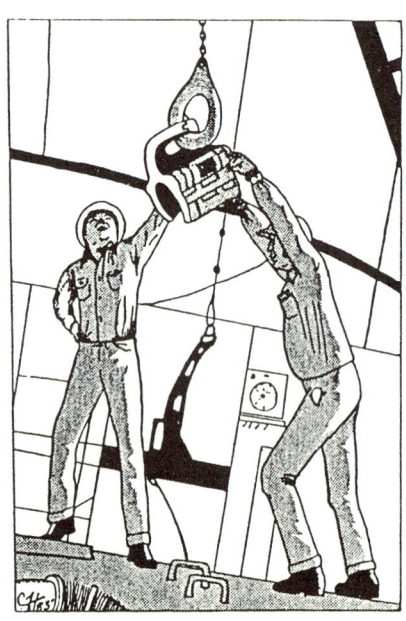

Rig Nine. William Rintoul

My real interest actually resides in the American migrant more than the American farmer. But outside of my connection with the Dustbowl Okies who wrote about stoop labor, short-handled hoes, and labor camp life experiences in the valley, I don't know of any others who tackle the subject of migrant life. My theory is that migrants are uneducated and therefore never reach a stage where they have poets or writers to speak of their plight. One country western singer of Oklahoma, James Talley, has several songs on migrants, coal miners, and even has released one album, *Tryin' Like the Devil,* of songs about the working man. The reason the Dustbowl Okies were so articulate was that they came from educated backgrounds. Their folks owned land in these states they came from. But the views of Rose, Haslam, McDaniel, and the Dustbowl artist Morine A. Stanley differ greatly from that of John Steinbeck. So the real Dustbowl literature did not emerge with *Grapes of Wrath.* It came thirty or forty years later in a new crop of writers and poets whose families had been caught up in the Dirty Thirties. In fact the migrant poems of Wilma Elizabeth McDaniel have still not been collected in one volume. Because of my present financial situation and inadequate distribution system I regret not being able to publish works that remain uncollected and unknown.

SIPAPU: Source of your contributors: their origin and ultimate literary destiny.

CUELHO: One thing that surprises new contributors who send me work is my informality. I am connected to friends in two ways: by a common rural background and by art. I tend not to have literary relationships based on business. In fact relationships that don't have some kind of personal touch beyond that of mere publishing—I drift away from such people. That's why my load of correspondence is so demanding. But the bottom line is that if you can't give of yourself then don't expect to receive much.

Fate was kind enough to deal me a younger brother with the same interests and talents as mine. Badger became fascinated by writing in his senior year in high school. It was his enthusiasm for literature that aroused my own curiosity about books. I started a daily journal in junior college. At twenty I was already writing short stories and I knew I wanted to be a novelist. As early as 21 after reading *Naked Came I,* the biography of Rodin, I knew I wanted to be an artist.

The first poet I met was Bob Goldtrap of Norman, Oklahoma. Bob lived in the Russian Hill district of Frisco. He once threw 200 of his early poems into the Mississippi River on the advice of another poet. I wrote a long poem to Goldtrap in my long-poem chapbook *A Caged Bird in Spring.* The title of this chapbook came directly from Van Gogh's letter to his brother Theo. In this same collection is a poem about Vincent that covers his life at the Borinage mining district where he decided to become a painter. What Van Gogh did with peasant life inspired me a great deal. I had the same kind of feel for it because of my rural background. Although I have not covered it so far, by what I have said one would get the impression that I'm a totally rural artist. That's not true: I've written satire like *Death's Legacy*. A lot of my canvasses come purely from my imagination. I suppose if one was to view my work on a percentage basis, about eight-five percent would be rural. I am speaking of the past 22 years: my future work will be almost all rural.

One of my other early friendships was with the farmgirl Patricia Elliott from Saskatoon, Saskatchewan. I doubt if there's any poet that I ever admired more. It was one of the major milestones in my life to publish her first book nine years after her death. With Bob Warden's help I finally got her between covers, *Here's to High Heels* (see *Small Press Review,* April, 1986; P.O. Box 100, Paradise, CA 95969).

I met Dave Carson in Billings. He was out of Oklahoma City and part Choctaw like Roxy. I rode a Greyhound once for 1000 miles to see him in Iowa City, Iowa. Laurel Speer, a pet friend of mine who was raised in L.A., but who now lives in Tucson was one of my early supporters. She reviewed a lot of my books in *Small Press Review:* "Art Cuelho: Aspects of the American West." I published one of Laurel's books: *Hokum: Visions of a Gringa*. But the first person to feature my poetry was Ben L. Hiatt of *Grande Ronde Review*. — One of my strongest friendships has been with the Lodi Lebanese writer Richard Dokey. I've published three of his books. The first was a valley novel called *Two Beer Sun*. I've published two of his short story collections which are still in print, and which focus on the farm and small town life. The first was *Birthright;* then came *Sundown*. One of the things that has strengthened my friendship with Dick is that he and his brother Jack and son Todd have come to Big Timber for the last five years to fish the Boulder River.

Gary Elder of Holmganger's Press just happened to be doing two first books of myself, and the poet and short-story writer of Fromberg, Montana, — Dean Phelps. I found out through Elder that Dean lived up the street from me, just three blocks, when I lived in Billings. He's the only writer in Montana whom I visit with. It's good to have a fellow artist just 81 miles down the road. Dean and I have been on many good drunks together. I have to tell you about one night when we got a little carried away. We'd got home when the bars closed and as it was our usual habit to talk and drink a couple more hours in my upstairs studio on Burnstead Drive. When Dean decided to stagger home I went out in the yard with him to say goodbye. We must have been so happy that we were singing at the moon. But what told the story the next day was the footsteps in the snow. There was this almost perfect tramped-down circle around this one tree where we had followed each other round and round, — shouting into the night. Those drunks were such a part of our ritual that I wrote a poem about it, called "Dean's Promised Land (Empty Beer Bottles and Crushed Cigarettes)". Phelps co-edited *Black Jack* #4.

Of course when I started *Valley Grapevine* a flood of personal friendships came out of that series. DeWayne Rail who teaches at Fresno City College adopted *Proud Harvest* into a literature course there. Jennifer Lagier, poet and librarian from Manteca has spread my flyers over several valley colleges and handed them out at poetry readings. Others from California who have supported me strongly include: the farmer Frank Cross of Chowchilla; Kenneth Funsten, reviewer for the L.A. *Times;* Billie Hensen; Doug Jensen; Margaret Kerbrat; Mary K. Mazotti; Faith Petric; Chuck Roner; Mary Moran; James X. Sawyer; and Martha Winnacher.

Some of my longtime supporters in the Southern Appalachians have been bookseller George Brosi; Garry Barker; John M. Clark; Wilma Horsley; Alice J. Kinder of Pikeville — she was the first person ever to do my literary and personal life story in a two-part article: "Art Cuelho Preserves Farm Heritage"; Thelma Scott Kizer; Parks Lanier; Louise Logan; William Paulk, and Patricia Shirley. I will be releasing an Appalachian book of poetry by Shirley on May 10th, 1986, called: *Pearl.*

Those supporters whom I have scattered across rural America are James A. Able, Jr., who has a column in *Hard Row to Hoe;* Brother Benet; Cathy Czapla; Lawrence Clayton; Lorraine S. DeGennaro; Walt Franklin; Willard Gellis; Sister Mary Ann Henn; Dennis Johnson; Glen McGuire; Kendell McCook, who has a column in *The Bread and Butter Chronicles;* Marion M. Poe; Ed Rielly; Bethany Schroeder, and Richard D. Woollatt.

My father has helped me through more than one financial crisis and at key times helped me out: as when I bought this new Olympia Startype typewriter.

SIPAPU: You cover distant regions, including the Appalachians. Yet your base is still in the West. What future do you see in becoming truly national, as we wish you might become?

CUELHO: Since my press has a focus on rural America it's understandable that my support is scattered across the fifty states. I've never had an ultimate goal of money profits. My ultimate goal of publishing is one, to make a living, and two, reach a point where I don't have to spend all my time trying to make money. Because the more business you have the less time you have to be an artist. I'm looking for a happy medium: a point in time when about half my time goes into my press, the other time devoted to my writing and painting. Of course, idealism is like junk food: it is only healthy in abstract form.

There is one very promising note about my press books: they don't find audiences just in hidden corners of rural America. The New York Public Library buys everything I publish. I've even gotten support from several European countries: Herbert Lang et Cie., AG., of Switzerland has bought several titles from me. A recent bookseller in Ireland bought every title in my 1985 catalog. The Soviet publisher Raduga (Moscow) asked permission to reprint two of William Rintoul's oilfield stories from *Roustabout,* in an anthology called *I Believe in Humanity.* Another of Rintoul's oilfield collections is *Rig Nine,* which I published.

It's only natural that if you have an anthology series in Central California or the Appalachians that you will generate support from those regions. However, one person in a certain city, with special clout, Jeff Shelley of Seattle told me last week that he was going to try to open up his city to Seven Buffaloes. Patricia Shirley works the Knoxville, Tennessee area. Gerald Haslam writes essays, attends western writing conferences and takes my catalogs and flyers to pass them around. Kendall McCook is promoting me in Dallas. Jim Wayne Miller gives workshops in his ten-state region and as far west as California. So the momentum from those who offer me support has penetrated many places in America. Such sales for my press are not a mere drop in the bucket for me because I am only one person with a family and have no one hired to do all the printing tasks. The nature of my true supporters is that they don't just buy one or two titles. They support the newsletter series and almost any project I start. With this in mind I don't think I have a whole lot farther to go before I have all that I can handle by myself.

I'm now working on the all-Alaska issue of *Hard Row to Hoe;* this will deal with Alaska's literary magazines and publishers. If I can make a connection with Hawaii that will open up new sales territory. The next step: contacting magazines and presses in foreign countries to see if there is any rural literature activity going on overseas.

I feel I have the knowledge to establish my press on a full-time basis. But as long as I hold my county job I don't have the necessary time to initiate my research, which is the backbone of my future publication. One of my major obstacles in the past was the release of too many titles with not enough depth in their distribution. I don't get many overlap sales: from one book or one author, to another. As a result, I have to devise a distribution plan for each book. I just released a book a month over the past four months. If I were to sit down and bind all those books, I wouldn't have any time to work on distribution. I've got some titles several years old without the covers on them yet. Because I have a one-man press there is no way I can launch a successful distribution beachhead and publish books—and work a job, too.

In practical terms I'm caught between the past and the future. The past is all those anthology series that I have yet to sell, plus all those individual author titles. I have to allow so much time to work on them. But I also can't forget about future books, because I've learned what and who will sell, and I'm concentrate on new books to create a cash flow. Because of the nature of book reviews you don't gain a whole lot of exposure at a time. Richard Dokey's *Sun-

down* review in the San Francisco *Chronicle* resulted in about 50 book orders, but the buyers bought only that book. Hardly any of them bought *Birthright*. Well, it's a slow meticulous process, this milking of the media. And that's why my press is just now coming out of the Dark Ages. I never catered to reviews in the past. I never even had stamps to send out review copies. Now I have so many review sources I have to choose which ones to send to. You see, I have more ideas on how to sell books than I have time to implement them. I have about fifteen different fronts I'm working on with my distribution and I give one a squirt of my time, the other a spurt of my energy and eventually it all comes together—the helter-skelter follies of Seven Buffaloes. It's a literary juggling act!

SIPAPU: Your criteria for inclusion in your mags/publications? Surely not everything that's rural is OK. You're not doing a literary version of *Countryside*, for example.

CUELHO: I don't have preconceived guidelines, but I do make judgments on rural work sent to me. When I collected *From Seedbed to Harvest* my spotlight was on labor in the fields, the cycle of the workday, and the rhythms of the seasons that go with plowing, planting, irrigation, cultivating, and finally harvesting. Well, there were dozens of people who had experience with gardening out behind their houses so they tried to pass themselves off as tillers of the soil. I had lots of bee and goat farmers. One well-known lady poet of New York City who had moved out West to join a literary community sent me a poem about a farmwife's struggle and then whipped the "F" word on me for not taking her self-styled brilliant work. The work itself wasn't all that bad, but the problem was, I already had taken a similar and better poem. The point here is: this lady poet had only the one poem to offer. If she had been a real rural poet as she was claiming she was, she would have sent me five to ten poems as most of the other contributors did. Sometimes contributors admit that their rural connection is not as a farmer, but if I'm impressed with their work and if it fits my theme, I accept it on its own merit.

But my standards are traditional insofar as I don't like maudlin poetry, but I like poems with honest nostalgia and straight-arrow sentiment. Some of the work I take is from common folk who don't have much literary or educational experience as writers. But there is something very genuine about their work, even though it might be raw or undisciplined at times. By way of contrast: a professional writer may have a better grip on an individual style, but he has taken all the juice out of the narrative and made it tame. There is balance to everything: I paint often with arbitrary colors, but it still has to make harmony to my naked eye. And if you can explain everything about your art, everything you make sound judgments on, then you have passed over into the realm of a philosopher, and are no longer a working artist. Spare me that day, Vincent!

I'm not all that hot on rhymed poetry either. And yet I'm a blues harmonica player and write songs that rhyme. About the only sure thing you can say about me is that I'm unpredictable in my likes and dislikes. I also make different quality decisions if the work is going into an anthology as opposed to a literary newsletter like *The Azorean Express*. The anthologies are more to showcase *Rural Cream*. The poems and stories in them have earned the right to a wider audience. That's why I've never been partial to the magazine format of *here today, gone tomorrow*. You mention *Countryside:* I must lead a sheltered life: I've never heard of them! This is not unusual because I have very little time to read; I've been a maverick all my life. I tend to attract writers, poets, and artists who fight battles on their own. I've only joined one organization: CCLM: (Coordinating Council of Literary Magazines), and I cringe every time I get one of their ballot sheets to vote for the members of the next Board. *I* don't know the Board members! What can literary organizations do for the only rural press in North America? One of the reasons I never got any small press grants from the NEA was, you had to declare yourself non-profit and in order to do this, — you had to pay three hundred dollars. I never had that kind of money in my poor poet-bum days. But CCLM kept *Black Jack* in existence for several years. I can't thank them enough.

It's not all that easy to explain how I make my critical judgments because they are mostly subjective. But being a poet, writer, and artist gives me more insight than if I were just an editor. I don't have much respect for non-creative critics. They always seem to send down proclamations from their ivory towers. They're afraid to take risks, spill the blood, fling the wild juices. They merely comment on the volcanic hot fires of creation after they have cooled. You want to be an important literary figure? Go out in the American Letters Swamp and wrestle with live alligators who haven't made a fresh kill lately.

I don't even like it when people address me as "Mr." I always just tell them to call me by my first name. I put it in a poem once, "A Drifter's Brand":

My name could be Utah,
Rainy Hunger, Lost Train;
my initials might be found
on a Great Northern boxcar.
You can just call me Art.

I don't want to be approached as some kind of wise old literary type. I've been in the lowest skid row bars and I've tried to understand tramps, migrants, the lost and the lonely; and sometimes it's how a poem or story comes across as a human experience, rather than being just well-crafted that impresses me. After all, I have to live up to this line of mine: "If I die without mercy, put my tombstone under the ground."

Where a lot of would-be contributors go haywire is in assuming that every editor West of the Mississippi can be impressed by a long list of their previous publication credits. They get off on the wrong foot with me as soon as I see those massive-attack three-page single-space vita sheets that list everything under the sun, including the fact that they talked to God personally last Tuesday on the telephone. I'm just as quick to take work from a complete unknown as someone with a name. I'm into literature and not in being stroked. I've learned long ago as a publisher that about 96 percent of the people you publish will never buy a single sample copy of your publication.

SIPAPU: Your future: where is the Seven Buffaloes stable of publications going from here?

CUELHO: I will probably be releasing more hardbacks. Jim Wayne Miller's poetry book *Nostalgia for 70* was my first hardback. *Vein of Words* by Miller will be released in hardback when I do the second printing. This selection is tailor-made for classroom adoption, in a course on how to write poetry. One section of its covers the poetry workshop experience. One of Jim's poems, from this collection, was included in "Pieces of a Puzzle," a 28-minute film produced as part of the Annenberg Project (on writing and rewriting) and distributed by Encyclopaedia Britannica Films, Inc.

I think the *American Farmer* series of poetry and prose will have enough success to allow me to bring out a new volume every year and a half.

One positive thing is that I don't see myself making the same mistakes as I made in the past. It's fine to come up with brainstorms, but you better have practical business visons to sell them to the public. I've never compromised my art or the work of others that I publish, but sometimes it is one's random methods or habits that slow one down. You have to have some kind of introspective feedback. Self-reflection perhaps is the key to how I will transform ideas in the future. One of the plans I'm working on right now is to have every book in my catalog reviewed. Then to circulate these reviews to libraries, bookstores, and individuals. You damn near have to treat books as you do children: give them a lot of individual attention. Anyone who says a book will sell itself is talking through his hat. It is quite often not the quality of the work that makes a best-seller. Or why would all the best-seller crap be on every news rack? They promote pulp writing in best-sellers. It's a media hype. The best a private press book publisher like myself can hope for is for books to sell steadily. I can't have a best-seller because I don't have money for advertising to create one. I accept literature for publication because of the beauty and truth of it. Commercial presses publish books because of the dollar investment. Same company selling shoe polish is also selling literature. New York City is not the seedbed for contemporary books. These past giants have grown self-serving. They've been incestuous with the money gods. I saw the writing on the wall years ago. Poets and writers would have to take the literary bull by the horns or be left in the dust. Can any one of us with visions afford just to twiddle our thumbs? My old visionary crawdad put it this way: "The desert wind holds all the high cards, but don't ever try to deny the joker in the quicksand."

SIPAPU: Montana! How did you get there, why do you stay there, and what does it do for you? Do you identify youself as a Montanan?

CUELHO: I like it better than my native valley because there isn't the rampant use of insecticides from crop dusters. The air in Sweetgrass County is clean. The Sierras were that way in the 1950s when I grew up. Now you rarely see the mountains for the red haze of smog.

There is no crime here either. In Fresno they have the largest concentration of Boat People. Someone is murdered there almost every night. Here we never lock our doors. The carpenters leave their tools on the ground at their job site. All the cops have to do here is chase the teenagers around for drinking beer and helping the town drunk out of the barpit.

I like the isolation of living out on the middle of the prairies. There are only 3700 people in this county about forty miles square. I like the location of the town, situated between the Boulder River and the Yellowstone River, which is the last undammed river in America. I like the elk in the Crazy Mountains, the antelope nestled down in the coulees, the coyotes out in the clear cold snowy horizon that looks as remote at times as the North Pole. I like the deer coming into town in the winter. I like the farmer and rancher friends I've made. Their land I can hunt and fish on. Their cottonwoods I clear out of their pastures for firewood. I like putting up 12 to 15 cords of wood each year. I like my children being raised in an area that still has a rural pace.

I don't identify myself as a typical Montanan; I never see myself as part of the mainstream or herd. I sided early with the plight of the American Indian. I always seem to be attracted to the underdog. White people here cannot understand why I sought a vision quest in the Sundance.

SIPAPU: Ethnic origins: is it easier being of Portuguese descent in Montana than in California's Great Central Valley? On what ethnic/geographic basis do you welcome contributors?

Home Valley. Art Cuelho, editor.

CUELHO: It was never a hardship being Portuguese in my hometown. Riverdale was dominated by Azorean farmers and dairymen. The connection of Azorean towns with valley towns like Tulare is common. They call them sister cities. Every summer the Soupas Festas are held in the various valley towns and native food is donated and cooked and there is a dance held and what I remember is the old Azorean country dances that the band played. They shout out the dance commands in Portuguese. I'd be out there stumbling around trying to follow by eye what my ear didn't understand. They always played the Azorean National Anthem too. These celebrations were not just for the Portuguese people. The entire community of Riverdale was invited.

My mother said that some people called them names where she grew up in the Lemoore area. My father said that he was never discriminated against in the Lanare area where he was raised. My Grandma Laureano hated the word *Portagee* and thought of it as a degrading word. Like the word *Okie* it finally became accepted and the old hateful meaning mostly died out of it. There always seem to be a few diehards for whom a *label* remains a *staple*.

I only knew of one Portuguese family in Montana. My father went to visit them in Fromberg this past summer. The man of the house had been a resident of Flores Island. So Azoreans always seek each other out.

I don't really welcome contributors on an ethnic basis because there's little that's Portuguese in American letters. I do seek every lead that's literary and Portuguese, whether it comes from Brazil, the Azores, or the mainland of Portugal. I still feel a bit cut off from the Azores and from Portugal because I don't correspond with contemporary poets and writers from my homeland. I will be making some attempt in 1986 to seek out some of these artists. The problem may be one of a language barrier since they do not write in English or speak it very well. I do have a complete set of Portuguese language records and will eventually learn the language before I visit the Azores.

The librarian and whaling historian, João Afonso, of Angra do Heroismo, Terceira Island, the Azores, ran across my farm poetry book *Evening Comes Slow to a Fieldhand,* in the E.P.E.C. Portuguese library in San Leandro, California. João reprinted my poem "Grandma Laureano" as a one-poem booklet. This poem and several others were translated into Portuguese and reprinted in three Azores newspapers. João Afonso had also introduced my work to a poet in Lisbon who was supposed to give me some literary mileage in Portugal, but he and his wife died in a car wreck and that ended my potential link to the Portuguese mainland. In today's mail the poet Teresina Pereira informed me that she was going to use my poems in her lectures in Brazil this summer, on American poetry.

Italian people married into our family and there was a community of Italians in Riverdale. My closest rural family in Big Timber, the Arlians, are Italians. Several contributor friends of mine have old ties to Italy. I seem to be linked to Italians more than to any other nationality, except Portuguese.

As far as geography goes I don't prefer one region over another. In fact I wish I was more familiar with most of them.

SIPAPU: Origin of your logo and of the name of your press? Your connection with Native Americans?

CUELHO: Marjorie Yellowtail, my Indian mother, gave me my adopted Crow name of Seven Buffaloes. We were driving towards Hardin to attend an Indian wedding. The ritual ceremony of singing four songs took place in the front seat of the station wagon. While Marjorie prayed she mentioned the Big Dipper and its seven stars and I felt pretty important to have a name that came out of the cosmos. By the way, she was using the dashboard for a drum and taking snorts of straight vodka out of a fifth bottle. I once took Marjorie to Great Falls with me and we liked to have never got there. She was familiar with certain kinds of herbs that grow in different areas and she was forever having me pull to the side of the road to check out the plant life there for possible personal use.

In the new *Pan Size* series of books I make reference to CRAWDAD KING PRODUCTIONS, which legally has nothing to do with my business.

But I whipped it in for my own personal status because I once caught 1500 crawdads in the slough out on the Wheatville farm and Larry Cassina (another Italian) and my closest friend in town called me THE CRAWDAD KING OF THE SAN JOAQUIN.

(Editor's note: Photograph and illustrations courtesy Art Cuelho. The illustrations are (obviously) from Seven Buffaloes Press books; among the illustrators, Roxy Gordon and Ada Morine Stanley should be mentioned. It wasn't always possible to match the right illustration with the right paragraph; for this the editor takes the blame. It rarely works out in any home-grown periodical. Footnotes supplied by the editor.)

LIBRARIES AND THE LIFE OF THE MIND: Such was the theme of the 87th Annual Conference of the California Library Association, Oakland, 15-20 November 1985. We weren't able to get to more than a few of the meetings, since it was our turn to "mind the store," but readers can judge for themselves how much mind was alive there.

"Librarians: an endangered species?" was to our ears one of the pseudo-questions the profession sets itself (others: "the paperless society" and "what about our image?"). However, the California State College Librarians' Chapter's program concerned the diminishing recruitment of librarians as an indicator of the public's diminishing need of them. Roger C. Greer, dean of the library school at the University of Southern California, described the decision to close that school on its fiftieth anniversary, as being based on declining job opportunities and declining enrollment. The school had become a drain on USC's resources instead of an asset, and a new Institute of Communication and Information Sciences was to be opened in Carlsbad, California. He asserted that library schools close because they aren't seen as academic or important; while the public doesn't value librarians because our science, technology, or "art" is not visible or understood. He wanted psychology and sociology to come to our aid. How is information transferred in society? How do individuals, groups, and organizations seek, process, and use information? How should information and communication organizations be designed and managed to deliver optimum services to a client population? How should a data base be designed? Such were his questions, over which he brooded; and we brooded silently over the fact that overquestioning breeds overkill; that what students want is help with a teacher's Mickey Mouse assignment, what young women want is another romance — ¼ of all books bought in the USA last year were of that genre; and what the old-timers want is information about somebody who arrived here from Sweden in 1848, because that pioneer immigrant was their great-great-grandfather. Librarians can get pretty theoretical, and so remote from reality, sometimes.

Marilyn Oberg, CSU/Hayward, took a feminist perspective, emphasizing the changes in libraries and library clientele in Reagan's America. Pessimistic over the future of libraries, she saw them as losing out to the private sector, with a resultant loss of librarians' control over their lives, jobs, and libraries. She urged a line of most resistance: the re-creation of ourselves as librarians, moving away from the semi-profession of the assistant or auxiliary. (Brooding again, we deemed it just as well that we are not too highly regarded. If we were on call twenty-four hours a day, like rural family doctors, or paid a hundred dollars an hour, like corporation lawyers, we wouldn't have the time or energy to produce this charming and indispensable newsletter.)

We moved thoughtfully away from this exercise in futurology to an Intellectual Freedom Committee and Government Relations Committee program on "Libraries and the First Amendment." Several bills to control pornography, in particular that which exploits children, have been introduced in the California Legislature, and Morris Polan (CSU/Los Angeles) had selected three speakers (not the ones mentioned in the program) to discuss two sides of the question. Jody Bush (Berkeley PL) gave a review of the history of porn, discussed the *Roth* decision (work is obscene if it violates community standards). Assembly Bill 365, then pending in the California Legislature, represents a shift to a Miller-type view as embodied in law, although she stated that libraries would be little affected.

Bernard Walter, Assistant District Attorney of San Francisco, gave a very forthright speech. He specializes in the prosecution of sex crimes, and opposes the American Civil Liberties Union position on pornography, since its purism and libertarianism ignore findings that porn is addictive and an individual's consumption of it escalates. For Walter, unbridled expression leads to anarchy, and he pointed out that there are three times as many porn shops in this country as there are McDonalds. (We avoid them *all.*) Like any other advertising, porn is effective over the long run, and its message is that women are dispensable and enjoy being victimized. What we are talking about is an $8-billion industry, which under *Roth* cannot be controlled. Asking that the California Library Association shift its traditional ground, he pointed out that the California law on obscenity is unique in the degree of obsolescence, compared with other states and Federal law.

Ellen Swartz of the ACLU chose to discuss porn involving adults only, and described the harassment prosecutions in Atlanta. She argued that the problem with *Miller* is that it forces a case-by-case examination of each title in each community.

At the end of the session a straw vote was taken: should CLA support a *Miller*-type law in California, or stay with its traditional hands-off freedom-of-the-press position? Support a *Miller*-type law: 40%; stay with traditional position, 60%.

We eventually drifted over to the program put on by the Librarians for Nuclear Arms Control. LNAC (we're going to call it "EL-nack") was discussing "The nuclear weapons dilemma: the role of librarians and the library profession," and apparently there was a statement or resolution at the beginning, that "librarians must take an active role in providing information and programs on the dangers and effects of nuclear war and nuclear proliferation" (we're quoting from the CLA official program, p. 57). We came in late, in time to hear the Reverend William Rankin, of St. Stephen's (Episcopal), Belvedere, urge librarians to humanize their jobs and take stands. He was a good speaker (it's a calling that calls for good speakers) and we were sorry not to have heard more of him. Lowell Smith, mayor of St. Helena, told us as a public official that public opinion on such matters is changing—there is a lot more local interest in international issues. St. Helena is a nuclear-free zone. Judith Sessions, of the Freedom to Read Foundation, who works at CSU/Chico, took a conservative point of view, stating that librarians might sign any petition or take any position when off work—she says she does a lot of that; but on the job they must commit themselves to the ALA position, as exemplified in the Library Bill of Rights: a balanced diversity of *all* points of view. She indicated the danger of radical librarians being *labelled* as radical librarians—eventually, to include *all* librarians.—Ernest Siegel, of Contra Costa PL (Pleasant Hill), took the liberal point of view, detailing his experiences at Contra Costa with a booklist on nuclear war and nuclear proliferation, which was well received with only a few protests; and with the use of library meeting rooms for anti-nuclear activists. His message seemed to be that the public is basically sympathetic to his way of thinking.

The above-described resolution was then submitted to a vote: and passed (though not unanimously). Victoria Kline announced that LNAC is now tax-exempt under 501(c)(3). Plans were laid for publicity and posters, and the suggestion of having a bookmobile on the Pro Peace March was mooted. (The following address was given us as a center for the organization of Pro Peace: 8150 Beverly Boulevard, Suite 203, Los Angeles, CA 90048, phone [213] 653-6245.)

CEREMONIES FOR BOB KAUFMAN: A.D. Winans wrote us a celebration of this Afro-Jewish American poet in our v. 13, no. 2, consecutive issue no. 26. Now comes his elegy:

It's January twelfth, 1986 [writes A.D. Winans]; I'm celebrating my fiftieth birthday, walking down Grant Avenue, in San Francisco's North Beach, when "Shig" stops me to say that fellow-poet Bob Kaufman is dead, three months short of 60, of emphysema.

My first reaction is shock: then rage. Again the heavy breath of death has blown past my increasingly vulnerable shoulders.

I find myself walking from bar to bar, informing first one, then another, of Bob's old friends. The reaction is mostly stunned silence, followed by "shit!" or "damn!" Truth is, that death is a silencer of conversations. At the Columbus Cafe I recall the words from an old Dylan song, "Everything went from bad to worse," which seem a fitting tribute to a fallen poet: "I was just too stubborn to be / governed by enforced insanity / Someone had to reach for the rising star / I guess it was up to me."

Bob Kaufman, "Beat" poet, a legend among North Beach poets and street people, was gone: along with the rage he expressed so well, — taunting his peers and the police alike, from the days of the Co-Existence Bagel Shop to our bleaker mid-Eighties. He will be duly recorded by literary historians as author of his last book of poems, *The Ancient Rain: Poems 1956-1978* (New Directions, 1981), but his *Abomunist Manifesto,* a folded broadside published by San Francisco's City Lights in 1959, was perhaps his most scathing attack against the conventional Establishment types whose descendants are today's "yuppies."

Someone said that Kaufman's ultimate ambition was to be completely forgotten, and for many in the Reagan era (and afterwords), he has already achieved this ambition: while his contemporaries age, librarians will collect and store his vision. But those who truly knew and respected him, will remember his work and pass this knowledge on. Even so, Kaufman was better known in France, where he was received as the Black American Rimbaud; in America he was simply "the original be-bop man," and in North Beach he had long been classed as a common drunk, a drug abuser, who long ago had forfeited the title of literary genius. But he retained that genius to the end.

Bitter and tragic that end was. Kaufman spent his last months at Our Lady of Perpetual Help Residential Care Center, located on Florida Street, San Francisco, where early in the morning of 12 January 1986, he died of emphysema complicated by cirrhosis of the liver, and the effect of too many hard drugs over too many hard years. "Death is hunting me down," he once told me: and that Sunday, the hunt ended.

Bob Kaufman was born 18 April 1925 to a Black Catholic mother and a German Jewish father. It was his first wife Eileen who encouraged him to put his verbal barbs down on paper. Along with William Margolis he founded the now legendary *Beatitude* magazine, sold on the streets in the heyday of the Beat generation. There are many who remember him for his clashes with the ex-police officer William Bigarini, who personally made war on all Beats, especially Kaufman. Kaufman tacked a poem to the Bagel Shop wall which said, "Adolf Hitler, bored with burning Jews and fooling around with Eva Braun, moved to San Francisco and became a cop." This poem, and several others, landed him in the City Jail where he was, allegedly, brutally beaten.

It became a North Beach folktale: Kaufman did not speak from the time President John F. Kennedy was assassinated until the end of the war in Vietnam. But in fact, the legend is without foundation. Bob spoke to many people: sometimes asking for a cigarette or a drink; occasionally breaking silence to engage a fellow-poet or friend in lively conversation. There is little doubt, however, that the assassinations of the Kennedys, Martin Luther King, Jr., Malcolm X, George Jackson, and others, caused him to retreat within himself: a refugee from the American "system." The last five years saw him banned from every bar in North Beach except the old Hawaiian Bar, across the street from the place where the old Co-Existence Bagel Shop had stood in his glory days. Here he could still stop for an occasional drink, smoke a cigarette, and trap a tourist into a hopeless argument with a "beatnik." Still, the Bob Kaufman of the 1980s was a tired Bob Kaufman. In a poem of 1965, he telegraphed his feelings:

my body is a torn mattress
dishevelled throbbing place
for the comings and goings
of loveless transients
before completely objective mirrors
I have shot myself with my eyes
but death refused my advances.

Two ceremonies marked Bob Kaufman's passing:

On Friday, 17 January, they came from all over — 250 poets and friends, to pay their respects to the most prominent Black Beat poet of our time. The predominantly white audience faced a Black priest and jazz group in Sacred Heart Church in San Francisco, near the Black Fillmore district. Lawrence Ferlinghetti read a letter from Allen Ginsberg, who was in New York and unable to attend the services; followed a moving poem by the poet Eugene Ruggles, lying incapacitated in the San Francisco Veterans' Administration hospital. Michael McClure read a Kaufman poem. It was odd, seeing Kaufman's memorial service inside a church, since he was a self-proclaimed atheist; but there were his friends, Lynne Wildey, who looked after Bob in his last years; and his modeling son Parker, who told us that services for Bob were being held simultaneously, to coincide with this one: in New York, France, the Netherlands, Belgium, West Germany. Afterwards, Jack Micheline read one of Kaufman's poems outside the church, to a large audience, while a mini-bus passed by, confused faces inside peering out at the unusual scene. At noon, some hundred of the mourners gathered at the Mirage Bar at 22nd and Guerrero Streets, for a sharing of camaraderie that lasted until nearly ten in the evening. There was a taped poetry reading in which Bob's poet friends, including myself, participated: remarkably free of the usual North Beach ego scenes. At ten, Parker, his friend Alix, and myself, retired to a nearby restaurant for dinner and the sharing of final recollections.

On Thursday, 23 January, I received telephone calls from Peter Alix, painter, and then from Parker, inviting me to a final celebration for Bob Kaufman. I politely declined, having ridden the "funeral train" one too many times, and preferring to pay my final respects in solitude and reflection. However, Peter later reported that this last ceremony was a good one: one that Kaufman would have liked. On a clear afternoon, a good crowd gathered to march along with a Dixieland band from the Cafe Trieste through Grant Avenue to Washington Square. Along the route, Kaufman's friends and poets paused at some of the bars and landmarks that Bob had visited and helped make famous. Jack Micheline, senior spokesman of the Kaufman crowd, was moved to write a new poem:

> Weaving a net of immortality
> his body a mass of scars
> the barrooms his playland
> and battlefield
> the streets his promenade of dreams
> his audience the derelicts of cities
> the uncrowned prince of words
> a warrior at rest
> his soul rising forever.

Well spoken, but Bob's mind was also a mass of scars, self-inflicted together with those inflicted by society; and his audience spanned beyond the derelicts, to include librarians, professors, middle-class workers. But it is true: Bob, like Jack, was a people's poet.

I'm told that at The Saloon, once known as the 1232 Club, saxophone sound blared at the passing crowd, from the jukebox. It was at the 1232 Club, where old "Johnny" once tended bar, that Bob and I shared many a drink and literary conversation, — Bob sometimes annoying the patrons with outbursts of language they could neither understand nor "feel." Finally, Bob was 86'd (= banned) from this bar, more for the sake of the tourists, than for the sake of his health.

The celebration continued down to the Marina Green, where the band played "Do you know what it means to miss New Orleans?" But, Bob was New Orleans, and — New York and Paris and San Francisco too. The question should be, — do you know what it will be like, to miss Bob Kaufman? Eileen, his wife, sent a letter written to Bob from Europe, after his death: "I heard you the night before the end, when you came to me and said, 'Goodbye, Eileen. I have always loved you, and hope it won't be so stormy the next time around.'"

Later that afternoon the crowd boarded boats to watch Kaufman's ashes being scattered on San Francisco Bay. The weather was peaceful: eyes wet as the sea. My heart was heavy as an anchor, heavy as the sheet round the body of a sailor. My thoughts there: my mind, if not my presence.

A simple, "so long, Bob," must be enough. May you be happier wherever you are. As you said in a poem, "When I die, I shall not stay dead." — A.D. WINANS

HOSE OF YOU who followed our denunciations of the "Holocaust didn't happen" lie in our last issue, and who also read Sanford Berman's article, "'In the Beginning': The Creationist Agenda," in *Library Journal*, 15 October 1985, and the letters pro and con following it, wondered where we stood, and where we would place creationism in our "typology of texts" (see our no. 32, p. 417). We'd place it in the category of minority theories, for reasons given below, but we didn't write letters to *LJ* for two reasons: one, Sandy is perfectly capable of fighting his own battles, and two, we want an occasion — a conference or a book review — to write upon, thus avoiding simply sounding off because it's a nice day for the speakers' platform. Now comes such an occasion: we were sent for review, from the California Academy of Sciences, Golden Gate Park, San Francisco 94118, a booklet by William J. Bennetta, a research associate there: *Crusade of the Credulous: A Collection of Articles About Contemporary Creationism and the Effects of that Movement on Public Education* ($2.00). Some of these articles we'd read in CAS's periodical, *Pacific Discovery*, but even if you are a member or your library subscribes, you'll want the two later articles appearing in print for the first time.

This splendid summary (36 pages) begins with a careful distinction between hypothesis, theory, and fact, showing their mutual relations (evolution is a theory, not a theory only, but also a fact, just as gravity is a theory and a fact), goes on to a history of the fundamentalist movement, emphasizing the trial before Judge William R. Overton in Little Rock, December 1981, by which Arkansas' creationist education act was overturned; reviews three books on the dispute; names textbooks to critique. The author's tune is lucid, patient, and professional, but his replies to standard creationist statements are devastating. He makes the point that the aim of the creationists is not actually the study of biology, but the control of schools — that is to say, that their aim is political, not scientific; that they indulge in half-truths, call inexpert witnesses, and misuse scientific terms. Above all, they endeavour, through controlling the textbook market, to impose on the whole country the beliefs of the most conservative part of the rural South.

Bennetta's booklet brings this all out, and throughout takes the scientist's point of view in answering creationists. Without having his scientific training, we might add the following points, which he or a contributor might wish to bring out in a second edition:

1. The theory of relativity, and the theory of quantum mechanics, are as widely supported by facts as the theory of evolution, or nearly so, and far

more disturbing to the fundamentalist than evolution, for if we understand the implications of Heinz R. Pagels's book, *The Cosmic Code* (Simon & Schuster 1982), both the structure of the galaxy and the infrastructure of the atom can only be described in terms of a given observer. Indeed, the observation of subatomic structure necessarily involves the interference of the observer. This suggests the implausibility of an omniscient God. But since none of us, save the physicists or astrophysicists, have the equipment or the mathematics to disprove their results, these implications are never explored. Besides, atoms and galaxies are not mentioned in the Bible.

2. The elements out of which we are made—hydrogen, oxygen, carbon, sulfur, nitrogen—are, with the exception of hydrogen, formed in stars in their later periods of development. This suggests that the fact that we are here is itself an indication that the universe is very old.

3. Most importantly, the literal interpretation of the Bible is only one form of interpretation—just one more "theory," if we may use that word. The booklet mentions the fact that fundamentalists do not speak for all Christians, and so far as evolution is concerned, that is true. The Catholic Church has no trouble with evolution at this time (see the *New Catholic Encyclopedia*, "Evolution"); neither does the Anglican Communion, nor the Methodists; we're not aware of objections from the churches of Calvinist descent; Quakers accept it without trouble (see Howard Haines Brinton, *Evolution and the Inward Light: Where Science and Religion Meet,* Wallingford, Pa., Pendle Hill, 1970). Objections to evolution come from some Lutherans, many Baptists, many Mormons (the Church has no official policy, from what a colleague has told us), Jehovah's Witnesses and Seventh-Day Adventists. This is a lot of people, but not everybody; and they shouldn't be running the whole educational show.

4. Yes, we did read the other side. We read large portions of Gleason Leonard Archer's *Encyclopedia of Bible Difficulties* (Grand Rapids, Zondervan, 1982), and found it so tortuous, its author so mean-spirited, so harsh and contemptuous of anyone who might disagree with him, that in our opinion he is in danger of mortal sin. His attempts to read the Bible literally would seem, in our eyes, to lead toward racism: Jews and other non-Christians face hell after death, whatever they may have suffered here—and in any case, Scriptural literalism and logic mixed together produce, as we see it, a heady brew called the *odium theologicum.*

5. To return to Berman and his conclusions: as we see it, Berman and Bennetta are right. Creation science is not science. The dispute is not between the Bible and the Book of Nature: both are open: it's what the churches will make of both of them, that will decide their thinking. Put "creation science" books in the 200s, and when readers object, hand them Bennetta's booklet. (Some newer works have lately come to hand on this controversy, but reviews will have to wait till later.) As we ended the homily on the Holocaust, let us end this homily with the injunction: KNOW WHAT YOU'RE TALKING ABOUT: READ.

17 : 2

This is number 34. The cartoons are by Bert Dodson, of Bradford, Vermont. He sent me a sample of cartoon strips, of his favorite character, NUKE. I interviewed him by mail (again, we've never met), ran the interview with a number of his cartoons, most of which drew the Bomb as a humorous, even sympathetic character (as Dodson said, "Herblock's" bomb is Nixonian, mine is Reaganesque") and McFarland picked it up. In 1988 they published a 128-page book, Nuke (A Book of Cartoons), *by Bert Dodson, and reprinted my interview in it. Dodson, born and bred in the Southwest, came to the Northeast, got involved in antiwar politics, and ended up drawing his version of the Bomb ("You need me!") in answer to questions from his young son. The publisher asked that I forbid the rerunning of the interview here: he wants you to* buy the book, get it?

This is a fuller coverage of the McCalden case, on a philosophical basis. The arguments here are presented in a revised and extended book, The Freedom to Lie, *with John Swan as co-author, published by McFarland in 1989.*

CARDINAL MAZARIN IS DEAD?! Most folks would gladly agree that the encounter of the California Library Association with David McCalden, the man who claims that the Holocaust did not happen, or at least that there are discrepancies between the official account and what he asserts, — was the most disruptive event to hit that Association since it was founded. It alienated CLA from the wider Jewish community, by pretending to take an important part of its history as a matter of academic debate; alienated Jewish and non-Jewish groups outside the Association, divided CLA membership, involved CLA in an expensive lawsuit, and might have suggested an earlier retirement to CLA's Executive Director Stefan B. Moses (we can't read his mind).

In the April 1986 issue of *Midstream* (New York), a monthly Jewish review sponsored by the Theodor Herzl Foundation, — two librarians, Mark Elliott and Michael McClintock, of Huntington Park Regional Library, Los Angeles, published a highly controversial yet short article, "Holocaust 'Revisionists' and the California Library Association." Here they took CLA and Moses to task for waffling on the question: whether David McCalden, who denies that Jews were gassed at Auschwitz, should have been allowed to staff a booth and present a program. In their article, they state, "To our knowledge, there has been no discussion by any library publication over the higher issues of anti-Semitism, integrity, and truth." We sent them our v. 16, no. 2; in the meanwhile, it appears that McCalden himself has held meetings to protest their article, which he finds, like ours, to be full of errors. But, let us recapitulate:

Our own belief is that CLA's involvement with David McCalden was a major blunder. It insulted the Jewish community by suggesting that CLA was willing to trivialize their history by making it a subject of academic debate (though the debate would have discussed banned books in general, it would have spilled over into a discussion of the contents of those books); it brought the Association into disrepute with other groups; divided its membership; and cost it an (initially) expensive lawsuit. Others see it simply as a defeat for free speech. Among these latter perhaps may be found John C. Swan, formerly of Wabash College, Crawfordsville, Indiana, but now head of Bennington College Library in Vermont, who published an article, "Untruth or Consequences," in the July issue of *Library Journal*. He also refers to the McCalden case, and his point is that as librarians, our cause is not truth, but freedom. "The commitment of librarians to truth as an absolute legal defense should never be confused with our basic professional commitment to the flow of all kinds of information without regard to its truth or falsehood. Truth may be, must be, an absolute defense under the law, but it has no such place in the selection, classification, storage, and weeding decisions made by librarians." Again, "the real world offers us a multiplicity of 'truths' compounded of desirability and appearance, often contradictory, sometimes in violent conflict with one another. As human beings we inevitably hold cause with one or many of these truths, but as librarians our cause is, in a very practical sense, not truth but freedom. Indeed, our truth *is* freedom, freedom of access, freedom for our patrons to draw upon our resources, to sort their own truths out of our carefully collected and managed mélange of truths, half-truths, untruths, and non-truths."

Without criticizing the CLA nor Moses, nor (at all!) supporting the views attributed to McCalden, Swan concludes that "We are committed both to the search for truth and to the freedom of expression of untruth," although he admits that "many people are ready to grant the untruth some theoretical place in the network of free debate, but no place that will somehow grant that untruth legitimacy." Swan makes a distinction between "intellectual purism" and his own position: "We are not defending the presence of untruth in our libraries just because it might turn out to be true. McCalden's arguments will never turn out to be true, and 'Creation science' will always be apologetics masquerading as criticism, but both have a place in our libraries." He winds up with this point: "The knowledge of truth and the knowledge of untruth, like the knowledge of good and evil, are indissolubly joined. Our cause, professionally and politically, is with both of them."

Swan's exposition of what we have come to call the "libertarian position" on intellectual freedom, and the responsibilities of librarians, is elegantly stated: but (for us) has a few defects. He confuses disagreement over facts with disagreement over moral judgments, and does not separate lies out from his category of "untruths." Consequently, his defense of intellectual freedom may be less adequate than at first appears.

With all due respect, we urge readers to consider these two statements:

(1) The Earth is round. (2) The Earth is flat.

We don't hesitate to say that the first is factually true, and the second factually false. However, while the second statement embodies an untruth, we do not "somehow grant that untruth legitimacy" by saying that "truth . . . has no such place in the selection, classification, storage, and weeding decisions made by librarians," and therefore make sure that we have *just as many* flat-earth books as round-earth books in our libraries, and that they are classed together in the same part of the classification devoted to geology. A librarian who solemnly made that decision, and acted upon it, would be an idiot-savant.

Notice: these two statements about the shape of the Earth, whether true or false: — are morally weightless: neutral. No consequences flow from them that could, or should, affect our actions. Now compare:

(3) Abortion is wrong. (4) Abortion is permissible, or necessary, under (certain [unspecified, at least this time]) conditions.

At once you unite! to disagree!! rising, scraping back your chairs. Wait!

Swan *correctly* notes that: "There are a lot of people who *know* that abortion is murder, and some of them liken abortion-on-demand to the Holocaust. They are about as interested in maintaining an open forum on the subject as most of us are interested in debating the Nazis." We suggest that Swan is *right* when he maintains that there are people who, carried away by their strong feelings on abortion, — call the first statement (3) about abortion, not a moral judgment open to debate, but a literal statement of fact. But we disagree with our friend, when he seems to imply, that if we are willing to debate the anti-abortionists, we should "debate the Nazis," too. Unfortunately two such debates, conducted according to Libraryland laws of fair play, would break down in confusion; for one debate is about moral judgements, the other about factual truths. They come from two different universes of discourse.

Now, consider the two following statements:
(5) The Earth is flat.   (6) The Holocaust didn't happen (or some modification of that statement, however expressed).

Both are false; but the first is morally weightless, while the second is loaded with moral, social, and political implications. To put them in the same category, as the utterances of kooks whom we may tolerate because in the "free marketplace of ideas"—both concepts will [probably] be discarded—is not to think clearly. Statement (5) has not been taken seriously for many years. Statement (6) appears to be believed, to some extent, and with modifications of detail, by a minority who, if they got wide acceptance for their ideas, would thereby get into power and establish a condition of things in which the free marketplace of ideas,—itself an idea,—would be suppressed. Statement (5) is one of Swan's "non-truths"; but Statement (6) is [we contend] a *lie*.

We define a *lie* as a deliberate falsehood uttered to deceive and hurt people. The concept of *lie* indeed the word "lie," is not deeply explored in Swan's article. Nor is it the source of much soul-searching in other periodical publications from Libraryland. May we suggest that the word "untruth" is a euphemism? We are told that "we must make it clear to our public that access means a professional responsibility to ... as much untruth as we can possibly manage." Perhaps there is room for another concept: Truth cannot simply endure the presence of a lie. It has to fight it and overcome it. The lie behind slavery led to the Civil Rights movement. The Reverend

Dr. Martin Luther King, Jr., was moved to oppose the lie of racism with his truth.

For, behind the Holocaust (which really happened!) — we discover another lie, the lie that made the Big Lie credible: the lie that Jews (and others: Romany, Slavs, blacks, gays) are subhuman: that *they* are the cause of *all the trouble in the world,* — and that, *therefore,* they must be eliminated. This lie, — believed by a whole nation and by many outside it, — caused the deaths of six million Jews *because they were Jews.*

As Robert Edward Herzstein, in his book: *The War that Hitler Won* (New York, Putnam's, 1978), — explaining why he has no separate chapter on anti-Jewish propaganda, says: "Anti-Jewish feeling permeated every level of the Nazi propaganda apparatus and mass media, even after the Nazis had 'evacuated' millions of Jews to the east. Since the enemy coalition was clearly a conspiracy, the arch-conspirator, the Jew, was portrayed as the mind behind the 'anti-world.' The Jews were responsible for German misery and German defeats. To have a chapter on the Jews would be to acknowledge anti–Semitism as a part of Nazi ideology, whereas it was its ultimate moral and historical guide" (introduction, p. 22).

Our own encounters with Jewish colleagues in the library profession as the McCalden crisis rose to its height made it plain to us that they would have agreed with Herzstein, that they saw anti–Semitism and its lies not as a "kook's theory" which ought to be tolerated in the search for truth, but as a deadly enemy which had murdered many of their kinfolk. They saw the CLA, or at least its leadership, not as honest souls waffling with a problem, but as insensitive opportunists. We have never seen merry young faces suddenly grow so grave, and even frightened, — within the comfortable walls of an American library.

However, besides the danger of the politically motivated lie, there is a certain sets of assumptions behind the libertarian position held by Swan (as we understand him) and (perhaps at least some other) librarians in the intellectual freedom field. We can glimpse it when he says: "the real world offers us a multiplicity of 'truths' compounded of desirability and appearance, often contradictory, sometimes in violent conflict with one another. As human beings we inevitably hold cause with one or many of these truths, but as librarians our cause is, in a very practical sense, not truth but freedom. Indeed, our truth *is* freedom, freedom of access, freedom for our patrons to draw upon our resources, to sort their own truths out of our carefully collected and managed mélange of truths, half-truths, untruths, and non-truths."

These noble words, to which, surely, many librarians might agree, conceal (perhaps a few) problems. The real world does not offer us anything: the universe is not a person, broadcasting opinions; it simply *is.* The multiplicity to which Swan refers, is not the world; it is only the number of statements made about the world; "Don't confuse the finger pointing at the moon, with the moon itself." Other assumptions? the patron has enough education, therefore enough knowledge of the truth (nowhere defined: *a priori?*) to make a selection from the librarian's "carefully collected" (but how?) "mélange." (Note, please, that we are talking about truth vs. untruths: we are speaking of the world of factual statements; we are not discussing moral debates, nor the autonomous world of magic, fantasy, art.) If it's a mélange, is it carefully collected and managed? If the librarian knows what the truth is, why the mélange?

Perhaps the story of truth behind the intellectual freedom position, as here deliberated by Swan, seems to resemble, if not necessary to derive from, the "pragmatic theory" of truth, as given by that quintessentially American philosopher, John Dewey. (For a good exposition of Dewey's theory of truth, see the article, "Pragmatic Theory of Truth," in *Encyclopedia of Philosophy* [Macmillan, 1967]. The article [v. 6, p. 427-430] is signed: Gertrude Ezorsky.) As given there, Dewey's pragmatic theory of truth tells us that truth emerges as the result of a search; an investigation which begins in doubt and uncertainty, — ending with the establishment of a *fact*. Truth has no prior existence (in Dewey's view, as we understand that interpretation) to the establishment of a fact; the fact does not stand "out there," but depends on the corroboration of supporting facts by ordered inquiry.

Since (according to Dewey) this process requires a free investigator; and since there are many inquirers: there will be many facts, — and many interpretations of those facts. Truth, therefore, (yours, ours, McCalden's) will be that much harder to pin down; becomes, at last, a mutable concept.

Perhaps it follows, for us as librarians: that if we could just get all the books together, all the various interpretations of the million texts which allude to the infinitude of facts, opinions, submissions published and unpublished: and let readers paw through this carefully collected mélange, — the readers will come up with "the Truth" on any subject. Such "Truth"—arrived at by reading and discussion—will be supplemented, corrected, added-to, subtracted-from, as more and more investigators read more and more books, argue and discuss them, on and on into the wee small hours, until the librarian closes the library and goes home to a well-deserved repose.

Swan himself does not mention Dewey's theory, nor our crude paraphrase thereof. But Carnap is quoted in the same *Encyclopedia of Philosophy* as saying that Dewey's theory of truth contradicts the law of excluded middle (which states: for every statement and proposition: either it is true, or its negation is true: either p or not-p. You deny the law of excluded middle? consider Voltaire's fellow who says, "Some believe the Cardinal Mazarin is dead, others believe he is still alive; as for me, I believe neither the one nor the other." (*Satirical Dictionary of Voltaire,* ed. Paul McPharlin; Mt. Vernon, Peter Pauper Press, c1945; p. 68, article "Liberty.")

Furthermore, a truth is not bound by time, as Carnap pointed out.

Cosmas Indicopleustes, a sixth-century traveller who sailed the coasts of the Indian Ocean, retired to a monastery in Alexandria, and there wrote a treatise called *Topographia Christiana,* in which he proved that the pernicious doctrines of the heathen philosophers were wrong, and that the Earth was flat. Before you laugh at poor Cosmas, reflect that it is not that "we know better," in some trivial way; it is that the Earth was never flat, was not flat when Cosmas was writing his treatise; and would not be flat even if he said it was in the pages of *Library Journal.* Experiment and experience determined us that the Earth is round; it was not settled by rhetorical exercise.

Here and now: let's entertain a hypothesis the contrary of Swan's: Freedom is dependent on truth, and a knowledge of truth is necessary for the intelligent exercise of freedom. If we know that we should drive on the right side of the road in the United States, and the left side in Britain, we have a good chance of driving safely; but if we never learned, or some liar has switched the signs around, — we are obliged to stay home: *we are not free to drive.* No wonder the Jews, and some librarians, were upset: CLA seemed to be playing fast and loose with truth. It was as if someone had switched the road signs around, telling us: "Open your minds! be tolerant! maybe it ought to be this way!" But the rules of the road are not for anyone's changing, and reality is not up for grabs.

To sum up: we have come to the conclusion that the current *defense* of intellectual freedom suffers from grave weaknesses, as exposed in CLA's experience with David McCalden and his "Truth Missions" group:

1) By making truth a thing to be settled by debate, the present theory leads to a violation of the law of the excluded middle: it is a logical fallacy to say that Cardinal Mazarin is neither dead nor alive.

2) The current libertarian theory of intellectual freedom detaches itself from reality, logical and political: we have no defense against manipulators, while we have no room for sensitivity toward the community which surrounds us.

3) Finally, the current theory of intellectual freedom contains a "liberal's paradox," arising out of that frequently-invoked phrase, "the free market-place of ideas." For the words "free market-place of ideas" are the name of an idea, the idea that it would be a good thing if there were a free market-place of ideas; and those words are also the name of a hypothetical universe of ideas, of which the chief characteristic, is that all the ideas in it are free, i.e.

immediately accessible without hindrance or exception — however repellent, absurd, and outmoded some buyers in the market may find them.

However, the phrase "there should be *no* free market-place of ideas," is also an idea; and it is the one idea which must be excluded forever from our free market-place of ideas. Why? because it the idea, "there should be no free market-place of ideas," is allowed to circulate freely, then it stands a chance of convincing many people of its truth; and therefore, the free market-place of ideas will be destroyed. On the other hand, if we exclude this negation of our idea from our free market-place of ideas, then we have created a market which is no longer free. Of course we all agree to ignore the pernicious idea: but to agree to ignore is to suppress and to exclude.

If we were masters of a world-ocean, and we admitted all manner of fishes to our ocean, saying "it's a free ocean, come and swim in it," we would still have to exclude the one fish who wanted to eat up all the other fish in the ocean: so we could no longer claim that our ocean was free.

(Actually, the free market-place of ideas was never that free. The ideas of many groups of people — women, African-Americans, gays, Native Peoples — were either suppressed or arbitrarily devalued in the market-place. Our contention is that CLA should not be perceived by anyone as being party to any such activity.)

In short, we can say, *loosely,* that the present defense of intellectual freedom contains or leads to one logical fallacy and one insoluble paradox. This is not good intellectual equipment with which to face the censors. In fact, we suggest that at least some of the censors dimly suspect this, and this is why they are hallooing and galloping after our tails. In the same issue of *Library Journal* in which Swan's article appears, there is another article, by Norman Poppel and Edwin M. Ashley: "Toward an Understanding of the Censor." In its homely wisdom we sense that some librarians understand that we not only need to understand the censor, we badly need to understand ourselves.

Meanwhile, there are all those outraged Jews, and bewildered librarians.

Last issue we suggested that ALA do a study of what racism and sexism do to a culture. But before they can do that, we need to understand what intellectual freedom is, what relation it bears to reality, how much of it is unconscious or concealed abuse of privilege, and how we justify using it. We need to understand that if freedom is indivisible, so is human dignity. This would result in a complete rewriting of the Library Bill of Rights: which, Poppel and Ashley suggest, isn't doing us much good anyway.

If that holy document is to be rewritten, we suggest that it should begin with the agreement that the world is round, and real; that the major events in its history did happen (the death of the Cardinal, the massacre of the Jews); and that racism is not just another theory, but a threat to the peace of the human household.

After that we may see not truth and untruth entwined, but truth and freedom, in a happier marriage. For (oddly) we find that it is a Book which tells us, "You shall know the truth, and the truth shall make you free."

WHEN YOU READ Douglas Curran's *In Advance of the Landing: Folk Concepts of Outer Space* (New York, Abbeville Press—price not easily visible), you will not be surprised to find that it has an introduction by Tom Wolfe, author of *The Electric Kool-aid Acid Test*. However, Wolfe's intro is only a small part of this book, which gives us little journeys to the homes and haunts of saucer-freaks. The author found them, in Ohio, Quebec, California, by showing local folks a rural model of a rocket or flying saucer, asking them, "Have you seen anything like this around here? Is anyone building something like this?" He was rewarded by finding a kind of naive scientific art: concrete saucers in San Bernardino, California, — UFO houses in Pensacola Beach, Florida. He spends some time with the life of George Adamski, whose home we remember seeing, at the foot of the road leading to Mount Palomar Observatory, — back in the fifties. Adamski came here with his parents from Poland in 1892, at the age of one; served his adopted country with the U.S. Cavalry on the Mexican border (1913-1916); held jobs at Yellowstone National Park, and elsewhere; only began to teach philosophy in 1926, and did not see his first UFO—a large cigar-shaped spacecraft—until 1946. His photographs, which we always saw as motel light fixtures, and his alleged contacts with the inhabitants of the planet Venus, brought him fame and even a meeting with HM Queen Juliana of The Netherlands; but as Adamski turned to spiritualism, and his longtime faithful secretary left him, his organization split, and he died in November 1965. Similar biographies and personal glimpses are given of a score of less-well-known true believers, accompanied by photographs and printed in a clear sans-serif type. In short: one of the sanest and most compassionate works we've seen on fringe-science and popular culture in many years.

Langdon Gilkey's *Creationism on Trial: Evolution and God at Little Rock* (Winston Press, $12.95) is an entirely different sort of exploration, not only because it is narrowly focused where Curran's work is wide-ranging, but because the author is a theologian from the Divinity School, University of Chicago. Gilkey was called as a witness on the evolutionists' side, in the challenge to the Arkansas law which mandated equal time for education according to the creation-science model, as against education in evolutionary science. The creationists lost their case, on the ground that their law constituted an establishment of a certain kind of religion; but Gilkey's book is far more concerned with philosophical implications, especially as regards the points of contact between science and religion. Gilkey sees both religion and science as intruding on each others' domains: scientists assuming that all "superstition" will be removed by a scientific education; the true-believers in religion confusing statements of fact, with positions of ultimate belief.

Considering Fascism, Naziism, Stalinism, &c., to be religious belief-systems in their own way, he sees the deliberate misuse of the methods and tools of science to be today's major threat; while insisting that a completely materialistic, non-spiritual view of life not only brings its believers to a dead end, but creates the very religious belief—sometimes taking bizarre and cruel forms—that it pretended to exorcise.

Calling for mutual respect between religion and science, asserting that their language and the objects of their reference are different, Gilkey asks for a mutual understanding and even collaboration between them, against those who—regardless of their political positions—would distort the meaning of either one (citing Shi'ite Iran as the latest example of such distortion). In short, Gilkey goes much farther than we did in reviewing Bennetta's book (*Crusade of the Credulous,* p. 459, last issue). Gilkey sees the mutual confusion and also the possibilities of understanding, not merely as a conflict between churches (although he sees this too, obviously), but as a mutual misunderstanding between scientists and believers in God's ultimate promise.

18 : 1

As of issue number 35, "the torch passes to a new generation." My nephew David Scott Peattie appoints himself production manager with his Macintosh computer and printer. I reprint here his description of East Bay publishing; I had divided the California small press landscape into several regions, covering mountain, desert, city and wheatfield among a number of contributors. The contributors were turned loose to describe their regions and, as it happened, this made for more headaches — some were prompt and demanded prompt publication and payment; others were "laid back" and the publication date fell behind as I waited for them.

A NEPOTISTIC JOURNEY THROUGH THE EAST BAY WITH DAVID PEATTIE: My first instinct is to say diversity is the key word in describing East Bay small press publishing. But in a way, that's a given. Small press publishing is always diverse. There are as many different types of small presses as there are small press publishers; presses tend to be reflective of the one or two people who run them. After talking to some of the key figures in the East Bay small press scene, I realized that in the Age of Information Access in which we live, geographic boundaries have relatively little to do with the difference between small presses. Back when the U.S. Postal Service made it possible to communicate between coasts (inexpensively) in just 3-5 days, it bridged the gap. Now, with access to the same information via a fiberoptic phone line, a switch of a CRT, or a satellite transmission, the gap narrows even more. Yet, at the same time, the East Bay does epitomize diversity, because it exemplifies an openness, an accepting attitude toward different types of cultures, belief systems, and styles. While elsewhere, a far-out, funky publishing idea might, at best, simply be tolerated, here in the East Bay, it will often thrive. Not all do — many of the small presses that sprang up during the Free Speech movement in the heyday of the 60s are now gone, and only those truly and seriously committed to publishing on a permanent level remain.

To truly examine the diversity of publishing in the East Bay, one would have to examine each and every small press and publication. Fulton's *International Directory* lists over 230 small presses and publications in the East Bay, covering everything from poetry to women's studies to media to New Age to computers to Jewish studies to punk publications. Obviously time and space prohibit such a study, but perhaps by delving into a few which are different in focus, style, size and age, we can get a brief glimpse of the true diversity of East Bay small press publishing.

Poetry Flash, a free monthly poetry review with a circulation of roughly 14,000, stands today as the pillar of the Bay Area poetry scene. It is reflective of the Bay Area and acts as a community poetry bulletin, calendar, and newsletter. But it also has writers of note from all over this country and others, making it much more than a local events calendar. Associate Editor Richard Silberg (who also conducts the poetry readings at Cody's bookstore in Berkeley) says of the tension between local and international coverage, "We're centered in the Bay Area and it's the Bay Area that is our first area of concern, but we want people who pick up the *Flash* to know what is going on *everywhere.*" Being located in Berkeley as it is has its advantages since the Bay Area is one of the top poetry hot spots, second only perhaps to New York, Boston or Paris. But the poetry community elsewhere does not share the broad-based communal spirit that the Bay Area does. For instance, *St. Mark's Newsletter*/Poetry Center (founded by Anne Waldman and now run by Jessica Hagidorn, originally from the Bay Area), the *Flash*'s sister publication in New York, while a viable poetry publication, does not come close to the size and quality of *Poetry Flash.* Silberg claims the *Flash* could only happen in the East Bay where there's a sense of community help and non-competitiveness; a sense of fairness. "People are open-minded here. [Laughing] There are many many people in the East Bay who have holes in their heads — I think that's important. There is a feeling of a cooking mixture, politically and in terms of social consciousness. But in other arts, the Bay Area is not the hot spot. Maybe because more than any other artists, poets can [or naturally choose to?] avoid focusing on money. There's no money anywhere for poetry, comparatively speaking — unlike painting, theatre, dancing, etc." Artists who feel the call of wealthy investors head down south to Los Angeles. While almost everyone is jumping on the bandwagon pointing to L.A. as the new mecca for the arts, Silberg notes that this is definitely not the case for poets and poetry: "L.A. seems to me essentially vulgar. Individuality does not flourish in L.A. It's a very image-conscious, money-conscious—well, hell, money talks everywhere—but it's a kind of artistically nouveau-riche city. That could change, but I think the main reason there's any art going on in L.A. is just the magnet of money. I don't think there's really a very fertile soil, as there is in New York, Boston, or San Francisco. The Bay Area is the hottest poetry spot in the country. It has more small presses than any comparable area. It's full of fine poets and there are more readings than any other place in the country. This place is really hopping and humming. It's like being at a nerve center."

This is a tradition that goes back beyond the Beat Explosion in the mid-1950s. There was *Circle Magazine* published by George Leite and Henry Miller, with Robert Duncan, Kenneth Rexroth, and Jack Spicer "having salons and doing their stuff." Both UC Berkeley and San Francisco State were, and continue to be, central to the poetry scene here. In November of 1955, at the Six Gallery reading (hosted by Kenneth Rexroth), Allen Ginsberg read *Howl* for the first time, and Michael McClure had his first public reading, joined by Philip Whalen, Gary Snyder, Philip Lamantia, and others. "*Howl* swept the country from there and North Beach became a poetic center."

Silberg speculates, "Maybe poetry is big here because there is a sense that the West Coast, northern California, was the last frontier, the last refuge for a lot of people in a forest fire or going to a new life, new possibilities . . . the free speech movement, the political excitement . . . hell, I'm just guessing now."

Arrival Magazine, a national literary-political-arts quarterly run out of Emerville, is the brain-child of 29-year-old entrepreneurial publisher Bill Katovsky. *Arrival* is a recent addition to the East Bay publishing scene, with its first issue out this past spring. Katovsky describes *Arrival* as a magazine for his generation, those who "grew up on the Flintstones and Dostoevsky's *Crime and Punishment,* the Jetsons, and Jay McInerney's *Bright Lights, Big City.*" Katovsky claims that the magazine challenges the big East Coast magazines such as *Harpers, Atlantic,* and the like.

While there are other publications which cover politics, arts, and the letters, Katovsky feels that there are none with the young, yet serious, tone that *Arrival* has. "We live in a de-politicized age where political issues affect us but we lack the efficacy to change them, or so we believe. . . . The 80s is an age of outright cynicism. We care about the horrible things that happen, but we expect it too." The magazine is geared to uncovering and examining the pluses and minuses of our society.

Katovsky sees the ideal reader of *Arrival* as 25 years old. "A lot of people that age are bright and intelligent but are put off by the conservative mags of the East Coast and the 'style-only' rags like *Interview* and *Detail*." He sees the East Coast magazines as having articles that are just plain too long to hold the interest of the reader: "A three hour article on education; a 25 page article on some canal lock. NO one is in the bathroom that long."

While *Arrival* boasts national distribution, many of the advertisements are from the Bay Area ranging from Dave's Smoke Shop of Berkeley to the UC Berkeley Art Museum to the Oasis of San Francisco. Also advertising are *Bomb* magazine of New York, Booksellers of Cleveland and Planet of Los Angeles. Katovsky would be the last to categorize *Arrival* as small press, although it's run out of a small studio flat with Katovsky, Emily Zukerberg (managing editor), and the receptionist, Rockee P. Boye, Katovsky's golden retriever. Katovsky says about the humble office space: "Well we are small in that sense. I think we're the only business where the distance from the floor to the ceiling is greater than from wall to wall. Cottage industry is a misnomer now; studio industry is more accurate. It's low overhead, but no window. This is our sarcophagus ... rent's cheap."

Being located in the East Bay is important to the tone of *Arrival*. While half the writers are from the East Coast, it's without many of the biases that New York–centered publications have. It could be possible to put out *Arrival* in New York, but Katovsky much prefers the East Bay to the East Coast. "The rent's cheap as I mentioned, but there's also the climate (both literal and figurative), the intellectual ambiance, a sense of community—not a big city—and openness, accepting, a climate for experimentation, a different vantage point. I thought a lot of people would be interested in getting involved out here and I was right. By having it here, I give the magazine a singular identity." While one might interpret that as meaning that he doesn't have any competition out here on the West Coast, Katovsky doesn't see any competition anywhere.

Bill Katovsky began his publishing career with *Tri-Athlete* magazine while still a graduate teaching assistant in political science at UC Berkeley. At the time, Katovsky was a tri-athlete himself and had even competed in the Hawaii Ironman Triathlon (a single day, 2.4-mile swim, 112-mile bike race, and 26-mile marathon). He considered it to be a trend-setting sports magazine, emphasizing where the sport was heading, rather than acting as a catalog for sports retailers. He has since sold *Tri-Athlete* (which presumably helped in starting *Arrival*) and sees *Arrival* as a wholly new challenge. "Before *Tri-Athlete,* I knew nothing about publishing, and this is totally new too."

Originally he had planned no fiction, only what he calls "creative nonfiction." "There are too many literary quarterlies out there. But Emily (Zukerberg) convinced me otherwise." The Summer issue features new fiction by David Foster Wallace (author of *Broom of the System*) and Philip

Graham. In the creative nonfiction department is an article, "Icons of the Modern Age," focusing on some of the pieces in the S.F. Museum of Modern Mythology.

Katovsky plans to eventually go monthly with *Arrival*. The quarterly issues have been to let investors know what it can be and, in fact, is. We're both potential and a reality." The magazine lives up to Katovsky's claim. The first two issues indicate that *Arrival* is a refreshing addition to the publishing scene, both locally and nationally, yet it's clear that there's even better to come....

Nolo Press is a publisher of legal self-help books located in the up-and-coming warehouse district of West Berkeley. Nolo has its roots in the early 70s when Ed Sherman and Ralph (now Jake) Warner ("recently retired legal aid lawyers" from Richmond) wrote *How to Do Your Own Divorce* (a result of changes in the California divorce law which simplified the procedure). Some 16 years and 50 titles later, Nolo Press is continuing to expand, including the quarterly newsletter, *Nolo News,* which acts as both a catalog and an up-to-date newsletter for the ever-changing legal field, as well as launching into the areas of legal software and audio cassettes (for wills and the expanding paralegal movement).

While Nolo started as primarily consumer books and has remained committed to that ideal, in recent years it has also begun publishing titles for tenants and landlords alike, small business and the entrepreneur in general. In the early 80s, Nolo even founded the Saturday Morning Law School which has taught over 1000 students at training sessions at Nolo. *The Divorce Book* has now sold over 350,000 copies and the *California Tenants Handbook* has sold over 200,000 copies, yet they still remain a small press in character. A visit to the 950 Parker Street bookstore will support the notion that Nolo is a publisher committed to helping the needs of the individual consumer at heart.

While former Associate Editor Carol Pladsen does not see Nolo as falling into any Berkeley stereotype, the anti-authoritarian/establishment side of Nolo (which prompted the California bar at one point to try to disbar Ed Sherman) still exists. Nolo Press and its founders see publishing simply as a method of information dispersal: legal information for the consumer. The only difference is that they're selling it at $9.50 per book rather than $100/hour or more.

According to Carol Pladsen, Nolo's success stems from several factors: 1) It has successfully found a niche, and is well-known as the best within that niche; 2) Quality versus Quantity; the press runs average 3500–4500; 3) Honesty in marketing. They have no flashy press kits and have never advertised in the usual sense. They are well-respected by the media (there are regular appearances on KCBS and they have been on *The Phil Donahue Show, Good Morning America;* yet they are willing to do interviews with drug store radio stations and small publications); 4) Employees. Everyone at Nolo is there because they want to be and feel good about the work that they do. It's very much a communal/family environment; and 5) Distribution. Nolo does about 28% of its sales from bookstores, 15% from libraries, and the remainder from its store and direct mail distribution.

Looking at the reasons for Nolo's success, one can see how a publisher like Nolo could neither have started nor lasted on the East Coast and remained what it is today. A publisher like Nolo whose primary philosophy is service for the individual could only have started and succeeded in Berkeley.

North Point Press is known as one of the most respected small presses in the country. But now they're financially successful too. While many East Bay publishers are different from the East Coast because of their far-out innovative approaches, North Point is different from East Coast publishers for exactly the opposite reason: they have returned to the old values of publishing that most of the big East Coast publishers have lost: quality in literary publishing.

North Point began in 1970 when William Turnbull met Jack Shoemaker. Turnbull, an avid book-lover who made his fortune building oil refineries in Europe under the Marshall Plan, retired at age 27 to pursue his love of the written word. It wasn't until he met with Shoemaker that he could embark on a publishing quest with someone who shared his editorial vision: succeeding at publishing serious literary works.

While everyone else was seeing the success of cookbooks, soft porn, sci-fi, mysteries, art and photography, they saw that they could publish and sell serious pieces of literature if handled with the care and attention that East Coast publishers could (or would?) no longer give. Jack Shoemaker, who has served on the literature panel of the National Endowment of the Arts, continues to run his own small press, Sand Dollar Press. It was Shoemaker who had the connections in publishing necessary to begin a successful quality small press.

North Point remains small (they total 12 employees in a small Albany house which was once a church) and the press runs average 4000–7000 per book. Many of their titles are quality reprints, the best example being Beryl Markham's *West With the Night* which continues to be their best seller (over a half million sold) — with a follow-up collection of her short stories just out. Originally they began with quite a few translations, but have cut the number down considerably. In addition, for reasons of cost and efficiency, they no longer handle fulfillment, which Strauss took over in 1983.

While Shoemaker believes that North Point could just as easily have started on the East Coast, both he and Turnbull are northern Californians at heart. In addition, it is the ability to maintain the character and integrity of a small press that is at the core of North Point's success. It may well be that being situated in low-key Albany has helped North Point to maintain the small press perspective.

Kingfisher is a small quarterly focusing on short stories (supplemented with poetry and artwork), edited by three women in Berkeley. Ruthie Singer and Barbara Schultz, both of whom work for architectural firms in the East Bay, met at UCSC as lit majors. They met up with Annie Barrows (who currently works at Oakland's *Artweek*) and the three decided that their 9–5 jobs were not enough: "Our creative faculties were going to pot so we decided we'd start a literary magazine in our spare time." What started as a part-time project mushroomed into a 90-page quarterly that took some 10 months to produce. Barrows claims, "If we had known how much it was going to take, we never would have tried. But we're glad we're doing it." While they may well retreat to a bi-annual format, the success of the first issue is astounding: "I don't know about Ruthie or Barbara, but I was pretty surprised at how well it turned out." *Kingfisher* is unique for a new literary publication in that it is not flashy or loud in approach. It has some outstanding short stories (especially Steve Bercu's "Valorous, Vaporous Pell") presented in a restrained, almost conservative format. Barrows believes that while other, flashier magazines may well catch on more quickly, a publication like *Kingfisher* will withstand the test of time.

According to Barrows, *Kingfisher* could not have succeeded anywhere but the East Bay. The small town atmosphere of the Bay Area helped. "Everyone seemed willing to help us. People would have scoffed at us in New York. While we may be out of the center of the literary world as New York sees it, we have breathing room to develop. People think, well, if you're not avant-garde, you're not literature and so no one's going to read you. It's that cocktail party attitude. Because of that, the West Coast is suffering from an inferiority complex." Barrows claims that while they distribute all over the country, the support from local bookstores was key in their success. "Melissa Mitinger at Cody's gave us great advice and support. And she works for *Zyzzyva* in San Francisco and there was no competitive spirit at all; more a sense of being a member of a literary community." The quarterly also got help from Wendy Lesser of *Threepenny Review* as well as Mary Ellen Padvorsky and Margaret Atwood. It may well be that the local support—physical, intellectual, and even emotional—is the key to the success of the East Bay's diverse small press scene.

[David Peattie works in Berkeley, California and helps his uncle publish *Sipapu*].

THE DOYEN OF THE SMALL PRESS CORPS is Len Fulton, who lives in Paradise, California, on a slope above the Valley. (For an interview with him, see *Sipapu,* v. 3, no. 2, consecutive issue no. 5.) Fulton's publishing company, Dustbooks, includes *Small Press Review* now in its 21st year, *The International Directory of Little Magazines and Small Presses* (now in its 23rd edition), *Small Press Record of Books in Print* (now in its 16th edition), *The Directory of Small Press and Magazine Editors and Publishers* (18th edition), and *Directory of Poetry Publishers* (3rd edition). Besides these publications are a number of poetry books including anthologies, some work by women, a travel book and a couple of novels by Fulton, bibliographies and books on publishing. Curiously enough, the only horse in this luxury stable of publications that seems to have bolted away in a cloud of dust is *Dust* itself, an occasional poetry magazine which Fulton started way back in the beginning of things (1954) which featured a number of fine writers before Fulton became as interested in the publishing process as in editorship. Fulton's interests were very much in the experimental form of literature, including concrete poetry, but his two novels, *The Grassman* and *Dark Other Adam Dreaming,* are in the traditional mode of narrative. In later years, Fulton has been active on the local irrigation district and now serves on the Butte County Board of Supervisors.

The time has long passed when Fulton knew most of the editors and publishers in his directories personally and could include photos of them on the cover and manifestos from them in the text. And it's been some time since he has written the editorials and reviews in *Small Press Review.* For some this has meant a lot of personal touch from a very personable man, but the ever-widening scope of small press publishing has meant an enormous increase in the scope of his operations. *Small Press Record of Books in Print,* which has author, title, publisher and subject indexes, now runs to over 1100 pages. Even the poetry publishers fill a 340 page volume, which includes definite statements from the editors on their likes and dislikes (e.g.: *pro*-Bukowski or *contra.* An editor has been defined as "one who knows exactly what [s]he likes but isn't quite sure.") *The International Directory of Little Magazines and Small Presses* has been criticized for including everything but the kitchen sink in it, and therefore losing its character as a guide to what is uniquely "small-press," e.g. off-beat literature and social change materials. This is not true, as Kitchen Sink Press (Princeton, Wisconsin) is indeed listed in the 23rd edition, and besides, Fulton does exclude material that he just doesn't like: "hate" literature and presses whose sole existence seems to be to publish an account of how great-grandma crossed the plains—vanity stuff, in short. Fulton, who gave up on other printers and maintains his own computers and print shop, is very much master of his own house and anyone who tries to a trip on him is quickly brushed off. Furthermore, there is for many small press outfits no other place where they find a listing: many of them are not in *PTLA* or the other publishers' directories, and the periodicals are not necessarily in *Ulrich's* or *New Serial Titles — NST* coming out too slowly anyway. Finally the statements by the publishers are frequently a joy to read and reveal the essential quirkiness of the whole small press scene (see, for example, *Quixote* and *Samisdat*).

If Len Fulton is no longer as personally visible on the small press scene as he was — he is no longer a member of COSMEP which he helped found, and his communications with his colleagues are mostly computerized printouts asking for updated information on their presses — he has shown a remarkable interest in libraries. A fat "library issue" is ready for each ALA conference, dealing with a small press theme; this year it was guest-edited by University of Southern California librarian Loss Pequeño Glazier, editor and publisher of *Oro Madre* and Ruddy Duck Press. Perhaps this interest is due to Len's realization that librarians are the best customers for his directories. Certainly it raises the question of what will happen to this vast and complex empire of bibliographic services once Len retires. Even though Fulton is not hob-nobbing with cronies in North Beach or Noe Valley, he nevertheless is a recognizable figure with enormous energy and an encyclopedic knowledge of his field. We have two copies of his books, one at home, one at the library, and reach for the "bible of the business" (as *The Wall Street Journal* called it) as often as your pastor reaches for his Scripture. For one assignment we had to go through the whole of the *International Directory* page by page, and other librarians find it is in frequent demand by local poets and writers. (At one point the president of the California Library Association was the director of the Butte County Library, and she found herself confronting Len Fulton on the supervisors' bench. Apparently she wasn't always happy with Len's position on libraries there.)

Certainly when Len Fulton comes to relinquish this empire — as Alexander the Great had to relinquish his — we suspect that it will leave a void which no one else could possibly fill. It would take a major corporation to do what he does, and major corporations are faceless and lack the motivation once the profit drops below a certain point. Nor would they do the job as well, nor would the small press community trust them. The Dustbooks enterprise might stagger on for a few years under Bowker or Wilson, but we expect they might drop it, clumsily. We hope not; but we fear.

This is why we end up this survey of California presses with best wishes for Dustbooks as it nears its quarter-century. To your health, Len. *Ad multos annos.*

18 : 2

We end with consecutive number 36 — the latest as this book goes to print.

Sipapu has fallen steadily behind, due originally to involvement with a short-lived small press organization ten years ago, but also due to the increasing number of publications requiring review or commentary. Only the intervention of nephew Dave Peattie as production manager has saved the periodical from disappearing into the Great Serbonian Bog.

The "language school of poetry" is now at its height, but who knows what will replace it? My own poetic manifesto (modest enough, certainly not alarming) concludes this survey of Sipapu's *eighteen years of publication.*

CLA 1987, SANTA CLARA: Monday, 16 November: "Rising early, in the morning," we managed to get to the 10:30 meeting of the meeting of the Bay Area Young Adult Librarians Chapter (they haven't yet styled themselves BAYALC, but it's only a question of time). This program was entirely devoted to the presentation of a film surrounding a branch of San Jose P.L. Entitled "Censorship: Beyond Books," it detailed the story of an attempt to stage a children's program on witchcraft in [what was perceived as] an increasingly suburban, therefore Christian and conservative, society. When children at a story hour near Halloween asked to see a "real witch," the librarian in charge found one, without considering that the supervisor of branch librarians would be out of town around the time that the witch would arrive. The librarian issued fliers, assuming few, if any, would turn up, but one boy carried the flier home to his mother, and the battle was on.

The film showed something that [as the librarian suggested] was right out of the movies. There were hundreds of picketers and police, a small group of witches or supporters of witches (or the right to be witches) and one lone picketer who was in favor of "live and let live." The witch, a plump, gentle lady named Zsuzanna Budapest, was escorted into the building by police, and interviewed by the press, along with the librarians, Teri Titus and

Caroline Ketman, who had invited her. Witch Budapest showed pictures of The Goddess in various cultures and civilizations; the audience inside was packed with Christians, one of whom pointed out that some of these pictures depicted idols mentioned and condemned in the Bible. The children never got to hear the witch at all.

The librarians pointed out that a lot of support was needed and very little gotten from the community. Ketman's phone was ringing all the time, and finally tired of threats and objurgations, she took it off the hook.

Our own estimate of the situation was that while the whole incident doesn't say much for the tolerance of San Jose suburbanites, it doesn't say much for the public relations skills of the librarians. An important function of librarians who are working with the community is to prevent this kind of thing from happening: either by deciding not to invite a witch — after all, she isn't an essential part of the library's program — or by contacting religious leaders and getting their support (or at least their tolerance). We should hate to be in charge of fund-raising and budgeting for the San Jose Public Library for the next few years. Some very angry people have long memories.

The California Poetry Bibliographers met over lunch and settled on the first draft of a Mission Statement, incorporating methods of electing officers and selecting meeting dates, and reading with interest the results of a preliminary survey showing which libraries are collecting archives and books in what geographical areas (e.g. UC Davis collects Northern California poets, mostly Gary Snyder and his circle; San Francisco State does all American poets but only on tapes; Stanford collects poets and writers, but only those who have some connection with the Stanford campus; the Archive for New Poetry at UC San Diego emphasizes experimental work, etc.). A panel on "How to Get Small Press Materials into Libraries" is planned for Fresno in November, and the "Poetry Czar" is selecting one or two local poets for the area. The "Reading Czar," or "Poetry Czar," Loss Glazer, we later learned, will be moving to SUNY Buffalo. For those who wonder why the library profession has suddenly developed a royal and imperial title, we explain that the term is really borrowed from sports, to indicate an impartial person whose decisions are to be accepted as final. We created that title (as chair) to distance ourselves from the choice of poets selected, so that nobody could use the position of chair to favor his friends. Of course the Czar could favor *his* friends, but as long as he doesn't give them Fabergé eggs at CLA's expense, that's his privilege. The relationship between chair and Czar is like that in an opera troupe between manager and impresario. (Nothing in the foregoing should be interpreted to indicate the impossibility of a Czarina. Quite the contrary!)

Dave Christy is the editor of **ALPHA BEAT SOUP**, 5110 Adam Street, Montreal, Quebec, Canada H1V 1W8 ($5/2 issues). This periodical deals entirely with Beat and post-Beat poets: John Clellon Holmes, Carl Solomon, of the first generation, and A.D. Winans and Lynne Savitt of the second. It seems incredible that this kind of poetry is still going; most of the voices seem terribly tired and the zest has gone out of living for many of them (a zest that made the early poems of this school, back in the sixties, fun to read). The fact that poetry has moved beyond this, through the language school of poetry and fortunately beyond that, seems to have escaped most of these writers. This periodical can be recommended for libraries wishing to collect in the world of poetry here represented; it was still the "in" kind of poetry when *Sipapu* got started; unfortunately, it is not "in" today. Sorry, it isn't us: it's that time moves on.

THE APOLOGY FOR THE "LANGUAGE" SCHOOL OF POETRY is made by Charles Bernstein in *Artifice of Absorption,* a long essay forming v. 4, no. 1 of *Paper Air* (P.O. Box 40034, Philadelphia, PA 19106, $24 for libraries). Bernstein makes his case by characterizing works of art as either dominated by "absorption" or "impermeability": absorptive works of art draw you into them, mesmerize you, surround you with a new reality: a Poe detective story is a classic example. Surface, non-conventional, rococo, decorative, non-realistic are characteristics of impermeable art; he gives a poem of Dickinson's as an example, but his own contributors in his magazine $L=A=N=G=U=A=G=E$ might do, or some of the work of e.e. cummings, or (dare we suggest it) the dialogue in the plays of Oscar Wilde. This is certainly not our favorite kind of poetry, but the erudite Mr. Bernstein almost convinces us, and persuades by an anti-absorptive device which actually absorbs us instead of putting us off: he breaks the essay up into lines of poetry, broken just where the reading voice would pause, indenting where text or quotation seem necessary. The result makes the essay easy for even the stubbornest to read and understand, and he points out that many early modern works, considered impermeable and therefore unreadable, are now easily read and enjoyed by their very familiarity, whereas the popular novels and poems of fifty years ago now seem tired and verbose. (This isn't wholly convincing; few sit down today and read *Finnegans Wake* with any sense of ease, while a major writer like Thomas Mann, for example, is still read with pleasure; as for Stravinsky's *Sacre du Printemps,* it was premiered decades ago, and it still scares the hell out of us every time we hear it.) At any rate, Bernstein has certainly done a service to all of us by making, plainly and nonpolemically, the case for his candidates, the poets of the "language" school.

Turn we now to Tom Clark, who in **THE GREAT NAROPA POETRY WARS** (see *Sipapu,* no. 23, p. 276) exposed the Naropa Institute and its brutal treatment of W.S. Merwin and his friend, and who now in *The Underground Forest* (21 Forest Avenue, Portland, ME 04101; $12/4 issues), v. 4, no. 4/v. 5, no. 1, goes after the language poets in "Stalin as Linguist." This turns out to be the latest report on a battle begun over an article of the same name in a 1985 issue of *Poetry Flash* (San Francisco), in which Clark's criticism of the "language" school brought bitter criticism of him in reply, scores of letters and threats to cancel ads to the magazine. In general, Clark's criticism of the language poets is that they are incomprehensible, contract the basis of poetry instead of expanding it, and that their criticism has taken priority over their poetry and is filled with jargon. This last we can certainly agree with; we have tried Kant and Joyce in our time, but find Jacques Derrida and his followers simply incomprehensible from the first sentence: such was our expereince with Derrida's *Glas*. The poetry itself, since it is deliberately anti-absorptive (to use Bernstein's term) has the same effect as the balls-and-pyramids style of certain Italian decorations of the 17th and 18th century: they hold the eye briefly, then one goes on for something else. And it is certainly true that while the Beats and others opened the door to poets and ways of writing poetry that had been suppressed or put down before, these critics have contracted the poetic ground; in order to be hailed, or published, you have to sound something like them—at least for some editors.

What seems to us necessary is to get past the tired Beat and past the new academy of the "language" poetry and to fall in love with the freshness of the visible world: the earth turned in the hand, the salt spray in the face, the bough breaking with abundance, the flash of a smile, the rise of the breast. And language is not for puzzle, but for music.

But we digress.

Index

Prepared by me with the advice and assistance of Maggie Horn and Thomas McFadden, for which I am extremely grateful. — N.P.

A

Able, James A., 445
Abnakis, 185
Absaroke (Crow Indians), 263, 434, 435, 437-438
Achebe, Chinua, 188
Ackerman, Page, 360
Adams, William F., 281
Adamski, George, 470
Adler, Allen, 423
Afonso, João, 452
African literature, 184, 188, 295-299
AIM (American Indian Movement), 185, 187, 262
Akwesasne Notes, 187
Alexander, Charles, 282
Alix, Peter, 458
Allan, W.P., 3, 7
Allen, Woody, 257
Alpha Beat Soup, 482-483
Alta, 57
Alternative Acquisitions Project, 225, 246
Alternative Press Center (APC), 407-414
Alternative Press Index (API), 401-414
Alternative Press Syndicate, 94, 101
Alternatives, 61
Alternatives in Print, 138, 139, 226-227
American Educator, 331
American Farmer series, 441, 449
American Indian Movement (AIM), 185, 187, 262
American Indians, 1, 6, 185-187, 223, 260-264
American Jewish Committee, 394, 415
American Library Association: Black Caucus, 207, 214; Conferences, 118, 152, 154, 178-179, 244-247, 266-270, 363, 397-399; Executive Board, 363; Government Documents Round Table, 398, 423; Intellectual Freedom Committee, 153-157, 213-215, 266, 363, 369, 378; Intellectual Freedom Round Table, 398, 423; Office of Intellectual Freedom, 214, 270, 369; Social Responsibilities Round Table *see* Social Responsibilities Round Table; Statement on the Freedom to Read, 267; Strategic Long-Range Planning, 397-398; Task Force on Alternatives in Print, 398, 423
Amerindians, 1, 6, 185-187, 223, 260-264
Amherst College, 303-304
Ananda, 61
Anaya, Rudolfo, 104
Ancient Rain, The, 277, 456
Anderson, John F., 69
Anderson, Sherwood, 433
Angel, Frank, 104
Antin, David, 287, 292
Antioch College, 48, 61
Anti-semitism, 420-421
Anvil, The, 23-27
AOXOMOXOA, 76
APC (Alternative Press Center), 407-414
API (Alternative Press Index), 401-414
Apollinaire, Guillaume, 320, 327
Appalachian writers, 439-440
Approaching Simone, 99
Appropriate technology, 168-174
Approval plans, 237-239
Arcade, 117, 179-180
Arce, Bayardo, 429

Archer, Gleonard Louison, 460-461
Argonaut (San Francisco), 279
Argüelles, José, 11
Argüelles, Miriam, 11, 100
Arlian, Dale, 436
Armstrong, David, 274
Arnold, David, 212
Arrival Magazine, 474
Ashbery, John, 292
Ashley, Edwin M., 469
Asian-American Librarians' Caucus, 199
Asian-American Writers Conference, 107-108
Asoma, 336
Association of American Publishers, 140, 141, 246, 271
Atwood, Margaret, 478
Auden, W.H., 143, 144, 156, 173, 178
Auschwitz, 419, 463
Australian Human Rights Commission, 424
Avalon Ballroom, 77
Avatar, The, 19
Ayala, John J., 58
Ayne, Blythe, 196-197, 206
Azorean-Americans, 430-434, 451-452
Azorean Express, 435, 442, 448

B

Babes in the Big House, 99
Bach, Johann Sebastian, 417
Bacon, Francis, 417
Baker, Chet, 402
Baker, Robert L., 244
Bakersfield Californian, 439
Baltimore Information Co-op (BIC), 412
Bamford, James, 416
Banks, Doris, 195
Banned Books Week, 383; *see also* Censorship
Bannerman, Helen, 266
BARC Notes, 70
Barker, Garry, 445
Barnes, Martin, 264
Barrett, Jane, 207
Barrows, Annie, 478
Baudelaire, Charles, 382
Baur-Heinhold, Margrete, 180-181
Bay Area (California), 472-479
Bay Area Reference Center, 69
Bay Area Social Responsibilities Round Table, 56, 166, 199, 207
Beat writers, 340-349, 474, 482-485; *see also* names of individual writers
Beatitude, 456
Behar, Sol, 3, 7
Bellinger, Bob, 57
Bender, Tom, 171
Benedict, Russell, 3, 58-59, 225
Benet, Brother, 445
Benetta, William J., 459-461
Bennett, John, 40, 133, 206
Bennington College, 143
Berger, Bennett, 290
Berger, Sidney, 132
Berkeley Barb, 35, 45, 274
Berkeley Con, 88
Berkeley Tribe, 35, 274
Berlet, Chip, 424
Berman, Sanford, 28-35, 42, 43-44, 57, 64-65, 111, 213, 226, 268, 274-276, 282, 459, 461-462; *The Joy of Cataloging*, 274-275
Bernstein, Charles, 483
Berrigan, Philip, 357, 359, 361
Berry, Wendell, 187
Beyond Baroque, 101, 146-149
Beyond Baroque (Venice, California), 142-150, 373
Biblarz, Dora, 90, 108-111
Bibliografie Bulletin, 371
BIC (Baltimore Information Co-op), 412
Bierce, Ambrose, 279
Big Dipper, 452
Big Timber (Montana), 430, 434, 450
Bigarini, William, 456
Bilingual education, 314-315; *see also* Multilingual education
Black, Alan, 361
Black Bart, 57, 134
Black Book Bulletin, 423
Black Box Magazine, 404-406
Black Caucus, 207, 214
Black Hills Alliance, 260-264
Black Jack, 435, 437, 438, 440, 441, 442, 448
Blackburn, Paul, 291
Blake, Fay, 110, 199-200
Blaser, Robin, 292
Blazek, Doug, 146
Bless Me, Ultima, 105
Blok, Ric, 216
Bloom, Marshall, 45
Blue, Jane, 375
Bly, Robert, 188, 285
Board, Mykel, 402
Bobker, Lee R., 214

Boll, Marilyn, 99
Bomb, 475
Book fairs, 117, 118, 136, 139, 150-152, 202, 423-424
Booklegger, 60, 111, 134, 162, 164, 167, 168
Borinquén, 333-337
Bowart, Walter, 256
Boys and Girls Grow Up, 404
Braden, Anne, 425
Braun, Eva, 457
Brazil, railroads in, 317-319
Bread and Butter Chronicles, 435, 442
Breit, Luke, 372, 375
Breslin, James E., 290
Bright, Susan, 272
Brighton Heads and Freaks, 66
Brilliant, Alan, 234
Brinton, Howard Haines, 460
Broccoli, Janice, 93
Brookings, Ernest Boyes, 403
Brooklyn College, 356
Brooklyn Public Library *Bulletin,* 244
Brosi, George, 445
Brother Antoninus, 287-289
Brown, Jerry, 197, 200
Brown, Otis, 404
Bruce, Lenny, 257
Bruchac, Carol, 190, 191
Bruchac, Joseph, 182, 184-193, 271, 272
Bruna, Dick, 270
Brutus, Dennis, 286, 295-299
Bryan, John, 151
Bucknell University, 359
Budapest, Zsuzsanna, 481-482
Buddhist Third-Class Junkmail Oracle, 50
Bufano, Benjamino, 151
Bukowski, Charles, 179-180
Bullock, Connie, 58
Burke, Clifford, 234-235
Burns, Creighton, 425
Burns, Grant, 350
Burns, Jerry, 37, 146
Burroughs, William, 346-347, 349
Bush, Jody, 454
Byler, Mary Colayne, 314

C

Caddie (film), 425
Café Trieste (San Francisco), 458
Cage and the Doorkey, The, 27
"Calabash, Mrs.," 381
Caldecott Medal, 306
California Conference on Ethnic Studies, 7
California Farm Observer, 264
California Library Association, 3, 56-58, 134-135, 193-202, 281, 392-396, 453-455, 481-482; Bay Area Young Adult Librarians Chapter, 481; California State College Librarians' Chapter, 453; Collection Development Chapter, 196, 197; Conference Planning Committee, 396; Council, 395; Forum on Publishers and Libraries, 177-178; Government Relations Committee, 454; Intellectual Freedom Committee, 59, 67, 201, 281, 393, 394, 396, 417, 454; Librarians', Publishers', and Vendors' Committee, 279, 281; *Newsletter,* 393-394; Palomar Chapter, 195-196
California Poetry Bibliographers, 482
California Quarterly (Los Angeles), 144
California State College (California, Pennsylvania), 343, 345
California State College at Stanislaus (Turlock, California), 363
California State University: Fresno, 439; Los Angeles, 374; Sacramento, 375; Sonoma, 415, 416, 417
California Writers' Club, 281
Calkins, Roger, 381
CALL (Current Awareness of Library Literature), 407
Callenbach, Ernest, 119-124
Callum, Diane, 302, 317-319, 427-429
CAMP (Combined Asian-American Resources Project), 107
Canadian Library Association, 423
Canadisc, 404
Canaselle, 335
Cannonade Press, 249
Captain Zero, 54
Cardenal, Ernesto, 429
Cardenas, Charlotte, 104
Cardona-Hina, Alvaro, 145
Carleton College, 407-408
Carnap, Rudolf, 467
Carousel, 400
Carson, Dave, 444
Carto, Elisabeth, 419
Carto, Willis, 419, 424
Case, Barbara, 194
Cassina, Larry, 453
Castro, Donaldo, 104

Cataloging-in-Publication (CIP), 132, 271
Cavallini, Ed, 56
CCLM (Coordinating Council of Literary Magazines), 146, 191, 273, 282, 435, 448
Censorship, 388, 395, 421
Center Pieces, 400
CERT (Council of Energy Resource Tribes), 263
Certification of librarians, 198-199
Chambers, Bradford, 270, 302-317, 331; *Chronicles of Black Protest,* 305
Chan, Jeff, 107
Chavez, Cesar, 60
Cheyenne, 263
Chicano publications, 56-57, 103-106
Childers, Thomas, 199
Children's literature, 302-317
Chin, Frank, 108
Chinaman, 108
Chinese Librarians' Association, 199
Chomsky, Noam, 425
Christensen, Peter, 442
Christy, Dave, 482
Chronicles of Black Protest, 305
Church of the Sub-Genius, 404
CIBC (Council on Interracial Books for Children), 152, 157, 199, 270, 305-317, 331-333, 418
Cifra, Kate, 132
CIP (Cataloging-in-Publication), 132, 271
Circle Magazine, 474
City of San Francisco Oracle, 11-20, 45, 60, 401
City on a Hill, 228, 229
Clark, John M., 445
Clark, Tom, 483-484; *The Great Naropa Poetry Wars,* 276
Class struggle (game), 218-220
Clausen, Andy, 146
Clayton, Lawrence, 445
Clear Creek, 95
Cleland, Richard, 271
Cleveland, Ohio, 50-51
Closest Penguins, The, 402-403
Coalition for the Right to Know, 281; *see also* Privatization of information; Right to Know
Coastlines, 143, 144-145
Coetts, Judith, 295
Co-Existence Bagel Shop (San Francisco), 456, 457

Cohen, Allen, 12-13, 18, 19
Cohen, David, 135, 178, 268
Cole, Richard, 227-228
Coleman, John, 170
Collazo, Oscar, 334
Collectors' Network, 225
Color My Cunt, 151
Columbus Café (San Francisco), 456
Combined Asian-American Resources Project (CAMP), 107
Comfort, Alex, 389
Committee of Small Press Editors and Publishers (COSMEP), 37, 52-53, 98, 101, 117, 131-136, 140, 146, 174-176, 186-187, 201-204, 243-244, 251, 270-273, 396-397, 421-422, 480
Committee to Defend Intellectual Honesty, 214
Commune papers, 60-63
Communitarian, 61
Communitarian Village, 63
Communities, 61, 63
Community Service, 61
Con Safos, 58
Concrete poetry, 326, 328; *see also* Visual poetry
Conde, David, 103
Conference on Freedom of Expression and Racist Propaganda (1982: Melbourne, Victoria), 424-425
Conference on the San Francisco Renaissance, 286-291
Confrontation, 101
Congress of American Parents and Teachers, 398
Connexions, 412
Connolly, Cyril, 289, 416
Conspiracy, 358, 361
Constitution of the United States: First Amendment, 213-214, 365, 370; Fourteenth Amendment, 370
Contemporary Culture Collection (Temple University), 223-227
Convocation: Women in Writing (conference), 98
Coordinating Council of Literary Magazines (CCLM), 146, 191, 273, 282, 435, 448
Coppel, Lynn M., 194
Correo Ambiental, 335
Corretjer, Juan Antonio, 333-334
Cosmas Indicopleustes, 468
COSMEP (Committee of Small Press Editors and Publishers), 37, 52-53,

98, 101, 117, 131-136, 140, 146, 174-176, 186-187, 201-204, 243-244, 251, 270-273, 396-397, 421-422, 480
Cosmic Code, The, 460
Cote, Carolyn, 100
Cottrell, Denise, 299
Council of Energy Resource Tribes (CERT), 263
Council on Interracial Books for Children (CIBC), 152, 157, 199, 270, 305-317, 331-333, 418
Country Joe and the Fish, 77
Countryside, 447, 448
Cowboy poets, 441
Craig, Paul, 172
Crater, Joseph Force, 381
"Crawdad King," 442, 452-453
Crawford, John, 396
Crayton, Jim, 57
CRAZY, 112
Creationism, 459-461, 464, 470-471
Creationism on Trial, 470
Creeley, Robert, 240, 292
Critchfield, Sue, 56, 57
Crockett, Ethel, 68-71, 177
Crooks, Joyce, 56
Cross, Frank, 445
Crow Indians, 263, 434, 435, 437-438
Crumb, R., 87, 88, 117, 152, 179-180, 264-265, 402
Cruz de los Pueblos, La, 336
Cuelho, Art, 430-453; *Road Ghost Lament,* 447
Cuelho, Michael Lynn, 438, 441
Culture, 423
Cumberland Journal, 401
Curiously Strong, 66
Curran, Douglas, 470
Current Awareness of Library Literature (CALL), 407
Czapla, Cathy, 445

D

D'Adamo, Chuck and Peggy, 408
Dahl, Barding, 143
Dakota, 186, 262
Dalkey, Victoria, 375
DAMP (Directory of Alternative Media Periodicals), 66
Dana, Joe, 12
Danky, James, 67, 225, 226, 246

Data Center (Oakland, California), 352-353, 363-365
Daumont, Lucas, 269
Davidson, Leigh, 272
Davidson, Michael, 286, 292, 407
Davis, Elizabeth Gould, 100
December Book, 211
Dee, Denise, 402-403
Defoe, Mark, 440
DeGennaro, Lorraine S., 445
Demac, Donna, 399, 423
Denúncia, La, 336
Derrida, Jacques, 484
De-selection in libraries, 193-195
Dewey, John, 467
Diary of Anne Frank, 420
Dickeman, Mildred, 57
Diego, José de, 335
Diné, 186, 262
Directory of Alternative & Radical Publications, 412
Directory of Alternative Media Periodicals (DAMP), 66
Directory of Little Magazines, 37, 38, 192, 479
Directory of Minority-Third World Publishers and Dealers, 135
Directory of Small Press and Magazine Editors and Publishers, 37, 38, 479
Disneyland, 56
Divergent Lines, 376
Divers Press, 240
Dobbs, Jenine, 98
Dodson, Bert, 426, 462
Dokey, Richard, 444, 447
Dollen, Charles, 22, 59, 60, 67-68
Dorian, Donna, 190
Dos Passos, John, 49
Douglas, Boyd, 359-360, 362
Dowd, Sheila T., 194
Dragon Brood, 206
Drexler, Rosalyn, 99
Drought, James, 348
Dubois, Paul, 103-106
Duncan, Robert, 287-288, 290, 292, 294, 474
Dunlap, John, 196
Duplex Planet, 403-404
Dust, 479
DUSTbooks, 36
Dustbowl, 442, 444

E

Earth (magazine), 95
East Village Other, 93, 256
East-West Journal, 206
Ecotopia, 119-124
Egan, Tim, 227
Elder, Gary, 444
Elliott, Mark, 463
Elliott, Patricia, 444
Ellsberg, Daniel, 46
Elms, Alan, 132
Emerson, Thomas, 213-214
Encyclopedia of Bible Difficulties, 460-461
Encyclopedia of Philosophy, 467
English, Dorothy, 56
Epting, Gary, 382
Erotica, 378-392; *see also* Fuck art; Pornography
Eshelman, William R., 4, 132
Eshleman, Clayton, 291, 292
Essary, Loris, 271, 272, 328, 331
Estren, Mark James, 86-88, 116
Eubanks, Jackie, 136-141, 174, 175, 202, 226, 423
Evergreen Review, 289
Everson, William, 287-289
Evolution, 459-461, 464, 470-471
Evolution and the Inward Light, 460
Excluded middle, law of, 467
Ezorsky, Gertrude, 467

F

Facts o' Life Funnies, 112
Factsheet Five, 402
Fairness Doctrine, 398
Family Dog, 77, 80
Fancher, Ed, 255
Fankuchen, Steve, 421
Farallones Institute, 169
Farmer-writers, 440
Farris, Michael, 266-267
Faulkner, Stanley, 306
Fausto, Tomás Ibarra, 105
Ferber, Ellen, 132, 177, 279
Fericano, Paul, 206
Ferlinghetti, Lawrence, 341, 346, 457
Feroe, Paul, 282
Field, Edward, 372
Fielding, Sybil, 109
Fife, Darlene, 72, 85-86
Fillmore Auditorium, 77, 80

First Guidebook to Prisons and Concentration Camps of the Soviet Union, The, 300-301
Five Chinese Brothers, 199
Flaherty, Joe, 202
Fletcher, Homer, 57
Flores, Azores, 451
Folsom, Franklin B., 306
Forcade, Tom, 45
Forster, E.M., 199
Fox, Hugh, 101-103, 146
Frank, Anne, 420
Frank, Edgar, 245
Franklin, Robert, 2
Franklin, Walt, 445
Frantz, John C., 271
Free, 42
Free market-place of ideas, 467-468
Freedom of Information Act, 366, 398
Freedom to Read Foundation, 367
Freep (Los Angeles Free Press), 44, 46, 93, 145, 274
Fresno (California), 433
Friends of Books and Comix, 57
From Seedbed to Harvest, 440-442, 447
Frumkin, Gene, 144
Fuchs, Jerry, 227
Fuck art, 389; *see also* Erotica; Pornography
Fujimoto, Isao, 260-264
Fulton, Len, 28, 36-42, 132, 145-146, 279
Funke, Michael, 84
Funsten, Kenneth, 445
Furness, Irene, 99
Further Fattening Adventures of Pudge, 114, 116
Futz (cat), 208

G

Gabler, Mel and Norma, 311, 367
Galbraith, Douglas, 2, 174
Galloway, R. Dean, 198, 360
Gamut competition, 328
Gargoyle, 349, 400
Garrett, Alexandra, 142-148, 150
Gavin, Camille, 439
Geisel, Theodore Seuss, 401
Gellis, Willard, 445
Gelpi, Albert, 291
Geography of Poets, A, 372
Gilbert, Elliot, 132
Gilkey, Langdon, 470

Gill, Eric, 385, 389
Gilroy *Dispatch*, 228
Ginger, Ann, 269
Ginsberg, Allen, 12, 17, 55, 247, 290, 320, 341, 346, 348, 457, 474
Girodias, Maurice, 349
Gitlin, Todd, 289
Glas, 484
Glazier, Loss Pequeño, 480, 482
Glide Publications, 150
Goddard, Joan, 56
GODORT (Government Documents Round Table), 398, 423
Going for Coffee, 442
Golden, Bruce, 195
Goldtrap, Bob, 443
Gonzales, Sylvia, 104
Goodall, Frank, 177-178, 279, 281
Goodwin, Guy, 358
Gordon, Roxy, 437-439, 444
Gosling, William A., 132
Gottlieb, Lou, 160-161
Gottstein, Karen, 272
Gottstein, Ruth, 57, 139, 174, 175, 273
Government Documents Round Table (GODORT), 398, 423
Graham, Bill, 77, 80
Graham, Philip, 475-476
Grassby, A.J., 424-425
Grateful Dead, 76, 77, 86
Great Falls (Montana), 452
Great Naropa Poetry Wars, The, 276
Great Speckled Bird, 45
Greek-Australians, 425
Greenberger, David, 403
Greenfield, Eloise, 156
Greer, Roger C., 453
Grenada, 364, 366
Grieger, Susan, 282
Griffin, Rick, 77, 79, 82, 87
Griffith, Bill, 180, 205-206
Grito del Norte, El, 58
Grito, El, 58
Grizzell, Patrick, 372, 374, 375
Ground Zero Press, 54
Guillen, Nicolas, 188

H

Hagidorn, Jessica, 473
Haight-Ashbury (San Francisco), 380
Halfbreed Chronicles, The, 426
Halford, Jay, 23-27
Hammond, Lorie, 299

Hannibal's Café (Sacramento), 372
Hard Row to Hoe, 441, 442
Hardin, Garrett, 170
Harms, Valerie, 98, 99
Harper's, 49, 388
Harris, LaDonna, 263
Harty, Sheila, 270
Haslam, Gerald, 438, 442, 443, 446
Hasselstrom, Linda, 435
Hawaiian Bar (San Francisco), 457
Hayakawa, S.I., 269, 270
Hazen, Deck, 227-229
Head, Robert, 42, 72, 85-86
Heads and Fists, 44
Heads & Freaks, 66
Heddle, Linda, 99
Helfand, Esther, 281
Helms, Chet, 77, 80
Henn, Mary Ann, 445
Hennepin County Library (Minnesota), 64, 268, 276
Hensen, Billie, 445
Herblock, 112
Herron, Carolyn, 146
Herzstein, Robert Edward, 466
Hewitt, Morgan, 439
Hiatt, Ben, 132-133, 439, 444
Higgins, Dick, 327, 331
Hill and Holler, 440, 441, 442
Hillman, Grady, 282
Hippie posters, 76-83
History of Underground Comics, A, 86-88, 116
Hitchcock, George, 287
Hitler, Adolf, 419, 457
Hodges, Kenneth, 93-98
Hodiosawnee, 186
Hoffman, Abbie, 425
Hogan, Ed, 350
Hogan, Judy, 133, 174, 226
Hohenstein, Nan, 272
Holmes, Fontayne, 281
Holmes, John Clellon, 349, 482
Holocaust, 383, 414, 417-421, 463, 466, 469
Holt, Rochelle, 99
Hoover, Jane, 361
Hoover Institution (Stanford, California), 418
Hopis, 223, 262
Horizon (London), 416-417
Horn, Maggie, 485
Horn, Zoia, 59, 352-370, 416
Horsley, Wilma, 445

How to Meet and Bed Girls, 202
Howard, Ed, 244
Howard, Peter, 234
Hoyem, Andrew, 320
Hudson, Howard P., 244
Human and Anti-human Values, 153–156, 213–215, 246, 313, 331–333
"Human Be-In," 45
Human Rights Commission (Australia), 424
Human Variation, 215
Huncke, Herbert, 346

I

Ibsen, Henrik, 196, 198
Idelson, Chuck, 84
IFRT (Intellectual Freedom Round Table), 398, 423
Immaculate Heart of Mary, Sisters of the, 373
In Advance of the Landing, 470
In the Night Kitchen, 302
Inada, Lawson, 107
Information-poor, 199
Information Unlimited, 134
Ins & Outs Press, 371
Institute for Historical Review, 419
Intellectual freedom, 156–157, 179, 203–204, 365–370, 417–423, 463–469
Intellectual Freedom Round Table (IFRT), 398, 423
Intercâmbio, 336–337
Intermediate Technology, 174
International Brotherhood of Teamsters, 63–64
Interracial Books for Children Bulletin, 152–153, 302, 306–308, 313, 331–333
Inter/VIEW, 258
Ippolito, Donna, 98, 99
Irby, Jane, 199
Iroquois, 186
Island Resources Foundation, 118, 204, 217

J

Jack, Alex: *Dragon Brood,* 206; *The New Age Dictionary,* 158–160, 206
Jack the Carpenter, 91

Jackson, George, 457
Jarvis-Gann Amendment (Proposition 13), 207, 217
Jefferson Airplane, 77
Jensen, Doug, 445
Jet Lag, 404
Jews, 417–420, 463, 466, 468, 469; *see also* Holocaust
Johansen, Deborah, 150
Johnsen, Gretchen, 400, 401
Johnson, Dennis, 445
Johnson, Thomas T., 419
Johnston, Alastair, 212
Jones, Penn, 133
Joplin, Janis, 45
Josephine, Helen, 165
Josey, E.J., 397
Joy of Cataloging, The, 274–275
Joy of Sex, The, 389

K

Kahane, Jack, 349
Kahle, Theodore, 132
Kaldron, 323–324, 329–330
Kamm, Sue, 393
Kanawha County (West Virginia), 156
Kaniecki, Michael, 402
Karle, Alice, 209
Kastan, Denise, 272
Katoff, Peter, 209, 212
Katovsky, Bill, 474–476
Katz, Judith, 99
Kaufman, Bob, 430, 455–459; *The Ancient Rain,* 277, 456; *Solitudes Crowded with Loneliness,* 277
Kaufman, Eileen, 456, 458
Kaufman, Parker, 457, 458
Keeping America Uninformed, 399, 423
Keiser, Jan, 370
Kelley, Alton, 77, 80
Kellum-Rose, Nancy, 132
Kemper, John D., 171
Kempton, Karl, 320
Kennedy, Adrienne, 99
Kennedy, John F., 457
Kennel, Nancy, 411
Kenyon Review, 290
Kerbrat, Margaret, 445
Kerouac, Jack, 292, 341, 346, 435
Ketman, Caroline, 482
Kimball, Kathleen, 99
Kimsey, Carolyn, 90, 93

Kinder, Alice J., 445
King, Martin Luther, Jr., 262, 457
Kingfisher, 478
Kinney, Jay, 117, 180, 204-205
Kinnick, B. Jo, 293
Kitchen, Dennis, 117
Kitchen Sink Press, 479
Kizer, Carolyn, 405
Kizer, Gary Allen, 439
Kizer, Thelma Scott, 445
KKK (Ku Klux Klan), 269
Klein, Binnie, 98
Kline, Victoria, 455
Kloefkorn, William, 285
Knight, Arthur, 340-349
Knight, Glee, 341, 346
Knight, Kit, 340-349
Know News, 111
Koenig, Herman, 171
Koestler, Arthur, 416
Kornblum, Allan, 350
Kreissman, Bernard, 415
Kruchkow, Diane, 90, 98, 101, 282
Ku Klux Klan (KKK), 269
Kunitz, Don, 132
Kunitz, Stanley, 143, 144, 405
Kunjufu, Jawenza, 226
Kunkin, Arthur, 44, 46, 145, 274
Kurtzman, Harvey, 87, 88
Kyger, Joanne, 291, 292

L

Labelling, 420, 455
Lacy Commission, 416
La Duke, Winona, 263
Lakota, 186, 262
Lamantia, Philip, 474
Lan, Dean, 107-108
Landing Signals, 372, 376
$L = A = N = G = U = A = G = E$, 483
Lanier, Parks, 445
LaRouche, Lyndon, 169, 331
LAUC (Librarians' Association of the University of California), 69-70
Laughlin, Stephen, 84
Lawrence, D.H., 388
Lawson, Todd, 266, 268, 272
Leahy, Diane, 272
Leamer, Laurence, 43-50
Leary, Timothy, 17, 257
Leaves of Twin Oaks, 61
Lee, Don L., 423

Lefcowitz, Allan, 400
Legion for the Survival of Freedom, 419
Leita, Carole, 134, 162-168
Leite, George, 474
Lemoore (California), 451
LeRoy Merritt Foundation, 363
Lesser, Wendy, 478
LeVeen, Phillip, 170
Levertov, Denise, 291
Levi, Steven C., 439, 440
Levine, Steve, 11-20
levy, d.a., 55
Lewis, Sam, 14
Liberation News Service, 45
Liberty Lobby, 419
Librarians' Association of the University of California (LAUC), 69-70
Librarians for Nuclear Arms Control, 455
Library Bill of Rights, 360, 363, 369, 370, 417, 419, 420, 455, 469
Library Journal, 70, 423
Library of Congress, 417
Lies, truth and untruth, 463
Lime Saddle, 60-63
Limelighters, The, 161
Línea Viva, 336
Linnaeus, Carolus, 72, 75
Literary Publishers of Southern California, 149, 175, 212
Little Black Sambo, 266
Lobster Tendencies, 402
Lobster Tendencies East, 402
Loercher, Donna, 99
Loewinsohn, Ron, 287, 290, 291
Logan, Louise, 445
Lomax, Alan, 441
London, Jack, 281, 435
Los Angeles: City Council, 394, 415, 418; Library Commission, 394, 415; Police Department, 394, 415, 463, 464
Los Angeles Free Press, 44, 46, 93, 145, 274
Los Angeles Times, 46, 394
Loyola University, Chicago, 423
Lullabies from Cochiti, 438
Lundborg, Louis, 171-172
Lurie, Janice, 126-130
Lurie, Tobie, 125-131
Lust, Vernon, 197
Luster, Helen, 145, 146
Lyons, Kit, 7

M

McAllister, Elizabeth, 357, 360, 361
McCalden, David, 393, 421-423, 463
McCann, Donnarae, 214, 245-246
McClintock, Michael, 463
McClure, Michael, 12, 286-288, 291, 349, 406, 457, 474
McCook, Kendall, 446
McDaniel, Wilma Elizabeth, 438, 442, 443
McDermott, Judy, 271
MacDonald, Eric, 196, 197
MacDonald, Peter, 263
McFadden, Thomas, 485
McGovern, Anne, 100
McGrath, Tom, 144
McGuire, Glen, 445
McHugh, Joe, 82
McIntyre, James, Cardinal, 373
Mackal, Roy P., 230-231
Mackenzie, Angus, 397
Mackey, Mary, 378, 382, 389
Mackintosh, Graham, 209
MacLuhan, Marshall, 35
McPhail, David, 83
Madison Kaleidoscope, 53, 54
Mahabudi, Haki, 423
Maharishi Mahesh Yogi, 217-218
Mahoney, Ron, 439
Mailer, Norman, 255
Maitreya, 100
Malcolm X, 457
Manhunt, 112
Margins, 101
Margolin, Malcolm, 230
Margolis, William, 456
Markham, Beryl, 477
Marqués, René, 334
Marrs, Lee, 111-116, 179; *Further Fattening Adventures of Pudge,* 114, 116
Marshall University, 441
Marshburn, Lawrence, 194
Martinez, Anna M., 196
Martinez, Delia, 268-269
Maskaleris, Gerta, 7
Matledge, Louise, 98
Maupin, Alfred A., 132
May, James Boyer, 144
Maytag, Ken, 234
Mazarin, Jules, Cardinal, 467, 468, 469
Mazotti, Mary K., 445
Means, Russell, 262-263
Medeiros, Walter P., 76-83

Medina, Luisín Lares, 333-337
Mehta, P.K., 170
Meiklejohn Civil Liberties Institute, 269
"Mei-Lin," 117, 179
Meltzer, David, 234, 287-289
Melville, Herman, 435
Mercurio, Janet, 260-264
Mermelstein, Mel, 419
Merwin, W.S., 276, 483
Métier, 390
Micheline, Jack, 457, 458
Michigan Arts Council, 285
Michigan Technological University, 285
Microforms, 196
Mid-Continent Forum for the Future of Literature, 282-285
Midstream, 463
Militant, 44
Miller, Henry, 388, 474
Miller, Jim Wayne, 436, 446, 449
Miller, Patrick, 389
Miller, Stanley ("Mouse"), 77, 80, 81
Miller, Warren, 439
Minnesota Library Association, 201
Minudri, Regina, 198
Mirage Bar (San Francisco), 457
Missouri Library Association, 407
"Mr. Natural," 264
"Mr. Toad," 180, 205
Mitinger, Melissa, 478
Moberg, Verne, 99
Modern Utopian, 61
Mollema, Peter, 393
Monsters of Loch Ness, The, 230-231
Montana, 449-450
Moore, John, 439
Moore, Lilian, 306
Moore, Marianne, 291
Moore, Mary, 372
Moral Majority, 267, 302, 311, 312, 367
Moral Re-Armament, 218
Moramarco, Fred, 290
Moran, Mary, 445
Morning Star Ranch, 83, 85, 160-161
Morning Star Scrapbook, 160-161
Morressy, John, 254
Morris, Richard, 146, 175, 202, 421
Morrisett, Elizabeth, 268
Moscoso, Victor, 77, 79, 81
Moscow Book Fair (1977), 202
Moses, Stefan B., 393, 396, 397, 415, 463, 464
Mother Earth News, 93-98
Mother Jones, 424

Mountain River Guild, 92
Mountains of California, The, 121
Movement for a New Society, 424
Mudfoot, Judyl, 207–213
Muir, John, 121
Multilingual education, 268–269; *see also* Bilingual education
Mungo, Ray, 45
Múñoz-Marín, Luís, 334
Musgrove, Margaret, 306
Muske, Carol, 190
Myers, Walter Dean, 305

N

NACLA (North American Congress on Latin America), 352
Nakano, Pat, 107
Napoleon III, 423
Naropa Institute (Boulder, Colorado), 483
National Anti-Klan Network, 269
National Clearinghouse for Bilingual Education, 315
National Conference of Christians and Jews, 305
National Endowment for the Arts, 191, 243, 448
National Endowment for the Humanities, 226
National Lawyers Guild, 424
National Nude Days, 277
National Organization Against Censorship, 367
National Organization for Women (NOW), 98, 166, 416
National Trade and Professional Associations of the United States, 422
National Women's Studies Association, 176
Native Americans, 1, 6, 185–187, 223, 260–264
Naturists, The, 277
Navahos, 186, 262
NEA (National Endowment for the Arts), 191, 243, 448
NEH (National Endowment for the Humanities), 226
Nelson, Ray, 281
Nelson, Willie, 441
Nemeth, Terry, 272
Neruda, Pablo, 188
Net Profit, 112
New, 145, 146

New Age Dictionary, The, 158–160, 206
New age papers, 11–20
New Catholic Encyclopedia, 460
New Mexico Highlands University, 103
New Orleans Review, 254
New Pages Exhibiting, 422
New Republic, 47
New Society Publishers, 423
New World Information Order, 398
New York Public Library, 355–356, 446
New York Review of Sex, 46
New York University, 304
Newberry Medal, 305
Newborn, Sasha, 207–210
Newsletter on Newsletters, 244
Newsletters, 146
Newsletters, 244–245
Newsweek, 46, 49
Nicaragua, 427–429
NOLA Express, 42, 72, 85–86
Nolo Press, 476–477
Noontide Press, 419
North American Congress on Latin America (NACLA), 352
North Devon Snail, 66
North Point Press, 241, 477–478
Nos, Tom, 380
Novak, Michael, 118
Novoa, Juan Bruce, 104
NOW (National Organization for Women), 98, 166, 416
Noyce, John, 66
Nuevo Dia, El, 334
"NUKE," 462

O

Oak, Mary, 299
Oberg, Marilyn, 454
Occult Laff Parade, 180
Odessa, Soviet Union, 353–354
Office of Intellectual Freedom (OIF), 214, 270, 369
Ohlone Way, The, 230
Ohlones, 230
Okie writers, 438, 441, 443
Oklahoma Dept. of Libraries *Source,* 244
Old Australians, 425
Old Mole (Boston), 46
O'Lexa, Elizabeth, 411
Ollman, Bertell, 218
On Beyond Zebra, 401
OP Magazine, 401

Oracle (San Francisco), 11-20, 45, 60, 401
Ortega, Phil, 103
Ortiz, Simon, 188
Osborne, Nancy Seale, 176-177
Osborne, R. Travis, 215
Other Scenes, 255, 256
Outlaw, The, 23, 27
Overton, William J., 459
OXOMOXO, 76, 81-82

P

P.O. Frisco, 11
Pacific Discovery, 451
Packwood, Bob (senator), 398
Padvorsky, Mary Ellen, 478
Pagels, Heinz R., 460
Palmer, Roger C., 67
Pan Size series, 441
Paperwork Reduction Act, 399
Parachute Manual, The, 250
Park, Charles, 267-268
Pattern poetry, 320-331
Paul Robeson, 156
Paulk, William, 445
Pay equity, 195-196, 200
Paycock Press, 400
Peabody, Richard, 349, 400
Peace Corps, 48
Peace movements, 248-249, 252, 299-300, 425-426
Peace Pilgrim, 337-339
Pearce, Roy Harvey, 290, 291, 293-294
Peattie, David Scott, 472-479, 481
Peattie, Malcolm R., 392
Peattie, Noel, 1-2, 108-111, 226
Penal Digest International, 27
Penchansky, Mimi, 226
Pennsylvania Library Association, 201
Pentagon Papers, 46, 365
People for the American Way, 367
Pepper, Elizabeth, 66
Perfecto, El, 112
Perloff, Marjorie, 287, 290
Perrin, Arnold, 282
Peterson, Claire, 150
Petric, Faith, 445
Phelps, Dean, 444-445
Phil Donahue Show, 476
Piombo, Akbar del (Norman Rubenstein), 349
Piper, Nelson, 286
Pladsen, Carol, 476

Plains Bookbus, 283-285
Plains Distribution Service, 283
Planet Drum Foundation, 372
Playboy, 220, 390
PLOP!, 112
Plotnik, Art: "Booktrucker," 181
Poe, Marion M., 445
Poet News, 374
Poet Tree, 373-376, 407
Poetry Czar, 482
Poetry Flash, 473, 484
"Pogo," 401
Polan, Morris, 194, 454
Pond, Lily, 378-392
Pooh, The (cat), 378, 382
Poppel, Norman, 469
Pornography, 220, 388-390, 392, 454-455; *see also* Erotica; Fuck art
Portuguese-Americans, 430-434, 451-452
Posters, rock concert, 76-83
Pound, Ezra, 291
Poynter, Dan, 248, 249-252, 271-272; *The Parachute Manual,* 250; *The Self-publishing Manual,* 252
Pragmatic theory of truth, 467
Precisely, 331
Presumptions, 389
Pride, Anne, 99, 133, 202
Print Mint, 12
Printers, 207-213
Prison papers, 23-27
Prison Project, 187, 189-190
Privatization of information, 398-400, 423-424; *see also* Right to Know
Progressive, The, 252
Progressive Action Center, 412
Pro Peace, 455
Proposition 13 (California), 207, 217
Proposition 18 (California), 67-68
Pruitt, Barbara, 60, 63-64
Psychedelic art, 76-83
Public Eye, 424
Publishing in California, 472-480
Publishing in the Netherlands, 216, 370-371
"Pudge," 111-117, 179
Puerto Rico, 333-337
Puzzle Palace, The, 416

Q

Quercus, 374, 375

R

Racism awareness, 152-157, 178-179, 203-204, 302-317, 331-333, 369-370; in Australia, 424-425
Radical Reader's Guide, 7
Rag, 45
Rags, 46, 47
Rain, 171, 372
Rains, John C., 358, 361
Rankin, William, 455
Ransom, John Crowe, 290
Raphael, Dan, 328
Rat, 45
Readings, 211
Reagan, Ronald, 423
Real Fun, 404
Red Mountain Tribe, 45
Redmond, Eugene, 133
Redwood Rancher, 341, 345
Regionalism, 372-373
Reinhardt, Madge, 202
Remick, Helen, 108, 110
Renya, Jose, 104
Resumén de Noticias, 337
Reweaving the Web of Life, 424
Rexroth, Kenneth, 289, 341, 474
Reynolds, Malvina, 162
Reznikoff, Charles, 291, 292
Rich, Adrienne, 292
Richardson, Joseph, 283
Rielly, Ed, 445
Rig Nine, 442, 446
Rig Talk, 442
Right to Know, 363-370, 400; *see also* Coalition for the Right to Know; Privatization of Information
Rintoul, William: *Rig Nine,* 442, 446; *Roustabout,* 446
Rip Off Comix, 180, 205
Rivera, Luis, 174, 226
Riverdale (California), 451
RJS, 50-56
Road Ghost Lament, 447
Robertson, Kell, 438
Roby, Jim, 380
Rochdale College, 408
Rock concert posters, 76-83; bibliography of, 82-83
Rockbottom, 209-210, 213
Rockee P. Boye (dog), 475
Rodefer, Stephen, 286
Rojas, Guillermo, 104
Rolling Stone, 47, 258

Rom, Pat, 362
Rominger, Richard, 169
Roner, Chuck, 445
Rose, Dorothy, 443; *Dustbowl,* 442, 444
Rose, Wendy, 426
Rothenburg, Jerome, 294
Roustabout, 446
Ruggles, Eugene, 457
Russo, Richard, 390

S

Sacramento (California), 375-376
Sacramento Bee, 374
Sacramento Poetry Center, 373-376, 407
Sacred Heart Church (San Francisco) 457
Saikaku, Ihara, 382
St. Helena (California), 455
St. Mark's Newsletter, 473
Saloon, The (San Francisco), 458
Salyer, Pat, 436
San Francisco Bay Area (California), 472-479
San Francisco Chronicle, 401
San Francisco International Book Fair, 150-152
San Francisco Oracle, 11-20, 45, 60, 401
San Francisco Phoenix, 152
San Joaquin Delta College (Stockton, California), 439
San Joaquin Valley (California), 430, 451-452
SAN-ROC (South African Non-Racial Olympic Committee), 296-297
Sand Creek, 187
Sand Dollar, 232, 235, 239-243, 417
Sandel, Betsy, 362
Santa Cruz *Goodtimes,* 229
Santa Cruz Independent, 227-229
Santa Cruz *Phoenix,* 229
Santa Cruz *Sentinel,* 227
Saroyan, William, 432
Savitt, Lynne, 483
Sawislak, Ellen, 423
Sawyer, James X., 445
Saxton, Catherine, 199
Schaefer, Jack, 196
Scherr, Max, 44
Schimmel, Nancy, 162, 165
Schmitz, Dennis, 375
Schoene alte Bibliotheken, 180-181

Schroeder, Bethany, 445
Schultz, Barbara, 478
Schumacher, E.F., 168-174, 206; *Small Is Beautiful,* 168
Scoblick, Tony, 361
Screw, 46
Scripps College, 109
Scrutton, Pam, 4
Seer, The, 19
Self-Publishing Manual, The, 252
Sendak, Maurice, 302
Serendipity Books, 234-235
Sessions, Judith, 416, 418, 455
Seuss, Dr., 401
Seven Buffaloes Press, 430, 435, 439, 445
Sexism awareness, 152-158, 178-179, 203-204, 213-215, 302-317, 331-333, 369-370
SF Official Bulletin, 70
Shakespeare, William, 417
Shange, Ntozake, 405
Shapiro, Karl, 374
SHARE (Sisters Have Resources Everywhere), 164
Shelley, Jeff, 446
Shelton, Gilbert, 87, 117, 180
Sherman, Ed, 476
Shifrin, Avraham, 300-301
Shirley, Patricia, 445, 446
Shoemaker, Jack, 232-243, 477-478
Shore, Elliott, 223-227, 246
Show-Me Libraries, 407
Shuttleworth, John and Jane, 93, 95, 97
Siegel, Ernest, 455
Silberg, Richard, 473-474
Silko, Leslie, 188-191
Silo, 144
Silvermarie, Sue, 100
Simon Wiesenthal Center, 419
Simon Wiesenthal Foundation (Los Angeles), 393, 396, 415
Singer, Ruthie, 478
Sioux, 186, 262
Sipapu, origin of name, 1, 6, 223, 426
Sisters Have Resources Everywhere (SHARE), 164
Skidmore College, 187, 192
Sklar, Holly, 425
Small Is Beautiful, 168
Small Press, 349-351
Small Press News, 90
Small Press Record of Books in Print, 37, 38, 479
Small Press Review, 37, 42, 101, 479

Smith, Elizabeth Martinez, 57-58
Smith, George Drury, 101, 146, 148-149, 150
Smith, Jan, 277
Smith, John, 10
Smith, Lowell, 455
Smith, Lynn, 281
Snyder, Gary, 12, 17, 122, 187, 233, 287-289, 292, 347, 372, 474
Social Responsibilities Round Table (SRRT), 363, 423; Action Council, 270; People's Librarian Task Force, 134; Task Force on Consciousness-Raising, 214, 270; Task Force on Ethnic Studies, 118, 135, 178, 268-269; Task Force on Tools for Consciousness-Raising, 270
Social responsibility, 156-157, 179, 203-204, 213-215, 331-333, 369-370, 417-423, 463-469
Socialist Workers Party, 133
Solitudes Crowded with Loneliness, 277
Solomon, Carl, 482
Song of Joe Raven, The, 439
Sonoma County *Bugle,* 83-85
Sontag, Frederick, 182
Sound Choice, 401
Sound poetry, 125-131
South African Non-Racial Olympic Committee (SAN-ROC), 296-297
Southern California Oracle, 12
Speaker, The (ALA film), 178, 182, 197-198, 200-201, 207, 213-215, 417
Speer, Laurel, 444
Spence, Mike, 7
Spencer, Sharon, 98
Spicer, Jack, 290, 293
Spiritual Community Guide, 65
SRRT see Social Responsibilities Round Table
SRRT Newsletter, 332
Stalnaker, Jean, 9
Stanley, Judith, 110
Stanley, Morine A., 443
Steele, Jack, 439
Steinbeck, John, 443
Stephens, Lele, 99
Steppes, 83, 84
Stevens, Walt & Tuck, 28
Stichting "Drukwerk in de Marge," 216, 370-371
Stilger, Robert, 7
Stjedarn, Kirsten, 270
Stone, Arlene, 202

Stone, Badger, 438, 441
Stoogism Anthology, 206
Studer, Norman, 305
Studies in Socialist Pedagogy, 218
Stump, 90-93
Subject headings, 28-35, 274-276, 417
Sumbi, Joyce, 57
Sundaz, 227
Swan, John C., 463-469
Swartz, Ellen, 454
Sweetgrass County (Montana), 436, 450
Swift, Jonathan, 398
Synergy, 7, 60, 68-71, 164

T

T-shirts, 217
Tablut (game), 72-75
Talbot, Elizabeth, 217
Talley, James, 443
Tanis, Norman, 201
Tapia, Betsy, 104
Task Force on Alternatives in Print, 398, 423
Taylor, Mildred, 305
Teamsters, 63-64
Technicalities, 332
Tell the American People, 424
Temple University, Contemporary Culture Collection at, 223-227
Ten Speed Press, 350
Terry, Megan, 98; *Approaching Simone,* 99; *Babes in the Big House,* 99
Texas Circuit, 272
Thelan, Ron, 12
Theodor Herzl Foundation, 463
Third World Press, 423
Thomas, Irv, 57
Three Mile Island Creamy Mushroom Dressing, 278
Tides Bookshop (Sausalito), 15
Time Bomb, 252
Tits and Clits, 151
Titus, Teri, 482
To Taste, 328
Tong, Ben, 108
Top Secret, 225
Torrance Public Library (California), 393
Torresola, Griselio, 334
Trace, 143-146
"Train of the dead" *(Trem dos Mortos),* 317-319

Transcendental Meditation, 217-218
Travis Air Force Base (Fairfield, California), 417
Trem dos Mortos, 317-319
Tri-Athlete, 475
Trina, 117
Trudell, John, 262
Truesdale, C.W., 282
Truman, Harry S, 334
Trumpet to Arms, A, 274
Truth Missions, 393, 395, 414-417, 419, 468
Tsang, Daniel, 226
Tsongas, George, 12-13, 20
Tung behind the i, 328
Turian, Pat, 199
Turnbull, William, 477-478
Turtle tags and pins, 118, 204, 217
Tusler, Anthony, 84
Tuten, Randy, 77
Twin Oaks, 61, 62
Typewriter, 320, 329
Typoglifs, 320-336; *see also* Concrete poetry

U

UFO's (Unidentified flying objects), 470
UFWU (United Farm Workers Union), 63-64
Underground comics, 86-89, 113, 179-180, 204-206
Underground Comics Festival (1974), 88-89, 114-115
Underground Forest, 483
Underground papers, 3, 7, 43-50, 53, 54, 333-337, 401-404
Underground Press Syndicate, 94
Unicorn Bookshop, 234
Unicorn Press, 234
Unidentified flying objects (UFO's), 470
United Farm Workers Union (UFWU), 63-64
United States: Central Intelligence Agency, 365; Constitution *see* Constitution of the United States; Customs Service, 427-429; Federal Communications Commission, 398; Federal Publishers Committee, 399; Information Agency, 367; Library of Congress, 417; National Security Agency, 416; Office of Management

and Budget, 399, 423; Temporary National Economic Committee, 50
U.S. Labor Party, 169
University of California, Davis, 132-133, 374, 428
University of California, Irvine, 374
University of California, San Diego, Archive for New Poetry, 286, 291-293
University of California, San Diego, Center for Music Experiment, 286, 291
University of the Pacific, 250
Unohoo, 160
Unspeakable Visions of the Individual, 340-349

V

Vallecillo, Al, 299
Vallejo, Cesar, 291, 292
Valley Grapevine, 435, 438, 441, 442
Van der Ryn, Sim, 169, 172
Vane, Norma, 133
Van Gogh, Vincent, 443
Van Sickle, Milton, 145
Van Slyke, Lyman, 170
Varanini, Emiliano, 173
Veaner, Allen B., 196
Venice (California), 142, 149
Verdad, La, 335
Vieques Island, 337
Village Idiot, 209-210
Village Voice, 255-257
Villanueva, Tino, 104
Vinciguerra, Theresa, 372-376, 383, 407
Vinz, Mark, 282, 284, 285
Vision Associates, 213-214
Visual poetry, 320-331
Viva, 112
Vocations for Social Change, 408
Vocero Informativo, El, 336
Voltaire, François Marie Arouet de, 467
Voz del Obrero, La, 336

W

Wagner, D.R., 146
Walden Three, 61
Waldman, Anne, 473
Waldport (Oregon), 289
Wall Street Journal, 480

Wallace, David Foster, 475
Walsh, Thomas James, (senator), 438
Walter, Bernard, 454
War That Hitler Won, The, 466
Warden, Robert Marine, 444; *Lullabies from Cochiti,* 438
Warhol, Andy, 257-258
WARN (Women of All Red Nations), 263
Warner, Ralph (Jake), 476
Waters, Nancy, 76
Watershed Foundation, 404-406
Watt, Kenneth, 172
Watts, Alan, 17
Waxman, Stephanie, 157-158
Wayman, Tom, 442
Weathermen, 45
Web process, 16-17
Weeding, 193-195
Weinstein, Bob, 84
Weird Mystery Tales, 112
Weisburd, Mel, 144
Welch, Lew, 12, 241, 286, 288, 291, 292
Wesling, Donald, 289
West, Celeste, 7, 60, 162, 164, 168, 268
West Coast Poetry Review, 320, 327, 331
West With the Night, 477
Western Independent Publishers (WIP), 211, 212, 283
Westreich, Bud, 132
Whalen, Philip, 290, 474
What Is a Girl? What Is a Boy?, 157-158
Wheat, Valerie, 111, 168
Wheatville (California), 433
Wheeler Ranch, 83, 85
Where Do We Go from Here?, 425
Whitman, Kimberly, 245
Whitson, Dick, 202
Wiese, Kurt, 199
Wilcock, John, 44, 66, 254-260
Wilcox, Laird, 7
Wildey, Lynne, 457
Wilkins, Bill, 271
Willard, Robert, 423
Williams, William Carlos, 290, 291
Wilson, Bill, 411
Wilson, S. Clay, 87, 88
Wilson, Wes, 77
Wilson Library Bulletin, 70, 75
Wimmen's Comix, 112, 114
Winans, A.D., 150-152, 175, 202, 272, 430, 455-459, 483
Winds of Change, 264-265
Winnacher, Martha, 445

Winters (California), 265, 286, 299–300
WIP (Western Independent Publishers), 211, 212, 283
Witches' Almanac, 66
Witness for Peace, 427
WLW (Women Library Workers), 165
WLW (Women Library Workers), 134–135, 162–168
WLW Newsletter, 165
Wolf, Dan, 255
Wolfe, Tom, 470
Woman's Day, 379
Women Library Workers (WLW), 165
Women Library Workers (WLW), 134–135, 162–168
Women of All Red Nations (WARN), 263
Women's Collection Development Conference, 108–111
Women's comics, 111–117
Women's conferences, 98–101, 108–111, 134–135, 176–177
Wood, Cliff, 132
Wood, John B., 194
Wood, Linda M., 395, 415
Woodard, Frederick, 246
Woodward, Kathleen, 294
Woollatt, Richard D., 445
Words that Wound, 424–425

World Government News, 217
Wounded Knee, 187, 262
Writers' Center (Glen Echo, Maryland), 400

X

X, Malcolm, 457

Y

Yashioka, Robert, 133
Yellow Silk, 378–392
Yellowtail, Marjorie, 452
Yellowtail, Robert Summers, 438
Yippies, 139, 176
Yu, Connie, 107, 199

Z

Z.Z. Top, 417
Zahir, 90, 98
Zeppa, Mary, 372, 375
Zero Population Growth, 169
Zippy, 180, 205
Zukerberg, Emily, 475